INTERMEDIATE
ALGEBRA
FOR COLLEGE STUDENTS
FIFTH EDITION

KEISER UNIVERSITY

with STUDENT SOLUTIONS MANUAL
DESIGNED BY BERNICE HERSMAN

JAMES STREETER
LATE PROFESSOR OF MATHEMATICS
CLACKAMAS COMMUNITY COLLEGE

DONALD HUTCHISON
CLACKAMAS COMMUNITY COLLEGE

BARRY BERGMAN
CLACKAMAS COMMUNITY COLLEGE

LOUIS HOELZLE
BUCKS COUNTY COMMUNITY COLLEGE

STEFAN BARRATO
CLACKAMAS COMMUNITY COLLEGE

IGNACIO BELLO
HILLSBOROUGH COMMUNITY COLLEGE
TAMPA, FLORIDA

 **Learning Solutions**

BOSTON BURR RIDGE, IL DUBUQUE, IA NEW YORK SAN FRANCISCO ST. LOUIS
BANGKOK BOGOTÁ CARACAS LISBON LONDON MADRID
MEXICO CITY MILAN NEW DELHI SEOUL SINGAPORE SYDNEY TAIPEI TORONTO

The McGraw-Hill Companies

INTERMEDIATE ALGEBRA FOR COLLEGE STUDENTS
FIFTH EDITION
KEISER UNIVERSITY
WITH STUDENT SOLUTIONS MANUAL
DESIGNED BY BERNICE HERSMAN

This book is a McGraw-Hill Custom Publishing textbook and contains select material from
Beginning Algebra, Fifth Edition by James Streeter, Donald Hutchison, Barry Bergman, and Louis Hoelzle. Copyright © 2001, 1998, 1993, 1989, 1986 by The McGraw-Hill Companies, Inc.
Basic Mathematical Skills with Geometry, Sixth Edition by Donald Hutchison, Barry Bergman, and Stefan Baratto.Copyright © 2005, 2001, 1998, 1993, 1989, 1986 by The McGraw-Hill Companies, Inc.
Intermediate Algebra, Fourth Edition by James Streeter, Donald Hutchison, Barry Bergman, and Louis Hoelzle. Copyright © 2001, 1998, 1993, 1989 by The McGraw-Hill Companies, Inc.
Algebra for College Students, Second Edition by Mark Dugopolski. Copyright © 2000 by The McGraw-Hill Companies, Inc.
Basic Mathematical Skills with Geometry, Sixth Edition by James Streeter, Donald Hutchison, Barry Bergman and Louis Hoelzle. Copyright © 2005, 2001 by The McGraw-Hill Companies, Inc.
Beginning Algebra, Sixth Edition by Donald Hutchison. Copyright © 2005 by The McGraw-Hill Companies, Inc.
Student Solutions Manual to accompany Beginning Algebra, Fifth Edition by James Streeter, Donald Hutchison, Barry Bergman, and Louis Hoelzle. Copyright © 2001 by The McGraw-Hill Companies, Inc.
Student Solutions Manual to accompany Intermediate Algebra, Fourth Edition by James Streeter, Donald Hutchison, Barry Bergman, and Louis Hoelzle. Copyright © 2001 by The McGraw-Hill Companies, Inc.
Student Solutions Manual to accompany Basic Math Skills with Geometry, Fifth Edition by James Streeter, Donald Hutchison, Barry Bergman, and Louis Hoelzle. Copyright © 2001 by The McGraw-Hill Companies, Inc.
Reprinted with permission of the publisher. Many custom published texts are modified versions or adaptations of our best-selling textbooks. Some adaptations are printed in black and white to keep prices at a minimum, while others are in color.

4 5 6 7 8 9 0 QDB QDB 13 12

ISBN-13: 978-0-07-763522-0
ISBN-10: 0-07-763522-1
PART OF:
ISBN-13: 978-0-07-763523-7
ISBN-10: 0-07-763523-X

Learning Solutions Consultant: Melani Theis
Learning Solutions Representative: Nada Mraovic
Production Editor: Kathy Phelan
Cover Design: Paul L. Illian
Printer/Binder: Quad/Graphics

Contents

AN ARITHMETIC REVIEW

0

INTRODUCTION

Cultures from all over the world have developed number systems and ways to record patterns in their natural surroundings. The Mayans in Central America had one of the most sophisticated number systems in the world in the twelfth century A.D. The Chinese numbering and recording system dates from around 1200 B.C.E. The oldest evidence of numerical record is in Africa, where a bone notched in numerical patterns and dating from about 35,000 B.C.E. was found in the Lebembo Mountains near modern-day Swaziland in southern Africa.

The roots of algebra developed among the Babylonians 4000 years ago in an area now part of the country of Iraq. The Babylonians developed ways to record useful numerical relationships so that they were easy to remember, easy to record, and helpful in solving problems. Archeologists have found many tables, such as one giving successive powers of a given number, 9^2, 9^3, 9^4, . . . , 9^n. The tables include instructions for solving problems in engineering, economics, city planning, and agriculture. The writing is on clay tablets. Some of the formulas developed by the Babylonians are still in use today.

You are about to embark on an exciting and useful endeavor: learning to use algebra to help you solve problems. It will take some time and effort, but do not be discouraged. Everyone can master this topic—people just like you have used it for many centuries! Today algebra is even more useful than in the past because it is used in nearly every field of human endeavor.

ANSWERS

1. _____

2. _____

3. _____

4. _____

5. _____ 6. _____

7. _____ 8. _____

9. _____ 10. _____

11. _____ 12. _____

13. _____ 14. _____ 15. _____

16. _____ 17. _____ 18. _____

19. _____

20. _____

21. _____

22. _____

23. _____

24. _____

25. _____

26. _____

27. _____

28. _____

0 **Pre-Test Chapter 0**

This pre-test will point out any difficulties you may be having with basic arithmetic. Do all the problems, then check your answers with those at the end of this section.

1. List all the factors of 42.

2. For the group of numbers 2, 3, 6, 7, 9, 17, 18, 21, and 23, list the prime and composite numbers.

Write the prime factorizations for each of the following numbers.

3. 60 **4.** 350

Find the greatest common factor (GCF) for each of the following groups of numbers.

5. 12 and 32 **6.** 24, 36, and 42

Perform the indicated operations.

7. $\dfrac{3}{5} \cdot \dfrac{25}{12}$ **8.** $\dfrac{6}{7} \div \dfrac{12}{21}$ **9.** $\dfrac{5}{6} + \dfrac{3}{4}$

10. $\dfrac{17}{18} - \dfrac{5}{9}$ **11.** $8.123 - 4.356$ **12.** $7.16 \cdot 3.19$

Evaluate the following expressions.

13. $21 - 3 \cdot 5$ **14.** $(16 - 12) \cdot 6$ **15.** $8 - 2^2$

16. $3 \cdot 4 - 2^2$ **17.** $(18 \div 9) \cdot 2 + 3^2$ **18.** $(15 - 12 + 5) \div 2^2$

Represent the integers on the number line shown.

19. $6, -8, 4, -2, 10$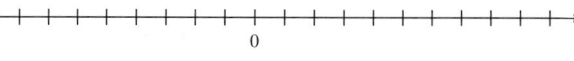

20. Place the following data set in ascending order: $5, -2, -4, 0, -1, 1$.

21. Determine the maximum and minimum of the following data set: $-4, 1, -5, 7, 3, 2$.

Evaluate:

22. $|-5|$ **23.** $|6|$ **24.** $|11 - 5|$

25. $|-11| - |5|$ **26.** $|4 + 5| - |6 - 3|$

Find the opposite of each of the following.

27. -16 **28.** 23

2

0.1 Addition

0.1 OBJECTIVES

1. Use the language of addition
2. Add single-digit numbers
3. Identify the properties of addition
4. Add groups of numbers with no carrying
5. Solve simple applications with no carrying
6. Add any group of numbers
7. Solve applications with some carrying

Overcoming Math Anxiety

Hint #1   Become familiar with your syllabus.

In the first class meeting, your instructor probably handed out a class syllabus. If you haven't done so already, you need to incorporate important information into your calendar and address book.

1. Write all important dates in your calendar. This includes homework due dates, quiz dates, test dates, and the date and time of the final exam. Never allow yourself to be surprised by any deadline!

2. Write your instructor's name, contact number, and office number in your address book. Also include the office hours. Make it a point to see your instructor early in the term. Although this is not the only person who can help clear up your confusion, he or she is the most important person.

3. Make note of other resources that are made available to you. These include CDs, video tapes, web pages, and tutoring.

Given all of these resources, it is important that you never let confusion or frustration mount. If you can't "get it" from the text, try another resource. All of the resources are there specifically for you, so take advantage of them!

The *natural* or *counting numbers* are the numbers we use to count objects.

The natural numbers are 1, 2, 3, . . .

When we include the number 0, we then have the set of *whole numbers.*

The whole numbers are 0, 1, 2, 3, . . .

Let's look at the operation of *addition* on the whole numbers.

NOTE The three dots (. . .) are called an **ellipsis**; they mean that the set continues the indicated pattern.

Definitions: Addition

Addition is the combining of two or more groups of the same kind of objects.

This concept is extremely important, as we will see in our later work with fractions. We can only combine or add numbers that represent the same kind of objects.

From your first encounter with arithmetic, you were taught to add "3 apples plus 2 apples."

On the other hand, you have probably encountered a phrase such as, "that's like combining apples and oranges." That is to say, what do you get when you add 3 apples and 2 oranges?

You could answer "5 fruits," or "5 objects," but you can't combine the apples and the oranges.

What if you walked 3 miles then walked 2 more miles? Clearly, you have now walked 3 miles + 2 miles = 5 miles. The addition was possible because you add groups of the same kind.

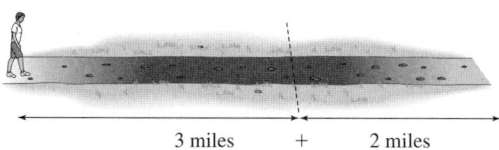

3 miles   +   2 miles

Each operation of arithmetic has its own special terms and symbols. The addition symbol + is read **plus.** When we write 3 + 4, 3 and 4 are called the **addends.**

We can use a number line to illustrate the addition process. To construct a number line, we pick a point on the line and label it 0. We then mark off evenly spaced units to the right, naming each point marked off with a successively larger whole number.

NOTE The first printed use of the symbol + dates back to 1500.

NOTE The point labeled 0 is called the **origin** of the number line.

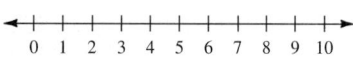

We use an arrowhead to show the number line continues.

Example 1

Representing Addition on a Number Line

Represent 3 + 4 on the number line.

To represent an addition, such as 3 + 4, on the number line, start by moving 3 spaces to the right of the origin. Then move 4 more spaces to the right to arrive at 7. The number 7 is called the *sum* of the addends.

NOTE Again, addition corresponds to combining groups of the same kind of objects.

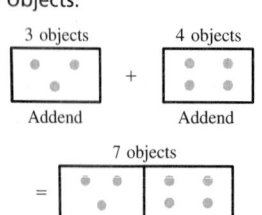

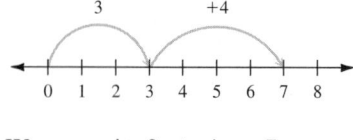

We can write 3 + 4 = 7

    Addend   Addend   Sum

   CHECK YOURSELF 1

Represent 5 + 6 on the number line.

A statement such as $3 + 4 = 7$ is one of the **basic addition facts.** These facts include the sum of every possible pair of digits. Before you can add larger numbers correctly and quickly, you must memorize these basic facts.

Basic Addition Facts

+	0	1	2	3	4	5	6	7	8	9
0	0	1	2	3	4	5	6	7	8	9
1	1	2	3	4	5	6	7	8	9	10
2	2	3	4	5	6	7	8	9	10	11
3	3	4	5	6	7	8	9	10	11	12
4	4	5	6	7	8	9	10	11	12	13
5	5	6	7	8	9	10	11	12	13	14
6	6	7	8	9	10	11	12	13	14	15
7	7	8	9	10	11	12	13	14	15	16
8	8	9	10	11	12	13	14	15	16	17
9	9	10	11	12	13	14	15	16	17	18

NOTE To find the sum $5 + 8$, start with the row labeled 5. Move along that row to the column headed 8 to find the sum, 13.

Examining the basic addition facts leads us to several important properties of addition on the whole numbers. For instance, we know that the sum $3 + 4$ is 7. What about the sum $4 + 3$? It is also 7. This is an illustration of the fact that addition is a **commutative** operation.

NOTE *Commute* means to move back and forth, as to school or work.

Rules and Properties: The Commutative Property of Addition

The order of two numbers around an addition sign *does not* affect the sum.

Example 2

Using the Commutative Property

NOTE The *order* does not affect the sum.

$8 + 5 = 5 + 8 = 13$

$6 + 9 = 9 + 6 = 15$

 CHECK YOURSELF 2

Show that the sum on the left equals the sum on the right.

$7 + 8 = 8 + 7$

If we wish to add *more* than two numbers, we can group them and then add. In mathematics this grouping is indicated by a set of parentheses ( ). This symbol tells us to perform the operation inside the parentheses first.

Example 3

Using the Associative Property

NOTE We add 3 and 4 as the first step and then add 5.

$(3 + 4) + 5 = 7 + 5 = 12$

We also have

NOTE Here we add 4 and 5 as the first step and then add 3. Again the final sum is 12.

$$3 + (4 + 5) = 3 + 9 = 12$$

Example 3 suggests the following property of whole numbers.

NOTE Above, the 4 could have been "associated" with the 3 or the 5.

> **Rules and Properties:**   The Associative Property of Addition
>
> The order in which several whole numbers are grouped *does not* affect the final sum when they are added.

CHECK YOURSELF 3

Find

$$(4 + 8) + 3 \qquad \text{and} \qquad 4 + (8 + 3)$$

The number 0 has a special property in addition.

> **Rules and Properties:**   The Additive Identity Property
>
> The sum of 0 and any whole number is just that whole number.

Because of this property, we call 0 the **identity** for the addition operation.

> **Example 4**

Adding Zero

Find the sum of **(a)** $3 + 0$ and **(b)** $0 + 8$.

(a) $3 + 0 = 3$

(b) $0 + 8 = 8$

CHECK YOURSELF 4

Find the sum.

(a) $4 + 0 =$ 　　　　　　　　　**(b)** $0 + 7 =$

Let's turn now to the process of adding larger numbers. We will apply the following rule.

> **Rules and Properties:**   Adding Digits of the Same Place Value
>
> We can add the digits of the same place value because they represent the same quantities.

Adding two numbers, such as 25 + 34, can be done in expanded form. Here we write out the place value for each digit.

NOTE Remember that
25 means 2 tens and 5 ones;
34 means 3 tens and 4 ones.

$$25 = 2 \text{ tens} + 5 \text{ ones}$$
$$+\ 34 = 3 \text{ tens} + 4 \text{ ones}$$
$$= 5 \text{ tens} + 9 \text{ ones}$$
$$= 59$$

Add down.

In actual practice, we use a more convenient short form to perform the addition.

Example 5

Adding Two Numbers

Add 352 + 546.

NOTE In using the short form, be very careful to line up the numbers correctly so that each column contains digits of the same place value.

Step 1 Add in the ones column.

$$\begin{array}{r} 352 \\ +\ 546 \\ \hline 8 \end{array}$$

Step 2 Add in the tens column.

$$\begin{array}{r} 352 \\ +\ 546 \\ \hline 98 \end{array}$$

Step 3 Add in the hundreds column.

$$\begin{array}{r} 352 \\ +\ 546 \\ \hline 898 \end{array}$$

 CHECK YOURSELF 5

Add.

$$\begin{array}{r} 245 \\ +\ 632 \end{array}$$

You have already seen that the word *sum* indicates addition. There are other words that also tell you to use the addition operation.

The *total* of 12 and 5 is written as

12 + 5 or 17

8 *more than* 10 is written as

10 + 8 or 18

12 *increased by* 3 is written as

12 + 3 or 15

Example 6

Translating Words That Indicate Addition

Find each of the following.

(a) 36 increased by 12.

36 increased by 12 is written as $36 + 12 = 48$.

(b) The total of 18 and 31.

The total of 18 and 31 is written as $18 + 31 = 49$.

 CHECK YOURSELF 6

Find each of the following.

(a) 43 increased by 25   **(b)** The total of 22 and 73

NOTE You may very well be able to do some of these problems in your head. Get into the habit of writing down *all* your work, rather than just an answer.

Now we consider applications, or word problems, that will use the operation of addition. An organized approach is the key to successful problem solving, and we would suggest the following strategy.

Step by Step: Solving Addition Applications

Step 1   Read the problem carefully to determine the given information and what you are asked to find.

Step 2   Decide upon the operation (in this case, addition) to be used.

Step 3   Write down the complete statement necessary to solve the problem and do the calculations.

Step 4   Write your answer as a complete sentence. Check to make sure you have answered the question of the problem and that your answer seems reasonable.

Let's work through an example, using these steps.

Example 7

Setting Up a Word Problem

Four sections of algebra were offered in the fall quarter, with enrollments of 33, 24, 20, and 22 students. What was the total number of students taking algebra?

Step 1   The given information is the number of students in each section. We want the total number.

Step 2   Since we wish a total, we use addition.

NOTE Remember to attach the proper unit (here "students") to your answer.

Step 3   Write $33 + 24 + 20 + 22 = 99$ students.

Step 4   There were 99 students taking algebra.

 CHECK YOURSELF 7

Elva Ramos won an election for city council with 3110 votes. Her two opponents had 1022 and 1211 votes. How many votes were cast in that election?

In the previous examples and exercises, the digits in each column added to 9 or less. Let's look at the situation in which a column has a two-digit sum. This will involve the process of **carrying.** Let's look at the process in expanded form.

Example 8

Adding in Expanded Form When Carrying Is Needed

$$
\begin{array}{r}
67 = 60 + 7 \\
+\, 28 = 20 + 8 \\
\hline
80 + 15
\end{array}
$$

We have written 15 ones as 1 ten and 5 ones.

or $\quad 80 + 10 + 5$ The 1 ten is then combined with the 8 tens.

or $\qquad 90 \quad + 5$

or $\qquad 95$

NOTE Of course this is true for any size number. The place value thousands is 10 times the place value hundreds, and so on.

The more convenient short form carries the excess units from one column to the next column left. Recall that the place value of the next column left is 10 times the value of the original column. It is this property of our decimal place-value system that makes carrying work. Let's look at the problem again, this time done in the short, or "carrying," form.

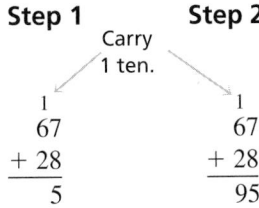

Step 1   **Step 2**

Carry 1 ten.

$$
\begin{array}{r}
\overset{1}{} \\
67 \\
+\, 28 \\
\hline
5
\end{array}
\qquad
\begin{array}{r}
\overset{1}{} \\
67 \\
+\, 28 \\
\hline
95
\end{array}
$$

Step 1: The sum of the digits in the ones column is 15, so write 5 and carry 1 to the tens column. **Step 2:** Now add in the tens column, being sure to include the carried 1.

 CHECK YOURSELF 8

Add.

$$
\begin{array}{r}
58 \\
+\, 36 \\
\end{array}
$$

The addition process often requires more than one carrying step, as is shown in Example 9.

Example 9

Adding in Short Form When Carrying Is Needed

Add 285 and 378.

$$
\begin{array}{r}
\overset{1}{} \\
285 \\
+\, 378 \\
\hline
3
\end{array}
$$
— Carry 1 ten.

The sum of the digits in the ones column is 13, so write 3 and carry 1 to the tens column.

Carry 1 hundred.
$$
\begin{array}{r}
1\,1 \\
285 \\
+\, 378 \\
\hline
63
\end{array}
$$

Now add in the tens column, being sure to include the carry. We have 16 tens, so write 6 in the tens place and carry 1 to the hundreds column.

$$
\begin{array}{r}
1\,1 \\
285 \\
+\, 378 \\
\hline
663
\end{array}
$$

Finally, add in the hundreds column.

CHECK YOURSELF 9

Add.

```
  479
+ 287
```

The carrying process is the same if we want to add more than two numbers.

Example 10

Adding in Short Form With Multiple Carrying Steps

Add 53, 2678, 587, and 27,009.

```
 1 1 2 2  ←——— Carries
      53          Add in the ones column: 3 + 8 + 7 + 9 = 27.
    2678          Write 7 in the sum and carry 2 to the tens column.
     587          Now add in the tens column, being sure to include
+ 27,009          the carry. The sum is 22. Write 2 tens and carry 2 to
  30,327          the hundreds column. Complete the addition by
                  adding in the hundreds column, the thousands
                  column, and the ten thousands column.
```

 CHECK YOURSELF 10

Add 46, 365, 7254, and 24,006.

CHECK YOURSELF ANSWERS

1.

$$5 + 6 = 11$$

2. 7 + 8 = 15 and 8 + 7 = 15
3. (4 + 8) + 3 = 12 + 3 = 15; 4 + (8 + 3) = 4 + 11 = 15   **4. (a)** 4; **(b)** 7
5. 877   **6. (a)** 68; **(b)** 95   **7.** 5343 votes   **8.** 94   **9.** 766   **10.** 31,671

1. In the statement $5 + 4 = 9$

   5 is called the
   4 is called the
   9 is called the

2. In the statement $7 + 8 = 15$

   7 is called the
   8 is called the
   15 is called the

ANSWERS

Name the property of addition that is illustrated. Explain your choice of property.

3. $5 + 8 = 8 + 5$

4. $2 + (7 + 9) = (2 + 7) + 9$

5. $(4 + 5) + 8 = 4 + (5 + 8)$

6. $9 + 7 = 7 + 9$

7. $4 + (7 + 6) = 4 + (6 + 7)$

8. $5 + 0 = 5$

9. $5 + (2 + 3) = (2 + 3) + 5$

10. $3 + (0 + 6) = (3 + 0) + 6$

Perform the indicated addition.

11.
```
  2792
+  205
```

12.
```
  5463
+  435
```

13.
```
  2345
+ 6053
```

14.
```
  3271
+ 4715
```

15.
```
  2531
+ 5354
```

16.
```
  5003
+ 4205
```

17.
```
  21,314
+ 43,042
```

18.
```
  12,325
+ 35,403
```

19.
```
  3490
   548
+   25
```

20.
```
   678
  4533
+   70
```

21.
```
  2289
    38
   578
+ 3489
```

22.
```
  3678
   259
    27
+ 2356
```

23.
```
  23,458
+ 32,623
```

24.
```
  52,591
+ 59,739
```

25.
```
  26,735
    259
   3056
+ 35,489
```

26.
```
  35,607
   2345
    456
+ 81,247
```

1. _____
2. _____
3. _____
4. _____
5. _____
6. _____
7. _____
8. _____
9. _____
10. _____
11. _____
12. _____
13. _____
14. _____
15. _____
16. _____
17. _____
18. _____
19. _____
20. _____
21. _____ 22. _____
23. _____ 24. _____
25. _____ 26. _____

In exercises 27 to 30, do the indicated addition.

27. $2 + 7 + 9$

28. $3 + 4 + 8$

29. $2 + 3 + 4 + 9$

30. $3 + 6 + 9 + 5$

31. Find the number that is 356 more than 1213.

32. Find the number that is 567 more than 2322.

33. Add 23, 2845, 5, and 589.

34. Find the sum of 3295, 9, 427, and 56.

35. What is the total of the five numbers 2195, 348, 640, 59, and 23,785?

36. Add 5637, 78, 690, 28, and 35,589.

37. Find the number that is 34 more than 125.

38. Find the total of 124 and 2351.

39. Find the total of the three numbers 23, 122, and 451.

40. Find the total of the three numbers 112, 24, and 532.

Solve each of the following addition applications.

41. Golf. A golfer shot a score of 42 on the first nine holes and a score of 46 on the second nine holes. What was her total score for the round?

42. Bowling. A bowler scored 201, 153, and 215 in three games. What was the total score for those games?

43. **Vacation mileage.** The Torres family drove 325 mi on the first day of a vacation trip and 273 mi on the second day. How far did they drive in those 2 days?

44. **Car purchase.** Susan Compton buys a car with a list price of $8250. She also orders an air conditioner for $445. What will the total cost be?

45. **Play attendance.** Four performances of a play had attendance figures of 230, 312, 244, and 213. How many people saw the play during this period?

46. **Airline travel.** An airline had 133, 115, 120, and 111 passengers on their four shuttle flights between Los Angeles and San Francisco during 1 day. What was the total number of passengers?

47. **Purchasing automobiles.** Tral bought a 1931 Model A for $5200, a 1964 Thunderbird convertible for $7100, and a 1959 Austin Healy Mark I for $7450. How much did he invest in the three cars?

48. **Consumer spending.** Oman bought a used Pentium 100 for $2120. In addition, he spent $379 for a printer and $589 for software. How much did he spend?

49. **Shipping.** Angelo's vineyard shipped 4200 pounds (lb) of grapes in August, 5970 lb in September, and 4850 lb in October. How many pounds were shipped?

50. **Total distance.** A salesman drove 68 miles (mi) on Tuesday, 114 mi on Thursday, and 79 mi on Friday. What was the mileage for those 3 days?

51. **Video rentals.** The following chart shows Family Video's monthly rentals for the first three months of 1996 by category of film. Complete the totals.

Category of Film	Jan.	Feb.	Mar.	Category Totals
Comedy	4568	3269	2189	_____
Drama	5612	4129	3879	_____
Action/Adventure	2654	3178	1984	_____
Musical	897	623	528	_____
Monthly Totals	_____	_____	_____	_____

43. _____
44. _____
45. _____
46. _____
47. _____
48. _____
49. _____
50. _____
51. _____

52. _____

53. _____

54. _____

55. _____

56. _____

57. _____

58. _____

59. _____

60. _____

61. _____

52. Business expenses. The following chart shows Regina's Dress Shop's expenses by department for the last three months of the year. Complete the totals.

Department	Oct.	Nov.	Dec.	Department Totals
Office	$31,714	$32,512	$30,826	_____
Production	85,146	87,479	81,234	_____
Sales	34,568	37,612	33,455	_____
Warehouse	16,588	11,368	13,567	_____
Monthly Totals	_____	_____	_____	_____

The following table ranks the top 10 areas for women-owned firms in the United States.

Metro Area	Number of Firms	Employment	Sales (in millions)
Los Angeles- Long Beach, Calif.	360,300	1,056,600	$181,455,900
New York	282,000	1,077,900	193,572,200
Chicago	260,200	1,108,800	161,200,900
Washington, D.C.	193,600	440,000	56,644,000
Philadelphia	144,600	695,900	90,231,000
Atlanta	138,700	331,800	50,206,800
Houston	136,400	560,100	78,180,300
Dallas	123,900	431,900	63,114,900
Detroit	123,600	371,400	50,060,700
Minneapolis- St. Paul, Minn.	119,600	337,400	51,063,400

53. How many firms in total are located in Washington, Philadelphia, and New York?

54. What is the total number of employees in all 10 of the areas listed?

55. What is the total sales for firms in Houston and Dallas?

56. How many firms in total are located in Chicago and Detroit?

The sequences below are called *arithmetic sequences*. Determine the pattern, and write the next four numbers in each sequence.

57. 5, 12, 19, 26, _____, _____, _____, _____

58. 8, 14, 20, 26, _____, _____, _____, _____

59. 7, 13, 19, 25, _____, _____, _____, _____

60. 9, 17, 25, 33, _____, _____, _____, _____

61. Fibonacci numbers occur in the sequence:

1, 1, 2, 3, 5, 8, 13, 21, 34, 55, . . .

This sequence begins with the numbers 1 and 1 again, and each subsequent number is obtained by adding the two preceding numbers.

Find the next four numbers in the sequence.

62. You can find more about Fibonacci numbers in an encyclopedia or on the World Wide Web. Do some research and find two examples in nature that exhibit the patterns displayed in the Fibonacci sequence.

63. A magic square is a square in which the sum along any row, column, or diagonal is the same. For example

35	10	15
0	20	40
25	30	5

Use the numbers 1 to 9 to form a magic square.

64. The following puzzle will give you a chance to practice some of your addition skills.

Across
1. $23 + 22$
3. $103 + 42$
6. $29 + 58 + 19$
8. $3 + 3 + 4$
9. $1480 + 1624$
11. $568 + 730$
13. $25 + 25$
14. $131 + 132$
16. The total of 121, 146, 119, and 132
17. The perimeter of a 4×6 rug

Down
1. The sum of 224,000, 155, and 186,000
2. $20 + 30$
4. $210 + 200$
5. $500,000 + 4730$
7. $130 + 509$
10. $90 + 92$
12. $100 + 101$
15. The perimeter of a 15×16 room

65. Adding of whole numbers is commutative. (The order in which you add does not affect the sum.) Can you think of two actions in your daily routine that are commutative? Explain. List two actions that are *not* commutative in your daily routine and explain.

66. Adding of whole numbers is associative. (The way you group whole numbers does not affect the final sum.) If you are following a recipe that lists 10 ingredients that need to be combined, do you think that adding these ingredients is associative? *Be daring!* Find a recipe and combine the ingredients in different orders. Tell the class what happens in each case. (Better yet, bring in the completed product for all to sample.)

67. Complete the following, using the given property.

    (a) Associative property of addition: $5 + (8 + 0) =$ _____

    (b) Commutative property of addition: $5 + (8 + 0) =$ _____

    (c) Additive identity property: $5 + (8 + 0) =$ _____

Answers for Pre-Test for Chapter 0

1. 1, 2, 3, 6, 7, 14, 21, 42   **2.** Prime: 2, 3, 7, 17, 23;
composite: 6, 9, 18, 21   **3.** $2 \times 2 \times 3 \times 5$ **4.** $2 \times 5 \times 5 \times 7$
5. 4   **6.** 6   **7.** $\frac{5}{4}$ **8.** $\frac{3}{2}$ **9.** $\frac{19}{12}$ **10.** $\frac{7}{18}$ **11.** 3.767   **12.** 22.8404
13. 6   **14.** 24   **15.** 4   **16.** 8   **17.** 13   **18.** 2

19.

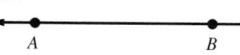

20. $-4, -2, -1, 0, 1, 5$ **21.** Max: 7; Min: -5 **22.** 5   **23.** 6
24. 6   **25.** 6   **26.** 6   **27.** 16   **28.** -23

Answers

1. 5 is the addend, 4 is the addend, 9 is the sum   **3.** Commutative property of
addition   **5.** Associative property of addition   **7.** Commutative property of
addition   **9.** Commutative property of addition   **11.** 2997   **13.** 8398
15. 7885   **17.** 64,356   **19.** 4063   **21.** 6394   **23.** 56,081
25. 65,539   **27.** 18   **29.** 18   **31.** 1569   **33.** 3462   **35.** 27,027
37. 159   **39.** 596   **41.** 88   **43.** 598 mi   **45.** 999 people
47. $19,750   **49.** 15,020 lb
51.

Category of Film	Jan.	Feb.	Mar.	Category Totals
Comedy	4568	3269	2189	**10,026**
Drama	5612	4129	3879	**13,620**
Action/Adventure	2654	3178	1984	**7816**
Musical	897	623	528	**2048**
Monthly Totals	**13,731**	**11,199**	**8580**	**33,510**

53. 620,200   **55.** $141,295,200   **57.** 33, 40, 47, 54
59. 31, 37, 43, 49   **61.** 89, 144, 233, 377
63.

8	3	4
1	5	9
6	7	2

65.

67. (a) $(5 + 8) + 0$;   **(b)** $(8 + 0) + 5$ or $5 + (0 + 8)$;   **(c)** $5 + 8$

0.2 Subtraction

0.2 OBJECTIVES

1. Use the language of subtraction
2. Subtract whole numbers without borrowing
3. Solve applications of simple subtraction
4. Use borrowing in subtracting whole numbers
5. Solve applications that require borrowing

Overcoming Math Anxiety

Hint #2   Don't procrastinate!

1. Do your math homework while you're still fresh. If you wait until too late at night, your tired mind will have all that much more difficulty understanding the concepts.

2. Do your homework the day it is assigned. The more recent the explanation is, the easier it is to recall.

3. When you've finished your homework, try reading the next section through once. This will give you a sense of direction when you next hear the material. This works whether you are in a lecture or lab setting.

Remember that, in a typical math class, you are expected to do two or three hours of homework for each weekly class hour. This means two or three hours per night. Schedule the time and stay to your schedule.

NOTE By *opposite* we mean that subtracting a number "undoes" an addition of that same number. Start with 1. Add 5 and then subtract 5. Where are you?

We are now ready to consider a second operation of arithmetic—subtraction. In Section 1.2, we described addition as the process of combining two or more groups of the same kind of objects. Subtraction can be thought of as the *opposite operation* to addition. Every arithmetic operation has its own notation. The symbol for subtraction, −, is called a **minus sign.**

When we write $8 - 5$, we wish to subtract 5 from 8. We call 5 the **subtrahend.** This is the number being subtracted. And 8 is the **minuend.** This is the number we are subtracting from. The **difference** is the result of the subtraction.

To find the *difference* of two numbers, we will assume that we wish to subtract the smaller number from the larger. Then we look for a number which, when added to the smaller number, will give us the larger number. For example,

$$8 - 5 = 3 \qquad \text{because} \qquad 3 + 5 = 8$$

This special relationship between addition and subtraction provides a method of checking subtraction.

Rules and Properties: Relationship Between Addition and Subtraction

The sum of the difference and the subtrahend must be equal to the minuend.

Example 1

Subtracting a Single-Digit Number

$12 - 5 = 7$

Check:

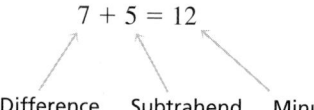

$7 + 5 = 12$

Difference   Subtrahend   Minuend

Our check works because $12 - 5$ asks for the number that must be added to 5 to get 12.

 CHECK YOURSELF 1

Subtract, and check your work.

$13 - 9 =$

The procedure for subtracting larger whole numbers is similar to the procedure for addition. We subtract digits of the same place value.

Example 2

Subtracting a Larger Number

Step 1	Step 2	Step 3
789	789	789
− 246	− 246	− 246
3	43	543

We subtract in the ones column, then in the tens column, and finally in the hundreds column.

To check: 789
            − 246 } Add
             543    $543 + 246 = 789$

The sum of the difference and the subtrahend must be the minuend.

CHECK YOURSELF 2

Subtract, and check your work.

  3468
− 2248

You know that the word *difference* indicates subtraction. There are other words that also tell you to use the subtraction operation. For instance, 5 *less than* 12 is written as

$12 - 5$ or 7

20 *decreased* by 8 is written as

$20 - 8$ or 12

Example 3

Translating Words That Indicate Subtraction

Find each of the following.

(a) 4 less than 11

4 less than 11 is written $11 - 4 = 7$.

(b) 27 decreased by 6

27 decreased by 6 is written $27 - 6 = 21$.

 CHECK YOURSELF 3

Find each of the following.

(a) 6 less than 19   **(b)** 18 decreased by 3

Units Analysis

This is the first in a series of essays that are designed to help you solve applications of mathematics. Questions in the exercise sets will require the skills that you build by reading these essays.

A number with a unit attached (like **7 feet** or **26 mpg**) is called a denominate number. Any genuine application of mathematics will involve denominate numbers.

When adding or subtracting denominate numbers, the units must be identical for both numbers. The sum or difference will have those same units.

Examples:

$4 + $9 = $13   (notice that, although we write the dollar sign first, we read it after the quantity, as in "four dollars")

7 feet + 9 feet = 16 feet
39 degrees − 12 degrees = 27 degrees
7 feet + 12 degrees yields no meaningful answer!

3 feet + 9 inches yields a meaningful result only if the 3 feet is converted into 36 inches. We will discuss conversion of units in later essays.

Now we consider subtraction word problems. The strategy is the same one presented in Section 0.1 for addition word problems. It is summarized with the following four basic steps.

Step by Step: Solving Subtraction Applications

Step 1 Read the problem carefully to determine the given information and what you are asked to find.

Step 2 Decide upon the operation (in this case, subtraction) to be used.

Step 3 Write down the complete statement necessary to solve the problem and do the calculations.

Step 4 Check to make sure you have answered the question of the problem and that your answer seems reasonable.

Let's work an example using these steps.

Example 4

Setting Up a Subtraction Word Problem

Tory has $37 in his wallet. He is thinking about buying a $24 pair of pants and a $10 shirt. If he buys them both, how much money will he have?

First we must add the cost of the pants and the shirt.

$24 + $10 = $34

Now, that amount must be subtracted from the $37.

$37 − $34 = $3

He will have $3 left.

✔ CHECK YOURSELF 4

Sonya has $97 left in her checking account. If she writes checks for $12, $32, and $21, how much will she have in the account?

Difficulties can arise in subtraction if one or more of the digits of the subtrahend are larger than the corresponding digits in the minuend. We will solve this problem by using a process called **borrowing.**

First, we'll look at an example in expanded form.

Example 5

Subtracting When Borrowing Is Needed

$$\begin{array}{r} 52 = 50 + 2 \\ -\ 27 = 20 + 7 \\ \hline \end{array}$$ Do you see that we cannot subtract in the ones column?

Regrouping, we borrow 1 ten in the minuend and write that ten as 10 ones:

$$\begin{array}{l} \qquad\qquad 50 \quad + 2 \\ \text{becomes} \quad 40 + 10 + 2 \\ \text{or} \qquad\quad 40 + \quad 12 \end{array}$$

We now have

$$\begin{array}{r} 52 = 40 + 12 \\ -\ 27 = 20 + \ 7 \\ \hline 20 + \ 5 \end{array}$$ We can now subtract as before.

or   25

In practice, we will use a more convenient short form for the subtraction.

$$\begin{array}{r} 52 \\ -\ 27 \\ \hline \end{array}$$ $$\begin{array}{r} 4\,1 \\ \not5 2 \\ -\ 27 \\ \hline 25 \end{array}$$ We indicate the fact that we have borrowed 1 ten by putting a slash through the 5 and then writing 4 tens. Add 10 ones to the original 2 ones to get 12 ones. We can then subtract.

Check: 25 + 27 = 52

✔ CHECK YOURSELF 5_____

Subtract, and check your work.

$$\begin{array}{r} 64 \\ -\ 38 \\ \hline \end{array}$$

Let's work through another subtraction example that will require a number of borrowing steps. Here, zero appears as a digit in the minuend.

Example 6

Subtracting When Borrowing Is Needed

Step 1

$$\begin{array}{r} {}^{4}\,\, \\ 405\overset{1}{3} \\ -\ 2365 \\ \hline 8 \end{array}$$

In this first step we borrow 1 ten. This is written as 10 ones and combined with the original 3 ones. We can then subtract in the ones column.

NOTE Here we borrow 1 thousand; this is written as 10 hundreds.

Step 2

$$\begin{array}{r} {}^{3}\,{}_{10}{}^{4}\, \\ 40\overset{1}{5}3 \\ -\ 2365 \\ \hline 8 \end{array}$$

We must borrow again to subtract in the tens column. There are no hundreds, and so we move to the thousands column.

NOTE We now borrow 1 hundred; this is written as 10 tens and combined with the remaining 4 tens.

Step 3

$$\begin{array}{r} 3\,9\,{}^{14}\, \\ 4\emptyset53 \\ -\ 2365 \\ \hline 8 \end{array}$$

The minuend is now renamed as 3 thousands, 9 hundreds, 14 tens, and 13 ones.

Step 4

$$\begin{array}{r} 9\,14 \\ 3\,10\,4\,1 \\ 4\emptyset53 \\ -\ 2365 \\ \hline 1688 \end{array}$$

The subtraction can now be completed.

To check our subtraction: 1688 + 2365 = 4053

✔ CHECK YOURSELF 6_____

Subtract, and check your work.

$$\begin{array}{r} 5024 \\ -\ 1656 \\ \hline \end{array}$$

You will need to use both addition and subtraction to solve some problems, as Example 7 illustrates.

Example 7

Solving a Subtraction Application

Bernard wants to buy a new piece of stereo equipment. He has $142 and can trade in his old amplifier for $135. How much more does he need if the new equipment costs $449?

First we must add to find out how much money Bernard has available. Then we subtract to find out how much more money he needs.

$142 + $135 = $277   The money available to Bernard

$449 − $277 = $172   The money Bernard still needs

CHECK YOURSELF 7

Martina spent $239 in airfare, $174 for lodging, and $108 for food on a business trip. Her company allowed her $375 for the expenses. How much of these expenses will she have to pay herself?

CHECK YOURSELF ANSWERS

1. $13 − 9 = 4$ **2.** 1220 **3. (a)** 13; **(b)** 15 **4.** $32
    Check: $4 + 9 = 13$

5. $\overset{5\,{}_1}{\cancel{6}}4$ To check:
     $\underline{-\ 38}$ $26 + 38 = 64$
       26

6. 3368 Check: $3368 + 1656 = 5024$

7. $239 521 ⟵ Total expenses
      174 $\underline{-\ 375}$ ⟵ Amount allowed
   $\underline{+\ 108}$ 146
     521 ⟵ Total expenses

0.2 **Exercises**

1. In the statement $9 - 6 = 3$
   9 is called the
   6 is called the
   3 is called the
   Write the related addition statement.

2. In the statement $7 - 5 = 2$
   5 is called the
   2 is called the
   7 is called the
   Write the related addition statement.

In exercises 3 to 26, do the indicated subtraction, and check your results by addition.

3.
$$\begin{array}{r} 347 \\ -\ 201 \\ \hline \end{array}$$

4.
$$\begin{array}{r} 575 \\ -\ 302 \\ \hline \end{array}$$

5.
$$\begin{array}{r} 689 \\ -\ 245 \\ \hline \end{array}$$

6.
$$\begin{array}{r} 598 \\ -\ 278 \\ \hline \end{array}$$

7.
$$\begin{array}{r} 3446 \\ -\ 2326 \\ \hline \end{array}$$

8.
$$\begin{array}{r} 5896 \\ -\ 3862 \\ \hline \end{array}$$

9.
$$\begin{array}{r} 64 \\ -\ 27 \\ \hline \end{array}$$

10.
$$\begin{array}{r} 73 \\ -\ 36 \\ \hline \end{array}$$

11.
$$\begin{array}{r} 627 \\ -\ 358 \\ \hline \end{array}$$

12.
$$\begin{array}{r} 642 \\ -\ 367 \\ \hline \end{array}$$

13.
$$\begin{array}{r} 6423 \\ -\ 3678 \\ \hline \end{array}$$

14.
$$\begin{array}{r} 5352 \\ -\ 2577 \\ \hline \end{array}$$

15.
$$\begin{array}{r} 6034 \\ -\ 2569 \\ \hline \end{array}$$

16.
$$\begin{array}{r} 5206 \\ -\ 1748 \\ \hline \end{array}$$

17.
$$\begin{array}{r} 4000 \\ -\ 2345 \\ \hline \end{array}$$

18.
$$\begin{array}{r} 6000 \\ -\ 4349 \\ \hline \end{array}$$

19.
$$\begin{array}{r} 33,486 \\ -\ 14,047 \\ \hline \end{array}$$

20.
$$\begin{array}{r} 53,487 \\ -\ 25,649 \\ \hline \end{array}$$

21.
$$\begin{array}{r} 29,400 \\ -\ 17,900 \\ \hline \end{array}$$

22.
$$\begin{array}{r} 53,500 \\ -\ 28,700 \\ \hline \end{array}$$

23.
$$\begin{array}{r} 59,000 \\ -\ 23,458 \\ \hline \end{array}$$

24.
$$\begin{array}{r} 41,000 \\ -\ 27,645 \\ \hline \end{array}$$

25.
$$\begin{array}{r} 3537 \\ -\ 2675 \\ \hline \end{array}$$

26.
$$\begin{array}{r} 4693 \\ -\ 2736 \\ \hline \end{array}$$

27. Find the number that is 25 less than 76.

28. Find the number that results when 58 is decreased by 23.

29. Find the number that is the difference between 97 and 43.

30. Find the number that is 125 less than 265.

31. Find the number that results when 298 is decreased by 47.

32. Find the number that is the difference between 167 and 57.

ANSWERS

1. _____

2. _____

3. _____

4. _____

5. _____

6. _____

7. _____

8. _____

9. _____

10. _____

11. _____

12. _____

13. _____

14.	15.
16.	17.
18.	19.
20.	21.
22.	23.
24.	25.
26.	27.
28.	29.
30.	31.

32. _____

33. _____

34. _____

35. _____

36. _____

37. _____

38. _____

39. _____

40. _____

41. _____

42. _____

43. _____

44. _____

45. _____

46. _____

47. _____

Based on units, determine if the following operations produce a meaningful result.

33. 8 miles − 4 miles

34. $560 + $314

35. 7 feet + 11 inches

36. 18°F − 6°C

37. 17 yards − 10 yards

38. 4 mi/hr + 6 ft/sec

In exercises 39 to 42, for various treks by a hiker in a mountainous region, the starting elevations and various changes are given. Determine the final elevation of the hiker in each case.

39. Starting elevation 1053 feet, increase of 123 feet, decrease of 98 feet, increase of 63 feet.

40. Starting elevation 1231 feet, increase of 213 feet, decrease of 112 feet, increase of 78 feet.

41. Starting elevation 7302 feet, decrease of 623 feet, decrease of 123 feet, increase of 307 feet.

42. Starting elevation 6907 feet, decrease of 511 feet, decrease of 203 feet, increase of 419 feet.

Solve the following applications.

43. Test scores. Shaka's score on a math test was 87 and Tony's score was 23 points less than Shaka's. What was Tony's score on the test?

44. New pay. Duardo's monthly pay of $879 was decreased by $175 for withholding. What amount of pay did he receive?

45. Number problem. The difference between two numbers is 134. If the larger number is 655, what is the smaller number?

46. Family budget. In Jason's monthly budget, he set aside $375 for housing, and $165 less than that for food. How much did he budget for food?

47. Consumer purchases. Inez has $228 in cash and wants to buy a television set that costs $449. How much more money does she need?

48. **Construction.** The Sears Tower in Chicago is 1454 feet (ft) tall. The Empire State Building is 1250 ft tall. How much taller is the Sears Tower than the Empire State Building?

49. **Education.** A college's enrollment was 2479 students in the fall of 1999 and 2653 students in the fall of 2000. What was the increase in enrollment?

50. **Net pay.** In one week, Margaret earned $278 in regular pay and $53 for overtime work, and $49 was deducted from her paycheck for income taxes and $18 for social security. What was her take-home pay?

51. **Savings.** Rafael opened a checking account and made deposits of $85 and $272. He wrote checks during the month for $35, $27, $89, and $178. What was his balance at the end of the month?

52. **Dieting.** Dalila is trying to limit herself to 1500 calories per day (cal/day). Her breakfast was 270 cal, her lunch was 450 cal, and her dinner was 820 cal. By how much was she *under* or *over* her diet?

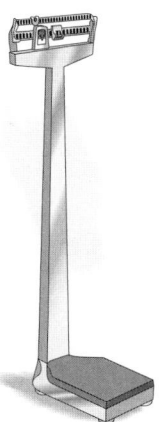

53. **Recreation.** A professional basketball team scored 98, 136, and 113 points in three games. If its opponents scored 102, 109, and 93 points, by how much did the team outscore its opponents?

54. **Checking account balance.** To keep track of a checking account, you must subtract the amount of each check from the current balance. Complete the following statement.

Beginning balance	$351
Check #1	29
Balance	
Check #2	139
Balance	
Check #3	75
Ending balance	

48. _____
49. _____
50. _____
51. _____
52. _____
53. _____
54. _____

55. **Expense accounts.** Complete the following record of a monthly expense account.

Monthly income	$1620
House payment	343
Balance	
Car payment	183
Balance	
Food	312
Balance	
Clothing	89
Amount remaining	

56. **Education.** A course outline states that you must have 540 points on five tests during the term to receive an A for the course. Your scores on the first four tests have been 95, 84, 82, and 89. How many points must you score on the 200-point final to receive an A?

57. **Travel.** Carmen's frequent-flyer program requires 30,000 miles (mi) for a free flight. During 1999 she accumulated 13,850 mi. In 2000 she took three more flights of 2800, 1475, and 4280 mi. How much further must she fly for her free trip?

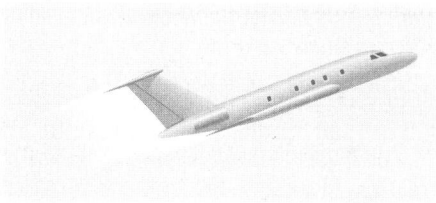

58. **Budget.** Peter, Paul, and Mary all submitted advertising budgets for a student government dance.

Ad Medium	Peter	Paul	Mary
Radio ads	$500	$600	$300
Newspaper ads	$150	$200	$150
Posters	$225	$250	$275
Hand bills	$175	$150	$250

If $900 is available for advertising, how much over budget would each student be?

59. **Farming.** The value of all crops in the Salinas Valley in 1998 was about $2 billion. The top four crops are listed below. (a) How much greater is the combined value of both types of lettuce than broccoli? (b) How much greater is the value of the lettuce and broccoli combined than the strawberries?

Crop	Crop value, in millions
Head lettuce	$360
Broccoli	$246
Leaf lettuce	$210
Strawberries	$198

Complete the magic squares.

60.

	7	2
	5	
8		

61.

4	3	
	5	
		6

62.

16	3		13
	10	11	
9	6	7	
			1

63.

7			14
2	13	8	11
16			
	6	15	

64. Efrain has lost track of his checking account transactions. He knows he started with $50 and has deposited $120, $85, and $120. He also knows he has withdrawn $200 and $55. He just can't remember the order in which he did all this.

(a) What is Efrain's balance after all these transactions?

(b) Does the order of the transactions make any difference from the math point of view?

(c) Does the order of transactions make any difference from the banking point of view?

Explain your answers.

65. Using the World Wide Web, determine the population of Arizona, California, Oregon, and Pennsylvania in each of the last three censuses.

(a) Find the total change in each state's population over this period.

(b) Which state shows the most change over the past three censuses?

(c) Write a brief essay describing the changes and any trends you see in this data. List any implications that they might have for future planning.

66. Describe in words each of the following equations. (Make sure you use a complete sentence.) Then exchange your sentence with other students and see if their interpretations result in the same equation you used.

(a) $69 - 23 = 46$ (b) $17 + 13 = 30$

67. Evaluate the following two expressions:

(1) $8 - (4 - 2)$ (2) $(8 - 4) - 2$

Do you obtain the same answer? What conclusion can you draw about subtraction and an associative property?

68.
_____

68. Think of any whole number.

Add 5.
Subtract 3.
Subtract two less than the original number.
What number do you end up with?
Check with other people. Does everyone have the same answer? Can you explain the results?

Answers

1. 9 is the minuend, 6 is the subtrahend, and 3 is the difference. $3 + 6 = 9$ **3.** 146
5. 444   **7.** 1120   **9.** 37   **11.** 269   **13.** 2745   **15.** 3465
17. 1655   **19.** 19,439   **21.** 11,500   **23.** 35,542   **25.** 862   **27.** 51
29. 54   **31.** 251   **33.** Yes   **35.** No   **37.** Yes   **39.** 1141 ft
41. 6863 ft   **43.** 64   **45.** 521   **47.** \$221   **49.** 174 students
51. \$28   **53.** 43 points   **55.** See exercise   **57.** 7595 mi
59. **(a)** \$324,000,000; **(b)** \$618,000,000

61.

4	3	8
9	5	1
2	7	6

63.

7	12	1	14
2	13	8	11
16	3	10	5
9	6	15	4

65.

67.

0.3 Multiplication

0.3 OBJECTIVES

1. Use the language of multiplication
2. Multiply whole numbers
3. Estimate products
4. Identify the properties of multiplication

Our work in this section deals with multiplication, another of the basic operations of arithmetic. Multiplication is closely related to addition. In fact, we can think of multiplication as a shorthand method for repeated addition. The symbol $\times$ is used to indicate multiplication.

3×4 can be interpreted as 3 rows of 4 objects. By counting we see that $3 \times 4 = 12$. Similarly, 4 rows of 3 means $4 \times 3 = 12$.

NOTE The use of the symbol $\times$ dates back to the 1600s.

The fact that $3 \times 4 = 4 \times 3$ is an example of the **commutative property of multiplication,** which is given below.

> **Rules and Properties:** The Commutative Property of Multiplication
>
> Given any two numbers, we can multiply them in either order and we get the same result.
>
> In symbols, we say $a \cdot b = b \cdot a$

NOTE The centered dot is the same as the times sign ($\times$). We use the centered dot when we are using letters to represent numbers, as we've done with *a* and *b* here. We do that so the times sign will not be confused with the letter *x*.

Example 1

Multiplying Single-Digit Numbers

3×5 means 5 multiplied by 3. It is read 3 *times* 5. To find 3×5, we can add 5 three times.

$$3 \times 5 = 5 + 5 + 5 = 15$$

In a multiplication problem such as $3 \times 5 = 15$, we call 3 and 5 the **factors.** The answer, 15, is the **product** of the factors, 3 and 5.

$$3 \times 5 = 15$$

Factor   Factor   Product

 CHECK YOURSELF 1

Name the factors and the product in the following statement.

$2 \times 9 = 18$

Statements such as $3 \times 4 = 12$ and $3 \times 5 = 15$ are called the **basic multiplication facts.** If you have difficulty with multiplication, it may be that you do not know some of these facts. The following table will help you review before you go on. Notice that, because of the commutative property, you need memorize only half of these facts!

Basic Multiplication Facts Table

×	0	1	2	3	4	5	6	7	8	9
0	0	0	0	0	0	0	0	0	0	0
1	0	1	2	3	4	5	6	7	8	9
2	0	2	4	6	8	10	12	14	16	18
3	0	3	6	9	12	15	18	21	24	27
4	0	4	8	12	16	20	24	28	32	36
5	0	5	10	15	20	25	30	35	40	45
6	0	6	12	18	24	30	36	42	48	54
7	0	7	14	21	28	35	42	49	56	63
8	0	8	16	24	32	40	48	56	64	72
9	0	9	18	27	36	45	54	63	72	81

Armed with these facts, you can become a better, and faster, problem solver. Take a look at the following example.

Example 2

Multiplying Instead of Counting

Find the total number of squares on the following checkerboard.

You could find the number of squares by counting them. If you counted one per second, it would take you just over a minute. You could make the job a little easier by simply counting the squares in one row (8), then adding $8 + 8 + 8 + 8 + 8 + 8 + 8 + 8$. Multiplication, which is simply repeated addition, allows you to find the total number of squares by multiplying 8×8. How long that takes depends on how well you know the basic multiplication facts! By now, you know that there are 64 squares on the checkerboard.

 CHECK YOURSELF 2

Find the number of windows on the displayed side of the building.

The next property involves *both* multiplication and addition.

Example 3

Using the Distributive Property

$$2 \times (3 + 4) = 2 \times 7 = 14$$ We have added 3 + 4 and then multiplied.

Also,

$$2 \times (3 + 4) = (2 \times 3) + (2 \times 4)$$ We have multiplied 2 × 3 and 2 × 4 as the first step.

$$= 6 + 8$$

$$= 14$$ The result is the same.

We see that $2 \times (3 + 4) = (2 \times 3) + (2 \times 4)$. This is an example of the **distributive property of multiplication over addition** because we distributed the multiplication (in this case by 2) over the "plus" sign.

Rules and Properties: The Distributive Property of Multiplication over Addition

To multiply a factor by a sum of numbers, multiply the factor by each number inside the parentheses. Then add the products. (The result will be the same if we find the sum then multiply.)

CHECK YOURSELF 3

Show that

$$3 \times (5 + 2) = (3 \times 5) + (3 \times 2)$$

Carrying must often be used to multiply larger numbers. Let's see how carrying works in multiplication by looking at an example in the expanded form.

Example 4

Multiplying by a Single-Digit Number

$$3 \times 25 = 3 \times (20 + 5)$$ We use the distributive property again.

$$= 3 \times 20 + 3 \times 5$$

$$= 60 \quad\quad + 15$$ Write the 15 as 10 + 5.

$$= 60 + 10 + 5$$ Carry 10 ones or 1 ten to the tens place.

$$= 70 + 5$$

$$= 75$$

Here is the same multiplication problem using the short form.

1 ←——— Carry

Step 1   25
           $\times$ 3
           ———
              5

Multiplying 3 $\times$ 5 gives us 15 ones. Write 5 ones and carry 1 ten.

1

Step 2   25
           $\times$ 3
           ———
             75

Now multiply 3 $\times$ 2 tens and add the carry to get 7, the tens digit of the product.

 CHECK YOURSELF 4

Multiply.

     34
$\times$ 6

Units Analysis

When multiplying a denominate number, like 6 feet, by an abstract number, like 5, the result has the same units as the denominate number. Some examples are

5 × 6 ft = 30 ft
3 × $7 = $21
9 × 4 A's = 36 A's

When multiplying two different denominate numbers, the units must also be multiplied. We will discuss this when we look at the area of a geometric figure.

NOTE Remember that it is best to write down the complete statement necessary for the solution of any application.

Let's review our discussion of applications, or word problems.

As you will see, the process of solving applications is the same no matter which operation is required for the solution. In fact, the four-step procedure we suggested in Section 1.2 can be effectively applied here.

Step by Step: Solving Applications

Step 1   Read the problem carefully to determine the given information and what you are asked to find.
Step 2   Decide upon the operation or operations to be used.
Step 3   Write down the complete statement necessary to solve the problem, and do the calculations.
Step 4   Check to make sure you have answered the question of the problem and that your answer seems reasonable.

Example 5

Solving an Application Involving Multiplication

A car rental agency orders a fleet of 7 new subcompact cars at a cost of $9258 per automobile. What will the company pay for the entire order?

Step 1 We know the number of cars and the price per car. We want to find the total cost.

Step 2 Multiplication is the best approach to the solution.

Step 3 Write

$7 \times \$9258 = \$64,806$ We could, of course, *add* $9258, the cost, 7 times, but multiplication is certainly more efficient.

Step 4 The total cost of the order is $64,806.

 CHECK YOURSELF 5

Tires sell for $47 apiece. What is the total cost for five tires?

To multiply by numbers with more than one digit, we must multiply each digit of the first factor by each digit of the second. To do this, we form a series of partial products and then add them to arrive at the final product.

Example 6

Multiplying by a Two-Digit Number

Multiply 56×47.

Step 1
$$\begin{array}{r} 4 \\ 56 \\ \times\ 47 \\ \hline 392 \end{array}$$
The first partial product is 7×56, or 392. Note that we had to carry 4 to the tens column.

Step 2
$$\begin{array}{r} 2 \\ \cancel{4} \\ 56 \\ \times\ 47 \\ \hline 392 \\ 2240 \end{array}$$
The second partial product is 40×56, or 2240. We must carry 2 during the process.

Step 3
$$\begin{array}{r} 2 \\ \cancel{4} \\ 56 \\ \times\ 47 \\ \hline 392 \\ 2240 \\ \hline 2632 \end{array}$$
We add the partial products for our final result.

CHECK YOURSELF 6

Multiply.

$$
\begin{array}{r}
38 \\
\times\ 76 \\
\end{array}
$$

NOTE The three partial products are formed when we multiply by the ones, tens, and then the hundreds digits.

If multiplication involves two three-digit numbers, another step is necessary. In this case we form three partial products. This will ensure that each digit of the first factor is multiplied by each digit of the second.

Example 7

Multiplying Two Three-Digit Numbers

Multiply.

$$
\begin{array}{r}
\scriptstyle 2\,2 \\
\scriptstyle 3\,3 \\
\scriptstyle 2\,2 \\
278 \\
\times\ 343 \\
\hline
834 \\
11120 \\
834\,00 \\
\hline
95,354 \\
\end{array}
$$

In forming the third partial product, we must multiply by 300. To indicate this, we shift that product *two* places left.

 CHECK YOURSELF 7

Multiply.

$$
\begin{array}{r}
352 \\
\times\ 249 \\
\end{array}
$$

Let's look at an example of multiplying by a number involving 0 as a digit. There are several ways to arrange the work, as our example shows.

Example 8

Multiplying Larger Numbers

Multiply 573×205.

Method 1

$$
\begin{array}{r}
\scriptstyle 1 \\
\scriptstyle 3\,1 \\
573 \\
\times\ 205 \\
\hline
2865 \\
0000 \\
114600 \\
\hline
117,465 \\
\end{array}
$$

We can write the second partial product as 0000 to indicate the multiplication by 0 in the tens place.

Let's look at a second approach to the problem.

Method 2

```
    1
   3 1
   573
 × 205
  2865
114600  ←
117,465
```

We can write a double 0 as our second step. If we place the third partial product on the same line, that product will be shifted *two* places left, indicating that we are multiplying by 200.

Because this second method is more compact, it is usually used.

 CHECK YOURSELF 8

Multiply.

```
   489
 × 304
```

The next example will lead us to another property of multiplication.

Example 9

Using the Associative Property

$(2 \times 3) \times 4 = 6 \times 4 = 24$

We do the multiplication in the parentheses first, $2 \times 3 = 6$. Then multiply 6×4.

Also,

$2 \times (3 \times 4) = 2 \times 12 = 24$

Here we multiply 3×4 as the first step. Then multiply 2×12.

We see that

$(2 \times 3) \times 4 = 2 \times (3 \times 4)$

The product is the same no matter which way we *group* the factors. This is called the **associative property** of multiplication.

> **Rules and Properties:** The Associative Property of Multiplication
>
> Multiplication is an *associative* operation. The way in which you group numbers in multiplication does not affect the final product.

 CHECK YOURSELF 9

Find the products.

(a) $(5 \times 3) \times 6$ **(b)** $5 \times (3 \times 6)$

There are some shortcuts that will let you simplify your work when you are multiplying by a number that ends in 0. Let's see what we can discover by looking at some examples.

Example 10

Multiplying by Ten

First we'll multiply by 10.

$$\begin{array}{r} 67 \\ \times\ 10 \\ \hline 670 \end{array}$$ $10 \times 67 = 670$

Next we'll multiply by 100.

$$\begin{array}{r} 537 \\ \times\ 100 \\ \hline 53{,}700 \end{array}$$ $100 \times 537 = 53{,}700$

Finally, we'll multiply by 1000.

$$\begin{array}{r} 489 \\ \times\ 1000 \\ \hline 489{,}000 \end{array}$$ $1000 \times 489 = 489{,}000$

 CHECK YOURSELF 10

Multiply.

$$\begin{array}{r} 257 \\ \times\ 100 \end{array}$$

Do you see a pattern? Rather than writing out the multiplication, there is an easier way! We call the numbers 10, 100, 1000, and so on, **powers of 10.**

Rules and Properties: Multiplying by Powers of 10

When a whole number is multiplied by a power of 10, the product is just that number followed by as many zeros as there are in the power of 10.

Example 11

Multiplying by Numbers That End in Zero

Multiply 400×678.

Write

$$\begin{array}{r} 678 \\ \times\quad 400 \end{array}$$ Shift 400 so that the two zeros are *to the right* of the digits above.

$$
\begin{array}{r}
33 \\
678 \\
\times \quad 400 \\
\hline
271{,}200
\end{array}
$$

Bring down the two zeros, then multiply 4×678 to find the product.

There is no mystery about why this works. We know that 400 is 4×100. In this method, we are multiplying 678 by 4 and then by 100, adding two zeros to the product by our earlier rule.

 CHECK YOURSELF 11

Multiply.

300×574

Your work in this section, together with our earlier rounding techniques, provides a convenient means of using estimation to check the reasonableness of our results in multiplication, as Example 12 illustrates.

Example 12

Estimating a Product by Rounding

Estimate the product below by rounding each factor to the nearest hundred.

$$
\begin{array}{rcr}
 & & \text{Rounded} \\
512 & \longrightarrow & 500 \\
\times\, 289 & \longrightarrow & \times\, 300 \\
\hline
 & & 150{,}000
\end{array}
$$

You might want to now find the *actual* product and use our estimate to see if your result seems reasonable.

 CHECK YOURSELF 12

Estimate the product by rounding each factor to the nearest hundred.

$$
\begin{array}{r}
689 \\
\times\, 425 \\
\hline
\end{array}
$$

Rounding the factors can be a very useful way of estimating the solution to an application problem.

Example 13

Estimating the Solution to a Multiplication Application

Bart is thinking of running an ad in the local newspaper for an entire year. The ad costs $19.95 per week. Approximate the annual cost of the ad.

Rounding the charge to $20 and rounding the number of weeks in a year to 50, we get

$50 \times 20 = 1000$

The ad would cost approximately $1000.

✔ CHECK YOURSELF 13

Phyllis is debating whether to join the health club for $450 per year or just pay $7 per visit. If she goes about once a week, approximately how much would she spend at $7 per visit?

CHECK YOURSELF ANSWERS

1. Factors 2, 9; product 18   **2.** 24   **3.** $3 \times 7 = 21$ and $15 + 6 = 21$
4. 204   **5.** $235   **6.** 2888   **7.** 87,648   **8.** 148,656   **9.** **(a)** 90; **(b)** 90
10. 25,700   **11.** 172,200   **12.** 280,000   **13.** $350

0.3 Exercises

1. Find 3×7 and 7×3 by repeated addition.

2. Find 4×5 and 5×4 by repeated addition.

3. If $6 \times 7 = 42$, we call 6 and 7 _____ of 42. And 42 is the _____ of 6 and 7.

4. If $5 \times 8 = 40$, we call 5 and 8 _____ of 40. And 40 is the _____ of 5 and 8.

5. Find the number of one foot square tiles in a floor that is 9 ft long and 12 ft wide.

6. Find the number of squares in a quilt that has four squares in each of four rows.

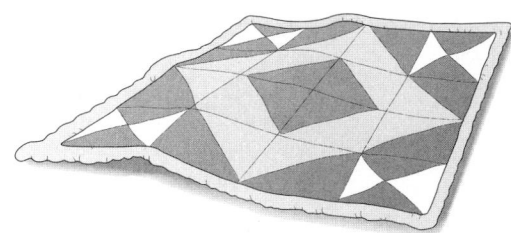

Multiply the following.

7. 8×3 yd

8. $9 \times \$15$

9. $6 \times 4°C$

10. 8×11 mi

Label the following as true or false.

11. 4×6 mi $= 24$

12. 3×52 sec $= 156$ sec

13. 8×22 hours $= 176$ hours

14. 9×15 days $= 135$

Name _____

Section _____ Date _____

ANSWERS

1. _____

2. _____

3. _____

4. _____

5. _____

6. _____

7. _____

8. _____

9. _____

10. _____

11. _____

12. _____

13. _____

14. _____

15. _____	16. _____
17. _____	18. _____
19. _____	20. _____
21. _____	22. _____
23. _____	24. _____
25. _____	26. _____
27. _____	28. _____
29. _____	30. _____
31. _____	32. _____
33. _____	34. _____
35. _____	36. _____
37. _____	38. _____
39. _____	40. _____
41. _____	42. _____
43. _____	
44. _____	
45. _____	
46. _____	
47. _____	
48. _____	
49. _____	
50. _____	
51. _____	
52. _____	
53. _____	
54. _____	
55. _____	
56. _____	

Multiply.

15. $\begin{array}{r} 5 \\ \times 3 \\ \hline \end{array}$

16. $\begin{array}{r} 7 \\ \times 4 \\ \hline \end{array}$

17. $\begin{array}{r} 8 \\ \times 1 \\ \hline \end{array}$

18. $\begin{array}{r} 9 \\ \times 5 \\ \hline \end{array}$

19. $\begin{array}{r} 6 \\ \times 0 \\ \hline \end{array}$

20. $\begin{array}{r} 6 \\ \times 6 \\ \hline \end{array}$

21. $\begin{array}{r} 2 \\ \times 9 \\ \hline \end{array}$

22. $\begin{array}{r} 1 \\ \times 7 \\ \hline \end{array}$

23. $\begin{array}{r} 23 \\ \times \ 2 \\ \hline \end{array}$

24. $\begin{array}{r} 32 \\ \times \ 3 \\ \hline \end{array}$

25. $\begin{array}{r} 48 \\ \times \ 4 \\ \hline \end{array}$

26. $\begin{array}{r} 53 \\ \times \ 5 \\ \hline \end{array}$

27. $\begin{array}{r} 508 \\ \times \ 6 \\ \hline \end{array}$

28. $\begin{array}{r} 903 \\ \times \ 9 \\ \hline \end{array}$

29. $\begin{array}{r} 523 \\ \times \ 8 \\ \hline \end{array}$

30. $\begin{array}{r} 635 \\ \times \ 7 \\ \hline \end{array}$

31. $\begin{array}{r} 2035 \\ \times \ 9 \\ \hline \end{array}$

32. $\begin{array}{r} 98 \\ \times 57 \\ \hline \end{array}$

33. $\begin{array}{r} 75 \\ \times 68 \\ \hline \end{array}$

34. $\begin{array}{r} 235 \\ \times 49 \\ \hline \end{array}$

35. $\begin{array}{r} 327 \\ \times 59 \\ \hline \end{array}$

36. $\begin{array}{r} 2364 \\ \times \ 67 \\ \hline \end{array}$

37. $\begin{array}{r} 4075 \\ \times \ 84 \\ \hline \end{array}$

38. $\begin{array}{r} 315 \\ \times 243 \\ \hline \end{array}$

39. $\begin{array}{r} 124 \\ \times 225 \\ \hline \end{array}$

40. $\begin{array}{r} 345 \\ \times 267 \\ \hline \end{array}$

41. $\begin{array}{r} 639 \\ \times 358 \\ \hline \end{array}$

42. $\begin{array}{r} 547 \\ \times 203 \\ \hline \end{array}$

43. $\begin{array}{r} 668 \\ \times 305 \\ \hline \end{array}$

44. $\begin{array}{r} 2458 \\ \times \ 135 \\ \hline \end{array}$

45. $\begin{array}{r} 3219 \\ \times \ 207 \\ \hline \end{array}$

46. $\begin{array}{r} 1208 \\ \times \ 305 \\ \hline \end{array}$

47. $\begin{array}{r} 2407 \\ \times \ 521 \\ \hline \end{array}$

48. $\begin{array}{r} 2534 \\ \times 3106 \\ \hline \end{array}$

49. $\begin{array}{r} 3158 \\ \times 2034 \\ \hline \end{array}$

50. $\begin{array}{r} 43 \\ \times 70 \\ \hline \end{array}$

51. $\begin{array}{r} 58 \\ \times 40 \\ \hline \end{array}$

52. $\begin{array}{r} 562 \\ \times 400 \\ \hline \end{array}$

53. $\begin{array}{r} 907 \\ \times 900 \\ \hline \end{array}$

54. $\begin{array}{r} 345 \\ \times 230 \\ \hline \end{array}$

55. $\begin{array}{r} 362 \\ \times 310 \\ \hline \end{array}$

56. $\begin{array}{r} 157 \\ \times 3200 \\ \hline \end{array}$

57. Find the product of 304 and 7.

58. Find the product of 409 and 4.

59. Find the product of 8 and 5679.

60. Find the product of 23,452 and 5.

61. What is the product of 21 and 551?

62. What is the product of 112 and 168?

63. What is the product of 135 and 507?

64. Find the product of 2409 and 68.

Name the property of addition and/or multiplication that is illustrated.

65. $5 \times 8 = 8 \times 5$

66. $3 \times (2 \times 5) = 3 \times (5 \times 2)$

67. $3 \times (4 + 9) = (3 \times 4) + (3 \times 9)$

68. $7 \times 6 = 6 \times 7$

69. $2 \times (3 \times 5) = (2 \times 3) \times 5$

70. $3 \times (2 + 8) = (3 \times 2) + (3 \times 8)$

71. $5 \times (6 + 2) = 5 \times (2 + 6)$

72. $2 \times (5 \times 7) = (2 \times 5) \times 7$

In exercises 73 to 75, complete the statement using the given property.

73. $7 + (3 \times 8) =$ \qquad Commutative property of multiplication

74. $9 \times (8 \times 5) =$ \qquad Associative property of multiplication

75. $3 \times (2 + 7) =$ \qquad Distributive property

Solve the following applications.

76. Number of seats. A small seminar room contains 12 rows of seats. Each row contains 7 seats. How many seats are in the room?

77. Transportation. A convoy company can transport 8 new cars on one of its trucks. If 34 truck shipments were made in one week, how many cars were shipped?

78. Printing. A computer printer can print 40 mailing labels per minute. How many labels can be printed in 1 hour (h)?

79. Parking. A rectangular parking lot has 14 rows of parking spaces and each row contains 24 spaces. How many cars can be parked in the lot?

57. _____
58. _____
59. _____
60. _____
61. _____
62. _____
63. _____
64. _____
65. _____
66. _____
67. _____
68. _____
69. _____
70. _____
71. _____
72. _____
73. _____
74. _____
75. _____
76. _____
77. _____
78. _____
79. _____

Answers

1. 21   **3.** Factors, product   **5.** 108 tiles   **7.** 24 yd   **9.** 24°C
11. False   **13.** True   **15.** 15   **17.** 8   **19.** 0   **21.** 18   **23.** 46
25. 192   **27.** 3048   **29.** 4184   **31.** 18,315   **33.** 5100   **35.** 19,293
37. 342,300   **39.** 27,900   **41.** 228,762   **43.** 203,740   **45.** 666,333
47. 1,254,047   **49.** 6,423,372   **51.** 2320   **53.** 816,300   **55.** 112,220
57. 2128   **59.** 45,432   **61.** 11,571   **63.** 68,445   **65.** Commutative
property of multiplication   **67.** Distributive property of multiplication over addition
69. Associative property of multiplication   **71.** Commutative property of addition
73. 7 + (8 × 3)   **75.** (3 × 2) + (3 × 7)   **77.** 272 cars   **79.** 336 cars

Division

0.4 OBJECTIVES

1. Use the language of division
2. Write a division problem as repeated subtraction
3. Divide whole numbers

We will now examine a fourth arithmetic operation, division. Just as multiplication was repeated addition, division is repeated subtraction. Division asks *how many times* one number is contained in another.

Example 1

Dividing by Using Subtraction

Joel needs to set up 48 chairs in the student union for a concert. If there is room for 8 chairs per row, how many rows will it take to set up all 48 chairs?

This problem can be solved by subtraction. Each row subtracts another 8 chairs.

48	40	32	24	16	8
-8	-8	-8	-8	-8	-8
40	32	24	16	8	0

Because 8 can be subtracted from 48 six times, there will be 6 rows.

This can also be seen as a division problem

$$48 \div 8 = 6 \quad \text{or} \quad 8\overline{)48}^{\,6} \quad \text{or} \quad \frac{48}{8} = 6$$

No matter which method we use, we call the 48 the **dividend,** the 8 the **divisor,** and the 6 the **quotient.**

 CHECK YOURSELF 1

Carlotta is creating a garden path made of bricks. She has 72 bricks. Each row will have 6 bricks in it. How many rows can she make?

Units Analysis

When dividing a denominate number by an abstract number, the result will get the units of the denominate number. Here are a couple of examples

76 trombones $\div$ 4 = 19 trombones

$55 $\div$ 11 = $5

When one denominate number is divided by another, the result will get the units of the dividend over the units of the divisor.

144 miles $\div$ 6 gallons = 24 miles/gallon (which we read as "miles per gallon")

$120 $\div$ 8 hours = 15 dollars/hour ("dollars per hour")

To solve a problem that requires division, you must first set up the problem as a division statement. The next example will illustrate this.

Example 2

Writing a Division Statement

Write a division statement that corresponds to the following situation. You need not do the division.

The staff at the Wok Inn Restaurant splits all tips at the end of each shift. Yesterday's evening shift collected a total of $224. How much should each of the seven employees get in tips?

$224 $\div$ 7 employees   (note that the units for the answer will be "dollars per employee")

 CHECK YOURSELF 2

Write a division statement that corresponds to the following situation. You need not do the division.

All nine sections of basic math skills at SCC (Sum Community College) are full. There are a total of 315 students in the classes. How many students are in each class? What are the units for the answer?

In the previous section, we used a rectangular array of stars to represent multiplication. These same arrays can represent division. Just as 3 $\times$ 4 = 12 and 4 $\times$ 3 = 12, so is it true that 12 $\div$ 3 = 4 and 12 $\div$ 4 = 3.

or
12 ÷ 3 = 4

or
12 ÷ 4 = 3

This relationship allows us to check our division results by doing multiplication.

Example 3

Checking Division by Using Multiplication

NOTE For a division problem to check, the *product* of the divisor and the quotient *must equal the dividend.*

(a) $7)\overline{21}$ Check: $7 \times 3 = 21$

(b) $48 \div 6 = 8$ Check: $6 \times 8 = 48$

CHECK YOURSELF 3

Complete the division statements, and check your results.

(a) $9)\overline{45}$ (b) $28 \div 7 =$

NOTE Because $36 \div 9 = 4$, we say that 36 is *exactly divisible* by 9.

In our examples so far, the product of the divisor and the quotient has been equal to the dividend. This means that the dividend is *exactly divisible* by the divisor. That is not always the case. Let's look at another example using repeated subtraction.

Example 4

Dividing by Using Subtraction, Leaving a Remainder

How many times is 5 contained in 23?

NOTE Notice that the remainder must be smaller than the divisor or we could subtract again.

23	18	13	8	We see that 5 is contained 4
− 5	− 5	− 5	− 5	times in 23, but 3 is "left over."
18	13	8	3	

23 is not exactly divisible by 5. The "left over" 3 is called the **remainder** in the division. To check the division operation when a remainder is involved, we have the following rule:

Definitions: Remainder

Dividend = divisor × quotient + remainder

CHECK YOURSELF 4

How many times is 7 contained in 38?

Example 5

Checking Division by a Single-Digit Number

Using the work of the previous example, we can write

NOTE Another way to write the result is

$$\begin{array}{r} 4\ r3 \\ 5\overline{)23} \end{array}$$ The "r" stands for remainder.

$$\begin{array}{r} 4 \\ 5\overline{)23} \end{array}$$ with remainder 3

To apply our previous rule, we have

NOTE Notice that the multiplication is done before the 3 is added.

Dividend ⟶ $23 = 5 \times 4 + 3$ ⟵ Remainder

with labels Divisor (5) and Quotient (4)

$23 = 20 + 3$

$23 = 23$ The division checks.

 CHECK YOURSELF 5

Evaluate $7\overline{)38}$. *Check your answer.*

We must be careful when 0 is involved in a division problem. There are two special cases.

Rules and Properties: Division and Zero

1. 0 divided by any whole number (except 0) is 0.
2. Division by 0 is undefined.

The first case involving zero occurs when we are dividing into zero.

Example 6

Dividing into Zero

$0 \div 5 = 0$ because $0 = 5 \times 0$.

 CHECK YOURSELF 6

(a) $0 \div 7 =$ **(b)** $0 \div 12 =$

Our second case illustrates what happens when 0 is the *divisor.* Here we have a special problem.

Example 7

Dividing by Zero

$8 \div 0 = ?$ This means that $8 = 0 \times ?$

Can 0 times some number ever be 8? From our multiplication facts, the answer is *no!* There is no answer to this problem, so we say that $8 \div 0$ is undefined.

CHECK YOURSELF 7

Decide whether each problem results in 0 or is undefined.

(a) $9 \div 0$ **(b)** $0 \div 9$ **(c)** $0 \div 15$ **(d)** $15 \div 0$

It is easy to divide when small whole numbers are involved, because much of the work can be done mentally. In working with larger numbers, we turn to a process called **long division.** This is a shorthand method for performing the steps of repeated subtraction.

To start, let's look at an example in which we subtract multiples of the divisor.

Example 8

NOTE With larger numbers, repeated subtraction is just too time-consuming to be practical.

Dividing by a Single-Digit Number

Divide 176 by 8.

Because 20 eights are 160, we know that there are at least 20 eights in 176.

Step 1 Write

$$\begin{array}{r} 20 \\ 8\overline{)176} \\ \text{20 eights} \longrightarrow 160 \\ \hline 16 \end{array}$$

Subtracting 160 is just a shortcut for subtracting eight 20 times.

After subtracting the 20 eights, or 160, we are left with 16. There are 2 eights in 16, and so we continue.

Step 2

$$\begin{array}{r} \left.\begin{array}{r} 2 \\ 20 \end{array}\right\} 22 \\ 8\overline{)176} \\ 160 \\ \hline 16 \\ \text{2 eights} \longrightarrow 16 \\ \hline 0 \end{array}$$

Adding 20 and 2 gives us the quotient, 22.

Subtracting the 2 eights, we have a 0 remainder. So $176 \div 8 = 22$

CHECK YOURSELF 8

Verify the results of Example 8, using multiplication.

The next step is to simplify this repeated-subtraction process one step further. The result will be the long-division method.

Example 9

Dividing by a Single-Digit Number

Divide 358 by 6.

The dividend is 358. We look at the first digit, 3. We cannot divide 6 into 3, and so we look at the *first two digits*, 35. There are 5 sixes in 35, and so we write 5 above the tens digit of the dividend.

$$\begin{array}{r} 5 \\ 6\overline{)358} \end{array}$$
When we place 5 as the tens digit, we really mean 5 tens, or 50.

Now multiply 5 × 6, place the product below 35, and subtract.

$$\begin{array}{r} 5 \\ 6\overline{)358} \\ \underline{30} \\ 5 \end{array}$$ We have actually subtracted 50 sixes (300) from 358.

Because the remainder, 5, is smaller than the divisor, 6, we bring down 8, the ones digit of the dividend.

$$\begin{array}{r} 5 \\ 6\overline{)358} \\ \underline{30} \\ 58 \end{array}$$

Now divide 6 into 58. There are 9 sixes in 58, and so 9 is the ones digit of the quotient. Multiply 9 × 6 and subtract to complete the process.

NOTE Because the 4 is smaller than the divisor, we have a remainder of 4.

$$\begin{array}{r} 59 \\ 6\overline{)358} \\ \underline{30}\downarrow \\ 58 \\ \underline{54} \\ 4 \end{array}$$ We now have:
358 ÷ 6 = 59 r4

NOTE Verify that this is true and that the division checks.

To check: 358 = 6 × 59 + 4

✔ **CHECK YOURSELF 9**

Divide 7$\overline{)453}$.

Long division becomes a bit more complicated when we have a two-digit divisor. It is now a matter of trial and error. We round the divisor and dividend to form a *trial divisor and a trial dividend*. We then estimate the proper quotient and must determine whether our estimate was correct.

Example 10

Dividing by a Two-Digit Number

Divide

38$\overline{)293}$

Round the divisor and dividend to the nearest ten. So 38 is rounded to 40, and 293 is rounded to 290. The trial divisor is then 40, and the trial dividend is 290.

NOTE Think: 4$\overline{)29}$

Now look at the nonzero digits in the trial divisor and dividend. They are 4 and 29. We know that there are 7 fours in 29, and so 7 is our first estimate of the quotient. Now let's see if 7 works.

$$\begin{array}{r} 7 \\ 38\overline{)293} \\ \underline{266} \\ 27 \end{array}$$ Your estimate

Multiply 7 × 38. The product, 266, is less than 293, and so we can subtract.

The remainder, 27, is less than the divisor, 38, and so the process is complete.

293 ÷ 38 = 7 r27

Check: 293 = 38 × 7 + 27   You should verify that this statement is true.

✔ CHECK YOURSELF 10

Divide.

$57\overline{)482}$

Because this process is based on estimation, we can't expect our first guess to always be right.

Example 11

Dividing by a Two-Digit Number

Divide

$54\overline{)428}$

NOTE Think: $5\overline{)43}^{\,8}$

Rounding to the nearest ten, we have a trial divisor of 50 and a trial dividend of 430.

Looking at the nonzero digits, how many fives are in 43? There are 8. This is our first estimate.

$$54\overline{)428}^{8}$$
$$\underline{432} \longleftarrow \text{Too large}$$

We multiply 8 × 54. Do you see what's wrong? The product, 432, is too large. We can't subtract. Our estimate of the quotient must be adjusted *downward*.

We adjust the quotient downward to 7. We can now complete the division.

$$54\overline{)428}^{7}$$
$$\underline{378}$$
$$50$$

We have

$428 \div 54 = 7\ r50$

Check: $428 = 54 \times 7 + 50$

✔ CHECK YOURSELF 11

Divide.

$63\overline{)557}$

We have to be careful when a 0 appears as a digit in the quotient. Let's look at an example in which this happens with a two-digit divisor.

Example 12

Dividing with Large Dividends

NOTE Our divisor, 32, will divide into 98, the first two digits of the dividend.

Divide

$32\overline{)9871}$

Rounding to the nearest ten, we have a trial divisor of 30 and a trial dividend of 100. Think, "How many threes are in 10?" There are 3, and this is our first estimate of the quotient.

$$
\begin{array}{r}
3 \\
32\overline{)9871} \\
96 \\
\hline
2
\end{array}
$$
Everything seems fine so far!

Bring down 7, the next digit of the dividend.

$$
\begin{array}{r}
30 \\
32\overline{)9871} \\
96 \\
\hline
27
\end{array}
$$
Now do you see the difficulty? We cannot divide 32 into 27, and so we place 0 in the tens place of the quotient to indicate this fact.

We continue by multiplying by 0. After subtraction, we bring down 1, the last digit of the dividend.

$$
\begin{array}{r}
30 \\
32\overline{)9871} \\
96 \\
\hline
27 \\
00 \\
\hline
271
\end{array}
$$

Another problem develops here. We round 32 to 30 for our trial divisor, and we round 271 to 270, which is the trial dividend at this point. Our estimate of the last digit of the quotient must be 9.

$$
\begin{array}{r}
309 \\
32\overline{)9871} \\
96 \\
\hline
27 \\
00 \\
\hline
271 \\
288
\end{array}
$$
←——— Too large

We can't subtract. The trial quotient must be adjusted downward to 8. We can now complete the division.

$$
\begin{array}{r}
308 \\
32\overline{)9871} \\
96 \\
\hline
27 \\
00 \\
\hline
271 \\
256 \\
\hline
15
\end{array}
$$

$9871 \div 32 = 308 \text{ r}15$

Check: $9871 = 32 \times 308 + 15$

 CHECK YOURSELF 12

Divide.

$43\overline{)8857}$

Because of the availability of the handheld calculator, it is rarely necessary that people find the exact answer when performing long division. On the other hand, it is frequently important that one be able to either estimate the result of long division, or confirm that a given answer (particularly from a calculator) is reasonable. As a result, the emphasis in this section will be to improve your estimation skills in division.

Let's divide a four-digit number by a two-digit number. Generally, we will round the divisor to the nearest ten and the dividend to the nearest hundred.

Example 13

Estimating the Result of a Division Application

The Ramirez family took a trip of 2394 miles (mi) in their new car, using 77 gallons (gal) of gas. Estimate their gas mileage (mi/gal).

Our estimate will be based on dividing 2400 by 80.

$$\frac{30}{80)\overline{2400}}$$

They got approximately 30 mi/gal.

 CHECK YOURSELF 13

Troy flew a light plane on a trip of 2844 mi that took 21 hours (h). What was his approximate speed in miles per hour (mi/h)?

As before, we may have to combine operations to solve an application of the mathematics you have learned.

Example 14

Estimating the Result of a Division Application

Charles purchases a new car for $8574. Interest charges will be $978. He agrees to make payments for 4 years. Approximately what should his payments be?

First, we find the amount that Charles owes:

$8574 + $978 = $9552

Now, to find the monthly payment, we divide that amount by 48 (months). To estimate the payment, we'll divide $9600 by 50 months.

$$\frac{192}{50)\overline{9600}}$$

The payments will be approximately $192 per month.

 CHECK YOURSELF 14

One $10 bag of fertilizer will cover 310 square feet. Approximately what would it cost to cover 2200 square feet?

CHECK YOURSELF ANSWERS

1. 12   2. 315 students ÷ 9 classes; students per class   3. (a) 5; 9 × 5 = 45;
(b) 4; 7 × 4 = 28   4. 5   5. 5 with remainder 3   6. (a) 0; (b) 0
7. (a) undefined; (b) 0; (c) 0; (d) undefined   8. 8 × 22 = 176
9. 64 with remainder 5   10. 8 with remainder 26   11. 8 with remainder 53
12. 205 with remainder 42   13. 140 mi/h   14. $70

0.4 Exercises

1. If $48 \div 8 = 6$, 8 is the _____, 48 is the _____, and 6 is the _____.

2. In the statement $5\overline{)45}^{\,9}$, 9 is the _____, 5 is the _____, and 45 is the _____.

3. Find $36 \div 9$ by repeated subtraction.

4. Find $40 \div 8$ by repeated subtraction.

5. Stefanie is planting rows of tomato plants. She wants to plant 63 plants with 9 plants per row. How many rows will she have?

6. Nick is designing a parking lot for a small office building. He must make room for 42 cars with 7 cars per row. How many rows should he plan for?

Divide the following. Identify the correct units for the quotient.

7. 36 pages $\div$ 4

8. $96 \div 8$

9. 4900 km $\div$ 7

10. 360 gal $\div$ 18

11. 160 miles $\div$ 4 hours

12. 264 ft $\div$ 3 sec

13. 3720 hours $\div$ 5 months

14. 560 calories $\div$ 7 grams

Divide using long division, and check your work.

15. $54 \div 9$

16. $21 \div 3$

17. $6\overline{)42}$

18. $7\overline{)63}$

19. $4\overline{)32}$

20. $56 \div 8$

21. $5\overline{)43}$

22. $40 \div 9$

23. $9\overline{)65}$

24. $6\overline{)51}$

25. $57 \div 8$

26. $74 \div 8$

27. $0 \div 5$

28. $5 \div 0$

29. $4 \div 0$

30. $0 \div 12$

31. $0 \div 6$

32. $18 \div 0$

ANSWERS

1. _____

2. _____

3. _____

4. _____

5. _____

6. _____

7. _____

8. _____

9. _____

10. _____

11. _____

12. _____

13. _____

14. _____

15. _____ 16. _____

17. _____ 18. _____

19. _____ 20. _____

21. _____ 22. _____

23. _____ 24. _____

25. _____ 26. _____

27. _____ 28. _____

29. _____

30. _____ 31. _____

32. _____

33. _____	
34. _____	
35. _____	
36. _____	
37. _____	
38. _____	
39. _____	
40. _____	
41. _____	
42. _____	
43. _____	
44. _____	
45. _____	
46. _____	
47. _____	
48. _____	
49. _____	
50. _____	
51. _____	52. _____
53. _____	54. _____
55. _____	56. _____
57. _____	58. _____
59. _____	60. _____
61. _____	62. _____
63. _____	64. _____
65. _____	
66. _____	
67. _____	

Divide.

33. $5\overline{)83}$ **34.** $9\overline{)78}$ **35.** $3\overline{)162}$

36. $4\overline{)232}$ **37.** $8\overline{)293}$ **38.** $7\overline{)346}$

39. $8\overline{)3136}$ **40.** $5\overline{)4938}$ **41.** $8\overline{)5438}$

42. $9\overline{)3527}$ **43.** $8\overline{)22,153}$ **44.** $5\overline{)43,287}$

45. $4\overline{)4351}$ **46.** $8\overline{)3251}$ **47.** $4\overline{)7321}$

48. $7\overline{)8923}$ **49.** $3\overline{)13,421}$ **50.** $4\overline{)34,093}$

51. $48\overline{)892}$ **52.** $54\overline{)372}$ **53.** $23\overline{)534}$

54. $67\overline{)939}$ **55.** $45\overline{)2367}$ **56.** $53\overline{)3480}$

57. $34\overline{)8748}$ **58.** $27\overline{)9335}$ **59.** $42\overline{)7902}$

60. $53\overline{)8729}$ **61.** $28\overline{)8547}$ **62.** $38\overline{)7892}$

63. $763\overline{)3071}$ **64.** $871\overline{)4321}$

Solve the following applications.

65. Counting. Ramon bought 56 bags of candy. There were 8 bags in each box. How many boxes were there?

66. Capacity. There are 32 students who are taking a field trip. If each car can hold 4 students, how many cars will be needed for the field trip?

67. Packaging. There are 63 candy bars in 7 boxes. How many candy bars are in each box?

68. Business. A total of 54 printers were shipped to 9 stores. How many printers were shipped to each store?

69. Recreation. Joaquin is putting pictures in an album. He can fit 8 pictures on each page. If he has 77 pictures, how many will be left over after he has filled the last 8-picture page?

70. Counting. Kathy is separating a deck of 52 cards into 6 equal piles. How many cards will be left over?

71. Recreation. Ticket receipts for a play were $552. If the tickets were $4 each, how many tickets were purchased?

72. Construction. Construction of a fence section requires 8 boards. If you have 256 boards available, how many sections can you build?

73. Business. The homeowners along a street must share the $2030 cost of new street lighting. If there are 14 homes, what amount will each owner pay?

74. Cost. A bookstore ordered 325 copies of a textbook at a cost of $7800. What was the cost to the store for an individual textbook?

ANSWERS

68. _____

69. _____

70. _____

71. _____

72. _____

73. _____

74. _____

75. _____

76. _____

77. _____

78. _____

79. _____

80. _____

81. _____

82. _____

83. _____

84. _____

75. Telephone calls. The records of an office show that 1702 calls were made in 1 day. If there are 37 phones in the office, how many calls were placed per phone?

76. Television costs. A television dealer purchased 23 sets, each the same model, for $5267. What was the cost of each set?

77. Computers. A computer printer can print 340 lines per minute (min). How long will it take to complete a report of 10,880 lines?

78. Distance. A train traveled 1364 mi in 22 h. What was the speed of the train? *Hint:* Speed is the distance traveled divided by the time.

79. Bonuses. A company distributes $16,488 in year-end bonuses. If each of the 36 employees receives the same amount, what bonus will each receive?

80. Complete the following number cross.

Across
1. 48 ÷ 4
3. 1296 ÷ 8
6. 2025 ÷ 5
8. 4 × 5
9. 11 × 11
12. 15 ÷ 3 × 111
14. 144 ÷ (2 × 6)
16. 1404 ÷ 6
18. 2500 ÷ 5
19. 3 × 5

Down
1. (12 + 16) ÷ 2
2. 67 × 3
4. 744 ÷ 12
5. 2600 ÷ 13
7. 6300 ÷ 12
10. 304 ÷ 2
11. 5 × (161 ÷ 7)
13. 9027 ÷ 17
15. 400 ÷ 20
17. 9 × 5

Estimate the result in the following division problems. (Remember to round divisors to the nearest ten and dividends to the nearest hundred.)

81. 810 divided by 38

82. 458 divided by 18

83. 4967 divided by 96

84. 3971 divided by 39

85. 8971 divided by 91

86. 3981 divided by 78

87. 3879 divided by 126

88. 8986 divided by 178

89. 3812 divided by 188

90. 5245 divided by 255

Solve the following applications.

91. Gas mileage. Jose drove 279 miles (mi) on 18 gallons of gas. Estimate his mileage. (*Hint:* Find the number of miles per gallon.)

92. Construction. A contractor can build a house in 27 days. Estimate how many houses can be built in 265 days.

93. Inheritances. Twelve people are to share equally in an estate totaling $26,875. Estimate how much money each person will receive.

94. Business. There is $365 left in the budget to purchase pens. If each box of pens costs $18, estimate the number of boxes of pens that can be ordered.

95. Monthly payments. Tara purchased a used car for $1850 by paying $275 down and the rest in equal monthly payments over a period of 18 months. Estimate the amount of her monthly payments.

96. Consumer purchases. Art has $275 to spend on shirts. If the cost of a shirt is $23, estimate the number of shirts that Art can buy.

97. You are going to recarpet your living room. You have budgeted $1500 for the carpet and installation.

(a) Determine how much carpet you will need to do the job. Draw a sketch to support your measurements.

(b) What is the highest price per square yard you can pay and still stay within budget?

(c) Go to a local store and determine the total cost of doing the job for three different grades of carpet. Be sure to include padding, labor costs, and any other expenses.

(d) What considerations (other than cost) would affect your decision about what type of carpet to install?

(e) Write a brief paragraph indicating your final decision, and give supporting reasons.

98. Division is the inverse operation of multiplication. Many daily activities have inverses. For each of the following activities, state the inverse activity:

(a) Spending money

(b) Going to sleep

(c) Turning down the volume on your CD player

(d) Getting dressed

ANSWERS

85. _____

86. _____

87. _____

88. _____

89. _____

90. _____

91. _____

92. _____

93. _____

94. _____

95. _____

96. _____

97. _____

98. _____

99.

100.

101.

102.

103.

99. If you have no money in your pocket and want to divide it equally among your four friends, how much does each person get? Use this situation to explain division of zero by a nonzero number.

100. Explain the difference between division by zero and division of zero by a natural number.

101. Division is not associative. For example, $8 \div 4 \div 2$ will produce different results if 8 is divided by 4 and then divided by 2 or if 8 is divided by the result of $4 \div 2$. In the following, place parentheses in the proper place so that the expression is true.

(a) $16 \div 8 \div 2 = 4$ (b) $16 \div 8 \div 2 = 1$

(c) $125 \div 25 \div 5 = 1$ (d) $125 \div 25 \div 5 = 25$

(e) Is there any situation in which the order of how the operation of division is performed produces the same result? Give an example.

102. Division is not commutative. For example, $15 \div 5 \neq 5 \div 15$. What must be true of the numbers a and b if $a \div b = b \div a$?

103. Your class goes to a local amusement park. A ride can carry 15 passengers in each cycle.

(a) If a new cycle starts every 5 min, how many cycles does the ride make every hour?

(b) How many passengers can ride every hour?

(c) How long would it take all the students in your class to complete the ride?

Answers

1. Divisor, dividend, quotient **3.** 4 **5.** 7 **7.** 9 pages **9.** 700 km
11. 40 miles/hour **13.** 744 hours/month **15.** 6 **17.** 7 **19.** 8
21. 8 r3 **23.** 7 r2 **25.** 7 r1 **27.** 0 **29.** Undefined **31.** 0
33. 16 r3 **35.** 54 **37.** 36 r5 **39.** 392 **41.** 679 r6 **43.** 2769 r1
45. 1087 r3 **47.** 1830 r1 **49.** 4473 r2 **51.** 18 r28 **53.** 23 r5
55. 52 r27 **57.** 257 r10 **59.** 188 r6 **61.** 305 r7 **63.** 4 r19
65. 7 boxes **67.** 9 bars **69.** 5 pictures **71.** 138 tickets **73.** $145
75. 46 calls **77.** 32 min **79.** $458 **81.** 20 **83.** 50
85. 100 **87.** 30 **89.** 20 **91.** 15 mi/gal **93.** $2700 **95.** $80
97.   **99.**   **101.**   **103.**

Decimals and Percents

 OBJECTIVES

1. Change a fraction to a decimal
2. Change a decimal to a fraction
3. Add and subtract decimals
4. Multiply and divide decimals
5. Change a percent to a fraction or decimal
6. Change a decimal or fraction to a percent

Because a fraction can be interpreted as division, you can divide the numerator of the fraction by its denominator to convert a fraction to a decimal. The result is called a **decimal equivalent.**

OBJECTIVE 1   **Example 1   Converting a Fraction to a Terminating Decimal**

Write $\dfrac{5}{8}$ as a decimal.

RECALL 5 can be written as 5.0, 5.00, 5.000, and so on. In this case, we continue the division by adding zeros to the dividend until a 0 remainder is reached.

$$
\begin{array}{r}
0.625 \\
8\overline{)5.000} \\
\underline{4\,8} \\
20 \\
\underline{16} \\
40 \\
\underline{40} \\
0
\end{array}
$$

Because $\dfrac{5}{8}$ means $5 \div 8$, divide 8 into 5.

We see that $\dfrac{5}{8} = 0.625$; 0.625 is the decimal equivalent of $\dfrac{5}{8}$.

 CHECK YOURSELF 1

Find the decimal equivalent of $\dfrac{7}{8}$.

If a decimal equivalent does not terminate, you can round the result to approximate the fraction to some specified number of decimal places. Consider Example 2.

Example 2   Converting a Fraction to a Decimal

Write $\dfrac{3}{7}$ as a decimal. Round the answer to the nearest thousandth.

$$
\begin{array}{r}
0.4285 \\
7\overline{)3.0000} \\
\underline{2\,8} \\
20 \\
\underline{14} \\
60 \\
\underline{56} \\
40 \\
\underline{35} \\
5
\end{array}
$$

In this example, we are choosing to round to three decimal places, so we must add enough zeros to carry the division to four decimal places.

So $\dfrac{3}{7} = 0.429$ (to the nearest thousandth).

 CHECK YOURSELF 2 _____

Find the decimal equivalent of $\dfrac{5}{11}$ to the nearest thousandth.

If a decimal equivalent does *not* terminate, it will *repeat* a sequence of digits. These decimals are called **repeating decimals.**

Example 3   Converting a Fraction to a Repeating Decimal

Write $\dfrac{5}{11}$ as a decimal.

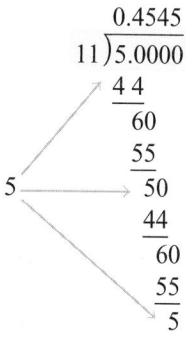

As soon as a remainder repeats itself, as 5 does here, the pattern of digits will repeat in the quotient.

$$\frac{5}{11} = 0.\overline{45}$$

$$= 0.4545\ldots$$

 CHECK YOURSELF 3 _____

Use the bar notation to write the decimal equivalent of $\dfrac{5}{7}$. (Be patient. You'll have to divide for a while to find the repeating pattern.)

To convert from a decimal to a fraction, write the decimal without the decimal point. This will be the **numerator** of the fraction. The **denominator** of the fraction is a 1 followed by as many zeros as there are places in the decimal. Examples 4 and 5 illustrate this process.

OBJECTIVE 2   **Example 4   Converting a Decimal to a Fraction**

$$0.7 = \frac{7}{10} \qquad\qquad 0.09 = \frac{9}{100} \qquad\qquad 0.257 = \frac{257}{1000}$$

One place   One zero   Two places   Two zeros   Three places   Three zeros

 CHECK YOURSELF 4 _____

Write as fractions.

(a) 0.3   **(b)** 0.311

When a decimal is converted to a fraction, the common fraction that results should be written in lowest terms.

Example 5   Converting a Decimal to a Fraction

Convert 0.395 to a fraction and write the result in lowest terms.

NOTE Divide the numerator and denominator by 5.

$$0.395 = \frac{395}{1000} = \frac{79}{200}$$

 CHECK YOURSELF 5 _____

Write 0.275 as a fraction.

Example 6 illustrates the addition and subtraction of decimals.

OBJECTIVE 3   ### Example 6   Adding or Subtracting Two Decimals

Perform the indicated operation.

(a) Add 2.356 and 15.6.

Aligning the decimal points, we get

$$\begin{array}{r} 2.356 \\ +15.600 \\ \hline 17.956 \end{array}$$ Although the zeros are not necessary, they ensure proper alignment.

(b) Subtract 3.84 from 8.1.

Again, we align the decimal points

$$\begin{array}{r} 8.10 \\ -3.84 \\ \hline 4.26 \end{array}$$ When subtracting, always add zeros so that the right columns line up.

 CHECK YOURSELF 6 _____

Perform the indicated operation.

(a) $34.76 + 2.419$ **(b)** $71.82 - 8.197$

Example 7 illustrates the multiplication of two decimal fractions.

OBJECTIVE 4   ### Example 7   Multiplying Two Decimals

Multiply 4.6 and 3.27

$$\begin{array}{r} 4.6 \\ \times\, 3.27 \\ \hline 322 \\ 920 \\ 13800 \\ \hline 15.042 \end{array}$$

It is not necessary to align decimals being multiplied. Note that the two factors have a total of three digits to the right of the decimal point.

The decimal point of the product is moved three digits to the left.

CHECK YOURSELF 7

Multiply 5.8 and 9.62.

We want now to look at division *by* decimals. Here is an example using a fractional form.

Example 8   Rewriting a Problem That Requires Dividing by a Decimal

Rewrite the division so that the divisor is a whole number.

$$2.57 \div 3.4 = \frac{2.57}{3.4}$$ Write the division as a fraction.

$$= \frac{2.57 \times 10}{3.4 \times 10}$$ We multiply the numerator and denominator by 10 so the divisor is a whole number. This *does not change* the value of the fraction.

$$= \frac{25.7}{34}$$ Multiplying by 10, shift the decimal point in the numerator and denominator *one place to the right*.

$$= 25.7 \div 34$$ Our division problem is rewritten so that the divisor is a whole number.

NOTE It's always easier to rewrite a division problem so that you're dividing by a whole number. Dividing by a whole number makes it easy to place the decimal point in the quotient.

So

$$2.57 \div 3.4 = 25.7 \div 34$$ After we multiply the numerator and denominator by 10, we see that 2.57 ÷ 3.4 is the same as 25.7 ÷ 34.

 CHECK YOURSELF 8

Rewrite the division problem so that the divisor is a whole number.

$$3.42 \div 2.5$$

NOTE Of course, multiplying by any whole-number power of 10 greater than 1 is just a matter of shifting the decimal point to the right.

Do you see the rule suggested by Example 8? We multiplied the numerator and the denominator (the dividend and the divisor) by 10. We made the divisor a whole number without altering the actual digits involved. All we did was shift the decimal point in the divisor and dividend the same number of places. This leads us to the following procedure.

Step by Step: To Divide by a Decimal

Step 1   Move the decimal point in the divisor *to the right,* making the divisor a whole number.
Step 2   Move the decimal point in the dividend to the right *the same number of places.* Add zeros if necessary.
Step 3   Place the decimal point in the quotient directly above the decimal point of the dividend.
Step 4   Divide as you would with whole numbers.

Let's look at an example of the use of our division rule.

Example 9   **Rounding the Result of Dividing by a Decimal**

Divide 1.573 by 0.48 and give the quotient to the nearest tenth.

Write

$$0.48\overline{)1.57\,3}$$

Shift the decimal points two places to the right to make the divisor a whole number.

Now divide:

NOTE Once the division statement is rewritten, place the decimal point in the quotient above that in the dividend.

$$
\begin{array}{r}
3.27 \\
48\overline{)157.30} \\
\underline{144} \\
13\,3 \\
\underline{9\,6} \\
3\,70 \\
\underline{3\,36} \\
34
\end{array}
$$

Add a 0 to carry the division to the hundredths place. In this case, we want to find the quotient to the nearest tenth.

Round 3.27 to 3.3. So

$1.573 \div 0.48 = 3.3$ (to the nearest tenth)

CHECK YOURSELF 9 _____

Divide, rounding the quotient to the nearest tenth.

$3.4 \div 1.24$

We have used fractions and decimals to name parts of a whole. **Percents** can also be used to accomplish this. The word *percent* means "for each hundred." We can think of percents as fractions whose denominators are 100. So 25% would be written as $\frac{25}{100}$ or in simplified form $\frac{1}{4}$.

Because there are different ways of naming the parts of a whole, you need to know how to change from one of these ways to another. First let's look at changing a percent to a fraction. Because a percent is a fraction or a ratio with denominator 100, we can use the following rule.

Rules and Properties: Changing a Percent to a Fraction

To change a percent to a fraction, replace the percent symbol with $\frac{1}{100}$.

The use of this rule is shown in Example 10.

OBJECTIVE 5   **Example 10   Changing a Percent to a Fraction**

Change each percent to a fraction.

(a) $7\% = 7\left(\dfrac{1}{100}\right) = \dfrac{7}{100}$

NOTE You can choose to write $\dfrac{25}{100}$ in simplest form.

(b) $25\% = 25\left(\dfrac{1}{100}\right) = \dfrac{25}{100} = \dfrac{1}{4}$

 CHECK YOURSELF 10 _____

Write 12% as a fraction.

In Example 10, we wrote percents as fractions by replacing the percent sign with $\dfrac{1}{100}$ and multiplying. How do we convert percents when we are working with decimals? Just move the decimal point two places to the left. This gives us a second rule for converting percents.

Rules and Properties: Changing a Percent to a Decimal

To change a percent to a decimal, replace the percent symbol with $\dfrac{1}{100}$. As a result of multiplying by $\dfrac{1}{100}$, the decimal point will move two places to the left.

Example 11   Changing a Percent to a Decimal

Change each percent to a decimal equivalent.

(a) $25\% = 25\left(\dfrac{1}{100}\right) = 0.25$ The decimal point in 25% is understood to be after the 5.

(b) $4.5\% = 4.5\left(\dfrac{1}{100}\right) = 0.045$ We must add a zero to move the decimal point.

NOTE A percent greater than 100 gives a decimal greater than 1.

(c) $130\% = 130\left(\dfrac{1}{100}\right) = 1.30$

 CHECK YOURSELF 11 _____

Write as decimals.

(a) 5%   **(b)** 3.9%   **(c)** 115%

Changing a decimal to a percent is the opposite of changing from a percent to a decimal. We reverse the process. Here is the rule:

> **Rules and Properties:**   Changing a Decimal to a Percent
>
> To change a decimal to a percent, move the decimal point *two* places to the *right* and attach the percent symbol.

OBJECTIVE 6   **Example 12   Changing a Decimal to a Percent**

Change each decimal to a percent equivalent.

(a) $0.18 = 18\%$
(b) $0.03 = 3\%$
(c) $1.25 = 125\%$

 CHECK YOURSELF 12

Change each decimal to a percent equivalent.

(a) 0.27   **(b)** 0.045   **(c)** 1.3

The following rule allows us to change fractions to percents.

> **Rules and Properties:**   Changing a Fraction to a Percent
>
> To change a fraction to a percent, write the decimal equivalent of the fraction. Move the decimal point two places to the right and attach the percent symbol.

Example 13   Changing a Fraction to a Percent

Change each fraction to a percent equivalent.

(a) $\dfrac{3}{5} = 0.60$ To find the decimal equivalent, just divide the denominator into the numerator.

Now write the percent.

$$\frac{3}{5} = 0.60 = 60\%$$

(b) $\dfrac{1}{8} = 0.125 = 12.5\%$ or $12\dfrac{1}{2}\%$

(c) $\dfrac{1}{3} = 0.\overline{3} = 0.33\overline{3} = 33.\overline{3}\%$ or $33\dfrac{1}{3}\%$

CHECK YOURSELF 13 _____

Change each fraction to a percent equivalent.

(a) $\dfrac{3}{4}$ **(b)** $\dfrac{3}{8}$ **(c)** $\dfrac{2}{3}$

Example 14 illustrates one of the many applications using decimals.

Example 14   An Application of Decimals

Lucetia's car gets approximately 20 miles per gallon (mi/gal) of fuel. If 1 gal of fuel costs $1.93, how much does it cost her to drive 125 mi?

$125 \div 20 = 6.25$ gal

$6.25 \cdot 1.93 = \$12.06$ (rounded)

 CHECK YOURSELF 14 _____

The art department has a budget of $195.75 to purchase art supplies. After purchasing 35 paintbrushes for $1.92 each, six jars of paint remover for $0.93 each, and four cans of blue paint for $2.95 each, how much money was left in the budget?

CHECK YOURSELF ANSWERS _____

1. 0.875   **2.** 0.455   **3.** $0.\overline{714285}$ **4. (a)** $\dfrac{3}{10}$; **(b)** $\dfrac{311}{1000}$ **5.** $\dfrac{11}{40}$

6. (a) 37.179; **(b)** 63.623   **7.** 55.796   **8.** $34.2 \div 25$ **9.** 2.7

10. $\dfrac{12}{100}$ or $\dfrac{3}{25}$ **11. (a)** 0.05; **(b)** 0.039; **(c)** 1.15   **12. (a)** $\dfrac{27}{100} = 27\%$;

(b) 4.5%; **(c)** 130%   **13. (a)** 75%; **(b)** 37.5%; **(c)** $66.\overline{6}\%$ or $66\dfrac{2}{3}\%$

14. $111.17

0.5 Exercises

Find the decimal equivalents for each of the following fractions.

1. $\dfrac{3}{4}$

2. $\dfrac{4}{5}$

3. $\dfrac{9}{20}$

4. $\dfrac{3}{10}$

5. $\dfrac{1}{5}$

6. $\dfrac{1}{8}$

7. $\dfrac{5}{16}$

8. $\dfrac{11}{20}$

9. $\dfrac{7}{10}$

10. $\dfrac{7}{16}$

11. $\dfrac{27}{40}$

12. $\dfrac{17}{32}$

Find the decimal equivalents rounded to the indicated place.

13. $\dfrac{5}{6}$ thousandth

14. $\dfrac{7}{12}$ hundredth

15. $\dfrac{4}{15}$ thousandth

Write the decimal equivalents, using the bar notation.

16. $\dfrac{1}{18}$

17. $\dfrac{4}{9}$

18. $\dfrac{3}{11}$

Write each of the following as a fraction. Write your answer in lowest terms.

19. 0.9

20. 0.3

21. 0.8

22. 0.6

23. 0.37

24. 0.97

25. 0.587

26. 0.379

27. 0.48

28. 0.75

29. 0.58

30. 0.65

Perform the indicated operations.

31. 7.1562 + 14.78

32. 6.2358 + 3.14

33. 11.12 + 8.3792

34. 6.924 + 5.2

35. 9.20 − 2.85

36. 17.345 − 11.12

ANSWERS

1. _____

2. _____

3. _____

4. _____

5. _____

6. _____

7. _____

8. _____

9. _____

10. _____

11. _____

12. _____

13. _____ 14. _____

15. _____ 16. _____

17. _____ 18. _____

19. _____ 20. _____

21. _____ 22. _____

23. _____ 24. _____

25. _____ 26. _____

27. _____ 28. _____

29. _____ 30. _____

31. _____ 32. _____

33. _____ 34. _____

35. _____ 36. _____

37. _____

38. _____

39. _____

40. _____

41. _____

42. _____

43. _____

44. _____

45. _____ 46. _____

47. _____ 48. _____

49. _____ 50. _____

51. _____ 52. _____

53. _____ 54. _____

55. _____ 56. _____

57. _____ 58. _____

59. _____ 60. _____

61. _____ 62. _____

63. _____ 64. _____

65. _____ 66. _____

67. _____ 68. _____

69. _____ 70. _____

71. _____ 72. _____

73. _____ 74. _____

75. _____ 76. _____

77. _____ 78. _____

79. _____ 80. _____

37. $18.234 - 13.64$ **38.** $21.983 - 9.395$ **39.** $3.21 \cdot 2.1$

40. $15.6 \cdot 7.123$ **41.** $6.29 \cdot 9.13$ **42.** $8.245 \cdot 3.1$

Divide.

43. $16.68 \div 6$ **44.** $43.92 \div 8$ **45.** $1.92 \div 4$

46. $5.52 \div 6$ **47.** $5.48 \div 8$ **48.** $2.76 \div 8$

49. $13.89 \div 6$ **50.** $21.92 \div 5$ **51.** $185.6 \div 32$

52. $165.6 \div 36$ **53.** $79.9 \div 34$ **54.** $179.3 \div 55$

55. $52\overline{)13.78}$ **56.** $76\overline{)26.22}$ **57.** $0.6\overline{)11.07}$

58. $0.8\overline{)10.84}$ **59.** $3.8\overline{)7.22}$ **60.** $2.9\overline{)13.34}$

61. $5.2\overline{)11.622}$ **62.** $6.4\overline{)3.616}$

Write as fractions.

63. 6% **64.** 17% **65.** 75%

66. 20% **67.** 65% **68.** 48%

69. 50% **70.** 52% **71.** 46%

72. 35% **73.** 66% **74.** 4%

Write as decimals.

75. 20% **76.** 70% **77.** 35%

78. 75% **79.** 39% **80.** 27%

81. 5%   **82.** 7%   **83.** 135%

84. 250%   **85.** 240%   **86.** 160%

Write each decimal as a percent.

87. 4.40   **88.** 5.13   **89.** 0.065

90. 0.095   **91.** 0.025   **92.** 0.085

93. 0.002   **94.** 0.008

Write each fraction as a percent.

95. $\dfrac{1}{4}$ **96.** $\dfrac{4}{5}$ **97.** $\dfrac{2}{5}$

98. $\dfrac{1}{2}$ **99.** $\dfrac{1}{5}$ **100.** $\dfrac{3}{4}$

101. $\dfrac{5}{8}$ **102.** $\dfrac{7}{8}$

103. Statistics. On a math quiz, Adam answered 18 of 20 questions correctly, or $\dfrac{18}{20}$ of the quiz. Write the decimal equivalent of this fraction.

18/20	Name: _Adam_
2 x 3 = _6_	5 x 4 = _20_
1 + 5 = _6_	3 x 4 = _12_
2 x 5 = _10_	5 x 2 = _10_
4 + 5 = _9_	5 + 4 = _9_
15 - 2 = _13_	15 - 4 = _11_
4 x 3 = _12_	✓8 x 3 = _22_
3 + 6 = _9_	6 + 3 = _9_
9 + 4 = _13_	5 + 6 = _11_
✓3 + 9 = _11_	6 + 9 = _15_
1 x 2 = _2_	2 x 1 = _2_

ANSWERS

81. _____
82. _____
83. _____
84. _____
85. _____
86. _____
87. _____
88. _____
89. _____
90. _____
91. _____
92. _____
93. _____
94. _____
95. _____
96. _____
97. _____
98. _____
99. _____
100. _____
101. _____
102. _____
103. _____

104. _____

105. _____

106. _____

107. _____

108. _____

109. _____

104. Statistics. In a weekend baseball tournament, Joel had 4 hits in 13 times at bat. That is, he hit safely $\frac{4}{13}$ of the time. Write the decimal equivalent for Joel's hitting, rounding to three decimal places. (That number is Joel's batting average.)

105. Business and finance. A restaurant bought 50 glasses at a cost of $39.90. What was the cost per glass to the nearest cent?

106. Business and finance. The cost of a case of 48 items is $28.20. What is the cost of an individual item to the nearest cent?

107. Business and finance. An office bought 18 hand-held calculators for $284. What was the cost per calculator to the nearest cent?

108. Business and finance. Al purchased a new refrigerator that cost $736.12 with interest included. He paid $100 as a down payment and agreed to pay the remainder in 18 monthly payments. What amount will he be paying per month?

109. Business and finance. The cost of a television set with interest is $490.64. If you make a down payment of $50 and agree to pay the balance in 12 monthly payments, what will be the amount of each monthly payment?

Answers

1. 0.75 **3.** 0.45 **5.** 0.2 **7.** 0.3125 **9.** 0.7 **11.** 0.675

13. 0.833 **15.** 0.267 **17.** $0.\overline{4}$ **19.** $\frac{9}{10}$ **21.** $\frac{4}{5}$ **23.** $\frac{37}{100}$

25. $\frac{587}{1000}$ **27.** $\frac{12}{25}$ **29.** $\frac{29}{50}$ **31.** 21.9362 **33.** 19.4992

35. 6.35 **37.** 4.594 **39.** 6.741 **41.** 57.4277 **43.** 2.78

45. 0.48 **47.** 0.685 **49.** 2.315 **51.** 5.8 **53.** 2.35 **55.** 0.265

57. 18.45 **59.** 1.9 **61.** 2.235 **63.** $\frac{3}{50}$ **65.** $\frac{3}{4}$ **67.** $\frac{13}{20}$

69. $\frac{1}{2}$ **71.** $\frac{23}{50}$ **73.** $\frac{33}{50}$ **75.** 0.2 **77.** 0.35 **79.** 0.39

81. 0.05 **83.** 1.35 **85.** 2.4 **87.** 440% **89.** 6.5% **91.** 2.5%

93. 0.2% **95.** 25% **97.** 40% **99.** 20% **101.** 62.5%

103. 0.9 **105.** $0.80 or 80¢ **107.** $15.78 **109.** $36.72

0.6 Prime Factorization

0.6 OBJECTIVES

1. Find the factors of a natural number
2. Determine whether a number is prime, composite, or neither
3. Find the prime factorization for a number
4. Find the GCF for two or more numbers

Overcoming Math Anxiety

Throughout this text, we will present you with a series of class-tested techniques that are designed to improve your performance in this math class.

Hint #3   Become familiar with your text book.

Perform each of the following tasks.

1. Use the Table of Contents.
2. Use the index to find the earliest reference to the term *mean*. (By the way, this term has nothing to do with the personality of either your instructor or the text book author!)
3. Find the answer to the first Check Yourself exercise.
4. Find the answers to the Self-Test.
5. Find the answers to the odd-numbered exercises.

Now you know where some of the most important features of the text are. When you have a moment of confusion, think about using one of these features to help you clear up that confusion.

How would you arrange the following list of objects: cow, dog, daisy, fox, lily, sunflower, cat, tulip?

Although there are many ways to arrange the objects, most people would break them into two groups, the animals and the flowers. In mathematics, we call a group of things that have something in common a *set*.

Definitions: Set

A **set** is a collection of objects.

We generally use braces to enclose the elements of a set.

{cow, dog, fox, cat}   or   {daisy, lily, sunflower, tulip}

Of course, in mathematics many (but not all) of the sets we are interested in are sets of numbers.

The numbers used to count things—1, 2, 3, 4, 5, and so on—are called the **natural (or counting) numbers.** The **whole numbers** consist of the natural numbers and zero—0, 1, 2, 3, 4, 5, and so on. They can be represented on a number line like the one shown. Zero (0) is considered the origin.

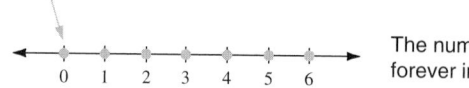

The origin

The number line continues forever in both directions.

NOTE The centered dot represents multiplication.

Any whole number can be written as a product of two whole numbers. For example, we say that 3 · 4 = 12. We call 3 and 4 **factors** of 12.

Definitions: Factor

A **factor** of a whole number is another whole number that will *divide exactly* into that number. This means that the division will have a remainder of 0.

NOTE 2 and 5 can also be called *divisors* of 10. They divide 10 exactly.

Example 1

Finding Factors

List all factors of 18.

3 · 6 = 18   Because 3 · 6 = 18, 3 and 6 are factors (or divisors) of 18.

NOTE This is a complete list of the factors. There are no other whole numbers that divide 18 exactly. Note that the factors of 18, except for 18 itself, are *smaller* than 18.

2 · 9 = 18   2 and 9 are also factors of 18.

1 · 18 = 18   1 and 18 are factors of 18.

1, 2, 3, 6, 9, and 18 are all the factors of 18.

✔ **CHECK YOURSELF 1***

List all the factors of 24.

NOTE A whole number greater than 1 will always have itself and 1 as factors. Sometimes these will be the *only* factors. For instance, 1 and 3 are the only factors of 3.

Listing factors leads us to an important classification of whole numbers. Any whole number larger than 1 is either a *prime* or a *composite* number. Let's look at the following definitions.

Definitions: Prime Number

A **prime number** is any whole number greater than 1 that has only 1 and itself as factors.

NOTE How large can a prime number be? There is no largest prime number. To date, the largest *known* prime is $2^{6972593} - 1$. This is a number with 2,098,960 digits, if you are curious. Of course, a computer had to be used to verify that a number of this size is prime. By the time you read this, someone may very well have found an even larger prime number.

As examples, 2, 3, 5, and 7 are prime numbers. Their only factors are 1 and themselves.
To check whether a number is prime, one approach is simply to divide the smaller primes, 2, 3, 5, 7, and so on, into the given number. If no factors other than 1 and the given number are found, the number is prime.

*Check Yourself answers appear at the end of each section throughout the book.

Here is the method known as the *sieve of Eratosthenes* for identifying prime numbers.

1. Write down a series of counting numbers, starting with the number 2. In the example below, we stop at 50.
2. Start at the number 2. Delete every second number after the 2.
3. Move to the number 3. Delete every third number after 3 (some numbers will be deleted twice).
4. Continue this process, deleting every fourth number after 4, every fifth number after 5, and so on.
5. When you have finished, the undeleted numbers are the prime numbers.

	2	3	~~4~~	5	~~6~~	7	~~8~~	~~9~~	~~10~~
11	~~12~~	13	~~14~~	~~15~~	~~16~~	17	~~18~~	19	20
~~21~~	~~22~~	23	~~24~~	~~25~~	26	~~27~~	28	29	~~30~~
31	~~32~~	~~33~~	~~34~~	~~35~~	36	37	~~38~~	~~39~~	~~40~~
41	~~42~~	43	~~44~~	~~45~~	~~46~~	47	~~48~~	~~49~~	~~50~~

The prime numbers less than 50 are 2, 3, 5, 7, 11, 13, 17, 19, 23, 29, 31, 37, 41, 43, and 47.

Example 2

Identifying Prime Numbers

Which of the following numbers are prime?

17 is a prime number. 1 and 17 are the only factors.

29 is a prime number. 1 and 29 are the only factors.

33 is *not* prime. 1, 3, 11, and 33 are all factors of 33.

Note: For two-digit numbers, if the number is *not* a prime, it will have one or more of the numbers 2, 3, 5, or 7 as factors.

CHECK YOURSELF 2

Which of the following numbers are prime numbers?

2, 6, 9, 11, 15, 19, 23, 35, 41

We can now define a second class of whole numbers.

NOTE This definition tells us that a composite number *does* have factors other than 1 and itself.

Definitions: Composite Number

A **composite number** is any whole number greater than 1 that is not prime.

Example 3

Identifying Composite Numbers

Which of the following numbers are composite?

18 is a composite number.	1, 2, 3, 6, 9, and 18 are all factors of 18.
23 is not a composite number.	1 and 23 are the only factors. This means that 23 is a *prime number.*
25 is a composite number.	1, 5, and 25 are factors.
38 is a composite number.	1, 2, 19, and 38 are factors.

 CHECK YOURSELF 3

Which of the following numbers are composite numbers?

2, 6, 10, 13, 16, 17, 22, 27, 31, 35

By the definitions of prime and composite numbers:

Rules and Properties: 0 and 1

The whole numbers 0 and 1 are neither prime nor composite.

To **factor a number** means to write the number as a product of its whole-number factors.

Example 4

Factoring a Composite Number

Factor the number 10.

$10 = 2 \cdot 5$

The order in which you write the factors does not matter, so $10 = 5 \cdot 2$ would also be correct.

Of course, $10 = 10 \cdot 1$ is also a correct statement. However, in this section we are interested in factors other than 1 and the given number.

Factor the number 21.

$21 = 3 \cdot 7$

CHECK YOURSELF 4

Factor 35.

In writing composite numbers as a product of factors, there may be several different possible factorizations.

Example 5

Factoring a Composite Number

Find three ways to factor 72.

NOTE There have to be at least two different factorizations, because a composite number has factors other than 1 and itself.

$$72 = 8 \cdot 9 \quad (1)$$
$$= 6 \cdot 12 \quad (2)$$
$$= 3 \cdot 24 \quad (3)$$

CHECK YOURSELF 5

Find three ways to factor 42.

We now want to write composite numbers as a product of their **prime factors.** Look again at the first factored line of Example 5. The process of factoring can be continued until all the factors are prime numbers.

Example 6

Factoring a Composite Number

NOTE This is often called a **factor tree.**

$$72 = \quad 8 \quad \cdot \quad 9$$
$$= \quad 2 \cdot 4 \quad \cdot 3 \cdot 3 \qquad \text{4 is still not prime, and so we continue by factoring 4.}$$
$$= 2 \cdot 2 \cdot 2 \cdot 3 \cdot 3 \qquad \text{72 is now written as a product of prime factors.}$$

When we write 72 as $2 \cdot 2 \cdot 2 \cdot 3 \cdot 3$, no further factorization is possible. This is called the *prime factorization* of 72.

NOTE Finding the prime factorization of a number will be important in our later work in adding fractions.

Now, what if we start with the second factored line from the same example, $72 = 6 \cdot 12$?

$$72 = \quad 6 \quad \cdot \quad 12 \qquad \text{Continue to factor 6 and 12.}$$
$$= 2 \cdot 3 \cdot \quad 3 \cdot 4 \qquad \text{Continue again to factor 4. Other choices for the factors of 12 are possible. As we shall see, the end result will be the same.}$$
$$= 2 \cdot 3 \cdot 3 \cdot 2 \cdot 2$$

No matter which pair of factors you start with, you will find the same prime factorization. In this case, there are three factors of 2 and two factors of 3. The order in which we write the factors does not matter.

CHECK YOURSELF 6

We could also write

72 = 2 · 36

Continue the factorization.

Rules and Properties: The Fundamental Theorem of Arithmetic

There is exactly one prime factorization for any composite number.

The method of the previous example will always work. However, an easier method for factoring composite numbers exists. This method is particularly useful when numbers get large, in which case factoring with a number tree becomes unwieldy.

Rules and Properties: Factoring by Division

NOTE The prime factorization is then the product of all the prime divisors and the final quotient.

To find the prime factorization of a number, divide the number by a series of primes until the final quotient is a prime number.

Example 7

Finding Prime Factors

To write 60 as a product of prime factors, divide 2 into 60 for a quotient of 30. Continue to divide by 2 again for the quotient 15. Because 2 won't divide exactly into 15, we try 3. Because the quotient 5 is prime, we are done.

$$
\begin{array}{ccc}
\dfrac{30}{2\overline{)60}} & \dfrac{15}{2\overline{)30}} & \dfrac{5}{3\overline{)15}} \quad \text{Prime}
\end{array}
$$

Our factors are the prime divisors and the final quotient. We have

$$60 = 2 \cdot 2 \cdot 3 \cdot 5$$

CHECK YOURSELF 7

Complete the process to find the prime factorization of 90.

$$
\dfrac{45}{2\overline{)90}} \qquad \dfrac{?}{?\overline{)45}}
$$

Remember to continue until the final quotient is prime.

Writing composite numbers in their completely factored form can be simplified if we use a format called **continued division.**

Example 8

Finding Prime Factors Using Continued Division

Use the continued-division method to divide 60 by a series of prime numbers.

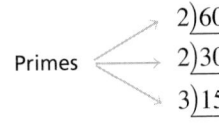

Primes

$$2\overline{)60}$$
$$2\overline{)30}$$
$$3\overline{)15}$$
$$5 \quad \text{Stop when the final quotient is prime.}$$

NOTE In each short division, we write the quotient *below* rather than above the dividend. This is just a convenience for the next division.

To write the factorization of 60, we include each divisor used and the final prime quotient. In our example, we have

$$60 = 2 \cdot 2 \cdot 3 \cdot 5$$

 CHECK YOURSELF 8

Find the prime factorization of 234.

We know that a factor or a divisor of a whole number divides that number exactly.

The factors or divisors of 20 are

$$1, 2, 4, 5, 10, 20$$

NOTE Again the factors of 20, other than 20 itself, are less than 20.

Each of these numbers divides 20 exactly, that is, with no remainder.

Our work in the rest of this section involves common factors or divisors. A **common factor** or **divisor** for two numbers is any factor that divides both the numbers exactly.

Example 9

Finding Common Factors

Look at the numbers 20 and 30. Is there a common factor for the two numbers?

First, we list the factors. Then we circle the ones that appear in both lists.

Factors

20: ①, ②, 4, ⑤, ⑩, 20

30: ①, ②, 3, ⑤, 6, ⑩, 15, 30

We see that 1, 2, 5, and 10 are common factors of 20 and 30. Each of these numbers divides both 20 and 30 exactly.

Our later work with fractions will require that we find the greatest common factor (GCF) of a group of numbers.

Definition: Greatest Common Factor

The **greatest common factor** (GCF) of a group of numbers is the *largest* number that will divide each of the given numbers exactly.

In the first part of Example 9, the common factors of the numbers 20 and 30 were listed as

1, 2, 5, 10   Common factors of 20 and 30

The GCF of the two numbers is then 10, because 10 is the *largest* of the four common factors.

 CHECK YOURSELF 9

List the factors of 30 and 36, and then find the GCF.

The method of Example 9 will also work in finding the GCF of a group of more than two numbers.

Example 10

Finding the GCF by Listing Factors

Find the GCF of 24, 30, and 36. We list the factors of each of the three numbers.

NOTE Looking at the three lists, we see that 1, 2, 3, and 6 are common factors.

24:    ①, ②, ③, 4, ⑥, 8, 12, 24
30:    ①, ②, ③, 5, ⑥, 10, 15, 30
36:    ①, ②, ③, 4, ⑥, 9, 12, 18, 36

6 is the GCF of 24, 30, and 36.

 CHECK YOURSELF 10

Find the GCF of 16, 24, and 32.

The process shown in Example 10 is very time-consuming when larger numbers are involved. A better approach to the problem of finding the GCF of a group of numbers uses the prime factorization of each number. Let's outline the process.

Finding the GCF

NOTE If there are no common prime factors, the GCF is 1.

Step 1   Write the prime factorization for each of the numbers in the group.
Step 2   Locate the prime factors that are *common* to all the numbers.
Step 3   The GCF will be the *product* of all the common prime factors.

Example 11

Finding the GCF

Find the GCF of 20 and 30.

Step 1   Write the prime factorizations of 20 and 30.

$20 = 2 \cdot 2 \cdot 5$

$30 = 2 \cdot 3 \cdot 5$

Step 2 Find the prime factors common to each number.

$20 = \circled{2} \cdot 2 \cdot \circled{5}$
$30 = \circled{2} \cdot 3 \cdot \circled{5}$ 2 and 5 are the common prime factors.

Step 3 Form the product of the common prime factors.

$2 \cdot 5 = 10$

10 is the greatest common factor.

CHECK YOURSELF 11

Find the GCF of 30 and 36.

To find the GCF of a group of more than two numbers, we use the same process.

Example 12

Finding the GCF

Find the GCF of 24, 30, and 36.

$24 = \circled{2} \cdot 2 \cdot 2 \cdot \circled{3}$
$30 = \circled{2} \cdot \circled{3} \cdot 5$
$36 = \circled{2} \cdot 2 \cdot \circled{3} \cdot 3$

2 and 3 are the prime factors common to *all three numbers.*

$2 \cdot 3 = 6$ is the GCF.

CHECK YOURSELF 12

Find the GCF of 15, 30, and 45.

Example 13

Finding the GCF

NOTE If two numbers, such as 15 and 28, have no common factor other than 1, they are called **relatively prime.**

Find the GCF of 15 and 28.

$15 = 3 \cdot 5$ There are no common prime factors
$28 = 2 \cdot 2 \cdot 7$ listed. But remember that 1 is a
            factor of every whole number.

The greatest common factor of 15 and 28 is 1.

CHECK YOURSELF 13

Find the greatest common factor of 30 and 49.

CHECK YOURSELF ANSWERS

1. 1, 2, 3, 4, 6, 8, 12, and 24.　　**2.** 2, 11, 19, 23, and 41 are prime numbers.

3. 6, 10, 16, 22, 27, and 35 are composite numbers.　　**4.** $5 \cdot 7$

5. $2 \cdot 21, 3 \cdot 14, 6 \cdot 7$　　**6.** $2 \cdot 2 \cdot 2 \cdot 3 \cdot 3$

7.

$$\begin{array}{ccccc}
45 & & 15 & & 5 \\
2\overline{)90} & \rightarrow & 3\overline{)45} & \rightarrow & 3\overline{)15}
\end{array}$$

8. $2 \cdot 3 \cdot 3 \cdot 13$

$90 = 2 \cdot 3 \cdot 3 \cdot 5$

9. 30: ①, ②, ③, 5, ⑥, 10, 15, 30

36: ①, ②, ③, 4, ⑥, 9, 12, 18, 36

6 is the GCF.

10. 16: ①, ②, ④, ⑧, 16

24: ①, ②, 3, ④, 6, ⑧, 12, 24

32: ①, ②, ④, ⑧, 16, 32

The GCF is 8.

11. $30 = ② \cdot ③ \cdot 5$

$36 = ② \cdot 2 \cdot ③ \cdot 3$

The GCF is $2 \cdot 3 = 6$.

12. 15　　**13.** GCF is 1; 30 and 49 are relatively prime.

0.6 Exercises

Name _____

Section _____ Date _____

List the factors of each of the following numbers.

1. 4

2. 6

3. 10

4. 12

5. 15

6. 21

7. 24

8. 32

9. 64

10. 66

11. 11

12. 37

Use the following list of numbers for Exercises 13 and 14.

0, 1, 15, 19, 23, 31, 49, 55, 59, 87, 91, 97, 103, 105

13. Which of the given numbers are prime?

14. Which of the given numbers are composite?

15. List all the prime numbers between 30 and 50.

16. List all the prime numbers between 55 and 75.

Find the prime factorization of each number.

17. 18

18. 22

19. 30

20. 35

21. 51

22. 42

23. 63

24. 94

ANSWERS

1. _____

2. _____

3. _____

4. _____

5. _____

6. _____

7. _____

8. _____

9. _____

10. _____

11. _____

12. _____

13. _____

14. _____

15. _____

16. _____

17. _____

18. _____

19. _____

20. _____

21. _____

22. _____

23. _____

24. _____

25. _____

26. _____

27. _____

28. _____

29. _____

30. _____

31. _____

32. _____

33. _____

34. _____

35. _____

36. _____

37. _____

38. _____

39. _____

40. _____

41. _____

42. _____

43. _____

44. _____

45. _____

46. _____

47. _____

48. _____

49. _____

50. _____

51. _____

52. _____

25. 70   **26.** 90

27. 66   **28.** 100

29. 130   **30.** 88

31. 315   **32.** 400

33. 225   **34.** 132

35. 189   **36.** 330

In later mathematics courses, you often will want to find factors of a number with a given sum or difference. The following problems use this technique.

37. Find two factors of 24 with a sum of 10.

38. Find two factors of 15 with a difference of 2.

39. Find two factors of 30 with a difference of 1.

40. Find two factors of 28 with a sum of 11.

Find the GCF for each of the following groups of numbers.

41. 4 and 6   **42.** 6 and 9

43. 10 and 15   **44.** 12 and 14

45. 21 and 24   **46.** 22 and 33

47. 20 and 21   **48.** 28 and 42

49. 18 and 24   **50.** 35 and 36

51. 18 and 54   **52.** 12 and 48

53. 36 and 48

54. 36 and 54

55. 84 and 105

56. 70 and 105

57. 45, 60, and 75

58. 36, 54, and 180

59. 12, 36, and 60

60. 15, 45, and 90

61. 105, 140, and 175

62. 32, 80, and 112

63. 25, 75, and 150

64. 36, 72, and 144

65. Prime numbers that differ by two are called *twin primes*. Examples are 3 and 5, 5 and 7, and so on. Find one pair of twin primes between 85 and 105.

66. The following questions refer to "twin primes" (see Exercise 65).

    (a) Search for, and make a list of several pairs of twin primes, in which the primes are greater than 3.

    (b) What do you notice about each number that lies *between* a pair of twin primes?

    (c) Write an explanation for your observation in part (b).

67. Obtain (or imagine that you have) a quantity of square tiles. Six tiles can be arranged in the shape of a rectangle in two different ways:

 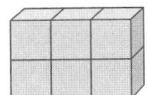

    (a) Record the dimensions of the rectangles shown above.

    (b) If you use seven tiles, how many different rectangles can you form?

    (c) If you use ten tiles, how many different rectangles can you form?

    (d) What kind of number (of tiles) permits *only one* arrangement into a rectangle? *More than* one arrangement?

68. The number 10 has four factors: 1, 2, 5, and 10. We can say that 10 has an even number of factors. Investigate several numbers to determine which numbers have an *even number* of factors and which numbers have an *odd number* of factors.

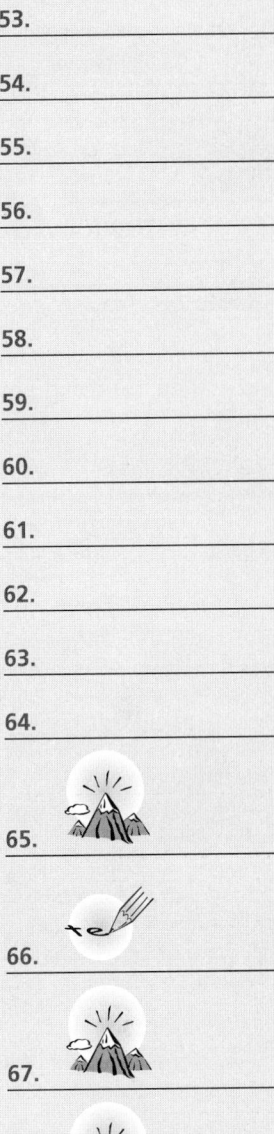

53. _____

54. _____

55. _____

56. _____

57. _____

58. _____

59. _____

60. _____

61. _____

62. _____

63. _____

64. _____

65. _____

66. _____

67. _____

68. _____

ANSWERS

69. _____

70. _____

71. _____

69. A natural number is said to be perfect if it is equal to the sum of its divisors.

    (a) Show that 28 is a perfect number.

    (b) Identify another perfect number less than 28.

70. Find the smallest natural number that is divisible by all of the following: 2, 3, 4, 6, 8, 9.

71. Suppose that a school has 1000 lockers and that they are all closed. A person passes through, opening every other locker, beginning with locker #2. Then another person passes through, changing every third locker (closing it if it is open, opening it if it is closed), starting with locker #3. Yet another person passes through, changing every fourth locker, beginning with locker #4. This process continues until 1000 people pass through.

    (a) At the end of this process, which locker numbers are closed?

    (b) Write an explanation for your answer to part (a).
       (Hint: It may help to attempt Exercise 68 first.)

Answers

We provide the answers for the odd numbered problems at the end of each Exercise set.

1. 1, 2, and 4   **3.** 1, 2, 5, and 10   **5.** 1, 3, 5, and 15

7. 1, 2, 3, 4, 6, 8, 12, and 24   **9.** 1, 2, 4, 8, 16, 32, and 64   **11.** 1 and 11

13. 19, 23, 31, 59, 97, 103   **15.** 31, 37, 41, 43, 47   **17.** $2 \cdot 3 \cdot 3$

19. $2 \cdot 3 \cdot 5$ **21.** $3 \cdot 17$ **23.** $3 \cdot 3 \cdot 7$ **25.** $2 \cdot 5 \cdot 7$ **27.** $2 \cdot 3 \cdot 11$

29. $2\overline{)130}$
    $5\overline{)65}$
      13
   $130 = 2 \cdot 5 \cdot 13$
      31. $3 \cdot 3 \cdot 5 \cdot 7$ **33.** $3 \cdot 3 \cdot 5 \cdot 5$

35. $3\overline{)189}$
    $3\overline{)63}$
    $3\overline{)21}$
      7
   $189 = 3 \cdot 3 \cdot 3 \cdot 7$
      37. 4, 6   **39.** 5, 6   **41.** 2   **43.** 5   **45.** 3

47. 1   **49.** 6   **51.** 18   **53.** 12   **55.** 21   **57.** 15   **59.** 12

61. 35   **63.** 25

65.   **67.**    **69.**   **71.**

0.7 Fractions

0.7 OBJECTIVES

1. Simplify a fraction
2. Multiply or divide two fractions
3. Add or subtract two fractions

This section provides a review of the basic operations, addition, subtraction, division, and multiplication, on fractions.

As mentioned in Section 0.1, the numbers used for counting are called the **natural numbers.** If we include zero in this group of numbers, we then call them the **whole numbers.**

The **numbers of ordinary arithmetic** consist of all the whole numbers and all fractions, whether they are proper fractions such as $\frac{1}{2}$ and $\frac{2}{3}$ or improper fractions such as $\frac{7}{2}$ or $\frac{19}{5}$.

Every number of ordinary arithmetic can be written in fraction form $\frac{a}{b}$.

The number 1 has many different fractional forms. Any fraction in which the numerator and denominator are the same (and not zero) is another name for the number one.

$$1 = \frac{2}{2} \qquad 1 = \frac{12}{12} \qquad 1 = \frac{257}{257}$$

Because these fractions are just different names for the same quantity, they are called **equivalent fractions.**

To write equivalent fractions, we use the **Fundamental Principle of Fractions (FPF).**

Rules and Properties: The Fundamental Principle of Fractions

$$\frac{a}{b} = \frac{a \cdot c}{b \cdot c} \text{ or } \frac{a \cdot c}{b \cdot c} = \frac{a}{b}, \text{ in which neither } b \text{ nor } c \text{ can equal zero.}$$

Example 1

Rewriting Fractions

Write three fractional representations for each number.

NOTE Each representation is a numeral, or name for the number. Each number has many names.

(a) $\frac{2}{3}$

We use the fundamental principle to multiply the numerator and denominator by the same number.

NOTE In each case, we have used the Fundamental Principle of Fractions with c equal to a different number.

$$\frac{2}{3} = \frac{2 \cdot 2}{3 \cdot 2} = \frac{4}{6}$$

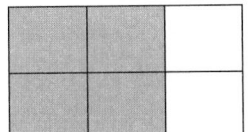 $\frac{4}{6}$

$$\frac{2}{3} = \frac{2 \cdot 3}{3 \cdot 3} = \frac{6}{9}$$

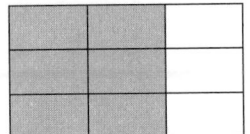 $\frac{6}{9}$

$$\frac{2}{3} = \frac{2 \cdot 10}{3 \cdot 10} = \frac{20}{30}$$

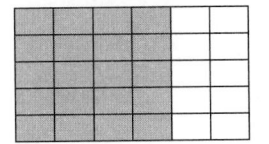 $\frac{20}{30}$

(b) 5

$$5 = \frac{5 \cdot 2}{1 \cdot 2} = \frac{10}{2}$$

$$5 = \frac{5 \cdot 3}{1 \cdot 3} = \frac{15}{3}$$

$$5 = \frac{5 \cdot 100}{1 \cdot 100} = \frac{500}{100}$$

 CHECK YOURSELF 1

Write three fractional representations for each number.

(a) $\frac{5}{8}$ **(b)** $\frac{4}{3}$ **(c)** 3

The simplest fractional representation for a number has the smallest numerator and denominator. Fractions written in this form are said to be **simplified.**

Example 2

Simplifying Fractions

Simplify each fraction.

(a) $\frac{22}{55}$ **(b)** $\frac{35}{45}$ **(c)** $\frac{24}{36}$

In each case, we first find the prime factors for the numerator and for the denominator.

(a) $\frac{22}{55} = \frac{2 \cdot 11}{5 \cdot 11}$

We then use the fundamental principle.

$$\frac{22}{55} = \frac{2 \cdot 11}{5 \cdot 11} = \frac{2}{5}$$

(b) $\frac{35}{45} = \frac{7 \cdot 5}{3 \cdot 3 \cdot 5} = \frac{7 \cdot 5}{9 \cdot 5}$

Using the fundamental principle to remove the common factor of 5 yields

$$\frac{35}{45} = \frac{7}{9}$$

(c) $\frac{24}{36} = \frac{2 \cdot 2 \cdot 2 \cdot 3}{2 \cdot 2 \cdot 3 \cdot 3}$

Removing the common factor $2 \cdot 2 \cdot 3$ yields

$\frac{2}{3}$

CHECK YOURSELF 2

Simplify each fraction.

(a) $\frac{21}{33}$ **(b)** $\frac{15}{30}$ **(c)** $\frac{12}{54}$

Rules and Properties: Multiplication of Fractions

NOTE This is how two fractions, under the operation of multiplication, become one fraction.

$$\frac{a}{b} \cdot \frac{c}{d} = \frac{a \cdot c}{b \cdot d}$$

When multiplying two fractions, rewrite them in factored form, and then simplify before multiplying.

Example 3

Multiplying Fractions

Find the product of the two fractions.

NOTE A product is the result from multiplication.

$$\frac{9}{2} \cdot \frac{4}{3}$$

$$\frac{9}{2} \cdot \frac{4}{3} = \frac{9 \cdot 4}{2 \cdot 3}$$

$$= \frac{3 \cdot 3 \cdot 2 \cdot 2}{2 \cdot 3}$$

$$= \frac{3 \cdot 2}{1}$$

$$= \frac{6}{1} \quad \text{The denominator of one is not necessary.}$$

$$= 6$$

 CHECK YOURSELF 3

Multiply and simplify each pair of fractions.

(a) $\dfrac{3}{5} \cdot \dfrac{10}{7}$ **(b)** $\dfrac{12}{5} \cdot \dfrac{10}{6}$

Rules and Properties: Division of Fractions

NOTE This is how two fractions, under the operation of division, become one fraction.

$$\frac{a}{b} \div \frac{c}{d} = \frac{a}{b} \cdot \frac{d}{c} = \frac{a \cdot d}{b \cdot c}$$

To divide two fractions, the divisor is inverted, then the fractions are multiplied.

Example 4

Dividing Fractions

Find the quotient of the two fractions.

NOTE A quotient is the result from division.

$$\frac{7}{3} \div \frac{5}{6}$$

$$\frac{7}{3} \div \frac{5}{6} = \frac{7}{3} \cdot \frac{6}{5} = \frac{7 \cdot 6}{3 \cdot 5}$$

$$= \frac{7 \cdot 2 \cdot 3}{3 \cdot 5} = \frac{7 \cdot 2}{5}$$

$$= \frac{14}{5}$$

CHECK YOURSELF 4

Find the quotient of the two fractions

$$\frac{9}{2} \div \frac{3}{5}$$

Rules and Properties: Addition of Fractions

NOTE This is how two fractions with the same denominator, under the operation of addition, become one fraction.

$$\frac{a}{b} + \frac{c}{b} = \frac{a+c}{b}$$

When adding two fractions, find the **least common denominator (LCD)** first. The least common denominator is the smallest number that both denominators evenly divide. If you have forgotten how to find the LCD, you might want to review the process from your arithmetic book. After rewriting the fractions with this denominator, add the numerators, then simplify the result.

Example 5

Adding Fractions

Find the sum of the two fractions.

NOTE A sum is the result from addition.

$$\frac{5}{8} + \frac{7}{12}$$ 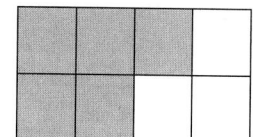 +

The LCD of 8 and 12 is 24. Each fraction should be rewritten as a fraction with that denominator.

$$\frac{5}{8} = \frac{15}{24}$$ Multiply the numerator and denominator by 3.

$$\frac{7}{12} = \frac{14}{24}$$ Multiply the numerator and denominator by 2.

$$\frac{5}{8} + \frac{7}{12} = \frac{15}{24} + \frac{14}{24} = \frac{29}{24}$$ This fraction cannot be simplified.

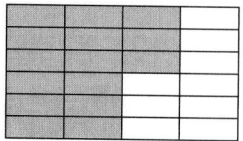 +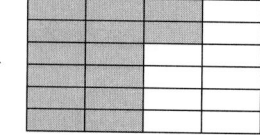

 CHECK YOURSELF 5

Find the sum for each pair of fractions.

(a) $\dfrac{4}{5} + \dfrac{7}{9}$ **(b)** $\dfrac{5}{6} + \dfrac{4}{15}$

Rules and Properties: Subtraction of Fractions

NOTE This is how two fractions with like denominators become one fraction under the operation of subtraction.

$$\frac{a}{b} - \frac{c}{b} = \frac{a - c}{b}$$

Subtracting fractions is treated exactly like adding them, except the numerator becomes the difference of the two numerators.

Example 6

Subtracting Fractions

Find the difference.

NOTE The difference is the result from subtraction.

$$\frac{7}{9} - \frac{1}{6}$$

The LCD is 18. We rewrite the fractions with that denominator.

$$\frac{7}{9} = \frac{14}{18}$$

$$\frac{1}{6} = \frac{3}{18}$$

$$\frac{7}{9} - \frac{1}{6} = \frac{14}{18} - \frac{3}{18} = \frac{11}{18} \qquad \text{This fraction cannot be simplified.}$$

 CHECK YOURSELF 6

Find the difference $\frac{11}{12} - \frac{5}{8}$.

Fractions with denominator 10 (or 100, 1000, etc.) can be written in **decimal form.** Example 7 demonstrates the addition or subtraction of decimal fractions.

Example 7   Converting a Fraction to a Mixed Number

Convert $\frac{17}{5}$ to a mixed number.

Divide 17 by 5.

$$\begin{array}{r} 3 \\ 5{\overline{)}17} \\ 15 \\ \hline 2 \end{array} \qquad \frac{17}{5} = 3\frac{2}{5}$$

Remainder

Original denominator

Quotient

 CHECK YOURSELF 7

Convert $\frac{32}{5}$ *to a mixed number.*

Example 8 illustrates how to convert a mixed number to an improper fraction.

Example 8   Converting Mixed Numbers to Improper Fractions

(a) Convert $3\frac{2}{5}$ to an improper fraction.

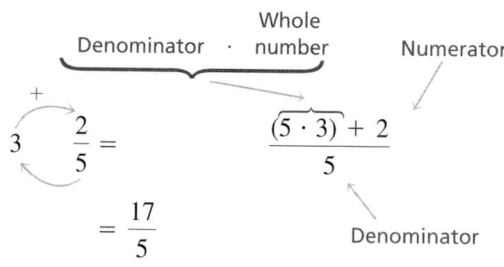

Multiply the denominator by the whole number ($5 \cdot 3 = 15$). Add the numerator. We now have 17.

Write 17 over the original denominator.

NOTE Multiply the denominator, 7, by the whole number, 4, and add the numerator, 5.

(b) Convert $4\frac{5}{7}$ to an improper fraction.

$$4\frac{5}{7} = \frac{(7 \cdot 4) + 5}{7} = \frac{33}{7}$$

✔ **CHECK YOURSELF 8**

Convert $5\frac{3}{8}$ to an improper fraction.

When multiplying two mixed numbers, it is usually easier to change the mixed numbers to improper fractions and then perform the multiplication.

CHECK YOURSELF ANSWERS

1. Answers will vary.   **2.** (a) $\frac{7}{11}$; (b) $\frac{1}{2}$; (c) $\frac{2}{9}$ **3.** (a) $\frac{6}{7}$; (b) 4

4. $\frac{15}{2}$ **5.** (a) $\frac{71}{45}$; (b) $\frac{11}{10}$ **6.** $\frac{7}{24}$ **7.** (a) 37.179; (b) 63.623   **8.** 55.796

Name _____

Section _____ Date _____

In Exercises 1 to 12, write three fractional representations for each number.

ANSWERS

1. $\dfrac{3}{7}$ **2.** $\dfrac{2}{5}$ **3.** $\dfrac{4}{9}$

4. $\dfrac{7}{8}$ **5.** $\dfrac{5}{6}$ **6.** $\dfrac{11}{13}$

7. $\dfrac{10}{17}$ **8.** $\dfrac{3}{7}$ **9.** $\dfrac{9}{16}$

10. $\dfrac{6}{11}$ **11.** $\dfrac{7}{9}$ **12.** $\dfrac{15}{16}$

Write each fraction in simplest form.

13. $\dfrac{8}{12}$ **14.** $\dfrac{12}{15}$ **15.** $\dfrac{10}{14}$

16. $\dfrac{15}{50}$ **17.** $\dfrac{12}{18}$ **18.** $\dfrac{28}{35}$

19. $\dfrac{35}{40}$ **20.** $\dfrac{21}{24}$ **21.** $\dfrac{11}{44}$

22. $\dfrac{10}{25}$ **23.** $\dfrac{12}{36}$ **24.** $\dfrac{18}{48}$

25. $\dfrac{24}{27}$ **26.** $\dfrac{30}{50}$ **27.** $\dfrac{32}{40}$

28. $\dfrac{17}{51}$ **29.** $\dfrac{75}{105}$ **30.** $\dfrac{62}{93}$

31. $\dfrac{48}{60}$ **32.** $\dfrac{48}{66}$ **33.** $\dfrac{105}{135}$

1. _____
2. _____
3. _____
4. _____
5. _____
6. _____
7. _____
8. _____
9. _____
10. _____
11. _____
12. _____

13. ___	14. ___	15. ___
16. ___	17. ___	18. ___
19. ___	20. ___	21. ___
22. ___	23. ___	24. ___
25. ___	26. ___	27. ___
28. ___	29. ___	30. ___
31. ___	32. ___	33. ___

34. _____ **35.** _____

36. _____ **37.** _____

38. _____

39. _____

40. _____

41. _____

42. _____

43. _____

44. _____

45. _____

46. _____ **47.** _____

48. _____ **49.** _____

50. _____ **51.** _____

52. _____ **53.** _____

54. _____ **55.** _____

56. _____ **57.** _____

58. _____

59. _____ **60.** _____

61. _____ **62.** _____

63. _____ **64.** _____

34. $\dfrac{54}{126}$ **35.** $\dfrac{15}{44}$ **36.** $\dfrac{10}{63}$

Multiply. Be sure to simplify each product.

37. $\dfrac{3}{4} \cdot \dfrac{7}{5}$ **38.** $\dfrac{2}{3} \cdot \dfrac{8}{5}$ **39.** $\dfrac{3}{5} \cdot \dfrac{5}{7}$

40. $\dfrac{6}{11} \cdot \dfrac{8}{6}$ **41.** $\dfrac{6}{13} \cdot \dfrac{4}{9}$ **42.** $\dfrac{5}{9} \cdot \dfrac{6}{11}$

43. $\dfrac{3}{11} \cdot \dfrac{7}{9}$ **44.** $\dfrac{7}{9} \cdot \dfrac{3}{5}$ **45.** $\dfrac{3}{10} \cdot \dfrac{5}{9}$

Divide. Write each result in simplest form.

46. $\dfrac{5}{21} \div \dfrac{25}{14}$ **47.** $\dfrac{1}{5} \div \dfrac{3}{4}$ **48.** $\dfrac{2}{5} \div \dfrac{1}{3}$

49. $\dfrac{2}{5} \div \dfrac{3}{4}$ **50.** $\dfrac{5}{8} \div \dfrac{3}{4}$ **51.** $\dfrac{8}{9} \div \dfrac{4}{3}$

52. $\dfrac{5}{9} \div \dfrac{8}{11}$ **53.** $\dfrac{7}{10} \div \dfrac{5}{9}$ **54.** $\dfrac{8}{9} \div \dfrac{11}{15}$

55. $\dfrac{8}{15} \div \dfrac{2}{5}$ **56.** $\dfrac{5}{27} \div \dfrac{15}{54}$

57. $\dfrac{5}{27} \div \dfrac{25}{36}$ **58.** $\dfrac{9}{28} \div \dfrac{27}{35}$

Add.

59. $\dfrac{2}{5} + \dfrac{1}{4}$ **60.** $\dfrac{2}{3} + \dfrac{3}{10}$ **61.** $\dfrac{2}{5} + \dfrac{7}{15}$

62. $\dfrac{3}{10} + \dfrac{7}{12}$ **63.** $\dfrac{3}{8} + \dfrac{5}{12}$ **64.** $\dfrac{5}{36} + \dfrac{7}{24}$

65. $\dfrac{2}{15} + \dfrac{9}{20}$

66. $\dfrac{9}{14} + \dfrac{10}{21}$

67. $\dfrac{7}{15} + \dfrac{13}{18}$

68. $\dfrac{12}{25} + \dfrac{19}{30}$

69. $\dfrac{1}{2} + \dfrac{1}{4} + \dfrac{1}{8}$

70. $\dfrac{1}{3} + \dfrac{1}{5} + \dfrac{1}{10}$

Subtract.

71. $\dfrac{8}{9} - \dfrac{3}{9}$

72. $\dfrac{9}{10} - \dfrac{6}{10}$

73. $\dfrac{5}{8} - \dfrac{1}{8}$

74. $\dfrac{11}{12} - \dfrac{7}{12}$

75. $\dfrac{7}{8} - \dfrac{2}{3}$

76. $\dfrac{5}{6} - \dfrac{3}{5}$

77. $\dfrac{11}{18} - \dfrac{2}{9}$

78. $\dfrac{5}{6} - \dfrac{1}{4}$

Convert the following fractions to mixed numbers.

79. $\dfrac{17}{4}$

80. $\dfrac{200}{11}$

Convert the following mixed numbers to fractions.

81. $3\dfrac{1}{4}$

82. $6\dfrac{3}{4}$

83. Sewing. Roseann is making shirts for her three children. One shirt requires $\dfrac{1}{2}$ yard of material, a second shirt requires $\dfrac{1}{3}$ yard of material, and the third shirt requires $\dfrac{1}{4}$ yard of material. How much material is required for all three shirts?

84. Hiking. Jose rode his trail bike for 10 miles. Two-thirds of the distance was over a mountain trail. How long is the mountain trail?

85. Salary. You make $240 a day on a job. What will you receive for working $\dfrac{2}{3}$ of a day?

© 2001 McGraw-Hill Companies

ANSWERS

65. _____

66. _____

67. _____

68. _____

69. _____

70. _____

71. _____ 72. _____

73. _____ 74. _____

75. _____ 76. _____

77. _____ 78. _____

79. _____ 80. _____

81. _____ 82. _____

83. _____

84. _____

85. _____

ANSWERS

86.

87.

88.

89.

90.

91.

92.

93.

94.

95.

86. Surveys. A survey has found that $\frac{3}{4}$ of the people in a city own pets. Of those who own pets, $\frac{2}{3}$ have cats. What fraction of those surveyed own cats?

Solve the following applications.

87. Map scales. The scale on a map is 1 inch (in.) = 200 miles (mi). What actual distance, in miles, does $\frac{3}{8}$ in. represent?

88. Salary. You make $90 a day on a job. What will you receive for working $\frac{3}{4}$ of a day?

89. Size. A lumberyard has a stack of 80 sheets of plywood. If each sheet is $\frac{3}{4}$ in. thick, how high will the stack be?

90. Family budget. A family uses $\frac{2}{5}$ of its monthly income for housing and utilities on average. If the family's monthly income is $1750, what is spent for housing and utilities? What amount remains?

91. Elections. Of the eligible voters in an election, $\frac{3}{4}$ were registered. Of those registered, $\frac{5}{9}$ actually voted. What fraction of those people who were eligible voted?

92. Surveys. A survey has found that $\frac{7}{10}$ of the people in a city own pets. Of those who own pets, $\frac{2}{3}$ have dogs. What fraction of those surveyed own dogs?

93. Area. A kitchen has dimensions $3\frac{1}{3}$ by $3\frac{3}{4}$ yards (yd). How many square yards (yd^2) of linoleum must be bought to cover the floor?

94. Distance. If you drive at an average speed of 52 miles per hour (mi/h) for $1\frac{3}{4}$ h, how far will you travel?

95. Distance. A jet flew at an average speed of 540 mi/h on a $4\frac{2}{3}$-h flight. What was the distance flown?

96. Area. A piece of land that has $11\frac{2}{3}$ acres is being subdivided for home lots. It is estimated that $\frac{2}{7}$ of the area will be used for roads. What amount remains to be used for lots?

97. Circumference. To find the approximate circumference or distance around a circle, we multiply its diameter by $\frac{22}{7}$. What is the circumference of a circle with a diameter of 21 in.?

98. Area. The length of a rectangle is $\frac{6}{7}$ yd, and its width is $\frac{21}{26}$ yd. What is its area in square yards?

99. Volume. Find the volume of a box that measures $2\frac{1}{4}$ in. by $3\frac{7}{8}$ in. by $4\frac{5}{6}$ in.

100. Topsoil. Nico wishes to purchase mulch to cover his garden. The garden measures $7\frac{7}{8}$ feet (ft) by $10\frac{1}{8}$ ft. He wants the mulch to be $\frac{1}{3}$ ft deep. How much mulch should Nico order if he must order a whole number of cubic feet?

101. Every fraction (rational number) has a corresponding decimal form that either terminates or repeats. For example, $\frac{5}{16} = 0.3125$ (the decimal form terminates), and $\frac{4}{11} = 0.363636........$ (the decimal form repeats). Investigate a number of fractions to determine which ones terminate and which ones repeat. (Hint: you can focus on the denominator; study the prime factorizations of several denominators.)

102. Complete the following sums:

$$\frac{1}{2} + \frac{1}{4} =$$

$$\frac{1}{2} + \frac{1}{4} + \frac{1}{8} =$$

$$\frac{1}{2} + \frac{1}{4} + \frac{1}{8} + \frac{1}{16} =$$

Based on these, predict the sum:

$$\frac{1}{2} + \frac{1}{4} + \frac{1}{8} + \frac{1}{16} + \frac{1}{32} + \frac{1}{64} + \frac{1}{128}$$

96. _____

97. _____

98. _____

99. _____

100. _____

101. _____

102. _____

Answers

1. $\frac{6}{14}, \frac{9}{21}, \frac{12}{28}$ **3.** $\frac{8}{18}, \frac{16}{36}, \frac{40}{90}$ **5.** $\frac{10}{12}, \frac{15}{18}, \frac{50}{60}$ **7.** $\frac{20}{34}, \frac{30}{51}, \frac{100}{170}$

9. $\frac{18}{32}, \frac{27}{48}, \frac{90}{160}$ **11.** $\frac{14}{18}, \frac{35}{45}, \frac{140}{180}$ **13.** $\frac{2}{3}$ **15.** $\frac{5}{7}$ **17.** $\frac{2}{3}$ **19.** $\frac{7}{8}$

Answers (*continued*)

21. $\frac{1}{4}$ **23.** $\frac{1}{3}$ **25.** $\frac{8}{9}$ **27.** $\frac{4}{5}$ **29.** $\frac{5}{7}$ **31.** $\frac{4}{5}$ **33.** $\frac{7}{9}$

35. $\frac{15}{44}$ **37.** $\frac{21}{20}$ **39.** $\frac{3}{7}$ **41.** $\frac{8}{39}$ **43.** $\frac{7}{33}$ **45.** $\frac{1}{6}$ **47.** $\frac{4}{15}$

49. $\frac{8}{15}$ **51.** $\frac{2}{3}$ **53.** $\frac{63}{50}$ **55.** $\frac{4}{3}$ **57.** $\frac{4}{15}$ **59.** $\frac{13}{20}$ **61.** $\frac{13}{15}$

63. $\frac{19}{24}$ **65.** $\frac{7}{12}$ **67.** $\frac{107}{90}$ **69.** $\frac{7}{8}$ **71.** $\frac{5}{9}$ **73.** $\frac{1}{2}$ **75.** $\frac{5}{24}$

77. $\frac{7}{18}$ **79.** $4\frac{1}{4}$ **81.** $\frac{13}{4}$ **83.** $\frac{13}{12}$ or $1\frac{1}{12}$ yds.   **85.** \$160   **87.** 75 mi.

89. 60 in. or 5 ft.   **91.** $\frac{5}{12}$ **93.** $12\frac{1}{2}$ yds.   **95.** 2520 mi.   **97.** 66 in. or $5\frac{1}{2}$ ft.

99. $42\frac{9}{64}$ in.^{3} **101.** Many answers

0.8 Exponents and the Order of Operations

 0.8 OBJECTIVES

1. Write a product of factors in exponential form
2. Evaluate an expression involving several operations

Often in mathematics we define symbols that allow us to write a mathematical statement in a more compact or "shorthand" form. This is an idea that you have encountered before. For example, the repeated addition:

$$5 + 5 + 5$$

NOTE
$5 + 5 + 5 = 15$
and
$3 \cdot 5 = 15$

can be rewritten as

$$3 \cdot 5$$

Thus multiplication is shorthand for repeated addition.

In algebra, we frequently have a number or variable that is repeated as a factor in an expression several times. For instance, we might have

$$5 \cdot 5 \cdot 5$$

To abbreviate this product, we write

NOTE A factor is a number or a variable that is being multiplied by another number or variable.

$$5 \cdot 5 \cdot 5 = 5^3$$

This is called **exponential notation** or **exponential form.** The exponent or power, here 3, indicates the number of times that the factor or base, here 5, appears in a product.

 C A U T I O N

Be careful: 5^3 is *not* the same as $5 \cdot 3$. Notice that
$5^3 = 5 \cdot 5 \cdot 5 = 125$ and
$5 \cdot 3 = 15$.

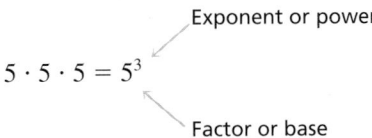

$$5 \cdot 5 \cdot 5 = 5^3$$

This is read "5 to the third power" or "5 cubed."

Example 1

Writing in Exponential Form

Write $3 \cdot 3 \cdot 3 \cdot 3$, using exponential form. The number 3 appears 4 times in the product, so

Four factors
of 3

$$3 \cdot 3 \cdot 3 \cdot 3 = 3^4$$

This is read "3 to the fourth power."

 CHECK YOURSELF 1

Rewrite each using exponential form.

(a) $4 \cdot 4 \cdot 4 \cdot 4 \cdot 4 \cdot 4$ **(b)** $7 \cdot 7 \cdot 7 \cdot 7$

To evaluate an arithmetic expression, you need to know the order in which the operations are done. To see why, simplify the expression $5 + 2 \cdot 3$.

CAUTION

Only one of these results can be correct.

Method 1 or *Method 2*

$\underbrace{5 + 2} \cdot 3$

Add first.

$5 + \underbrace{2 \cdot 3}$

Multiply first.

$= 7 \cdot 3$
$= 21$

$= 5 + 6$
$= 11$

Because we get different answers depending on how we do the problem, the language of mathematics would not be clear if there were no agreement on which method is correct. The following rules tell us the order in which operations should be done.

Step by Step: The Order of Operations

NOTE Parentheses and brackets are both grouping symbols. Later we will see that fraction bars and radicals are also grouping symbols.

Step 1 Evaluate all expressions inside grouping symbols first.
Step 2 Evaluate all expressions involving exponents.
Step 3 Do any multiplication or division in order, working from left to right.
Step 4 Do any addition or subtraction in order, working from left to right.

Example 2

Evaluating Expressions

Evaluate $5 + 2 \cdot 3$.

There are no parentheses or exponents, so start with step 3: First multiply and then add.

$5 + 2 \cdot 3$

Multiply first.

$= 5 + 6$

Then add.

NOTE Method 2 shown above is the correct one.

$= 11$

 CHECK YOURSELF 2

Evaluate the following expressions.

(a) $20 - 3 \cdot 4$ **(b)** $9 + 6 \div 3$

When there are no parentheses, evaluate the exponents first.

Example 3

Evaluating Expressions

Evaluate $5 \cdot 3^2$.

$5 \cdot 3^2 = 5 \cdot 9$

Evaluate the power first.

$= 45$

 CHECK YOURSELF 3

Evaluate $4 \cdot 2^4$.

Both scientific and graphing calculators correctly interpret the order of operations. This is demonstrated in Example 4.

Example 4

Using a Calculator to Evaluate Expressions

Use your scientific or graphing calculator to evaluate each expression. Round the answer to the nearest tenth.

(a) $24.3 + 6.2 \cdot 3.53$

When evaluating expressions by hand, you must consider the order of operations. In this case, the multiplication must be done first, then the addition. With a calculator, you need only enter the expression correctly. The calculator is programmed to follow the order of operations.

Entering   24.3 $\boxed{+}$ 6.2 $\boxed{\times}$ 3.53 $\boxed{\text{ENTER}}$

> **NOTE** With most graphing calculators, the final command is $\boxed{\text{ENTER}}$. With most other scientific calculators; the key is marked $\boxed{=}$.

yields the evaluation 46.186. Rounding to the nearest tenth, we have 46.2.

(b) $2.45^3 - 49 \div 8000 + 12.2 \cdot 1.3$

Some calculators use the carat (^) to designate powers. Others use the symbol x^y (or y^x).

Entering 2.45 $\boxed{\wedge}$ 3 $\boxed{-}$ 49 $\boxed{\div}$ 8000 $\boxed{+}$ 12.2 $\boxed{\times}$ 1.3 $\boxed{\text{ENTER}}$

or   2.45 $\boxed{y^x}$ 3 $\boxed{-}$ 49 $\boxed{\div}$ 8000 $\boxed{+}$ 12.2 $\boxed{\times}$ 1.3 $\boxed{=}$

yields the evaluation 30.56. Rounding to the nearest tenth, we have 30.6.

CHECK YOURSELF 4

Use your scientific or graphing calculator to evaluate each expression.

(a) $67.89 - 4.7 \cdot 12.7$ **(b)** $4.3 \cdot 55.5 - 3.75^3 + 8007 \div 1600$

Operations inside grouping symbols are done first.

Example 5

Evaluating Expressions

Evaluate $(5 + 2) \cdot 3$.
    Do the operation inside the parentheses as the first step.

$(5 + 2) \cdot 3 = 7 \cdot 3 = 21$

────── Add.

CHECK YOURSELF 5

Evaluate $4 \cdot (9 - 3)$.

The principle is the same when more than two "levels" of operations are involved.

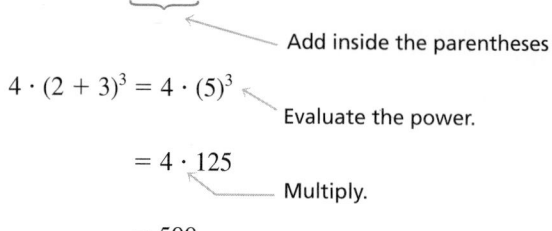

Example 6

(a) Evaluate $4 \cdot (2 + 3)^3$.

Add inside the parentheses first.

$$4 \cdot (2 + 3)^3 = 4 \cdot (5)^3$$

Evaluate the power.

$$= 4 \cdot 125$$

Multiply.

$$= 500$$

(b) Evaluate $5 \cdot (7 - 3)^2 - 10$.

Evaluate the expression inside the parentheses.

$$5 \cdot (7 - 3)^2 - 10 = 5(4)^2 - 10$$

Evaluate the power.

$$= 5 \cdot 16 - 10$$

Multiply.

$$= 80 - 10 = 70$$

Subtract.

 CHECK YOURSELF 6

Evaluate.

(a) $4 \cdot 3^3 - 8 \cdot 11$ **(b)** $12 + 4 \cdot (2 + 3)^2$

CHECK YOURSELF ANSWERS

1. (a) 4^6; **(b)** 7^4 **2. (a)** 8; **(b)** 11   **3.** 64   **4. (a)** 8.2; **(b)** 190.92   **5.** 24
6. (a) 20; **(b)** 112

0.8 Exercises

Write each expression in exponential form.

1. $7 \cdot 7 \cdot 7 \cdot 7$

2. $2 \cdot 2 \cdot 2 \cdot 2 \cdot 2 \cdot 2$

3. $6 \cdot 6 \cdot 6 \cdot 6 \cdot 6$

4. $4 \cdot 4 \cdot 4 \cdot 4 \cdot 4 \cdot 4 \cdot 4$

5. $8 \cdot 8 \cdot 8 \cdot 8 \cdot 8 \cdot 8 \cdot 8 \cdot 8 \cdot 8 \cdot 8$

6. $10 \cdot 10 \cdot 10$

7. $15 \cdot 15 \cdot 15 \cdot 15 \cdot 15 \cdot 15$

8. $31 \cdot 31 \cdot 31 \cdot 31 \cdot 31 \cdot 31 \cdot 31 \cdot 31 \cdot 31 \cdot 31$

Evaluate each of the following expressions.

9. $7 + 2 \cdot 6$

10. $10 - 4 \cdot 2$

11. $(7 + 2) \cdot 6$

12. $(10 - 4) \cdot 2$

13. $12 - 8 \div 4$

14. $10 + 20 \div 5$

15. $(12 - 8) \div 4$

16. $(10 + 20) \div 5$

17. $8 \cdot 7 + 2 \cdot 2$

18. $48 \div 8 - 4 \div 2$

19. $8 \cdot (7 + 2) \cdot 2$

20. $48 \div (8 - 4) \div 2$

21. $3 \cdot 5^2$

22. $5 \cdot 2^3$

23. $(3 \cdot 5)^2$

24. $(5 \cdot 2)^3$

25. $4 \cdot 3^2 - 2$

26. $3 \cdot 2^4 - 8$

ANSWERS

1. _____
2. _____
3. _____
4. _____
5. _____
6. _____
7. _____
8. _____
9. _____
10. _____
11. _____
12. _____
13. _____
14. _____
15. _____
16. _____
17. _____
18. _____
19. _____
20. _____
21. _____
22. _____
23. _____
24. _____
25. _____
26. _____

27. _____

28. _____

29. _____

30. _____

31. _____

32. _____

33. _____

34. _____

35. _____

36. _____

37. _____

38. _____

39. _____

40. _____

41. _____

42. _____

43. _____

44. _____

45. _____

46. _____

47. _____

48. _____

49. _____

50. _____

51. _____

52. _____

53. _____

54. _____

27. $7 \cdot (2^3 - 5)$ **28.** $4 \cdot (3^2 - 7)$

29. $3 \cdot 2^4 - 6 \cdot 2$ **30.** $4 \cdot 2^3 - 5 \cdot 6$

31. $(2 \cdot 4)^2 - 8 \cdot 3$ **32.** $(3 \cdot 2)^3 - 7 \cdot 3$

33. $4 \cdot (2 + 6)^2$ **34.** $3 \cdot (8 - 4)^2$

35. $(4 \cdot 2 + 6)^2$ **36.** $(3 \cdot 8 - 4)^2$

37. $3 \cdot (4 + 3)^2$ **38.** $5 \cdot (4 - 2)^3$

39. $3 \cdot 4 + 3^2$ **40.** $5 \cdot 4 - 2^3$

41. $4 \cdot (2 + 3)^2 - 25$ **42.** $8 + 2 \cdot (3 + 3)^2$

43. $(4 \cdot 2 + 3)^2 - 25$ **44.** $8 + (2 \cdot 3 + 3)^2$

Evaluate using your calculator. Round your answer to the nearest tenth.

45. $(1.2)^3 \div 2.0736 \cdot 2.4 + 1.6935 - 2.4896$

46. $(5.21 \cdot 3.14 - 6.2154) \div 5.12 - 0.45625$

47. $1.23 \cdot 3.169 - 2.05194 + (5.128 \cdot 3.15 - 10.1742)$

48. $4.56 + (2.34)^4 \div 4.7896 \cdot 6.93 \div 27.5625 - 3.1269 + (1.56)^2$

49. Population doubling. Over the last 2000 years, the Earth's population has doubled approximately 5 times. Write this last factor in exponential form.

50. Volume of a cube. The volume of a cube with each edge of length 9 in. is given by $9 \cdot 9 \cdot 9$. Write the volume using exponential notation.

Insert grouping symbols in the proper place so that the given value of the expression is obtained.

51. $36 \div 4 + 2 - 4;\ 2$ **52.** $48 \div 3 \cdot 2 - 2 \cdot 3;\ 2$

53. $6 + 9 \div 3 + 16 - 4 \cdot 2;\ 29$

54. $5 - 3 \cdot 2 + 8 \cdot 5 - 2;\ 28$

Answers

1. 7^4 **3.** 6^5 **5.** 8^{10} **7.** 15^6 **9.** 19   **11.** 54   **13.** 10
15. 1   **17.** 60   **19.** 144   **21.** 75   **23.** 225   **25.** 34   **27.** 21
29. 36   **31.** 40   **33.** 256   **35.** 196   **37.** 147   **39.** 21   **41.** 75
43. 96   **45.** 1.2   **47.** 7.8   **49.** 2^5 **51.** $36 \div (4 + 2) - 4$
53. $(6 + 9) \div 3 + (16 - 4) \cdot 2$

THE LANGUAGE OF ALGEBRA

1

INTRODUCTION

Anthropologists and archeologists investigate modern human cultures and societies as well as cultures that existed so long ago that their characteristics must be inferred from objects found buried in lost cities or villages. When some interesting object is found, such as the Babylonian tablets mentioned in Chapter 0, often the first questions that arise are "How old is this? When did this culture flourish?" With methods such as carbon dating, it has been established that large, organized cultures existed around 3000 B.C.E. in Egypt, 2800 B.C.E. in India, no later than 1500 B.C.E. in China, and around 1000 B.C.E. in the Americas.

How long ago was 1500 B.C.E.? Which is older, an object from 3000 B.C.E. or an object from 500 A.D.*? Using the Christian notation for dates, we have to count A.D. years and B.C.E. years differently. An object from 500 A.D. is $2000 - 500$ years old, or about 1500 years old. But an object from 3000 B.C.E. is $2000 + 3000$ years old, or about 5000 years old. Why subtract in the first case but add in the other? Because of the way years are counted before the Christian era (B.C.E.) and after the birth of Christ (A.D.), the B.C.E. dates must be considered as *negative* numbers.

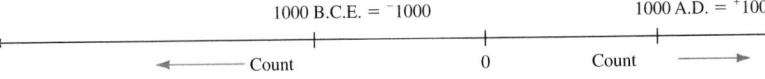

1000 B.C.E. = ⁻1000   1000 A.D. = ⁺1000

← Count   0   Count →

Very early on, the Chinese accepted the idea that a number could be negative; they used red calculating rods for positive numbers and black for negative numbers. Hindu mathematicians in India worked out the arithmetic of negative numbers as long ago as 400 A.D., but western mathematicians did not recognize this idea until the sixteenth century. It would be difficult today to think of measuring things such as temperature, altitude, and money without using negative numbers.

*A.D. stands for the Latin *Anno Domini*, which means "in the year of the Lord."

ANSWERS

1. _____

2. _____

3. _____

4. _____

5. _____

6. _____

7. _____

8. _____

9. _____

10. _____

11. _____

12. _____

13. _____

14. _____

15. _____

16. _____

17. _____

18. _____

19. _____

20. _____ 21. _____

22. _____

23. _____

24. _____

25. _____

1 **Pre-Test Chapter 1**

Write each of the following using symbols.

1. 8 less than x

2. the quotient when w is divided by the product of x and 17

Identify which are expressions and which are not.

3. $7x - 5 = 11$

4. $3x - 2(x + 1)$

Identify the property that is illustrated by the following statements.

5. $8 \cdot 9 = 9 \cdot 8$

6. $3(4 + 2) = 3 \cdot 4 + 3 \cdot 2$

7. $9 + (1 + 7) = (9 + 1) + 7$

Perform the indicated operations.

8. $-7 + (-3)$ **9.** $8 + (-9)$ **10.** $(-3) + (-2)$

11. $-\dfrac{7}{4} + \dfrac{3}{4}$ **12.** $8 - 11$ **13.** $-8 - 11$

14. $9 - (-3)$ **15.** $6 + (-6)$ **16.** $(-7)(-3)$

17. $(3.5)(4)$ **18.** $(3)\left(\dfrac{1}{6}\right)$ **19.** $\dfrac{-27 + 6}{-3}$

Evaluate the following expressions,

20. $5 - 4^2 \cdot 3 \div 6$ **21.** $(45 - 3 \cdot 5) + 5^2$

22. If $x = -2$, $y = 7$, and $w = -4$, evaluate the expression $\dfrac{x^2 y}{w}$.

Combine like terms.

23. $5w^2 t + 3w^2 t$ **24.** $4a^2 - 3a + 5 + 7a - 2 - 5a^2$

Divide.

25. $\dfrac{96x^3 y^5}{8x^2 y^3}$

From Arithmetic to Algebra

 OBJECTIVES

1. Represent addition, subtraction, multiplication, and division by using the symbols of algebra
2. Identify algebraic expressions

Overcoming Math Anxiety

Throughout this text, we will present you with a series of class-tested techniques that are designed to improve your performance in this math class.

Hint #4   Become familiar with your syllabus.

In the first class meeting, your instructor probably handed out a class syllabus. If you haven't done so already, you need to incorporate important information into your calendar and address book.

1. Write all important dates in your calendar. This includes homework due dates, quiz dates, test dates, and the date and time of the final exam. Never allow yourself to be surprised by any deadline!

2. Write your instructor's name, contact number, and office number in your address book. Also include the office hours. Make it a point to see your instructor early in the term. Although this is not the only person who can help clear up your confusion, it is the most important person.

3. Make note of other resources that are made available to you. This includes CDs, video tapes, web pages, and tutoring.

Given all of these resources, it is important that you never let confusion or frustration mount. If you can't "get it" from the text, try another resource. All of the resources are there specifically for you, so take advantage of them!

In arithmetic, you learned how to do calculations with numbers by using the basic operations of addition, subtraction, multiplication, and division.

In algebra, you will still use numbers and the same four operations. However, you will also use letters to represent numbers. Letters such as x, y, L, or W are called **variables** when they represent numerical values.

Here we see two rectangles whose lengths and widths are labeled with numbers.

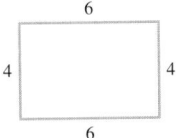 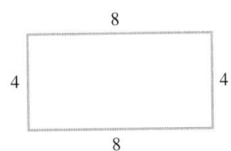

If we need to represent the length and width of *any* rectangle, we can use the variables L and W.

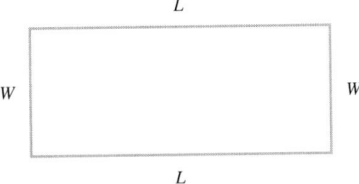

NOTE In arithmetic:
+ denotes addition
− denotes subtraction
× denotes multiplication
÷ denotes division.

You are familiar with the four symbols (+, −, ×, ÷) used to indicate the fundamental operations of arithmetic.

Let's look at how these operations are indicated in algebra. We begin by looking at addition.

Definitions: Addition

$x + y$ means the *sum* of x and y or *x plus y.*

Example 1

Writing Expressions That Indicate Addition

(a) *The sum of a and* 3 is written as $a + 3$.

(b) *L plus W* is written as $L + W$.

(c) 5 *more than m* is written as $m + 5$.

(d) *x increased by* 7 is written as $x + 7$.

CHECK YOURSELF 1

Write, using symbols.

(a) The sum of y and 4   **(b)** *a* plus *b*

(c) 3 more than x **(d)** *n* increased by 6

Let's look at how subtraction is indicated in algebra.

Definitions: Subtraction

$x − y$ means the *difference* of x and y or *x minus y.*

Example 2

Writing Expressions That Indicate Subtraction

(a) *r minus s* is written as $r − s$.

(b) *The difference of m and* 5 is written as $m − 5$.

(c) *x decreased by* 8 is written as $x − 8$.

(d) 4 *less than a* is written as $a − 4$.

CHECK YOURSELF 2

Write, using symbols.

(a) *w* minus *z*   **(b)** The difference of *a* and 7

(c) *y* decreased by 3   **(d)** 5 less than *b*

You have seen that the operations of addition and subtraction are written exactly the same way in algebra as in arithmetic. This is not true in multiplication because the sign $\times$ looks like the letter x. So in algebra we use other symbols to show multiplication to avoid any confusion. Here are some ways to write multiplication.

NOTE x and y are called the **factors** of the product xy.

Definitions: Multiplication

A centered dot	$x \cdot y$	
Parentheses	$(x)(y)$	These all indicate the *product* of x and y or x times y.
Writing the letters next to each other	xy	

Example 3

Writing Expressions That Indicate Multiplication

NOTE You can place letters next to each other or numbers and letters next to each other to show multiplication. But you *cannot* place numbers side by side to show multiplication: 37 means the number "thirty-seven," not 3 times 7.

(a) The product of 5 and a is written as $5 \cdot a$, $(5)(a)$, or $5a$. The last expression, $5a$, is the shortest and the most common way of writing the product.

(b) 3 times 7 can be written as $3 \cdot 7$ or $(3)(7)$.

(c) Twice z is written as $2z$.

(d) The product of 2, s, and t is written as $2st$.

(e) 4 more than the product of 6 and x is written as $6x + 4$.

 CHECK YOURSELF 3

Write, using symbols.

(a) m times n

(b) The product of h and b

(c) The product of 8 and 9

(d) The product of 5, w, and y

(e) 3 more than the product of 8 and a

Before we move on to division, let's look at how we can combine the symbols we have learned so far.

NOTE Not every collection of symbols is an expression.

Definitions: Expression

An **expression** is a meaningful collection of numbers, variables, and signs of operation.

Example 4

Identifying Expressions

(a) $2m + 3$ is an expression. It means that we multiply 2 and m, then add 3.

(b) $x + \cdot + 3$ is not an expression. The three operations in a row have no meaning.

(c) $y = 2x - 1$ is not an expression. The equals sign is not an operation sign.

(d) $3a + 5b - 4c$ is an expression. Its meaning is clear.

CHECK YOURSELF 4

Identify which are expressions and which are not.

(a) $7 - \cdot x$

(b) $6 + y = 9$

(c) $a + b - c$

(d) $3x - 5yz$

To write more complicated products in algebra, we need some "punctuation marks." Parentheses ( ) mean that an expression is to be thought of as a single quantity. Brackets [ ] are used in exactly the same way as parentheses in algebra. Look at the following example showing the use of these signs of grouping.

Example 5

Expressions with More Than One Operation

(a) 3 times the sum of a and b is written as

NOTE This can be read as "3 times the quantity a plus b."

$$\underbrace{3(a + b)}$$

The sum of a and b is a single quantity, so it is enclosed in parentheses.

NOTE No parentheses are needed here because the 3 multiplies *only* the a.

(b) The sum of 3 times a and b is written as $3a + b$.

(c) 2 times the difference of m and n is written as $2(m - n)$.

(d) The product of s plus t and s minus t is written as $(s + t)(s - t)$.

(e) The product of b and 3 less than b is written as $b(b - 3)$.

CHECK YOURSELF 5

Write, using symbols.

(a) Twice the sum of p and q

(b) The sum of twice p and q

(c) The product of a and the quantity $b - c$

(d) The product of x plus 2 and x minus 2

(e) The product of x and 4 more than x

NOTE In algebra the fraction form is usually used.

Now let's look at the operation of division. In arithmetic, you use the division sign $\div$, the long division symbol $\overline{)}\,$, and the fraction notation. For example, to indicate the quotient when 9 is divided by 3, you could write

$$9 \div 3 \quad \text{or} \quad 3\overline{)9} \quad \text{or} \quad \frac{9}{3}$$

Definitions: Division

$\dfrac{x}{y}$ means *x divided by y* or *the quotient of x and y*.

Example 6

Writing Expressions That Indicate Division

(a) *m* divided by 3 is written as $\dfrac{m}{3}$.

(b) The quotient of *a* plus *b* divided by 5 is written as $\dfrac{a+b}{5}$.

(c) The sum *p* plus *q* divided by the difference *p* minus *q* is written as $\dfrac{p+q}{p-q}$.

 CHECK YOURSELF 6

Write, using symbols.

(a) *r* divided by *s*
(b) The quotient when *x* minus *y* is divided by 7
(c) The difference *a* minus 2 divided by the sum *a* plus 2

Notice that we can use many different letters to represent variables. In Example 6 the letters *m*, *a*, *b*, *p*, and *q* represented different variables. We often choose a letter that reminds us of what it represents, for example, *L* for *length* or *W* for *width*.

Example 7

Writing Geometric Expressions

(a) *Length* times *width* is written $L \cdot W$.

(b) One-half of *altitude* times *base* is written $\dfrac{1}{2} a \cdot b$.

(c) *Length* times *width* times *height* is written $L \cdot W \cdot H$.

(d) Pi (π) times *diameter* is written πd.

 CHECK YOURSELF 7

Write each geometric expression, using symbols.

(a) Two times *length* plus two times *width*   **(b)** Two times pi (π) times *radius*

CHECK YOURSELF ANSWERS

1. (a) $y + 4$; **(b)** $a + b$; **(c)** $x + 3$; **(d)** $n + 6$ **2. (a)** $w - z$; **(b)** $a - 7$; **(c)** $y - 3$; **(d)** $b - 5$ **3. (a)** mn; **(b)** hb; **(c)** $8 \cdot 9$ or $(8)(9)$; **(d)** $5wy$; **(e)** $8a + 3$

4. (a) Not an expression; **(b)** not an expression; **(c)** an expression; **(d)** an expression

5. (a) $2(p + q)$; **(b)** $2p + q$; **(c)** $a(b - c)$; **(d)** $(x + 2)(x - 2)$; **(e)** $x(x + 4)$

6. (a) $\dfrac{r}{s}$; **(b)** $\dfrac{x - y}{7}$; **(c)** $\dfrac{a - 2}{a + 2}$ **7. (a)** $2L + 2W$; **(b)** $2\pi r$

1.1 <u>**Exercises**</u>

Write each of the following phrases, using symbols.

ANSWERS

1. The sum of *c* and *d*

2. *a* plus 7

3. *w* plus *z*

4. The sum of *m* and *n*

5. *x* increased by 2

6. 3 more than *b*

7. 10 more than *y*

8. *m* increased by 4

9. *a* minus *b*

10. 5 less than *s*

11. *b* decreased by 7

12. *r* minus 3

13. 6 less than *r*

14. *x* decreased by 3

15. *w* times *z*

16. The product of 3 and *c*

17. The product of 5 and *t*

18. 8 times *a*

19. The product of 8, *m*, and *n*

20. The product of 7, *r*, and *s*

21. The product of 3 and the quantity *p* plus *q*

22. The product of 5 and the sum of *a* and *b*

23. Twice the sum of *x* and *y*

24. 3 times the sum of *m* and *n*

25. The sum of twice *x* and *y*

1. _____

2. _____

3. _____

4. _____

5. _____

6. _____

7. _____

8. _____

9. _____

10. _____

11. _____

12. _____

13. _____

14. _____

15. _____

16. _____

17. _____

18. _____

19. _____

20. _____

21. _____

22. _____

23. _____

24. _____

25. _____

26. _____

27. _____

28. _____

29. _____

30. _____

31. _____

32. _____

33. _____

34. _____

35. _____

36. _____

37. _____

38. _____

39. _____

40. _____

41. _____

42. _____

43. _____

44. _____

45. _____

46. _____

47. _____

48. _____

49. _____

50. _____

51. _____

26. The sum of 3 times m and n

27. Twice the difference of x and y

28. 3 times the difference of c and d

29. The quantity a plus b times the quantity a minus b

30. The product of x plus y and x minus y

31. The product of m and 3 less than m

32. The product of a and 7 more than a

33. x divided by 5

34. The quotient when b is divided by 8

35. The quotient of a plus b, divided by 7

36. The difference x minus y, divided by 9

37. The difference of p and q, divided by 4

38. The sum of a and 5, divided by 9

39. The sum of a and 3, divided by the difference of a and 3

40. The difference of m and n, divided by the sum of m and n

Write each of the following phrases, using symbols. Use the variable x to represent the number in each case.

41. 5 more than a number

42. A number increased by 8

43. 7 less than a number

44. A number decreased by 10

45. 9 times a number

46. Twice a number

47. 6 more than 3 times a number

48. 5 times a number, decreased by 10

49. Twice the sum of a number and 5

50. 3 times the difference of a number and 4

51. The product of 2 more than a number and 2 less than that same number

52. The product of 5 less than a number and 5 more than that same number

53. The quotient of a number and 7

54. A number divided by 3

55. The sum of a number and 5, divided by 8

56. The quotient when 7 less than a number is divided by 3

57. 6 more than a number divided by 6 less than that same number

58. The quotient when 3 less than a number is divided by 3 more than that same number

Write each of the following geometric expressions using symbols.

59. Four times the length of a side (s)

60. $\dfrac{4}{3}$ times π times the cube of the radius (r)

61. The radius (r) squared times the height (h) times π

62. Twice the length (L) plus twice the width (W)

63. One-half the product of the height (h) and the sum of two unequal sides (b_1 and b_2)

64. Six times the length of a side (s) squared

Identify which are expressions and which are not.

65. $2(x + 5)$

66. $4 + (x - 3)$

67. $4 + \div m$

68. $6 + a = 7$

69. $2b = 6$

70. $x(y + 3)$

71. $2a + 5b$

72. $4x + \cdot 7$

73. Population growth. The Earth's population has doubled in the last 40 years. If we let x represent the Earth's population 40 years ago, what is the population today?

74. Species extinction. It is estimated that the Earth is losing 4000 species of plants and animals every year. If S represents the number of species living last year, how many species are on Earth this year?

75. Interest. The simple interest (I) earned when a principal (P) is invested at a rate (r) for a time (t) is calculated by multiplying the principal times the rate times the time. Write a formula for the interest earned.

52. _____

53. _____

54. _____

55. _____

56. _____

57. _____

58. _____

59. _____

60. _____

61. _____

62. _____

63. _____

64. _____

65. _____

66. _____

67. _____

68. _____

69. _____

70. _____

71. _____

72. _____

73. _____

74. _____

75. _____

76. _____

77. _____

a. _____

b. _____

c. _____

d. _____

e. _____

f. _____

76. **Kinetic energy.** The kinetic energy of a particle of mass m is found by taking one-half of the product of the mass and the square of the velocity (v). Write a formula for the kinetic energy of a particle.

77. Rewrite the following algebraic expressions in English phrases. Exchange papers with another student to edit your writing. Be sure the meaning in English is the same as in algebra. These expressions are not complete sentences, so your English does not have to be in complete sentences. Here is an example.

Algebra: $2(x - 1)$

English: We could write "One less than a number is doubled." Or we might write "A number is diminished by one and then multiplied by two."

(a) $n + 3$ **(b)** $\dfrac{x + 2}{5}$ **(c)** $3(5 + a)$ **(d)** $3 - 4n$ **(e)** $\dfrac{x + 6}{x - 1}$

*Getting Ready

Evaluate the following:

(a) $8 - (5 + 2)$ (b) $(8 - 5) + 2$ (c) $16 \div 4 \cdot 2$

(d) $16 \div (4 \cdot 2)$ (e) $6 \cdot 2$ (f) $2 \cdot 6$

Pre-Test for Chapter 1
1. $x - 8$ **2.** $\dfrac{w}{17x}$ **3.** No **4.** Yes **5.** Commutative property of multiplication
6. Distributive property **7.** Associative property of addition **8.** -10 **9.** -1
10. -5 **11.** -1 **12.** -3 **13.** -19
14. 12 **15.** 0 **16.** 21 **17.** 14 **18.** $\dfrac{1}{2}$ **19.** 7 **20.** -3 **21.** 55

22. -7 **23.** $8w^2t$ **24.** $-a^2 + 4a + 3$ **25.** $12xy^2$

Answers

1. $c + d$ **3.** $w + z$ **5.** $x + 2$ **7.** $y + 10$ **9.** $a - b$
11. $b - 7$ **13.** $r - 6$ **15.** wz **17.** $5t$ **19.** $8mn$ **21.** $3(p + q)$
23. $2(x + y)$ **25.** $2x + y$ **27.** $2(x - y)$ **29.** $(a + b)(a - b)$

31. $m(m - 3)$ **33.** $\dfrac{x}{5}$ **35.** $\dfrac{a + b}{7}$ **37.** $\dfrac{p - q}{4}$ **39.** $\dfrac{a + 3}{a - 3}$

41. $x + 5$ **43.** $x - 7$ **45.** $9x$ **47.** $3x + 6$ **49.** $2(x + 5)$

51. $(x + 2)(x - 2)$ **53.** $\dfrac{x}{7}$ **55.** $\dfrac{x + 5}{8}$ **57.** $\dfrac{x + 6}{x - 6}$

59. $4s$ **61.** $\pi r^2 h$ **63.** $\dfrac{1}{2}h(b_1 + b_2)$ **65.** Expression

67. Not an expression **69.** Not an expression **71.** Expression

73. $2x$ **75.** $I = Prt$ **77.** **a.** 1 **b.** 5 **c.** 8

d. 2 **e.** 12 **f.** 12

*Exercises headed "Getting Ready for . . ." are designed to help you prepare for material in the next section of the text.

Positive and Negative Integers

 OBJECTIVES

1. Represent integers on a number line
2. Order signed numbers
3. Evaluate numerical expressions involving absolute value

When numbers are used to represent physical quantities (altitudes, temperatures, and amounts of money are examples), it may be necessary to distinguish between *positive* and *negative* quantities. It is convenient to represent these quantities with plus (+) or minus (−) signs. For instance,

The altitude of Mount Whitney is 14,495 feet (ft) *above* sea level (+14,495).

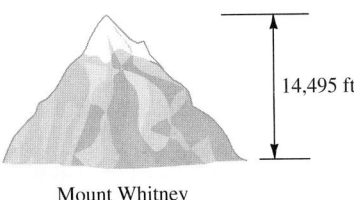

14,495 ft

Mount Whitney

The altitude of Death Valley is 282 ft *below* sea level (−282).

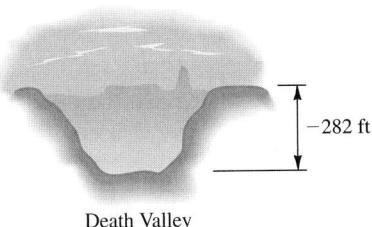

−282 ft

Death Valley

The temperature in Chicago is 10° *below* zero (−10°).

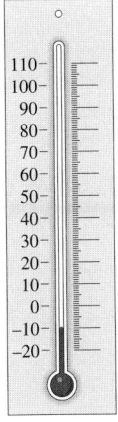

An account could show a *gain* of $100 (+100), or a *loss* of $100 (−100).

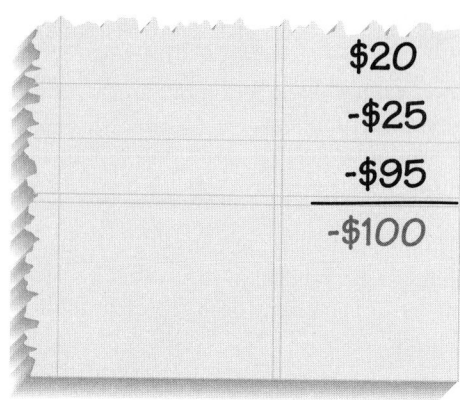

These numbers suggest the need to extend the whole numbers to include both positive numbers (like +100) and negative numbers (like −282).

To represent the negative numbers, we extend the number line to the *left* of zero and name equally spaced points.

Numbers used to name points to the right of zero are positive numbers. They are written with a positive (+) sign or with no sign at all.

+6 and 9 are positive numbers

Numbers used to name points to the left of zero are negative numbers. They are always written with a negative (−) sign.

−3 and −20 are negative numbers

Read "negative 3."

Positive and negative numbers considered together are **signed numbers.**

Here is the number line extended to include both positive and negative numbers.

NOTE 0 is not considered a signed number.

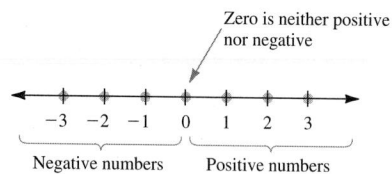

The numbers used to name the points shown on the number line above are called the **integers.** The integers consist of the natural numbers, their negatives, and the number 0. We can represent the set of integers by

NOTE The dots are called *ellipses* and indicate that the pattern continues.

$$\{\ldots, -3, -2, -1, 0, 1, 2, 3, \ldots\}$$

Example 1

Representing Integers on the Number Line

Represent the following integers on the number line shown.

$-3, -12, 8, 15, -7$

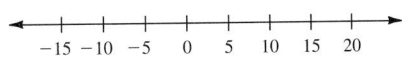

CHECK YOURSELF 1

Represent the following integers on a number line.

$-1, -9, 4, -11, 8, 20$

The set of numbers on the number line is *ordered.* The numbers get smaller moving to the left on the number line and larger moving to the right.

When a set of numbers is written from smallest to largest, the numbers are said to be in *ascending order.*

Example 2

Ordering Signed Numbers

Place each set of numbers in ascending order.

(a) $9, -5, -8, 3, 7$

From smallest to largest, the numbers are

$-8, -5, 3, 7, 9$ Note that this is the order in which the numbers appear on a number line as we move from left to right.

(b) $3, -2, 18, -20, -13$

From smallest to largest, the numbers are

$-20, -13, -2, 3, 18$

 CHECK YOURSELF 2

Place each set of numbers in ascending order.

(a) $12, -13, 15, 2, -8, -3$ **(b)** $3, 6, -9, -3, 8$

The least and greatest numbers in a set are called the **extreme values.** The least element is called the **minimum** and the greatest element is called the **maximum.**

Example 3

Labeling Extreme Values

For each set of numbers, determine the minimum and maximum values.

(a) $9, -5, -8, 3, 7$

From our previous ordering of these numbers, we see that -8, the least element, is the minimum, and 9, the greatest element, is the maximum.

(b) $3, -2, 18, -20, -13$

-20 is the minimum and 18 is the maximum.

 CHECK YOURSELF 3

For each set of numbers, determine the minimum and maximum values.

(a) $12, -13, 15, 2, -8, -3$ **(b)** $3, 6, -9, -3, 8$

Integers are not the only kind of signed numbers. Decimals and fractions can also be thought of as signed numbers.

Example 4

Identifying Signed Numbers that are Integers

Which of the following signed numbers are also integers?

(a) 145 is an integer.
(b) -28 is an integer.
(c) 0.35 is not an integer.
(d) $-\dfrac{2}{3}$ is not an integer.

 CHECK YOURSELF 4

Which of the following signed numbers are also integers?

-23 1054 -0.23 0 -500 $-\dfrac{4}{5}$

Sometimes we refer to the negative of a number as its "opposite." But what is the opposite of the opposite of a number? It is the number itself. The next example illustrates.

Example 5

Find the Opposite for Each Number

(a) 5   The opposite of 5 is −5.

(b) −9   The opposite of −9 is 9.

CHECK YOURSELF 5

Find the opposite for each number.

(a) 17   **(b)** −12

An important idea for our work in this chapter is the **absolute value** of a number. This represents the distance of the point named by the number from the origin on the number line.

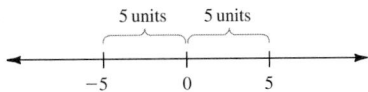

The absolute value of 5 is 5. The absolute value of −5 is also 5.

The **absolute value** of a positive number or zero is itself. The absolute value of a negative number is its opposite.

In symbols we write

$$|5| = 5 \qquad \text{and} \qquad |-5| = 5$$

Read "the absolute   Read "the absolute
value of 5."   value of negative 5."

The absolute value of a number does *not* depend on whether the number is to the right or to the left of the origin, but on its *distance* from the origin.

Example 6

Simplifying Absolute Value Expressions

(a) $|7| = 7$

(b) $|-7| = 7$

(c) $-|-7| = -7$

This is the *negative,* or opposite, of the absolute value of negative 7.

(d) $|-10| + |10| = 10 + 10 = 20$

Absolute value bars serve as another set of grouping symbols, so do the operation *inside* first.

(e) $|8 - 3| = |5| = 5$

(f) $|8| - |3| = 8 - 3 = 5$

Here, evaluate the absolute values, then subtract.

✔ **CHECK YOURSELF 6**

Evaluate.

(a) $|8|$ **(b)** $|-8|$ **(c)** $-|-8|$

(d) $|-9| + |4|$ **(e)** $|9 - 4|$ **(f)** $|9| - |4|$

CHECK YOURSELF ANSWERS

1.

2. (a) $-13, -8, -3, 2, 12, 15$

   (b) $-9, -3, 3, 6, 8$

3. (a) minimum is -13; maximum is 15 **(b)** minimum is -9; maximum is 8

4. $-23, 1054, 0,$ and -500 **5. (a)** -17;   **(b)** 12

6. (a) 8;   **(b)** 8;   **(c)** -8;   **(d)** 13;   **(e)** 5;   **(f)** 5

1.2 Exercises

Represent each quantity with a signed number.

1. An altitude of 400 feet (ft) above sea level

2. An altitude of 80 ft below sea level

3. A loss of $200

4. A profit of $400

5. A decrease in population of 25,000

6. An increase in population of 12,500

Represent the integers on the number lines shown.

7. 5, −15, 18, −8, 3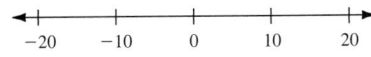

8. −18, 4, −5, 13, 9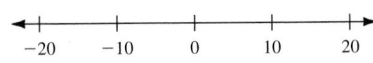

Which numbers in the following sets are integers?

9. $\left\{5, -\dfrac{2}{9}, 175, -234, -0.64\right\}$

10. $\left\{-45, 0.35, \dfrac{3}{5}, 700, -26\right\}$

Place each of the following sets in ascending order.

11. 3, −5, 2, 0, −7, −1, 8

12. −2, 7, 1, −8, 6, −1, 0

13. 9, −2, −11, 4, −6, 1, 5

14. 23, −18, −5, −11, −15, 14, 20

15. −6, 7, −7, 6, −3, 3

16. 12, −13, 14, −14, 15, −15

For each set, determine the maximum and minimum values.

17. 5, −6, 0, 10, −3, 15, 1, 8

18. 9, −1, 3, 11, −4, 2, 5, −2

19. 21, −15, 0, 7, −9, 16, −3, 11

20. −22, 0, 22, −31, 18, −5, 3

21. 3, 0, 1, −2, 5, 4, −1

22. 2, 7, −3, 5, −10, −5

Find the opposite of each number.

23. 15

24. 18

ANSWERS

1. _____
2. _____
3. _____
4. _____
5. _____
6. _____
7. _____
8. _____
9. _____
10. _____
11. _____
12. _____
13. _____
14. _____
15. _____
16. _____
17. _____
18. _____
19. _____
20. _____
21. _____
22. _____
23. _____
24. _____

25. _____

26. _____

27. _____

28. _____

29. _____

30. _____

31. _____

32. _____

33. _____

34. _____

35. _____

36. _____

37. _____

38. _____

39. _____

40. _____

41. _____

42. _____

43. _____

44. _____

45. _____

46. _____

47. _____

48. _____

49. _____

50. _____

51. _____

52. _____

25. 11   **26.** 34

27. -19 **28.** -5

29. -7 **30.** -54

Evaluate.

31. $|17|$ **32.** $|28|$

33. $|-10|$ **34.** $|-7|$

35. $-|3|$ **36.** $-|5|$

37. $-|-8|$ **38.** $-|-13|$

39. $|-2|+|3|$ **40.** $|4|+|-3|$

41. $|-9|+|9|$ **42.** $|11|+|-11|$

43. $|4|-|-4|$ **44.** $|5|-|-5|$

45. $|15|-|8|$ **46.** $|11|-|3|$

47. $|15-8|$ **48.** $|11-3|$

49. $|-9|+|2|$ **50.** $|-7|+|4|$

51. $|-8|-|-7|$ **52.** $|-9|-|-4|$

Label each statement as true or false.

53. All whole numbers are integers.

54. All nonzero integers are signed numbers.

55. All integers are whole numbers.

56. All signed numbers are integers.

57. All negative integers are whole numbers.

58. Zero is neither positive nor negative.

Place absolute value bars in the proper location on the left side of the expression so that the equation is true.

59. $6 + (-2) = 4$

60. $8 + (-3) = 5$

61. $6 + (-2) = 8$

62. $8 + (-3) = 11$

Represent each quantity with a signed number.

63. Soil erosion. The erosion of 5 centimeters (cm) of topsoil from an Iowa corn field.

64. Soil formation. The formation of 2.5 cm of new topsoil on the African savanna.

65. Checking accounts. The withdrawal of $50 from a checking account.

66. Saving accounts. The deposit of $200 in a savings account.

67. Temperature. The temperature change pictured.

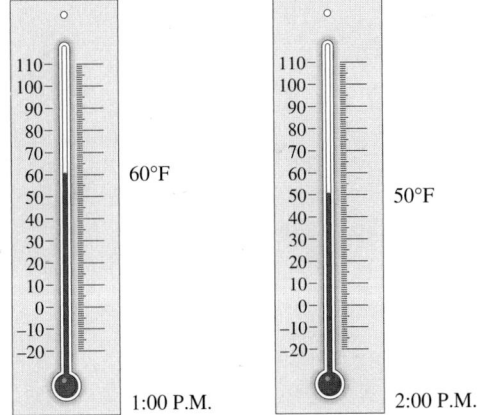

1:00 P.M.　　　2:00 P.M.

68. Stocks. An increase of 75 points in the Dow-Jones average.

ANSWERS

53. _____

54. _____

55. _____

56. _____

57. _____

58. _____

59. _____

60. _____

61. _____

62. _____

63. _____

64. _____

65. _____

66. _____

67. _____

68. _____

69. _____

70. _____

71. _____

72. _____

73. _____

74. _____

75. _____

76. _____

77. _____

69. Baseball. An eight-game losing streak by the local baseball team.

70. Population. An increase of 25,000 in the population of the city.

71. Positive trade balance. A country exported \$90,000,000 more than it imported, creating a positive trade balance.

72. Negative trade balance. A country exported \$60,000,000 less than it imported, creating a negative trade balance.

For each collection of numbers given in exercises 73 to 76, answer the following:

(a) Which number is smallest?

(b) Which number lies farthest from the origin?

(c) Which number has the largest absolute value?

(d) Which number has the smallest absolute value?

73. $-6, 3, 8, 7, -2$

74. $-8, 3, -5, 4, 9$

75. $-2, 6, -1, 0, 2, 5$

76. $-9, 0, -2, 3, 6$

77. Simplify each of the following:

$$-(-7) \qquad -(-(-7)) \qquad -(-(-(-7)))$$

Based on your answers, generalize your results.

Answers

1. 400 or $(+400)$ **3.** -200 **5.** $-25,000$

7.
$$\begin{array}{c} -15 \quad -8 \qquad 3\ 5 \qquad\qquad 18 \\ \leftarrow\!+\!-\!\bullet\!-\!+\!\bullet\!-\!-\!+\!-\!\bullet\bullet\!-\!+\!-\!-\!\bullet\!+\!\rightarrow \\ -20 \quad -10 \quad\ 0 \quad\ 10 \quad\ 20 \end{array}$$
   9. $5, 175, -234$

11. $-7, -5, -1, 0, 2, 3, 8$ **13.** $-11, -6, -2, 1, 4, 5, 9$

15. $-7, -6, -3, 3, 6, 7$ **17.** Max: 15; Min: -6 **19.** Max: 21, Min: -15

21. Max: 5; Min: -2 **23.** -15 **25.** -11 **27.** 19   **29.** 7   **31.** 17

33. 10   **35.** -3 **37.** -8 **39.** 5   **41.** 18   **43.** 0   **45.** 7

47. 7   **49.** 11   **51.** 1   **53.** True   **55.** False   **57.** False

59. $|6 + (-2)| = 4$ **61.** $|6| + |-2| = 8$ **63.** -5 **65.** -50

67. $-10°F$ **69.** -8 **71.** $+90,000,000$

73. $-6; 8; 8; -2$ **75.** $-2; 6; 6; 0$ **77.**

1.3 Properties of Signed Numbers

1.3 OBJECTIVES

1. Recognize applications of the commutative property
2. Recognize applications of the associative property
3. Recognize applications of the distributive property

All that we do in algebra is based on the rules for the operations introduced in Section 1.1. We call these rules **properties of the real numbers.** In this section we consider those properties that we will use in the remainder of this chapter.

The **commutative properties** tell us that we can add or multiply in any order.

Rules and Properties: The Commutative Properties

If a and b are any numbers,

1. $a + b = b + a$ Commutative property of addition
2. $a \cdot b = b \cdot a$ Commutative property of multiplication

---

NOTE All integers, decimals, and fractions that we see in this course are real numbers.

Example 1

Identifying the Commutative Properties

(a) $5 + 9 = 9 + 5$ and $x + 7 = 7 + x$

These are applications of the commutative property of addition.

(b) $5 \cdot 9 = 9 \cdot 5$

This is an application of the commutative property of multiplication.

 CHECK YOURSELF 1

Identify the property being applied.

(a) $7 + 3 = 3 + 7$ **(b)** $7 \cdot 3 = 3 \cdot 7$
(c) $a + 4 = 4 + a$ **(d)** $x \cdot 2 = 2 \cdot x$

We also want to be able to change the grouping in simplifying expressions. This is possible because of the **associative properties.** Numbers or variables can be grouped in any manner to find a sum or a product.

Rules and Properties: The Associative Properties

If a, b, and c are any numbers,

1. $a + (b + c) = (a + b) + c$ Associative property of addition
2. $a \cdot (b \cdot c) = (a \cdot b) \cdot c$ Associative property of multiplication

---

Example 2

Demonstrating the Associative Properties

(a) Show that $2 + (3 + 8) = (2 + 3) + 8$.

NOTE Remember, we always do the operation in the parentheses first.

$2 + \underbrace{(3 + 8)}_{\text{Add first.}}$ $\qquad$ $\underbrace{(2 + 3)}_{\text{Add first.}} + 8$

$= 2 + 11$ $\qquad$ $= 5 + 8$

$= 13$ $\qquad$ $= 13$

So

$$2 + (3 + 8) = (2 + 3) + 8$$

(b) Show that $\frac{1}{3} \cdot (6 \cdot 5) = \left(\frac{1}{3} \cdot 6\right) \cdot 5$.

$\frac{1}{3} \cdot \underbrace{(6 \cdot 5)}_{\text{Multiply first.}}$ $\qquad$ $\underbrace{\left(\frac{1}{3} \cdot 6\right)}_{\text{Multiply first.}} \cdot 5$

$= \frac{1}{3} \cdot (30)$ $\qquad$ $= (2) \cdot 5$

$= 10$ $\qquad$ $= 10$

So

$$\frac{1}{3} \cdot (6 \cdot 5) = \left(\frac{1}{3} \cdot 6\right) \cdot 5$$

CHECK YOURSELF 2

Show that the following statements are true.

(a) $3 + (4 + 7) = (3 + 4) + 7$

(b) $3 \cdot (4 \cdot 7) = (3 \cdot 4) \cdot 7$

(c) $\left(\frac{1}{5} \cdot 10\right) \cdot 4 = \frac{1}{5} \cdot (10 \cdot 4)$

The **distributive property** involves addition and multiplication together. We can illustrate this property with an application.

REMEMBER: The area of a rectangle is the product of its length and width:

$A = L \cdot W$

Suppose that we want to find the total of the two areas shown in the following figure.

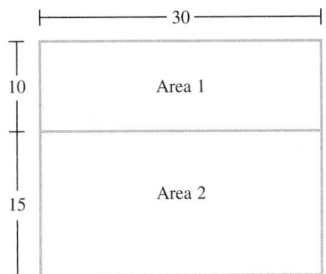

We can find the total area by multiplying the length by the overall width, which is found by adding the two widths. [or] We can find the total area as a sum of the two areas.

Length	Overall Width	(Area 1) Length · Width		(Area 2) Length · Width
30	· (10 + 15)	30 · 10	+	30 · 15
= 30 · 25		= 300 + 450		
= 750		= 750		

So

$30 \cdot (10 + 15) = 30 \cdot 10 + 30 \cdot 15$

This leads us to the following property.

Rules and Properties: The Distributive Property

NOTE Notice the pattern.

$a(b + c) = a \cdot b + a \cdot c$

We "distributed" the multiplication "over" the addition.

If a, b, and c are any numbers,

$a(b + c) = a \cdot b + a \cdot c$ and $(b + c)a = b \cdot a + c \cdot a$

Example 3

Using the Distributive Property

Use the distributive property to simplify (remove the parentheses in) the following.

NOTE $5(3 + 4) = 5 \cdot 7 = 35$ or

$5 \cdot 3 + 5 \cdot 4 = 15 + 20 = 35$

(a) $5(3 + 4)$

$5(3 + 4) = 5 \cdot 3 + 5 \cdot 4$

$= 15 + 20 = 35$

(b) $8(x + y)$

NOTE Because the variables are different, $8x + 8y$ cannot be simplified further.

$8(x + y) = 8x + 8y$

(c) $2(3x + 5)$

$2(3x + 5) = 2 \cdot 3x + 2 \cdot 5$

$= 6x + 10$

NOTE It is also true that

$\frac{1}{3}(9 + 12) = \frac{1}{3}(21) = 7$

(d) $\frac{1}{3}(9 + 12) = \frac{1}{3} \cdot 9 + \frac{1}{3} \cdot 12$

$= 3 + 4 = 7$

CHECK YOURSELF 3

Use the distributive property to simplify (remove the parentheses).

(a) $4(6 + 7)$ **(b)** $9(m + n)$

(c) $3(5a + 7)$ **(d)** $\frac{1}{5}(10 + 15)$

Example 4 requires that you identify which property is being demonstrated. Look for patterns that will help you remember each of the properties.

Example 4

Identifying Properties

Name the property demonstrated.

(a) $3(x + 2) = 3x + 3 \cdot 2$ demonstrates the distributive property.
(b) $2 + (3 + 5) = (2 + 3) + 5$ demonstrates the associative property of addition.
(c) $3 \cdot 5 = 5 \cdot 3$ demonstrates the commutative property of multiplication.

CHECK YOURSELF 4

Name the property demonstrated.

(a) $2 \cdot (3 \cdot 5) = (2 \cdot 3) \cdot 5$

(b) $4(a + b) = 4a + 4b$

(c) $x + 8 = 8 + x$

CHECK YOURSELF ANSWERS

1. (a) Commutative property of addition; **(b)** commutative property of multiplication; **(c)** commutative property of addition; **(d)** commutative property of multiplication
2. (a) $3 + (4 + 7) = 3 + 11 = 14$ **(b)** $3 \cdot (4 \cdot 7) = 3 \cdot 28 = 84$
    $(3 + 4) + 7 = 7 + 7 = 14$ $(3 \cdot 4) \cdot 7 = 12 \cdot 7 = 84$

(c) $\left(\frac{1}{5} \cdot 10\right) \cdot 4 = 2 \cdot 4 = 8$

$\frac{1}{5} \cdot (10 \cdot 4) = \frac{1}{5} \cdot 40 = 8$

3. (a) $4 \cdot 6 + 4 \cdot 7 = 24 + 28 = 52$; **(b)** $9m + 9n$; **(c)** $15a + 21$;

(d) $\frac{1}{5} \cdot 10 + \frac{1}{5} \cdot 15 = 2 + 3 = 5$

4. (a) Associative property of multiplication; **(b)** distributive property; **(c)** commutative property of addition

Identify the property that is illustrated by each of the following statements.

1. $5 + 9 = 9 + 5$

2. $6 + 3 = 3 + 6$

3. $2 \cdot (3 \cdot 5) = (2 \cdot 3) \cdot 5$

4. $3 \cdot (5 \cdot 6) = (3 \cdot 5) \cdot 6$

5. $10 \cdot 5 = 5 \cdot 10$

6. $8 \cdot 4 = 4 \cdot 8$

7. $8 + 12 = 12 + 8$

8. $6 + 2 = 2 + 6$

9. $(5 \cdot 7) \cdot 2 = 5 \cdot (7 \cdot 2)$

10. $(8 \cdot 9) \cdot 2 = 8 \cdot (9 \cdot 2)$

11. $9 \cdot 8 = 8 \cdot 9$

12. $6 \cdot 4 = 4 \cdot 6$

13. $2(3 + 5) = 2 \cdot 3 + 2 \cdot 5$

14. $5 \cdot (4 + 6) = 5 \cdot 4 + 5 \cdot 6$

15. $5 + (7 + 8) = (5 + 7) + 8$

16. $8 + (2 + 9) = (8 + 2) + 9$

17. $(10 + 5) + 9 = 10 + (5 + 9)$

18. $(5 + 5) + 3 = 5 + (5 + 3)$

19. $7 \cdot (3 + 8) = 7 \cdot 3 + 7 \cdot 8$

20. $5 \cdot (6 + 8) = 5 \cdot 6 + 5 \cdot 8$

Verify that each of the following statements is true by evaluating each side of the equation separately and comparing the results.

21. $7 \cdot (3 + 4) = 7 \cdot 3 + 7 \cdot 4$

22. $4 \cdot (5 + 1) = 4 \cdot 5 + 4 \cdot 1$

23. $2 + (9 + 8) = (2 + 9) + 8$

24. $6 + (15 + 3) = (6 + 15) + 3$

25. $5 \cdot (6 \cdot 3) = (5 \cdot 6) \cdot 3$

26. $2 \cdot (9 \cdot 10) = (2 \cdot 9) \cdot 10$

1. _____
2. _____
3. _____
4. _____
5. _____
6. _____
7. _____
8. _____
9. _____
10. _____
11. _____
12. _____
13. _____
14. _____
15. _____
16. _____
17. _____
18. _____
19. _____
20. _____
21. _____
22. _____
23. _____
24. _____
25. _____
26. _____

27. _____

28. _____

29. _____

30. _____

31. _____

32. _____

33. _____

34. _____

35. _____

36. _____

37. _____

38. _____

39. _____

40. _____

41. _____

42. _____

43. _____

44. _____

45. _____

46. _____

47. _____

48. _____

49. _____

50. _____

51. _____

52. _____

53. _____

54. _____

27. $5 \cdot (2 + 8) = 5 \cdot 2 + 5 \cdot 8$

28. $3 \cdot (10 + 2) = 3 \cdot 10 + 3 \cdot 2$

29. $(3 + 12) + 8 = 3 + (12 + 8)$

30. $(8 + 12) + 7 = 8 + (12 + 7)$

31. $(4 \cdot 7) \cdot 2 = 4 \cdot (7 \cdot 2)$

32. $(6 \cdot 5) \cdot 3 = 6 \cdot (5 \cdot 3)$

33. $\dfrac{1}{2} \cdot (2 + 6) = \dfrac{1}{2} \cdot 2 + \dfrac{1}{2} \cdot 6$

34. $\dfrac{1}{3} \cdot (6 + 9) = \dfrac{1}{3} \cdot 6 + \dfrac{1}{3} \cdot 9$

35. $\left(\dfrac{2}{3} + \dfrac{1}{6}\right) + \dfrac{1}{3} = \dfrac{2}{3} + \left(\dfrac{1}{6} + \dfrac{1}{3}\right)$

36. $\dfrac{3}{4} + \left(\dfrac{5}{8} + \dfrac{1}{2}\right) = \left(\dfrac{3}{4} + \dfrac{5}{8}\right) + \dfrac{1}{2}$

37. $(2.3 + 3.9) + 4.1 = 2.3 + (3.9 + 4.1)$

38. $(1.7 + 4.1) + 7.6 = 1.7 + (4.1 + 7.6)$

39. $\dfrac{1}{2} \cdot (2 \cdot 8) = \left(\dfrac{1}{2} \cdot 2\right) \cdot 8$

40. $\dfrac{1}{5} \cdot (5 \cdot 3) = \left(\dfrac{1}{5} \cdot 5\right) \cdot 3$

41. $\left(\dfrac{3}{5} \cdot \dfrac{5}{6}\right) \cdot \dfrac{4}{3} = \dfrac{3}{5} \cdot \left(\dfrac{5}{6} \cdot \dfrac{4}{3}\right)$

42. $\dfrac{4}{7} \cdot \left(\dfrac{21}{16} \cdot \dfrac{8}{3}\right) = \left(\dfrac{4}{7} \cdot \dfrac{21}{16}\right) \cdot \dfrac{8}{3}$

43. $2.5 \cdot (4 \cdot 5) = (2.5 \cdot 4) \cdot 5$

44. $4.2 \cdot (5 \cdot 2) = (4.2 \cdot 5) \cdot 2$

Use the distributive property to remove the parentheses in each of the following expressions. Then simplify your result where possible.

45. $2(3 + 5)$

46. $5(4 + 6)$

47. $3(x + 5)$

48. $5(y + 8)$

49. $4(w + v)$

50. $7(c + d)$

51. $2(3x + 5)$

52. $3(7a + 4)$

53. $\dfrac{1}{3} \cdot (15 + 9)$

54. $\dfrac{1}{6} \cdot (36 + 24)$

Use the properties of addition and multiplication to complete each of the following statements.

55. $5 + 7 = \quad + 5$

56. $(5 + 3) + 4 = 5 + (\quad + 4)$

57. $(8)(3) = (3)(\quad)$

58. $8(3 + 4) = 8 \cdot 3 + \quad \cdot 4$

59. $7(2 + 5) = 7 \cdot \quad + 7 \cdot 5$

60. $4 \cdot (2 \cdot 4) = (\quad \cdot 2) \cdot 4$

Use the indicated property to write an expression that is equivalent to each of the following expressions.

61. $3 + 7$ (commutative property of addition)

62. $2(3 + 4)$ (distributive property)

63. $5 \cdot (3 \cdot 2)$ (associative property of multiplication)

64. $(3 + 5) + 2$ (associative property of addition)

65. $2 \cdot 4 + 2 \cdot 5$ (distributive property)

66. $7 \cdot 9$ (commutative property of multiplication)

Evaluate each of the following pairs of expressions. Then answer the given question.

67. $8 - 5$ and $5 - 8$
Do you think subtraction is commutative?

68. $12 \div 3$ and $3 \div 12$
Do you think division is commutative?

69. $(12 - 8) - 4$ and $12 - (8 - 4)$
Do you think subtraction is associative?

70. $(48 \div 16) \div 4$ and $48 \div (16 \div 4)$
Do you think division is associative?

71. $3(6 - 2)$ and $3 \cdot 6 - 3 \cdot 2$
Do you think multiplication is distributive over subtraction?

72. $\dfrac{1}{2}(16 - 10)$ and $\dfrac{1}{2} \cdot 16 - \dfrac{1}{2} \cdot 10$

Do you think multiplication is distributive over subtraction?

In Exercises 73 and 74, complete the statement using

  (a) the distributive property,
  (b) the commutative property of addition,
  (c) the commutative property of multiplication.

ANSWERS

55. _____

56. _____

57. _____

58. _____

59. _____

60. _____

61. _____

62. _____

63. _____

64. _____

65. _____

66. _____

67. _____

68. _____

69. _____

70. _____

71. _____

72. _____

73.

74.

75.

76.

77.

78.

a.

b.

c.

d.

e.

f.

73. $5 \cdot (3 + 4) =$

74. $6 \cdot (5 + 4) =$

In Exercises 75 to 78, identify the property that is used.

75. $5 + (6 + 7) = (5 + 6) + 7$

76. $5 + (6 + 7) = 5 + (7 + 6)$

77. $4 \cdot (3 + 2) = 4 \cdot (2 + 3)$

78. $4 \cdot (3 + 2) = (3 + 2) \cdot 4$

 Getting Ready

Find each sum.

(a) $3 + (8 + 9)$

(b) $6 + (12 + 3)$

(c) $(3 + 8) + (9 + 4)$

(d) $15 - 11 - (2 + 1)$

(e) $\dfrac{3}{5} + \dfrac{4}{15}$

(f) $\dfrac{12}{27} - \dfrac{2}{9}$

Answers

1. Commutative property of addition   **3.** Associative property of multiplication
5. Commutative property of multiplication   **7.** Commutative property of addition
9. Associative property of multiplication
11. Commutative property of multiplication
13. Distributive property   **15.** Associative property of addition
17. Associative property of addition   **19.** Distributive property   **21.** $49 = 49$
23. $19 = 19$ **25.** $90 = 90$ **27.** $50 = 50$ **29.** $23 = 23$ **31.** $56 = 56$
33. $4 = 4$ **35.** $\dfrac{7}{6} = \dfrac{7}{6}$ **37.** $10.3 = 10.3$ **39.** $8 = 8$ **41.** $\dfrac{2}{3} = \dfrac{2}{3}$
43. $50 = 50$ **45.** 16 **47.** $3x + 15$ **49.** $4w + 4v$ **51.** $6x + 10$
53. 8 **55.** 7 **57.** 8 **59.** 2 **61.** $7 + 3$ **63.** $(5 \cdot 3) \cdot 2$
65. $2 \cdot (4 + 5)$ **67.** No   **69.** No   **71.** Yes   **73. (a)** $5 \cdot 3 + 5 \cdot 4$
(b) $5 \cdot (4 + 3)$ **(c)** $(3 + 4) \cdot 5$ **75.** Associative property of addition
77. Commutative property of addition   **a.** 20 **b.** 21 **c.** 24 **d.** 1
e. $\dfrac{13}{15}$ **f.** $\dfrac{2}{9}$

Adding and Subtracting Signed Numbers

1.4 **OBJECTIVES**

1. Use a number line to add signed numbers
2. Add two signed numbers
3. Find the median of a set of signed numbers
4. Find the difference of two signed numbers
5. Find the range of a set of signed numbers

In Section 1.2 we introduced the idea of signed numbers. Now we will examine the four arithmetic operations (addition, subtraction, multiplication, and division) and see how those operations are performed when signed numbers are involved. We start by considering addition.

An application may help. As before, let's represent a gain of money as a positive number and a loss as a negative number.

If you gain $3 and then gain $4, the result is a gain of $7:

$$3 + 4 = 7$$

If you lose $3 and then lose $4, the result is a loss of $7:

$$-3 + (-4) = -7$$

If you gain $3 and then lose $4, the result is a loss of $1:

$$3 + (-4) = -1$$

If you lose $3 and then gain $4, the result is a gain of $1:

$$-3 + 4 = 1$$

The number line can be used to illustrate the addition of signed numbers. Starting at the origin, we move to the *right* for positive numbers and to the *left* for negative numbers.

Example 1

Adding Signed Numbers

(a) Add $(-3) + (-4)$.

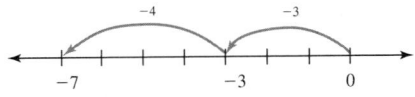

Start at the origin and move 3 units to the left. Then move 4 more units to the left to find the sum. From the number line we see that the sum is

$$(-3) + (-4) = -7$$

(b) Add $\left(-\dfrac{3}{2}\right) + \left(-\dfrac{1}{2}\right)$.

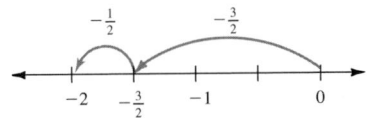

As before, we start at the origin. From that point move $\frac{3}{2}$ units left. Then move another $\frac{1}{2}$ unit left to find the sum. In this case

$$\left(-\frac{3}{2}\right) + \left(-\frac{1}{2}\right) = -2$$

 CHECK YOURSELF 1

Add.

(a) $(-4) + (-5)$

(b) $(-3) + (-7)$

(c) $(-5) + (-15)$

(d) $\left(-\frac{5}{2}\right) + \left(-\frac{3}{2}\right)$

You have probably noticed some helpful patterns in the previous examples. These patterns will allow you to do the work mentally without having to use the number line. Look at the following rule.

Rules and Properties: Adding Signed Numbers Case 1: Same Sign

NOTE This means that the sum of two positive numbers is positive and the sum of two negative numbers is negative. We first encountered absolute values in Section 1.2.

If two numbers have the same sign, add their absolute values. Give the sum the sign of the original numbers.

Let's again use the number line to illustrate the addition of two numbers. This time the numbers will have *different* signs.

Example 2

Adding Signed Numbers

(a) Add $3 + (-6)$.

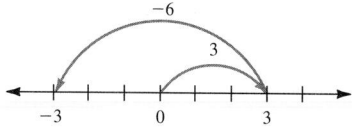

First move 3 units to the right of the origin. Then move 6 units to the left.

$$3 + (-6) = -3$$

(b) Add $-4 + 7$.

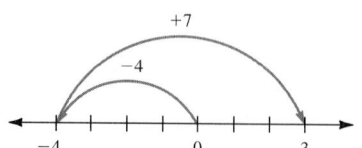

This time move 4 units to the left of the origin as the first step. Then move 7 units to the right.

$$-4 + 7 = 3$$

 CHECK YOURSELF 2

Add.

(a) $7 + (-5)$ **(b)** $4 + (-8)$ **(c)** $-\dfrac{1}{3} + \dfrac{16}{3}$ **(d)** $-7 + 3$

You have no doubt noticed that, in adding a positive number and a negative number, sometimes the sum is positive and sometimes it is negative. This depends on which of the numbers has the larger absolute value. This leads us to the second part of our addition rule.

NOTE Again, we first encountered absolute values in Section 1.2.

> **Rules and Properties: Adding Signed Numbers Case 2: Different Signs**
>
> If two numbers have different signs, subtract their absolute values, the smaller from the larger. Give the result the sign of the number with the larger absolute value.

Example 3

Adding Signed Numbers

(a) $7 + (-19) = -12$
Because the two numbers have different signs, subtract the absolute values ($19 - 7 = 12$). The sum has the sign ($-$) of the number with the larger absolute value, -19.

(b) $-\dfrac{13}{2} + \dfrac{7}{2} = -3$

Subtract the absolute values $\left(\dfrac{13}{2} - \dfrac{7}{2} = \dfrac{6}{2} = 3\right)$. The sum has the sign ($-$) of the number with the larger absolute value, $-\dfrac{13}{2}$.

(c) $-8.2 + 4.5 = -3.7$

NOTE Remember, **signed numbers** can be fractions and decimals as well as integers.

Subtract the absolute values ($8.2 - 4.5 = 3.7$). The sum has the sign ($-$) of the number with the larger absolute value, -8.2.

CHECK YOURSELF 3

Add mentally.

(a) $5 + (-14)$ **(b)** $-7 + (-8)$ **(c)** $-8 + 15$

(d) $7 + (-8)$ **(e)** $-\dfrac{2}{3} + \left(-\dfrac{7}{3}\right)$ **(f)** $5.3 + (-2.3)$

In Section 1.3 we discussed the commutative, associative, and distributive properties. There are two other properties of addition that we should mention. First, the sum of any number and 0 is always that number. In symbols,

Rules and Properties: Additive Identity Property

For any number a,

$$a + 0 = 0 + a = a$$

NOTE No number loses its identity after addition with 0. Zero is called the **additive identity**.

Example 4

Adding Signed Numbers

Add.

(a) $9 + 0 = 9$

(b) $0 + \left(-\dfrac{5}{4}\right) = -\dfrac{5}{4}$

(c) $(-25) + 0 = -25$

 CHECK YOURSELF 4

Add.

(a) $8 + 0$ **(b)** $0 + \left(-\dfrac{8}{3}\right)$ **(c)** $(-36) + 0$

NOTE The opposite of a number is also called the **additive inverse** of that number.

NOTE 3 and -3 are opposites.

Recall that every number has an *opposite*. It corresponds to a point the same distance from the origin as the given number, but in the opposite direction.

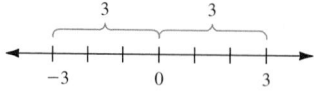

The opposite of 9 is -9.
The opposite of -15 is 15.

Our second property states that the sum of any number and its opposite is 0.

Rules and Properties: Additive Inverse Property

© 2001 McGraw-Hill Companies

NOTE Here $-a$ represents the opposite of the number a. The sum of any number and its opposite, or additive inverse, is 0.

For any number a, there exists a number $-a$ such that

$$a + (-a) = (-a) + a = 0$$

Example 5

Adding Signed Numbers

(a) $9 + (-9) = 0$

(b) $-15 + 15 = 0$

(c) $(-2.3) + 2.3 = 0$

(d) $\dfrac{4}{5} + \left(-\dfrac{4}{5}\right) = 0$

 CHECK YOURSELF 5

Add.

(a) $(-17) + 17$

(b) $12 + (-12)$

(c) $\dfrac{1}{3} + \left(-\dfrac{1}{3}\right)$

(d) $(-1.6) + 1.6$

In Section 1.2 we saw that the least and greatest elements of a set were called the minimum and maximum. The middle value of an ordered set is called the **median.** The median is sometimes used to represent an average of the set of numbers.

Example 6

Finding the Median

Find the median for each set of numbers.

(a) $9, -5, -8, 3, 7$

First, rewrite the set in ascending order.

$-8, -5, 3, 7, 9$

The median is then the element that has just as many numbers to its right as it has to its left. In this set, 3 is the median, because there are two numbers that are larger (7 and 9) and two numbers that are smaller (-8 and -5).

(b) $3, -2, 18, -20, -13$

First, rewrite the set in ascending order.

$-20, -13, -2, 3, 18$

The median is then the element that is exactly in the middle. The median for this set is -2.

CHECK YOURSELF 6

Find the median for each set of numbers.

(a) $-3, 2, 7, -6, -1$ **(b)** $5, 1, -10, 2, -20$

In the previous example, each set had an odd number of elements. If we had an even number of elements, there would be no single middle number.

To find the median from a set with an even number of elements, add the two middle numbers and divide their sum by 2.

Example 7

Finding the Median

Find the median for each set of numbers.

(a) $-3, 3, -8, 4, -1, -7, 5, 9$

First, rewrite the set in ascending order.

$-8, -7, -3, -1, 3, 4, 5, 9$

Add the middle two numbers (-1 and 3), then divide their sum by 2.

$$\frac{(-1) + (3)}{2} = \frac{2}{2} = 1$$

The median is 1.

(b) $8, 3, -2, 4, -5, -7$

Rewrite the set in ascending order.

$-7, -5, -2, 3, 4, 8$

The median is one-half the sum of the middle two numbers.

$$\frac{-2 + 3}{2} = \frac{1}{2} = 0.5$$

CHECK YOURSELF 7

Find the median for each set of numbers.

(a) $2, -5, 15, 8, 3, -4$
(b) $8, 3, 6, -8, 9, -7$

To begin our discussion of subtraction when signed numbers are involved, we can look back at a problem using natural numbers. Of course, we know that

$8 - 5 = 3$ (1)

From our work in adding signed numbers, we know that it is also true that

$$8 + (-5) = 3 \tag{2}$$

Comparing equations (1) and (2), we see that the results are the same. This leads us to an important pattern. Any subtraction problem can be written as a problem in addition. Subtracting 5 is the same as adding the opposite of 5, or -5. We can write this fact as follows:

$$8 - 5 = 8 + (-5) = 3$$

This leads us to the following rule for subtracting signed numbers.

Rules and Properties: Subtracting Signed Numbers

1. Rewrite the subtraction problem as an addition problem by
   a. Changing the minus sign to a plus sign.
   b. Replacing the number being subtracted with its opposite.
2. Add the resulting signed numbers as before.
   In symbols,

   $$a - b = a + (-b)$$

NOTE This is the *definition* of subtraction.

Example 8 illustrates the use of this definition while subtracting.

Example 8

Subtracting Signed Numbers

Subtraction   *Addition*

Change the subtraction symbol (−) to an addition symbol (+).

(a) $15 - 7 = 15 + (-7)$

Replace 7 with its opposite, -7.

$$= 8$$

(b) $9 - 12 = 9 + (-12) = -3$

(c) $-6 - 7 = -6 + (-7) = -13$

(d) $-\dfrac{3}{5} - \dfrac{7}{5} = -\dfrac{3}{5} + \left(-\dfrac{7}{5}\right) = -\dfrac{10}{5} = -2$

(e) $2.1 - 3.4 = 2.1 + (-3.4) = -1.3$

(f) Subtract 5 from -2. We write the statement as $-2 - 5$ and proceed as before:

$$-2 - 5 = -2 + (-5) = -7$$

CHECK YOURSELF 8

Subtract.

(a) $18 - 7$ **(b)** $5 - 13$ **(c)** $-7 - 9$

(d) $-\dfrac{5}{6} - \dfrac{7}{6}$ **(e)** $-2 - 7$ **(f)** $5.6 - 7.8$

The subtraction rule is used in the same way when the number being subtracted is negative. Change the subtraction to addition. Replace the negative number being subtracted with its opposite, which is positive. Example 9 will illustrate this principle.

Example 9

Subtracting Signed Numbers

Subtraction   *Addition*

Change the subtraction to an addition.

(a) $5 - (-2) = 5 + (+2) = 5 + 2 = 7$

Replace -2 with its opposite, $+2$ or 2.

(b) $7 - (-8) = 7 + (+8) = 7 + 8 = 15$

(c) $-9 - (-5) = -9 + 5 = -4$

(d) $-12.7 - (-3.7) = -12.7 + 3.7 = -9$

(e) $-\dfrac{3}{4} - \left(-\dfrac{7}{4}\right) = -\dfrac{3}{4} + \left(+\dfrac{7}{4}\right) = \dfrac{4}{4} = 1$

(f) Subtract -4 from -5. We write

$-5 - (-4) = -5 + 4 = -1$

 CHECK YOURSELF 9

Subtract.

(a) $8 - (-2)$ **(b)** $3 - (-10)$ **(c)** $-7 - (-2)$

(d) $-9.8 - (-5.8)$ **(e)** $7 - (-7)$

Given a set of numbers, the **range** is the difference between the maximum and the minimum.

Example 10

Finding the Range

Find the range for each set of numbers.

(a) $5, -2, -7, 9, 3$

Rewrite the set in ascending order. The maximum is 9, the minimum is -7. The range is the difference.

$$9 - (-7) = 9 + 7 = 16$$

The range is 16.

(b) $3, 8, -17, 12, -2$

Rewrite the set in ascending order. The maximum is 12. The minimum is -17. The range is $12 - (-17) = 29$.

 CHECK YOURSELF 10

Find the range for each set of numbers.

(a) $2, -4, 7, -3, -1$ **(b)** $-3, 4, -7, 5, 9, -4$

Your scientific calculator can be used to do arithmetic with signed numbers. Before we look at an example, there are some keys on your calculator with which you should become familiar.

There are two similar keys you must find on the calculator. The first is used for subtraction ($\boxed{-}$) and is usually found in the right column of calculator keys. The second will "change the sign" of a number. It is usually a $\boxed{+/-}$ and is found on the bottom row.

We will use these keys in our next example.

NOTE Some graphing calculators have a negative sign $\boxed{(-)}$ that acts to change the sign of a number.

 ### Example 11

Subtracting Signed Numbers

NOTE If you have a graphing calculator, the key sequence will be

$\boxed{(-)}$ 12.43 $\boxed{-}$ 3.516 $\boxed{\text{ENTER}}$

Using your calculator, find the difference.

(a) $-12.43 - 3.516$

Enter the 12.43 and push the $\boxed{+/-}$ to make it negative. Then push $\boxed{-}$ 3.516 $\boxed{=}$. The result should be -15.946.

(b) $23.56 - (-4.7)$

The key sequence is

23.56 $\boxed{-}$ 4.7 $\boxed{+/-}$ $\boxed{=}$

The answer should be 28.26.

✔ CHECK YOURSELF 11

Use your calculator to find the difference.

(a) $-13.46 - 5.71$

(b) $-3.575 - (-6.825)$

CHECK YOURSELF ANSWERS

1. **(a)** -9; **(b)** -10; **(c)** -20; **(d)** -4 2. **(a)** 2; **(b)** -4; **(c)** 5; **(d)** -4

3. **(a)** -9; **(b)** -15; **(c)** 7; **(d)** -1; **(e)** -3; **(f)** 3 4. **(a)** 8; **(b)** $-\dfrac{8}{3}$; **(c)** -36

5. **(a)** 0; **(b)** 0; **(c)** 0; **(d)** 0 6. **(a)** -1; **(b)** 1 7. **(a)** 2.5; **(b)** 4.5

8. **(a)** 11; **(b)** -8; **(c)** -16; **(d)** -2; **(e)** -9; **(f)** -2.2

9. **(a)** 10; **(b)** 13; **(c)** -5; **(d)** -4; **(e)** 14 10. **(a)** $7 - (-4) = 11$;

(b) $9 - (-7) = 16$ 11. **(a)** -19.17; **(b)** 3.25

1.4 Exercises

Add.

1. $3 + 6$

2. $5 + 9$

3. $11 + 5$

4. $8 + 7$

5. $\dfrac{3}{4} + \dfrac{5}{4}$

6. $\dfrac{7}{3} + \dfrac{8}{3}$

7. $\dfrac{1}{2} + \dfrac{4}{5}$

8. $\dfrac{2}{3} + \dfrac{5}{9}$

9. $(-2) + (-3)$

10. $(-1) + (-9)$

11. $\left(-\dfrac{3}{5}\right) + \left(-\dfrac{7}{5}\right)$

12. $\left(-\dfrac{3}{5}\right) + \dfrac{12}{5}$

13. $\left(-\dfrac{1}{2}\right) + \left(-\dfrac{3}{8}\right)$

14. $\left(-\dfrac{4}{7}\right) + \left(-\dfrac{3}{14}\right)$

15. $(-1.6) + (-2.3)$

16. $(-3.5) + (-2.6)$

17. $9 + (-3)$

18. $10 + (-4)$

19. $\dfrac{3}{4} + \left(-\dfrac{1}{2}\right)$

20. $\dfrac{2}{3} + \left(-\dfrac{1}{6}\right)$

21. $\left(-\dfrac{4}{5}\right) + \dfrac{9}{20}$

22. $\left(-\dfrac{11}{6}\right) + \dfrac{5}{12}$

ANSWERS

1. _____
2. _____
3. _____
4. _____
5. _____
6. _____
7. _____
8. _____
9. _____
10. _____
11. _____
12. _____
13. _____
14. _____
15. _____
16. _____
17. _____
18. _____
19. _____
20. _____
21. _____
22. _____

23. _____

24. _____

25. _____

26. _____

27. _____

28. _____

29. _____

30. _____

31. _____

32. _____

33. _____

34. _____

35. _____

36. _____

37. _____

38. _____

39. _____

40. _____

41. _____

42. _____

43. _____

44. _____

45. _____

46. _____

47. _____

48. _____

49. _____

50. _____

23. $-11.4 + 13.4$

24. $-5.2 + 9.2$

25. $-3.6 + 7.6$

26. $-2.6 + 4.9$

27. $-9 + 0$

28. $-15 + 0$

29. $7 + (-7)$

30. $12 + (-12)$

31. $-4.5 + 4.5$

32. $\left(-\dfrac{2}{3}\right) + \dfrac{2}{3}$

33. $7 + (-9) + (-5) + 6$

34. $(-4) + 6 + (-3) + 0$

35. $7 + (-3) + 5 + (-11)$

36. $-\dfrac{6}{5} + \left(-\dfrac{13}{5}\right) + \dfrac{4}{5}$

37. $-\dfrac{3}{2} + \left(-\dfrac{7}{4}\right) + \dfrac{1}{4}$

38. $\dfrac{1}{3} + \left(-\dfrac{5}{6}\right) + \left(-\dfrac{1}{2}\right)$

39. $2.3 + (-5.4) + (-2.9)$

40. $-5.4 + (-2.1) + (-3.5)$

Subtract.

41. $21 - 13$

42. $36 - 22$

43. $82 - 45$

44. $103 - 56$

45. $\dfrac{15}{7} - \dfrac{8}{7}$

46. $\dfrac{17}{8} - \dfrac{9}{8}$

47. $7.9 - 5.4$

48. $11.7 - 4.5$

49. $8 - 10$

50. $14 - 19$

51. $24 - 45$

52. $136 - 352$

53. $\dfrac{7}{6} - \dfrac{19}{6}$

54. $\dfrac{5}{9} - \dfrac{32}{9}$

55. $7.8 - 11.6$

56. $14.3 - 25.5$

57. $-5 - 3$

58. $-15 - 8$

59. $-9 - 14$

60. $-8 - 12$

61. $-\dfrac{2}{5} - \dfrac{7}{10}$

62. $-\dfrac{5}{9} - \dfrac{7}{18}$

63. $-3.4 - 4.7$

64. $-8.1 - 7.6$

65. $5 - (-11)$

66. $7 - (-5)$

67. $7 - (-12)$

68. $3 - (-10)$

69. $\dfrac{3}{4} - \left(-\dfrac{3}{2}\right)$

70. $\dfrac{5}{6} - \left(-\dfrac{7}{6}\right)$

71. $\dfrac{6}{7} - \left(-\dfrac{5}{14}\right)$

72. $\dfrac{11}{16} - \left(-\dfrac{7}{8}\right)$

73. $8.3 - (-5.7)$

74. $6.5 - (-4.3)$

75. $8.9 - (-11.7)$

76. $14.5 - (-24.6)$

77. $-36 - (-24)$

78. $-28 - (-11)$

51. _____

52. _____

53. _____

54. _____

55. _____

56. _____

57. _____

58. _____

59. _____

60. _____

61. _____

62. _____

63. _____

64. _____

65. _____

66. _____

67. _____

68. _____

69. _____

70. _____

71. _____

72. _____

73. _____

74. _____

75. _____

76. _____

77. _____

78. _____

79. _____

80. _____

81. _____

82. _____

83. _____

84. _____

85. _____

86. _____

87. _____

88. _____

89. _____

90. _____

91. _____

92. _____

93. _____

94. _____

95. _____

96. _____

97. _____

98. _____

99. _____

100. _____

101. _____

102. _____

103. _____

104. _____

105. _____

106. _____

79. $-19 - (-27)$

80. $-11 - (-16)$

81. $\left(-\dfrac{3}{4}\right) - \left(-\dfrac{11}{4}\right)$

82. $-\dfrac{1}{2} - \left(-\dfrac{5}{8}\right)$

83. $-12.7 - (-5.7)$

84. $-5.6 - (-2.6)$

85. $-6.9 - (-10.1)$

86. $-3.4 - (-7.6)$

Use your calculator to evaluate each expression.

87. $-4.1967 - 5.2943$

88. $5.3297 - (-4.1897)$

89. $-4.1623 - (-3.1468)$

90. $(-3.6829) - 4.5687$

91. $-6.3267 + 8.6789$

92. $-6.6712 + 5.3245$

Find the median for each of the following sets.

93. $1, 3, 5, 7, 9$

94. $2, 4, 6, 8, 10$

95. $8, 7, 2, 25, 5, 13, 3$

96. $53, 23, 34, 21, 32, 30, 32$

Determine the range for each of the following sets.

97. $2, 7, 9, 15, 24$

98. $4, 8, 11, 15, 27$

99. $-4, -3, 2, 7, 9$

100. $-7, -2, 1, 8, 11$

101. $\dfrac{7}{8}, 2, -\dfrac{1}{2}, -8, \dfrac{3}{4}$

102. $3, \dfrac{5}{6}, -7, -\dfrac{1}{3}, \dfrac{2}{3}$

103. $3, 2, -5, 6, -3$

104. $1, -9, 7, -2, 3$

Solve the following problems.

105. Checking account. Amir has $100 in his checking account. He writes a check for $23 and makes a deposit of $51. What is his new balance?

106. Checking account. Olga has $250 in her checking account. She deposits $52 and then writes a check for $77. What is her new balance?

Bal: _____ 250

Dep: _____ 52

CK # 1111: _____ 77

107. **Football yardage.** On four consecutive running plays, Ricky Watters of the Seattle Seahawks gained 23 yards, lost 5 yards, gained 15 yards, and lost 10 yards. What was his net yardage change for the series of plays?

108. **VISA balance.** Ramon owes $780 on his VISA account. He returns three items costing $43.10, $36.80, and $125.00 and receives credit on his account. Next, he makes a payment of $400. He then makes a purchase of $82.75. How much does Tom still owe?

109. **Temperature.** The temperature at noon on a June day was 82°. It fell by 12° in the next 4 hours. What was the temperature at 4:00 P.M.?

110. **Mountain climbing.** Chia is standing at a point 6000 feet (ft) above sea level. She descends to a point 725 ft lower. What is her distance above sea level?

111. **Checking account.** Omar's checking account was overdrawn by $72. He wrote another check for $23.50. How much was his checking account overdrawn after writing the check?

112. **Personal finance.** Angelo owed his sister $15. He later borrowed another $10. What positive or negative number represents his current financial condition?

113. **Education.** A local community college had a decrease in enrollment of 750 students in the fall of 1999. In the spring of 2000, there was another decrease of 425 students. What was the total decrease in enrollment for both semesters?

114. **Temperature.** At 7 A.M., the temperature was −15°F. By 1 P.M., the temperature had increased by 18°F. What was the temperature at 1 P.M.?

115. **Education.** Ezra's scores on five tests taken in a mathematics class were 87, 71, 95, 81, and 90. What was the range of his scores?

107. _____

108. _____

109. _____

110. _____

111. _____

112. _____

113. _____

114. _____

115. _____

Answers

1. 9   **3.** 16   **5.** 2   **7.** $\dfrac{13}{10}$ **9.** -5 **11.** -2 **13.** $-\dfrac{7}{8}$

15. -3.9 **17.** 6   **19.** $\dfrac{1}{4}$ **21.** $-\dfrac{7}{20}$ **23.** 2   **25.** 4   **27.** -9

29. 0   **31.** 0   **33.** -1 **35.** -2 **37.** -3 **39.** -6 **41.** 8

43. 37   **45.** 1   **47.** 2.5   **49.** -2 **51.** -21 **53.** -2 **55.** -3.8

57. -8 **59.** -23 **61.** $-\dfrac{11}{10}$ **63.** -8.1 **65.** 16   **67.** 19

69. $\dfrac{9}{4}$ **71.** $\dfrac{17}{14}$ **73.** 14   **75.** 20.6   **77.** -12 **79.** 8   **81.** 2

83. -7 **85.** 3.2   **87.** -9.491 **89.** -1.0155 **91.** 2.3522

93. 5   **95.** 7   **97.** 22   **99.** 13   **101.** 10   **103.** 11   **105.** $128

107. 23 yards   **109.** 70°   **111.** $95.50   **113.** 1175   **115.** 24

Operations and Properties

1. Represent the four arithmetic operations using variables
2. Evaluate expressions using the order of operations
3. Recognize and apply the properties of addition
4. Recognize and apply the properties of multiplication
5. Recognize and apply the distributive property

NOTE Francois Viete (1540–1603), a French mathematician, first introduced the practice of using letters to represent known and unknown quantities.

The process of combining two elements of a set to produce a third element is called a **binary operation.** There are four basic binary operations: addition, subtraction, multiplication, and division. In algebra, we write these operations as follows:

$x + y$ is called the sum of x and y, or x plus y.

$x - y$ is called the difference of x and y, or x minus y.

NOTE We do not use a multiplication sign $\times$ because of the possible confusion with the letter x.

xy (or $x \cdot y$) is the product of x and y, or x times y.

$\dfrac{x}{y}$ (or $x \div y$) is the quotient of x and y, or x divided by y.

NOTE The symbols $+$ and $-$ first appeared in print in a book by Johann Widman (1489). The symbol $\times$ dates to a text by William Oughtred (1631).

Each of the above is an example of an **expression.** An expression is a meaningful collection of numbers, variables, and operations.

Algebraic expressions frequently involve more than one of the operation symbols that we have seen thus far in this section. For instance, when we are given an expression to evaluate such as

$2 + 3 \cdot 4$

we must agree on the order in which the indicated operations are to be performed. If we don't, we can end up with different results after the evaluation. For instance, if we were to add first, in this case we would have

$\underset{\substack{\text{Add} \\ \text{first}}}{\underline{2 + 3}} \cdot 4 = \underset{\substack{\text{Then} \\ \text{multiply}}}{\underline{5 \cdot 4}} = 20$

However, if we multiply first, we have

$2 + \underset{\text{Multiply}}{\underline{3 \cdot 4}} = \underset{\text{Then add}}{\underline{2 + 12}} = 14$

Because we get different answers depending on the order in which we do the operations, the language of algebra would not be clear unless we agreed on which of the methods of evaluation shown above is correct.

To avoid this difficulty, we will agree that the multiplication in an expression such as

NOTE This means that $2 + 3 \cdot 4 = 14$ and the second approach shown above is the correct one.

$2 + 3 \cdot 4$

should always be done *before* the addition.

© 2001 McGraw-Hill Companies

NOTE An algorithm is a step-by-step process for solving a problem.

We refer to our procedure as the **order of operations.** The following algorithm gives us a set of rules, defining the order in which the operations should be performed.

NOTE The most common grouping symbols are parentheses, brackets, fraction bars, absolute value signs, and radicals.

Rules and Properties: Order of Operations

1. Simplify within the innermost grouping symbol, and work outward until all grouping symbols are removed.
2. Evaluate any expressions involving exponents.
3. Perform any multiplication and division, working from left to right.
4. Then do any addition and subtraction, again working left to right.

Example 1

Evaluating Expressions

Evaluate each expression.

(a) $2 \cdot 4 + 3 = 8 + 3$ Multiply first.

$\qquad\qquad = 11$ Then do the addition.

(b) $2(4 + 3) = 2 \cdot 7$ Simplify within the grouping symbol.

$\qquad\qquad = 14$ Then multiply.

NOTE Remember:

$7^2 = 7 \cdot 7 = 49$

Two factors

$2^3 = 2 \cdot 2 \cdot 2 = 8$

Three factors

(c) $2(4 + 3)^2 = 2(7)^2$ Add inside the parentheses.

$\qquad\qquad = 2 \cdot 49$ Evaluate the power.

$\qquad\qquad = 98$ Multiply.

(d) $3 + 5 \cdot 2^3 - 3 = 3 + 5 \cdot 8 - 3$ Evaluate the power.

$\qquad\qquad = 3 + 40 - 3$ Multiply.

$\qquad\qquad = 43 - 3$ Add and then subtract—from left to right.

$\qquad\qquad = 40$

 CHECK YOURSELF 1

Evaluate each expression.

(a) $50 - 6 \cdot 8$ **(b)** $3(25 - 20)$

(c) $3(25 - 20)^2$ **(d)** $17 + 2 \cdot 3^3$

There are several properties of the two primary operations, addition and multiplication, that are very important in the study of algebra. The following table describes several of those properties for real numbers a, b, and c.

Property	Addition	Multiplication
Closure	$a + b \in R$	$a \cdot b \in R$
Associative	$(a + b) + c = a + (b + c)$	$(a \cdot b) \cdot c = a \cdot (b \cdot c)$
Commutative	$a + b = b + a$	$a \cdot b = b \cdot a$
Identity	$a + 0 = a$	$a \cdot 1 = a$
Inverse	$a + (-a) = 0$	$a \cdot \dfrac{1}{a} = 1$

NOTE The multiplicative inverse of *a* is also called the *reciprocal* of *a*. This is the property that allows us to *define division* by any nonzero number.

Example 2 illustrates the use of the properties introduced above.

Example 2

Identifying Properties of Multiplication

State the property used to justify each statement.

NOTE The *grouping* has been changed.

(a) $2 + (3 + b) = (2 + 3) + b$
Associative property of addition

NOTE Because $\frac{3}{2}$ is the reciprocal of $\frac{2}{3}$.

(b) $\left(\frac{2}{3}\right)\left(\frac{3}{2}\right) = 1$
Multiplicative inverse

(c) $(-3)(-4)$ is a real number
Closure property of multiplication

(d) $1(5) = 5$
Multiplicative identity

NOTE Only the *order* has been changed.

(e) $2 + (x + y) = 2 + (y + x)$
Commutative property of addition

✔ CHECK YOURSELF 2

State the property used to justify each statement.

(a) $(9)(-7)$ is a real number

(b) $2 + x + y = 2 + y + x$

(c) $\left(\frac{1}{3} \cdot 3\right)xy = 1 \cdot xy$

(d) $0 + x + y = x + y$

(e) $12(3ab) = (12 \cdot 3)ab$

In addition to the specific properties for addition and multiplication, we have one property that involves both operations.

Rules and Properties: Distributive Property

For any real numbers *a*, *b*, and *c*,

$a(b + c) = ab + ac$

In words, multiplication distributes *over* addition.

The following example illustrates the use of the distributive property.

Example 3

Using the Distributive Property

Use the distributive property to simplify each expression.

NOTE "Distribute" the multiplication by 4 over $3x$ and 7.
Simplify.

(a) $4(3x + 7) = 4(3x) + 4(7)$
$$= 12x + 28$$

(b) $7(3x + 2y + 5) = 7(3x) + 7(2y) + 7(5)$
$$= 21x + 14y + 35$$

 CHECK YOURSELF 3

Use the distributive property to simplify each expression.

(a) $5(4a + 5)$ **(b)** $4(2x^2 + 5x)$
(c) $6(4a + 3b + 7c)$ **(d)** $5(p + 5q)$

One of the most important uses of the distributive property relates to the combining of like terms. Example 4 illustrates.

Example 4

Combining Like Terms

Combine all like terms.

(a) $2x + 5x = (2 + 5)x = 7x$
(b) $3a + 4b + 7a - 3b = (3 + 7)a + (4 - 3)b = 10a + b$

CHECK YOURSELF 4

Combine all like terms.

(a) $3x + 12x$ **(b)** $2a + b + 7a - b$
(c) $2x^2 + 9x + 2 + x^2 - 3x$

CHECK YOURSELF ANSWERS

1. **(a)** 2; **(b)** 15; **(c)** 75; **(d)** 71
2. **(a)** Closure property of multiplication; **(b)** commutative property of addition; **(c)** multiplicative inverse; **(d)** additive identity; **(e)** associative property of multiplication
3. **(a)** $20a + 25$; **(b)** $8x^2 + 20x$; **(c)** $24a + 18b + 42c$; **(d)** $5p + 25q$
4. **(a)** $15x$; **(b)** $9a$; **(c)** $3x^2 + 6x + 2$

(1.5) **Exercises**

Translate each of the following statements, using symbols.

1. The sum of 10 and x

2. x plus 5

3. 12 more than p

4. The sum of m and 25

5. n increased by 1

6. s increased by 3

7. m minus 14

8. 5 less than b

9. Subtract 1 from x.

10. 25 minus a

11. The product of m and n

12. The quotient of b and 2

13. s divided by 4

14. 7 times b

15. 2 times the difference of c and d

16. Twice the sum of a and b

17. 4 less than the product of r and s

18. 11 more than 2 times w

19. The sum of c and 4, divided by d

20. The difference of m and 2, divided by n

Apply the order-of-operations algorithm to evaluate the following expressions.

21. $5 + 4 \cdot 6$

22. $7 + 5 \cdot 3$

23. $7(8 - 2)$

24. $3(12 - 7)$

25. $6(8 - 4)^2$

26. $4(12 - 6)^2$

27. $(4 + 3)(5 + 3)$

28. $(5 + 6)(3 + 1)$

29. $4 + 3 \cdot 5 + 2$

30. $5 + 6 \cdot 2 + 1$

31. $(7 + 5)(7 - 5)$

32. $(12 + 3)(12 - 3)$

33. $7 + 5 \cdot 7 - 5$

34. $11 + 2 \cdot 11 - 3$

35. $9^2 - 5^2$

36. $12^2 - 3^2$

37. $(9 - 5)^2$

38. $(11 - 2)^2$

ANSWERS

1. _____

2. _____

3. _____

4. _____

5. _____

6. _____

7. _____

8. _____

9. _____

10. _____

11. _____ 12. _____

13. _____ 14. _____

15. _____ 16. _____

17. _____ 18. _____

19. _____ 20. _____

21. _____ 22. _____

23. _____ 24. _____

25. _____ 26. _____

27. _____ 28. _____

29. _____ 30. _____

31. _____ 32. _____

33. _____ 34. _____

35. _____ 36. _____

37. _____ 38. _____

39. _____ 40. _____

41. _____ 42. _____

43. _____ 44. _____

45. _____ 46. _____

47. _____ 48. _____

49. _____ 50. _____

51. _____ 52. _____

53. _____ 54. _____

55. _____ 56. _____

57. _____ 58. _____

59. _____ 60. _____

61. _____ 62. _____

63. _____ 64. _____

65. _____ 66. _____

67. _____ 68. _____

69. _____

70. _____

71. _____

72. _____

73. _____

74. _____

75. _____

76. _____

77. _____

78. _____

39. $16 \div 2^3 \cdot 2 - 3 + 11$

40. $10 - 3 \cdot 8 \div 4 + 3$

41. $-12 - 8 \div 4$

42. $48 \div 8 - 14 \div 2$

43. $(2^3 + 3)^2 + 12 \div 3 \cdot 2$

44. $(4 \cdot 3 + 13) \div 5 \cdot 3^2$

45. $3[35 - 3(6 - 2)^2]$

46. $3[14 - 2(5 - 3)^3]$

47. $\dfrac{5 - 15}{2 + 3}$

48. $\dfrac{4 - (-8)}{2 - 5}$

49. $\dfrac{-6 + 18}{-2 - 4}$

50. $\dfrac{-4 - 21}{3 - 8}$

51. $\dfrac{(5)(-12)}{(-3)(5)}$

52. $\dfrac{(-8)(-3)}{(2)(-4)}$

In each exercise, apply the commutative and associative properties to rewrite the expression. Then simplify the result.

53. $(b + 5) + 3$

54. $(x + 2) + 8$

55. $8 + (6 + a)$

56. $10 + (2 + y)$

57. $(2x + 5) + 12$

58. $(2w + 2) + 10$

59. $8 + (p + 6)$

60. $6 + (2m + 12)$

61. $(8 + a) + (-8)$

62. $-2 + (p + 2)$

63. $2(8x)$

64. $6(2b)$

65. $\dfrac{1}{4}(4w)$

66. $6p\left(\dfrac{1}{6}\right)$

67. $\left(\dfrac{2}{7}\right)\left(\dfrac{7}{2}\right)\left(\dfrac{1}{m}\right)m$

68. $\left(\dfrac{3}{4}\right)(b)\left(\dfrac{4}{3}\right)$

In each exercise apply the distributive property to rewrite the expression. Then simplify the result when possible.

69. $5(2m + 3)$

70. $2(4p + 5)$

71. $4a(a + 4)$

72. $6b(b + 5)$

73. $\dfrac{1}{2}(4a + 10)$

74. $\dfrac{1}{3}(6y + 15)$

75. $5(3a + 2b + 4)$

76. $6(3m + 6n + 7)$

77. $\dfrac{1}{2}(4a + 6b + 2c)$

78. $\dfrac{2}{3}(3x + 6y + 9z)$

In each exercise, apply the distributive property to simplify the expression.

79. $8b + 2b$

80. $10a + 2a$

81. $3m + 4m + m$

82. $b + 11b + 3b$

83. $\frac{2}{3}a + \frac{4}{3}a$

84. $\frac{2}{5}b + \frac{8}{5}b$

85. $\frac{1}{2}a + \frac{1}{3}a$

86. $\frac{3}{4}m + \frac{5}{6}m$

In each exercise, apply the appropriate properties to rewrite the expression. Then simplify the result.

87. $6x + (2 + 3x)$

88. $5p + (3 + 9p)$

89. $8y + (2y + 5)$

90. $8m + (3 + 4m)$

91. $2x + 9 + 4x + 6$

92. $2a + 1 + 9a + 7$

93. $3b + 2b + 5 + 4b$

94. $6x + 7 + 8x + 10$

95. $3 + 7y + (-3) + y$

96. $w + (-7) + 2w + 7$

97. $2 + 3(2y + 1) + 3y$

98. $5 + 2(3b + 3) + 4b$

99. $2y^2 + 3y(2 + y) + 3y$

100. $5n + 3n(n + 2) + 2n^2$

State the property used to justify the following statements.

101. $2 + 8 = 8 + 2$

102. $3 \cdot 6$ is a real number

103. $2(y + 5) = 2y + 10$

104. $6(2x) = (6 \cdot 2)x$

105. $4 + (5 + 6) = (4 + 5) + 6$

106. $4 + (5 + 6) = (5 + 6) + 4$

107. $18b + 6 + 12b = 18b + 12b + 6$

108. $18b + (12b + 6) = (18b + 12b) + 6$

109. $(18b + 12b) + 6 = (18 + 12)b + 6$

110. $\left(\frac{2}{7}\right)\left(\frac{7}{2}\right) = 1$

111. $\frac{3}{5} + \left(-\frac{3}{5}\right) = 0$

112. $(y + 3)(y + 2) = y(y + 2) + 3(y + 2)$

79.	80.
81.	82.
83.	84.
85.	86.
87.	88.
89.	90.
91.	92.
93.	94.
95.	96.
97.	
98.	
99.	
100.	
101.	
102.	
103.	
104.	
105.	
106.	
107.	
108.	
109.	
110.	
111.	
112.	

113. _____

114. _____

115. _____

116. _____

117. _____

118. _____

119. _____

120. _____

121. _____

122. _____

123. _____

124. _____

125. _____

126. _____

127. _____

128. _____

Determine whether each statement is true or false. If it is false, rewrite the right side of the equation to make it a true statement.

113. $3 + 5(y + 4) = 3 + 5y + 4$ **114.** $10 + 5x + 5 = 5(2 + x + 5)$

115. $7b + 8b = 15b$ **116.** $3a + (10 + 2a) = (3a + 2a) + 10$

117. $4(3w + 3) = 12w + 7$ **118.** $\frac{1}{5}y + \frac{2}{5}y = \frac{3}{10}y$

119. $3m + 4m + 1 = 7m + 1$ **120.** $3b + 2b + 5 = 10b$

121. $6y + (-6)y = 0$ **122.** $4b + (-4b) = b$

123. $2n + 6n = 8n^2$ **124.** $3a + a = 3a^2$

125. A local baker observed that the sales in her store in May were twice the sales in April. She also observed that the sales in June were three-fourths the sales in April. Use variables to describe the sales of the bakery in each of the 3 months.

126. Computer Corner noted that the sales of computers in August were three-fourths of the sales of computers in July. The sales of computers in September were five-sixths of the sales of computers in July. Use variables to describe the number of computers sold in each of the 3 months.

127. Create an example to show that subtraction of signed numbers is *not* commutative.

128. Create an example to show that division of signed numbers is *not* associative.

Answers

1. $10 + x$ **3.** $p + 12$ **5.** $n + 1$ **7.** $m - 14$ **9.** $x - 1$ **11.** mn

13. $\frac{s}{4}$ **15.** $2(c - d)$ **17.** $rs - 4$ **19.** $\frac{c + 4}{d}$ **21.** 29 **23.** 42

25. 96 **27.** 56 **29.** 21 **31.** 24 **33.** 37 **35.** 56 **37.** 16

39. 12 **41.** -14 **43.** 129 **45.** -39 **47.** -2 **49.** -2

51. 4 **53.** $b + 8$ **55.** $14 + a$ **57.** $2x + 17$ **59.** $p + 14$ **61.** a

63. $16x$ **65.** w **67.** 1 **69.** $10m + 15$ **71.** $4a^2 + 16a$

73. $2a + 5$ **75.** $15a + 10b + 20$ **77.** $2a + 3b + c$ **79.** $10b$ **81.** $8m$

83. $2a$ **85.** $\frac{5}{6}a$ **87.** $9x + 2$ **89.** $10y + 5$ **91.** $6x + 15$

93. $9b + 5$ **95.** $8y$ **97.** $9y + 5$ **99.** $5y^2 + 9y$

101. Commutative property of addition   **103.** Distributive property

105. Associative property of addition   **107.** Commutative property of addition

109. Distributive property   **111.** Additive inverse   **113.** False, $3 + 5y + 20$

115. True   **117.** False, $12w + 12$ **119.** True   **121.** True

123. False, $8n$ **125.** April: x; May: $2x$; June: $\frac{3}{4}x$ **127.**

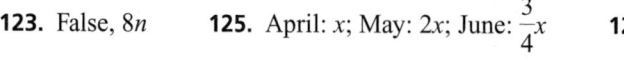

1.6 Multiplying and Dividing Signed Numbers

1.6 OBJECTIVES

1. Find the product of two signed numbers
2. Find the quotient of two signed numbers

When you first considered multiplication in arithmetic, it was thought of as repeated addition. Let's see what our work with the addition of signed numbers can tell us about multiplication when signed numbers are involved. For example,

$$3 \cdot 4 = \underbrace{4 + 4 + 4}_{} = 12$$

We interpret multiplication as repeated addition to find the product, 12.

Now, consider the product $(3)(-4)$:

$$(3)(-4) = (-4) + (-4) + (-4) = -12$$

Looking at this product suggests the first portion of our rule for multiplying signed numbers. The product of a positive number and a negative number is negative.

> **Rules and Properties:** Multiplying Signed Numbers Case 1: Different Signs
>
> The product of two numbers with different signs is negative.

To use this rule in multiplying two numbers with different signs, multiply their absolute values and attach a negative sign.

Example 1

Multiplying Signed Numbers

Multiply.

(a) $(5)(-6) = -30$

The product is negative.

(b) $(-10)(10) = -100$

(c) $(8)(-12) = -96$

NOTE Multiply together numerators and then denominators and reduce.

(d) $\left(-\dfrac{3}{4}\right)\left(\dfrac{2}{5}\right) = -\dfrac{3}{10}$

 CHECK YOURSELF 1

Multiply.

(a) $(-7)(5)$ **(b)** $(-12)(9)$ **(c)** $(-15)(8)$ **(d)** $\left(-\dfrac{4}{7}\right)\left(\dfrac{14}{5}\right)$

The product of two negative numbers is harder to visualize. The following pattern may help you see how we can determine the sign of the product.

NOTE This number is decreasing by 1.

$$(3)(-2) = -6$$

$$(2)(-2) = -4$$

$$(1)(-2) = -2$$ Do you see that the product is *increasing* by 2 each time?

$$(0)(-2) = 0$$

NOTE $(-1)(-2)$ is the opposite of -2.

$$(-1)(-2) = 2$$

What should the product $(-2)(-2)$ be? Continuing the pattern shown, we see that

$$(-2)(-2) = 4$$

This suggests that the product of two negative numbers is positive. That is the case. We can extend our multiplication rule.

NOTE If you would like a more detailed explanation, see the discussion at the end of this section.

Rules and Properties: Multiplying Signed Numbers Case 2: Same Sign

The product of two numbers with the same sign is positive.

Example 2

Multiplying Signed Numbers

Multiply.

(a) $9 \cdot 7 = 63$ The product of two positive numbers (same sign, +) is positive.

(b) $(-8)(-5) = 40$ The product of two negative numbers (same sign, −) is positive.

(c) $\left(-\dfrac{1}{2}\right)\left(-\dfrac{1}{3}\right) = \dfrac{1}{6}$

 CHECK YOURSELF 2

Multiply.

(a) $10 \cdot 12$ **(b)** $(-8)(-9)$ **(c)** $\left(-\dfrac{2}{3}\right)\left(-\dfrac{6}{7}\right)$

Two numbers, 0 and 1, have special properties in multiplication.

Rules and Properties: Multiplicative Identity Property

NOTE The number 1 is called the **multiplicative identity** for this reason.

The product of 1 and any number is that number. In symbols,

$$a \cdot 1 = 1 \cdot a = a$$

> **Rules and Properties:** Multiplicative Property of Zero
>
> The product of 0 and any number is 0. In symbols,
>
> $a \cdot 0 = 0 \cdot a = 0$

Example 3

Multiplying Signed Numbers

Find each product.

(a) $(1)(-7) = -7$

(b) $(15)(1) = 15$

(c) $(-7)(0) = 0$

(d) $0 \cdot 12 = 0$

(e) $\left(-\dfrac{4}{5}\right)(0) = 0$

 CHECK YOURSELF 3

Multiply.

(a) $(-10)(1)$ **(b)** $(0)(-17)$ **(c)** $\left(\dfrac{5}{7}\right)(1)$ **(d)** $(0)\left(\dfrac{3}{4}\right)$

Before we continue, consider the following equivalent fractions:

$$-\frac{1}{a} = \frac{-1}{a} = \frac{1}{-a}$$

Any of these forms can occur in the course of simplifying an expression. The first form is generally preferred.

To complete our discussion of the properties of multiplication, we state the following.

> **Rules and Properties:** Multiplicative Inverse Property
>
> For any number a, where $a \neq 0$, there is a number $\dfrac{1}{a}$ such that
>
> $a \cdot \dfrac{1}{a} = 1$

NOTE $\dfrac{1}{a}$ is called the **multiplicative inverse,** or the **reciprocal,** of a. The product of any nonzero number and its reciprocal is 1.

Example 4 illustrates this property.

Example 4

Multiplying Signed Numbers

(a) $3 \cdot \dfrac{1}{3} = 1$ The reciprocal of 3 is $\dfrac{1}{3}$.

(b) $-5\left(-\dfrac{1}{5}\right) = 1$ The reciprocal of -5 is $\dfrac{1}{-5}$ or $-\dfrac{1}{5}$.

(c) $\dfrac{2}{3} \cdot \dfrac{3}{2} = 1$ The reciprocal of $\dfrac{2}{3}$ is $\dfrac{1}{\frac{2}{3}}$, or $\dfrac{3}{2}$.

✓ CHECK YOURSELF 4

Find the multiplicative inverse (or the reciprocal) of each of the following numbers.

(a) 6   **(b)** −4   **(c)** $\dfrac{1}{4}$ **(d)** $-\dfrac{3}{5}$

You know from your work in arithmetic that multiplication and division are related operations. We can use that fact, and our work of the last section, to determine rules for the division of signed numbers. Every division problem can be stated as an equivalent multiplication problem. For instance,

$$\frac{15}{5} = 3 \qquad \text{because} \qquad 15 = 5 \cdot 3$$

$$\frac{-24}{6} = -4 \qquad \text{because} \qquad -24 = (6)(-4)$$

$$\frac{-30}{-5} = 6 \qquad \text{because} \qquad -30 = (-5)(6)$$

The examples above illustrate that because the two operations are related, the rule of signs that we stated in the last section for multiplication is also true for division.

Rules and Properties: Dividing Signed Numbers

1. The quotient of two numbers with different signs is negative.
2. The quotient of two numbers with the same sign is positive.

Again, the rule is easy to use. To divide two signed numbers, divide their absolute values. Then attach the proper sign according to the rule above.

Example 5

Dividing Signed Numbers

Divide.

(a) Positive ⟶ / Positive ⟶ $\dfrac{28}{7} = 4$ ⟵ Positive

(b) Negative ⟶ / Negative ⟶ $\dfrac{-36}{-4} = 9$ ⟵ Positive

(c) Negative ⟶ / Positive ⟶ $\dfrac{-42}{7} = -6$ ⟵ Negative

(d) Positive ⟶ / Negative ⟶ $\dfrac{75}{-3} = -25$ ⟵ Negative

(e) Positive ⟶ / Negative ⟶ $\dfrac{15.2}{-3.8} = -4$ ⟵ Negative

CHECK YOURSELF 5

Divide.

(a) $\dfrac{-55}{11}$ **(b)** $\dfrac{80}{20}$ **(c)** $\dfrac{-48}{-8}$ **(d)** $\dfrac{144}{-12}$ **(e)** $\dfrac{-13.5}{-2.7}$

You should be very careful when 0 is involved in a division problem. Remember that 0 divided by any nonzero number is just 0. Recall that

$$\frac{0}{-7} = 0 \qquad \text{because} \qquad 0 = (-7)(0)$$

However, if zero is the *divisor,* we have a special problem. Consider

$$\frac{9}{0} = ?$$

This means that $9 = 0 \cdot ?$.

Can 0 times a number ever be 9? No, so there is no solution.

Because $\dfrac{9}{0}$ cannot be replaced by any number, we agree that *division by 0 is not allowed.*

We say that

Rules and Properties: Division by Zero

Division by 0 is undefined.

Example 6

Dividing Signed Numbers

Divide, if possible.

(a) $\dfrac{7}{0}$ is undefined.

(b) $\dfrac{-9}{0}$ is undefined.

(c) $\dfrac{0}{5} = 0$

(d) $\dfrac{0}{-8} = 0$

Note: The expression $\dfrac{0}{0}$ is called an **indeterminate form.** You will learn more about this in later mathematics classes.

 CHECK YOURSELF 6

Divide if possible.

(a) $\dfrac{0}{3}$ **(b)** $\dfrac{5}{0}$ **(c)** $\dfrac{-7}{0}$ **(d)** $\dfrac{0}{-9}$

The fraction bar serves as a *grouping symbol.* This means that all operations in the numerator and denominator should be performed separately. Then the division is done as the last step. Example 7 illustrates this property.

Example 7

Dividing Signed Numbers

Evaluate each expression.

(a) $\dfrac{(-6)(-7)}{3} = \dfrac{42}{3} = 14$ Multiply in the numerator, then divide.

(b) $\dfrac{3 + (-12)}{3} = \dfrac{-9}{3} = -3$ Add in the numerator, then divide.

(c) $\dfrac{-4 + (2)(-6)}{-6 - 2} = \dfrac{-4 + (-12)}{-6 - 2}$ Multiply in the numerator. Then add in the numerator and subtract in the denominator.

$= \dfrac{-16}{-8} = 2$ Divide as the last step.

CHECK YOURSELF 7

Evaluate each expression.

(a) $\dfrac{-4 + (-8)}{6}$ (b) $\dfrac{3 - (2)(-6)}{-5}$ (c) $\dfrac{(-2)(-4) - (-6)(-5)}{(-4)(11)}$

Evaluating fractions with a calculator poses a special problem. Example 8 illustrates this problem.

Example 8

Using a Calculator to Divide

Use your scientific calculator to evaluate each fraction.

(a) $\dfrac{4}{2 - 3}$

As you can see, the correct answer should be -4. To get this answer with your calculator, you must place the denominator in parentheses. The key stroke sequence will be

4 ÷ (2 − 3) =

(b) $\dfrac{-7 - 7}{3 - 10}$

In this problem, the correct answer is 2. This can be found on your calculator by placing the numerator in parentheses and then placing the denominator in parentheses. The key stroke sequence will be

$\boxed{(}\ 7\ \boxed{+/-}\ \boxed{-}\ 7\ \boxed{)}\ \boxed{\div}\ \boxed{(}\ 3\ \boxed{-}\ 10\ \boxed{)}\ \boxed{=}$

When evaluating a fraction with a calculator, it is safest to use parentheses in both the numerator and the denominator.

✔ **CHECK YOURSELF 8**

Evaluate using your calculator.

(a) $\dfrac{-8}{5 - 7}$ **(b)** $\dfrac{-3 - 2}{-13 + 23}$

Example 9

Multiplying Signed Numbers

Evaluate each expression.

(a) $7(-9 + 12)$ Evaluate inside the parentheses first.

$= 7(3) = 21$

(b) $(-8)(-7) - 40$ Multiply first, then subtract.

$= 56 - 40$

$= 16$

(c) $(-5)^2 - 3$ Evaluate the power first.

$= (-5)(-5) - 3$ Note that $(-5)^2 = (-5)(-5)$
$\qquad\qquad\qquad\qquad\qquad = 25$

$= 25 - 3$

$= 22$

(d) $-5^2 - 3$ Note that $-5^2 = -25$. The power applies *only* to the 5.

$= -25 - 3$

$= -28$

✔ **CHECK YOURSELF 9**

Evaluate each expression.

(a) $8(-9 + 7)$ **(b)** $(-3)(-5) + 7$
(c) $(-4)^2 - (-4)$ **(d)** $-4^2 - (-4)$

NOTE Here is a more detailed explanation of why the product of two negative numbers is positive.

Rules and Properties: The Product of Two Negative Numbers

From our earlier work, we know that the sum of a number and its opposite is 0:

$$5 + (-5) = 0$$

Multiply both sides of the equation by -3:

$$(-3)[5 + (-5)] = (-3)(0)$$

Because the product of 0 and any number is 0, on the right we have 0.

$$(-3)[5 + (-5)] = 0$$

We use the distributive property on the left.

$$(-3)(5) + (-3)(-5) = 0$$

We know that $(-3)(5) = -15$, so the equation becomes

$$-15 + (-3)(-5) = 0$$

We now have a statement of the form

$$-15 + \square = 0$$

in which $\square$ is the value of $(-3)(-5)$. We also know that $\square$ is the number that must be added to -15 to get 0, so $\square$ is the opposite of -15, or 15. This means that

$$(-3)(-5) = 15 \qquad \text{The product is positive!}$$

It doesn't matter what numbers we use in this argument. The resulting product of two negative numbers will always be positive.

CHECK YOURSELF ANSWERS

1. **(a)** -35; **(b)** -108; **(c)** -120; **(d)** $-\dfrac{8}{5}$ 2. **(a)** 120; **(b)** 72; **(c)** $\dfrac{4}{7}$

3. **(a)** -10; **(b)** 0; **(c)** $\dfrac{5}{7}$; **(d)** 0   4. **(a)** $\dfrac{1}{6}$; **(b)** $-\dfrac{1}{4}$; **(c)** 4; **(d)** $-\dfrac{5}{3}$

5. **(a)** -5; **(b)** 4; **(c)** 6; **(d)** -12; **(e)** 5   6. **(a)** 0; **(b)** undefined; **(c)** undefined; **(d)** 0

7. **(a)** -2; **(b)** -3; **(c)** $\dfrac{1}{2}$ 8. **(a)** 4; **(b)** -0.5 9. **(a)** -16; **(b)** 22;

(c) 20; **(d)** -12

1.6 Exercises

Multiply.

1. $4 \cdot 10$

2. $3 \cdot 14$

3. $(5)(-12)$

4. $(10)(-2)$

5. $(-8)(9)$

6. $(-12)(3)$

7. $(4)\left(-\dfrac{3}{2}\right)$

8. $(9)\left(-\dfrac{2}{3}\right)$

9. $\left(-\dfrac{1}{4}\right)(8)$

10. $\left(-\dfrac{3}{2}\right)(4)$

11. $(3.25)(-4)$

12. $(5.4)(-5)$

13. $(-8)(-7)$

14. $(-9)(-8)$

15. $(-5)(-12)$

16. $(-7)(-3)$

17. $(-9)\left(-\dfrac{2}{3}\right)$

18. $(-6)\left(-\dfrac{3}{2}\right)$

19. $(-1.25)(-12)$

20. $(-1.5)(-20)$

21. $(0)(-18)$

22. $(-17)(0)$

23. $(15)(0)$

24. $(0)(25)$

25. $\left(-\dfrac{11}{12}\right)(0)$

26. $\left(-\dfrac{8}{9}\right)(0)$

ANSWERS

1. _____
2. _____
3. _____
4. _____
5. _____
6. _____
7. _____
8. _____
9. _____
10. _____
11. _____
12. _____
13. _____
14. _____
15. _____
16. _____
17. _____
18. _____
19. _____
20. _____
21. _____
22. _____
23. _____
24. _____
25. _____
26. _____

27. _____

28. _____

29. _____

30. _____

31. _____

32. _____

33. _____

34. _____

35. _____

36. _____

37. _____

38. _____

39. _____

40. _____

41. _____

42. _____

43. _____

44. _____

45. _____

46. _____

47. _____

48. _____

49. _____

50. _____

51. _____

52. _____

53. _____

54. _____

55. _____

56. _____

27. $(-3.57)(0)$

28. $(-2.37)(0)$

29. $\left(-\dfrac{3}{2}\right)\left(-\dfrac{2}{3}\right)$

30. $\left(-\dfrac{4}{5}\right)\left(-\dfrac{5}{4}\right)$

31. $\left(\dfrac{4}{7}\right)\left(-\dfrac{7}{4}\right)$

32. $\left(\dfrac{8}{9}\right)\left(-\dfrac{9}{8}\right)$

Divide.

33. $\dfrac{-20}{-4}$

34. $\dfrac{70}{14}$

35. $\dfrac{48}{6}$

36. $\dfrac{-24}{8}$

37. $\dfrac{50}{-5}$

38. $\dfrac{-32}{-8}$

39. $\dfrac{-52}{4}$

40. $\dfrac{56}{-7}$

41. $\dfrac{-75}{-3}$

42. $\dfrac{-60}{15}$

43. $\dfrac{0}{-8}$

44. $\dfrac{-125}{-25}$

45. $\dfrac{-9}{-1}$

46. $\dfrac{-10}{0}$

47. $\dfrac{-96}{-8}$

48. $\dfrac{-20}{2}$

49. $\dfrac{18}{0}$

50. $\dfrac{0}{8}$

51. $\dfrac{-17}{1}$

52. $\dfrac{-27}{-1}$

53. $\dfrac{-144}{-16}$

54. $\dfrac{-150}{6}$

55. $\dfrac{-29.4}{4.9}$

56. $\dfrac{-25.9}{-3.7}$

57. $\dfrac{-8}{32}$

58. $\dfrac{-6}{-30}$

59. $\dfrac{24}{-16}$

60. $\dfrac{-25}{10}$

61. $\dfrac{-28}{-42}$

62. $\dfrac{-125}{-75}$

Perform the indicated operations.

63. $\dfrac{(-6)(-3)}{2}$

64. $\dfrac{(-9)(5)}{-3}$

65. $\dfrac{(-8)(2)}{-4}$

66. $\dfrac{(7)(-8)}{-14}$

67. $\dfrac{24}{-4-8}$

68. $\dfrac{36}{-7+3}$

69. $\dfrac{-12-12}{-3}$

70. $\dfrac{-14-4}{-6}$

71. $\dfrac{55-19}{-12-6}$

72. $\dfrac{-11-7}{-14+8}$

73. $\dfrac{7-5}{2-2}$

74. $\dfrac{10-6}{4-4}$

Do the indicated operations. Remember the rules for the order of operations.

75. $5(7-2)$

76. $7(8-5)$

77. $2(5-8)$

78. $6(14-16)$

79. $-3(9-7)$

80. $-6(12-9)$

81. $-3(-2-5)$

82. $-2(-7-3)$

83. $(-2)(3)-5$

84. $(-6)(8)-27$

ANSWERS

57. _____

58. _____

59. _____

60. _____

61. _____

62. _____

63. _____

64. _____

65. _____

66. _____

67. _____

68. _____

69. _____

70. _____

71. _____

72. _____

73. _____

74. _____

75. _____

76. _____

77. _____

78. _____

79. _____

80. _____

81. _____

82. _____

83. _____

84. _____

85. _____

86. _____

87. _____

88. _____

89. _____

90. _____

91. _____

92. _____

93. _____

94. _____

95. _____

96. _____

97. _____

98. _____

99. _____

100. _____

101. _____

102. _____

103. _____

104. _____

105. _____

106. _____

107. _____

108. _____

109. _____

110. _____

111. _____

112. _____

85. $4(-7) - 5$

86. $(-3)(-9) - 11$

87. $(-5)(-2) - 12$

88. $(-7)(-3) - 25$

89. $(3)(-7) + 20$

90. $(2)(-6) + 8$

91. $-4 + (-3)(6)$

92. $-5 + (-2)(3)$

93. $7 - (-4)(-2)$

94. $9 - (-2)(-7)$

95. $(-7)^2 - 17$

96. $(-6)^2 - 20$

97. $(-5)^2 + 18$

98. $(-2)^2 + 10$

99. $-6^2 - 4$

100. $-5^2 - 3$

101. $(-4)^2 - (-2)(-5)$

102. $(-3)^3 - (-8)(-2)$

103. $(-8)^2 - 5^2$

104. $(-6)^2 - 4^2$

105. $(-6)^2 - (-3)^2$

106. $(-8)^2 - (-4)^2$

107. $-8^2 - 5^2$

108. $-6^2 - 3^2$

109. $-8^2 - (-5)^2$

110. $-9^2 - (-6)^2$

111. Basketball. You score 23 points a game for 11 straight games. What is the total number of points that you scored?

112. Gambling. In Atlantic City, Nick played the slot machines for 12 hours. He lost $45 an hour. Use signed numbers to represent the change in Nick's financial status at the end of the 12 hours.

113. **Stocks.** Suppose you own 35 shares of stock. If the price increases $1.25 per share, how much money have you made?

114. **Checking account.** Your bank charges a flat service charge of $3.50 per month on your checking account. You have had the account for 3 years. How much have you paid in service charges?

115. **Temperature.** The temperature is −6°F at 5:00 in the evening. If the temperature drops 2°F every hour, what is the temperature at 1:00 A.M.?

116. **Dieting.** A woman lost 42 pounds (lb). If she lost 3 lb each week, how long has she been dieting?

117. **Mowing lawns.** Patrick worked all day mowing lawns and was paid $9 per hour. If he had $125 at the end of a 9-hour day, how much did he have before he started working?

118. **Unit pricing.** A 4.5-lb can of food costs $8.91. What is the cost per pound?

119. **Investment.** Suppose that you and your two brothers bought equal shares of an investment for a total of $20,000 and sold it later for $16,232. How much did each person lose?

120. **Temperature.** Suppose that the temperature outside is dropping at a constant rate. At noon, the temperature is 70°F and it drops to 58°F at 5:00 P.M. How much did the temperature change each hour?

121. **Test tube count.** A chemist has 84 ounces (oz) of a solution. He pours the solution into test tubes. Each test tube holds $\frac{2}{3}$ oz. How many test tubes can he fill?

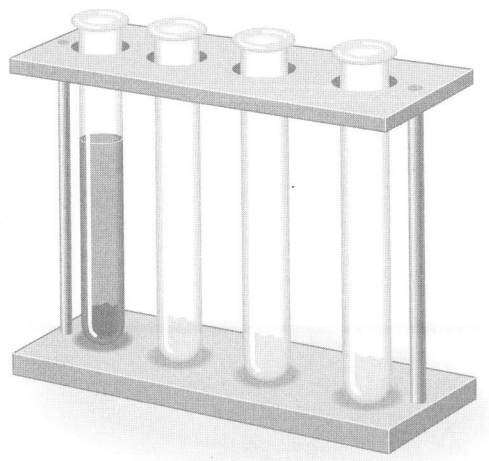

113. _____

114. _____

115. _____

116. _____

117. _____

118. _____

119. _____

120. _____

121. _____

Use your calculator to evaluate each expression.

122. $\dfrac{7}{4-5}$

123. $\dfrac{-8}{-4+2}$

124. $\dfrac{-6-9}{-4+1}$

125. $\dfrac{-10+4}{-7+10}$

126. Some animal ecologists in Minnesota are planning to reintroduce a group of animals into a wilderness area. The animals, a mammal on the endangered species list, will be released into an area where they once prospered and where there is an abundant food supply. But, the animals will face predators. The ecologists expect the number of mammals to grow about 25 percent each year but that 30 of the animals will die from attacks by predators and hunters.

　The ecologists need to decide how many animals they should release to establish a stable population. Work with other students to try several beginning populations and follow the numbers through 8 years. Is there a number of animals that will lead to a stable population? Write a letter to the editor of your local newspaper explaining how to decide what number of animals to release. Include a formula for the number of animals next year based on the number this year. Begin by filling out this table to track the number of animals living each year after the release:

No. Initially Released	Year							
	1	2	3	4	5	6	7	8
20	+___ −___ =_____							
100	+___ −___ =_____							
200	+___ −___ =_____							

Getting Ready

(a) $\dfrac{6 \cdot 2 + 8}{5 - 3}$

(b) $\dfrac{4 \cdot 5 - 8}{8 - 4 \div 2}$

(c) $\dfrac{-8 + 3 \cdot 2}{-12 \div 6}$

(d) $\dfrac{-3^2 - (-4 - 1)}{-2 \cdot 2}$

(e) $8 \div 4 - 3 \cdot 2$

(f) $6^2 - 18 \div 2 \cdot 3$

Answers

1. 40　　**3.** −60　　**5.** −72　　**7.** −6　　**9.** −2　　**11.** −13　　**13.** 56
15. 60　　**17.** 6　　**19.** 15　　**21.** 0　　**23.** 0　　**25.** 0　　**27.** 0
29. 1　　**31.** −1　　**33.** 5　　**35.** 8　　**37.** −10　　**39.** −13　　**41.** 25
43. 0　　**45.** 9　　**47.** 12　　**49.** Undefined　　**51.** −17　　**53.** 9　　**55.** −6
57. $-\dfrac{1}{4}$　　**59.** $-\dfrac{3}{2}$　　**61.** $\dfrac{2}{3}$　　**63.** 9　　**65.** 4　　**67.** −2　　**69.** 8
71. −2　　**73.** Undefined　　**75.** 25　　**77.** −6　　**79.** −6　　**81.** 21
83. −11　　**85.** −33　　**87.** −2　　**89.** −1　　**91.** −22　　**93.** −1　　**95.** 32
97. 43　　**99.** −40　　**101.** 6　　**103.** 39　　**105.** 27　　**107.** −89
109. −89　　**111.** 253 points　　**113.** $43.75　　**115.** −22°F　　**117.** $44
119. $1256　　**121.** 126　　**123.** 4　　**125.** −2　　**a.** 10　　**b.** 2　　**c.** 1
d. 1　　**e.** −4　　**f.** 9

 1.7 Evaluating Algebraic Expressions

1.7 OBJECTIVES

1. Evaluate algebraic expressions given any signed number value for the variables
2. Use a calculator to evaluate algebraic expressions
3. Find the sum of a set of signed numbers
4. Interpret summation notation

In applying algebra to problem solving, you will often want to find the value of an algebraic expression when you know certain values for the letters (or variables) in the expression. Finding the value of an expression is called *evaluating the expression* and uses the following steps.

Step by Step: To Evaluate an Algebraic Expression

Step 1 Replace each variable by the given number value.
Step 2 Do the necessary arithmetic operations, following the rules for order of operations.

Example 1

Evaluating Algebraic Expressions

Suppose that $a = 5$ and $b = 7$.

(a) To evaluate $a + b$, we replace a with 5 and b with 7.

$$a + b = 5 + 7 = 12$$

(b) To evaluate $3ab$, we again replace a with 5 and b with 7.

$$3ab = 3 \cdot 5 \cdot 7 = 105$$

 CHECK YOURSELF 1

If x = 6 and y = 7, evaluate.

(a) $y - x$ **(b)** $5xy$

We are now ready to evaluate algebraic expressions that require following the rules for the order of operations.

Example 2

Evaluating Algebraic Expressions

Evaluate the following expressions if $a = 2$, $b = 3$, $c = 4$, and $d = 5$.

CAUTION

This is different from
$(3c)^2 = (3 \cdot 4)^2$
$= 12^2 = 144$

(a) $5a + 7b = 5 \cdot 2 + 7 \cdot 3$ Multiply first.

$\qquad\qquad = 10 + 21 = 31$ Then add.

(b) $3c^2 = 3 \cdot 4^2$ Evaluate the power.

$\qquad\quad = 3 \cdot 16 = 48$ Then multiply.

(c) $7(c + d) = 7(4 + 5)$ Add inside the parentheses.

$\qquad\qquad = 7 \cdot 9 = 63$

(d) $5a^4 - 2d^2 = 5 \cdot 2^4 - 2 \cdot 5^2$ Evaluate the powers.

$\qquad\qquad\quad = 5 \cdot 16 - 2 \cdot 25$ Multiply.

$\qquad\qquad\quad = 80 - 50 = 30$ Subtract.

✔ **CHECK YOURSELF 2**

If $x = 3$, $y = 2$, $z = 4$, and $w = 5$, evaluate the following expressions.

(a) $4x^2 + 2$ **(b)** $5(z + w)$ **(c)** $7(z^2 - y^2)$

To evaluate algebraic expressions when a fraction bar is used, do the following: Start by doing all the work in the numerator, then do the work in the denominator. Divide the numerator by the denominator as the last step.

Example 3

Evaluating Algebraic Expressions

If $p = 2$, $q = 3$, and $r = 4$, evaluate:

(a) $\dfrac{8p}{r}$

NOTE As we mentioned in Section 1.6, the fraction bar is a grouping symbol, like parentheses. Work first in the numerator and then in the denominator.

Replace p with 2 and r with 4.

$$\frac{8p}{r} = \frac{8 \cdot 2}{4} = \frac{16}{4} = 4 \qquad \text{Divide as the last step.}$$

(b) $\dfrac{7q + r}{p + q} = \dfrac{7 \cdot 3 + 4}{2 + 3}$ Now evaluate the top and bottom separately.

$$= \frac{21 + 4}{2 + 3} = \frac{25}{5} = 5$$

✔ **CHECK YOURSELF 3**

Evaluate the following if $c = 5$, $d = 8$, and $e = 3$.

(a) $\dfrac{6c}{e}$ **(b)** $\dfrac{4d + e}{c}$ **(c)** $\dfrac{10d - e}{d + e}$

Example 4 shows how a scientific calculator can be used to evaluate algebraic expressions.

Example 4

Using a Calculator to Evaluate Expressions

Use a scientific calculator to evaluate the following expressions.

(a) $\dfrac{4x + y}{z}$ if $x = 2$, $y = 1$, and $z = 3$

Replace x with 2, y with 1, and z with 3:

$$\frac{4x + y}{z} = \frac{4 \cdot 2 + 1}{3}$$

Now, use the following keystrokes:

$$\boxed{(} \; 4 \; \boxed{\times} \; 2 \; \boxed{+} \; 1 \; \boxed{)} \; \boxed{\div} \; 3 \; \boxed{=}$$

The display will read 3.

(b) $\dfrac{7x - y}{3z - x}$ if $x = 2$, $y = 6$, and $z = 2$

$$\frac{7x - y}{3z - x} = \frac{7 \cdot 2 - 6}{3 \cdot 2 - 2}$$

Use the following keystrokes:

$$\boxed{(} \; 7 \; \boxed{\times} \; 2 \; \boxed{-} \; 6 \; \boxed{)} \; \boxed{\div} \; \boxed{(} \; 3 \; \boxed{\times} \; 2 \; - \; 2 \; \boxed{)} \; \boxed{=}$$

The display will read 2.

 CHECK YOURSELF 4

Use a scientific calculator to evaluate the following if $x = 2$, $y = 6$, and $z = 5$.

(a) $\dfrac{2x + y}{z}$ 　　　　　　　　　　　　　　 **(b)** $\dfrac{4y - 2z}{x}$

Example 5

Evaluating Expressions

Evaluate $5a + 4b$ if $a = -2$ and $b = 3$.

Replace *a* with −2 and *b* with 3.

NOTE Remember the rules for the order of operations. Multiply first, then add.

$$5a + 4b = 5(-2) + 4(3)$$
$$= -10 + 12$$
$$= 2$$

 CHECK YOURSELF 5

Evaluate $3x + 5y$ if $x = -2$ and $y = -5$.

We follow the same rules no matter how many variables are in the expression.

Example 6

Evaluating Expressions

Evaluate the following expressions if $a = -4$, $b = 2$, $c = -5$, and $d = 6$.

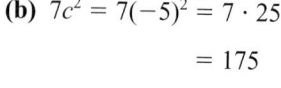

This becomes $-(-20)$, or $+20$.

(a) $7a - 4c = 7(-4) - 4(-5)$

$= -28 + 20$

$= -8$

Evaluate the power first, then multiply by 7.

C A U T I O N

When a squared variable is replaced by a negative number, square the negative.

$(-5)^2 = (-5)(-5) = 25$

↑

The exponent applies to -5!

$-5^2 = -(5 \cdot 5) = -25$

↑

The exponent applies only to 5!

(b) $7c^2 = 7(-5)^2 = 7 \cdot 25$

$= 175$

(c) $b^2 - 4ac = 2^2 - 4(-4)(-5)$

$= 4 - 4(-4)(-5)$

$= 4 - 80$

$= -76$

Add inside the parentheses first.

(d) $b(a + d) = 2(-4 + 6)$

$= 2(2)$

$= 4$

 CHECK YOURSELF 6

Evaluate if $p = -4$, $q = 3$, and $r = -2$.

(a) $5p - 3r$ **(b)** $2p^2 + q$ **(c)** $p(q + r)$

(d) $-q^2$ **(e)** $(-q)^2$

If an expression involves a fraction, remember that the fraction bar is a grouping symbol. This means that you should do the required operations first in the numerator and then the denominator. Divide as the last step.

Example 7

Evaluating Expressions

Evaluate the following expressions if $x = 4$, $y = -5$, $z = 2$, and $w = -3$.

(a) $\dfrac{z - 2y}{x} = \dfrac{2 - 2(-5)}{4} = \dfrac{2 + 10}{4}$

$= \dfrac{12}{4} = 3$

(b) $\dfrac{3x - w}{2x + w} = \dfrac{3(4) - (-3)}{2(4) + (-3)} = \dfrac{12 + 3}{8 + (-3)}$

$\qquad = \dfrac{15}{5} = 3$

 CHECK YOURSELF Z

Evaluate if m = −6, n = 4, and p = −3.

(a) $\dfrac{m + 3n}{p}$

(b) $\dfrac{4m + n}{m + 4n}$

     When an expression is evaluated by a calculator, the same order of operations is followed.

	Algebraic Notation	Calculator Notation
Addition	$6 + 2$	6 $\boxed{+}$ 2
Subtraction	$4 - 8$	4 $\boxed{-}$ 8
Multiplication	$(3)(-5)$	3 $\boxed{\times}$ $\boxed{(-)}$ 5 or 3 $\boxed{\times}$ 5 $\boxed{+/-}$
Division	$\dfrac{8}{6}$	8 $\boxed{\div}$ 6
Exponential	3^4	3^4 or 3 $\boxed{y^x}$ 4

In many applications, you will need to find the sum of a set of numbers that you are working with. In mathematics, the shorthand symbol for "sum of" is the Greek letter Σ (capital sigma, the "S" of the Greek alphabet). The expression Σx, in which x refers to all the numbers in a given set, means the sum of all the numbers in that set.

Example 8

Summing a Set

Find Σx for the following set of numbers:

$-2, -6, 3, 5, -4$

$\Sigma x = -2 + (-6) + 3 + 5 + (-4)$

$\quad = (-8) + 3 + 5 + (-4)$

$\quad = (-8) + 8 + (-4)$

$\quad = -4$

CHECK YOURSELF 8

Find Σx for each set of numbers.

(a) $-3, 4, -7, -9, 8$

(b) $-2, 6, -5, -3, 4, 7$

CHECK YOURSELF ANSWERS

1. (a) 1; (b) 210   2. (a) 38; (b) 45; (c) 84   3. (a) 10; (b) 7; (c) 7
4. (a) 2; (b) 7   5. -31 6. (a) -14; (b) 35; (c) -4; (d) -9; (e) 9
7. (a) -2; (b) -2 8. (a) -7; (b) 7

1.7 <u>**Exercises**</u>

Evaluate each of the expressions if $a = -2$, $b = 5$, $c = -4$, and $d = 6$.

1. $3c - 2b$

2. $4c - 2b$

3. $8b + 2c$

4. $7a - 2c$

5. $-b^2 + b$

6. $(-b)^2 + b$

7. $3a^2$

8. $6c^2$

9. $c^2 - 2d$

10. $3a^2 + 4c$

11. $2a^2 + 3b^2$

12. $4b^2 - 2c^2$

13. $2(a + b)$

14. $5(b - c)$

15. $4(2a - d)$

16. $6(3c - d)$

17. $a(b + 3c)$

18. $c(3a - d)$

19. $\dfrac{6d}{c}$

20. $\dfrac{8b}{5c}$

21. $\dfrac{3d + 2c}{b}$

22. $\dfrac{2b + 3d}{2a}$

1. _____

2. _____

3. _____

4. _____

5. _____

6. _____

7. _____

8. _____

9. _____

10. _____

11. _____

12. _____

13. _____

14. _____

15. _____

16. _____

17. _____

18. _____

19. _____

20. _____

21. _____

22. _____

23. _____

24. _____

25. _____

26. _____

27. _____

28. _____

29. _____

30. _____

31. _____

32. _____

33. _____

34. _____

35. _____

36. _____

37. _____

38. _____

39. _____

40. _____

41. _____

42. _____

43. _____

44. _____

45. _____

46. _____

23. $\dfrac{2b - 3a}{c + 2d}$

24. $\dfrac{3d - 2b}{5a + d}$

25. $d^2 - b^2$

26. $c^2 - a^2$

27. $(d - b)^2$

28. $(c - a)^2$

29. $(d - b)(d + b)$

30. $(c - a)(c + a)$

31. $d^3 - b^3$

32. $c^3 + a^3$

33. $(d - b)^3$

34. $(c + a)^3$

35. $(d - b)(d^2 + db + b^2)$

36. $(c + a)(c^2 - ac + a^2)$

37. $b^2 + a^2$

38. $d^2 - a^2$

39. $(b + a)^2$

40. $(d - a)^2$

41. $a^2 + 2ad + d^2$

42. $b^2 - 2bc + c^2$

Use your calculator to evaluate each expression if $x = -2.34$, $y = -3.14$, and $z = 4.12$. Round your answer to the nearest tenth.

43. $x + yz$

44. $y - 2z$

45. $x^2 - z^2$

46. $x^2 + y^2$

47. $\dfrac{xy}{z - x}$

48. $\dfrac{y^2}{zy}$

49. $\dfrac{2x + y}{2x + z}$

50. $\dfrac{x^2 y^2}{xz}$

For the following data sets, evaluate Σx.

51. $1, 2, 3, 7, 8, 9, 11$

52. $2, 4, 5, 6, 10, 11, 12$

53. $-5, -3, -1, 2, 3, 4, 8$

54. $-4, -2, -1, 5, 7, 8, 10$

55. $3, 2, -1, -4, -3, 8, 6$

56. $3, -4, 2, -1, 2, -7, 9$

57. $-\dfrac{1}{2}, -\dfrac{3}{4}, 2, 3, \dfrac{1}{4}, \dfrac{3}{2}, -1$

58. $-\dfrac{1}{3}, -\dfrac{5}{3}, -1, 1, 3, \dfrac{2}{3}, \dfrac{5}{3}$

59. $-2.5, -3.2, 2.6, -1, 2, 4, -3$

60. $-2.4, -3.1, -1.7, 3, 1, 2, 5$

In each of the following problems, decide if the given values make the statement true or false.

61. $x - 7 = 2y + 5; x = 22, y = 5$

62. $3(x - y) = 6; x = 5, y = -3$

63. $2(x + y) = 2x + y; x = -4, y = -2$

64. $x^2 - y^2 = x - y; x = 4, y = -3$

65. Electrical resistance. The formula for the total resistance in a parallel circuit is given by the formula $R_T = R_1 R_2/(R_1 + R_2)$. Find the total resistance if $R_1 = 6$ ohms (Ω) and $R_2 = 10\ \Omega$.

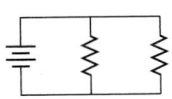

66. Area. The formula for the area of a triangle is given by $A = \dfrac{1}{2}ab$. Find the area of a triangle if $a = 4$ centimeters (cm) and $b = 8$ cm.

ANSWERS

47. _____
48. _____
49. _____
50. _____
51. _____
52. _____
53. _____
54. _____
55. _____
56. _____
57. _____
58. _____
59. _____
60. _____
61. _____
62. _____
63. _____
64. _____
65. _____
66. _____

67. _____

68. _____

69. _____

70. _____

71. _____

72. _____

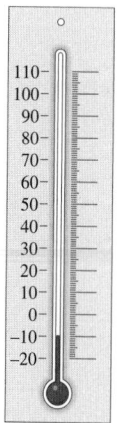

73. _____

67. Perimeter. The perimeter of a rectangle of length L and width W is given by the formula $P = 2L + 2W$. Find the perimeter when $L = 10$ inches (in.) and $W = 5$ in.

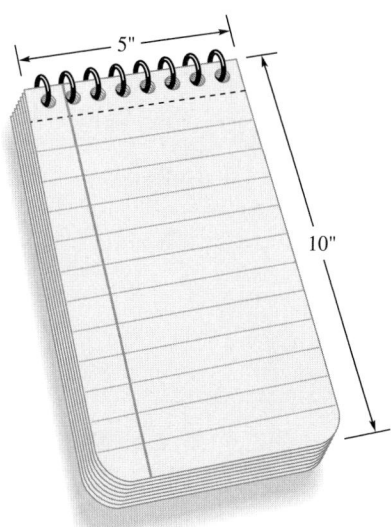

68. Simple interest. The simple interest I on a principal of P dollars at interest rate r for time t, in years, is given by $I = Prt$. Find the simple interest on a principal of $6000 at 8 percent for 3 years. (**Note:** 8% = 0.08)

69. Simple interest. Use the simple interest formula to find the principal if the total interest earned was $150 and the rate of interest was 4% for 2 years.

70. Simple interest. Use the simple interest formula to find the rate of interest if $10,000 earns $1500 interest in 3 years.

71. Temperature conversion. The formula that relates Celsius and Fahrenheit temperature is $F = \dfrac{9}{5}C + 32$. If the temperature of the day is $-10°C$, what is the Fahrenheit temperature?

72. Geometry. If the area of a circle whose radius is r is given by $A = \pi r^2$, where $\pi = 3.14$, find the area when $r = 3$ meters (m).

73. Write an English interpretation of each of the following algebraic expressions.

(a) $(2x^2 - y)^3$

(b) $3n - \dfrac{n-1}{2}$

(c) $(2n+3)(n-4)$

74. Is $a^n + b^n = (a + b)^n$? Try a few numbers and decide if you think this is true for all numbers, for some numbers, or never true. Write an explanation of your findings and give examples.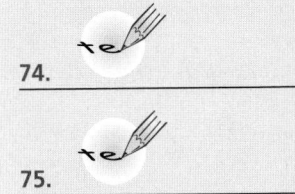

75. Enjoyment of patterns in art, music, and language is common to all cultures, and many cultures also delight in and draw spiritual significance from patterns in numbers. One such set of patterns is that of the "magic" square. One of these squares appears in a famous etching by Albrecht Dürer, who lived from 1471 to 1528 in Europe. He was one of the first artists in Europe to use geometry to give perspective, a feeling of three dimensions, in his work.

The magic square in his work is this one:

16	3	2	13
5	10	11	8
9	6	7	12
4	15	14	1

Why is this square "magic"? It is magic because every row, every column, and both diagonals add to the same number. In this square there are sixteen spaces for the numbers 1 through 16.

Part 1: What number does each row and column add to?

Write the square that you obtain by adding -17 to each number. Is this still a magic square? If so, what number does each column and row add to? If you add 5 to each number in the original magic square, do you still have a magic square? You have been studying the operations of addition, multiplication, subtraction, and division with integers and with rational numbers. What operations can you perform on this magic square and still have a magic square? Try to find something that will not work. Use algebra to help you decide what will work and what won't. Write a description of your work and explain your conclusions.

Part 2: Here is the oldest published magic square. It is from China, about 250 B.C.E. Legend has it that it was brought from the River Lo by a turtle to the Emperor Yii, who was a hydraulic engineer.

4	9	2
3	5	7
8	1	6

Check to make sure that this is a magic square. Work together to decide what operation might be done to every number in the magic square to make the sum of each row, column, and diagonal the *opposite* of what it is now. What would you do to every number to cause the sum of each row, column, and diagonal to equal zero?

a. _____

b. _____

c. _____

d. _____

e. _____

f. _____

 Getting Ready

(a) $(8 + 9) - 5$

(b) $15 - 4 - 11$

(c) $5(4 + 3) - 9$

(d) $-3(5 - 7) + 11$

(e) $-6(-9 + 7) - 4$

(f) $8 - 7(-2 - 6)$

Answers

1. -22 **3.** 32 **5.** -20 **7.** 12 **9.** 4 **11.** 83 **13.** 6

15. -40 **17.** 14 **19.** -9 **21.** 2 **23.** 2 **25.** 11 **27.** 1

29. 11 **31.** 91 **33.** 1 **35.** 91 **37.** 29 **39.** 9 **41.** 16

43. -15.3 **45.** -11.5 **47.** 1.1 **49.** 14.0 **51.** 41 **53.** 8

55. 11 **57.** $\dfrac{9}{2}$ **59.** -1.1 **61.** True   **63.** False   **65.** $3.75 \ \Omega$

67. 30 in.   **69.** $\$1875$ **71.** $14°F$ **73.**   **75.**

a. 12 **b.** 0 **c.** 26 **d.** 17 **e.** 8 **f.** 64

1.8 Adding and Subtracting Terms

1.8 OBJECTIVES

1. Identify terms and like terms
2. Combine like terms
3. Add algebraic expressions
4. Subtract algebraic expressions

To find the perimeter of (or the distance around) a rectangle, we add 2 times the length and 2 times the width. In the language of algebra, this can be written as

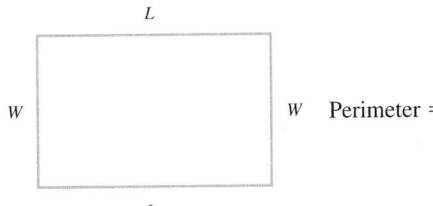

Perimeter $= 2L + 2W$

We call $2L + 2W$ an **algebraic expression,** or more simply an **expression.** Recall from Section 1.1 that an expression allows us to write a mathematical idea in symbols. It can be thought of as a meaningful collection of letters, numbers, and operation signs.

Some expressions are

$$5x^2 \qquad\qquad 3a + 2b \qquad\qquad 4x^3 + (-2y) + 1$$

In algebraic expressions, the addition and subtraction signs break the expressions into smaller parts called *terms.*

> **Definitions:** Term
>
> A **term** is a number, or the product of a number and one or more variables, raised to a power.

In an expression, each sign ($+$ or $-$) is a part of the term that follows the sign.

> **Example 1**

Identifying Terms

(a) $5x^2$ has one term.

(b) $\underbrace{3a}_{\text{Term}} + \underbrace{2b}_{\text{Term}}$ has two terms: $3a$ and $2b$.

NOTE This could also be written as $4x^3 - 2y + 1$

(c) $\underbrace{4x^3}_{\text{Term}} + \underbrace{(-2y)}_{\text{Term}} + \underbrace{1}_{\text{Term}}$ has three terms: $4x^3$, $-2y$, and 1.

 CHECK YOURSELF 1

List the terms of each expression.

(a) $2b^4$ **(b)** $5m + 3n$ **(c)** $2s^2 - 3t - 6$

Note that a term in an expression may have any number of factors. For instance, $5xy$ is a term. It has factors of 5, x, and y. The number factor of a term is called the **numerical coefficient.** So for the term $5xy$, the numerical coefficient is 5.

Example 2

Identifying the Numerical Coefficient

(a) $4a$ has the numerical coefficient 4.

(b) $6a^3b^4c^2$ has the numerical coefficient 6.

(c) $-7m^2n^3$ has the numerical coefficient -7.

(d) Because $1 \cdot x = x$, the numerical coefficient of x is understood to be 1.

CHECK YOURSELF 2

Give the numerical coefficient for each of the following terms.

(a) $8a^2b$ **(b)** $-5m^3n^4$ **(c)** y

If terms contain exactly the *same letters* (or variables) raised to the *same powers*, they are called **like terms.**

Example 3

Identifying Like Terms

(a) The following are like terms.

$6a$ and $7a$

$5b^2$ and b^2 Each pair of terms has the same letters, with each letter raised to the same power—the numerical coefficients can be any number.

$10x^2y^3z$ and $-6x^2y^3z$

$-3m^2$ and m^2

(b) The following are *not* like terms.

Different letters

$6a$ and $7b$

Different exponents

$5b^2$ and b^3

Different exponents

$3x^2y$ and $4xy^2$

CHECK YOURSELF 3

Circle the like terms.

$5a^2b$ ab^2 a^2b $-3a^2$ $4ab$ $3b^2$ $-7a^2b$

Like terms of an expression can always be combined into a single term. Look at the following:

$$\underbrace{2x}_{x + x + x + x + x + x} + \underbrace{5x}_{x + x + x + x + x + x} = \underbrace{7x}_{}$$

Rather than having to write out all those x's, try

NOTE Here we use the distributive property from Section 1.3.

$$2x + 5x = (2 + 5)x = 7x$$

In the same way,

NOTE You don't have to write all this out—just do it mentally!

$$9b + 6b = (9 + 6)b = 15b$$

and $10a + (-4a) = (10 + (-4))a = 6a$

This leads us to the following rule.

Step by Step: To Combine Like Terms

To combine like terms, use the following steps.

Step 1   Add or subtract the numerical coefficients.
Step 2   Attach the common variables.

Example 4

Combining Like Terms

Combine like terms.*

(a) $8m + 5m = (8 + 5)m = 13m$
(b) $5pq^3 - 4pq^3 = 5pq^3 + (-4pq^3) = 1pq^3 = pq^3$

NOTE Remember that when any factor is multiplied by 0, the product is 0.

(c) $7a^3b^2 - 7a^3b^2 = 7a^3b^2 + (-7a^3b^2) = 0a^3b^2 = 0$

 CHECK YOURSELF 4

Combine like terms.

(a) $6b + 8b$
(b) $12x^2 - 3x^2$
(c) $8xy^3 - 7xy^3$
(d) $9a^2b^4 - 9a^2b^4$

Let's look at some expressions involving more than two terms. The idea is just the same.

Example 5

Combining Like Terms

NOTE The distributive property can be used over any number of like terms.

Combine like terms.

(a) $5ab - 2ab + 3ab$

$$= 5ab + (-2ab) + 3ab$$

$$= (5 + (-2) + 3)ab = 6ab$$

*When an example requires simplification of an expression, that expression will be screened. The simplification will then follow the equals sign.

Only like terms can be combined.

(b) $8x - 2x \quad + 5y$

$(8 + (-2))x + 5y$

$= 6x \qquad + 5y$

Like terms   Like terms

NOTE With practice you won't be writing out these steps, but doing it mentally.

(c) $5m + 8n \quad + 4m - 3n$ Here we have used the associative and commutative properties.

$= (5m + 4m) + (8n + (-3n))$

$= \quad 9m \quad + \quad 5n$

(d) $4x^2 + 2x - 3x^2 + x$

$= (4x^2 + (-3x^2)) + (2x + x)$

$= x^2 + 3x$

As these examples illustrate, combining like terms often means changing the grouping and the order in which the terms are written.

CHECK YOURSELF 5

Combine like terms.

(a) $4m^2 - 3m^2 + 8m^2$ **(b)** $9ab + 3a - 5ab$ **(c)** $4p + 7q + 5p - 3q$

As you have seen in arithmetic, subtraction can be performed directly. As this is the form used for most of mathematics, we will use that form throughout this text. Just remember, by using negative numbers, you can always rewrite a subtraction problem as an addition problem.

Example 6

Combining Like Terms

Combine the like terms.

(a) $2xy - 3xy + 5xy$ **(b)** $5a - 2b + 7b - 8a$

$= (2 - 3 + 5)xy$ $= (5a - 8a) + (-2b + 7b)$

$= 4xy$ $= -3a + 5b$

CHECK YOURSELF 6

Combine like terms.

(a) $4ab + 5ab - 3ab - 7ab$ **(b)** $2x - 7y - 8x - y$

CHECK YOURSELF ANSWERS

1. (a) $2b^4$; **(b)** $5m, 3n$; **(c)** $2s^2, -3t, -6$ **2. (a)** 8; **(b)** -5; **(c)** 1

3. The like terms are $5a^2b$, a^2b, and $-7a^2b$ **4. (a)** $14b$; **(b)** $9x^2$; **(c)** xy^3; **(d)** 0

5. (a) $9m^2$; **(b)** $4ab + 3a$; **(c)** $9p + 4q$ **6. (a)** $-ab$; **(b)** $-6x - 8y$

Exercises

List the terms of the following expressions.

1. $5a + 2$

2. $7a - 4b$

3. $4x^3$

4. $3x^2$

5. $3x^2 + 3x - 7$

6. $2a^3 - a^2 + a$

Circle the like terms in the following groups of terms.

7. $5ab, 3b, 3a, 4ab$

8. $9m^2, 8mn, 5m^2, 7m$

9. $4xy^2, 2x^2y, 5x^2, -3x^2y, 5y, 6x^2y$

10. $8a^2b, 4a^2, 3ab^2, -5a^2b, 3ab, 5a^2b$

Combine the like terms.

11. $3m + 7m$

12. $6a^2 + 8a^2$

13. $7b^3 + 10b^3$

14. $7rs + 13rs$

15. $21xyz + 7xyz$

16. $4mn^2 + 15mn^2$

17. $9z^2 - 3z^2$

18. $7m - 6m$

19. $5a^3 - 5a^3$

20. $13xy - 9xy$

21. $19n^2 - 18n^2$

22. $7cd - 7cd$

23. $21p^2q - 6p^2q$

24. $17r^3s^2 - 8r^3s^2$

25. $10x^2 - 7x^2 + 3x^2$

26. $13uv + 5uv - 12uv$

ANSWERS

1. _____
2. _____
3. _____
4. _____
5. _____
6. _____
7. _____
8. _____
9. _____
10. _____
11. _____
12. _____
13. _____
14. _____
15. _____
16. _____
17. _____
18. _____
19. _____
20. _____
21. _____
22. _____
23. _____
24. _____
25. _____
26. _____

27.	
28.	
29.	
30.	
31.	
32.	
33.	
34.	
35.	
36.	
37.	
38.	
39.	
40.	
41.	
42.	
43.	
44.	
45.	
46.	
47.	
48.	
49.	
50.	
51.	
52.	

27. $9a - 7a + 4b$

28. $5m^2 - 3m + 6m^2$

29. $7x + 5y - 4x - 4y$

30. $6a^2 + 11a + 7a^2 - 9a$

31. $4a + 7b + 3 - 2a + 3b - 2$

32. $5p^2 + 2p + 8 + 4p^2 + 5p - 6$

33. $\dfrac{2}{3}m + 3 + \dfrac{4}{3}m$

34. $\dfrac{1}{5}a - 2 + \dfrac{4}{5}a$

35. $\dfrac{13}{5}x + 2 - \dfrac{3}{5}x + 5$

36. $\dfrac{17}{12}y + 7 + \dfrac{7}{12}y - 3$

37. $2.3a + 7 + 4.7a + 3$

38. $5.8m + 4 - 2.8m + 11$

Perform the indicated operations.

39. Find the sum of $5a^4$ and $8a^4$.

40. Find the sum of $9p^2$ and $12p^2$.

41. Subtract $12a^3$ from $15a^3$.

42. Subtract $5m^3$ from $18m^3$.

43. Subtract $4x$ from the sum of $8x$ and $3x$.

44. Subtract $8ab$ from the sum of $7ab$ and $5ab$.

45. Subtract $3mn^2$ from the sum of $9mn^2$ and $5mn^2$.

46. Subtract $4x^2y$ from the sum of $6x^2y$ and $12x^2y$.

Use the distributive property to remove the parentheses in each expression. Then simplify by combining like terms.

47. $2(3x + 2) + 4$

48. $3(4z + 5) - 9$

49. $5(6a - 2) + 12a$

50. $7(4w - 3) - 25w$

51. $4s + 2(s + 4) + 4$

52. $5p + 4(p + 3) - 8$

53. Write a paragraph explaining the difference between n^2 and $2n$.

54. Complete the explanation: "x^3 and $3x$ are not the same because . . ."

55. Complete the statement: "$x + 2$ and $2x$ are different because . . ."

56. Write an English phrase for each algebraic expression below:

    (a) $2x^3 + 5x$ **(b)** $(2x + 5)^3$ **(c)** $6(n + 4)^2$

57. Work with another student to complete this exercise. Place $>$, $<$, or $=$ in the blank in these statements.

    1^2 ____ 2^1 What happens as the table of numbers is extended? Try more examples.

    2^3 ____ 3^2

    3^4 ____ 4^3 What sign seems to occur the most in your table? $>$, $<$, or $=$?

    4^5 ____ 5^4 Write an algebraic statement for the pattern of numbers in this table. Do you think this is a pattern that continues? Add more lines to the table and extend the pattern to the general case by writing the pattern in algebraic notation. Write a short paragraph stating your conjecture.

58. Work with other students on this exercise.

Part 1: Evaluate the three expressions $\dfrac{n^2 - 1}{2}, n, \dfrac{n^2 + 1}{2}$ using odd values of n: 1, 3, 5, 7, etc. Make a chart like the one below and complete it.

n	$a = \dfrac{n^2 - 1}{2}$	$b = n$	$c = \dfrac{n^2 + 1}{2}$	a^2	b^2	c^2
1						
3						
5						
7						
9						
11						
13						

Part 2: The numbers a, b, and c that you get in each row have a surprising relationship to each other. Complete the last three columns and work together to discover this relationship. You may want to find out more about the history of this famous number pattern.

Getting Ready

Write the following using exponential notation.

(a) $4 \cdot 4 \cdot 4$ (b) $6 \cdot 6 \cdot 6 \cdot 6 \cdot 6 \cdot 6$

(c) $3 \cdot 3 \cdot 3 \cdot 3 \cdot 3$ (d) $(-2) \cdot (-2) \cdot (-2)$

(e) $(-8) \cdot (-8) \cdot (-8) \cdot (-8)$ (f) $9 \cdot 9 \cdot 9 \cdot 9 \cdot 9 \cdot 9 \cdot 9 \cdot 9$

Answers

1. $5a, 2$ **3.** $4x^3$ **5.** $3x^2, 3x, -7$ **7.** $5ab, 4ab$ **9.** $2x^2y, -3x^2y, 6x^2y$
11. $10m$ **13.** $17b^3$ **15.** $28xyz$ **17.** $6z^2$ **19.** 0 **21.** n^2
23. $15p^2q$ **25.** $6x^2$ **27.** $2a + 4b$ **29.** $3x + y$ **31.** $2a + 10b + 1$
33. $2m + 3$ **35.** $2x + 7$ **37.** $7a + 10$ **39.** $13a^4$ **41.** $3a^3$
43. $7x$ **45.** $11mn^2$ **47.** $6x + 8$ **49.** $42a - 10$ **51.** $6s + 12$

53.   **55.**   **57.**   **a.** 4^3 **b.** 6^6 **c.** 3^5

d. $(-2)^3$ **e.** $(-8)^4$ **f.** 9^8

 **1.9 Solving Equations by the Addition Property**

1.9 OBJECTIVES

1. Determine whether a given number is a solution for an equation
2. Use the addition property to solve an equation

Overcoming Math Anxiety

Throughout this text, we will present you with a series of class-tested techniques that are designed to improve your performance in this math class.

Hint #5   Don't Procrastinate!

1. Do your math homework while you're still fresh. If you wait until too late at night, your tired mind will have much more difficulty understanding the concepts.

2. Do your homework the day it is assigned. The more recent the explanation is, the easier it is to recall.

3. When you've finished your homework, try reading the next section through one time. This will give you a sense of direction when you next hear the material. This works whether you are in a lecture or lab setting.

Remember that, in a typical math class, you are expected to do two or three hours of homework for each weekly class hour. This means two or three hours per night. Schedule the time and stay to your schedule.

In this chapter you will begin working with one of the most important tools of mathematics, the equation. The ability to recognize and solve various types of equations is probably the most useful algebraic skill you will learn. We will continue to build upon the methods of this chapter throughout the remainder of the text. To start, let's describe what we mean by an *equation*.

Definitions: Equation

An **equation** is a mathematical statement that two expressions are equal.

Some examples are $3 + 4 = 7$, $x + 3 = 5$, $P = 2L + 2W$.

As you can see, an equals sign ($=$) separates the two equal expressions. These expressions are usually called the *left side* and the *right side* of the equation.

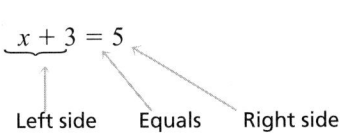

$$x + 3 = 5$$

Left side   Equals   Right side

NOTE An equation such as

$x + 3 = 5$

is called a **conditional equation** because it can be either true or false depending on the value given to the variable.

Just as the balance scale may be in balance or out of balance, an equation may be either true or false. For instance, $3 + 4 = 7$ is true because both sides name the same number. What about an equation such as $x + 3 = 5$ that has a letter or variable on one side? Any number can replace x in the equation. However, only one number will make this equation a true statement.

$$\text{If } x = 2 \begin{cases} 1 & 1 + 3 = 5 \text{ is false} \\ 2 & 2 + 3 = 5 \text{ is true} \\ 3 & 3 + 3 = 5 \text{ is false} \end{cases}$$

The number 2 is called the **solution** (or *root*) of the equation $x + 3 = 5$ because substituting 2 for x gives a true statement.

Definitions: Solution

A **solution** for an equation is any value for the variable that makes the equation a true statement.

Example 1

Verifying a Solution

(a) Is 3 a solution for the equation $2x + 4 = 10$?

To find out, replace x with 3 and evaluate $2x + 4$ on the left.

Left side   *Right side*

$$2 \cdot 3 + 4 \quad \overset{?}{=} \quad 10$$
$$6 + 4 \quad \overset{?}{=} \quad 10$$
$$10 \quad = \quad 10$$

Because $10 = 10$ is a true statement, 3 is a solution of the equation.

(b) Is 5 a solution of the equation $3x - 2 = 2x + 1$?

To find out, replace x with 5 and evaluate each side separately.

NOTE Remember the rules for the order of operation. Multiply first; then add or subtract.

Left side   *Right side*

$$3 \cdot 5 - 2 \quad \overset{?}{=} \quad 2 \cdot 5 + 1$$
$$15 - 2 \quad \overset{?}{=} \quad 10 + 1$$
$$13 \quad \neq \quad 11$$

Because the two sides do not name the same number, we do not have a true statement, and 5 is not a solution.

 CHECK YOURSELF 1

For the equation

$2x - 1 = x + 5$

(a) Is 4 a solution?   **(b)** Is 6 a solution?

You may be wondering whether an equation can have more than one solution. It certainly can. For instance,

NOTE This is an example of a **quadratic equation.**

$$x^2 = 9$$

has two solutions. They are 3 and -3 because

$$3^2 = 9 \quad \text{and} \quad (-3)^2 = 9$$

In this chapter, however, we will always work with *linear equations in one variable.* These are equations that can be put into the form

$$ax + b = 0$$

in which the variable is x, a and b are any numbers, and a is not equal to 0. In a linear equation, the variable can appear only to the first power. No other power (x^2, x^3, etc.) can appear. Linear equations are also called **first-degree equations.** The degree of an equation in one variable is the highest power to which the variable appears.

Rules and Properties: Linear Equations

Linear equations in one variable are equations that can be written in the form

$$ax + b = 0 \qquad a \neq 0$$

Every such equation will have exactly one solution.

Example 2

Identifying Expressions and Equations

Label each of the following as an expression, a linear equation, or an equation that is not linear.

(a) $4x + 5$ is an expression
(b) $2x + 8 = 0$ is a linear equation
(c) $3x^2 - 9 = 0$ is an equation that is not linear
(d) $5x = 15$ is a linear equation

 CHECK YOURSELF 2

Label each as an expression, a linear equation, or an equation that is not linear.

(a) $2x^2 = 8$ **(b)** $2x - 3 = 0$ **(c)** $5x - 10$ **(d)** $2x + 1 = 7$

It is not difficult to find the solution for an equation such as $x + 3 = 8$ by guessing the answer to the question "What plus 3 is 8?" Here the answer to the question is 5, and that is also the solution for the equation. But for more complicated equations you are going to need something more than guesswork. A better method is to transform the given equation to an *equivalent equation* whose solution can be found by inspection. Let's make a definition.

Definitions: Equivalent Equations

Equations that have the same solution are called **equivalent equations**.

The following are all equivalent equations:

$$2x + 3 = 5 \qquad 2x = 2 \qquad \text{and} \qquad x = 1$$

They all have the same solution, 1. We say that a linear equation is *solved* when it is transformed to an equivalent equation of the form

NOTE In some cases we'll write the equation in the form

$\Box = x$

The number will be our solution when the equation has the variable isolated on the left or on the right.

$$x = \Box$$

The variable is alone on the left side.   The right side is some number, the solution.

The addition property of equality is the first property you will need to transform an equation to an equivalent form.

Rules and Properties: The Addition Property of Equality

If $a = b$

then $a + c = b + c$

In words, adding the same quantity to both sides of an equation gives an equivalent equation.

REMEMBER An equation is a statement that the two sides are equal. Adding the same quantity to both sides does not change the equality or "balance."

Recall that we said that a true equation was like a scale in balance.

The addition property is equivalent to adding the same weight to both sides of the scale. It will remain in balance.

Example 3

Using the Addition Property to Solve an Equation

Solve

$$x - 3 = 9$$

Remember that our goal is to isolate x on one side of the equation. Because 3 is being subtracted from x, we can add 3 to remove it. We must use the addition property to add 3 to both sides of the equation.

NOTE To check, replace x with 12 in the original equation:

$x - 3 \overset{?}{=} 9$

$12 - 3 \overset{?}{=} 9$

$9 = 9$

Because we have a true statement, 12 is the solution.

$$
\begin{array}{rcl}
x - 3 &=& 9 \\
\underline{+3} & & \underline{+3} \\
x & = & 12
\end{array}
$$

$\left\{\begin{array}{l}\text{Adding 3 "undoes" the} \\ \text{subtraction and leaves} \\ x \text{ alone on the left.}\end{array}\right.$

Because 12 is the solution for the equivalent equation $x = 12$, it is the solution for our original equation.

  CHECK YOURSELF 3

Solve and check.

$$x - 5 = 4$$

The addition property also allows us to add a negative number to both sides of an equation. This is really the same as subtracting the same quantity from both sides.

Example 4

Using the Addition Property to Solve an Equation

Solve

$$x + 5 = 9$$

NOTE Recall our comment that we could write an equation in the equivalent forms $x = \square$ or $\square = x$, in which $\square$ represents some number. Suppose we have an equation like

$12 = x + 7$

Adding -7 will isolate x *on the right:*

$$
\begin{array}{rcl}
12 &=& x + 7 \\
\underline{-7} & & \underline{-7} \\
5 &=& x
\end{array}
$$

and the solution is 5.

In this case, 5 is *added* to x on the left. We can use the addition property to add a -5 to both sides. Because $5 + (-5) = 0$, this will "undo" the addition and leave the variable x alone on one side of the equation.

$$
\begin{array}{rcl}
x + 5 &=& 9 \\
\underline{-5} & & \underline{-5} \\
x & = & 4
\end{array}
$$

The solution is 4. To check, replace x with 4:

$$4 + 5 = 9 \qquad \text{(True)}$$

CHECK YOURSELF 4

Solve and check.

$$x + 6 = 13$$

What if the equation has a variable term on both sides? You will have to use the addition property to add or subtract a term involving the variable to get the desired result.

Example 5

Using the Addition Property to Solve an Equation

Solve

$$5x = 4x + 7$$

We will start by adding $-4x$ to both sides of the equation. Do you see why? Remember that an equation is solved when we have an equivalent equation of the form $x = \square$.

NOTE Recall that adding $-4x$ is identical to subtracting $4x$.

$$
\begin{array}{rl}
5x = & 4x + 7 \\
\underline{-4x} & \underline{-4x} \\
x = & 7
\end{array}
\left\{ \begin{array}{l} \text{Adding } -4x \text{ to both} \\ \text{sides } removes\ 4x \\ \text{from the right.} \end{array} \right.
$$

To check: Because 7 is a solution for the equivalent equation $x = 7$, it should be a solution for the original equation. To find out, replace x with 7:

$$5 \cdot 7 \overset{?}{=} 4 \cdot 7 + 7$$
$$35 \overset{?}{=} 28 + 7$$
$$35 = 35 \qquad \text{(True)}$$

 CHECK YOURSELF 5

Solve and check.

$$7x = 6x + 3$$

You may have to apply the addition property more than once to solve an equation. Look at Example 6.

Example 6

Using the Addition Property to Solve an Equation

Solve

$$7x - 8 = 6x$$

We want all variables on *one* side of the equation. If we choose the left, we add $-6x$ to both sides of the equation. This will remove $6x$ from the right:

$$
\begin{array}{rl}
7x - 8 = & 6x \\
\underline{-6x} & \underline{-6x} \\
x - 8 = & 0
\end{array}
$$

We want the variable alone, so we add 8 to both sides. This isolates x on the left.

$$
\begin{array}{rl}
x - 8 = & 0 \\
\underline{+ 8} & \underline{+8} \\
x \quad = & 8
\end{array}
$$

The solution is 8. We'll leave it to you to check this result.

CHECK YOURSELF 6

Solve and check.

$9x + 3 = 8x$

Often an equation will have more than one variable term *and* more than one number. You will have to apply the addition property twice in solving these equations.

Example 7

Using the Addition Property to Solve an Equation

Solve

$5x - 7 = 4x + 3$

We would like the variable terms on the left, so we start by adding $-4x$ to remove the $4x$ term from the right side of the equation:

$$\begin{array}{rcl} 5x - 7 = & 4x + 3 \\ \underline{-4x} & \underline{-4x} \\ x - 7 = & 3 \end{array}$$

Now, to isolate the variable, we add 7 to both sides.

$$\begin{array}{rcl} x - 7 = & 3 \\ \underline{+7} & \underline{+7} \\ x & = 10 \end{array}$$

NOTE You could just as easily have added 7 to both sides and *then* added $-4x$. The result would be the same. In fact, some students prefer to combine the two steps.

The solution is 10. To check, replace x with 10 in the original equation:

$$5 \cdot 10 - 7 \stackrel{?}{=} 4 \cdot 10 + 3$$
$$43 = 43 \quad \text{(True)}$$

CHECK YOURSELF 7

Solve and check.

(a) $4x - 5 = 3x + 2$ **(b)** $6x + 2 = 5x - 4$

NOTE Remember, by *simplify* we mean to combine all like terms.

In solving an equation, you should always simplify each side as much as possible before using the addition property.

Example 8

Combining Like Terms and Solving the Equation

Solve

Like terms   Like terms

$5 + 8x - 2 = 2x - 3 + 5x$

Because like terms appear on each side of the equation, we start by combining the numbers on the left (5 and -2). Then we combine the like terms ($2x$ and $5x$) on the right. We have

$$3 + 8x = 7x - 3$$

Now we can apply the addition property, as before:

$$
\begin{array}{rrl}
3 + 8x = & 7x - 3 & \\
-7x = & -7x & \text{Add } -7x. \\
\hline
3 + x = & -3 & \\
-3 & -3 & \text{Add } -3. \\
\hline
x = & -6 & \text{Isolate } x.
\end{array}
$$

The solution is -6. To check, always return to the original equation. That will catch any possible errors in simplifying. Replacing x with -6 gives

$$5 + 8(-6) - 2 \stackrel{?}{=} 2(-6) - 3 + 5(-6)$$

$$5 - 48 - 2 \stackrel{?}{=} -12 - 3 - 30$$

$$-45 = -45 \quad \text{(True)}$$

 CHECK YOURSELF 8

Solve and check.

(a) $3 + 6x + 4 = 8x - 3 - 3x$ **(b)** $5x + 21 + 3x = 20 + 7x - 2$

We may have to apply some of the properties discussed in Section 1.3 in solving equations. Example 9 illustrates the use of the distributive property to clear an equation of parentheses.

Example 9

Using the Distributive Property and Solving Equations

Solve

NOTE $2(3x + 4)$
$= 2(3x) + 2(4)$
$= 6x + 8$

$$2(3x + 4) = 5x - 6$$

Applying the distributive property on the left, we have

$$6x + 8 = 5x - 6$$

We can then proceed as before:

$$
\begin{array}{rrl}
6x + 8 = & 5x - 6 & \\
-5x & -5x & \text{Add } -5x. \\
\hline
x + 8 = & -6 & \\
-8 & -8 & \text{Add } -8. \\
\hline
x = & -14 &
\end{array}
$$

NOTE Remember that
$x = -14$ and $-14 = x$
are equivalent equations.

The solution is -14. We will leave the checking of this result to the reader.
Remember: Always return to the original equation to check.

CHECK YOURSELF 9

Solve and check each of the following equations.

(a) $4(5x - 2) = 19x + 4$ **(b)** $3(5x + 1) = 2(7x - 3) - 4$

Given an expression such as

$$-2(x - 5)$$

the distributive property can be used to create the equivalent expression.

$$-2x + 10$$

The distribution of a negative number is used in Example 10.

Example 10

Distributing a Negative Number

Solve each of the following equations.

(a) $-2(x - 5) = -3x + 2$

$$
\begin{array}{rll}
-2x + 10 &= -3x + 2 & \text{Distribute the } -2. \\
\underline{+3x \quad\quad +3x} & & \text{Add } 3x. \\
x + 10 &= \quad\quad 2 & \\
\underline{\quad -10 = \quad -10} & & \text{Add } -10. \\
x &= \quad -8 &
\end{array}
$$

(b) $-3(3x + 5) = -5(2x - 2)$

$$
\begin{array}{rll}
-9x - 15 &= -5(2x - 2) & \text{Distribute the } -3. \\[4pt]
-\ 9x - 15 &= -10x + 10 & \text{Distribute the } -5. \\
\underline{+10x \quad\quad +10x} & & \text{Add } 10x. \\
x - 15 &= \quad\quad 10 & \\
\underline{\quad +15 \quad\quad +15} & & \text{Add } 15. \\
x &= \quad\quad 25 &
\end{array}
$$

CHECK YOURSELF 10

Solve each of the following.

(a) $-2(x - 3) = -x + 5$ **(b)** $-4(2x - 1) = -3(3x + 2)$

When parentheses are preceded only by a negative, or by the minus sign, we say that we have a silent negative one. Example 11 illustrates this case.

Example 11

Distributing the Silent Negative One

Solve

$$-(2x + 3) = -3x + 7$$

$$-1(2x + 3) = -3x + 7$$

$$(-1)(2x) + (-1)(3) = -3x + 7$$

$$
\begin{array}{rcl}
-2x - 3 & = & -3x + 7 \\
+3x & & +3x \\
\hline
x - 3 & = & 7 \\
+ 3 & & + 3 \\
\hline
x & = & 10
\end{array}
$$

Add 3x.

Add 3.

CHECK YOURSELF 11

Solve $-(3x + 2) = -2x - 6.$

CHECK YOURSELF ANSWERS

1. **(a)** 4 is not a solution; **(b)** 6 is a solution
2. **(a)** Nonlinear equation; **(b)** linear equation; **(c)** expression; **(d)** linear equation
3. 9   **4.** 7   **5.** 3   **6.** −3   **7. (a)** 7; **(b)** −6   **8. (a)** −10; **(b)** −3
9. **(a)** 12; **(b)** −13   **10. (a)** 1; **(b)** −10   **11.** 4

Is the number shown in parentheses a solution for the given equation?

1. $x + 4 = 9$ (5)

2. $x + 2 = 11$ (8)

3. $x - 15 = 6$ (−21)

4. $x - 11 = 5$ (16)

5. $5 - x = 2$ (4)

6. $10 - x = 7$ (3)

7. $4 - x = 6$ (−2)

8. $5 - x = 6$ (−3)

9. $3x + 4 = 13$ (8)

10. $5x + 6 = 31$ (5)

11. $4x - 5 = 7$ (2)

12. $2x - 5 = 1$ (3)

13. $5 - 2x = 7$ (−1)

14. $4 - 5x = 9$ (−2)

15. $4x - 5 = 2x + 3$ (4)

16. $5x + 4 = 2x + 10$ (4)

17. $x + 3 + 2x = 5 + x + 8$ (5)

18. $5x - 3 + 2x = 3 + x - 12$ (−2)

19. $\dfrac{3}{4}x = 20$ (18)

20. $\dfrac{3}{5}x = 24$ (40)

21. $\dfrac{3}{5}x + 5 = 11$ (10)

22. $\dfrac{2}{3}x + 8 = -12$ (−6)

Label each of the following as an expression or a linear equation.

23. $2x + 1 = 9$

24. $7x + 14$

25. $2x - 8$

26. $5x - 3 = 12$

ANSWERS

1. _____

2. _____

3. _____

4. _____

5. _____

6. _____

7. _____

8. _____

9. _____

10. _____

11. _____

12. _____

13. _____

14. _____

15. _____

16. _____

17. _____

18. _____

19. _____

20. _____

21. _____

22. _____

23. _____

24. _____

25. _____

26. _____

27. _____

28. _____

29. _____

30. _____

31. _____

32. _____

33. _____

34. _____

35. _____

36. _____

37. _____

38. _____

39. _____

40. _____

41. _____

42. _____

43. _____

44. _____

45. _____

46. _____

47. _____

48. _____

49. _____

50. _____

51. _____

52. _____

53. _____

54. _____

27. $7x + 2x + 8 - 3$

28. $x + 5 = 13$

29. $2x - 8 = 3$

30. $12x - 5x + 2 + 5$

Solve and check the following equations.

31. $x + 9 = 11$

32. $x - 4 = 6$

33. $x - 8 = 3$

34. $x + 11 = 15$

35. $x - 8 = -10$

36. $x + 5 = 2$

37. $x + 4 = -3$

38. $x - 5 = -4$

39. $11 = x + 5$

40. $x + 7 = 0$

41. $4x = 3x + 4$

42. $7x = 6x - 8$

43. $11x = 10x - 10$

44. $9x = 8x + 5$

45. $6x + 3 = 5x$

46. $12x - 6 = 11x$

47. $8x - 4 = 7x$

48. $9x - 7 = 8x$

49. $2x + 3 = x + 5$

50. $3x - 2 = 2x + 1$

51. $4x - \dfrac{3}{5} = 3x + \dfrac{1}{10}$

52. $5\left(x - \dfrac{3}{4}\right) = 4x + \dfrac{3}{8}$

53. $\dfrac{7}{8}(x - 2) = \dfrac{3}{4} - \dfrac{1}{8}x$

54. $\dfrac{5}{6}(3x - 2) = \dfrac{3}{2}(x + 1)$

55. $3x - 0.54 = 2(x - 0.15)$

56. $7x + 0.125 = 6x - 0.289$

57. $6x + 3(x - 0.2789) = 4(2x + 0.3912)$

58. $9x - 2(3x - 0.124) = 2x + 0.965$

59. $3x - 5 + 2x - 7 + x = 5x + 2$

60. $5x + 8 + 3x - x + 5 = 6x - 3$

61. $5x - (0.345 - x) = 5x + 0.8713$

62. $-3(0.234 - x) = 2(x + 0.974)$

63. $3(7x + 2) = 5(4x + 1) + 17$

64. $5(5x + 3) = 3(8x - 2) + 4$

65. $\dfrac{5}{4}x - 1 = \dfrac{1}{4}x + 7$

66. $\dfrac{7}{5}x + 3 = \dfrac{2}{5}x - 8$

67. $\dfrac{9}{2}x - \dfrac{3}{4} = \dfrac{7}{2}x + \dfrac{5}{4}$

68. $\dfrac{11}{3}x + \dfrac{1}{6} = \dfrac{8}{3}x + \dfrac{19}{6}$

69. Which of the following is equivalent to the equation $5x - 7 = 4x - 12$?

    a. $9x = 19$ **b.** $9x - 7 = -12$ **c.** $x = -18$ **d.** $x - 7 = -12$

70. Which of the following is equivalent to the equation $12x - 6 = 8x + 14$?

    a. $4x - 6 = 14$ **b.** $x = 20$ **c.** $20x = 20$ **d.** $4x = 8$

71. Which of the following is equivalent to the equation $7x + 5 = 12x - 10$?

    a. $5x = -15$ **b.** $7x - 5 = 12x$ **c.** $-5 = 5x$ **d.** $7x + 15 = 12x$

True or false?

72. Every linear equation with one variable has exactly one solution.

73. Isolating the variable on the right side of the equation will result in a negative solution.

74. An algebraic equation is a complete sentence. It has a subject, a verb, and a predicate. For example, $x + 2 = 5$ can be written in English as "Two more than a number is five." Or, "A number added to two is five." Write an English version of the following equations. Be sure you write complete sentences and that the sentences express the same idea as the equations. Exchange sentences with another student, and see if your interpretation of each other's sentences result in the same equation.

    (a) $2x - 5 = x + 1$ **(b)** $2(x + 2) = 14$

    (c) $n + 5 = \dfrac{n}{2} - 6$ **(d)** $7 - 3a = 5 + a$

75. Complete the following explanation in your own words: "The difference between $3(x - 1) + 4 - 2x$ and $3(x - 1) + 4 = 2x$ is . . . ."

ANSWERS

55.

56.

57.

58.

59.

60.

61.

62.

63.

64.

65.

66.

67.

68.

69.

70.

71.

72.

73.

74.

75.

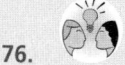

76.

a.

b.

c.

d.

e.

f.

g.

h.

76. "Surprising Results!" Work with other students to try this experiment. Each person should do the following six steps mentally, not telling anyone else what their calculations are:

    (a) Think of a number.   **(b)** Add 7.

    (c) Multiply by 3.   **(d)** Add 3 more than the original number.

    (e) Divide by 4.   **(f)** Subtract the original number.

What number do you end up with? Compare your answer with everyone else's. Does everyone have the same answer? Make sure that everyone followed the directions accurately. How do you explain the results? Algebra makes the explanation clear. Work together to do the problem again, using a variable for the number. Make up another series of computations that give "surprising results."

Getting Ready

Multiply.

(a) $\left(\dfrac{1}{3}\right)(3)$

(b) $(-6)\left(-\dfrac{1}{6}\right)$

(c) $(7)\left(\dfrac{1}{7}\right)$

(d) $\left(-\dfrac{1}{4}\right)(-4)$

(e) $\left(\dfrac{3}{5}\right)\left(\dfrac{5}{3}\right)$

(f) $\left(\dfrac{7}{8}\right)\left(\dfrac{8}{7}\right)$

(g) $\left(-\dfrac{4}{7}\right)\left(-\dfrac{7}{4}\right)$

(h) $\left(-\dfrac{6}{11}\right)\left(-\dfrac{11}{6}\right)$

Answers

1. Yes   **3.** No   **5.** No   **7.** Yes   **9.** No   **11.** No   **13.** Yes
15. Yes   **17.** Yes   **19.** No   **21.** Yes   **23.** Linear equation
25. Expression   **27.** Expression   **29.** Linear equation   **31.** 2
33. 11   **35.** -2 **37.** -7 **39.** 6   **41.** 4   **43.** -10 **45.** -3
47. 4   **49.** 2   **51.** $\dfrac{7}{10}$ **53.** $\dfrac{5}{2}$ **55.** 0.24   **57.** 2.4015   **59.** 14
61. 1.2163   **63.** 16   **65.** 8   **67.** 2   **69.** d   **71.** d   **73.** False
75.   a. 1   b. 1   c. 1   d. 1   e. 1   f. 1   g. 1

h. 1

Solving Equations by the Multiplication Property

 OBJECTIVES

1. Determine whether a given number is a solution for an equation
2. Use the multiplication property to solve equations
3. Find the mean for a given set

Let's look at a different type of equation. For instance, what if we want to solve an equation like the following?

$6x = 18$

Using the addition property of the last section won't help. We will need a second property for solving equations.

> **Rules and Properties:** The Multiplication Property of Equality
>
> If $a = b$ then $ac = bc$ where $c \neq 0$
>
> In words, multiplying both sides of an equation by the same nonzero number gives an equivalent equation.

NOTE Again, as long as you do the *same* thing to *both* sides of the equation, the "balance" is maintained.

NOTE Do you see why the number cannot be 0? Multiplying by 0 gives $0 = 0$. We have lost the variable!

Again, we return to the image of the balance scale. We start with the assumption that a and b have the same weight.

The multiplication property tells us that the scale will be in balance as long as we have the same number of "a weights" as we have of "b weights."

Let's work through some examples, using this second rule.

Example 1

Solving Equations by Using the Multiplication Property

Solve

$6x = 18$

Here the variable x is multiplied by 6. So we apply the multiplication property and multiply both sides by $\frac{1}{6}$. Keep in mind that we want an equation of the form

NOTE

$\frac{1}{6}(6x) = \left(\frac{1}{6} \cdot 6\right)x$

$\qquad = 1 \cdot x,\ \text{or}\ x$

We then have x alone on the left, which is what we want.

$x = \square$

$\frac{1}{6}(6x) = \left(\frac{1}{6}\right)18$

We can now simplify.

$1 \cdot x = 3 \qquad \text{or} \qquad x = 3$

The solution is 3. To check, replace x with 3:

$6 \cdot 3 \stackrel{?}{=} 18$

$\quad 18 = 18 \qquad \text{(True)}$

CHECK YOURSELF 1

Solve and check.

$8x = 32$

In Example 1 we solved the equation by multiplying both sides by the reciprocal of the coefficient of the variable.

Example 2 illustrates a slightly different approach to solving an equation by using the multiplication property.

Example 2

Solving Equations by Using the Multiplication Property

Solve

$5x = -35$

NOTE Because division is defined in terms of multiplication, we can also divide both sides of an equation by the same nonzero number.

The variable x is multiplied by 5. We *divide* both sides by 5 to "undo" that multiplication:

$\frac{5x}{5} = \frac{-35}{5}$

$\quad x = -7$
Note that the right side reduces to -7. Be careful with the rules for signs.

We will leave it to you to check the solution.

CHECK YOURSELF 2

Solve and check.

$7x = -42$

Example 3

Solving Equations by Using the Multiplication Property

Solve

$-9x = 54$

In this case, x is multiplied by -9, so we divide both sides by -9 to isolate x on the left:

$$\frac{-9x}{-9} = \frac{54}{-9}$$

$$x = -6$$

The solution is -6. To check:

$$(-9)(-6) \stackrel{?}{=} 54$$

$$54 = 54 \qquad \text{(True)}$$

CHECK YOURSELF 3

Solve and check.

$-10x = -60$

Example 4 illustrates the use of the multiplication property when fractions appear in an equation.

Example 4

Solving Equations by Using the Multiplication Property

(a) Solve

$$\frac{x}{3} = 6$$

Here x is *divided* by 3. We will use multiplication to isolate x.

$$3\left(\frac{x}{3}\right) = 3 \cdot 6$$

> This leaves x alone on the left because
> $$3\left(\frac{x}{3}\right) = \frac{3}{1} \cdot \frac{x}{3} = \frac{x}{1} = x$$

$$x = 18$$

To check:

$$\frac{18}{3} \stackrel{?}{=} 6$$

$$6 = 6 \qquad \text{(True)}$$

(b) Solve

$$\frac{x}{5} = -9$$

$$5\left(\frac{x}{5}\right) = 5(-9)$$ Because x is divided by 5, multiply both sides by 5

$$x = -45$$

The solution is -45. To check, we replace x with -45:

$$\frac{-45}{5} \overset{?}{=} -9$$

$$-9 = -9$$ (True)

The solution is verified.

 CHECK YOURSELF 4

Solve and check.

(a) $\dfrac{x}{7} = 3$ 　　　　　　　　　　 **(b)** $\dfrac{x}{4} = -8$

When the variable is multiplied by a fraction that has a numerator other than 1, there are two approaches to finding the solution.

Example 5

Solving Equations by Using Reciprocals

Solve

$$\frac{3}{5}x = 9$$

One approach is to multiply by 5 as the first step.

$$5\left(\frac{3}{5}x\right) = 5 \cdot 9$$

$$3x = 45$$

Now we divide by 3.

$$\frac{3x}{3} = \frac{45}{3}$$

$$x = 15$$

To check:

$$\frac{3}{5} \cdot 15 \overset{?}{=} 9$$

$$9 = 9$$ (True)

A second approach combines the multiplication and division steps and is generally a bit more efficient. We multiply by $\dfrac{5}{3}$.

$$\dfrac{5}{3}\left(\dfrac{3}{5}x\right) = \dfrac{5}{3} \cdot 9$$

$$x = \dfrac{5}{\underset{1}{\cancel{3}}} \cdot \dfrac{\overset{3}{\cancel{9}}}{1} = 15$$

So $x = 15$, as before.

 CHECK YOURSELF 5

Solve and check.

$$\dfrac{2}{3}x = 18$$

You may sometimes have to simplify an equation before applying the methods of this section. Example 6 illustrates this property.

Example 6

Combining Like Terms and Solving Equations

Solve and check:

$$3x + 5x = 40$$

Using the distributive property, we can combine the like terms on the left to write

$$8x = 40$$

We can now proceed as before.

$$\dfrac{8x}{8} = \dfrac{40}{8} \qquad \text{Divide by 8.}$$

$$x = 5$$

The solution is 5. To check, we return to the original equation. Substituting 5 for x yields

$$3 \cdot 5 + 5 \cdot 5 \overset{?}{=} 40$$

$$15 + 25 \overset{?}{=} 40$$

$$40 = 40 \qquad \text{(True)}$$

The solution is verified.

✔ **CHECK YOURSELF 6**

Solve and check.

$7x + 4x = -66$

An **average** is a value that is representative of a set of numbers. One kind of average is the *mean*.

Definitions: Mean

The **mean** of a set is the sum of the set divided by the number of elements in the set. The mean is written as $\bar{x}$ (sometimes called "x-bar"). In mathematical symbols, we say

$$\bar{x} = \frac{\Sigma x}{n}$$

⟵ The sum of the set

⟵ The number of elements in the set

Example 7

Finding the Mean

Find the mean for each set of numbers.

(a) $2, -3, 5, 4, 7$

We begin by finding Σx.

$\Sigma x = 2 + (-3) + 5 + 4 + 7 = 15$

Next we find n.

$n = 5$ Remember that n is the number of elements in the set.

Finally, we substitute our numbers into the equation.

$$\bar{x} = \frac{\Sigma x}{n} = \frac{15}{5} = 3$$

The mean of the set is 3.

(b) $-4, 7, 9, -3, 6, -2, -3, 8$

First find Σx.

$\Sigma x = (-4) + 7 + 9 + (-3) + 6 + (-2) + (-3) + 8 = 18$

Next find n.

$n = 8$

Substitute these numbers into the equation

$$\bar{x} = \frac{\Sigma x}{n} = \frac{18}{8} = \frac{9}{4} \text{ (or 2.25)}$$

The mean of this set is $\frac{9}{4}$ or 2.25

CHECK YOURSELF 7

Find the mean for each set of numbers.

(a) $5, -2, 6, 3, -2$

(b) $6, -2, 3, 8, 5, -6, 1, -3$

Example 8

Finding the Mean

During a week in February the low temperature in Fargo, North Dakota, was recorded each day. The results are presented in the following table. Find both the median and the mean for the set of numbers.

M	T	W	Th	F	Sa	Su
-11	-17	-15	-18	-20	-2	20

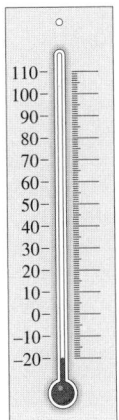

NOTE You can review the discussion of the median in Section 1.4.

To find the median we place the numbers in ascending order:

$$-20 \quad -18 \quad -17 \quad -15 \quad -11 \quad -2 \quad 20$$

The median is the middle value, so the median is -15 degrees.

To find the mean, we first find Σx.

$$\Sigma x = (-11) + (-17) + (-15) + (-18) + (-20) + (-2) + 20 = -63$$

Then, given that $n = 7$, we use the equation for the mean.

$$\bar{x} = \frac{\Sigma x}{n} = \frac{-63}{7} = -9$$

The mean is -9.

Which average was more appropriate? There is really no "right" answer to that question. In this case, the median would probably be preferred by most statisticians. It yields a temperature that was actually the low temperature on Wednesday of that week, so it is more representative of the set of low temperatures.

CHECK YOURSELF 8

The low temperatures in Anchorage, Alaska, for one week in January are given in the following table. Compute both the median and the mean low temperature for that week.

M	T	W	Th	F	Sa	Su
6	−10	−12	−22	−28	−26	−27

CHECK YOURSELF ANSWERS

1. 4 **2.** −6 **3.** 6 **4.** (a) 21; (b) −32 **5.** 27 **6.** −6
7. (a) 2; (b) 1.5 **8.** mean = −17, median = −22

1.10 Exercises

Name _____

Section _____ Date _____

Solve for x and check your result.

1. $5x = 20$

2. $6x = 30$

3. $9x = 54$

4. $6x = -42$

5. $63 = 9x$

6. $66 = 6x$

7. $4x = -16$

8. $-3x = 27$

9. $-9x = 72$

10. $10x = -100$

11. $6x = -54$

12. $-7x = 49$

13. $-4x = -12$

14. $52 = -4x$

15. $-42 = 6x$

16. $-7x = -35$

17. $-6x = -54$

18. $-4x = -24$

19. $\dfrac{x}{2} = 4$

20. $\dfrac{x}{3} = 2$

21. $\dfrac{x}{5} = 3$

22. $\dfrac{x}{8} = 5$

23. $6 = \dfrac{x}{7}$

24. $6 = \dfrac{x}{3}$

25. $\dfrac{x}{5} = -4$

26. $\dfrac{x}{7} = -5$

27. $-\dfrac{x}{3} = 8$

28. $-\dfrac{x}{4} = -3$

29. $\dfrac{2}{3}x = 0.9$

30. $\dfrac{4}{5}x = 8$

31. $\dfrac{3}{4}x = -15$

32. $\dfrac{3}{5}x = 10 - \dfrac{6}{5}$

33. $-\dfrac{5}{6}x = -15$

34. $5x + 4x = 36$

35. $16x - 9x = -16.1$

36. $4x - 2x + 7x = 36$

1.	2.
3.	4.
5.	6.
7.	8.
9.	10.
11.	12.
13.	14.
15.	16.
17.	18.
19.	20.
21.	22.
23.	24.
25.	26.
27.	28.
29.	30.
31.	32.
33.	34.
35.	36.

37. _____

38. _____

39. _____

40. _____

41. _____

42. _____

43. _____

44. _____

45. _____

46. _____

47. _____

48. _____

49. _____

50. _____

a. _____

b. _____

c. _____

d. _____

e. _____

f. _____

g. _____

h. _____

Once again, certain equations involving decimal fractions can be solved by the methods of this section. For instance, to solve $2.3x = 6.9$ we simply use our multiplication property to divide both sides of the equation by 2.3. This will isolate x on the left as desired. Use this idea to solve each of the following equations for x.

37. $3.2x = 12.8$

38. $5.1x = -15.3$

39. $-4.5x = 3.51$

40. $-8.2x = -31.078$

41. $1.3x + 2.8x = 12.3$

42. $2.7x + 5.4x = -16.2$

Find the median and the mean of each data set.

43. 2, 3, 4, 5, 6

44. 1, 3, 8, 10, 18

45. $-3, -1, 2, 4, 6, 10$

46. $-5, -2, 1, 4, 6, 8$

47. $-\dfrac{3}{2}, -1, 2, \dfrac{5}{2}, 3, 7$

48. $-\dfrac{4}{3}, -\dfrac{1}{3}, \dfrac{2}{3}, 5, 6$

49. Average weight. Kareem bought four bags of candy. The weights of the bags were 16 ounces (oz), 21 oz, 18 oz, and 15 oz. Find the median and the mean weight of the bags of candy.

50. Average savings. Jose has savings accounts for each of his five children. They contain $215, $156, $318, $75, and $25. Find the median and the mean amount of money per account.

 Getting Ready

Use the distributive property to remove the parentheses in the following expressions.

(a) $2(x - 3)$ (b) $3(a + 4)$ (c) $5(2b + 1)$ (d) $3(3p - 4)$

(e) $7(3x - 4)$ (f) $-4(5x + 4)$ (g) $-3(4x - 3)$ (h) $-5(3y - 2)$

Answers

1. 4   **3.** 6   **5.** 7   **7.** -4 **9.** -8 **11.** -9 **13.** 3   **15.** -7
17. 9   **19.** 8   **21.** 15   **23.** 42   **25.** -20 **27.** -24 **29.** 1.35
31. -20 **33.** 18   **35.** -2.3 **37.** 4   **39.** -0.78 **41.** 3
43. 4   **45.** 3   **47.** 2   **49.** Mean: 17.5, Median: 17 oz.   **a.** $2x - 6$
b. $3a + 12$ **c.** $10b + 5$ **d.** $9p - 12$ **e.** $21x - 28$
f. $-20x - 16$ **g.** $-12x + 9$ **h.** $-15y + 10$

Combining the Rules to Solve Equations

 **OBJECTIVES**

1. Combine the addition and multiplication properties to solve an equation
2. Solve equations that contain parentheses
3. Solve equations that contain fractions
4. Recognize identities
5. Recognize equations with no solutions

In each example thus far, either the addition property or the multiplication property was used in solving an equation. Often, finding a solution will require the use of both properties.

OBJECTIVE 1 | **Example 1   Solving Equations**

(a) Solve

$$4x - 5 = 7$$

Here x is *multiplied* by 4. The result, $4x$, then has 5 subtracted from it (or -5 added to it) on the left side of the equation. These two operations mean that both properties must be applied in solving the equation.

Because the variable term is already on the left, we start by adding 5 to both sides:

$$\begin{array}{rcr} 4x - 5 = & 7 \\ + 5 & +5 \\ \hline 4x = & 12 \end{array}$$

We now divide both sides by 4:

$$\frac{4x}{4} = \frac{12}{4}$$

$$x = 3$$

The solution is 3. To check, replace x with 3 in the original equation. Be careful to follow the rules for the order of operations.

$$4 \cdot 3 - 5 \stackrel{?}{=} 7$$
$$12 - 5 \stackrel{?}{=} 7$$
$$7 = 7 \quad \text{(True)}$$

(b) Solve

$$\begin{array}{rcr} 3x + 8 = & -4 \\ - 8 & -8 \end{array} \quad \text{Add } -8 \text{ to both sides.}$$
$$\begin{array}{rcr} \hline 3x = & -12 \end{array}$$

Now divide both sides by 3 to isolate x on the left.

$$\frac{3x}{3} = \frac{-12}{3}$$

$$x = -4$$

The solution is -4. We leave the check of this result to you.

CHECK YOURSELF 1 _____

Solve and check.

(a) $6x + 9 = -15$ **(b)** $5x - 8 = 7$

The variable may appear in any position in an equation. Just apply the rules carefully as you try to write an equivalent equation, and you will find the solution.

Example 2   Solving Equations

Solve

$$3 - 2x = \quad 9$$
$$\underline{-3 \qquad\quad -3} \quad \text{First add } -3 \text{ to both sides.}$$
$$-2x = \quad 6$$

NOTE $\dfrac{-2}{-2} = 1$, so we divide by -2 to isolate x on the left.

Now divide both sides by -2. This will leave x alone on the left.

$$\frac{-2x}{-2} = \frac{6}{-2}$$
$$x = -3$$

The solution is -3. We leave it to you to check this result.

CHECK YOURSELF 2 _____

Solve and check.

$10 - 3x = 1$

You may also have to combine multiplication with addition or subtraction to solve an equation. Consider Example 3.

Example 3   Solving Equations

(a) Solve

$$\frac{x}{5} - 3 = 4$$

To get the x term alone, we first add 3 to both sides.

$$\frac{x}{5} - 3 = \quad 4$$
$$\underline{\quad + 3 \quad +3}$$
$$\frac{x}{5} \qquad = \quad 7$$

Now, to undo the division multiply both sides of the equation by 5.

$$5\left(\frac{x}{5}\right) = 5 \cdot 7$$
$$x = 35$$

The solution is 35. Return to the original equation to check the result.

$$\frac{35}{5} - 3 \overset{?}{=} 4$$

$$7 - 3 \overset{?}{=} 4$$

$$4 = 4 \qquad \text{(True)}$$

(b) Solve

$$\frac{2}{3}x + 5 = 13$$

$$\underline{\phantom{\frac{2}{3}x} -5 \quad -5} \qquad \text{First add } -5 \text{ to both sides.}$$

$$\frac{2}{3}x \quad\;\; = 8$$

Now multiply both sides by $\dfrac{3}{2}$, the reciprocal of $\dfrac{2}{3}$.

$$\left(\frac{3}{2}\right)\left(\frac{2}{3}x\right) = \left(\frac{3}{2}\right)8$$

or

$$x = 12$$

The solution is 12. We leave it to you to check this result.

 CHECK YOURSELF 3

Solve and check.

(a) $\dfrac{x}{6} + 5 = 3$ \qquad\qquad\qquad **(b)** $\dfrac{3}{4}x - 8 = 10$

You learned how to solve certain equations when the variable appeared on both sides. Example 4 will show you how to extend that work when using the multiplication and addition properties of equality.

Example 4   Solving an Equation

Solve

$$6x - 4 = 3x - 2$$

First add 4 to both sides. This will undo the subtraction on the left.

$$6x - 4 = 3x - 2$$

$$\underline{ +4 \qquad\;\; +4}$$

$$6x \qquad = 3x + 2$$

Now add $-3x$ so that the terms in x will only be on the left side.

$$6x = \quad 3x + 2$$

$$\underline{-3x \quad -3x}$$

$$3x = \qquad\;\; 2$$

Finally divide by 3.

$$\frac{3x}{3} = \frac{2}{3}$$

$$x = \frac{2}{3}$$

Check:

$$6\left(\frac{2}{3}\right) - 4 \stackrel{?}{=} 3\left(\frac{2}{3}\right) - 2$$

$$4 - 4 \stackrel{?}{=} 2 - 2$$

$$0 = 0 \quad \text{(True)}$$

The basic idea is to use our two properties to form an equivalent equation with the x isolated. Here we added 4 and then subtracted $3x$. You can do these steps in either order. Try it for yourself the other way. In either case, the multiplication property is then used as the *last step* in finding the solution.

CHECK YOURSELF 4 _____

Solve and check.

$7x - 5 = 3x + 5$

Next, we look at two approaches to solving equations in which the coefficient on the right side is greater than the coefficient on the left side.

Example 5 Solving an Equation (Two Methods)

Solve $4x - 8 = 7x + 7$.

Method 1

$$
\begin{array}{rcl}
4x - 8 & = & 7x + 7 \\
+ 8 & & + 8 \\
\hline
4x & = & 7x + 15 \\
-7x & & -7x \\
\hline
-3x & = & 15
\end{array}
$$

Adding 8 will leave the x term alone on the left.

Adding $-7x$ will get the variable terms on the left.

$$\frac{-3x}{-3} = \frac{15}{-3}$$

Dividing by -3 will isolate x on the left.

$$x = -5$$

We'll let you check this result.

To avoid a negative coefficient (in this example, -3), some students prefer a different approach.

This time we work toward having the number on the *left* and the x term on the *right*, or $\square = x$.

Method 2

NOTE It is usually easier to isolate the variable term on the side that will result in a positive coefficient.

$$4x - 8 = 7x + 7$$
$$\underline{\quad -7 \qquad -7\quad}$$ Add -7.
$$4x - 15 = 7x$$
$$\underline{-4x \qquad\quad -4x\quad}$$ Add $-4x$ to get the variables on the right.
$$-15 = 3x$$

$$\frac{-15}{3} = \frac{3x}{3}$$ Divide by 3 to isolate x on the right.

$$-5 = x$$

Because $-5 = x$ and $x = -5$ are equivalent equations, it really makes no difference; the solution is still -5! You can use whichever approach you prefer.

CHECK YOURSELF 5

Solve $5x + 3 = 9x - 21$ by finding equivalent equations of the form $x = \square$ and $\square = x$ to compare the two methods of finding the solution.

It may also be necessary to remove grouping symbols in solving an equation.

OBJECTIVE 2   **Example 6   Solving Equations That Contain Parentheses**

Solve.

NOTE
$5(x - 3)$
$= 5(x + (-3))$
$= 5x + 5(-3)$
$= 5x + (-15)$
$= 5x - 15$

$$5(x - 3) - 2x = x + 7$$ First, apply the distributive property.
$$5x - 15 - 2x = x + 7$$ Combine like terms.
$$3x - 15 = x + 7$$
$$\underline{\quad + 15 \qquad + 15\quad}$$ Add 15.
$$3x = x + 22$$
$$\underline{-x \quad -x\quad}$$ Add $-x$.
$$2x = 22$$ Divide by 2.
$$x = 11$$

The solution is 11. To check, substitute 11 for x in the original equation. Again note the use of our rules for the order of operations.

$$5((11) - 3) - 2 \cdot (11) \overset{?}{=} (11) + 7$$ Simplify terms in parentheses.
$$5 \cdot 8 - 2 \cdot 11 \overset{?}{=} 11 + 7$$ Multiply.
$$40 - 22 \overset{?}{=} 11 + 7$$ Add and subtract.
$$18 = 18$$ A true statement.

CHECK YOURSELF 6

Solve and check.

$$7(x + 5) - 3x = x - 7$$

We will now look at equations that contain fractions with different denominators. To solve an equation involving fractions, the first step is to multiply both sides of the equation by the **least common multiple (LCM)** of all denominators in the equation. Recall that the **LCM** of a set of numbers is the *smallest* number into which all the numbers will divide evenly.

OBJECTIVE 3   **Example 7**   **Solving an Equation That Contains Fractions**

Solve

$$\frac{x}{2} - \frac{2}{3} = \frac{5}{6}$$

First, multiply each side by 6, the LCM of 2, 3, and 6.

$$6\left(\frac{x}{2} - \frac{2}{3}\right) = 6\left(\frac{5}{6}\right) \qquad \text{Apply the distributive property.}$$

$$6\left(\frac{x}{2}\right) - 6\left(\frac{2}{3}\right) = 6\left(\frac{5}{6}\right) \qquad \text{Simplify.}$$

$$3x - 4 = 5$$

Next, isolate the variable x on the left side.

$$3x = 9$$
$$x = 3$$

The solution can be checked by returning to the original equation.

CHECK YOURSELF 7 _____

Solve and check.

$$\frac{x}{4} - \frac{4}{5} = \frac{19}{20}$$

Example 8   **Solving an Equation That Contains Fractions**

Solve

$$\frac{2x - 1}{5} + 1 = \frac{x}{2}$$

First multiply each side by 10, the LCM of 5 and 2.

$$10\left(\frac{2x - 1}{5} + 1\right) = 10\left(\frac{x}{2}\right) \qquad \text{Apply the distributive property on the left and reduce.}$$

$$10\left(\frac{2x - 1}{5}\right) + 10(1) = 10\left(\frac{x}{2}\right)$$

$$2(2x - 1) + 10 = 5x$$

$$4x - 2 + 10 = 5x \qquad \text{Next, isolate } x \text{ on the right side.}$$

$$4x + 8 = 5x$$

$$8 = x \qquad \text{The solution to the original equation is 8.}$$

CHECK YOURSELF 8 _____

Solve and check.

$$\frac{3x + 1}{4} - 2 = \frac{x + 1}{3}$$

An equation that is true for any value of x is called an **identity.**

OBJECTIVE 4 **Example 9 Solving an Equation**

Solve the equation $2(x - 3) = 2x - 6$.

$$
\begin{array}{rcl}
2(x - 3) = & 2x - 6 \\
2x - 6 = & 2x - 6 \\
\underline{-2x \qquad -2x} \\
-6 = & -6
\end{array}
$$

NOTE We could ask the question "For what values of x does $-6 = -6$?"

The statement $-6 = -6$ is true for any value of x. The original equation is an identity.

 CHECK YOURSELF 9 _____

Solve the equation $3(x - 4) - 2x = x - 12$.

There are also equations for which there are no solutions.

OBJECTIVE 5 **Example 10 Solving an Equation**

Solve the equation $3(2x - 5) - 4x = 2x + 1$.

$$
\begin{array}{rcl}
3(2x - 5) - 4x = & 2x + 1 \\
6x - 15 \ - 4x = & 2x + 1 \\
2x - 15 = & 2x + 1 \\
\underline{-2x \qquad -2x} \\
-15 = 1
\end{array}
$$

NOTE We could ask the question "For what values of x does $-15 = 1$?"

These two numbers are never equal. The original equation has no solutions.

 CHECK YOURSELF 10 _____

Solve the equation $2(x - 5) + x = 3x - 3$.

NOTE Such an outline of steps is sometimes called an **algorithm.**

Step by Step: Solving Linear Equations

Step 1   Use the distributive property to remove any grouping symbols. Then simplify by combining like terms on each side of the equation.

Step 2   Add or subtract the same term on each side of the equation until the variable term is on one side and a number is on the other.

Step 3   Multiply or divide both sides of the equation by the same nonzero number so that the variable is alone on one side of the equation. If no variable remains, determine whether the original equation is an identity or whether it has no solutions.

Step 4   Check the solution in the original equation.

CHECK YOURSELF ANSWERS _____

1. (a) -4; **(b)** 3   **2.** 3   **3. (a)** -12; **(b)** 24   **4.** $\dfrac{5}{2}$ **5.** 6   **6.** -14

7. 7   **8.** 5   **9.** The equation is an identity, x can be any real number.
10. There are no solutions.

1.11 Exercises

Name _____

Section _____ Date _____

Solve for x and check your result.

1. $3x + 2 = 14$

2. $3x - 1 = 17$

3. $3x - 2 = 7$

4. $7x + 9 = 37$

5. $4x + 7 = 35$

6. $7x - 8 = 13$

7. $2x + 9 = 5$

8. $6x + 25 = -5$

9. $4 - 7x = 18$

10. $8 - 5x = -7$

11. $5 - 3x = 11$

12. $5 - 4x = 25$

13. $\dfrac{x}{2} + 1 = 5$

14. $\dfrac{x}{5} - 3 = 2$

15. $\dfrac{x}{5} - 3 = 4$

16. $\dfrac{x}{5} + 3 = 8$

17. $\dfrac{2}{3}x + 5 = 17$

18. $\dfrac{3}{4}x - 5 = 4$

19. $\dfrac{3}{4}x - 2 = 16$

20. $\dfrac{5}{7}x + 4 = 14$

21. $5x = 2x + 9$

22. $7x = 18 - 2x$

23. $3x = 10 - 2x$

24. $11x = 7x + 20$

25. $9x + 2 = 3x + 38$

26. $8x - 3 = 4x + 17$

27. $4x - 8 = x - 14$

28. $6x - 5 = 3x - 29$

29. $5x + 7 = 2x - 3$

30. $9x + 7 = 5x - 3$

31. $7x - 3 = 9x + 5$

32. $5x - 2 = 8x - 11$

33.
_____

34.
_____

35.
_____

36.
_____

37.
_____

38.
_____

39.
_____

40.
_____

41.
_____

42.
_____

43.
_____

44.
_____

45.
_____

46.
_____

47. _____ 48. _____

49. _____ 50. _____

51. _____ 52. _____

53. _____ 54. _____

55.
_____

56.
_____

57.
_____

58.
_____

59.
_____

60.
_____

61.
_____

62.
_____

63.
_____

33. $5x + 4 = 7x - 8$

34. $2x + 23 = 6x - 5$

35. $2x - 3 + 5x = 7 + 4x + 2$

36. $8x - 7 - 2x = 2 + 4x - 5$

37. $6x + 7 - 4x = 8 + 7x - 26$

38. $7x - 2 - 3x = 5 + 8x + 13$

39. $9x - 2 + 7x + 13 = 10x - 13$

40. $5x + 3 + 6x - 11 = 8x + 25$

41. $2(x + 3) = 8$

42. $-3(x - 1) = 4(x + 2) + 2$

43. $7(2x - 1) - 5x = x + 25$

44. $9(3x + 2) - 10x = 12x - 7$

45. $3x + 2(4x - 3) = 6x - 9$

46. $7x + 3(2x + 5) = 10x + 17$

47. $\dfrac{8}{3}x - 3 = \dfrac{2}{3}x + 15$

48. $\dfrac{12}{5}x + 7 = 31 - \dfrac{3}{5}x$

49. $\dfrac{2x}{5} - \dfrac{x}{3} = \dfrac{7}{15}$

50. $\dfrac{2x}{7} - \dfrac{3x}{5} = \dfrac{6}{35}$

51. $5.3x - 7 = 2.3x + 5$

52. $9.8x + 2 = 3.8x + 20$

53. $\dfrac{5x - 3}{4} - 2 = \dfrac{x}{3}$

54. $\dfrac{6x - 1}{5} - \dfrac{2x}{3} = 3$

55. $5(x + 1) - 4x = x - 5$

56. $-4(2x - 3) = -8x + 5$

57. $6x - 4x + 1 = 12 + 2x - 11$

58. $-2x + 5x - 9 = 3(x - 4) - 5$

59. $-4(x + 2) - 11 = 2(-2x - 3) - 13$

60. $4(-x - 2) + 5 = -2(2x + 7)$

61. Create an equation of the form $ax + b = c$ that has 2 as a solution.

62. Create an equation of the form $ax + b = c$ that has 7 as a solution.

63. The equation $3x = 3x + 5$ has no solution, whereas the equation $7x + 8 = 8$ has zero as a solution. Explain the difference between a solution of zero and no solution.

64. Construct an equation for which every real number is a solution.

In exercises 65 to 68, find the length of each side of the figure for the given perimeter.

65.

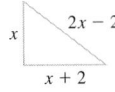

$2x - 2$
x
$x + 2$

$P = 24$ in.

66.

$3x - 4$
x

$P = 32$ cm

67.

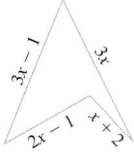

$3x - 1$
$3x$
$2x - 1$
$x + 2$

$P = 90$ in.

68.

$4x + 5$
$3x - 2$

$P = 34$ cm

Getting Ready

Divide.

(a) $\dfrac{3b}{3}$

(b) $\dfrac{5x}{5}$

(c) $\dfrac{4xy}{4x}$

(d) $\dfrac{6a^2 b}{6a^2}$

(e) $\dfrac{7mn^2}{7n^2}$

(f) $\dfrac{\pi ab}{\pi a}$

(g) $\dfrac{srt}{sr}$

(h) $\dfrac{x^2 yz}{x^2 z}$

64. _____

65. _____

66. _____

67. _____

68. _____

a. _____

b. _____

c. _____

d. _____

e. _____

f. _____

g. _____

h. _____

Answers

1. 4   **3.** 3   **5.** 7   **7.** -2 **9.** -2 **11.** -2 **13.** 8
15. 35   **17.** 18   **19.** 24   **21.** 3   **23.** 2   **25.** 6   **27.** -2

29. $-\dfrac{10}{3}$ **31.** -4 **33.** 6   **35.** 4   **37.** 5   **39.** -4 **41.** 1

43. 4   **45.** $-\dfrac{3}{5}$ **47.** 9   **49.** 7   **51.** 4   **53.** 3

55. No solution   **57.** Identity   **59.** Identity   **61.** $6x + 5 = 17$
63. ✐   **65.** 6 in., 8 in., 10 in.   **67.** 12 in., 19 in., 29 in., 30 in.

a. b **b.** x **c.** y **d.** b **e.** m **f.** b **g.** t **h.** y

1.12 Solving Applications with Proportions

1.12 OBJECTIVE

1. Solving an application with proportions.

Now that you have learned how to find an unknown value in a proportion, let's see how this can be used in the solution of applications.

The following equation is a special kind of equation involving fractions:

$$\frac{t}{4} = \frac{1}{2}$$

An equation of the form $\frac{a}{b} = \frac{c}{d}$ is said to be in **proportion form,** or more simply it is called a **proportion.** This type of equation occurs often enough in algebra that it is worth developing some special methods for its solution. First, we will need some definitions.

A **ratio** is a means of comparing two quantities. A ratio can be written as a fraction. For instance, the ratio of 2 to 3 can be written as $\frac{2}{3}$. A statement that two ratios are equal is called a *proportion.* A proportion has the form

$$\frac{a}{b} = \frac{c}{d}$$

In the proportion above, a and d are called the **extremes** of the proportion, and b and c are called the **means.**

A useful property of proportions is easily developed. If

$$\frac{a}{b} = \frac{c}{d}$$

NOTE bd is the LCD of the denominators.

and we multiply both sides by $b \cdot d$, then

$$\left(\frac{a}{b}\right)bd = \left(\frac{c}{d}\right)bd \qquad \text{or} \qquad ad = bc$$

Rules and Properties: Proportions

If $\frac{a}{b} = \frac{c}{d}$ then $ad = bc$

In words:

In any proportion, the product of the extremes (ad) is equal to the product of the means (bc).

Because a proportion is a special kind of fractional equation, this rule gives us an alternative approach to solving equations that are in the proportion form.

Example 1

Solving a Proportion

Solve the equations for x.

NOTE The extremes are x and 15. The means are 5 and 12.

(a) $\dfrac{x}{5} = \dfrac{12}{15}$

Set the product of the extremes equal to the product of the means.

$15x = 5 \cdot 12$

$15x = 60$

$x = 4$

Our solution is 4. You can check as before, by substituting in the original proportion.

(b) $\dfrac{x + 3}{10} = \dfrac{x}{7}$

Set the product of the extremes equal to the product of the means. Be certain to use parentheses with a numerator with more than one term.

$7(x + 3) = 10x$

$7x + 21 = 10x$

$21 = 3x$

$7 = x$

We will leave the checking of this result to the reader.

 CHECK YOURSELF 1

Solve for x.

(a) $\dfrac{x}{8} = \dfrac{3}{4}$ 　　　　　　　　　　　**(b)** $\dfrac{x - 1}{9} = \dfrac{x + 1}{12}$

Step by Step: Solving Applications of Proportions

Step 1 Read the problem carefully to determine the given information.
Step 2 Write the proportion necessary to solve the problem. Use a letter to represent the unknown quantity. Be sure to include the units in writing the proportion.
Step 3 Solve, answer the question of the original problem, and check the proportion as before.

Example 2

Medical Assisting

Dr. Kelly prescribes 50 mg of Keflix. On hand you have 300 mg in 12cc of bacteriostatic water. How much will you give? This uses

$$\frac{Dosage\ ordered\ (mg)}{Units\ given\ (cc)} = \frac{Known\ dosage\ (mg)}{Known\ units\ (cc)}.$$

Answer: You need to carefully read the question and try to pair up each of the numbers with something in the formula. The units (mg and cc) give a clue for instance, since Dr. Kelly prescribed 50 mg of Keflix, that must be the *Dosage ordered (**mg**)*. The 300 **mg** must be the *known dosage (**mg**)*. Also, the 12 **cc** must be the *known units (**cc**)*. That leaves the *Units given (**cc**)* to be how much we will give, and since we do not know what this is (yet), we will call this x.

This is what we get when we substitute in the values: $\dfrac{50\ mg}{x} = \dfrac{300\ mg}{12\ cc}$.

Cross multiply to get 50 *mg* 12 *cc* = x 300 *mg*

Simplify: 600 mg cc = 300x mg

Divide both sides by 300 mg: $\dfrac{600\ mg\ cc}{300\ mg} = \dfrac{300x\ mg}{300\ mg}$

Simplifying, we get 2 cc = x, so we need to give 2 cc's of the Keflix. Notice the mg's canceled out on both sides of the equation.

Example 3

Radiation Technology

Maria receives 88 mRads of x-ray dosage standing 6 feet away from an x-ray machine. What dose would she receive at 9 feet away? This uses the

"Inverse Square Law" which is $\dfrac{Dose\ 1}{Dose\ 2} = \dfrac{(Distance\ 2)^2}{(Distance\ 1)^2}$

Answer: After carefully reading the problem, you realize you need to find out what *Dose 1, Dose 2, Distance 1* and *Distance 2* are so you can plug them into the proportion. It seems that the 6 feet and the 9 feet are the distances (because you measure distance using feet!), and the 88 mRads must be a dose. Since the 6 feet "goes with" the 88 mRads, we call the 6 feet "*Distance 1*" and the 88 mRads "*Dose 1.*" We could have called them both "*Distance 2*" and "*Dose 2*" respectively and the problem would still work fine.

This leaves the 9 feet to be "*Distance 2.*" So what is *Dose 2*? *Dose 2* is what we are trying to find, the dosage she would receive if she was standing 9 feet away. Since we do not yet know what that dosage is, we call it x.

So now we have: $\dfrac{88\ m\ Rads}{x} = \dfrac{(9\ feet)^2}{(6\ feet)^2}$. The best thing to do now is take care of the squares: $\dfrac{88\ m\ Rads}{x} = \dfrac{81\ feet^2}{36\ feet^2}$.

Cross multiply: 88 *mrads* 36 *feet*^{2} = 81*x feet*^{2}

or 3168 *mrads feet*^{2} = 81*x feet*^{2}

Divide both sides by 81 *feet*^{2} to get $\dfrac{3168 \ mrads \ feet^2}{81 \ feet^2} = x$

Simplify to get approximately 39 mrads. Notice the *feet*^{2} cancel out.

Note this answer makes some sense, since if you are further away, the second dose should be weaker than the original dose. Here we got 39 mrads, which is weaker than the original 88 mrads.

Example 4

Using a Proportion to Find an Unknown Value

In a shipment of 400 parts, 14 are found to be defective. How many defective parts should be expected in a shipment of 1000?
   Assume that the ratio of defective parts to the total number remains the same.

$$\frac{14 \text{ defective}}{400 \text{ total}} = \frac{x \text{ defective}}{1000 \text{ total}}$$ We have decided to let *x* be the unknown number of defective parts.

Multiply:

$400x = 14{,}000$

Divide by the coefficient, 400.

$x = 35$

35 defective parts should be expected in the shipment.
   Checking the original proportion, we get

$14 \cdot 1000 \overset{?}{=} 400 \cdot 35$

$14{,}000 = 14{,}000$

 CHECK YOURSELF 4

An investment of $3000 earned $330 for 1 year. How much will an investment of $10,000 earn at the same rate for 1 year?

Let's look at an application involving fractions in the proportion.

Example 5

Using Proportions to Find an Unknown Value

The scale on a map is given as $\frac{1}{4}$ inch (in.) = 3 miles (mi). The distance between two towns is 4 in. on the map. How far apart are the towns in miles?

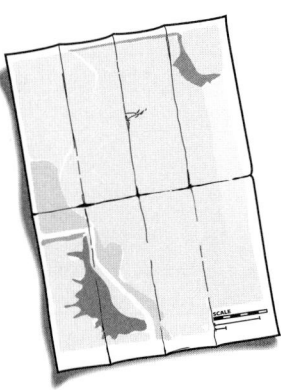

NOTE We could divide both sides by $\frac{1}{4}$:

$$\frac{\frac{1}{4} \cdot x}{\frac{1}{4}} = \frac{3 \cdot 4}{\frac{1}{4}}$$

$$x = \frac{3 \cdot 4}{\frac{1}{4}}$$

$$x = \frac{12}{\frac{1}{4}}$$

then invert and multiply

$$x = \frac{12}{1} \cdot \frac{4}{1}$$

$$= 48$$

For this solution we use the fact that the ratio of inches (on the map) to miles remains the same.

$$\frac{\frac{1}{4} \text{ in.}}{3 \text{ mi}} = \frac{4 \text{ in.}}{x \text{ mi}}$$

$$\frac{1}{4} \cdot x = 3 \cdot 4$$

$$4\left(\frac{1}{4}\right) \cdot x = 4 \cdot 3 \cdot 4$$

$$1 \cdot x = 4 \cdot 3 \cdot 4$$

$$x = 48 \text{ (mi)}$$

 CHECK YOURSELF 5

Jack drives 125 *mi in* $2\frac{1}{2}$ *hours (h). At the same rate, how far will he be able to travel in 4 h? (Hint: Write* $2\frac{1}{2}$ *as an improper fraction.)*

We may also find decimals in the solution of an application.

Example 6

Using Proportions to Find an Unknown Value

Jill works 4.2 h and receives $21. How much will she get if she works 10 h?

The ratio of hours worked to the amount of pay remains the same.

$$\frac{4.2 \text{ h}}{\$21} = \frac{10 \text{ h}}{\$a} \qquad \text{Let } a \text{ be the unknown amount of pay.}$$

$$4.2a = 210$$

$$\frac{4.2a}{4.2} = \frac{210}{4.2}$$ Divide both sides by 4.2.

$$a = \$50$$

 CHECK YOURSELF 6

A piece of cable 8.5 centimeters (cm) long weighs 68 grams (g). What will a 10-cm length of the same cable weigh?

In Example 7 we must convert the units stated in the problem.

Example 7

Using Proportions to Find an Unknown Value

A machine can produce 15 tin cans in 2 minutes (min). At this rate how many cans can it make in an 8-h period?

In writing a proportion for this problem, we must write the times involved in terms of the same units.

$$\frac{15 \text{ cans}}{2 \text{ min}} = \frac{x \text{ cans}}{480 \text{ min}}$$ Because 1 h is 60 min, convert 8 h to 480 min.

$$2x = 15 \cdot 480$$

or $$2x = 7200$$

$$x = 3600 \text{ cans}$$

 CHECK YOURSELF 7

Instructions on a can of film developer call for 2 ounces (oz) of concentrate to 1 quart (qt) of water. How much of the concentrate is needed to mix with 1 gallon (gal) of water? (4 qt = 1 gal.)

An important use of proportions is in solving problems involving *similar* geometric figures. These are figures that have the same shape and whose corresponding sides are proportional. For instance, in the similar triangles shown below,

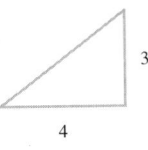 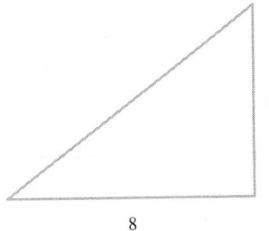

a proportion involving corresponding sides is

$$\frac{3}{4} = \frac{6}{8}$$

Example 8

Solving an Application Using Similar Triangles

If a 6-foot-tall man casts a shadow that is 10 feet long, how tall is a tree that casts a shadow that is 140 feet long?

Let's look at a picture of the two triangles involved.

NOTE Connect the top of the tree to the end of the shadow to create a triangle. Connecting the top of the man to the end of his shadow creates a similar triangle.

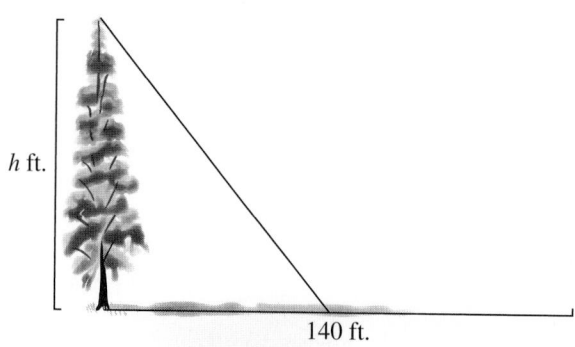

h ft.

140 ft.

6 ft.
10 ft.

From the similar triangles, we have the proportion

$$\frac{6}{10} = \frac{h}{140}$$

Using the proportion rule, we have $6 \cdot 140 = 10 \cdot h$

$$10 \cdot h = 840$$

$$\frac{10 \cdot h}{10} = \frac{840}{10}$$

$$h = 84$$

The tree is 84 feet tall.

✔ CHECK YOURSELF 8

If a woman who is $5\frac{1}{2}$ feet tall casts a shadow that is 3 feet long, how tall is a building that casts a shadow that is 90 feet long?

CHECK YOURSELF ANSWERS

1. (a) $x = 6$; **(b)** $x = 7$ **4.** $1100   **5.** $\dfrac{125 \text{ mi}}{\dfrac{5}{2}\text{ h}} = \dfrac{x \text{ mi}}{4 \text{ h}}$

$$\frac{5}{2}x = 500 \qquad \text{Divide both sides by } \frac{5}{2}$$

$$x = 200 \text{ mi}$$

6. 80 g   **7.** 8 oz   **8.** 165 feet tall

 **1.12** **Exercises**

Name _____

Section _____ Date _____

Solve each of the following equations for *x*.

ANSWERS

1. $\dfrac{x}{11} = \dfrac{12}{33}$

2. $\dfrac{4}{x} = \dfrac{16}{20}$

3. $\dfrac{5}{8} = \dfrac{20}{x}$

4. $\dfrac{x}{10} = \dfrac{9}{30}$

5. $\dfrac{4x}{5} = 8$

6. $\dfrac{3x}{4} = 6$

7. $\dfrac{x}{5} = \dfrac{3}{15}$

8. $\dfrac{5}{8} = \dfrac{10}{x}$

9. $\dfrac{3}{x} = \dfrac{9}{12}$

10. $\dfrac{-5x}{6} = \dfrac{10}{3}$

11. $\dfrac{3x}{4} = -6$

1. _____

2. _____

3. _____

4. _____

5. _____

6. _____

7. _____

8. _____

9. _____

10. _____

11. _____

12. _____

13. _____

Solve the following applications.

12. Legal Studies: John Doe (plaintiff) was not wearing his seatbelt while driving down the highway. Susan Smith (defendant), while traveling the opposite direction, veers into plaintiff's lane and causes a head on collision. Plaintiff sues on the basis of personal injury, and the jury awards the plaintiff $100,000. The jury also finds the plaintiff was 20% at fault and the defendant was 80% at fault. The plaintiff's amount will be reduced by his percentage of fault.

a) How much does each party get? Use $\dfrac{percentage}{100} = \dfrac{amount\ awarded}{total\ amount\ awarded}$.

b) Lawyers get 33% of the defendant's and plaintiff's award. Now how much does each party get?

13. Radiation Technology: Maria receives 100 mRads of x-ray dosage standing 5 feet away from an x-ray machine. What dose would she receive at 10 feet away? This uses the "Inverse Square Law" which is $\dfrac{Dose\ 1}{Dose\ 2} = \dfrac{(Distance\ 2)^2}{(Distance\ 1)^2}$

14. _____

15. _____

16. _____

17. _____

18. _____

19. _____

20. _____

21. _____

22. _____

23. _____

24. _____

14. **Radiation Technology:** A radiograph is taken at 5 mAs at 40 inches with acceptable density. A new radiograph is need at 72 inches, what is the new mAs?

    This uses the "Exposure Maintenance Law: $\dfrac{First\ mAs}{Second\ mAs} = \dfrac{(Distance\ 1)^2}{(Distance\ 2)^2}$

15. **Medical Assisting:** Dr. Kelly prescribes 200 mg of Keflix. On hand you have 1000 mg in 5cc of bacteriostatic water. How much will you give? This uses
    $$\frac{Dosage\ ordered\ (mgs)}{Units\ given\ (cc's)} = \frac{known\ dosage\ (mgs)}{known\ units\ (cc's)}$$

16. **Histology:** Dr. Washington wants you to prepare 50 ml of 2% sodium thiosulfate from a 5% solution by adding bacteriostatic water. How much 5% solution and how much bacteriostatic water do you need to combine? This uses
    $\dfrac{Beginning\ percentage}{Desired\ percentage} = \dfrac{Desired\ volume}{Beginning\ volume}$ to calculate how much of the
    5% solution you need, then you add enough bacteriostatic water to fill it out to the 50ml.

17. **Nursing:** Dr. Wolfe prescribes 5 mg IV (intravenously) of Lopressor. Your supply is .5 Liter of 2 mg/ml solution. How many ml will you administer? Use the formula from problem 15, and be careful! You don't want to overdose the patient!

18. **Criminal Justice:** If a 2010 Mustang's skid is 95 feet long when it is going 40 miles per hour, how fast was the car going if the skid is 145 feet long? Use
    $\dfrac{First\ speed}{(First\ skid\ length)^2} = \dfrac{Second\ speed}{(Second\ skid\ length)^2}.$

19. **OTA:** Your goal was to increase your patient's grip strength by 20%. The initial grip strength was 60 pounds. Just now the reassessment was 78 pounds. Has the patient met her goal? Use $\dfrac{Percentage\ increase}{100} = \dfrac{Grip\ strength\ increase}{Beginning\ grip\ strength}.$

20. **Book purchases.** If 12 books are purchased for $40, how much will you pay for 18 books at the same rate?

21. **Construction.** If an 8-foot (ft) two-by-four costs 96¢, what should a 12-ft two-by-four cost?

22. **Consumer affairs.** A box of 18 tea bags is marked 90¢. At that price, what should a box of 48 tea bags cost?

23. **Consumer affairs.** Cans of orange juice are marked 2 for 93¢. What would the price of a case of 24 cans be?

24. **Workload.** A worker can complete the assembly of 15 tape players in 6 hours (h). At this rate, how many can the worker complete in a 40-h workweek?

25. **Consumer affairs.** If 3 pounds (lb) of apples cost 90¢, what will 10 lb cost?

26. **Elections.** The ratio of yes to no votes in an election was 3 to 2. How many no votes were cast if there were 2880 yes votes?

27. **College enrollment.** The ratio of men to women at a college is 7 to 5. How many women students are there if there are 3500 men?

28. **Photography.** A photograph 5 inches (in.) wide by 6 in. high is to be enlarged so that the new width is 15 in. What will be the height of the enlargement?

29. **Shift work.** Meg's job is assembling lawn chairs. She can put together 55 chairs in 4 h. At this rate, how many chairs can she assemble in an 8-h shift?

30. **Distance.** Christy can travel 110 miles (mi) in her new car on 5 gallons (gal) of gas. How far can she travel on a full tank, which has 12 usable gal?

31. **Property taxes.** The Changs purchased an $80,000 home, and the property taxes were $1400. If they make improvements and the house is now valued at $120,000, what will the new property tax be?

32. **Distance.** A car travels 165 mi in 3 h. How far will it travel in 8 h if it continues at the same speed?

33. **Consumer affairs.** A battery pack is on sale at 2 for $3. At this rate, how much will 7 packs cost?

34. **Manufacturing.** The ratio of teeth on a smaller gear to those on a larger gear is 3 to 7. If the smaller gear has 15 teeth, how many teeth does the larger gear have?

35. **Consumer affairs.** A store has T-shirts on sale at 2 for $5.50. At this rate, what will five shirts cost?

25. _____

26. _____

27. _____

28. _____

29. _____

30. _____

31. _____

32. _____

33. _____

34. _____

35. _____

36. _____

37. _____

38. _____

39. _____

40. _____

41. _____

42. _____

43. _____

Using the given map, find the distances between the cities named in exercises 17 to 20.

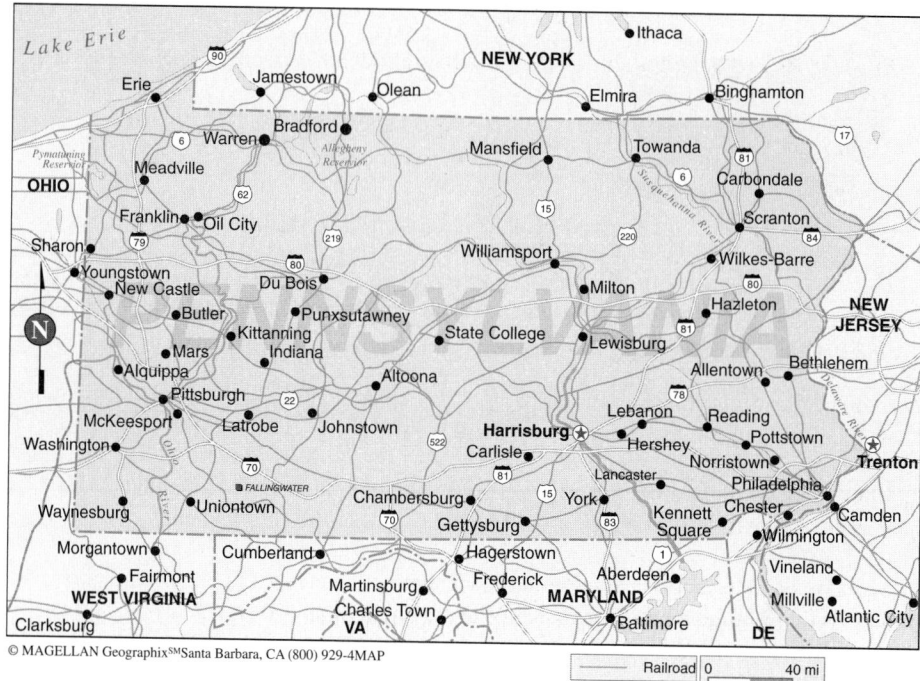

© MAGELLAN Geographix℠Santa Barbara, CA (800) 929-4MAP

Railroad 0 ——— 40 mi

36. Find the distance from Harrisburg to Philadelphia.

37. Find the distance from Punxsutawney (home of the groundhog) to State College (home of the Nittany Lions).

38. Find the distance from Gettysburg to Meadville.

39. Find the distance from Scranton to Waynesburg.

40. Manufacturing. An inspection reveals 30 defective parts in a shipment of 500. How many defective parts should be expected in a shipment of 1200?

41. Investments. You invest $4000 in a stock that pays a $180 dividend in 1 year. At the same rate, how much will you need to invest to earn $270?

42. Football. A football back ran 212 yards (yd) in the first two games of the season. If he continues at the same pace, how many yards should he gain in the 11-game season?

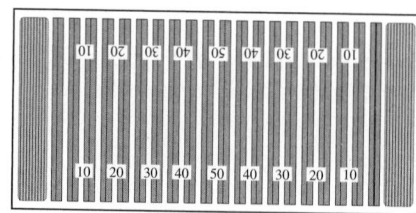

43. Cooking. A 6-lb roast will serve 14 people. What size roast is needed to serve 21 people?

44. **Lawn care.** A 2-lb box of grass seed is supposed to cover 2500 square feet (ft^2) of lawn. How much seed will you need for 8750 ft^2 of lawn?

45. **Fencing.** A 6-ft fence post casts a 9-ft shadow. How tall is a nearby pole that casts a 15-ft shadow?

46. **Lighting.** A 9-ft light pole casts a 15-ft shadow. Find the height of a nearby tree that is casting a 40-ft shadow.

47. **Construction.** On the blueprint of the Wilsons' new home, the scale is 5 in. equals 7 ft. What will be the actual length of a bedroom if it measures 10 in. long on the blueprint?

48. **Distance.** The scale on a map is $\frac{1}{2}$ in. = 50 mi. If the distance between two towns on the map is 6 in., how far apart are they in miles?

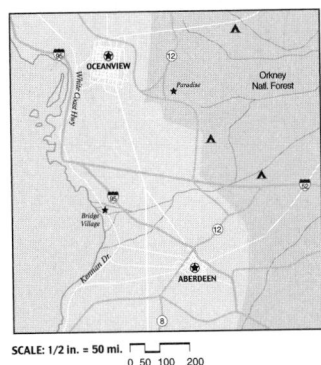

49. **Science.** A metal bar expands $\frac{1}{4}$ in. for each 12°F rise in temperature. How much will it expand if the temperature rises 48°F?

50. **Car maintenance.** Your car burns $2\frac{1}{2}$ quarts (qt) of oil on a trip of 5000 mi. How many quarts should you expect to use when driving 7200 mi?

51. **Lighting.** A 6-ft person casts a $7\frac{1}{2}$-ft shadow. If the shadow of a nearby pole is 30 ft long, how tall is the pole?

52. **Manufacturing.** A piece of tubing 10.5 centimeters (cm) long weighs 35 grams (g). What is the weight of a piece of the same tubing that is 15 cm long?

44 _____

45. _____

46. _____

47. _____

48. _____

49. _____

50. _____

51. _____

52. _____

53. _____

54. _____

55. _____

56. _____

57. _____

58. _____

59. _____

60. _____

61. _____

53. Salary. Jane works 7.75 h and receives $38.75 pay. What will she receive at the same rate if she works 12 h?

54. Sales tax. The sales tax on an item costing $80 is $5.20. What will the tax be for an item costing $150?

55. Conversion. If 8 kilometers (km) is approximately 4.8 mi, how many kilometers will equal 12 mi?

56. Timing. You find that your watch gains 2 minutes (min) in 6 h. How much will it gain in 3 days?

57. Painting. If 2 qt of paint will cover 225 ft², how many square feet will 2 gal cover? (1 gal = 4 qt)

58. Construction. Directions on a box of 4 cups of wallpaper paste are to mix the contents with 5 qt of water. To mix a smaller batch using 1 cup of paste, how much water (in ounces) should be added? (1 qt = 32 oz)

59. Film processing. A film processing machine can develop three rolls of film every 8 min. At this rate, how many rolls can be developed in a 4-h period?

60. Carpooling. Approximately 7 out of every 10 people in the U.S. workforce drive to work alone. During morning rush hour there are 115,000 cars on the streets of a medium-sized city. How many of these cars have one person in them?

61. Carpooling. Approximately 15 out of every 100 people in the U.S. workforce carpool to work. There are an estimated 320,000 people in the workforce of a given city. How many of these people are in car pools?

Use a proportion to find the unknown side, labeled *x*, in each of the following pairs of similar figures.

62.
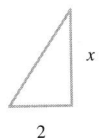 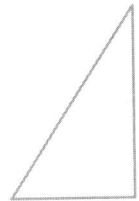

63.
 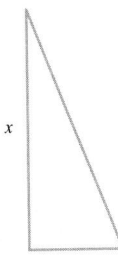

64.
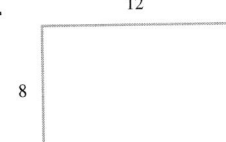

65.
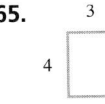 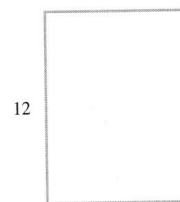

ANSWERS

62. _____

63. _____

64. _____

65. _____

66. _____

66. A recipe for 12 servings lists the following ingredients:

12 cups ziti	7 cups spaghetti sauce	4 cups ricotta cheese
$\frac{1}{2}$ cup parsley	1 teaspoon garlic powder	$\frac{1}{2}$ teaspoon pepper
4 cups mozzarella cheese	2 tablespoons parmesan cheese	

Determine the amount of ingredients necessary to serve 5 people.

Answers

1. 4   **3.** 32   **5.** 10   **7.** 1   **9.** 4   **11.** −8   **13.** 25 mRads

15. 1 cc   **17.** 2.5 or $2\frac{1}{2}$ ml   **19.** Yes–grip strength increase is 30%

21. $1 44   **23.** $11 16   **25.** $3 00   **27.** 2500 women   **29.** 110 chairs

31. $2100   **33.** $10.50   **35.** $13.75   **37.** 65 mi.   **39.** 285 mi.   **41.** $6000

43. 9 lb.   **45.** 10 ft   **47.** 14 ft   **49.** 1 in.   **51.** 24 ft   **53.** $60

55. 20 km   **57.** 900 ft^2 **59.** 90 rolls   **61.** 48,000 people   **63.** 15   **65.** 9

1.13 Absolute Value Equations and Inequalities

 OBJECTIVES

1. Solve an absolute value equation in one variable
2. Solve an absolute value inequality in one variable

Equations and inequalities may involve the absolute value notation in their statements. In this section we build on our work with absolute value for the necessary solution techniques.

Recall that the absolute value of x, written $|x|$, is the distance between x and 0 on the number line. Consider, for example, the absolute value equation

NOTE Technically we mean the distance between the *point corresponding* to x and the *point corresponding* to 0, the origin.

$$|x| = 4$$

This means that the distance between x and 0 is 4, as is pictured below.

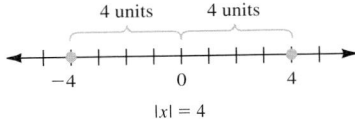

As the sketch illustrates, $x = 4$ and $x = -4$ are the two solutions for the equation.

This observation suggests the more general statement.

 CAUTION

p must be positive because an equation such as $|x - 2| = -3$ has no solution. The absolute value of a quantity must always be equal to a nonnegative number.

Rules and Properties: Absolute Value Equations—Property 1

For any positive number p, if

$$|x| = p$$

then

$$x = p \quad \text{or} \quad x = -p$$

This property allows us to "translate" an equation involving absolute value to two linear equations that we can then solve separately. The following example illustrates.

Example 1

Solving an Absolute Value Equation

Solve for x:

$$|3x - 2| = 4$$

From Property 1 we know that $|3x - 2| = 4$ is equivalent to the equations

$$3x - 2 = 4 \quad \text{or} \quad 3x - 2 = -4$$

NOTE Add 2.

$$3x = 6 \qquad\qquad 3x = -2$$

NOTE Divide by 3.

$$x = 2 \qquad\qquad x = -\frac{2}{3}$$

CAUTION

Be Careful! A common mistake is to solve *only* the equation $3x - 2 = 4$. You must solve *both* of the equivalent equations to find the two required solutions.

The solutions are $-\dfrac{2}{3}$ and 2. These solutions are easily checked by replacing x with $-\dfrac{2}{3}$ and 2 in the original absolute value equation.

CHECK YOURSELF 1

Solve for x.

$$|4x + 1| = 9$$

An equation involving absolute value may have to be rewritten before you can apply Property 1. Consider the following example.

Example 2

Solving an Absolute Value Equation

Solve for x:

$$|2 - 3x| + 5 = 10$$

To use Property 1, we must first isolate the absolute value on the left side of the equation. This is easily done by subtracting 5 from both sides for the result:

$$|2 - 3x| = 5$$

We can now proceed as before by using Property 1.

$2 - 3x = 5$ or	$2 - 3x = -5$

NOTE Subtract 2.

$$-3x = 3 \qquad\qquad -3x = -7$$

NOTE Divide by -3.

$$x = -1 \qquad\qquad x = \dfrac{7}{3}$$

The solution set is $\left\{-1, \dfrac{7}{3}\right\}$.

CHECK YOURSELF 2

Solve for x.

$$|5 - 2x| - 4 = 7$$

In some applications more than one absolute value is involved in an equation. Consider an equation of the form

$$|x| = |y|$$

Because the absolute values of x and y are equal, x and y are the same distance from 0. This means they are either *equal* or *opposite in sign*. This leads to a second general property of absolute value equations.

Rules and Properties: Absolute Value Equations—Property 2

If

$$|x| = |y|$$

then

$$x = y \quad \text{or} \quad x = -y$$

Let's look at an application of this second property in our next example.

Example 3

Solving an Absolute Value Equation

Solve for x:

$$|3x - 4| = |x + 2|$$

By Property 2, we can write

$$3x - 4 = x + 2 \quad \text{or} \quad 3x - 4 = -(x + 2)$$

$$3x - 4 = -x - 2$$

$$3x = x + 6 \qquad\qquad 3x = -x + 2$$

$$2x = 6 \qquad\qquad 4x = 2$$

$$x = 3 \qquad\qquad x = \frac{1}{2}$$

The solution set is $\left\{ \dfrac{1}{2}, 3 \right\}$.

 CHECK YOURSELF 3

Solve for x.

$$|4x - 1| = |x + 5|$$

We started this section by noting that the solution set for the equation

$$|x| = 4$$

consists of those numbers whose distance from the origin is equal to 4. Similarly, the solution set for the absolute value inequality

$$|x| < 4$$

consists of those numbers whose distance from the origin is *less than* 4, that is, all numbers between -4 and 4. The solution set is pictured below.

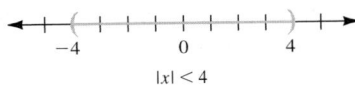

NOTE The solution set would be

$\{x|-4 < x < 4\}$

The solution set can be described by the compound inequality

$-4 < x < 4$

and this suggests the following general statement.

Rules and Properties: Absolute Value Inequalities—Property 1

For any positive number p, if

$|x| < p$

then

$-p < x < p$

Let's look at an application of Property 1 in solving an absolute value inequality.

Example 4

Solving an Absolute Value Inequality

Solve and graph the solution set of

$|2x - 3| < 5$

NOTE With Property 1 we can *translate* an absolute value inequality to an inequality *not* involving absolute value that can be solved by our earlier methods.

From Property 1, we know that the given absolute value inequality is equivalent to the compound inequality

$-5 < 2x - 3 < 5$

Solving as before, we isolate the variable in the center term.

$-2 < 2x < 8$ Add 3 to all three parts.

$-1 < \ x < 4$ Divide by 2.

The solution set is

$\{x|-1 < x < 4\}$

The graph is shown below.

NOTE Notice that the solution is an open interval on the number line.

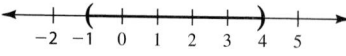

 CHECK YOURSELF 4

Solve and graph the solution set.

$|3x - 4| \leq 8$

We know that the solution set for the absolute value inequality

$|x| < 4$

consists of those numbers whose distance from the origin is *less than* 4. Now consider the solution set for

$|x| > 4$

It must consist of those numbers whose distance from the origin is *greater than* 4. The solution set is pictured below.

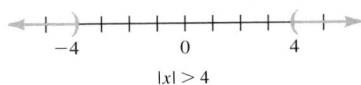

$$|x| > 4$$

The solution set can be described by the compound inequality

$$x < -4 \quad \text{or} \quad x > 4$$

and this suggests the following general statement.

Rules and Properties: Absolute Value Inequalities—Property 2

For any positive number p, if

$$|x| > p$$

then

$$x < -p \quad \text{or} \quad x > p$$

Let's apply Property 2 to the solution of an absolute value inequality.

Example 5

Solving an Absolute Value Inequality

Solve and graph the solution set of

$$|5x - 2| > 8$$

From Property 2, we know that the given absolute value inequality is equivalent to the compound inequality

$$5x - 2 < -8 \quad \text{or} \quad 5x - 2 > 8$$

NOTE Again we *translate* the absolute value inequality to the compound inequality *not* involving absolute value.

Solving as before, we have

NOTE Add 2.

$$5x < -6 \quad \text{or} \quad 5x > 10$$

NOTE Divide by 5.

$$x < -\frac{6}{5} \qquad x > 2$$

NOTE You could describe the solution set as

$$\left\{ x \,\middle|\, x < -\frac{6}{5} \right\} \cup \{x \mid x > 2\}$$

The solution set is $\left\{ x \,\middle|\, x < -\dfrac{6}{5} \text{ or } x > 2 \right\}$ and the graph is shown below.

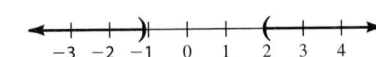

✓ **CHECK YOURSELF 5**

Solve and graph the solution set.

$$|3 - 2x| \geq 9$$

The following chart summarizes our discussion of absolute value inequalities.

NOTE As before, *p* must be a positive number.

Type of Inequality	Equivalent Inequality	Graph of Solution Set
$\lvert ax + b \rvert < p$	$-p < ax + b < p$	
$\lvert ax + b \rvert > p$	$ax + b < -p$ or $ax + b > p$	

CHECK YOURSELF ANSWERS

1. $\left\{ -\dfrac{5}{2}, 2 \right\}$ 2. $\{-3, 8\}$ 3. $\left\{ 2, -\dfrac{4}{5} \right\}$

4. $\left\{ x \,\middle|\, -\dfrac{4}{3} \le x \le 4 \right\}$

5. $\{ x \mid x \le -3 \text{ or } x \ge 6 \}$

Name _____

Section _____ Date _____

Solve each of the following absolute value equations.

1. $|x| = 5$

2. $|x| = 7$

3. $|x| = 10$

4. $|x| = 22$

5. $|x| = -8$

6. $|x| = -11$

7. $|x - 2| = 3$

8. $|x + 5| = 6$

9. $|x + 6| = 0$

10. $|x - 3| = 0$

11. $|3 - x| = 7$

12. $|5 - x| = 4$

13. $|2x - 3| = 9$

14. $|3x + 5| = 11$

15. $|5 - 4x| = 1$

16. $|3 - 6x| = 9$

17. $\left|\dfrac{1}{2}x + 5\right| = 7$

18. $\left|\dfrac{2}{3}x - 4\right| = 6$

19. $\left|4 - \dfrac{3}{4}x\right| = 8$

20. $\left|3 - \dfrac{2}{5}x\right| = 9$

21. $|3x + 1| = -2$

22. $|5x - 2| = -3$

Rewrite each of the following absolute value equations, and then solve the equations.

23. $|x| - 3 = 2$

24. $|x| + 4 = 6$

25. $|x| + 4 = 12$

26. $|x| - 9 = 13$

ANSWERS

1. _____

2. _____

3. _____

4. _____

5. _____

6. _____

7. _____

8. _____

9. _____

10. _____

11. _____

12. _____

13. _____

14. _____

15. _____

16. _____

17. _____

18. _____

19. _____

20. _____

21. _____

22. _____

23. _____

24. _____

25. _____

26. _____

27. _____

28. _____

29. _____

30. _____

31. _____

32. _____

33. _____

34. _____

35. _____

36. _____

37. _____

38. _____

39. _____

40. _____

41. _____

42. _____

43. _____

44. _____

45. _____

46. _____

47. _____

48. _____

49. _____

50. _____

27. $|x| + 7 = -3$

28. $|x| - 2 = -5$

29. $|x - 2| + 3 = 5$

30. $|x + 5| - 2 = 5$

31. $|2x - 3| - 1 = 6$

32. $|3x + 5| + 2 = 4$

33. $\left| \dfrac{1}{2}x + 2 \right| - 3 = 5$

34. $\left| \dfrac{1}{3}x - 4 \right| + 3 = 9$

35. $8 - |x - 4| = 5$

36. $10 - |2x + 1| = 3$

37. $|3x - 2| + 4 = 3$

38. $|5x - 3| + 5 = 3$

Solve each of the following absolute value equations.

39. $|2x - 1| = |x + 3|$

40. $|3x + 1| = |2x - 3|$

41. $|5x - 2| = |2x + 4|$

42. $|7x - 3| = |2x + 7|$

43. $|x - 2| = |x + 1|$

44. $|x + 3| = |x - 2|$

45. $|2x - 5| = |2x - 3|$

46. $|3x + 1| = |3x - 1|$

47. $|x - 2| = |2 - x|$

48. $|x - 4| = |4 - x|$

Find and graph the solution set for each of the following absolute value inequalities.

49. $|x| < 5$

50. $|x| > 3$

51. $|x| \geq 7$

52. $|x| \leq 4$

53. $|x - 4| > 2$

54. $|x + 5| < 3$

55. $|x + 6| \leq 4$

56. $|x - 7| \geq 5$

57. $|3 - x| > 5$

58. $|5 - x| < 3$

59. $|x - 7| < 0$

60. $|x + 5| \geq 0$

61. $|2x - 5| < 3$

62. $|3x - 1| > 8$

63. $|3x + 4| \geq 5$

64. $|2x + 3| \leq 9$

65. $|5x - 3| > 7$

66. $|6x - 5| < 13$

67. $|2 - 3x| < 11$

68. $|3 - 2x| \geq 11$

69. $|3 - 5x| \geq 7$

70. $|7 - 3x| < 13$

71. $\left| \dfrac{3}{4}x - 5 \right| < 7$

72. $\left| \dfrac{2}{3}x + 5 \right| \geq 3$

On some popular calculators there is a special absolute value function key. It is usually labeled "abs." To register an absolute value, you press this key and then put the desired expression in parentheses. For the expression $|x + 3|$, enter abs($x + 3$). Rewrite each expression in calculator form.

73. $|x + 2|$

74. $|x - 2|$

75. $|2x - 3|$

76. $|5x + 7|$

51. _____

52. _____

53. _____

54. _____

55. _____

56. _____

57. _____

58. _____

59. _____

60. _____

61. _____

62. _____

63. _____

64. _____

65. _____

66. _____

67. _____

68. _____

69. _____

70. _____

71. _____

72. _____

73. _____

74. _____

75. _____

76. _____

77. _____

78. _____

79. _____

80. _____

77. $|3x + 2| - 4$

78. $|4x - 7| + 2$

79. $2|3x - 1|$

80. $-3|2x + 8|$

Answers

1. $\{-5, 5\}$ **3.** $\{-10, 10\}$ **5.** No solution   **7.** $\{-1, 5\}$ **9.** $\{-6\}$

11. $\{-4, 10\}$ **13.** $\{-3, 6\}$ **15.** $\left\{1, \dfrac{3}{2}\right\}$ **17.** $\{-24, 4\}$ **19.** $\left\{-\dfrac{16}{3}, 16\right\}$

21. No solution   **23.** $\{-5, 5\}$ **25.** $\{-8, 8\}$ **27.** No solution   **29.** $\{0, 4\}$

31. $\{-2, 5\}$ **33.** $\{-20, 12\}$ **35.** $\{1, 7\}$ **37.** No solution   **39.** $\left\{-\dfrac{2}{3}, 4\right\}$

41. $\left\{-\dfrac{2}{7}, 2\right\}$ **43.** $\left\{\dfrac{1}{2}\right\}$ **45.** $\{2\}$ **47.** All real numbers

49. $\{x \mid -5 < x < 5\}$

51. $\{x \mid x \leq -7 \text{ or } x \geq 7\}$

53. $\{x \mid x < 2 \text{ or } x > 6\}$

55. $\{x \mid -10 \leq x \leq -2\}$

57. $\{x \mid x < -2 \text{ or } x > 8\}$

59. No solution

61. $\{x \mid 1 < x < 4\}$

63. $\left\{x \mid x \leq -3 \text{ or } x \geq \dfrac{1}{3}\right\}$

65. $\left\{x \mid x < -\dfrac{4}{5} \text{ or } x > 2\right\}$

67. $\left\{x \mid -3 < x < \dfrac{13}{3}\right\}$

69. $\left\{x \mid x \leq -\dfrac{4}{5} \text{ or } x \geq 2\right\}$

71. $\left\{x \mid -\dfrac{8}{3} < x < 16\right\}$

73. abs(x + 2)   **75.** abs(2 * x - 3)   **77.** abs(3 * x + 2) - 4

79. 2 * abs(3 * x - 1)

1.14 Inequalities—An Introduction

1. Use the notation of inequalities
2. Graph the solution set of an inequality
3. Solve an inequality and graph the solution set

As pointed out in the introduction to this chapter, an equation is just a statement that two expressions are equal. In algebra, an **inequality** is a statement that one expression is less than or greater than another. Four new symbols are used in writing inequalities. The use of two of them is illustrated in Example 1.

> ### Example 1
>
> **Reading the Inequality Symbol**

NOTE To help you remember, the "arrowhead" always points toward the smaller quantity.

$5 < 8$ is an inequality read "5 is less than 8."

$9 > 6$ is an inequality read "9 is greater than 6."

✔ **CHECK YOURSELF 1**

Fill in the blanks, using the symbols $<$ and $>$.

(a) 12 _____ 8

(b) 20 _____ 25

Like an equation, an inequality can be represented by a balance scale. Note that, in each case, the inequality arrow points to the side that is "lighter."

$2x < 4x - 3$

NOTE The 2x side is less than the 4x − 3 side, so it is "lighter."

$5x - 6 > 9$

Just as was the case with equations, inequalities that involve variables may be either true or false depending on the value that we give to the variable. For instance, consider the inequality

$x < 6$

$$\text{If } x = \begin{cases} 3 & 3 < 6 \text{ is true} \\ 5 & 5 < 6 \text{ is true} \\ -10 & -10 < 6 \text{ is true} \\ 8 & 8 < 6 \text{ is false} \end{cases}$$

Therefore 3, 5, and -10 are some *solutions* for the inequality $x < 6$; they make the inequality a true statement. You should see that 8 is *not* a solution. We call the set of all solutions the **solution set** for the inequality. Of course, there are many possible solutions.

Because there are so many solutions (an infinite number, in fact), we certainly do not want to try to list them all! A convenient way to show the solution set of an inequality is with the use of a number line.

Example 2

Solving Inequalities

To graph the solution set for the inequality $x < 6$, we want to include all real numbers that are "less than" 6. This means all numbers *to the left* of 6 on the number line. We then start at 6 and draw an arrow extending left, as shown:

NOTE The left arrow indicates the direction of the *solution*.

Note: The **open circle** at 6 means that we do not include 6 in the solution set (6 is not less than itself). The colored arrow shows all the numbers in the solution set, with the arrowhead indicating that the solution set continues indefinitely to the left.

 CHECK YOURSELF 2

Graph the solution set of $x < -2$.

Two other symbols are used in writing inequalities. They are used with inequalities such as

$x \geq 5$ and $x \leq 2$

Here $x \geq 5$ is really a combination of the two statements $x > 5$ and $x = 5$. It is read "x is greater than or equal to 5." The solution set includes 5 in this case.

The inequality $x \leq 2$ combines the statements $x < 2$ and $x = 2$. It is read "x is less than or equal to 2."

Example 3

Graphing Inequalities

NOTE Here the filled-in circle means that we want to include 5 in the solution set. This is often called a **closed** circle.

The solution set for $x \geq 5$ is graphed as follows.

CHECK YOURSELF 3

Graph the solution sets.

(a) $x \leq -4$ **(b)** $x \geq 3$

You have learned how to graph the solution sets of some simple inequalities, such as $x < 8$ or $x \geq 10$. Now we will look at more complicated inequalities, such as

$2x - 3 < x + 4$

This is called a **linear inequality in one variable.** Only one variable is involved in the inequality, and it appears only to the first power. Fortunately, the methods used to solve this type of inequality are very similar to those we used earlier in this chapter to solve linear equations in one variable. Here is our first property for inequalities.

Rules and Properties: The Addition Property of Inequality

If $a < b$ then $a + c < b + c$

In words, adding the same quantity to both sides of an inequality gives an **equivalent inequality.**

NOTE Equivalent inequalities have exactly the same solution sets.

Again, we can use the idea of a balance scale to see the significance of this property. If we add the same weight to both sides of an unbalanced scale, it stays unbalanced.

Example 4

Solving Inequalities

NOTE The inequality is solved when an equivalent inequality has the form

$x <$ ☐   or $x >$ ☐

Solve and graph the solution set for $x - 8 < 7$.
    To solve $x - 8 < 7$, add 8 to both sides of the inequality by the addition property.

$$x - 8 <\ \ \ 7$$
$$\underline{+\ 8\ \ \ \ \ +8}$$
$$x \ \ \ \ \ \ < 15 \quad \text{(The inequality is solved)}$$

The graph of the solution set is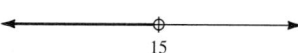

 CHECK YOURSELF 4

Solve and graph the solution set for

$x - 9 > -3$

Example 5

Solving Inequalities

Solve and graph the solution set for $4x - 2 \geq 3x + 5$.
First, we add $-3x$ to both sides of the inequality.

NOTE We added $-3x$ and then added 2 to both sides. If these steps are done in the other order, the resulting inequality will be the same.

$$
\begin{array}{rcl}
4x - 2 & \geq & 3x + 5 \\
-3x & & -3x \\
\hline
x - 2 & \geq & 5 \\
+ 2 & & + 2 \\
\hline
x & \geq & 7
\end{array}
$$

Now we add 2 to both sides.

The graph of the solution set is

 CHECK YOURSELF 5

Solve and graph the solution set.

$7x - 8 \leq 6x + 2$

You will also need a rule for multiplying on both sides of an inequality. Here you'll have to be a bit careful. There is a difference between the multiplication property for inequalities and that for equations. Look at the following:

$2 < 7$ (A true inequality)

Let's multiply both sides by 3.

$$
\begin{array}{c}
2 < 7 \\
3 \cdot 2 < 3 \cdot 7 \\
6 < 21 \quad \text{(A true inequality)}
\end{array}
$$

Now we multiply both sides by -3.

$$
\begin{array}{c}
2 < 7 \\
(-3)(2) < (-3)(7) \\
-6 < -21 \quad \text{(\textit{Not} a true inequality)}
\end{array}
$$

Let's try something different.

$$
\begin{array}{c}
2 < 7 \\
(-3)(2) > (-3)(7) \\
-6 > -21
\end{array}
$$

Change the "sense" of the inequality: $<$ becomes $>$.
(This is now a true inequality.)

This suggests that multiplying both sides of an inequality by a negative number changes the "sense" of the inequality.

We can state the following general property.

Rules and Properties: The Multiplication Property of Inequality

If $a < b$ then $ac < bc$ when $c > 0$
and $ac > bc$ when $c < 0$

In words, multiplying both sides of an inequality by the same *positive* number gives an equivalent inequality.

When both sides of an inequality are multiplied by the same *negative* number, it is necessary to *reverse the sense* of the inequality to give an equivalent inequality.

Example 6

Solving and Graphing Inequalities

(a) Solve and graph the solution set for $5x < 30$.

Multiplying both sides of the inequality by $\dfrac{1}{5}$ gives

$$\frac{1}{5}(5x) < \frac{1}{5}(30)$$

Simplifying, we have

$$x < 6$$

The graph of the solution set is

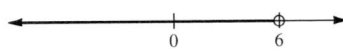

(b) Solve and graph the solution set for $-4x \geq 28$.

In this case we want to multiply both sides of the inequality by $-\dfrac{1}{4}$ to leave x alone on the left.

$$\left(-\frac{1}{4}\right)(-4x) \leq \left(-\frac{1}{4}\right)(28)$$

Reverse the sense of the inequality because you are multiplying by a negative number!

or $\qquad x \leq -7$

The graph of the solution set is

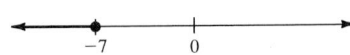

 CHECK YOURSELF 6

Solve and graph the solution sets:

(a) $7x > 35$ **(b)** $-8x \leq 48$

Example 7 illustrates the use of the multiplication property when fractions are involved in an inequality.

Example 7

Solving and Graphing Inequalities

(a) Solve and graph the solution set for

$$\frac{x}{4} > 3$$

Here we multiply both sides of the inequality by 4. This will isolate x on the left.

$$4\left(\frac{x}{4}\right) > 4(3)$$

$$x > 12$$

The graph of the solution set is

(b) Solve and graph the solution set for

$$-\frac{x}{6} \geq -3$$

In this case, we multiply both sides of the inequality by -6:

NOTE Note that we reverse the sense of the inequality because we are multiplying by a negative number.

$$(-6)\left(-\frac{x}{6}\right) \leq (-6)(-3)$$

$$x \leq 18$$

The graph of the solution set is

✔ CHECK YOURSELF 7

Solve and graph the solution sets for the following inequalities.

(a) $\dfrac{x}{5} \leq 4$ **(b)** $-\dfrac{x}{3} < -7$

Example 8

Solving and Graphing Inequalities

(a) Solve and graph the solution set for $5x - 3 < 2x$.

First, add 3 to both sides to undo the subtraction on the left.

$$\begin{array}{ll} 5x - 3 < 2x & \\ \underline{+3+3} & \text{Add 3 to both sides to undo the subtraction.} \\ 5x < 2x + 3 & \end{array}$$

Now add $-2x$, so that only the number remains on the right.

$$\begin{array}{ll} 5x < 2x + 3 & \\ \underline{+(-2x)+(-2x)} & \text{Add } -2x \text{ to isolate the number on the right.} \\ 3x < 3 & \end{array}$$

NOTE Note that the multiplication property also allows us to divide both sides by a nonzero number.

Next *divide* both sides by 3.

$$\frac{3x}{3} < \frac{3}{3}$$

$$x < 1$$

The graph of the solution set is

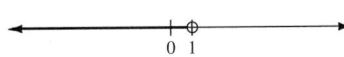

(b) Solve and graph the solution set for $2 - 5x < 7$.

$$
\begin{array}{rcl}
2 - 5x &<& 7 \\
-2 & & -2 \qquad \text{Add } -2. \\
\hline
-5x &<& 5
\end{array}
$$

$$\frac{-5x}{-5} > \frac{5}{-5} \qquad \text{Divide by } -5. \text{ Be sure to reverse the}$$
$$\text{sense of the inequality.}$$

or $x > -1$

The graph is

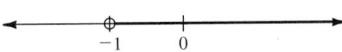

CHECK YOURSELF 8

Solve and graph the solution sets.

(a) $4x + 9 \geq x$ 　　　　　　　　　　　 **(b)** $5 - 6x < 41$

As with equations, we will collect all variable terms on one side and all constant terms on the other.

Example 9

Solving and Graphing Inequalities

Solve and graph the solution set for $5x - 5 \geq 3x + 4$.

$$
\begin{array}{rcl}
5x - 5 &\geq& 3x + 4 \\
+5 & & +5 \qquad \text{Add } 5. \\
\hline
5x &\geq& 3x + 9 \\
-3x & & -3x \qquad \text{Add } -3x. \\
\hline
2x &\geq& 9
\end{array}
$$

$$\frac{2x}{2} \geq \frac{9}{2} \qquad \text{Divide by } 2.$$

$$x \geq \frac{9}{2}$$

The graph of the solution set is

CHECK YOURSELF 9

Solve and graph the solution set for

$8x + 3 < 4x - 13$

Be especially careful when negative coefficients occur in the solution process.

Example 10

Solving and Graphing Inequalities

Solve and graph the solution set for $2x + 4 < 5x - 2$.

$$
\begin{array}{rcl}
2x + 4 & < & 5x - 2 \\
-4 & & -4 \qquad \text{Add } -4.
\end{array}
$$

$$
\begin{array}{rcl}
2x & < & 5x - 6 \\
-5x & & -5x \qquad \text{Add } -5x.
\end{array}
$$

$$
\begin{array}{rcl}
-3x & < & -6
\end{array}
$$

$$
\dfrac{-3x}{-3} > \dfrac{-6}{-3} \qquad \text{Divide by } -3, \text{ and reverse the sense of the inequality.}
$$

$$
x > 2
$$

The graph of the solution set is

CHECK YOURSELF 10

Solve and graph the solution set.

$5x + 12 \geq 10x - 8$

The solution of inequalities may also require the use of the distributive property.

Example 11

Solving and Graphing Inequalities

Solve and graph the solution set for

$5(x - 2) \geq -8$

Applying the distributive property on the left yields

$5x - 10 \geq -8$

Solving as before yields

$$
\begin{array}{rcl}
5x - 10 & \geq & -8 \\
+10 & & +10 \qquad \text{Add } 10.
\end{array}
$$

$$
5x \geq 2
$$

$$
\text{or} \qquad x \geq \dfrac{2}{5} \qquad \text{Divide by } 5.
$$

The graph of the solution set is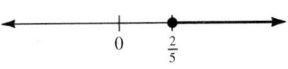

 CHECK YOURSELF 11

Solve and graph the solution set.

$4(x + 3) < 9$

Some applications are solved by using an inequality instead of an equation. Example 12 illustrates such an application.

Example 12

Solving an Application with Inequalities

Mohammed needs a mean score of 92 or higher on four tests to get an A. So far his scores are 94, 89, and 88. What score on the fourth test will get him an A?

NOTE What do you need to find?

Step 1   We are looking for the score that will, when combined with the other scores, give Mohammed an A.

NOTE Assign a letter to the unknown.
NOTE Write an inequality.

Step 2   Let x represent a fourth-test score that will get him an A.

Step 3   The inequality will have the mean on the left side, which must be greater than or equal to the 92 on the right.

$$\frac{94 + 89 + 88 + x}{4} \geq 92$$

NOTE Solve the inequality.

Step 4   First, multiply both sides by 4:

$94 + 89 + 88 + x \geq 368$

Then add the test scores:

$183 + 88 + x \geq 368$

$271 + x \geq 368$

Subtracting 271 from both sides,

$x \geq 97$

Step 5   To check the solution, we find the mean of the four test scores, 94, 89, 88, and 97.

$$\frac{94 + 89 + 88 + 97}{4} = \frac{368}{4} = 92$$

 CHECK YOURSELF 12

Felicia needs a mean score of at least 75 on five tests to get a passing grade in her health class. On her first four tests she has scores of 68, 79, 71, and 70. What score on the fifth test will give her a passing grade?

The following outline (or algorithm) summarizes our work in this section.

Step by Step: Solving Linear Inequalities

Step 1   Remove any grouping symbols and combine any like terms appearing on either side of the inequality.

Step 2   Apply the addition property to write an equivalent inequality with the variable term on one side of the inequality and the number on the other.

Step 3   Apply the multiplication property to write an equivalent inequality with the variable isolated on one side of the inequality. Be sure to reverse the sense of the inequality if you multiply or divide by a negative number. The set of solutions derived in step 3 can then be graphed on a number line.

CHECK YOURSELF ANSWERS

1. (a) $>$; (b) $<$ **2.**

3. (a)   ;   (b)

4. $x > 6$ **5.** $x \leq 10$

6. (a) $x > 5$;   (b) $x \geq -6$

7. (a) $x \leq 20$;   (b) $x > 21$

8. (a) $x \geq -3$;   (b) $x > -6$

9. $x < -4$ **10.** $x \leq 4$

11. $x < -\dfrac{3}{4}$ **12.** 87 or greater

Name _____

Section _____ Date _____

Complete the statements, using the symbol $<$ or $>$.

1. 5 _____ 10

2. 9 _____ 8

3. 7 _____ -2

4. 0 _____ -5

5. 0 _____ 4

6. -10 _____ -5

7. -2 _____ -5

8. -4 _____ -11

Write each inequality in words.

9. $x < 3$

10. $x \leq -5$

11. $x \geq -4$

12. $x < -2$

13. $-5 \leq x$

14. $2 < x$

Graph the solution set of each of the following inequalities.

15. $x > 2$

16. $x < -3$

17. $x < 9$

18. $x > 4$

19. $x > 1$

20. $x < -2$

21. $x < 8$

22. $x > 3$

23. $x > -5$

24. $x < -4$

ANSWERS

1. _____

2. _____

3. _____

4. _____

5. _____

6. _____

7. _____

8. _____

9. _____

10. _____

11. _____

12. _____

13. _____

14. _____

15. _____

16. _____

17. _____

18. _____

19. _____

20. _____

21. _____

22. _____

23. _____

24. _____

25. _____

26. _____

27. _____

28. _____

29. _____

30. _____

31. _____

32. _____

33. _____

34. _____

35. _____

36. _____

37. _____

38. _____

39. _____

40. _____

41. _____

42. _____

43. _____

44. _____

45. _____

46. _____

47. _____

48. _____

25. $x \geq 9$

26. $x \geq 0$

27. $x < 0$

28. $x \leq -3$

Solve and graph the solution set of each of the following inequalities.

29. $x - 7 < 6$

30. $x + 5 \leq 4$

31. $x + 8 \geq 10$

32. $x - 11 > -14$

33. $5x < 4x + 7$

34. $3x \geq 2x - 4$

35. $6x - 8 \leq 5x$

36. $3x + 2 > 2x$

37. $4x - 3 \geq 3x + 5$

38. $5x + 2 \leq 4x - 6$

39. $7x + 5 < 6x - 4$

40. $8x - 7 > 7x + 3$

41. $3x \leq 9$

42. $5x > 20$

43. $5x > -35$

44. $7x \leq -21$

45. $-6x \geq 18$

46. $-9x < 45$

47. $-10x < -60$

48. $-12x \geq -48$

49. $\dfrac{x}{4} > 5$

50. $\dfrac{x}{3} \le -3$

51. $-\dfrac{x}{2} \ge -3$

52. $-\dfrac{x}{5} < 4$

53. $\dfrac{2x}{3} < 6$

54. $\dfrac{3x}{4} \ge -9$

55. $5x > 3x + 8$

56. $4x \le x - 9$

57. $5x - 2 > 3x$

58. $7x + 3 \ge 2x$

59. $3 - 2x > 5$

60. $5 - 3x \le 17$

61. $2x \ge 5x + 18$

62. $3x < 7x - 28$

63. $5x - 3 \le 3x + 15$

64. $8x + 7 > 5x + 34$

65. $9x + 7 > 2x - 28$

66. $10x - 5 \le 8x - 25$

67. $7x - 5 < 3x + 2$

68. $5x - 2 \ge 2x - 7$

69. $5x + 7 > 8x - 17$

70. $4x - 3 \le 9x + 27$

71. $3x - 2 \le 5x + 3$

72. $2x + 3 > 8x - 2$

ANSWERS

49. _____

50. _____

51. _____

52. _____

53. _____

54. _____

55. _____

56. _____

57. _____

58. _____

59. _____

60. _____

61. _____

62. _____

63. _____

64. _____

65. _____

66. _____

67. _____

68. _____

69. _____

70. _____

71. _____

72. _____

73. _____

74. _____

75. _____

76. _____

77. _____

78. _____

79. _____

80. _____

81. _____

82. _____

83. _____

84. _____

85. _____

86. _____

87. _____

88. _____

89. _____

73. $4(x + 7) \leq 2x + 31$

$\longleftarrow\hspace{3cm}\longrightarrow$

74. $6(x - 5) > 3x - 26$

$\longleftarrow\hspace{3cm}\longrightarrow$

75. $2(x - 7) > 5x - 12$

$\longleftarrow\hspace{3cm}\longrightarrow$

76. $3(x + 4) \leq 7x + 7$

$\longleftarrow\hspace{3cm}\longrightarrow$

Translate the following statements into inequalities. Let x represent the number in each case.

77. 5 more than a number is greater than 3.

78. 3 less than a number is less than or equal to 5.

79. 4 less than twice a number is less than or equal to 7.

80. 10 more than a number is greater than negative 2.

81. 4 times a number, decreased by 15, is greater than that number.

82. 2 times a number, increased by 28, is less than or equal to 6 times that number.

Match each inequality on the right with a statement on the left.

83. x is nonnegative   **a.** $x \geq 0$

84. x is negative   **b.** $x \geq 5$

85. x is no more than 5   **c.** $x \leq 5$

86. x is positive   **d.** $x > 0$

87. x is at least 5   **e.** $x < 5$

88. x is less than 5   **f.** $x < 0$

89. Panda population. There are fewer than 1000 wild giant pandas left in the bamboo forests of China. Write an inequality expressing this relationship.

90. _____

91. _____

92. _____

93. _____

94. _____

95. _____

96. _____

97. _____

90. **Forestry.** Let C represent the amount of Canadian forest and M represent the amount of Mexican forest. Write an inequality showing the relationship of the forests of Mexico and Canada if Canada contains at least 9 times as much forest as Mexico.

91. **Test scores.** To pass a course with a grade of B or better, Liza must have an average of 80 or more. Her grades on three tests are 72, 81, and 79. Write an inequality representing the score that Liza must get on the fourth test to obtain a B average or better for the course.

92. **Test scores.** Sam must have an average of 70 or more in his summer course to obtain a grade of C. His first three test grades were 75, 63, and 68. Write an inequality representing the score that Sam must get in the last test to get a C grade.

93. **Commission.** Juanita is a salesperson for a manufacturing company. She may choose to receive $500 or 5 percent commission on her sales as payment for her work. How much does she need to sell to make the 5 percent offer a better deal?

94. **Telephone costs.** The cost for a long distance telephone call is $0.36 for the first minute and $0.21 for each additional minute or portion thereof. The total cost of the call cannot exceed $3. Write an inequality representing the number of minutes a person could talk without exceeding $3.

95. **Geometry.** The perimeter of a rectangle is to be no greater than 250 centimeters (cm) and the length must be 105 cm. Find the maximum width of the rectangle.

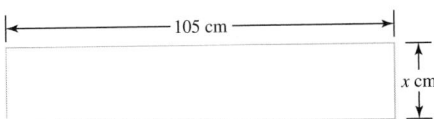

96. **Recreation.** Sarah bowled 136 and 189 in her first two games. What must she bowl in her third game to have an average of at least 170?

97. You are the office manager for a small company. You need to acquire a new copier for the office. You find a suitable one that leases for $250 a month from the copy machine company. It costs 2.5¢ per copy to run the machine. You purchase paper for $3.50 a ream (500 sheets). If your copying budget is no more than $950 per month, is this machine a good choice? Write a brief recommendation to the Purchasing Department. Use equations and inequalities to explain your recommendation.

98. _____

98. Your aunt calls to ask your help in making a decision about buying a new refrigerator. She says that she found two that seem to fit her needs, and both are supposed to last at least 14 years, according to *Consumer Reports.* The initial cost for one refrigerator is $712, but it only uses 88 kilowatt-hours (kWh) per month. The other refrigerator costs $519 and uses an estimated 100 kWh/per month. You do not know the price of electricity per kilowatt-hour where your aunt lives, so you will have to decide what in cents per kilowatt-hour will make the first refrigerator cheaper to run for its 14 years of expected usefulness. Write your aunt a letter explaining what you did to calculate this cost, and tell her to make her decision based on how the kilowatt-hour rate she has to pay in her area compares with your estimation.

Answers

1. $5 < 10$ **3.** $7 > -2$ **5.** $0 < 4$ **7.** $-2 > -5$ **9.** x is less than 3

11. x is greater than or equal to -4 **13.** -5 is less than or equal to x

15.

17.

19.

21.

23.

25.

27.

29. $x < 13$

31. $x \geq 2$

33. $x < 7$

35. $x \leq 8$

37. $x \geq 8$

39. $x < -9$

41. $x \leq 3$

43. $x > -7$

45. $x \leq -3$

47. $x > 6$

49. $x > 20$

51. $x \leq 6$

53. $x < 9$

55. $x > 4$

57. $x > 1$

59. $x < -1$

61. $x \leq -6$

63. $x \leq 9$

65. $x > -5$

67. $x < \dfrac{7}{4}$

69. $x < 8$

71. $x \geq -\dfrac{5}{2}$

73. $x \leq \dfrac{3}{2}$

75. $x < -\dfrac{2}{3}$

77. $x + 5 > 3$ **79.** $2x - 4 \leq 7$

81. $4x - 15 > x$ **83.** a **85.** c **87.** b **89.** $P < 1000$ **91.** $x \geq 88$

93. $> \$10{,}000$ **95.** 20 cm **97.**

1.15 Interval Notation and Graphs

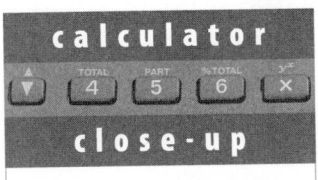
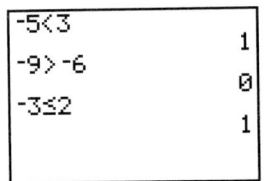
If an inequality involves a variable, then which real numbers can be used in place of the variable to obtain a correct statement? The set of all such numbers is the **solution set** to the inequality. For example, $x < 3$ is correct if x is replaced by any number that lies to the left of 3 on the number line:

$$1.5 < 3, \qquad 0 < 3, \qquad \text{and} \qquad -2 < 3$$

The set of real numbers to the left of 3 is written in set notation as $\{x \mid x < 3\}$, in **interval notation** as $(-\infty, 3)$, and graphed in Fig. 1.142:

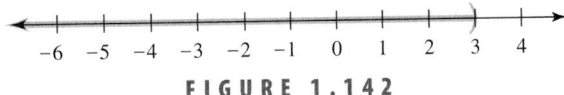

FIGURE 1.142

Note that $-\infty$ (negative infinity) is not a number, but it indicates that there is no end to the real numbers less than 3. The parenthesis used next to the 3 in the interval notation and on the graph means that 3 is not included in the solution set to $x < 3$.

An inequality such as $x \geq 1$ is satisfied by 1 and any real number that lies to the right of 1 on the number line. The solution set to $x \geq 1$ is written in set notation as $\{x \mid x \geq 1\}$, in interval notation as $[1, \infty)$, and graphed in Fig. 1.143:

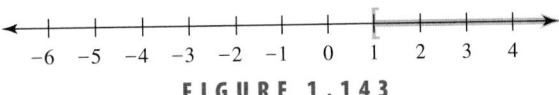

FIGURE 1.143

The bracket used next to the 1 in the interval notation and on the graph means that 1 is in the solution set to $x \geq 1$.

The solution set to an inequality can be stated symbolically with set notation and interval notation, or visually with a graph. Interval notation is popular because it is simpler to write than set notation. The interval notation and graph for each of the four basic inequalities is summarized as follows.

Basic Interval Notation (k any real number)		
Inequality	**Solution Set with Interval Notation**	**Graph**
$x > k$	(k, ∞)	
$x \geq k$	$[k, \infty)$	
$x < k$	$(-\infty, k)$	
$x \leq k$	$(-\infty, k]$	

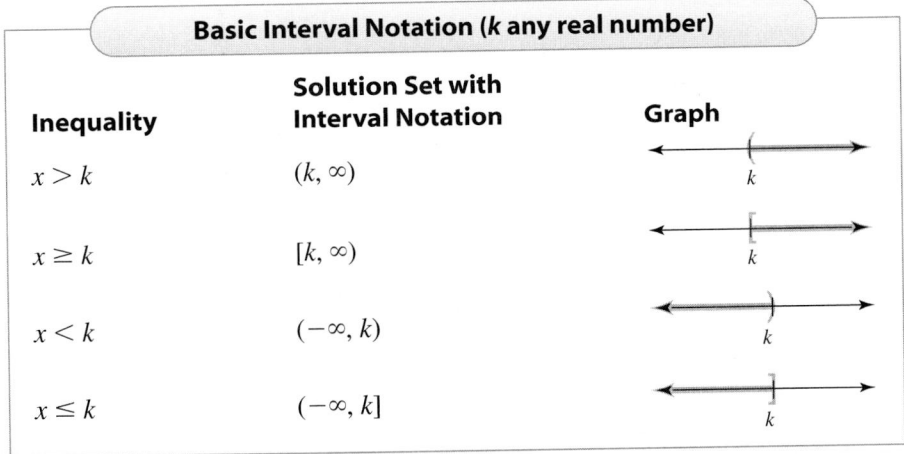

Note that a bracket is used next to k if k is in the interval and a parenthesis when k is not in the interval. A parenthesis is always used on the infinite end of the interval because ∞ is not a number that might or might not be in the interval.

EXAMPLE 2

Interval notation and graphs

Write the solution set to each inequality in interval notation and graph it.

a) $x > -5$

b) $x \le 2$

Solution

a) The solution set to the inequality $x > -5$ is $\{x \mid x > -5\}$. The solution set is the interval of all numbers to the right of -5 on the number line. This set is written in interval notation as $(-5, \infty)$, and it is graphed in Fig. 1.144.

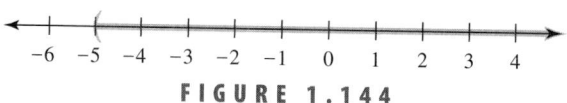

FIGURE 1.144

b) The solution set to $x \le 2$ is $\{x \mid x \le 2\}$. This set includes 2 and all real numbers to the left of 2. Because 2 is included, we use a bracket at 2. The interval notation for this set is $(-\infty, 2]$. The graph is shown in Fig. 1.145.

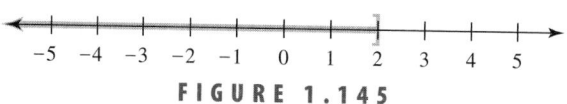

FIGURE 1.145

Solving Linear Inequalities

We define a linear equation as an equation of the form $ax + b = 0$. If we replace the equality symbol in a linear equation with an inequality symbol, we have a linear inequality.

Linear Inequality

A **linear inequality** in one variable x is any inequality of the form $ax + b < 0$, where a and b are real numbers, with $a \ne 0$. In place of $<$ we may also use $\le$, $>$, or $\ge$.

Inequalities that can be rewritten as $ax + b > 0$ are also called linear inequalities.

Equivalent inequalities have the same solution set. Any real number can be added to or subtracted from each side of an inequality to get an equivalent inequality. For example, if $x + 2 < 8$ then we can subtract 2 from each side to get $x < 6$. If $x - 3 > 4$, then we can add 3 to each side to get $x > 7$.

We can also multiply or divide each side of an inequality by any nonzero real number to get an equivalent inequality. However, multiplying or dividing by a negative number reverses the inequality. To understand why, multiply each side of $5 < 6$ by -1. The correct result is $-5 > -6$.

These properties of inequality are summarized as follows.

Properties of Inequality

Addition Property of Inequality
If the same number is added to both sides of an inequality, then the solution set to the inequality is unchanged.

Multiplication Property of Inequality
If both sides of an inequality are multiplied by the same *positive number,* then the solution set to the inequality is unchanged.

If both sides of an inequality are multiplied by the same *negative number* and *the inequality symbol is reversed,* then the solution set to the inequality is unchanged.

Because subtraction is defined in terms of addition, the addition property of inequality also allows us to subtract the same number from both sides. Because division is defined in terms of multiplication, the multiplication property of inequality also allows us to divide both sides by the same nonzero real number *as long as we reverse the inequality symbol when dividing by a negative number.*

In the next example we use the properties of inequality to solve an inequality in the same manner that we solve equations.

E X A M P L E   3   **Solving inequalities**

Solve each inequality. State and graph the solution set.

a) $2x - 7 < -1$ **b)** $5 - 3x < 11$

Solution

a) We proceed exactly as we do when solving equations:

$$2x - 7 < -1 \quad \text{Original inequality}$$
$$2x < 6 \quad \text{Add 7 to each side.}$$
$$x < 3 \quad \text{Divide each side by 2.}$$

The solution set is written in set notation as $\{x \mid x < 3\}$ and in interval notation as $(-\infty, 3)$. The graph is shown in Fig. 1.146.

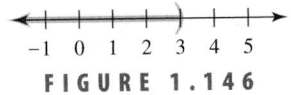

FIGURE 1.146

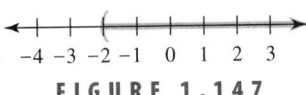

FIGURE 1.147

b) We divide by a negative number to solve this inequality.

$$5 - 3x < 11 \quad \text{Original equation}$$
$$-3x < 6 \quad \text{Subtract 5 from each side.}$$
$$x > -2 \quad \text{Divide each side by } -3 \text{ and reverse the inequality symbol.}$$

The solution set is written in set notation as $\{x \mid x > -2\}$ and in interval notation as $(-2, \infty)$. The graph is shown in Fig. 1.147.

---

calculator close-up

To check the solution to Example 3(b), press the Y = key and let $y_1 = 5 - 3x$.

```
Plot1 Plot2 Plot3
\Y1■5-3X
\Y2=
\Y3=
\Y4=
\Y5=
\Y6=
\Y7=
```

Press TBLSET to set the starting point for x and the distance between the x-values.

```
TABLE SETUP
 TblStart=0
 △Tbl=1
Indpnt: Auto Ask
Depend: Auto Ask
```

Now press TABLE and scroll through values of x until y_1 gets smaller than 11.

```
  X  │ Y1 │
 -4  │ 17 │
 -3  │ 14 │
 -2  │ 11 │
 -1  │  8 │
  0  │  5 │
  1  │  2 │
  2  │ -1 │
Y1■5-3X
```

This table supports the conclusion that if $x > -2$, then $5 - 3x < 11$.

EXAMPLE 4

Solving inequalities

Solve $\frac{8 + 3x}{-5} \geq -4$. State and graph the solution set.

Solution

$$\frac{8 + 3x}{-5} \geq -4 \qquad \text{Original inequality}$$

$$-5\left(\frac{8 + 3x}{-5}\right) \leq -5(-4) \qquad \text{Multiply each side by } -5 \text{ and reverse the inequality symbol.}$$

$$8 + 3x \leq 20 \qquad \text{Simplify.}$$

$$3x \leq 12 \qquad \text{Subtract 8 from each side.}$$

$$x \leq 4 \qquad \text{Divide each side by 3.}$$

The solution set is $(-\infty, 4]$, and its graph is shown in Fig. 1.148.

```
◄──┼────┼────┼────┼────┼────┼────┼────┼────┼────┤────┼──►
  -5   -4   -3   -2   -1    0    1    2    3    4    5
```

FIGURE 1.148

EXAMPLE 5

An inequality with fractions

Solve $\frac{1}{2}x - \frac{2}{3} \leq x + \frac{4}{3}$. State and graph the solution set.

Solution

First multiply each side of the inequality by 6, the LCD:

$$\frac{1}{2}x - \frac{2}{3} \leq x + \frac{4}{3} \qquad \text{Original inequality}$$

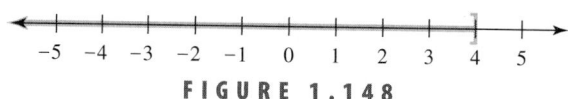

Multiplying by positive 6 does not reverse the inequality.

$$3x - 4 \le 6x + 8 \qquad \text{Distributive property}$$

$$3x \le 6x + 12 \qquad \text{Add 4 to each side.}$$

$$-3x \le 12 \qquad \text{Subtract } 6x \text{ from each side.}$$

$$x \ge -4 \qquad \text{Divide each side by } -3 \text{ and reverse the inequality.}$$

The solution set is the interval $[-4, \infty)$. Its graph is shown in Fig. 1.149.

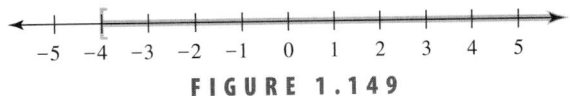

FIGURE 1.149

Applications

Inequalities have applications just as equations do. To use inequalities, we must be able to translate a verbal problem into an algebraic inequality. Inequality can be expressed verbally in a variety of ways.

E X A M P L E   6

Writing inequalities

Identify the variable and write an inequality that describes the situation.

a) Chris paid more than $200 for a suit.

b) A candidate for president must be at least 35 years old.

c) The capacity of an elevator is at most 1500 pounds.

d) The company must hire no fewer than 10 programmers.

Solution

a) If c is the cost of the suit in dollars, then $c > 200$.

b) If a is the age of the candidate in years, then $a \ge 35$.

c) If x is the capacity of the elevator in pounds, then $x \le 1500$.

d) If n represents the number of programmers and n is not less than 10, then $n \ge 10$.

In Example 6(d) we know that n is not less than 10. So there are exactly two other possibilities: n is greater than 10 or equal to 10. If $x \ne 4$, then either $x > 4$ or $x < 4$. If w is not greater than 5, then $w \le 5$. The fact that there are only three possibilities when comparing two numbers is called the **trichotomy property.**

Trichotomy Property

For any two real numbers a and b, exactly one of the following is true:

$$a < b, \qquad a = b, \qquad \text{or} \qquad a > b$$

We follow the same steps to solve problems involving inequalities as we do to solve problems involving equations.

E X A M P L E   7

Price range

Lois plans to spend less than $500 on an electric dryer, including the 9% sales tax and a $64 setup charge. In what range is the selling price of the dryer that she can afford?

Solution

If we let x represent the selling price in dollars for the dryer, then the amount of sales tax is $0.09x$. Because her total cost must be less than $500, we can write the following inequality:

$$x + 0.09x + 64 < 500$$

$$1.09x < 436 \qquad \text{Subtract 64 from each side.}$$

$$x < \frac{436}{1.09} \qquad \text{Divide each side by 1.09.}$$

$$x < 400$$

The selling price of the dryer must be less than $400. ∎

Note that if we had written the equation $x + 0.09x + 64 = 500$ for the last example, we would have gotten $x = 400$. We could then have concluded that the selling price must be less than $400. This would certainly solve the problem, but it would not illustrate the use of inequalities. The original problem describes an inequality, and we should solve it as an inequality.

E X A M P L E   8

Paying off the mortgage

Tessie owns a piece of land on which she owes $12,760 to a bank. She wants to sell the land for enough money to at least pay off the mortgage. The real estate agent gets 6% of the selling price, and her city has a $400 real estate transfer tax paid by the seller. What should the range of the selling price be for Tessie to get at least enough money to pay off her mortgage?

Solution

If x is the selling price in dollars, then the commission is $0.06x$. We can write an inequality expressing the fact that the selling price minus the real estate commission minus the $400 tax must be at least $12,760:

$$x - 0.06x - 400 \geq 12,760$$

$$0.94x - 400 \geq 12,760 \qquad 1 - 0.06 = 0.94$$

$$0.94x \geq 13,160 \qquad \text{Add 400 to each side.}$$

$$x \geq \frac{13,160}{0.94} \qquad \text{Divide each side by 0.94.}$$

$$x \geq 14,000$$

The selling price must be at least $14,000 for Tessie to pay off the mortgage. ∎

WARM-UPS

True or false? Explain your answer.

1. $0 < 0$ 2. $-300 > -2$ 3. $-60 \leq -60$
4. The inequality $6 < x$ is equivalent to $x < 6$.
5. The inequality $-2x < 10$ is equivalent to $x < -5$.
6. The solution set to $3x \geq -12$ is $(-\infty, -4]$.
7. The solution set to $-x > 4$ is $(-\infty, -4)$.
8. If x is no larger than 8, then $x \leq 8$.

9. If m is any real number, then exactly one of the following is true: $m < 0$, $m = 0$, or $m > 0$.

10. The number -2 is a member of the solution set to the inequality $3 - 4x \le 11$.

1.14   EXERCISES

Reading and Writing   After reading this section, write out the answers to these questions. Use complete sentences.

1. What is an inequality?

2. What symbols are used to express inequality?

3. What does it mean when we say that a is less than b?

4. What is a linear inequality?

5. How does solving linear inequalities differ from solving linear equations?

6. What verbal phrases are used to indicate an inequality?

Determine whether each inequality is true or false. See Example 1.

7. $-3 < -9$ **8.** $-8 > -7$

9. $0 \le 8$ **10.** $-6 \ge -8$

11. $(-3)20 > (-3)40$ **12.** $(-1)(-3) < (-1)(5)$

13. $9 - (-3) \le 12$ **14.** $(-4)(-5) + 2 \ge 21$

Determine whether each inequality is satisfied by the given number.

15. $2x - 4 < 8, -3$ **16.** $5 - 3x > -1, 6$

17. $2x - 3 \le 3x - 9, 5$ **18.** $6 - 3x \ge 10 - 2x, -4$

19. $5 - x < 4 - 2x, -1$ **20.** $3x - 7 \ge 3x - 10, 9$

Write the solution set in interval notation and graph it. See Example 2.

21. $x \le -1$

22. $x \ge -7$

23. $x > 20$

24. $x < 30$

25. $3 \le x$

26. $-2 > x$

27. $x < 2.3$

28. $x \le 4.5$

Rewrite each set in interval notation.

29. $\{x \mid x > 1\}$ **30.** $\{x \mid x < 3\}$

31. $\{x \mid x \le -3\}$ **32.** $\{x \mid x \ge -2\}$

33. $\{x \mid x < 5\}$ **34.** $\{x \mid x > -7\}$

35. $\{x \mid x \ge -4\}$ **36.** $\{x \mid x \le -9\}$

Fill in the blank with an inequality symbol so that the two statements are equivalent.

37. $x + 5 > 12$ **38.** $2x - 3 \le -4$ **39.** $-x < 6$
     x ___ 7 $2x$ ___ -1 x ___ -6

40. $-5 \ge -x$ **41.** $-2x \ge 8$ **42.** $-5x > -10$
     5 ___ x x ___ -4 x ___ 2

43. $4 < x$ **44.** $-9 \le -x$
     x ___ 4 x ___ 9

Solve each of the following inequalities. Express the solution set in interval notation and graph it. See Examples 3–5.

45. $7x > -14$

46. $4x \leq -8$

47. $-3x \leq 12$

48. $-2x > -6$

49. $2x - 3 > 7$

50. $3x - 2 < 6$

51. $3 - 5x \leq 18$

52. $5 - 4x \geq 19$

53. $\dfrac{x - 3}{-5} < -2$

54. $\dfrac{2x - 3}{4} > 6$

55. $\dfrac{5 - 3x}{4} \leq 2$

56. $\dfrac{7 - 5x}{-2} \geq -1$

57. $3 - \dfrac{1}{4}x \geq 2$

58. $5 - \dfrac{1}{3}x > 2$

59. $\dfrac{1}{4}x - \dfrac{1}{2} < \dfrac{1}{2}x - \dfrac{2}{3}$

60. $\dfrac{1}{3}x - \dfrac{1}{6} < \dfrac{1}{6}x - \dfrac{1}{2}$

61. $\dfrac{y - 3}{2} > \dfrac{1}{2} - \dfrac{y - 5}{4}$

62. $\dfrac{y - 1}{3} - \dfrac{y + 1}{5} > 1$

Solve each inequality and graph the solution set.

63. $2x + 3 > 2(x - 4)$

64. $-2(5x - 1) \leq -5(5 + 2x)$

65. $-4(2x - 5) \leq 2(6 - 4x)$

66. $-3(2x - 1) \leq 2(5 - 3x)$

67. $-\dfrac{1}{2}(x - 6) < \dfrac{1}{2}x + 2$

68. $-3\left(\dfrac{1}{2}x - \dfrac{1}{4}\right) > \dfrac{x}{2} - \dfrac{1}{4}$

69. $4.273 + 2.8x \leq 10.985$

70. $1.064 < 5.94 - 3.2x$

71. $3.25x - 27.39 > 4.06 + 5.1x$

72. $4.86(3.2x - 1.7) > 5.19 - x$

Identify the variable and write an inequality that describes each situation. See Example 6.

73. Tony is taller than 6 feet.

74. Glenda is under 60 years old.

75. Wilma makes less than $80,000 per year.

76. Bubba weighs over 80 pounds.

77. The maximum speed for the Concorde is 1450 miles per hour (mph).

78. The minimum speed on the freeway is 45 mph.

79. Julie can afford at most $400 per month.

80. Fred must have at least a 3.2 grade point average.

81. Burt is no taller than 5 feet.

82. Ernie cannot run faster than 10 mph.

83. Tina makes no more than $8.20 per hour.

84. Rita will not take less than $12,000 for the car.

Solve each problem by using an inequality. See Examples 7 and 8.

85. *Car shopping.* Jennifer is shopping for a new car. In addition to the price of the car, there is an 8% sales tax and a $172 title and license fee. If Jennifer decides that she will spend less than $10,000 total, then what is the price range for the car?

86. *Sewing machines.* Charles wants to buy a sewing machine in a city with a 10% sales tax. He has at most $700 to spend. In what price range should he look?

87. *Truck shopping.* Linda and Bob are shopping for a new truck in a city with a 9% sales tax. There is also an $80 title and license fee to pay. They want to get a good truck and plan to spend at least $10,000. What is the price range for the truck?

88. *Curly's contribution.* Larry, Curly, and Moe are going to buy their mother a color television set. Larry has a better job than Curly and agrees to contribute twice as much as Curly. Moe is unemployed and can spare only $50. If the kind of television Mama wants costs at least $600, then what is the price range for Curly's contribution?

89. *Renting a Mustang.* Hillary can rent a Ford Mustang from Alpha Car Rental for $45 per day with no charge for miles. From Beta Car Rental she can get the same car for $35 per day plus 25 cents per mile. For what number of daily miles is Beta cheaper?

90. *Renting a Cadillac.* George can rent a Cadillac from Gamma Car Rental for $50 per day plus 35 cents per mile. He can get the same car from Delta Car Rental for $35 per day plus 45 cents per mile. For what number of daily miles is Delta cheaper?

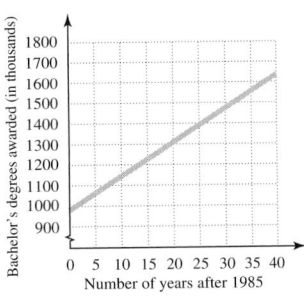 

FIGURE FOR EXERCISE 91

91. *Bachelor's degrees.* The graph shows the number of bachelor's degrees awarded in the United States each year since 1985 (National Center for Education Statistics, www.nces.ed.gov).
a) Has the number of bachelor's degrees been increasing or decreasing since 1985?
b) The formula $B = 16.45n + 980.20$ can be used to approximate the number of degrees awarded in thousands in the year 1985 + n. What is the first year in which the number of bachelor's degrees will exceed 1.3 million?

92. *Master's degrees.* In 1985, 15.9% of all degrees awarded in U.S. higher education were master's degrees (National Center for Education Statistics). If the formulas $M = 7.79n + 287.87$ and $T = 30.95n + 1808.22$ give the number of master's degrees and the total number of higher education degrees awarded in thousands, respectively, in the year 1985 + n, then what is the first year in which more than 20% of all degrees awarded will be master's degrees?

93. *Weighted average.* Professor Jorgenson gives only a midterm exam and a final exam. The semester average is computed by taking $\frac{1}{3}$ of the midterm exam score plus $\frac{2}{3}$ of the final exam score. The grade is determined from the semester average by using the grading scale given in the table. If Stanley scored only 56 on the midterm, then for what range of scores on the final exam would he get a C or better in the course?

Grading	Scale
90–100	A
80–89	B
70–79	C
60–69	D

TABLE FOR EXERCISES 93 AND 94

94. *C or better.* Professor Brown counts her midterm as $\frac{2}{3}$ of the grade and her final as $\frac{1}{3}$ of the grade. Wilbert scored only 56 on the midterm. If Professor Brown also uses the grading scale given in the table, then what range of scores on the final exam would give Wilbert a C or better in the course?

ANSWERS

1. An inequality is a sentence that expresses inequality between two algebraic expressions.

2. To express inequality we use the symbols $<$, $\leq$, $>$, and $\geq$.

3. If a is less than b, then a lies to the left of b on the number line.

4. A linear inequality is an inequality of the form $ax + b > 0$ or with any of the other inequality symbols used in place of $>$.

5. When you multiply or divide by a negative number, the inequality symbol is reversed.

6. We can verbally indicate inequality with words like "less than," "at least," "greater than," and "at most."

7. F **8.** F **9.** T **10.** T **11.** T **12.** F **13.** T

14. T **15.** Yes **16.** No **17.** No **18.** Yes

19. No **20.** Yes

21. $(-\infty, -1]$

22. $[-7, \infty)$

23. $(20, \infty)$

24. $(-\infty, 30)$

25. $[3, \infty)$

26. $(-\infty, -2)$

27. $(-\infty, 2.3)$

28. $(-\infty, 4.5]$

29. $(1, \infty)$ **30.** $(-\infty, 3)$ **31.** $(-\infty, -3]$ **32.** $[-2, \infty)$

33. $(-\infty, 5)$ **34.** $(-7, \infty)$ **35.** $[-4, \infty)$ **36.** $(-\infty, -9)$

37. $>$ **38.** $\leq$ **39.** $>$ **40.** $\leq$ **41.** $\leq$ **42.** $<$

43. $>$ **44.** $\leq$

45. $(-2, \infty)$

46. $(-\infty, -2]$

47. $[-4, \infty)$

48. $(-\infty, 3)$

49. $(5, \infty)$

50. $\left(-\infty, \frac{8}{3}\right)$

51. $[-3, \infty)$

52. $\left(-\infty, -\frac{7}{2}\right]$

53. $(13, \infty)$

54. $\left(\frac{27}{2}, \infty\right)$

55. $[-1, \infty)$

56. $[1, \infty)$

57. $(-\infty, 4]$

58. $(-\infty, 9)$

59. $\left(\frac{2}{3}, \infty\right)$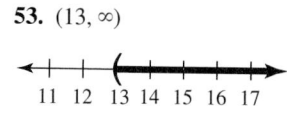

60. $(-\infty, -2)$

61. $\left(\dfrac{13}{3}, \infty\right)$

62. $\left(\dfrac{23}{2}, \infty\right)$

63. $(-\infty, \infty)$

64. $\varnothing$

65. $\varnothing$

66. $(-\infty, \infty)$

67. $(1, \infty)$

68. $\left(-\infty, \dfrac{1}{2}\right)$

69. $(-\infty, 2.397]$

70. $(-\infty, 1.52375)$

71. $(-\infty, -17)$

72. $(0.8127, \infty)$

73. x = Tony's height, $x > 6$ feet

74. a = Glenda's age, $a < 60$ years

75. s = Wilma's salary, $s < \$80{,}000$

76. w = Bubba's weight, $w > 80$ pounds

77. v = speed of the Concorde, $v \le 1450$ mph

78. s = speed, $s \ge 45$ mph

79. a = amount Julie can afford, $a \le \$400$

80. a = Fred's grade point average, $a \ge 3.2$

81. b = Burt's height, $b \le 5$ feet

82. r = Ernie's speed, $r \le 10$ mph

83. t = Tina's hourly wage, $t \le \$8.20$

84. s = selling price, $s \ge \$12{,}000$

85. x = price of car, $x < \$9100$

86. x = price of sewing machine, $x \le \$636.36$

87. x = price of truck, $x \ge \$9100.92$

88. x = Curly's contribution, $x \ge \$183.33$

89. $[0, 40)$ **90.** $[0, 150)$

91. a) Increasing   **b)** 2005   **92.** 2031

93. x = final exam score, $x \ge 77$

1.16 Multiplying and Dividing Terms

1. Find the product of two algebraic terms
2. Find the quotient of two algebraic terms

Remember that the exponent tells us how many times the base is to be used as a factor.

Exponent

↓

$$2^5 = 2 \cdot 2 \cdot 2 \cdot 2 \cdot 2 = 32$$

Base   The fifth power of 2

NOTE In general,

$$x^m = \underbrace{x \cdot x \cdots \cdot x}_{m \text{ factors}}$$

where m is a natural number.
Natural numbers are the numbers we use for counting: 1, 2, 3, and so on.

The notation can also be used when you are working with letters or variables.

$$x^4 = \underbrace{x \cdot x \cdot x \cdot x}_{4 \text{ factors}}$$

Now look at the product $x^2 \cdot x^3$.

$$x^2 \cdot x^3 = (x \cdot x)(x \cdot x \cdot x) = \underbrace{x \cdot x \cdot x \cdot x \cdot x}_{} = x^5$$

2 factors + 3 factors = 5 factors

So

NOTE Note that the exponent of x^5 is the *sum* of the exponents in x^2 and x^3.

$$x^2 \cdot x^3 = x^{2+3} = x^5$$

This leads us to the following property of exponents.

Rules and Properties: Property 1 of Exponents

For any positive integers m and n and any real number a,

$$a^m \cdot a^n = a^{m+n}$$

In words, to multiply expressions with the same base, keep the base and add the exponents.

Example 1

Using the First Property of Exponents

(a) $a^5 \cdot a^7 = a^{5+7} = a^{12}$

(b) $x \cdot x^8 = x^1 \cdot x^8 = x^{1+8} = x^9$ $x = x^1$

(c) $3^2 \cdot 3^4 = 3^{2+4} = 3^6$

(d) $y^2 \cdot y^3 \cdot y^5 = y^{2+3+5} = y^{10}$

(e) $x^3 \cdot y^4$ *cannot* be simplified. The bases are not the same.

CAUTION

The product is *not* 9^6. The base does not change.

✔ CHECK YOURSELF 1

Multiply.

(a) $b^6 \cdot b^8$　　　　**(b)** $y^7 \cdot y$　　　　**(c)** $2^3 \cdot 2^4$　　　　**(d)** $a^2 \cdot a^4 \cdot a^3$

Suppose that numerical coefficients (other than 1) are involved in a product. To find the product, multiply the coefficients and then use the first property of exponents to combine the variables.

NOTE Note that although we have several factors, this is still a single term.

$$2x^3 \cdot 3x^5 = (2 \cdot 3)(x^3 \cdot x^5) \qquad \text{Multiply the coefficients.}$$
$$= 6x^{3+5} \qquad\qquad \text{Add the exponents.}$$
$$= 6x^8$$

You may have noticed that we have again changed the order and grouping. This method uses the commutative and associative properties of Section 1.2.

Example 2

Using the First Property of Exponents

Multiply.

NOTE Again we have written out all the steps. You can do the multiplication mentally with practice.

(a) $5a^4 \cdot 7a^6 = (5 \cdot 7)(a^4 \cdot a^6) = 35a^{10}$

(b) $y^2 \cdot 3y^3 \cdot 6y^4 = (1 \cdot 3 \cdot 6)(y^2 \cdot y^3 \cdot y^4) = 18y^9$

(c) $2x^2y^3 \cdot 3x^5y^2 = (2 \cdot 3)(x^2 \cdot x^5)(y^3 \cdot y^2) = 6x^7y^5$

✔ CHECK YOURSELF 2

Multiply.

(a) $4x^3 \cdot 7x^5$　　　　**(b)** $3a^2 \cdot 2a^4 \cdot 2a^5$　　　　**(c)** $3m^2n^4 \cdot 5m^3n$

What about dividing expressions when exponents are involved? For instance, what if we want to divide x^5 by x^2? We can use the following approach to division:

$$\frac{x^5}{x^2} = \frac{\overbrace{x \cdot x \cdot x \cdot x \cdot x}^{5 \text{ factors}}}{\underbrace{x \cdot x}_{2 \text{ factors}}} = \frac{x \cdot x \cdot x \cdot x \cdot x}{x \cdot x}$$

We can divide by 2 factors of x.

$$= \overbrace{x \cdot x \cdot x}^{3 \text{ factors}} = x^3$$

So

NOTE Note that the exponent of x^3 is the *difference* of the exponents in x^5 and x^2.

$$\frac{x^5}{x^2} = x^{5-2} = x^3$$

This leads us to a second property of exponents.

Rules and Properties: Property 2 of Exponents

For any positive integers m and n, where m is greater than n, and any real number a, where a is not equal to zero,

$$\frac{a^m}{a^n} = a^{m-n}$$

In words, to divide expressions with the same base, keep the base and subtract the exponents.

Example 3

Using the Second Property of Exponents

Divide the following.

(a) $\dfrac{y^7}{y^3} = y^{7-3} = y^4$

(b) $\dfrac{m^6}{m} = \dfrac{m^6}{m^1} = m^{6-1} = m^5$ Apply the second property to each variable separately.

(c) $\dfrac{a^3 b^5}{a^2 b^2} = a^{3-2} \cdot b^{5-2} = ab^3$

✔ CHECK YOURSELF 3

Divide.

(a) $\dfrac{m^9}{m^6}$ (b) $\dfrac{a^8}{a}$ (c) $\dfrac{a^3 b^5}{a^2}$ (d) $\dfrac{r^5 s^6}{r^3 s^2}$

If numerical coefficients are involved, just divide the coefficients and then use the second law of exponents to divide the variables. Look at Example 4.

Example 4

Using the Second Property of Exponents

Divide the following.

Subtract the exponents.

(a) $\dfrac{6x^5}{3x^2} = 2x^{5-2} = 2x^3$

6 divided by 3

20 divided by 5

(b) $\dfrac{20a^7b^5}{5a^3b^4} = 4a^{7-3} \cdot b^{5-4}$

Again apply the second property to each variable separately.

$= 4a^4b$

 CHECK YOURSELF 4

Divide.

(a) $\dfrac{4x^3}{2x}$ **(b)** $\dfrac{20a^6}{5a^2}$ **(c)** $\dfrac{24x^5y^3}{4x^2y^2}$

CHECK YOURSELF ANSWERS

1. **(a)** b^{14}; **(b)** y^8; **(c)** 2^7; **(d)** a^9 **2.** **(a)** $28x^8$; **(b)** $12a^{11}$; **(c)** $15m^5n^5$

3. **(a)** m^3; **(b)** a^7; **(c)** ab^5; **(d)** r^2s^4 **4.** **(a)** $2x^2$; **(b)** $4a^4$; **(c)** $6x^3y$

1.16 Exercises

Multiply.

1. $x^5 \cdot x^7$

2. $b^2 \cdot b^4$

3. $5 \cdot 5^5$

4. $y^6 \cdot y^4$

5. $a^9 \cdot a$

6. $3^4 \cdot 3^5$

7. $z^{10} \cdot z^3$

8. $x^7 \cdot x$

9. $p^5 \cdot p^7$

10. $s^6 \cdot s^9$

11. $x^3 y \cdot x^2 y^4$

12. $m^2 n^3 \cdot mn^4$

13. $w^5 \cdot w^2 \cdot w$

14. $x^5 \cdot x^4 \cdot x^6$

15. $m^3 \cdot m^2 \cdot m^4$

16. $r^3 \cdot r \cdot r^5$

17. $a^3 b \cdot a^2 b^2 \cdot ab^3$

18. $w^2 z^3 \cdot wz \cdot w^3 z^4$

19. $p^2 q \cdot p^3 q^5 \cdot pq^4$

20. $c^3 d \cdot c^4 d^2 \cdot cd^5$

21. $3a^6 \cdot 2a^3$

22. $5s^6 \cdot s^4$

23. $x^2 \cdot 3x^5$

24. $2m^4 \cdot 6m^7$

1. _____

2. _____

3. _____

4. _____

5. _____

6. _____

7. _____

8. _____

9. _____

10. _____

11. _____

12. _____

13. _____

14. _____

15. _____

16. _____

17. _____

18. _____

19. _____

20. _____

21. _____

22. _____

23. _____

24. _____

25. _____

26. _____

27. _____

28. _____

29. _____

30. _____

31. _____

32. _____

33. _____

34. _____

35. _____

36. _____

37. _____

38. _____

39. _____

40. _____

41. _____

42. _____

43. _____

44. _____

45. _____

46. _____

47. _____

48. _____

49. _____

50. _____

51. _____

52. _____

25. $5m^3n^2 \cdot 4mn^3$

26. $7x^2y^5 \cdot 6xy^4$

27. $6x^3y \cdot 9xy^5$

28. $5a^3b \cdot 10ab^4$

29. $2a^2 \cdot a^3 \cdot 3a^7$

30. $4x^5 \cdot 2x^3 \cdot 3x^2$

31. $3c^2d \cdot 4cd^3 \cdot 2c^5d$

32. $5p^2q \cdot p^3q^2 \cdot 3pq^3$

33. $5m^2 \cdot m^3 \cdot 2m \cdot 3m^4$

34. $3a^3 \cdot 2a \cdot a^4 \cdot 2a^5$

35. $2r^3s \cdot rs^2 \cdot 3r^2s \cdot 5rs$

36. $6a^2b \cdot ab \cdot 3ab^3 \cdot 2a^2b$

Divide.

37. $\dfrac{a^9}{a^6}$

38. $\dfrac{m^8}{m^2}$

39. $\dfrac{y^{10}}{y^4}$

40. $\dfrac{b^9}{b^4}$

41. $\dfrac{p^{15}}{p^{10}}$

42. $\dfrac{s^{18}}{s^{12}}$

43. $\dfrac{x^5y^3}{x^2y^2}$

44. $\dfrac{s^5t^4}{s^3t^2}$

45. $\dfrac{6m^3}{3m}$

46. $\dfrac{8x^5}{4x}$

47. $\dfrac{24a^7}{6a^4}$

48. $\dfrac{25x^9}{5x^8}$

49. $\dfrac{26m^8n}{13m^6}$

50. $\dfrac{30a^4b^5}{6b^4}$

51. $\dfrac{28w^3z^5}{7wz}$

52. $\dfrac{48p^6q^7}{8p^4q}$

53. $\dfrac{18x^3y^4z^5}{9xy^2z^2}$

54. $\dfrac{25a^5b^4c^3}{5a^4bc^2}$

Simplify each of the following expressions where possible.

55. $2a^3b \cdot 3a^2b$

56. $2xy^3 \cdot 3xy^2$

57. $2a^3b + 3a^2b$

58. $2xy^3 + 3xy^2$

59. $2x^2y^3 \cdot 3x^2y^3$

60. $5a^3b^2 \cdot 10a^3b^2$

61. $2x^2y^3 + 3x^2y^3$

62. $5a^3b^2 + 10a^3b^2$

63. $\dfrac{8a^2b \cdot 6a^2b}{2ab}$

64. $\dfrac{6x^2y^3 \cdot 9x^2y^3}{3x^2y^2}$

65. $\dfrac{8a^2b + 6a^2b}{2ab}$

66. $\dfrac{6x^2y^3 + 9x^2y^3}{3x^2y^2}$

67. Complete the following statements:

    (a) a^n is negative when _____ because _____.

    (b) a^n is positive when _____ because _____.

              (give all possibilities)

68. "Earn Big Bucks!" reads an ad for a job. "You will be paid 1 cent for the first day and 2 cents for the second day, 4 cents for the third day, 8 cents for the fourth day, and so on, doubling each day. Apply now!" What kind of deal is this—where is the big money offered in the headline? The fine print at the bottom of the ad says: "Highly qualified people may be paid \$1,000,000 for the first 28 working days if they choose." Well, *that* does sound like big bucks! Work with other students to decide which method of payment is better and how much better. You may want to make a table and try to find a formula for the first offer.

69. An oil spill from a tanker in pristine Prince Williams Sound in Alaska begins in a circular shape only 2 ft across. The area of the circle is $A = \pi r^2$. Make a table to decide what happens to the area if the diameter is doubling each hour. How large will the spill be in 24 h?

2 ft

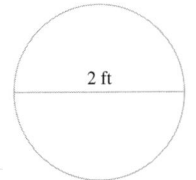

53. _____

54. _____

55. _____

56. _____

57. _____

58. _____

59. _____

60. _____

61. _____

62. _____

63. _____

64. _____

65. _____

66. _____

67. _____

68. _____

69. _____

Answers

1. x^{12} **3.** 5^6 **5.** a^{10} **7.** z^{13} **9.** p^{12} **11.** x^5y^5 **13.** w^8

15. m^9 **17.** a^6b^6 **19.** p^6q^{10} **21.** $6a^9$ **23.** $3x^7$ **25.** $20m^4n^5$

27. $54x^4y^6$ **29.** $6a^{12}$ **31.** $24c^8d^5$ **33.** $30m^{10}$ **35.** $30r^7s^5$ **37.** a^3

39. y^6 **41.** p^5 **43.** x^3y **45.** $2m^2$ **47.** $4a^3$ **49.** $2m^2n$

51. $4w^2z^4$ **53.** $2x^2y^2z^3$ **55.** $6a^5b^2$ **57.** Cannot simplify   **59.** $6x^4y^6$

61. $5x^2y^3$ **63.** $24a^3b$ **65.** $7a$ **67.**   **69.**

Exponents and Polynomials

 ## OBJECTIVES

1. Recognize the five properties of exponents
2. Use the properties to simplify expressions
3. Identify types of polynomials
4. Find the degree of a polynomial
5. Write a polynomial in descending exponent form
6. Evaluate a polynomial

Overcoming Math Anxiety

Hint #6   Preparing for a Test

Preparation for a test really begins on the first day of class. Everything you have done in class and at home has been part of that preparation. However, there are a few things that you should focus on in the last few days before a scheduled test.

1. Plan your test preparation to end at least 24 hours before the test. The last 24 hours is too late, and besides, you will need some rest before the test.

2. Go over your homework and class notes with pencil and paper in hand. Write down all of the problem types, formulas, and definitions that you think might give you trouble on the test.

3. The day before the test, take the page(s) of notes from step 2, and transfer the most important ideas to a 3 × 5 card.

4. Just before the test, review the information on the card. You will be surprised at how much you remember about each concept.

5. Understand that, if you have been successful at completing your homework assignments, you can be successful on the test. This is an obstacle for many students, but it is an obstacle that can be overcome. Truly anxious students are often surprised that they scored as well as they did on a test. They tend to attribute this to blind luck. It is not. It is the first sign that you really do "get it." Enjoy the success.

Recall that the exponent notation indicates repeated multiplication and that the exponent tells us how many times the base is to be used as a factor.

Exponent
↓
$$3^5 = \underbrace{3 \cdot 3 \cdot 3 \cdot 3 \cdot 3}_{\text{5 factors}} = 243$$
↑
Base

Now, we will look at the properties of exponents.

The first property is used when multiplying two values with the same base.

Rules and Properties: Property 1 of Exponents

For any real number a and positive integers m and n,

$$a^m \cdot a^n = a^{m+n}$$

For example,

$$2^5 \cdot 2^7 = 2^{12}$$

The second property is used when dividing two values with the same base.

Rules and Properties: Property 2 of Exponents

For any real number a and positive integers m and n, with $m > n$,

$$a^m/a^n = a^{m-n}$$

For example,

$$2^{12}/2^7 = 2^5$$

NOTE Notice that this means that the base, x^2, is used as a factor *4* times.

Consider the following:

$$(x^2)^4 = x^2 \cdot x^2 \cdot x^2 \cdot x^2 = x^8$$

This leads us to our third property for exponents.

Rules and Properties: Property 3 of Exponents

For any real number a and positive integers m and n,

$$(a^m)^n = a^{m \cdot n}$$

For example,

$$(2^3)^2 = 2^{3 \cdot 2} = 2^6$$

The use of this new property is illustrated in Example 1.

Example 1

Using the Third Property of Exponents

 CAUTION

Be careful! Be sure to distinguish between the correct use of Property 1 and Property 3.

$(x^4)^5 = x^{4 \cdot 5} = x^{20}$

but

$x^4 \cdot x^5 = x^{4+5} = x^9$

Simplify each expression.

(a) $(x^4)^5 = x^{4 \cdot 5} = x^{20}$

Multiply the exponents.

(b) $(2^3)^4 = 2^{3 \cdot 4} = 2^{12}$

CHECK YOURSELF 1

Simplify each expression.

(a) $(m^5)^6$ **(b)** $(m^5)(m^6)$ **(c)** $(3^2)^4$ **(d)** $(3^2)(3^4)$

NOTE Here the base is $3x$.

Suppose we now have a product raised to a power. Consider an expression such as

$$(3x)^4$$

We know that

$$(3x)^4 = (3x)(3x)(3x)(3x)$$
$$= (3 \cdot 3 \cdot 3 \cdot 3)(x \cdot x \cdot x \cdot x)$$
$$= 3^4 \cdot x^4 = 81x^4$$

Note that the power, here 4, has been applied to each factor, 3 and x. In general, we have

Rules and Properties: Property 4 of Exponents

For any real numbers a and b and positive integer m,

$$(ab)^m = a^m b^m$$

For example,

$$(3x)^3 = 3^3 \cdot x^3 = 27x^3$$

The use of this property is shown in Example 2.

Example 2

NOTE Notice that $(2x)^5$ and $2x^5$ are entirely different expressions. For $(2x)^5$, the base is $2x$, so we raise each factor to the fifth power. For $2x^5$, the base is x, and so the exponent applies only to x.

Using the Fourth Property of Exponents

Simplify each expression.

(a) $(2x)^5 = 2^5 \cdot x^5 = 32x^5$

(b) $(3ab)^4 = 3^4 \cdot a^4 \cdot b^4 = 81a^4b^4$

(c) $5(2r)^3 = 5 \cdot 2^3 \cdot r^3 = 40r^3$

 CHECK YOURSELF 2

Simplify each expression.

(a) $(3y)^4$ **(b)** $(2mn)^6$ **(c)** $3(4x)^2$ **(d)** $5x^3$

We may have to use more than one of our properties in simplifying an expression involving exponents. Consider Example 3.

Example 3

NOTE To help you understand each step of the simplification, we refer to the property being applied. Make a list of the properties now to help you as you work through the remainder of this and the next section.

Using the Properties of Exponents

Simplify each expression.

(a) $(r^4s^3)^3 = (r^4)^3 \cdot (s^3)^3$ Property 4

$$= r^{12}s^9$$ Property 3

(b) $(3x^2)^2 \cdot (2x^3)^3$

$$= 3^2(x^2)^2 \cdot 2^3 \cdot (x^3)^3$$ Property 4

$$= 9x^4 \cdot 8x^9$$ Property 3

$$= 72x^{13}$$ Multiply the coefficients and apply Property 1.

(c) $\dfrac{(a^3)^5}{a^4} = \dfrac{a^{15}}{a^4}$ Property 3

$= a^{11}$ Property 2

 CHECK YOURSELF 3

Simplify each expression.

(a) $(m^5n^2)^3$ 　　　　　 **(b)** $(2p)^4(4p^2)^2$ 　　　　　 **(c)** $\dfrac{(s^4)^3}{s^5}$

We have one final exponent property to develop. Suppose we have a quotient raised to a power. Consider the following:

$$\left(\frac{x}{3}\right)^3 = \frac{x}{3} \cdot \frac{x}{3} \cdot \frac{x}{3} = \frac{x \cdot x \cdot x}{3 \cdot 3 \cdot 3} = \frac{x^3}{3^3}$$

Note that the power, here 3, has been applied to the numerator x and to the denominator 3. This gives us our fifth property of exponents.

Rules and Properties: Property 5 of Exponents

For any real numbers a and b, when b is not equal to 0, and positive integer m,

$$\left(\frac{a}{b}\right)^m = \frac{a^m}{b^m}$$

For example,

$$\left(\frac{2}{5}\right)^3 = \frac{2^3}{5^3} = \frac{8}{125}$$

Example 4 illustrates the use of this property. Again note that the other properties may also have to be applied in simplifying an expression.

Example 4

Using the Fifth Property of Exponents

Simplify each expression.

(a) $\left(\dfrac{3}{4}\right)^3 = \dfrac{3^3}{4^3} = \dfrac{27}{64}$ Property 5

(b) $\left(\dfrac{x^3}{y^2}\right)^4 = \dfrac{(x^3)^4}{(y^2)^4}$ Property 5

$= \dfrac{x^{12}}{y^8}$ Property 3

(c) $\left(\dfrac{r^2s^3}{t^4}\right)^2 = \dfrac{(r^2s^3)^2}{(t^4)^2}$ Property 5

$= \dfrac{(r^2)^2(s^3)^2}{(t^4)^2}$ Property 4

$= \dfrac{r^4s^6}{t^8}$ Property 3

✔ CHECK YOURSELF 4

Simplify each expression.

(a) $\left(\dfrac{2}{3}\right)^4$ (b) $\left(\dfrac{m^3}{n^4}\right)^5$ (c) $\left(\dfrac{a^2 b^3}{c^5}\right)^2$

The following table summarizes the five properties of exponents that were discussed in this section:

General Form	Example
1. $a^m a^n = a^{m+n}$	$x^2 \cdot x^3 = x^5$
2. $\dfrac{a^m}{a^n} = a^{m-n}$ $(m > n)$	$\dfrac{5^7}{5^3} = 5^4$
3. $(a^m)^n = a^{mn}$	$(z^5)^4 = z^{20}$
4. $(ab)^m = a^m b^m$	$(4x)^3 = 4^3 x^3 = 64x^3$
5. $\left(\dfrac{a}{b}\right)^m = \dfrac{a^m}{b^m}$	$\left(\dfrac{2}{3}\right)^6 = \dfrac{2^6}{3^6} = \dfrac{64}{729}$

Our work in this chapter deals with the most common kind of algebraic expression, a *polynomial*. To define a polynomial, let's recall our earlier definition of the word *term*.

Definitions: Term

A **term** is a number or the product of a number and one or more variables.

For example, x^5, $3x$, $-4xy^2$, and 8 are terms. A **polynomial** consists of one or more terms in which the only allowable exponents are the whole numbers, 0, 1, 2, 3, . . . and so on. These terms are connected by addition or subtraction signs.

Definitions: Numerical Coefficient

NOTE In a polynomial, terms are separated by + and − signs.

In each term of a polynomial, the number is called the **numerical coefficient**, or more simply the **coefficient**, of that term.

Example 5

Identifying Polynomials

(a) $x + 3$ is a polynomial. The terms are x and 3. The coefficients are 1 and 3.
(b) $3x^2 - 2x + 5$, or $3x^2 + (-2x) + 5$, is also a polynomial. Its terms are $3x^2$, $-2x$, and 5. The coefficients are 3, −2, and 5.
(c) $5x^3 + 2 - \dfrac{3}{x}$ is *not* a polynomial because of the division by x in the third term.

CHECK YOURSELF 5

Which of the following are polynomials?

(a) $5x^2$ **(b)** $3y^3 - 2y + \dfrac{5}{y}$ **(c)** $4x^2 - 2x + 3$

Certain polynomials are given special names because of the number of terms that they have.

> **NOTE** The prefix *mono-* means 1. The prefix *bi-* means 2. The prefix *tri-* means 3. There are no special names for polynomials with four or more terms.

Definitions: Monomial, Binomial, and Trinomial

A polynomial with one term is called a **monomial.**
A polynomial with two terms is called a **binomial.**
A polynomial with three terms is called a **trinomial.**

Example 6

Identifying Types of Polynomials

(a) $3x^2y$ is a monomial. It has one term.
(b) $2x^3 + 5x$ is a binomial. It has two terms, $2x^3$ and $5x$.
(c) $5x^2 - 4x + 3$, or $5x^2 + (-4x) + 3$, is a trinomial. Its three terms are $5x^2$, $-4x$, and 3.

CHECK YOURSELF 6

Classify each of these as a monomial, binomial, or trinomial.

(a) $5x^4 - 2x^3$ **(b)** $4x^7$ **(c)** $2x^2 + 5x - 3$

> **NOTE** Remember, in a polynomial the allowable exponents are the whole numbers 0, 1, 2, 3, and so on. The degree will be a whole number.

We also classify polynomials by their *degree.* The **degree** of a polynomial that has only one variable is the highest power appearing in any one term.

Example 7

Classifying Polynomials by Their Degree

The highest power
(a) $5x^3 - 3x^2 + 4x$ has degree 3.

The highest power
(b) $4x - 5x^4 + 3x^3 + 2$ has degree 4.

> **NOTE** We will see in the next section that $x^0 = 1$.

(c) $8x$ has degree 1. (Because $8x = 8x^1$)
(d) 7 has degree 0.

Note: Polynomials can have more than one variable, such as $4x^2y^3 + 5xy^2$. The degree is then the sum of the highest powers in any single term (here $2 + 3$, or 5). In general, we will be working with polynomials in a single variable, such as x.

CHECK YOURSELF 7

Find the degree of each polynomial.

(a) $6x^5 - 3x^3 - 2$ **(b)** $5x$ **(c)** $3x^3 + 2x^6 - 1$ **(d)** 9

Working with polynomials is much easier if you get used to writing them in **descending-exponent form** (sometimes called *descending-power form*). This simply means that the term with the highest exponent is written first, then the term with the next highest exponent, and so on.

Example 8

Writing Polynomials in Descending Order

The exponents get smaller
from left to right.

(a) $5x^7 - 3x^4 + 2x^2$ is in descending-exponent form.

(b) $4x^4 + 5x^6 - 3x^5$ is *not* in descending-exponent form. The polynomial should be written as

$5x^6 - 3x^5 + 4x^4$

Notice that the degree of the polynomial is the power of the *first*, or *leading*, term once the polynomial is arranged in descending-exponent form.

CHECK YOURSELF 8

Write the following polynomials in descending-exponent form.

(a) $5x^4 - 4x^5 + 7$ **(b)** $4x^3 + 9x^4 + 6x^8$

A polynomial can represent any number. Its value depends on the value given to the variable.

Example 9

Evaluating Polynomials

Given the polynomial

$3x^3 - 2x^2 - 4x + 1$

(a) Find the value of the polynomial when $x = 2$.

Substituting 2 for x, we have

NOTE Again note how the rules for the order of operations are applied.

$3(2)^3 - 2(2)^2 - 4(2) + 1$

$= 3(8) - 2(4) - 4(2) + 1$

$= 24 - 8 - 8 + 1$

$= 9$

CAUTION

Be particularly careful when dealing with powers of negative numbers!

(b) Find the value of the polynomial when $x = -2$.

Now we substitute -2 for x.

$3(-2)^3 - 2(-2)^2 - 4(-2) + 1$

$= 3(-8) - 2(4) - 4(-2) + 1$

$= -24 - 8 + 8 + 1$

$= -23$

 CHECK YOURSELF 9

Find the value of the polynomial

$4x^3 - 3x^2 + 2x - 1$

When

(a) $x = 3$ **(b)** $x = -3$

CHECK YOURSELF ANSWERS

1. (a) m^{30}; **(b)** m^{11}; **(c)** 3^8; **(d)** 3^6 **2. (a)** $81y^4$; **(b)** $64m^6n^6$; **(c)** $48x^2$; **(d)** $5x^3$

3. (a) $m^{15}n^6$; **(b)** $256p^8$; **(c)** s^7 **4. (a)** $\dfrac{16}{81}$; **(b)** $\dfrac{m^{15}}{n^{20}}$; **(c)** $\dfrac{a^4b^6}{c^{10}}$

5. (a) and **(c)** are polynomials.   **6. (a)** Binomial; **(b)** monomial; **(c)** trinomial

7. (a) 5; **(b)** 1; **(c)** 6; **(d)** 0   **8. (a)** $-4x^5 + 5x^4 + 7$; **(b)** $6x^8 + 9x^4 + 4x^3$

9. (a) 86; **(b)** -142

1.17 Exercises

Use Property 3 of exponents to simplify each of the following expressions.

1. $(x^2)^3$

2. $(a^5)^3$

3. $(m^4)^4$

4. $(p^7)^2$

5. $(2^4)^2$

6. $(3^3)^2$

7. $(5^3)^5$

8. $(7^2)^4$

Use the five properties of exponents to simplify each of the following expressions.

9. $(3x)^3$

10. $(4m)^2$

11. $(2xy)^4$

12. $(5pq)^3$

13. $5(3ab)^3$

14. $4(2rs)^4$

15. $\left(\dfrac{3}{4}\right)^2$

16. $\left(\dfrac{2}{3}\right)^3$

17. $\left(\dfrac{x}{5}\right)^3$

18. $\left(\dfrac{a}{2}\right)^5$

19. $(2x^2)^4$

20. $(3y^2)^5$

21. $(a^8b^6)^2$

22. $(p^3q^4)^2$

23. $(4x^2y)^3$

24. $(4m^4n^4)^2$

25. $(3m^2)^4(m^3)^2$

26. $(y^4)^3(4y^3)^2$

27. $\dfrac{(x^4)^3}{x^2}$

28. $\dfrac{(m^5)^3}{m^6}$

29. $\dfrac{(s^3)^2(s^2)^3}{(s^5)^2}$

30. $\dfrac{(y^5)^3(y^3)^2}{(y^4)^4}$

31. $\left(\dfrac{m^3}{n^2}\right)^3$

32. $\left(\dfrac{a^4}{b^3}\right)^4$

33. $\left(\dfrac{a^3b^2}{c^4}\right)^2$

34. $\left(\dfrac{x^5y^2}{z^4}\right)^3$

Which of the following expressions are polynomials?

35. $7x^3$

36. $5x^3 - \dfrac{3}{x}$

37. $4x^4y^2 - 3x^3y$

38. 7

39. -7

40. $4x^3 + x$

41. $\dfrac{3 + x}{x^2}$

42. $5a^2 - 2a + 7$

ANSWERS

1. _____   2. _____
3. _____   4. _____
5. _____   6. _____
7. _____   8. _____
9. _____   10. _____
11. _____   12. _____
13. _____   14. _____
15. _____   16. _____
17. _____   18. _____
19. _____   20. _____
21. _____   22. _____
23. _____   24. _____
25. _____   26. _____
27. _____   28. _____
29. _____   30. _____
31. _____   32. _____
33. _____   34. _____
35. _____
36. _____
37. _____
38. _____
39. _____
40. _____
41. _____
42. _____

43. _____

44. _____

45. _____

46. _____

47. _____

48. _____

49. _____

50. _____

51. _____

52. _____

53. _____

54. _____

55. _____

56. _____

57. _____

58. _____

59. _____

60. _____

61. _____

62. _____

63. _____

64. _____

65. _____ 66. _____

67. _____ 68. _____

69. _____ 70. _____

71. _____ 72. _____

For each of the following polynomials, list the terms and the coefficients.

43. $2x^2 - 3x$

44. $5x^3 + x$

45. $4x^3 - 3x + 2$

46. $7x^2$

Classify each of the following as a monomial, binomial, or trinomial where possible.

47. $7x^3 - 3x^2$

48. $4x^7$

49. $7y^2 + 4y + 5$

50. $2x^2 + 3xy + y^2$

51. $2x^4 - 3x^2 + 5x - 2$

52. $x^4 + \dfrac{5}{x} + 7$

53. $6y^8$

54. $4x^4 - 2x^2 + 5x - 7$

55. $x^5 - \dfrac{3}{x^2}$

56. $4x^2 - 9$

Arrange in descending-exponent form if necessary, and give the degree of each polynomial.

57. $4x^5 - 3x^2$

58. $5x^2 + 3x^3 + 4$

59. $7x^7 - 5x^9 + 4x^3$

60. $2 + x$

61. $4x$

62. $x^{17} - 3x^4$

63. $5x^2 - 3x^5 + x^6 - 7$

64. 5

Find the values of each of the following polynomials for the given values of the variable.

65. $6x + 1, x = 1$ and $x = -1$

66. $5x - 5, x = 2$ and $x = -2$

67. $x^3 - 2x, x = 2$ and $x = -2$

68. $3x^2 + 7, x = 3$ and $x = -3$

69. $3x^2 + 4x - 2, x = 4$ and $x = -4$

70. $2x^2 - 5x + 1, x = 2$ and $x = -2$

71. $-x^2 - 2x + 3, x = 1$ and $x = -3$

72. $-x^2 - 5x - 6, x = -3$ and $x = -2$

Indicate whether each of the following statements is always true, sometimes true, or never true.

73. A monomial is a polynomial.

74. A binomial is a trinomial.

75. The degree of a trinomial is 3.

76. A trinomial has three terms.

77. A polynomial has four or more terms.

78. A binomial must have two coefficients.

Solve the following problems.

79. Write x^{12} as a power of x^2.

80. Write y^{15} as a power of y^3.

81. Write a^{16} as a power of a^2.

82. Write m^{20} as a power of m^5.

83. Write each of the following as a power of 8. (Remember that $8 = 2^3$.)

$2^{12}, 2^{18}, (2^5)^3, (2^7)^6$

84. Write each of the following as a power of 9.

$3^8, 3^{14}, (3^5)^8, (3^4)^7$

85. What expression raised to the third power is $-8x^6y^9z^{15}$?

86. What expression raised to the fourth power is $81x^{12}y^8z^{16}$?

The formula $(1 + R)^Y = G$ gives us useful information about the growth of a population. Here R is the rate of growth expressed as a decimal, y is the time in years, and G is the growth factor. If a country has a 2 percent growth rate for 35 years, then it will double its population:

$(1.02)^{35} \approx 2$

87. a. With this growth rate, how many doublings will occur in 105 years? How much larger will the country's population be?

b. The less developed countries of the world had an average growth rate of 2 percent in 1986. If their total population was 3.8 billion, what will their population be in 105 years if this rate remains unchanged?

88. The United States has a growth rate of 0.7 percent. What will be its growth factor after 35 years?

89. Write an explanation of why $(x^3)(x^4)$ is *not* x^{12}.

90. Your algebra study partners are confused. "Why isn't $x^2 \cdot x^3 = 2x^5$?", they ask you. Write an explanation that will convince them.

ANSWERS

73. _____

74. _____

75. _____

76. _____

77. _____

78. _____

79. _____

80. _____

81. _____

82. _____

83. _____

84. _____

85. _____

86. _____

87. _____

88. _____

89. _____

90. _____

91. _____

92. _____

93. _____

94. _____

95. _____

96. _____

97. _____

98. _____

99. _____

100. _____

101. _____

102. _____

103. _____

104. _____

105. _____

106. _____

Capital italic letters such as P or Q are often used to name polynomials. For example, we might write $P(x) = 3x^3 - 5x^2 + 2$ in which $P(x)$ is read "P of x." The notation permits a convenient shorthand. We write $P(2)$, read "P of 2," to indicate the value of the polynomial when $x = 2$. Here

$$P(2) = 3(2)^3 - 5(2)^2 + 2$$
$$= 3 \cdot 8 - 5 \cdot 4 + 2$$
$$= 6$$

Use the information above in the following problems.

If $P(x) = x^3 - 2x^2 + 5$ and $Q(x) = 2x^2 + 3$, find:

91. $P(1)$ **92.** $P(-1)$ **93.** $Q(2)$ **94.** $Q(-2)$

95. $P(3)$ **96.** $Q(-3)$ **97.** $P(0)$

98. $Q(0)$ **99.** $P(2) + Q(-1)$ **100.** $P(-2) + Q(3)$

101. $P(3) - Q(-3) \div Q(0)$ **102.** $Q(-2) \div Q(2) \cdot P(0)$

103. $|Q(4)| - |P(4)|$ **104.** $\dfrac{P(-1) + Q(0)}{P(0)}$

105. Cost of typing. The cost, in dollars, of typing a term paper is given as 3 times the number of pages plus 20. Use y as the number of pages to be typed and write a polynomial to describe this cost. Find the cost of typing a 50-page paper.

106. Manufacturing. The cost, in dollars, of making suits is described as 20 times the number of suits plus 150. Use s as the number of suits and write a polynomial to describe this cost. Find the cost of making seven suits.

107. Revenue. The revenue, in dollars, when x pairs of shoes are sold is given by $3x^2 - 95$. Find the revenue when 12 pairs of shoes are sold. What is the average revenue per pair of shoes?

108. Manufacturing. The cost in dollars of manufacturing w wing nuts is given by the expression $0.07w + 13.3$. Find the cost when 375 wing nuts are made. What is the average cost to manufacture one wing nut?

109. Suppose that when you were born, a rich uncle put $500 in the bank for you. He never deposited money again, but the bank paid 5 percent interest on the money every year on your birthday. How much money was in the bank after 1 year? After 2 years? After 1 year (as you know), the amount is $500 + 500(0.05)$, which can be written as $500(1 + 0.05)$ because of the distributive property. $1 + 0.05 = 1.05$, so after 1 year the amount in the bank was $500(1.05)$. After 2 years, this amount was again multiplied by 1.05. How much is in the bank today? Complete the following chart.

Birthday	Computation	Amount
0 (Day of Birth)		$500
1	$500(1.05)	
2	$500(1.05)(1.05)	
3	$500(1.05)(1.05)(1.05)	
4	$500(1.05)^4	
5	$500(1.05)^5	
6		
7		
8		

Write a formula for the amount in the bank on your nth birthday. About how many years does it take for the money to double? How many years for it to double again? Can you see any connection between this and the rules for exponents? Explain why you think there may or may not be a connection.

110. Work with another student to correctly complete the statements:

(a) $\dfrac{m^3}{n^3} < 1$ when . . .

$\dfrac{m^3}{n^3} > 1$ when . . .

$\dfrac{m^3}{n^3} = 1$ when . . .

$\dfrac{m^3}{n^3} < 0$ (is negative) when . . .

$\dfrac{m^3}{n^3} = 0$ when . . .

(b) $\dfrac{a^x}{a^y} > 1$ when . . .

$\dfrac{a^x}{a^y} = 1$ when . . .

$\dfrac{a^x}{a^y} < 1$ when . . .

$\dfrac{a^x}{a^y} = 0$ when . . .

$\dfrac{a^x}{a^y} < 0$ when . . .

a. _____

b. _____

c. _____

d. _____

e. _____

f. _____

g. _____

h. _____

 Getting Ready

Reduce each of the following fractions to simplest form.

(a) $\dfrac{m^3}{m^5}$ (b) $\dfrac{x^7}{x^{10}}$ (c) $\dfrac{a^3}{a^9}$ (d) $\dfrac{y^4}{y^8}$

(e) $\dfrac{x^3}{x^3}$ (f) $\dfrac{b^5}{b^5}$ (g) $\dfrac{s^7}{s^7}$ (h) $\dfrac{r^{10}}{r^{10}}$

Answers

1. x^6 **3.** m^{16} **5.** 2^8 **7.** 5^{15} **9.** $27x^3$ **11.** $16x^4y^4$ **13.** $135a^3b^3$

15. $\dfrac{9}{16}$ **17.** $\dfrac{x^3}{125}$ **19.** $16x^8$ **21.** $a^{16}b^{12}$ **23.** $64x^6y^3$ **25.** $81m^{14}$

27. x^{10} **29.** s^2 **31.** $\dfrac{m^9}{n^6}$ **33.** $\dfrac{a^6b^4}{c^8}$ **35.** Polynomial

37. Polynomial **39.** Polynomial **41.** Not a polynomial
43. $2x^2, -3x; 2, -3$ **45.** $4x^3, -3x, 2; 4, -3, 2$ **47.** Binomial
49. Trinomial **51.** Not classified **53.** Monomial **55.** Not a polynomial
57. $4x^5 - 3x^2; 5$ **59.** $-5x^9 + 7x^7 + 4x^3; 9$ **61.** $4x; 1$
63. $x^6 - 3x^5 + 5x^2 - 7; 6$ **65.** $7, -5$ **67.** $4, -4$ **69.** $62, 30$
71. $0, 0$ **73.** Always **75.** Sometimes **77.** Sometimes **79.** $(x^2)^6$
81. $(a^2)^8$ **83.** $8^4, 8^6, 8^5, 8^{14}$ **85.** $-2x^2y^3z^5$
87. (a) Three doublings, 8 times as large; **(b)** 30.4 billion **89.**

91. 4 **93.** 11 **95.** 14 **97.** 5 **99.** 10 **101.** 7 **103.** -2

105. $3y + 20$, \$170 **107.** \$337, \$28.08 **109.** **a.** $\dfrac{1}{m^2}$ **b.** $\dfrac{1}{x^3}$

c. $\dfrac{1}{a^6}$ **d.** $\dfrac{1}{y^4}$ **e.** 1 **f.** 1 **g.** 1 **h.** 1

 **1.18 Negative Exponents and Scientific Notation**

© 2001 McGraw-Hill Companies

1.18 OBJECTIVES

1. Evaluate expressions involving zero or a negative exponent
2. Simplify expressions involving zero or a negative exponent
3. Write a decimal number in scientific notation
4. Solve an application of scientific notation

In Section 1.17, we discussed exponents.

We now want to extend our exponent notation to include 0 and negative integers as exponents.

First, what do we do with x^0? It will help to look at a problem that gives us x^0 as a result. What if the numerator and denominator of a fraction have the same base raised to the same power and we extend our division rule? For example,

$$\frac{a^5}{a^5} = a^{5-5} = a^0 \tag{1}$$

NOTE By Property 2,

$$\frac{a^m}{a^n} = a^{m-n}$$

when $m > n$. Here m and n are *both* 5 so $m = n$.

But from our experience with fractions we know that

$$\frac{a^5}{a^5} = 1 \tag{2}$$

By comparing equations (1) and (2), it seems reasonable to make the following definition:

NOTE As was the case with $\frac{0}{0}$, 0^0 will be discussed in a later course.

> **Definitions:** Zero Power
>
> For any number a, $a \neq 0$,
>
> $$a^0 = 1$$
>
> In words, any expression, except 0, raised to the 0 power is 1.

Example 1 illustrates the use of this definition.

> **Example 1**
>
> **Raising Expressions to the Zero Power**

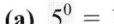 **CAUTION**

In part (d) the 0 exponent applies only to the x and *not* to the factor 6, because the base is x.

Evaluate. Assume all variables are nonzero.

(a) $5^0 = 1$

(b) $27^0 = 1$

(c) $(x^2 y)^0 = 1$ if $x \neq 0$ and $y \neq 0$

(d) $6x^0 = 6 \cdot 1 = 6$ if $x \neq 0$

 **CHECK YOURSELF 1**

Evaluate. Assume all variables are nonzero.

(a) 7^0 (b) $(-8)^0$ (c) $(xy^3)^0$ (d) $3x^0$

The second property of exponents allows us to define a negative exponent. Suppose that the exponent in the denominator is *greater than* the exponent in the numerator. Consider the expression $\dfrac{x^2}{x^5}$.

Our previous work with fractions tells us that

NOTE Divide the numerator and denominator by the two common factors of *x*.

$$\frac{x^2}{x^5} = \frac{x \cdot x}{x \cdot x \cdot x \cdot x \cdot x} = \frac{1}{x^3} \qquad (1)$$

However, if we extend the second property to let *n* be greater than *m*, we have

REMEMBER: $\dfrac{a^m}{a^n} = a^{m-n}$

$$\frac{x^2}{x^5} = x^{2-5} = x^{-3} \qquad (2)$$

Now, by comparing equations (1) and (2), it seems reasonable to define x^{-3} as $\dfrac{1}{x^3}$. In general, we have this result:

Definitions: Negative Powers

NOTE John Wallis (1616–1703), an English mathematician, was the first to fully discuss the meaning of 0 and negative exponents.

For any number *a*, $a \neq 0$, and any positive integer *n*,

$$a^{-n} = \frac{1}{a^n}$$

Example 2

Rewriting Expressions That Contain Negative Exponents

Rewrite each expression, using only positive exponents.

Negative exponent in numerator

(a) $x^{-4} = \dfrac{1}{x^4}$

Positive exponent in denominator

(b) $m^{-7} = \dfrac{1}{m^7}$

(c) $3^{-2} = \dfrac{1}{3^2}$ or $\dfrac{1}{9}$

(d) $10^{-3} = \dfrac{1}{10^3}$ or $\dfrac{1}{1000}$

 **CAUTION**

(e) $2x^{-3} = 2 \cdot \dfrac{1}{x^3} = \dfrac{2}{x^3}$

The −3 exponent applies only to *x*, because *x* is the base.

(f) $\dfrac{a^5}{a^9} = a^{5-9} = a^{-4} = \dfrac{1}{a^4}$

(g) $-4x^{-5} = -4 \cdot \dfrac{1}{x^5} = -\dfrac{4}{x^5}$

✔ CHECK YOURSELF 2

Write, using only positive exponents.

(a) a^{-10} **(b)** 4^{-3} **(c)** $3x^{-2}$ **(d)** $\dfrac{x^5}{x^8}$

We will now allow negative integers as exponents in our first property for exponents. Consider Example 3.

Example 3

Simplifying Expressions Containing Exponents

NOTE $a^m \cdot a^n = a^{m+n}$ for *any* integers *m* and *n*. So add the exponents.

Simplify (write an equivalent expression that uses only positive exponents).

(a) $x^5 x^{-2} = x^{5+(-2)} = x^3$

Note: An alternative approach would be

NOTE By definition

$x^{-2} = \dfrac{1}{x^2}$

$$x^5 x^{-2} = x^5 \cdot \frac{1}{x^2} = \frac{x^5}{x^2} = x^3$$

(b) $a^7 a^{-5} = a^{7+(-5)} = a^2$

(c) $y^5 y^{-9} = y^{5+(-9)} = y^{-4} = \dfrac{1}{y^4}$

✔ CHECK YOURSELF 3

Simplify (write an equivalent expression that uses only positive exponents).

(a) $x^7 x^{-2}$ **(b)** $b^3 b^{-8}$

Example 4 shows that all the properties of exponents introduced in the last section can be extended to expressions with negative exponents.

Example 4

Simplifying Expressions Containing Exponents

Simplify each expression.

(a) $\dfrac{m^{-3}}{m^4} = m^{-3-4}$ Property 2

$\qquad\quad = m^{-7} = \dfrac{1}{m^7}$

(b) $\dfrac{a^{-2}b^6}{a^5 b^{-4}} = a^{-2-5}b^{6-(-4)}$ Apply Property 2 to each variable.

$\qquad\quad = a^{-7}b^{10} = \dfrac{b^{10}}{a^7}$

NOTE This could also be done by using Property 4 first, so

$(2x^4)^{-3} = 2^{-3} \cdot (x^4)^{-3} = 2^{-3}x^{-12}$

$= \dfrac{1}{2^3 x^{12}}$

$= \dfrac{1}{8x^{12}}$

(c) $(2x^4)^{-3} = \dfrac{1}{(2x^4)^3}$ Definition of the negative exponent

$= \dfrac{1}{2^3(x^4)^3}$ Property 4

$= \dfrac{1}{8x^{12}}$ Property 3

(d) $\dfrac{(y^{-2})^4}{(y^3)^{-2}} = \dfrac{y^{-8}}{y^{-6}}$ Property 3

$= y^{-8-(-6)}$ Property 2

$= y^{-2} = \dfrac{1}{y^2}$

CHECK YOURSELF 4

Simplify each expression.

(a) $\dfrac{x^5}{x^{-3}}$ **(b)** $\dfrac{m^3 n^{-5}}{m^{-2} n^3}$ **(c)** $(3a^3)^{-4}$ **(d)** $\dfrac{(r^3)^{-2}}{(r^{-4})^2}$

Let us now take a look at an important use of exponents, scientific notation.

We begin the discussion with a calculator exercise. On most calculators, if you multiply 2.3 times 1000, the display will read

2300

Multiply by 1000 a second time. Now you will see

2300000.

Multiplying by 1000 a third time will result in the display

NOTE This must equal 2,300,000,000.

2.3   09   or   2.3   E09

And multiplying by 1000 again yields

2.3   12   or   2.3   E12

NOTE Consider the following table:

$2.3 = 2.3 \times 10^0$
$23 = 2.3 \times 10^1$
$230 = 2.3 \times 10^2$
$2300 = 2.3 \times 10^3$
$23{,}000 = 2.3 \times 10^4$
$230{,}000 = 2.3 \times 10^5$

Can you see what is happening? This is the way calculators display very large numbers. The number on the left is always between 1 and 10, and the number on the right indicates the number of places the decimal point must be moved to the right to put the answer in standard (or decimal) form.

This notation is used frequently in science. It is not uncommon in scientific applications of algebra to find yourself working with very large or very small numbers. Even in the time of Archimedes (287–212 B.C.E.), the study of such numbers was not unusual. Archimedes estimated that the universe was 23,000,000,000,000,000 m in diameter, which is the approximate distance light travels in $2\dfrac{1}{2}$ years. By comparison, Polaris (the North Star) is actually 680 light-years from the earth. Example 6 will discuss the idea of light-years.

In scientific notation, Archimedes's estimate for the diameter of the universe would be

2.3×10^{16} m

In general, we can define scientific notation as follows.

Definitions: Scientific Notation

Any number written in the form

$a \times 10^n$

in which $1 \le a < 10$ and n is an integer, is written in scientific notation.

Example 5

Using Scientific Notation

Write each of the following numbers in scientific notation.

NOTE Notice the pattern for writing a number in scientific notation.

(a) $120{,}000. = 1.2 \times 10^5$

5 places   The power is 5.

(b) $88{,}000{,}000. = 8.8 \times 10^7$

7 places   The power is 7.

NOTE The exponent on 10 shows the *number of places* we must move the decimal point. A positive exponent tells us to move right, and a negative exponent indicates to move left.

(c) $520{,}000{,}000. = 5.2 \times 10^8$

8 places

(d) $4{,}000{,}000{,}000. = 4 \times 10^9$

9 places

(e) $0.0005 = 5 \times 10^{-4}$ If the decimal point is to be moved to the left, the exponent will be negative.

4 places

NOTE To convert back to standard or decimal form, the process is simply reversed.

(f) $0.0000000081 = 8.1 \times 10^{-9}$

9 places

 CHECK YOURSELF 5

Write in scientific notation.

(a) 212,000,000,000,000,000   **(b)** 0.00079
(c) 5,600,000   **(d)** 0.0000007

Example 6

An Application of Scientific Notation

(a) Light travels at a speed of 3.05×10^8 meters per second (m/s). There are approximately 3.15×10^7 s in a year. How far does light travel in a year?

We multiply the distance traveled in 1 s by the number of seconds in a year. This yields

NOTE Notice that
$9.6075 \times 10^{15} \approx 10 \times 10^{15} = 10^{16}$

$$(3.05 \times 10^8)(3.15 \times 10^7) = (3.05 \cdot 3.15)(10^8 \cdot 10^7)$$
$$= 9.6075 \times 10^{15}$$

Multiply the coefficients, and add the exponents.

For our purposes we round the distance light travels in 1 year to 10^{16} m. This unit is called a **light-year,** and it is used to measure astronomical distances.

(b) The distance from earth to the star Spica (in Virgo) is 2.2×10^{18} m. How many light-years is Spica from earth?

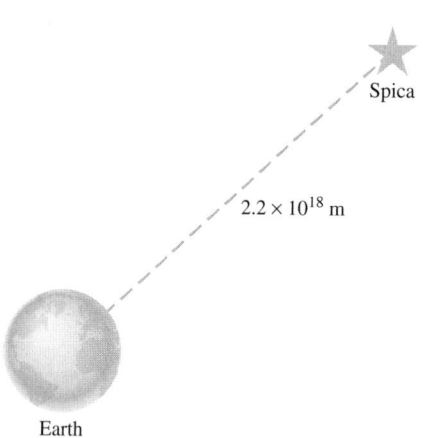

Spica

2.2×10^{18} m

Earth

NOTE We divide the distance (in meters) by the number of meters in 1 light-year.

$$\frac{2.2 \times 10^{18}}{10^{16}} = 2.2 \times 10^{18-16}$$
$$= 2.2 \times 10^2 = 220 \text{ light-years}$$

✔ CHECK YOURSELF 6

The farthest object that can be seen with the unaided eye is the Andromeda galaxy. This galaxy is 2.3×10^{22} m from earth. What is this distance in light-years?

CHECK YOURSELF ANSWERS

1. (a) 1; **(b)** 1; **(c)** 1; **(d)** 3   **2. (a)** $\dfrac{1}{a^{10}}$; **(b)** $\dfrac{1}{4^3}$ or $\dfrac{1}{64}$; **(c)** $\dfrac{3}{x^2}$; **(d)** $\dfrac{1}{x^3}$

3. (a) x^5; **(b)** $\dfrac{1}{b^5}$ **4. (a)** x^8; **(b)** $\dfrac{m^5}{n^8}$; **(c)** $\dfrac{1}{81a^{12}}$; **(d)** r^2

5. (a) 2.12×10^{17}; **(b)** 7.9×10^{-4}; **(c)** 5.6×10^6; **(d)** 7×10^{-7}

6. 2,300,000 light-years

1.18 Exercises

Evaluate (assume the variables are nonzero).

1. 4^0

2. $(-7)^0$

3. $(-29)^0$

4. 75^0

5. $(x^3y^2)^0$

6. $7m^0$

7. $11x^0$

8. $(2a^3b^7)^0$

9. $(-3p^6q^8)^0$

10. $-7x^0$

Write each of the following expressions using positive exponents; simplify when possible.

11. b^{-8}

12. p^{-12}

13. 3^{-4}

14. 2^{-5}

15. 5^{-2}

16. 4^{-3}

17. 10^{-4}

18. 10^{-5}

19. $5x^{-1}$

20. $3a^{-2}$

21. $(5x)^{-1}$

22. $(3a)^{-2}$

23. $-2x^{-5}$

24. $3x^{-4}$

25. $(-2x)^{-5}$

26. $(3x)^{-4}$

Use Properties 1 and 2 to simplify each of the following expressions. Write your answers with positive exponents only.

27. a^5a^3

28. m^5m^7

29. x^8x^{-2}

30. $a^{12}a^{-8}$

31. b^7b^{-11}

32. y^5y^{-12}

33. x^0x^5

34. $r^{-3}r^0$

35. $\dfrac{a^8}{a^5}$

ANSWERS	
1.	2.
3.	4.
5.	6.
7.	8.
9.	10.
11.	12.
13.	14.
15.	16.
17.	18.
19.	20.
21.	22.
23.	24.
25.	26.
27.	28.
29.	30.
31.	32.
33.	34.
35.	

36. _____

37. _____

38. _____

39. _____

40. _____

41. _____

42. _____

43. _____

44. _____

45. _____

46. _____

47. _____

48. _____

49. _____

50. _____

51. _____

52. _____

53. _____

54. _____

55. _____

56. _____

57. _____

58. _____

59. _____

36. $\dfrac{m^9}{m^4}$ **37.** $\dfrac{x^7}{x^9}$ **38.** $\dfrac{a^3}{a^{10}}$

39. $\dfrac{r^{-3}}{r^5}$ **40.** $\dfrac{x^3}{x^{-5}}$ **41.** $\dfrac{x^{-4}}{x^{-5}}$

42. $\dfrac{p^{-6}}{p^{-3}}$

Simplify each of the following expressions. Write your answers with positive exponents only.

43. $\dfrac{m^5 n^{-3}}{m^{-4} n^5}$ **44.** $\dfrac{p^{-3} q^{-2}}{p^4 q^{-3}}$ **45.** $(2a^{-3})^4$

46. $(3x^2)^{-3}$ **47.** $(x^{-2} y^3)^{-2}$ **48.** $(a^5 b^{-3})^{-3}$

49. $\dfrac{(r^{-2})^3}{r^{-4}}$ **50.** $\dfrac{(y^3)^{-4}}{y^{-6}}$ **51.** $\dfrac{(x^{-3})^3}{(x^4)^{-2}}$

52. $\dfrac{(m^4)^{-3}}{(m^{-2})^4}$ **53.** $\dfrac{(a^{-3})^2(a^4)}{(a^{-3})^{-3}}$ **54.** $\dfrac{(x^2)^{-3}(x^{-2})}{(x^2)^{-4}}$

In exercises 55 to 58, express each number in scientific notation.

55. The distance from the earth to the sun: 93,000,000 mi.

56. The diameter of a grain of sand: 0.000021 m.

57. The diameter of the sun: 130,000,000,000 cm.

58. The number of molecules in 22.4 L of a gas: 602,000,000,000,000,000,000,000 (Avogadro's number).

59. The mass of the sun is approximately 1.98×10^{30} kg. If this were written in standard or decimal form, how many 0s would follow the digit 8?

60. Archimedes estimated the universe to be 2.3×10^{19} millimeters (mm) in diameter. If this number were written in standard or decimal form, how many 0s would follow the digit 3?

In exercises 61 to 64, write each expression in standard notation.

61. 8×10^{-3} **62.** 7.5×10^{-6} **63.** 2.8×10^{-5} **64.** 5.21×10^{-4}

In exercises 65 to 68, write each of the following in scientific notation.

65. 0.0005   **66.** 0.000003   **67.** 0.00037   **68.** 0.000051

In exercises 69 to 72, compute the expressions using scientific notation, and write your answer in that form.

69. $(4 \times 10^{-3})(2 \times 10^{-5})$ **70.** $(1.5 \times 10^{-6})(4 \times 10^{2})$

71. $\dfrac{9 \times 10^{3}}{3 \times 10^{-2}}$ **72.** $\dfrac{7.5 \times 10^{-4}}{1.5 \times 10^{2}}$

In exercises 73 to 78, perform the indicated calculations. Write your result in scientific notation.

73. $(2 \times 10^{5})(4 \times 10^{4})$ **74.** $(2.5 \times 10^{7})(3 \times 10^{5})$ **75.** $\dfrac{6 \times 10^{9}}{3 \times 10^{7}}$

76. $\dfrac{4.5 \times 10^{12}}{1.5 \times 10^{7}}$ **77.** $\dfrac{(3.3 \times 10^{15})(6 \times 10^{15})}{(1.1 \times 10^{8})(3 \times 10^{6})}$ **78.** $\dfrac{(6 \times 10^{12})(3.2 \times 10^{8})}{(1.6 \times 10^{7})(3 \times 10^{2})}$

In 1975 the population of Earth was approximately 4 billion and doubling every 35 years. The formula for the population P in year Y for this doubling rate is

$$P \text{ (in billions)} = 4 \times 2^{(Y-1975)/35}$$

79. What was the approximate population of Earth in 1960?

80. What will Earth's population be in 2025?

The United States population in 1990 was approximately 250 million, and the average growth rate for the past 30 years gives a doubling time of 66 years. The above formula for the United States then becomes

$$P \text{ (in millions)} = 250 \times 2^{(Y-1990)/66}$$

81. What was the approximate population of the United States in 1960?

82. What will be the population of the United States in 2025 if this growth rate continues?

ANSWERS

60. _____

61. _____

62. _____

63. _____

64. _____

65. _____

66. _____

67. _____

68. _____

69. _____

70. _____

71. _____

72. _____

73. _____

74. _____

75. _____

76. _____

77. _____

78. _____

79. _____

80. _____

81. _____

82. _____

83. _____

84. _____

85. _____

86. _____

87. _____

a. _____

b. _____

c. _____

d. _____

e. _____

f. _____

g. _____

h. _____

83. Megrez, the nearest of the Big Dipper stars, is 6.6×10^{17} m from Earth. Approximately how long does it take light, traveling at 10^{16} m/year, to travel from Megrez to Earth?

84. Alkaid, the most distant star in the Big Dipper, is 2.1×10^{18} m from Earth. Approximately how long does it take light to travel from Alkaid to Earth?

85. The number of liters (L) of water on Earth is 15,500 followed by 19 zeros. Write this number in scientific notation. Then use the number of liters of water on Earth to find out how much water is available for each person on Earth. The population of Earth is 6 billion.

86. If there are 6×10^9 people on Earth and there is enough freshwater to provide each person with 8.79×10^5 L, how much freshwater is on Earth?

87. The United States uses an average of 2.6×10^6 L of water per person each year. The United States has 3.2×10^8 people. How many liters of water does the United States use each year?

 Getting Ready

Combine like terms where possible.

(a) $8m + 7m$

(b) $9x - 5x$

(c) $9m^2 - 8m$

(d) $8x^2 - 7x^2$

(e) $5c^3 + 15c^3$

(f) $9s^3 + 8s^3$

(g) $8c^2 - 6c + 2c^2$

(h) $8r^3 - 7r^2 + 5r^3$

Answers

1. 1 **3.** 1 **5.** 1 **7.** 11 **9.** 1 **11.** $\dfrac{1}{b^8}$ **13.** $\dfrac{1}{81}$

15. $\dfrac{1}{25}$ **17.** $\dfrac{1}{10,000}$ **19.** $\dfrac{5}{x}$ **21.** $\dfrac{1}{5x}$ **23.** $-\dfrac{2}{x^5}$

25. $-\dfrac{1}{32x^5}$ **27.** a^8 **29.** x^6 **31.** $\dfrac{1}{b^4}$ **33.** x^5 **35.** a^3 **37.** $\dfrac{1}{x^2}$

39. $\dfrac{1}{r^8}$ **41.** x **43.** $\dfrac{m^9}{n^8}$ **45.** $\dfrac{16}{a^{12}}$ **47.** $\dfrac{x^4}{y^6}$ **49.** $\dfrac{1}{r^2}$ **51.** $\dfrac{1}{x}$

53. $\dfrac{1}{a^{11}}$ **55.** 9.3×10^7 mi **57.** 1.3×10^{11} cm **59.** 28 **61.** 0.008

63. 0.000028 **65.** 5×10^{-4} **67.** 3.7×10^{-4} **69.** 8×10^{-8}
71. 3×10^5 **73.** 8×10^9 **75.** 2×10^2 **77.** 6×10^{16}
79. 2.97 billion **81.** 182 million **83.** 66 years
85. 1.55×10^{23} L; 2.58×10^{13} L **87.** 8.32×10^{14} L **a.** $15m$ **b.** $4x$
c. $9m^2 - 8m$ **d.** x^2 **e.** $20c^3$ **f.** $17s^3$ **g.** $10c^2 - 6c$ **h.** $13r^3 - 7r^2$

An Introduction to Graphing

2

INTRODUCTION

Graphs are used to discern patterns and trends that may be difficult to see when looking at a list of numbers or other kinds of data. The word *graph* comes from Latin and Greek roots and means "to draw a picture." This is just what a graph does in mathematics: It draws a picture of a relationship between two or more variables. But, as in art, these graphs can be difficult to interpret without a little practice and training. This chapter is the beginning of that training. And the training is important because graphs are used in every field in which numbers are used.

In the field of pediatric medicine, there has been controversy about the use of somatotropin (human growth hormone) to help children whose growth has been impeded by various health problems. The reason for the controversy is that many doctors are giving this expensive drug therapy to children who are simply shorter than average or shorter than their parents want them to be. The question of which children are not growing normally because of some serious health defect and need the therapy and which children are healthy and simply small of stature and thus should not be subjected to this treatment has been vigorously argued by professionals here and in Europe, where the therapy is being used.

Some of the measures used to distinguish between the two groups are blood tests and age and height measurements. The age and height measurements are graphed and monitored over several years of a child's life to monitor the rate of growth. If during a certain period the child's rate of growth slows to below 4.5 centimeters per year, this indicates that something may be seriously wrong. The graph can also indicate if the child's size fits within a range considered normal at each age of the child's life.

2 **Pre-Test Chapter 2**

Determine which of the ordered pairs are solutions for the given equations.

1. $x - y = 12$ (15, 3), (9, 6), (18, 6)

2. $3x + 2y = 6$ (1, 2), (0, 3), (2, 0)

3. Complete the ordered pairs so that each is a solution for the given equation.

$2x + y = 5$ (1,), (0,), (, 11)

4. Find three solutions for each of the following equations.

$2x - 3y = 8$ $6x + y = 11$

5. Give the coordinates of the points graphed below

6. Plot the points with the given coordinates. S(−1, 2), T(3, 0)

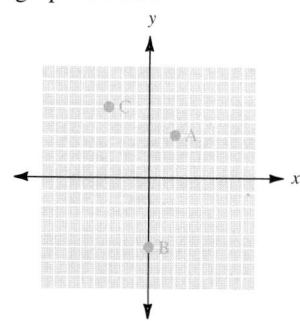   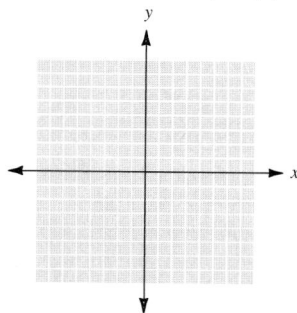

Graph each of the following equations.

7. $x + y = 5$ **8.** $y = \dfrac{1}{2}x - 1$ **9.** $y = -2$

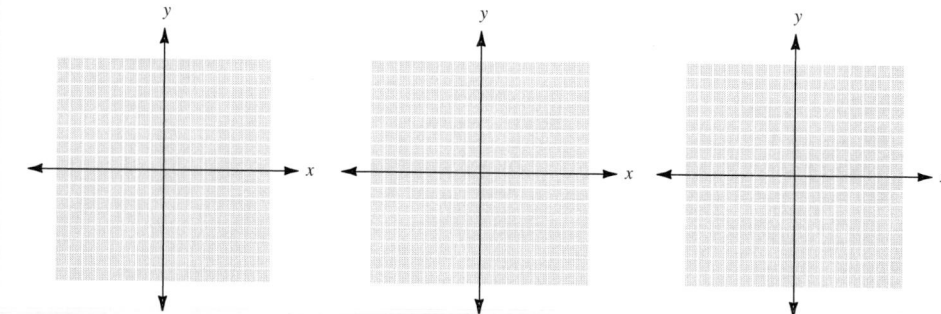

Find the slope of the line through the following pairs of points.

10. (−2,5) and (5,12)   **11.** (−1,−3) and (7,−11)

12. Find the constant of variation, k, if y varies directly with x and $y = 56$ when $x = 7$.

Find the slope of the line for the following equations.

13. $y = 4x - 5$ **14.** $y = -\dfrac{2}{5}x + 7$

15. Pete's commission varies directly as the number of appliances he sells. If his commission last month was $800 and he sold 20 appliances, what would his salary be if he sold 25 appliances?

The Rectangular Coordinate System

 OBJECTIVES

1. Give the coordinates of a set of points on the plane
2. Graph the points corresponding to a set of ordered pairs

We know that ordered pairs could be used to write the solutions of equations in two variables. The next step is to graph those ordered pairs as points in a plane.

Because there are two numbers (one for x and one for y), we will need two number lines. One line is drawn horizontally, and the other is drawn vertically; their point of intersection (at their respective zero points) is called the *origin*. The horizontal line is called the *x* **axis,** and the vertical line is called the *y* **axis.** Together the lines form the **rectangular coordinate system.**

The axes divide the plane into four regions called **quadrants,** which are numbered (usually by Roman numerals) counterclockwise from the upper right.

NOTE This system is also called the **cartesian coordinate system,** named in honor of its inventor, René Descartes (1596–1650), a French mathematician and philosopher.

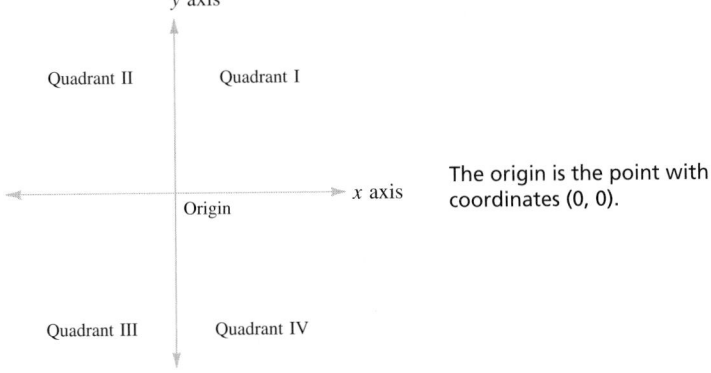

The origin is the point with coordinates (0, 0).

We now want to establish correspondences between ordered pairs of numbers (x, y) and points in the plane.

For any ordered pair

$$(x, y)$$

x coordinate y coordinate

the following are true:

1. If the x coordinate is

Positive, the point corresponding to that pair is located x units to the *right* of the y axis.
Negative, the point is x units to the *left* of the y axis.
Zero, the point is on the y axis.

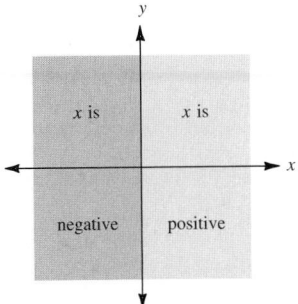

2. If the *y* coordinate is

Positive, the point is *y* units *above* the *x* axis.
Negative, the point is *y* units *below* the *x* axis.
Zero, the point is on the *x* axis.

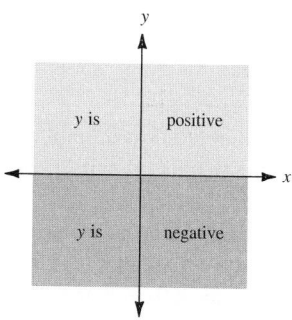

Example 1 illustrates how to use these guidelines to give coordinates to points in the plane.

Example 1

Identifying the Coordinates for a Given Point

Give the coordinates for the given point

(a)

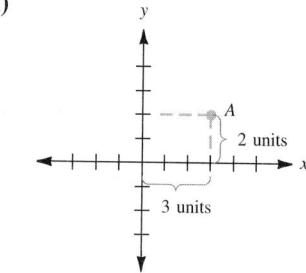

Point *A* is 3 units to the *right* of the *y* axis and 2 units *above* the *x* axis. Point *A* has coordinates (3, 2).

(b)

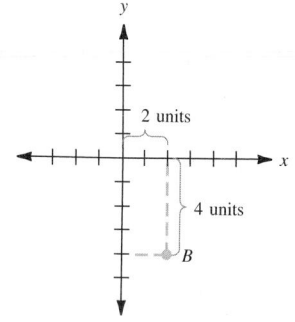

Point *B* is 2 units to the *right* of the *y* axis and 4 units *below* the *x* axis. Point *B* has coordinates (2, −4).

(c)

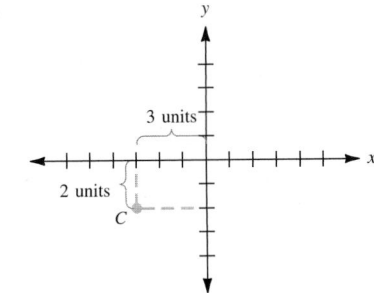

Point *C* is 3 units to the *left* of the *y* axis and 2 units *below* the *x* axis. *C* has coordinates $(-3, -2)$.

(d)

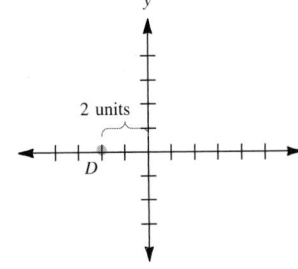

Point *D* is 2 units to the *left* of the *y* axis and *on* the *x* axis. Point *D* has coordinates $(-2, 0)$.

 CHECK YOURSELF 1

Give the coordinates of points P, Q, R, and S.

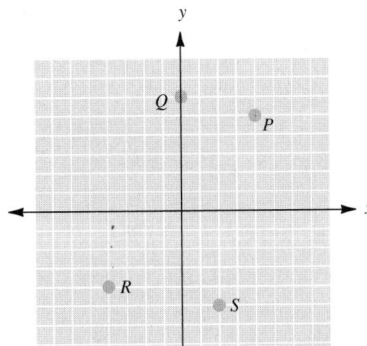

P _____

Q _____

R _____

S _____

Reversing the process above will allow us to graph (or plot) a point in the plane given the coordinates of the point. You can use the following steps.

NOTE The graphing of individual points is sometimes called **point plotting**.

Step by Step: To Graph a Point in the Plane

Step 1   Start at the origin.
Step 2   Move right or left according to the value of the *x* coordinate.
Step 3   Move up or down according to the value of the *y* coordinate.

Example 2

Graphing Points

(a) Graph the point corresponding to the ordered pair (4, 3).

Move 4 units to the right on the *x* axis. Then move 3 units up from the point you stopped at on the *x* axis. This locates the point corresponding to (4, 3).

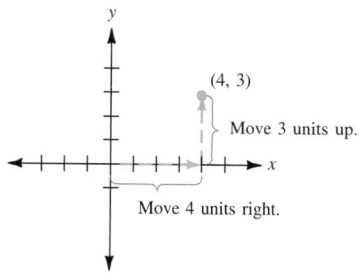

(b) Graph the point corresponding to the ordered pair (−5, 2).

In this case move 5 units *left* (because the *x* coordinate is negative) and then 2 units *up*.

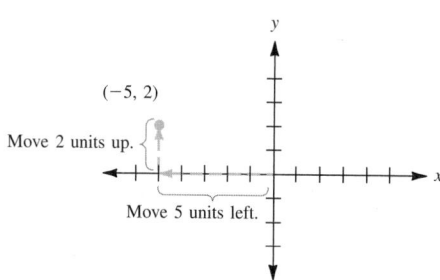

(c) Graph the point corresponding to (−4, −2).

Here move 4 units *left* and then 2 units *down* (the *y* coordinate is negative).

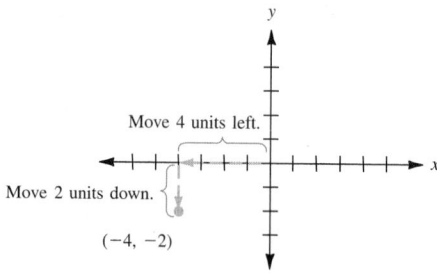

NOTE Any point on an axis will have 0 for one of its coordinates.

(d) Graph the point corresponding to $(0, -3)$.

There is *no* horizontal movement because the *x* coordinate is 0. Move 3 units *down*.

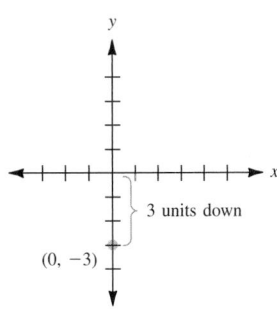

(e) Graph the point corresponding to $(5, 0)$.

Move 5 units *right*. The desired point is on the *x* axis because the *y* coordinate is 0.

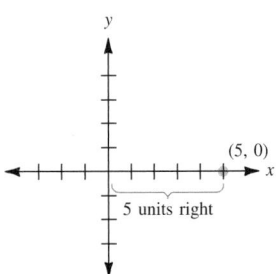

 CHECK YOURSELF 2

Graph the points corresponding to M(4, 3), N(−2, 4), P(−5, −3), and Q(0, −3).

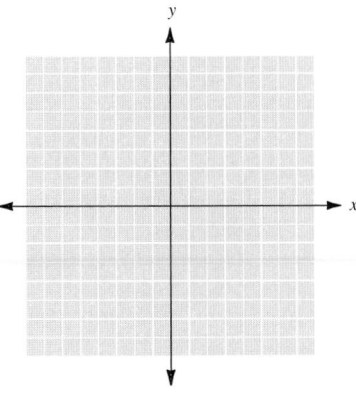

CHECK YOURSELF ANSWERS

1. $P(4, 5)$, $Q(0, 6)$, $R(-4, -4)$, and $S(2, -5)$

2.

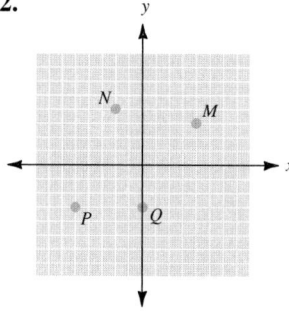

2.1 Exercises

Give the coordinates of the points graphed below.

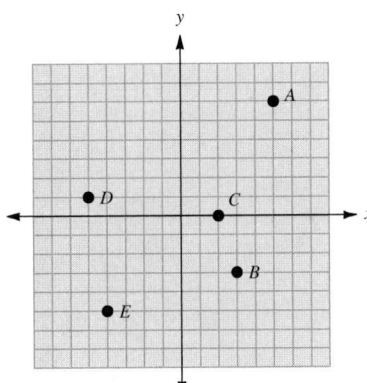

1. *A*

2. *B*

3. *C*

4. *D*

5. *E*

Give the coordinates of the points graphed below.

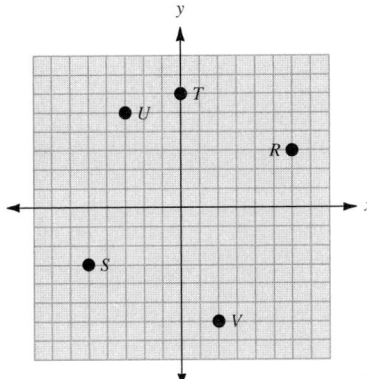

6. *R*

7. *S*

8. *T*

9. *U*

10. *V*

Plot points with the following coordinates on the graph below.

11. $M(5, 3)$

12. $N(0, -3)$

13. $P(-2, 6)$

14. $Q(5, 0)$

15. $R(-4, -6)$

16. $S(-3, -4)$

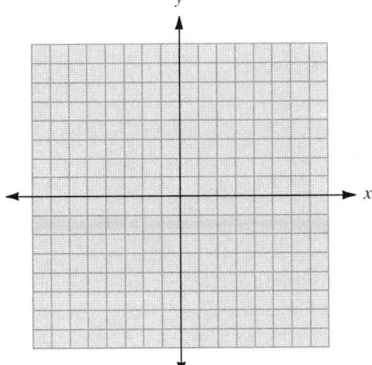

ANSWERS

1. _____

2. _____

3. _____

4. _____

5. _____

6. _____

7. _____

8. _____

9. _____

10. _____

11. _____

12. _____

13. _____

14. _____

15. _____

16. _____

17. _____

18. _____

19. _____

20. _____

21. _____

22. _____

23. _____

24. _____

Plot points with the following coordinates on the graph below.

17. $F(-3, -1)$ **18.** $G(4, 3)$

19. $H(5, -2)$ **20.** $I(-3, 0)$

21. $J(-5, 3)$ **22.** $K(0, 6)$

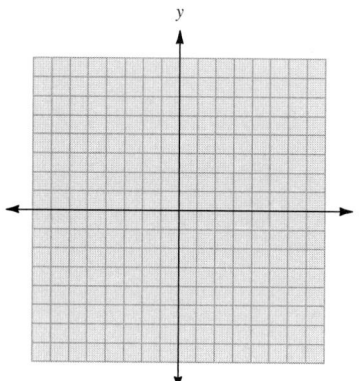

23. Graph points with coordinates (2, 3), (3, 4), and (4, 5) below. What do you observe? Can you give the coordinates of another point with the same property?

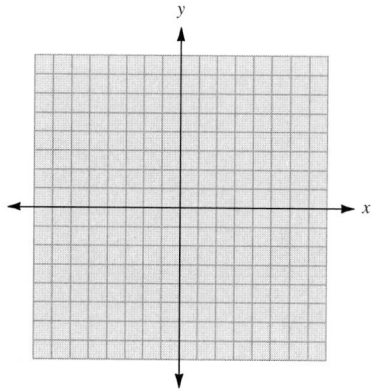

24. Graph points with coordinates $(-1, 4)$, $(0, 3)$, and $(1, 2)$ below. What do you observe? Can you give the coordinates of another point with the same property?

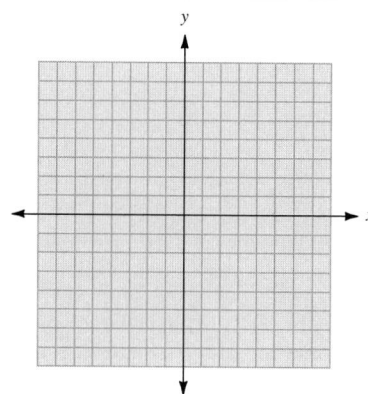

25. Graph points with coordinates $(-1, 3)$, $(0, 0)$, and $(1, -3)$ below. What do you observe? Can you give the coordinates of another point with the same property?

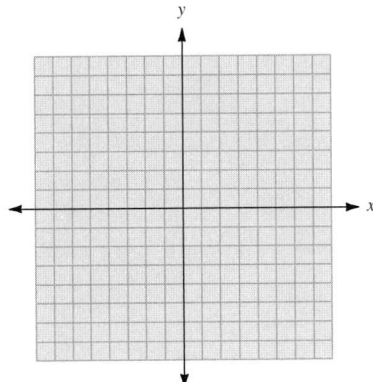

26. Graph points with coordinates $(1, 5)$, $(-1, 3)$, and $(-3, 1)$ below. What do you observe? Can you give the coordinates of another point with the same property?

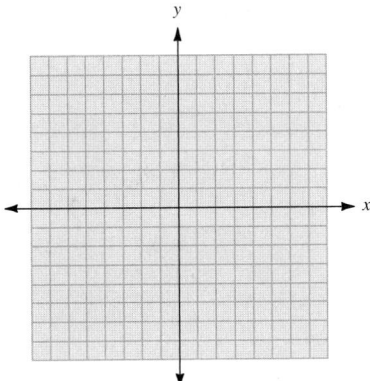

27. Environment. A local plastics company is sponsoring a plastics recycling contest for the local community. The focus of the contest is collecting plastic milk, juice, and water jugs. The company will award $200 plus the current market price of the jugs collected to the group that collects the most jugs in a single month. The number of jugs collected and the amount of money won can be represented as an ordered pair.

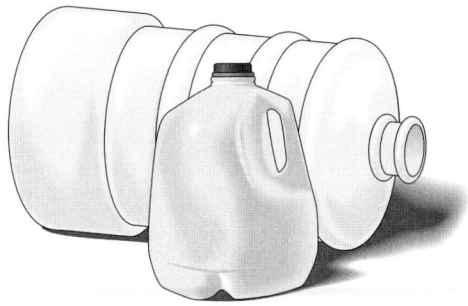

(a) In April, group A collected 1500 pounds (lb) of jugs to win first place. The prize for the month was $350. On the graph on the next page, x represents the pounds of jugs and y represents the amount of money that the group won. Graph the point that represents the winner for April.

(b) In May, group *B* collected 2300 lb of jugs to win first place. The prize for the month was $430. Graph the point that represents the May winner on the same axis you used in part (a).

(c) In June, group *C* collected 1200 lb of jugs to win the contest. The prize for the month was $320. Graph the point that represents the June winner on the same axis as used before.

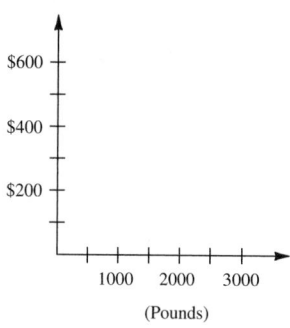

28. Education. The table gives the hours, x, that Damien studied for five different math exams and the resulting grades, y. Plot the data given in the table.

x	4	5	5	2	6
y	83	89	93	75	95

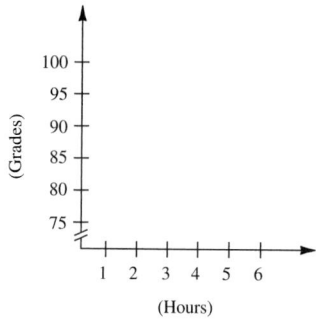

29. Science. The table gives the average temperature y (in degrees Fahrenheit) for the first 6 months of the year, x. The months are numbered 1 through 6, with 1 corresponding to January. Plot the data given in the table.

x	1	2	3	4	5	6
y	4	14	26	33	42	51

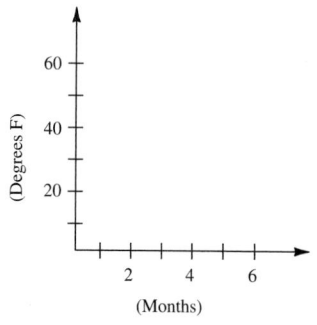

30. Business. The table gives the total salary of a salesperson, y, for each of the four quarters of the year, x. Plot the data given in the table.

x	1	2	3	4
y	$6000	$5000	$8000	$9000

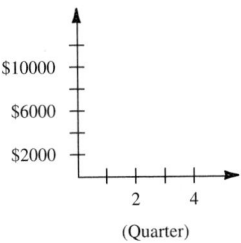

(Quarter)

31. Sports. The table shows the number of runs scored by the New York Yankees in the 1999 World Series.

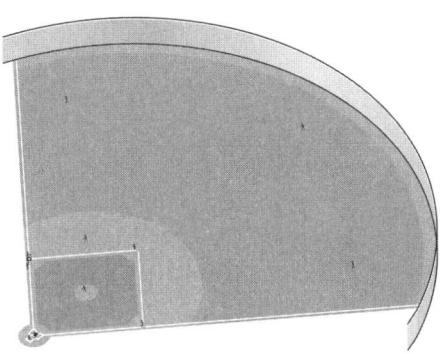

Game	1	2	3	4
Runs	4	7	6	4

Plot the data given in the table.

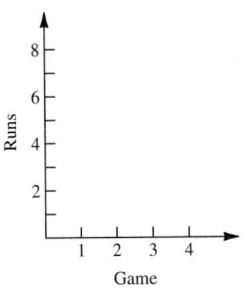

32. **Sports.** The following table shows the number of wins and total points for the five teams in the Atlantic Division of the National Hockey League in the early part of the 1999–2000 season.

Team	Wins	Points
New Jersey Devils	5	12
Philadelphia Flyers	4	10
New York Rangers	4	9
Pittsburgh Penguins	2	6
New York Islanders	2	5

Plot the data given in the table.

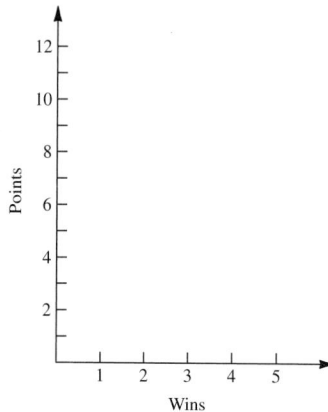

33. How would you describe a rectangular coordinate system? Explain what information is needed to locate a point in a coordinate system.

34. Some newspapers have a special day that they devote to automobile ads. Use this special section or the Sunday classified ads from your local newspaper to find all the want ads for a particular automobile model. Make a list of the model year and asking price for 10 ads, being sure to get a variety of ages for this model. After collecting the information, make a scatter plot of the age and the asking price for the car.

    Describe your graph, including an explanation of how you decided which variable to put on the vertical axis and which on the horizontal axis. What trends or other information are given by the graph?

35. The map shown on the next page uses letters and numbers to label a grid that helps to locate a city. For instance, Salem is located at E-4.

    (a) Find the coordinates for the following: White Swan, Newport, and Wheeler.

    (b) What cities correspond to the following coordinates: A2, F4, and A5?

 Getting Ready

Solve each of the following equations.

(a) $2x - 2 = 6$

(b) $2 - 5x = 12$

(c) $7y + 10 = -11$

(d) $-3 + 5x = 1$

(e) $6 - 3x = 8$

(f) $-4y + 6 = 3$

Answers for Pre-Test for Chapter 2

1. $(15, 3)$; $(18, 6)$ **2.** $(0, 3)$; $(2, 0)$ **3.** $(1, 3)$; $(0, 5)$; $(-3, 11)$
4. Answers vary **5.** $A(2, 3)$ $B(0, -5)$ $C(-3, 5)$

6.

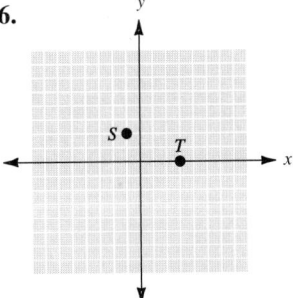

7.

8.

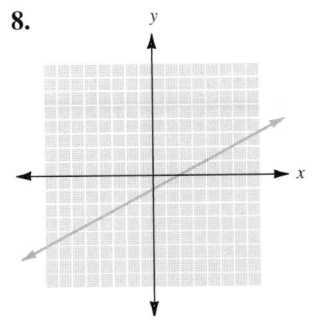

9.

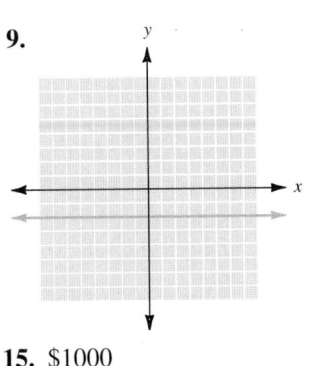

10. 1 **11.** -1 **12.** 8 **13.** 4 **14.** $-\dfrac{2}{5}$ **15.** $\$1000$

Answers

1. $(5, 6)$ **3.** $(2, 0)$ **5.** $(-4, -5)$ **7.** $(-5, -3)$ **9.** $(-3, 5)$

11–21.

23. The points lie on a line; $(1, 2)$

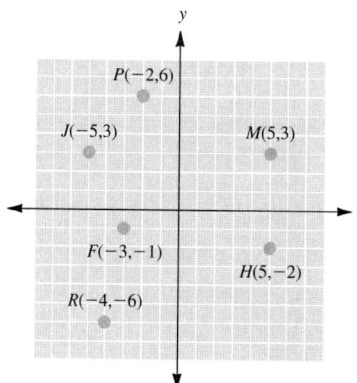

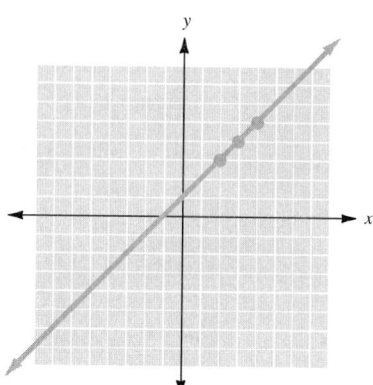

25. The points lie on a line; $(2, -6)$

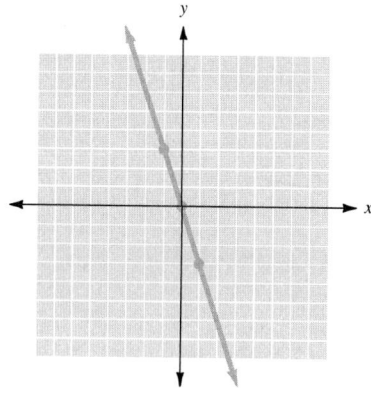

27. **(a)** $(1500, 350)$; **(b)** $(2300, 430)$; **(c)** $(1200, 320)$

29.

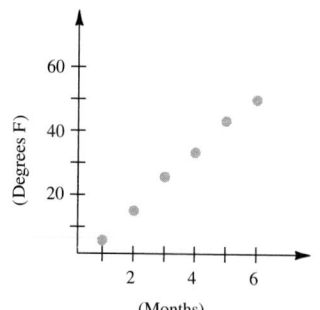

31.

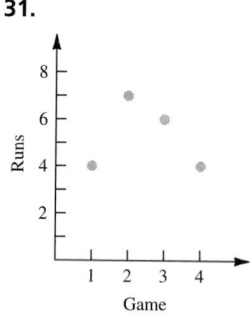

33.

35. **(a)** B7, F2, C2; **(b)** Oysterville, Sweet Home, Mineral

a. 4 **b.** -2 **c.** -3 **d.** $\dfrac{4}{5}$ **e.** $-\dfrac{2}{3}$ **f.** $\dfrac{3}{4}$

 # Graphing Linear Equations

 OBJECTIVES

1. Graph a linear equation by plotting points
2. Graph a linear equation by the intercept method
3. Graph a linear equation by solving the equation for *y*

We are now ready to combine our work of the previous sections. In Section 2.1, ordered pairs were graphed in the plane. Putting these ideas together will let us graph certain equations. Example 1 illustrates this approach.

Example 1

Graphing a Linear Equation

Graph $x + 2y = 4$.

Step 1 Find some solutions for $x + 2y = 4$. To find solutions, we choose any convenient values for x, say $x = 0$, $x = 2$, and $x = 4$. Given these values for x, we can substitute and then solve for the corresponding value for y. So

NOTE We are going to find *three* solutions for the equation. We'll point out why shortly.

If $x = 0$, then $y = 2$, so $(0, 2)$ is a solution.
If $x = 2$, then $y = 1$, so $(2, 1)$ is a solution.
If $x = 4$, then $y = 0$, so $(4, 0)$ is a solution.

A handy way to show this information is in a table such as this:

NOTE The table is just a convenient way to display the information. It is the same as writing (0, 2), (2, 1), and (4, 0).

x	y
0	2
2	1
4	0

Step 2 We now graph the solutions found in step 1.

$x + 2y = 4$

x	y
0	2
2	1
4	0

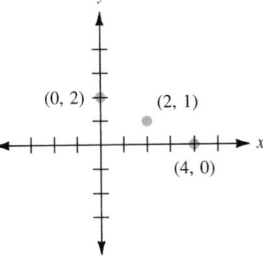

What pattern do you see? It appears that the three points lie on a straight line, and that is in fact the case.

Step 3 Draw a straight line through the three points graphed in step 2.

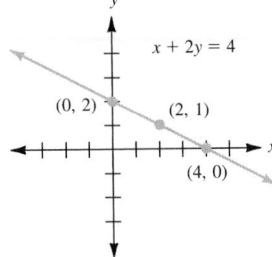

NOTE The arrows on the end of the line mean that the line extends indefinitely in either direction.

The line shown is the **graph** of the equation $x + 2y = 4$. It represents *all* of the ordered pairs that are solutions (an infinite number) for that equation.

Every ordered pair that is a solution will have its graph on this line. Any point on the line will have coordinates that are a solution for the equation.

Note: Why did we suggest finding *three* solutions in step 1? Two points determine a line, so technically you need only two. The third point that we find is a check to catch any possible errors.

 CHECK YOURSELF 1

Graph $2x - y = 6$, using the steps shown in Example 1.

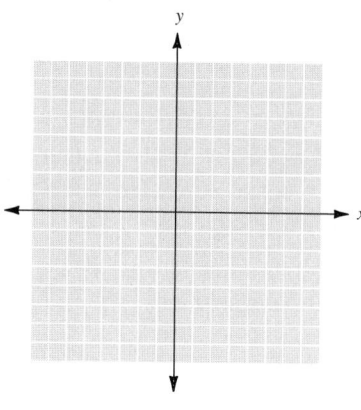

Let's summarize. An equation that can be written in the form

$$Ax + By = C$$

in which A, B, and C are real numbers and A and B cannot both be 0 is called a **linear equation in two variables.** The graph of this equation is a *straight line*.

The steps of graphing follow.

Step by Step: To Graph a Linear Equation

Step 1 Find at least three solutions for the equation, and put your results in tabular form.
Step 2 Graph the solutions found in step 1.
Step 3 Draw a straight line through the points determined in step 2 to form the graph of the equation.

Example 2

Graphing a Linear Equation

Graph $y = 3x$.

Step 1 Some solutions are

x	y
0	0
1	3
2	6

Step 2   Graph the points.

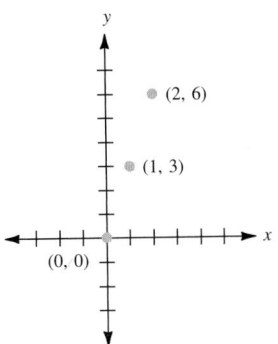

NOTE Notice that connecting any two of these points produces the same line.

Step 3   Draw a line through the points.

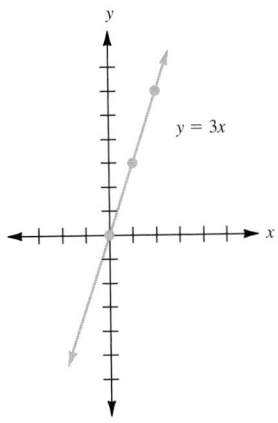

CHECK YOURSELF 2

Graph the equation y = −2x after completing the table of values.

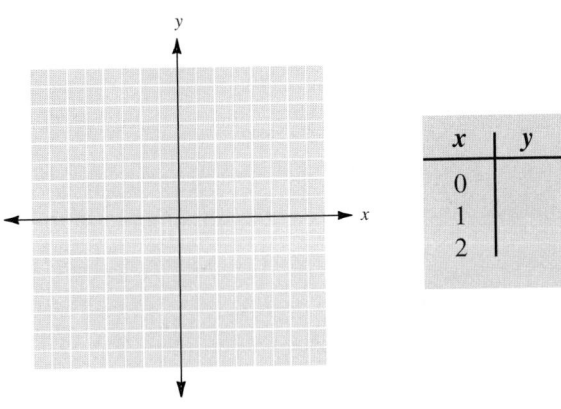

Let's work through another example of graphing a line from its equation.

Example 3

Graphing a Linear Equation

Graph $y = 2x + 3$.

Step 1   Some solutions are

x	y
0	3
1	5
2	7

Step 2   Graph the points corresponding to these values.

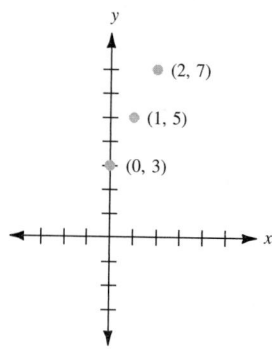

Step 3   Draw a line through the points.

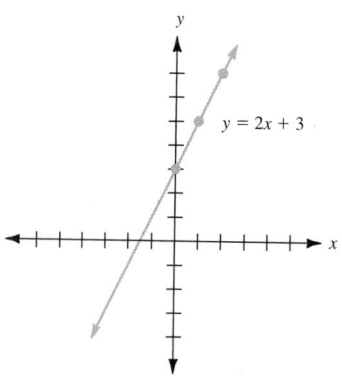

$y = 2x + 3$

✔ CHECK YOURSELF 3

Graph the equation y = 3x − 2 after completing the table of values.

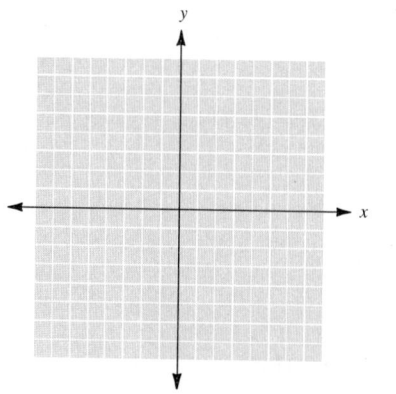

x	y
0	
1	
2	

In graphing equations, particularly when fractions are involved, a careful choice of values for x can simplify the process. Consider Example 4.

Example 4

Graphing a Linear Equation

Graph

$$y = \frac{3}{2}x - 2$$

As before, we want to find solutions for the given equation by picking convenient values for x. Note that in this case, choosing *multiples of 2* will avoid fractional values for y and make the plotting of those solutions much easier. For instance, here we might choose values of $-2, 0,$ and 2 for x.

Step 1   If $x = -2$:

$$y = \frac{3}{2}(-2) - 2$$

$$= -3 - 2 = -5$$

If $x = 0$:

$$y = \frac{3}{2}(0) - 2$$

$$= 0 - 2 = -2$$

If $x = 2$:

$$y = \frac{3}{2}(2) - 2$$

$$= 3 - 2 = 1$$

In tabular form, the solutions are

x	y
-2	-5
0	-2
2	1

NOTE Suppose we do *not* choose a multiple of 2, say, $x = 3$. Then

$$y = \frac{3}{2}(3) - 2$$

$$= \frac{9}{2} - 2$$

$$= \frac{5}{2}$$

$\left(3, \dfrac{5}{2}\right)$ is still a valid solution, but we must graph a point with fractional coordinates.

Step 2   Graph the points determined above.

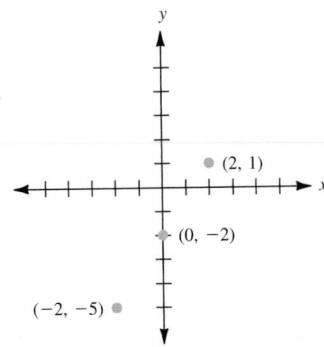

Step 3   Draw a line through the points.

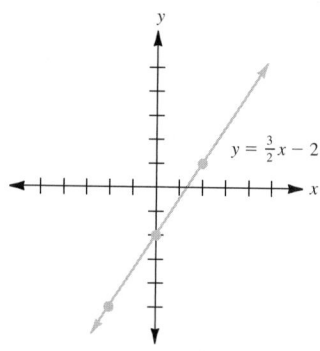

$$y = \frac{3}{2}x - 2$$

✔ **CHECK YOURSELF 4**

Graph the equation $y = -\dfrac{1}{3}x + 3$ *after completing the table of values.*

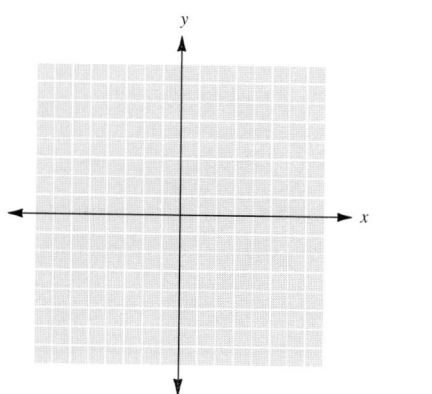

x	y
-3	
0	
3	

Some special cases of linear equations are illustrated in Examples 5 and 6.

Example 5

Graphing an Equation That Results in a Vertical Line

Graph $x = 3$.

The equation $x = 3$ is equivalent to $x + 0 \cdot y = 3$. Let's look at some solutions.

If $y = 1$:   If $y = 4$:   If $y = -2$:

$x + 0 \cdot 1 = 3$ $x + 0 \cdot 4 = 3$ $x + 0(-2) = 3$

$x = 3$ $x = 3$ $x = 3$

In tabular form,

x	y
3	1
3	4
3	-2

What do you observe? The variable x has the value 3, regardless of the value of y. Look at the graph on the following page.

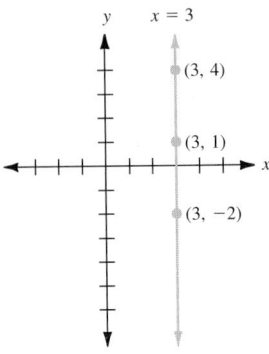

The graph of $x = 3$ is a vertical line crossing the x axis at $(3, 0)$.

Note that graphing (or plotting) points in this case is not really necessary. Simply recognize that the graph of $x = 3$ *must* be a vertical line (parallel to the y axis) that intercepts the x axis at $(3, 0)$.

 CHECK YOURSELF 5

Graph the equation $x = -2$.

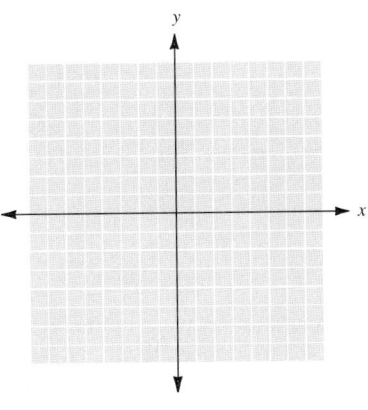

Example 6 is a related example involving a horizontal line.

Example 6

Graphing an Equation That Results in a Horizontal Line

Graph $y = 4$.

Because $y = 4$ is equivalent to $0 \cdot x + y = 4$, any value for x paired with 4 for y will form a solution. A table of values might be

x	y
-2	4
0	4
2	4

Here is the graph.

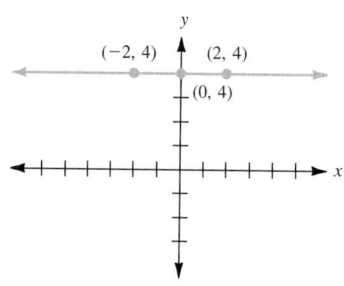

This time the graph is a horizontal line that crosses the *y* axis at (0, 4). Again the graphing of points is not required. The graph of $y = 4$ *must* be horizontal (parallel to the *x* axis) and intercepts the *y* axis at (0, 4).

 CHECK YOURSELF 6

Graph the equation $y = -3$.

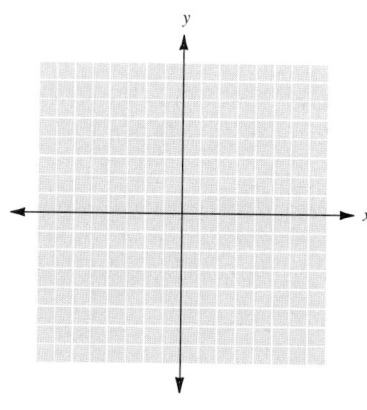

The following box summarizes our work in the previous two examples:

Definitions: Vertical and Horizontal Lines

1. The graph of $x = a$ is a *vertical line* crossing the *x* axis at (*a*, 0).
2. The graph of $y = b$ is a *horizontal line* crossing the *y* axis at (0, *b*).

To simplify the graphing of certain linear equations, some students prefer the **intercept method** of graphing. This method makes use of the fact that the solutions that are easiest to find are those with an *x* coordinate or a *y* coordinate of 0. For instance, let's graph the equation

$$4x + 3y = 12$$

NOTE With practice, all this can be done mentally, which is the big advantage of this method.

First, let $x = 0$ and solve for *y*.

$$4 \cdot 0 + 3y = 12$$
$$3y = 12$$
$$y = 4$$

So (0, 4) is one solution. Now we let $y = 0$ and solve for *x*.

$$4x + 3 \cdot 0 = 12$$
$$4x = 12$$
$$x = 3$$

A second solution is (3, 0).

The two points corresponding to these solutions can now be used to graph the equation.

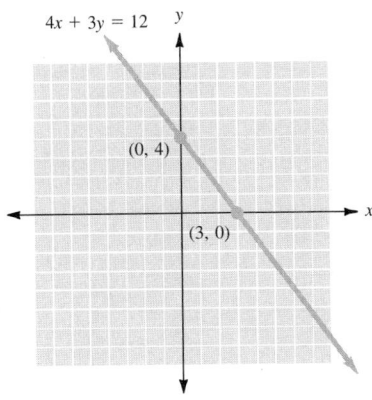

The ordered pair (3, 0) is called the **x intercept,** and the ordered pair (0, 4) is the **y intercept** of the graph. Using these points to draw the graph gives the name to this method. Let's look at a second example of graphing by the intercept method.

Example 7

Using the Intercept Method to Graph a Line

Graph $3x - 5y = 15$, using the intercept method.

To find the x intercept, let $y = 0$.

$$3x - 5 \cdot 0 = 15$$
$$x = 5$$

The x intercept is (5, 0)

To find the y intercept, let $x = 0$.

$$3 \cdot 0 - 5y = 15$$
$$y = -3$$

The y intercept is (0, −3)

So (5, 0) and (0, −3) are solutions for the equation, and we can use the corresponding points to graph the equation.

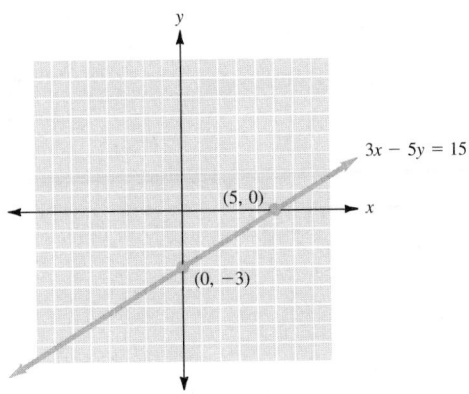

✔ CHECK YOURSELF 7

Graph $4x + 5y = 20$, using the intercept method.

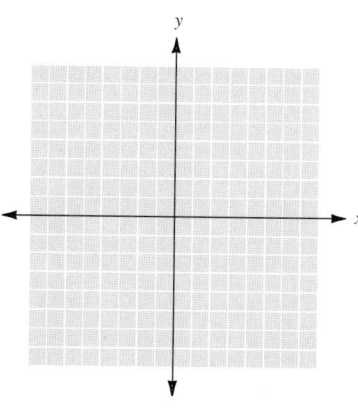

NOTE Finding the third "checkpoint" is always a good idea.

This all looks quite easy, and for many equations it is. What are the drawbacks? For one, you don't have a third checkpoint, and it is possible for errors to occur. You can, of course, still find a third point (other than the two intercepts) to be sure your graph is correct. A second difficulty arises when the x and y intercepts are very close to one another (or are actually the same point—the origin). For instance, if we have the equation

$$3x + 2y = 1$$

the intercepts are $\left(\dfrac{1}{3}, 0\right)$ and $\left(0, \dfrac{1}{2}\right)$. It is hard to draw a line accurately through these intercepts, so choose other solutions farther away from the origin for your points.

Let's summarize the steps of graphing by the intercept method for appropriate equations.

Step by Step: Graphing a Line by the Intercept Method

Step 1   To find the x intercept: Let $y = 0$, then solve for x.
Step 2   To find the y intercept: Let $x = 0$, then solve for y.
Step 3   Graph the x and y intercepts.
Step 4   Draw a straight line through the intercepts.

A third method of graphing linear equations involves **solving the equation for y.** The reason we use this extra step is that it often will make finding solutions for the equation much easier. Let's look at an example.

Example 8

Graphing a Linear Equation

Graph $2x + 3y = 6$.

Rather than finding solutions for the equation in this form, we solve for y.

NOTE Remember that solving for y means that we want to leave y isolated on the left.

$$2x + 3y = 6$$

$$3y = 6 - 2x \qquad \text{Subtract } 2x.$$

$$y = \frac{6 - 2x}{3} \qquad \text{Divide by 3.}$$

or $\quad y = 2 - \dfrac{2}{3}x$

Now find your solutions by picking convenient values for x.

If $x = -3$:

$y = 2 - \dfrac{2}{3}(-3)$

$= 2 + 2 = 4$

So $(-3, 4)$ is a solution.

If $x = 0$:

$y = 2 - \dfrac{2}{3} \cdot 0$

$= 2$

So $(0, 2)$ is a solution.

If $x = 3$:

$y = 2 - \dfrac{2}{3} \cdot 3$

$= 2 - 2 = 0$

So $(3, 0)$ is a solution.

We can now plot the points that correspond to these solutions and form the graph of the equation as before.

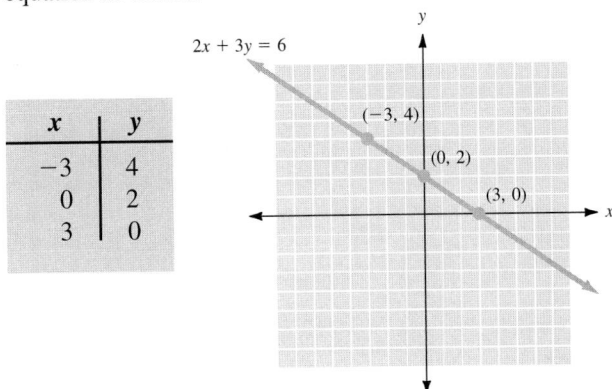

x	y
-3	4
0	2
3	0

 CHECK YOURSELF 8

Graph the equation $5x + 2y = 10$. Solve for y to determine solutions.

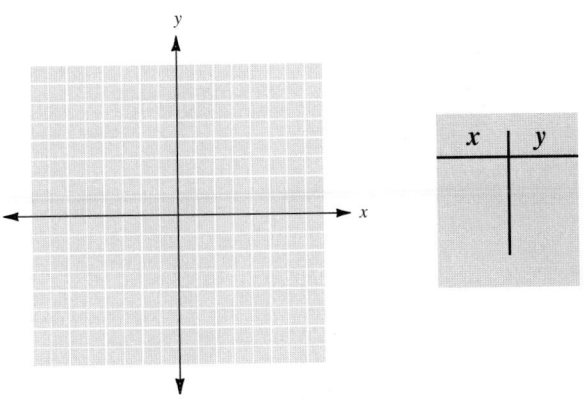

x	y

CHECK YOURSELF ANSWERS

1.

x	y
1	−4
2	−2
3	0

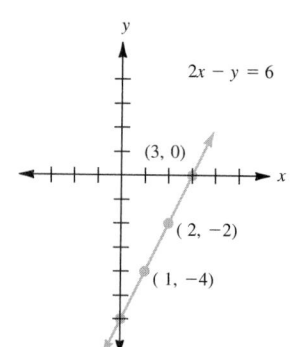

2.

x	y
0	0
1	−2
2	−4

3.

x	y
0	−2
1	1
2	4

4.

x	y
−3	4
0	3
3	2

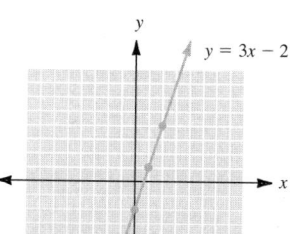

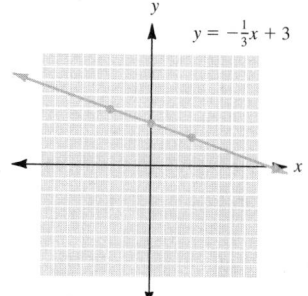

5.

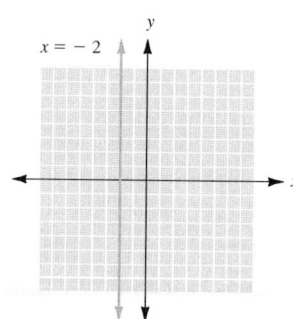

6.

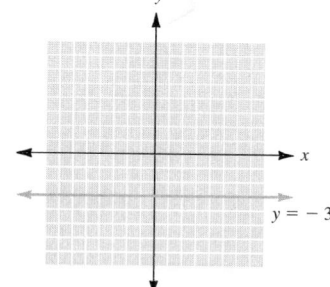

7.

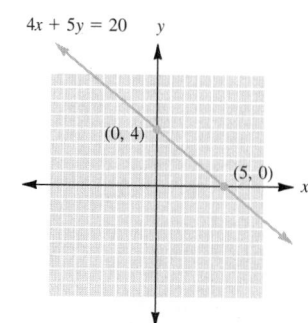

8.

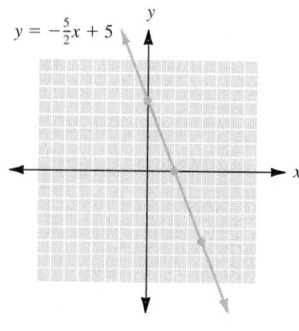

2.2 Exercises

Graph each of the following equations.

1. $x + y = 6$

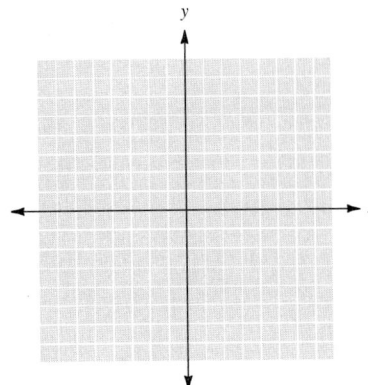

2. $x - y = 5$

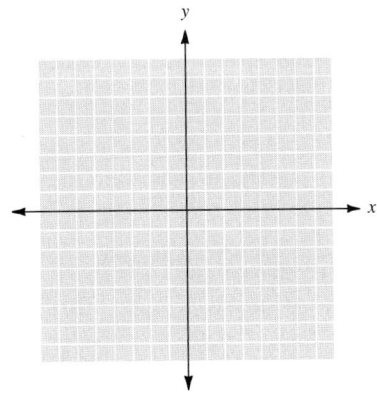

3. $x - y = -3$

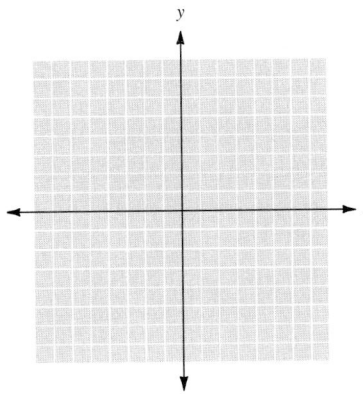

4. $x + y = -3$

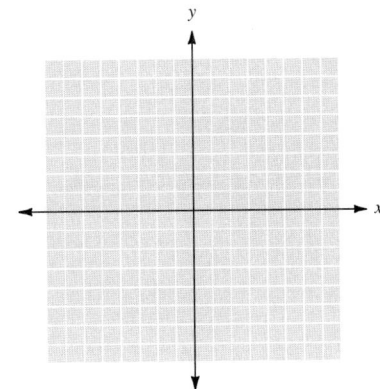

5. $2x + y = 2$

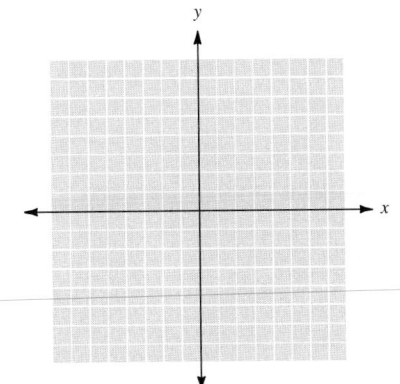

6. $x - 2y = 6$

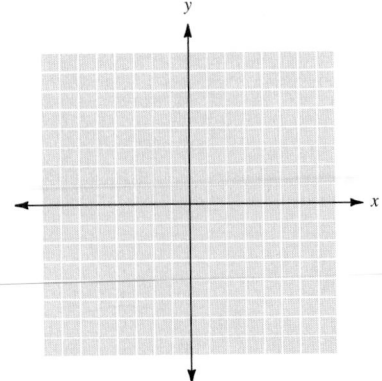

7. $3x + y = 0$

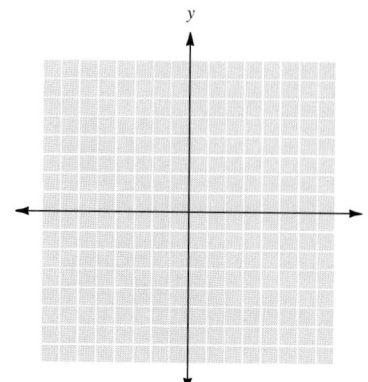

8. $3x - y = 6$

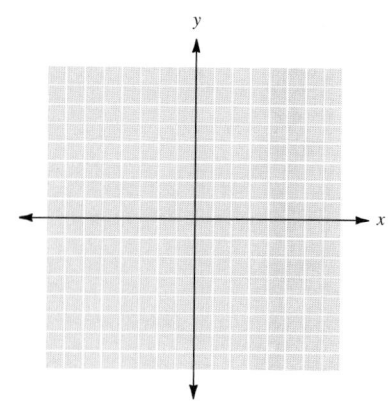

9. $x + 4y = 8$

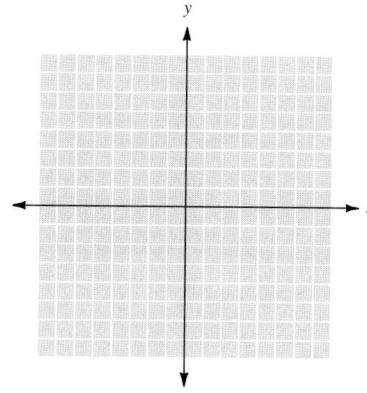

10. $2x - 3y = 6$

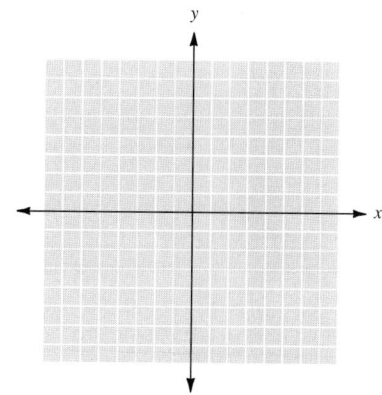

11. $y = 5x$

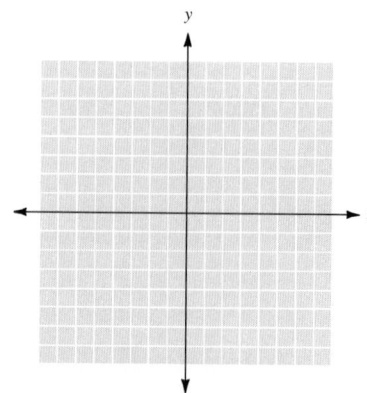

12. $y = -4x$

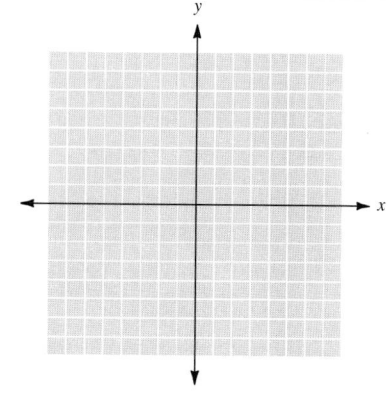

13. $y = 2x - 1$

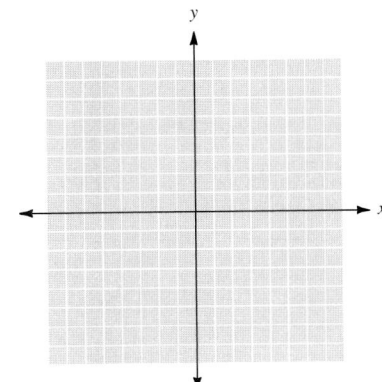

14. $y = 4x + 3$

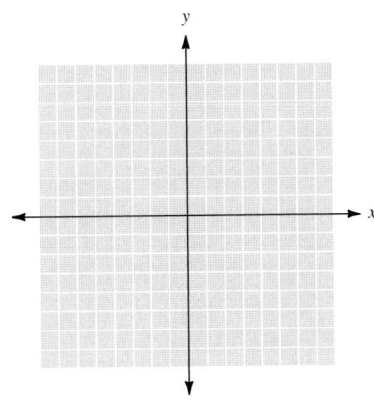

13. _____

14. _____

15. _____

16. _____

17. _____

18. _____

15. $y = -3x + 1$

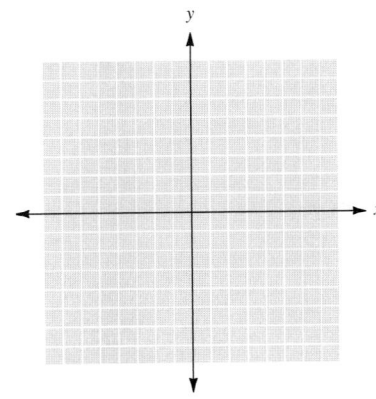

16. $y = -3x - 3$

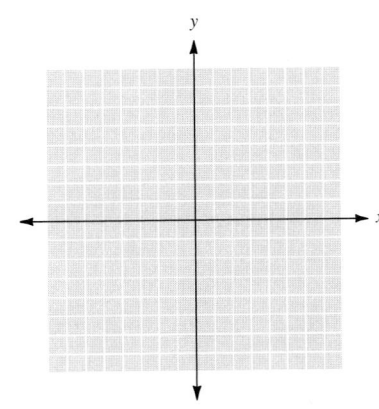

17. $y = \dfrac{1}{3}x$

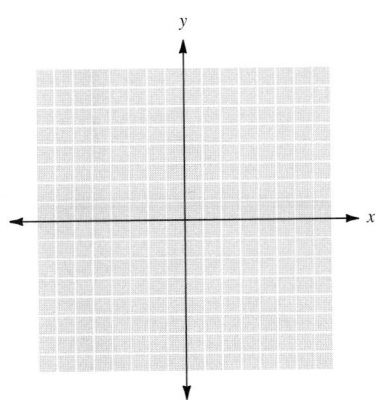

18. $y = -\dfrac{1}{4}x$

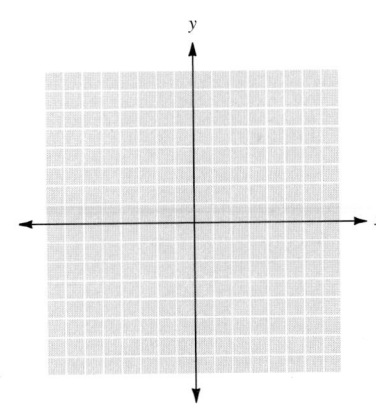

19. $y = \dfrac{2}{3}x - 3$

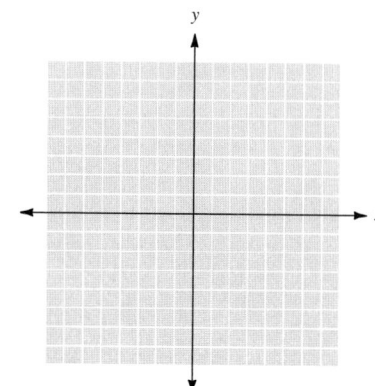

20. $y = \dfrac{3}{4}x + 2$

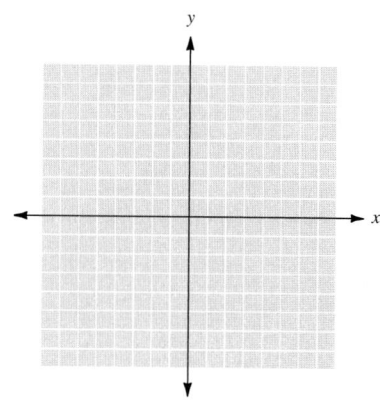

21. $x = 5$

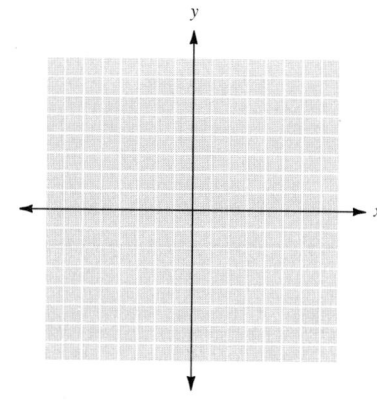

22. $y = -3$

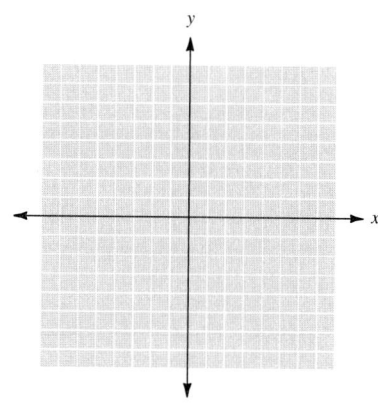

23. $y = 1$

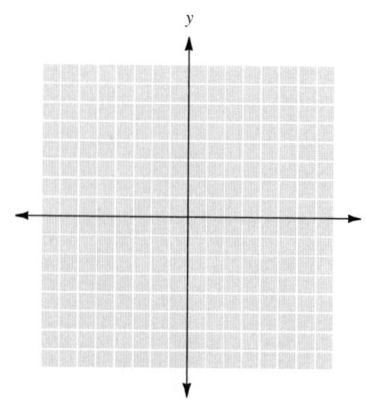

24. $x = -2$

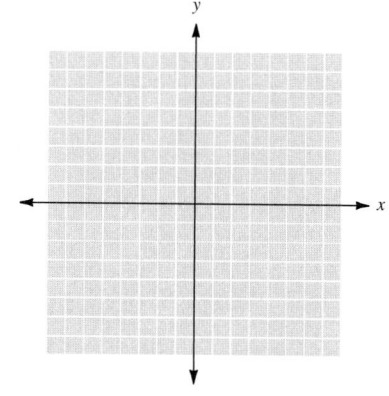

Graph each of the following equations, using the intercept method.

25. $x - 2y = 4$

26. $6x + y = 6$

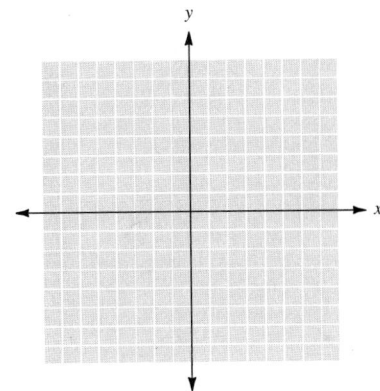

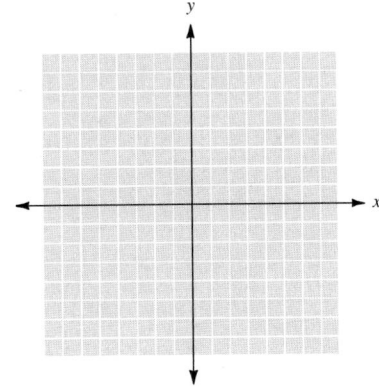

27. $5x + 2y = 10$

28. $2x + 3y = 6$

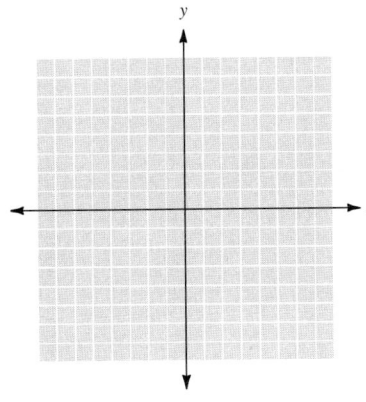

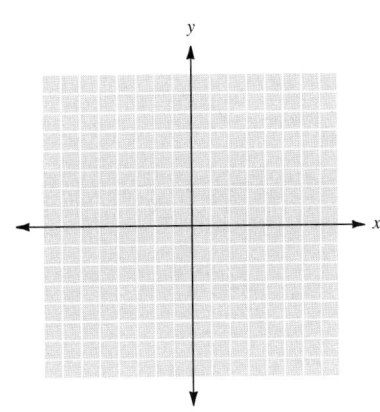

29. $3x + 5y = 15$

30. $4x + 3y = 12$

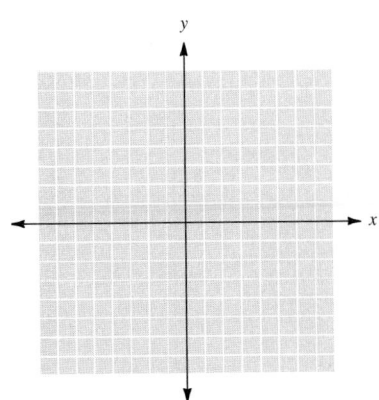

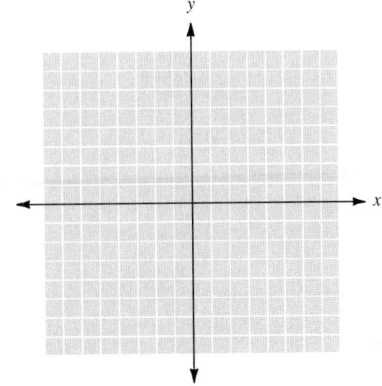

ANSWERS

25. _____

26. _____

27. _____

28. _____

29. _____

30. _____

Graph each of the following equations by first solving for y.

31. $x + 3y = 6$

32. $x - 2y = 6$

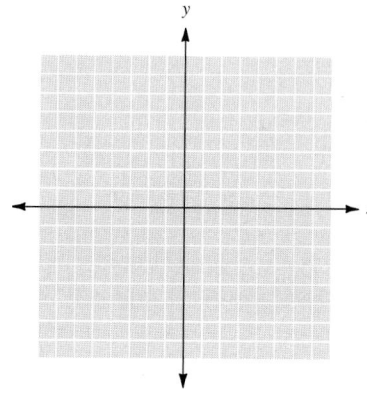

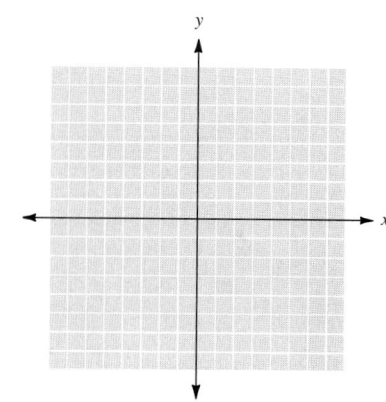

33. $3x + 4y = 12$

34. $2x - 3y = 12$

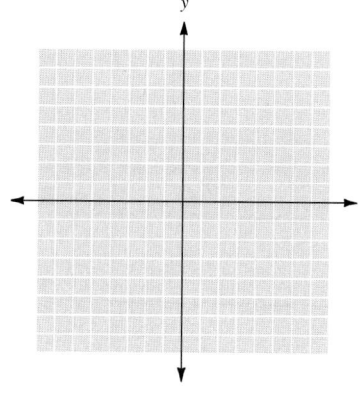

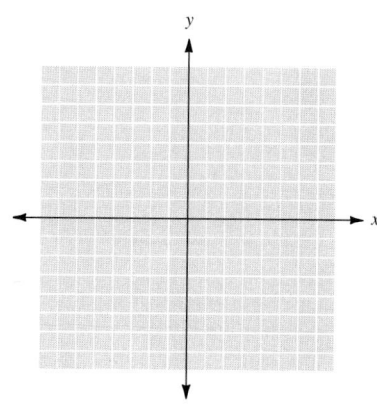

35. $5x - 4y = 20$

36. $7x + 3y = 21$

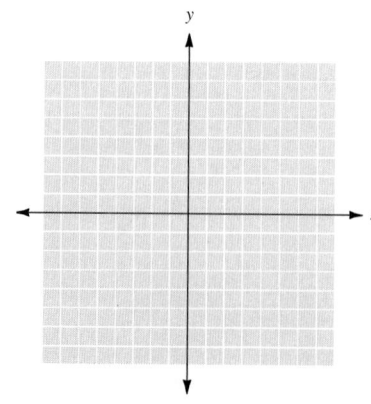

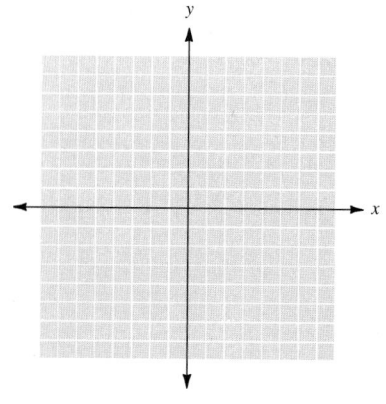

Write an equation that describes the following relationships between x and y. Then graph each relationship.

37. y is twice x.

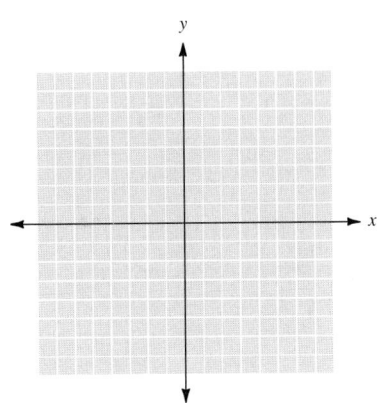

38. y is 3 times x.

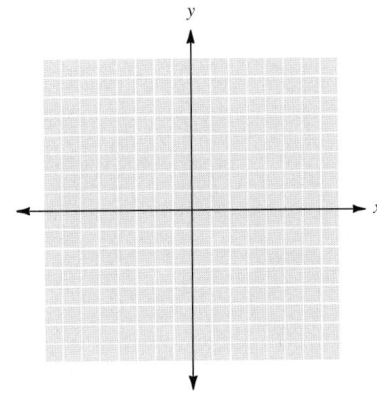

39. y is 3 more than x.

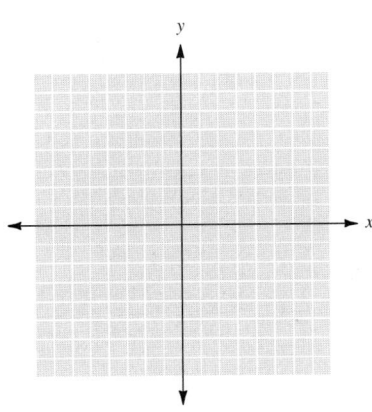

40. y is 2 less than x.

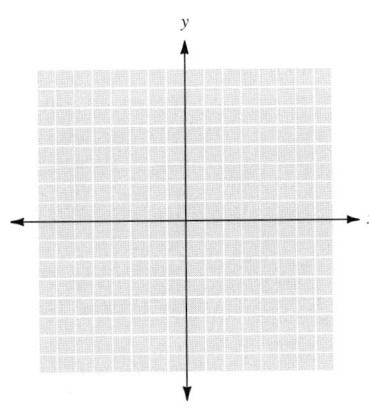

41. y is 3 less than 3 times x.

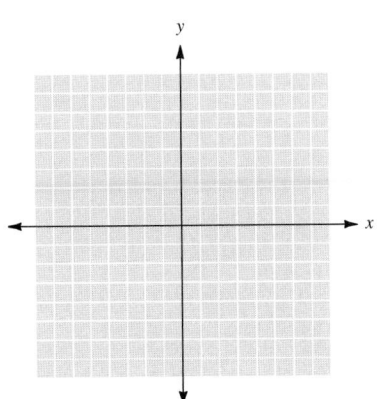

42. y is 4 more than twice x.

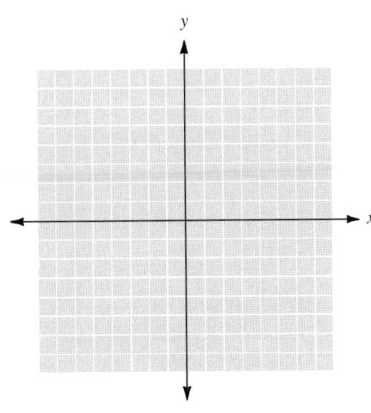

43. The difference of x and the product of 4 and y is 12.

44. The difference of twice x and y is 6.

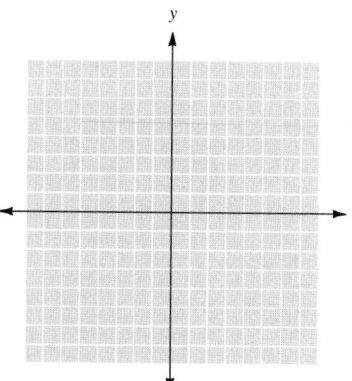

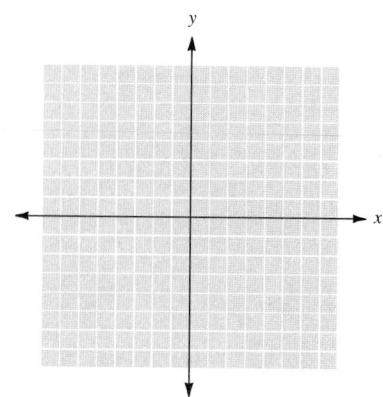

Graph each pair of equations on the same axes. Give the coordinates of the point where the lines intersect.

45. $x + y = 4$
$x - y = 2$

46. $x - y = 3$
$x + y = 5$

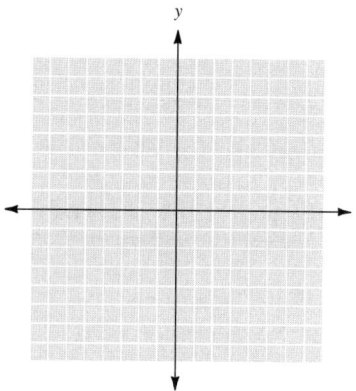

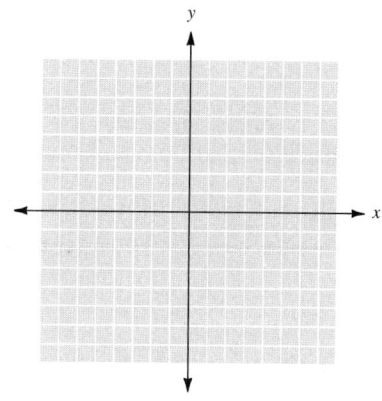

47. Graph of winnings. The equation $y = 0.10x + 200$ describes the amount of winnings a group earns for collecting plastic jugs in the recycling contest described in exercise 27 at the end of Section 2.1. Sketch the graph of the line on the coordinate system below.

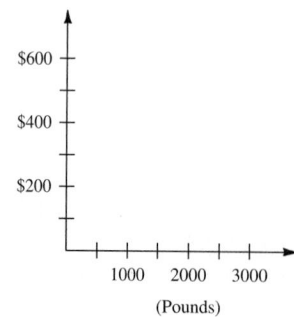

48. Minimum values. The contest sponsor will award a prize only if the winning group in the contest collects 100 lb of jugs or more. Use your graph in exercise 47 to determine the minimum prize possible.

49. Fundraising. A high school class wants to raise some money by recycling newspapers. They decide to rent a truck for a weekend and to collect the newspapers from homes in the neighborhood. The market price for recycled newsprint is currently $11 per ton. The equation $y = 11x - 100$ describes the amount of money the class will make, in which y is the amount of money made in dollars, x is the number of tons of newsprint collected, and 100 is the cost in dollars to rent the truck.

(a) Using the axes below, draw a graph that represents the relationship between newsprint collected and money earned.

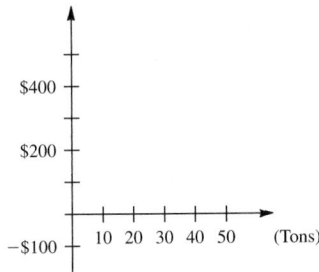

(b) The truck is costing the class $100. How many tons of newspapers must the class collect to break even on this project?

(c) If the class members collect 16 tons of newsprint, how much money will they earn?

(d) Six months later the price of newsprint is $17 dollars a ton, and the cost to rent the truck has risen to $125. Write the equation that describes the amount of money the class might make at that time.

50. Production costs. The cost of producing a number of items x is given by $C = mx + b$, in which b is the fixed cost and m is the variable cost (the cost of producing one more item).

(a) If the fixed cost is $40 and the variable cost is $10, write the cost equation.

(b) Graph the cost equation.

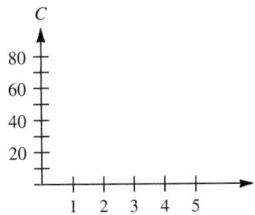

(c) The revenue generated from the sale of x items is given by $R = 50x$. Graph the revenue equation on the same set of axes as the cost equation.

(d) How many items must be produced for the revenue to equal the cost (the break-even point)?

Graph each set of equations on the same coordinate system. Do the lines intersect? What are the y intercepts?

51. $y = 3x$
$\quad\;\; y = 3x + 4$
$\quad\;\; y = 3x - 5$

52. $y = -2x$
$\quad\;\;\; y = -2x + 3$
$\quad\;\;\; y = -2x - 5$

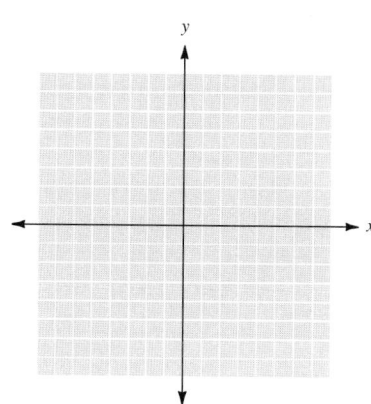

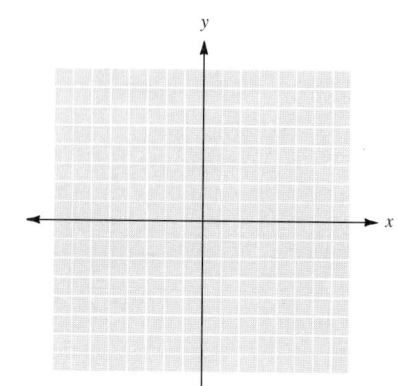

 Getting Ready

Evaluate the following expressions.

(a) $\dfrac{7 - 3}{8 - 4}$ (b) $\dfrac{-9 - 5}{-4 - 3}$ (c) $\dfrac{4 - (-2)}{6 - 2}$ (d) $\dfrac{-4 - (-4)}{8 - 2}$

Answers

1. $x + y = 6$ **3.** $x - y = -3$ **5.** $2x + y = 2$

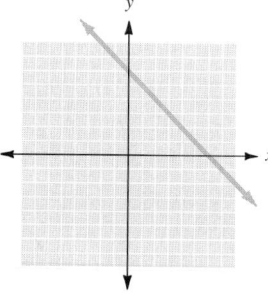   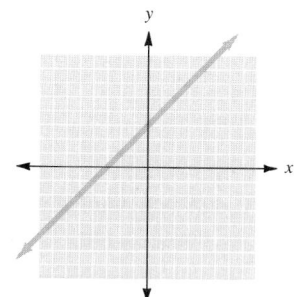   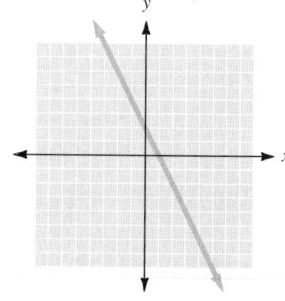

7. $3x + y = 0$ **9.** $x + 4y = 8$ **11.** $y = 5x$

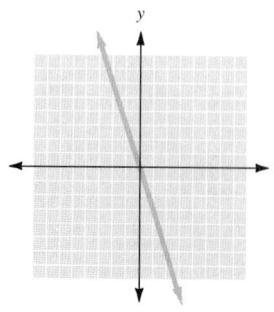   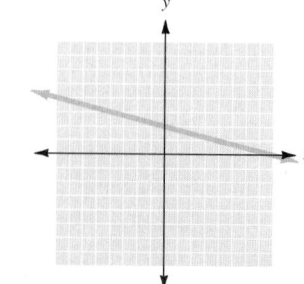   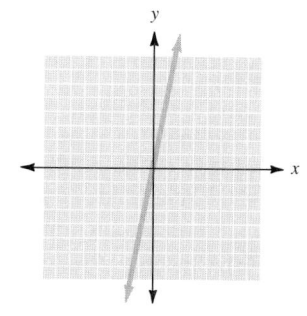

13. $y = 2x - 1$

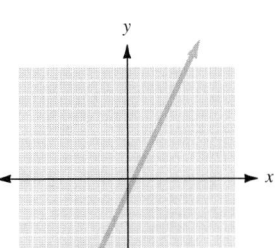

15. $y = -3x + 1$

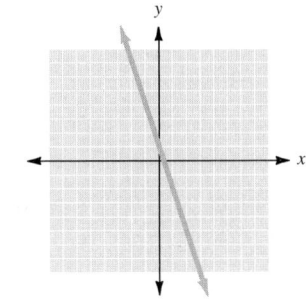

17. $y = \dfrac{1}{3}x$

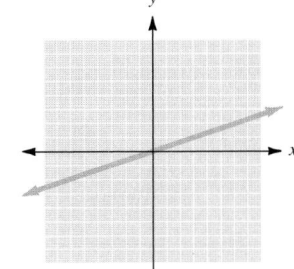

19. $y = \dfrac{2}{3}x - 3$

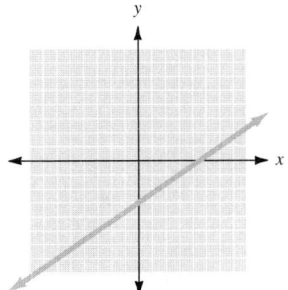

21. $x = 5$

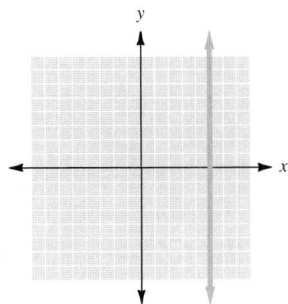

23. $y = 1$

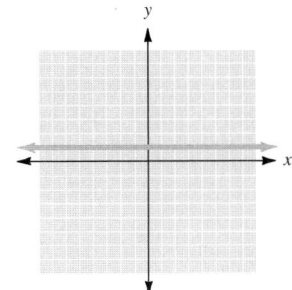

25. $x - 2y = 4$

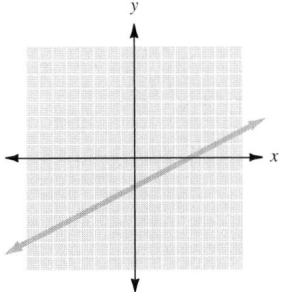

27. $5x + 2y = 10$

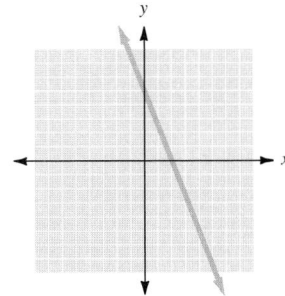

29. $3x + 5y = 15$

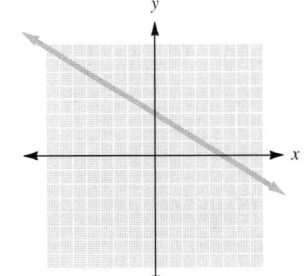

31. $y = 2 - \dfrac{x}{3}$

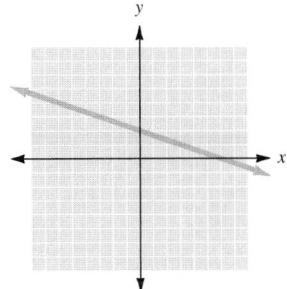

33. $y = 3 - \dfrac{3}{4}x$

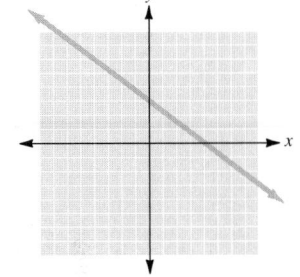

35. $y = -5 + \dfrac{5}{4}x$

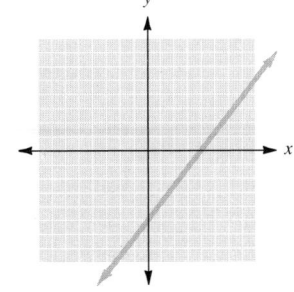

37. $y = 2x$ **39.** $y = x + 3$ **41.** $y = 3x - 3$

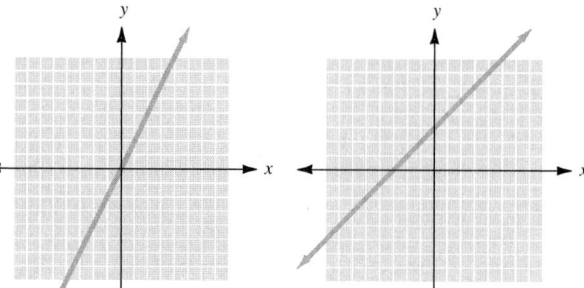

43. $x - 4y = 12$ **45.** $(3, 1)$ **47.** Graph

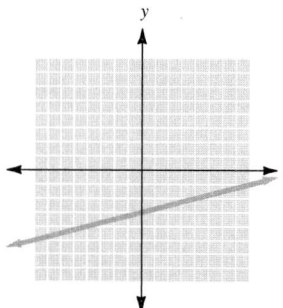 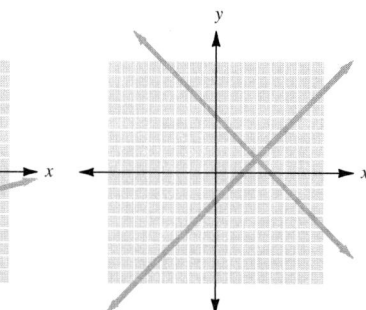 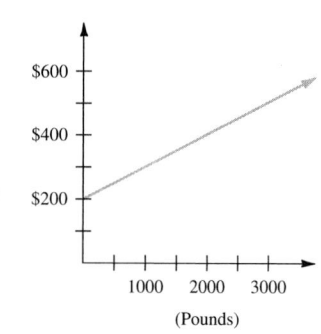

49. (a) Graph; **(b)** $\dfrac{100}{11}$ or ≈ 9 tons;

(c) \$76; **(d)** $y = 17x - 125$

51. The lines do not intersect. The y intercepts are $(0, 0)$, $(0, 4)$, and $(0, -5)$.

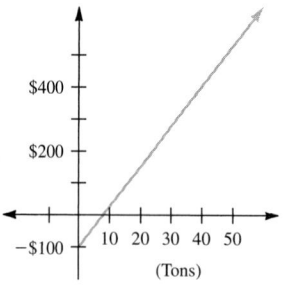 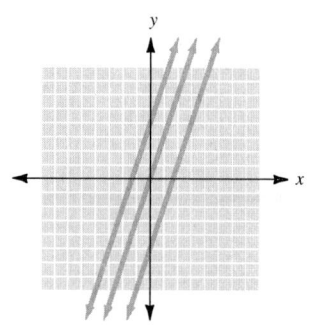

a. 1   **b.** 2   **c.** $\dfrac{3}{2}$ **d.** 0

2.3 The Slope of a Line

2.3 OBJECTIVES

1. Find the slope of a line through two given points
2. Find the slope of a line from its graph

We saw in Section 2.2 that the graph of an equation such as

$$y = 2x + 3$$

is a straight line. In this section we want to develop an important idea related to the equation of a line and its graph, called the **slope** of a line. Finding the slope of a line gives us a numerical measure of the "steepness" or inclination of that line.

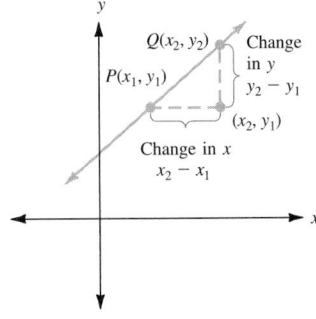

NOTE Recall that an equation such as $y = 2x + 3$ is a *linear equation in two variables*. Its graph is always a straight line.

To find the slope of a line, we first let $P(x_1, y_1)$ and $Q(x_2, y_2)$ be any two distinct points on that line. The **horizontal change** (or the change in x) between the points is $x_2 - x_1$. The **vertical change** (or the change in y) between the points is $y_2 - y_1$.

NOTE x_1 is read "x sub 1," x_2 is read "x sub 2," and so on. The 1 in x_1 and the 2 in x_2 are called **subscripts**.

We call the ratio of the vertical change, $y_2 - y_1$, to the horizontal change, $x_2 - x_1$, the *slope* of the line as we move along the line from P to Q. That ratio is usually denoted by the letter m, and so we have the following formula:

NOTE The difference $x_2 - x_1$ is sometimes called the **run** between points P and Q. The difference $y_2 - y_1$ is called the **rise**. So the slope may be thought of as "rise over run."

Definitions: The Slope of a Line

If $P(x_1, y_1)$ and $Q(x_2, y_2)$ are any two points on a line, then m, the slope of the line, is given by

$$m = \frac{\text{vertical change}}{\text{horizontal change}} = \frac{y_2 - y_1}{x_2 - x_1} \quad \text{when } x_2 \neq x_1$$

This definition provides exactly the numerical measure of "steepness" that we want. If a line "rises" as we move from left to right, the slope will be positive—the steeper the line, the larger the numerical value of the slope. If the line "falls" from left to right, the slope will be negative.

Let's proceed to some examples.

Example 1

Finding the Slope

Find the slope of the line containing points with coordinates (1, 2) and (5, 4).

Let $P(x_1, y_1) = (1, 2)$ and $Q(x_2, y_2) = (5, 4)$. By the definition of slope, we have

$$m = \frac{y_2 - y_1}{x_2 - x_1} = \frac{4 - 2}{5 - 1} = \frac{2}{4} = \frac{1}{2}$$

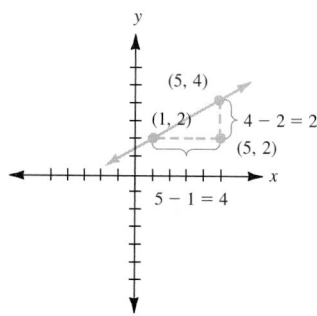

Note: We would have found the same slope if we had reversed P and Q and subtracted in the other order. In that case, $P(x_1, y_1) = (5, 4)$ and $Q(x_2, y_2) = (1, 2)$, so

$$m = \frac{2 - 4}{1 - 5} = \frac{-2}{-4} = \frac{1}{2}$$

It makes no difference which point is labeled (x_1, y_1) and which is (x_2, y_2). The resulting slope will be the same. You must simply stay with your choice once it is made and *not* reverse the order of the subtraction in your calculations.

 CHECK YOURSELF 1

Find the slope of the line containing points with coordinates (2, 3) and (5, 5).

By now you should be comfortable subtracting negative numbers. Let's apply that skill to finding a slope.

Example 2

Finding the Slope

Find the slope of the line containing points with the coordinates $(-1, -2)$ and $(3, 6)$.
  Again, applying the definition, we have

$$m = \frac{6 - (-2)}{3 - (-1)} = \frac{6 + 2}{3 + 1} = \frac{8}{4} = 2$$

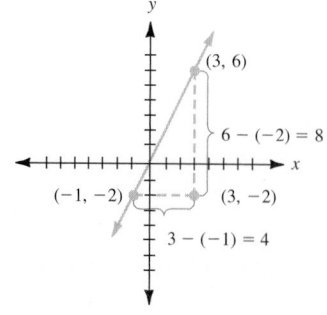

The figure below compares the slopes found in the two previous examples. Line l_1, from Example 1, had slope $\dfrac{1}{2}$. Line l_2, from Example 2, had slope 2. Do you see the idea of slope measuring steepness? The greater the slope, the more steeply the line is inclined upward.

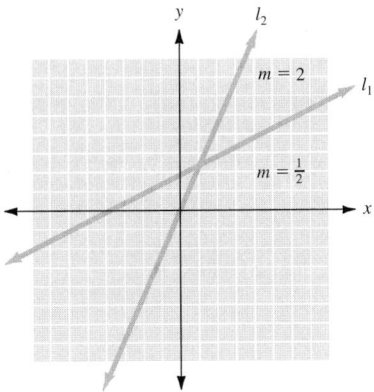

✔ CHECK YOURSELF 2

Find the slope of the line containing points with coordinates $(-1, 2)$ and $(2, 7)$. Draw a sketch of this line and the line of Check Yourself 1. Compare the lines and the two slopes.

Let's look at lines with a negative slope.

Example 3

Finding the Slope

Find the slope of the line containing points with coordinates $(-2, 3)$ and $(1, -3)$.
    By the definition,

$$m = \frac{-3 - 3}{1 - (-2)} = \frac{-6}{3} = -2$$

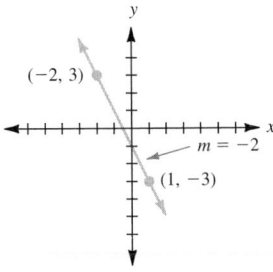

This line has a *negative* slope. The line *falls* as we move from left to right.

✔ CHECK YOURSELF 3

Find the slope of the line containing points with coordinates $(-1, 3)$ and $(1, -3)$.

We have seen that lines with positive slope rise from left to right and lines with negative slope fall from left to right. What about lines with a slope of zero? A line with a slope of 0 is especially important in mathematics.

Example 4

Finding the Slope

Find the slope of the line containing points with coordinates $(-5, 2)$ and $(3, 2)$.
  By the definition,

$$m = \frac{2 - 2}{3 - (-5)} = \frac{0}{8} = 0$$

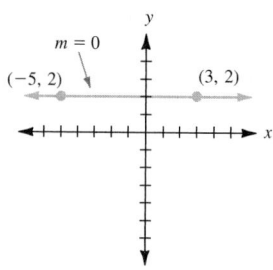

The slope of the line is 0. In fact, that will be the case for any horizontal line. Because any two points on the line have the same y coordinate, the vertical change $y_2 - y_1$ must always be 0, and so the resulting slope is 0.

✓ CHECK YOURSELF 4

Find the slope of the line containing points with coordinates $(-2, -4)$ and $(3, -4)$.

Because division by 0 is undefined, it is possible to have a line with an undefined slope.

Example 5

Finding the Slope

Find the slope of the line containing points with coordinates $(2, -5)$ and $(2, 5)$.
  By the definition,

$$m = \frac{5 - (-5)}{2 - 2} = \frac{10}{0} \qquad \text{Remember that division by zero is undefined.}$$

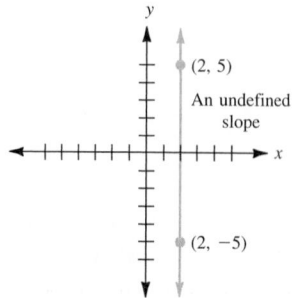

We say that the vertical line has an undefined slope. On a vertical line, any two points have the same x coordinate. This means that the horizontal change $x_2 - x_1$ must always be 0 and because division by 0 is undefined, the slope of a vertical line will always be undefined.

 CHECK YOURSELF 5

Find the slope of the line containing points with the coordinates $(-3, -5)$ and $(-3, 2)$.

Given the graph of a line, we can find the slope of that line. Example 6 illustrates this.

Example 6

Finding the Slope from the Graph

Find the slope of the line graphed below.

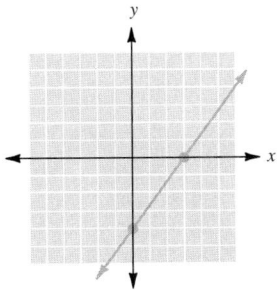

We can find the slope by identifying any two points. It is almost always easiest to use the x and y intercepts. In this case, those intercepts are $(3, 0)$ and $(0, -4)$.

Using the definition of slope, we find

$$m = \frac{0 - (-4)}{3 - 0} = \frac{4}{3}$$

The slope of the line is $\frac{4}{3}$.

 CHECK YOURSELF 6

Find the slope of the line graphed below.

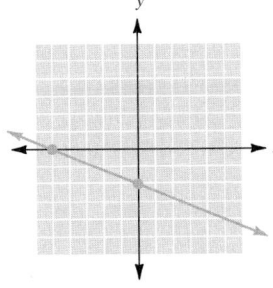

In Section 2.2, we saw that a line could be drawn from two ordered pairs. Given equations of the form $y = kx$, it is fairly easy to find two ordered pairs. In the next example, we will use those ordered pairs to find the graph of the equation.

Example 7

Graphing an Equation of the Form $y = kx$

(a) Find the graph of the equation $y = -2x$.

From the table to the right, we know that the ordered pairs $(0, 0)$ and $(1, -2)$ are solutions to the equation.

x	y
0	0
1	-2

The graph is displayed below

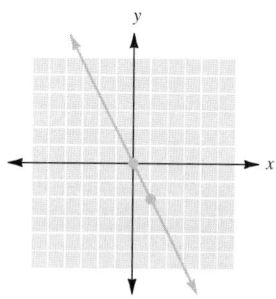

Note that the slope of the line that passes through the points $(0, 0)$ and $(1, -2)$ is

$$m = \frac{0 - (-2)}{0 - 1} = \frac{2}{-1} = -2$$

(b) Find the graph of the equation $y = \frac{1}{3}x$.

From the table to the right, we know that the ordered pairs $(0, 0)$ and $(3, 1)$ are solutions to the equation.

x	y
0	0
3	1

The graph is displayed below

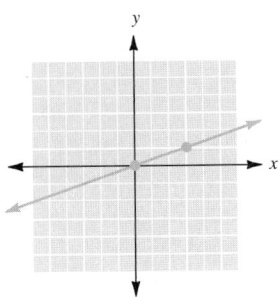

Note that the slope of the line that passes through the points $(0, 0)$ and $(3, 1)$ is

$$m = \frac{0 - 1}{0 - 3} = \frac{1}{3}$$

 CHECK YOURSELF 7

Find the graph of the equation $y = -\frac{1}{2}x$.

In Example 7, we noted that the slope of the line for the equation $y = -2x$ is -2, and the slope of the line for the equation $y = \frac{1}{3}x$ is $\frac{1}{3}$. This leads us to the following observation.

The slope of a line for an equation of the form $y = kx$ will always be k. Because k is the slope, we generally write the form as

$$y = mx$$

Note that $(0, 0)$ will be a solution for any equation of this form. As a result, the line for an equation of the form $y = mx$ will always pass through the origin.

The following sketch summarizes the results of our previous examples.

NOTE As the slope gets closer to 0, the line gets "flatter."

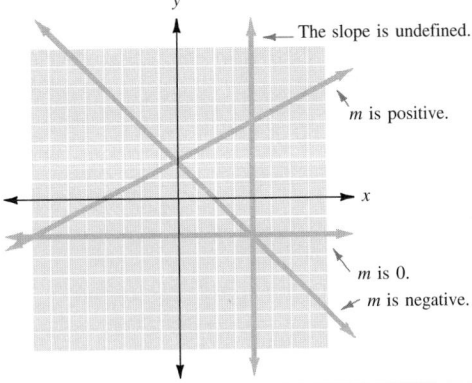

The slope is undefined.

m is positive.

m is 0.
m is negative.

Four lines are illustrated in the figure. Note that

1. The slope of a line that rises from left to right is positive.
2. The slope of a line that falls from left to right is negative.
3. The slope of a horizontal line is 0.
4. A vertical line has an undefined slope.

CHECK YOURSELF ANSWERS

1. $m = \dfrac{2}{3}$ **2.** $m = \dfrac{5}{3}$

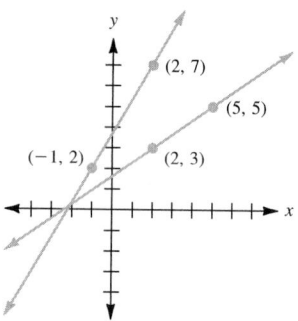

3. $m = -3$ **4.** $m = 0$ **5.** m is undefined   **6.** $m = -\dfrac{2}{5}$

7.

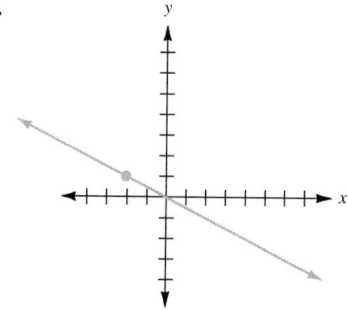

(Note: Your second point could have been $(-2, 1)$ or $(2, -1)$.)

2.3 Exercises

Find the slope of the line through the following pairs of points.

1. $(5, 7)$ and $(9, 11)$

2. $(4, 9)$ and $(8, 17)$

3. $(-2, -5)$ and $(2, 15)$

4. $(-3, 2)$ and $(0, 17)$

5. $(-2, 3)$ and $(3, 7)$

6. $(-3, -4)$ and $(3, -2)$

7. $(-3, 2)$ and $(2, -8)$

8. $(-6, 1)$ and $(2, -7)$

9. $(3, 3)$ and $(5, 0)$

10. $(-2, 4)$ and $(3, 1)$

11. $(5, -4)$ and $(5, 2)$

12. $(-5, 4)$ and $(2, 4)$

13. $(-4, -2)$ and $(3, 3)$

14. $(-5, -3)$ and $(-5, 2)$

15. $(-3, -4)$ and $(2, -4)$

16. $(-5, 7)$ and $(2, -2)$

17. $(-1, 7)$ and $(2, 3)$

18. $(-4, -2)$ and $(6, 4)$

In exercises 19 to 24, two points are shown. Find the slope of the line through the given points.

19.

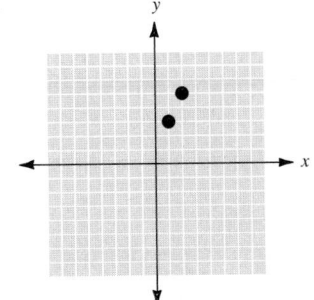

20.

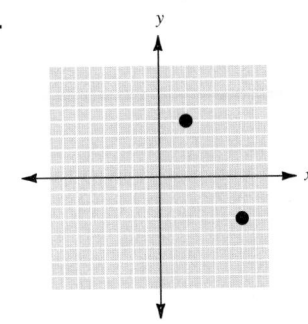

ANSWERS

1. _____

2. _____

3. _____

4. _____

5. _____

6. _____

7. _____

8. _____

9. _____

10. _____

11. _____

12. _____

13. _____

14. _____

15. _____

16. _____

17. _____

18. _____

19. _____

20. _____

21.

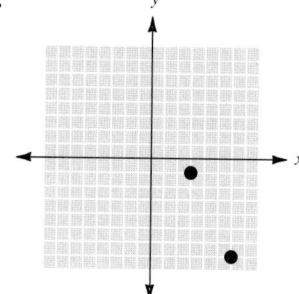

22.

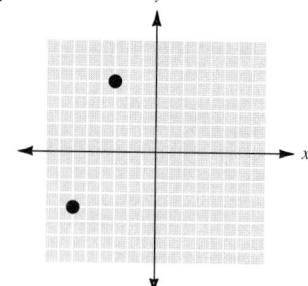

23.

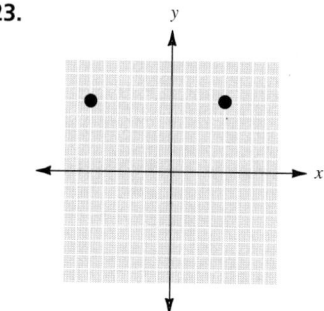

24.

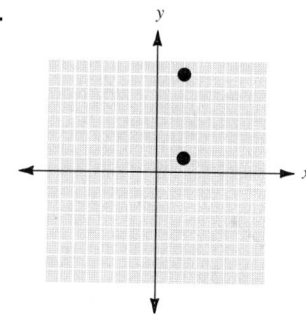

In exercises 25 to 30, find the slope of the lines graphed.

25.

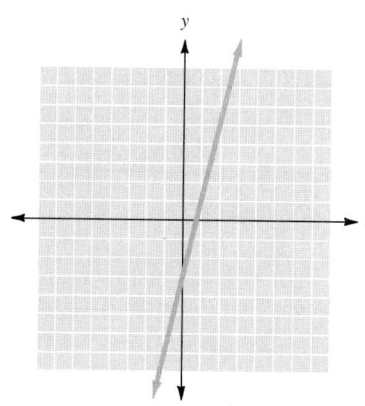

26.

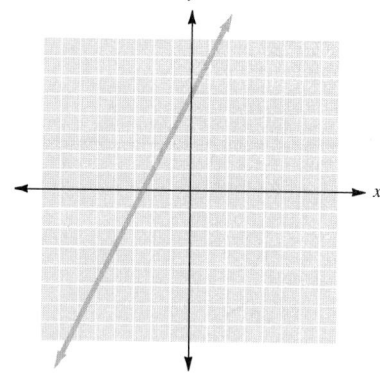

27.

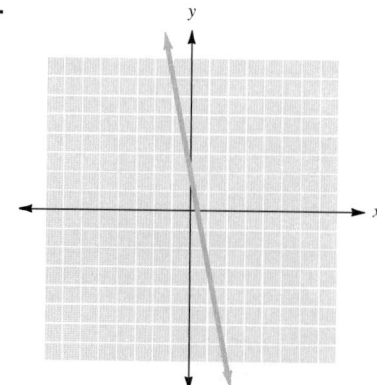

28.

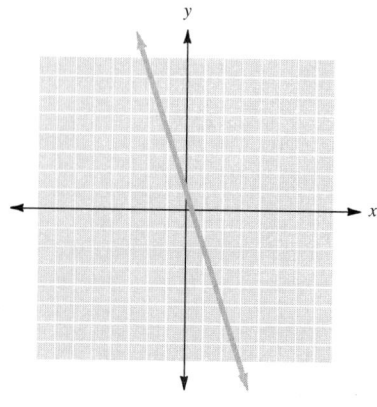

29.

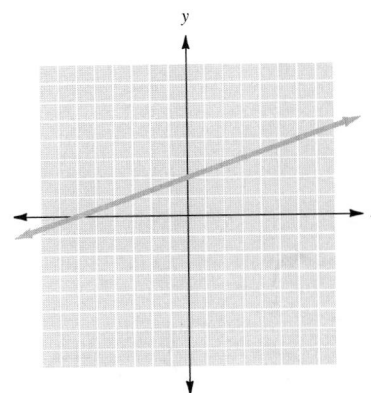

30.

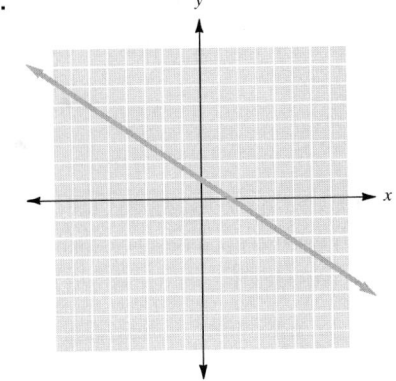

29. _____

30. _____

31. _____

32. _____

33. _____

34. _____

35. _____

36. _____

Find the graph of the following equations.

31. $y = -4x$

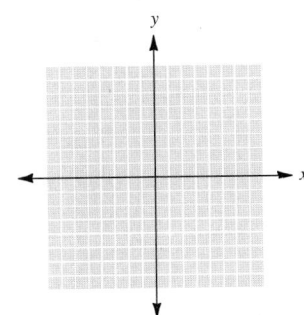

32. $y = 3x$

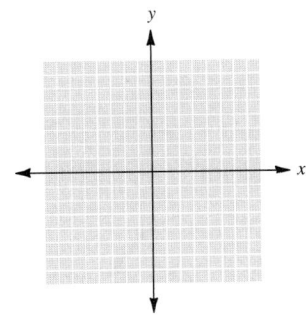

33. $y = \dfrac{2}{3}x$

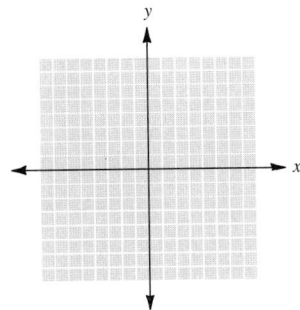

34. $y = -\dfrac{3}{4}x$

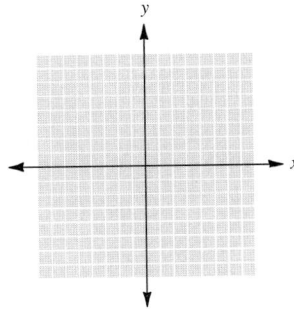

35. $y = \dfrac{5}{4}x$

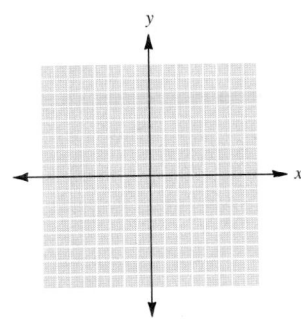

36. $y = -\dfrac{4}{5}x$

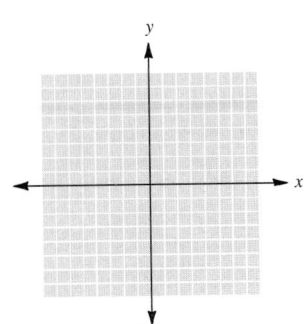

37. (a) _____

 (b) _____

 (c) _____

38. (a) _____

 (b) _____

 (c) _____

39. (a) _____

 (b) _____

 (c) _____

40. (a) _____

 (b) _____

 (c) _____

41. (a) _____

 (b) _____

 (c) _____

 (d) _____

42. (a) _____

 (b) _____

 (c) _____

 (d) _____

43. (a) _____

 (b) _____

 (c) _____

 (d) _____

44. (a) _____

 (b) _____

 (c) _____

 (d) _____

37. Consider the equation $y = 2x - 5$.

 (a) Complete the following table:

x	y
3	
4	

 (b) Use the ordered pairs found in part (a) to calculate the slope of the line.

 (c) What do you observe concerning the slope found in part (b) and the given equation?

38. Repeat exercise 37 for $y = \dfrac{3}{2}x + 5$ and

x	y
2	
4	

39. Repeat exercise 37 for $y = -\dfrac{1}{3}x + 2$ and

x	y
3	
6	

40. Repeat exercise 37 for $y = -4x - 6$ and

x	y
−1	
−3	

41. Consider the equation: $y = 2x + 3$

 (a) Complete the following table of values, and plot the resulting points.

Point	x	y
A	5	
B	6	
C	7	
D	8	
E	9	

 (b) As the x coordinate changes by 1 (for example, as you move from point A to point B), how much do the corresponding y coordinates change?

 (c) Is your answer to part (b) the same if you move from B to C? from C to D? from D to E?

 (d) Describe the "growth rate" of the line using these observations. Complete the following statement: When the x value grows by 1 unit, the y value _____.

42. Repeat exercise 41 using: $y = 2x + 5$

43. Repeat exercise 41 using: $y = -4x + 50$

44. Repeat exercise 41 using: $y = -4x + 40$

In the following exercises, (a) plot the given point; (b) using the given slope, move from the point plotted in (a) to plot a new point; (c) draw the line that passes through the points plotted in (a) and (b).

45. $(3, 1)$, $m = 2$

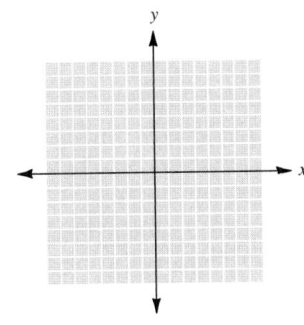

46. $(-1, 4)$, $m = -2$

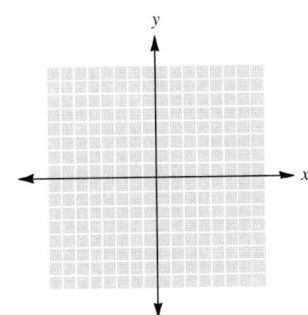

47. $(-2, -1)$, $m = -4$

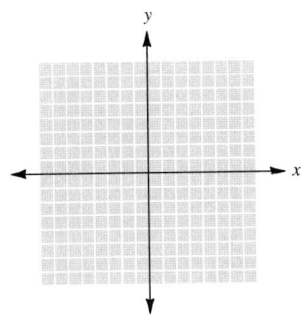

48. $(-3, 5)$, $m = 2$

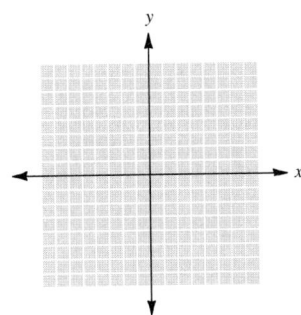

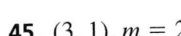 **Getting Ready**

Solve each equation for x.

(a) $25 = 5x$ (b) $36 = -12x$ (c) $-49 = -7x$

(d) $14 = 3x$ (e) $-24 = 9x$ (f) $72 = -24x$

Answers

1. 1 **3.** 5 **5.** $\dfrac{4}{5}$ **7.** -2 **9.** $-\dfrac{3}{2}$ **11.** Undefined   **13.** $\dfrac{5}{7}$

15. 0 **17.** $-\dfrac{4}{3}$ **19.** 2 **21.** -2 **23.** 0 **25.** 4 **27.** -5 **29.** $\dfrac{1}{3}$

31. $y = -4x$

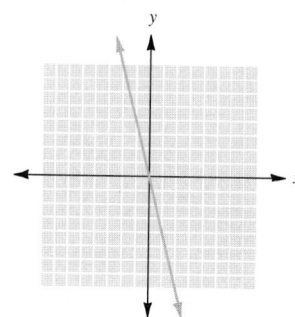

33. $y = \frac{2}{3}x$

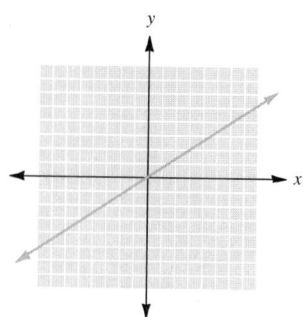

35. $y = \frac{5}{4}x$ **37. (a)** (3, 1), (4, 3); **(b)** 2; **(c)** slope equals coefficient of x

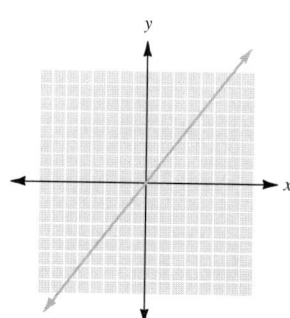

39. (a) (3, 1), (6, 0); **(b)** $-\frac{1}{3}$; **(c)** slope equals coefficient of x

41. (a) (5, 13), (6, 15), (7, 17), (8, 19), (9, 21); **(b)** 2; **(c)** Yes; **(d)** increases by 2

43. (a) (5, 30), (6, 26), (7, 22), (8, 18), (9, 14); **(b)** 4; **(c)** Yes; **(d)** decreases by 4

45.

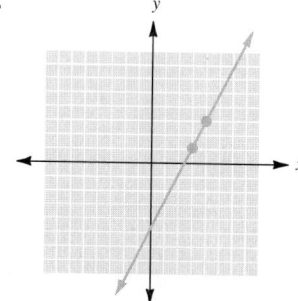

47.

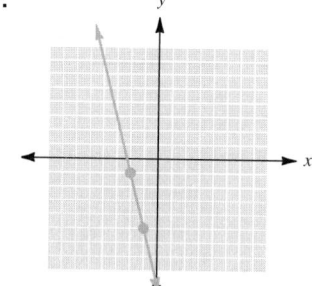

a. 5   **b.** −3   **c.** 7   **d.** $\frac{14}{3}$ **e.** $-\frac{8}{3}$ **f.** −3

2.4 The Slope-Intercept Form

2.4 OBJECTIVES

1. Find the slope and y intercept from the equation of a line
2. Given the slope and y intercept, write the equation of a line
3. Use the slope and y intercept to graph a line

In Chapter 2, we use two points to find the slope of a line. In this chapter we will use the slope to find the graph of an equation.

First, we want to consider finding the equation of a line when its slope and y intercept are known.

Suppose that the y intercept of a line is $(0, b)$. Then the point at which the line crosses the y axis has coordinates $(0, b)$. Look at the sketch at left.

Now, using any other point (x, y) on the line and using our definition of slope, we can write

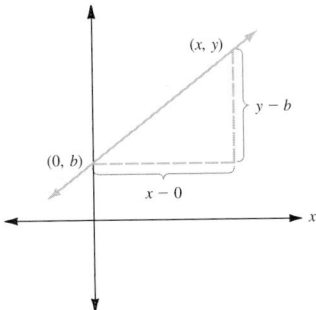

Change in y.

$$m = \frac{y - b}{x - 0} \qquad (1)$$

Change in x.

or

$$m = \frac{y - b}{x} \qquad (2)$$

Multiplying both sides of equation (2) by x, we have

$$mx = y - b \qquad (3)$$

Finally, adding b to both sides of equation (3) gives

$$mx + b = y$$

or

$$y = mx + b \qquad (4)$$

We can summarize the above discussion as follows:

NOTE In this form, the equation is *solved for y.* The coefficient of x will give you the slope of the line, and the constant term gives the y intercept.

Definitions: The Slope-Intercept Form for a Line

An equation of the line with slope m and y intercept $(0, b)$ is

$$y = mx + b$$

Example 1

Finding the Slope and y Intercept

Find the slope and y intercept for the graph of the equation

$$y = -\frac{2}{3}x - 5$$

$$\underset{m}{\uparrow} \qquad \underset{b}{\uparrow}$$

The slope of the line is $-\frac{2}{3}$; the y intercept is $(0, -5)$.

CHECK YOURSELF 1

Find the slope and y intercept for the graph of each of the following equations.

(a) $y = -3x - 7$

(b) $y = \dfrac{3}{4}x + 5$

As Example 2 illustrates, we may have to solve for y as the first step in determining the slope and the y intercept for the graph of an equation.

Example 2

Finding the Slope and *y* Intercept

Find the slope and y intercept for the graph of the equation

$3x + 2y = 6$

First, we must solve the equation for y.

NOTE If we write the equation as

$$y = \frac{-3x + 6}{2}$$

it is more difficult to identify the slope and the intercept.

$3x + 2y = 6$

$2y = -3x + 6$ Add $(-3x)$ to both sides.

$y = -\dfrac{3}{2}x + 3$ Divide each term by 2.

The equation is now in slope-intercept form. The slope is $-\dfrac{3}{2}$, and the y intercept is $(0, 3)$.

CHECK YOURSELF 2

Find the slope and y intercept for the graph of the equation

$2x - 5y = 10$

As we mentioned earlier, knowing certain properties of a line (namely, its slope and y intercept) will also allow us to write the equation of the line by using the slope-intercept form. Example 3 illustrates this approach.

Example 3

Writing the Equation of a Line

Write the equation of a line with slope $-\dfrac{3}{4}$ and y intercept $(0, -3)$.

We know that $m = -\dfrac{3}{4}$ and $b = -3$. In this case,

$$y = \underset{m}{-\dfrac{3}{4}}x + \underset{b}{(-3)}$$

or

$$y = -\dfrac{3}{4}x - 3$$

which is the desired equation.

> ✔ **CHECK YOURSELF 3**
>
> *Write the equation of a line with the following:*
>
> **(a)** slope -2 and *y* intercept $(0, 7)$ **(b)** slope $\dfrac{2}{3}$ and *y* intercept $(0, -3)$

We can also use the slope and *y* intercept of a line in drawing its graph. Consider Example 4.

Example 4

Graphing a Line

Graph the line with slope $\dfrac{2}{3}$ and *y* intercept $(0, 2)$.

Because the *y* intercept is $(0, 2)$, we begin by plotting the point $(0, 2)$. Because the horizontal change (or run) is 3, we move 3 units to the right *from that y intercept.* Then because the vertical change (or rise) is 2, we move 2 units up to locate another point on the desired graph. Note that we will have located that second point at $(3, 4)$. The final step is to simply draw a line through that point and the *y* intercept.

NOTE

$m = \dfrac{2}{3} = \dfrac{\text{rise}}{\text{run}}$

The line rises from left to right because the slope is positive.

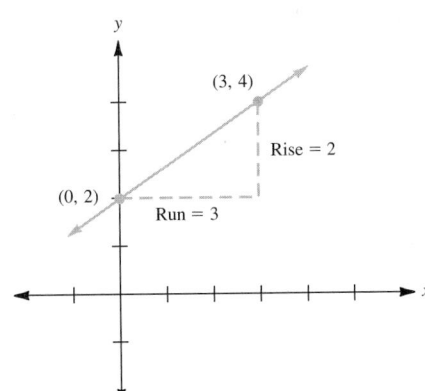

The equation of this line is $y = \dfrac{2}{3}x + 2$.

> ✔ **CHECK YOURSELF 4**
>
> *Graph the equation of a line with slope $\dfrac{3}{5}$ and y intercept $(0, -2)$.*

> **Step by Step: Graphing by Using the Slope-Intercept Form**
>
> **Step 1**   Write the original equation of the line in slope-intercept form.
> **Step 2**   Determine the slope *m* and the *y* intercept $(0, b)$.
> **Step 3**   Plot the *y* intercept at $(0, b)$.
> **Step 4**   Use *m* (the change in *y* over the change in *x*) to determine a second point on the desired line.
> **Step 5**   Draw a line through the two points determined above to complete the graph.

You have now seen two methods for graphing lines: the slope-intercept method and the intercept method. When you graph a linear equation, you should first decide which is the appropriate method.

Example 5

Selecting an Appropriate Graphing Method

Decide which of the two methods for graphing lines—the intercept method or the slope-intercept method—is more appropriate for graphing equations (a), (b), and (c).

(a) $2x - 5y = 10$

Because both intercepts are easy to find, you should choose the intercept method to graph this equation.

(b) $2x + y = 6$

This equation can be quickly graphed by either method. As it is written, you might choose the intercept method. It can, however, be rewritten as $y = -2x + 6$. In that case the slope-intercept method is more appropriate.

(c) $y = \dfrac{1}{4}x - 4$

Because the equation is in slope-intercept form, that is the more appropriate method to choose.

CHECK YOURSELF 5

Which would be more appropriate for graphing each equation, the intercept method or the slope-intercept method?

(a) $x + y = -2$ **(b)** $3x - 2y = 12$ **(c)** $y = -\dfrac{1}{2}x - 6$

CHECK YOURSELF ANSWERS

1. **(a)** Slope is -3, y intercept is $(0, -7)$; **(b)** Slope is $\dfrac{3}{4}$, y intercept is $(0, 5)$

2. $y = \dfrac{2}{5}x - 2$; the slope is $\dfrac{2}{5}$; the y intercept is $(0, -2)$

3. **(a)** $y = -2x + 7$; **(b)** $y = \dfrac{2}{3}x - 3$

4.

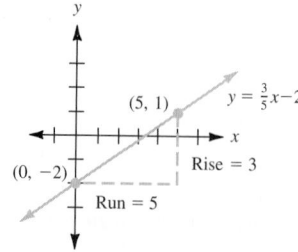

5. **(a)** Either; **(b)** intercept; **(c)** slope-intercept

2.4 Exercises

Name _____

Section _____ Date _____

Find the slope and y intercept of the line represented by each of the following equations.

1. $y = 3x + 5$

2. $y = -7x + 3$

3. $y = -2x - 5$

4. $y = 5x - 2$

5. $y = \dfrac{3}{4}x + 1$

6. $y = -4x$

7. $y = \dfrac{2}{3}x$

8. $y = -\dfrac{3}{5}x - 2$

9. $4x + 3y = 12$

10. $2x + 5y = 10$

11. $y = 9$

12. $2x - 3y = 6$

13. $3x - 2y = 8$

14. $x = 5$

Write the equation of the line with given slope and y intercept. Then graph each line, using the slope and y intercept.

15. Slope: 3; y intercept: (0, 5)

16. Slope: -2; y intercept: (0, 4)

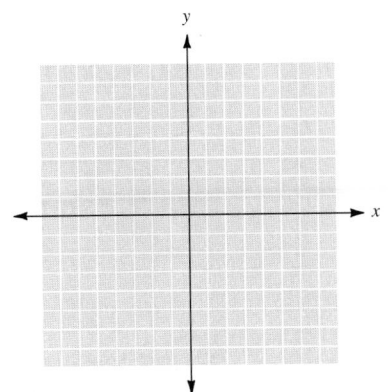

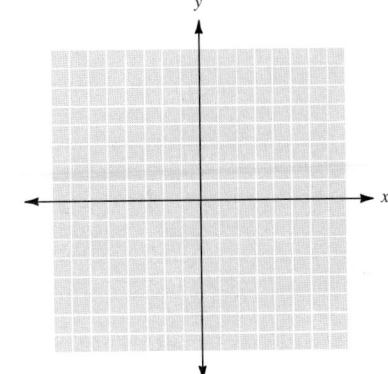

ANSWERS

1. _____

2. _____

3. _____

4. _____

5. _____

6. _____

7. _____

8. _____

9. _____

10. _____

11. _____

12. _____

13. _____

14. _____

15. _____

16. _____

17. Slope: -3; y intercept: $(0, 4)$

18. Slope: 5; y intercept: $(0, -2)$

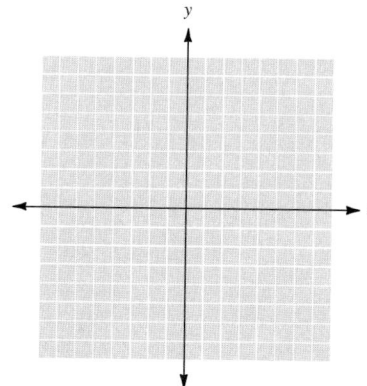

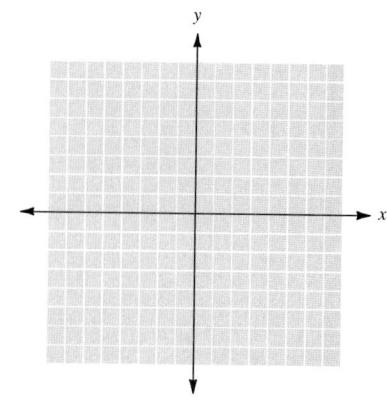

19. Slope: $\dfrac{1}{2}$; y intercept: $(0, -2)$

20. Slope: $-\dfrac{3}{4}$; y intercept: $(0, 8)$

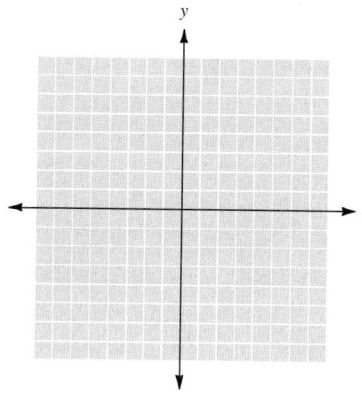

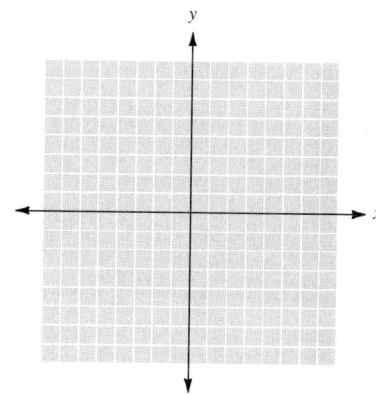

21. Slope: $-\dfrac{2}{3}$; y intercept: $(0, 0)$

22. Slope: $\dfrac{2}{3}$; y intercept: $(0, -2)$

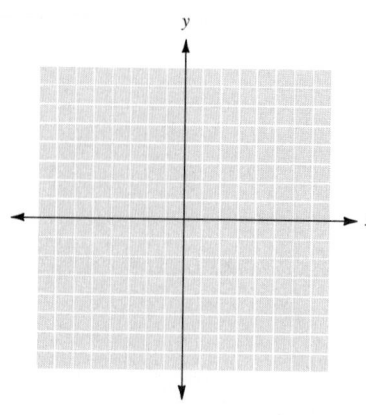

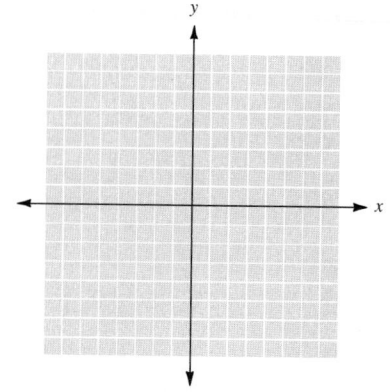

23. Slope: $\dfrac{3}{4}$; y intercept: $(0, 3)$

24. Slope: -3; y intercept: $(0, 0)$

23. _____

24. _____

25. _____

26. _____

27. _____

28. _____

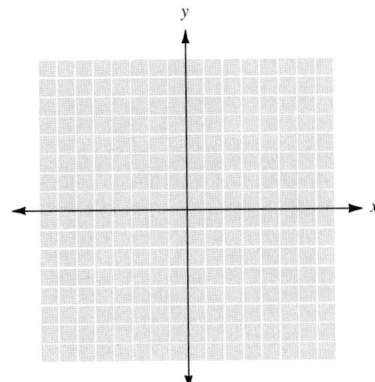

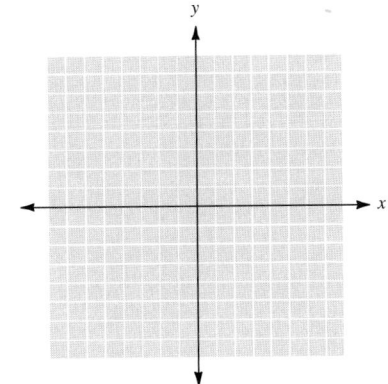

In exercises 25 to 32, match the graph with one of the equations below.

(a) $y = 2x$, **(b)** $y = x + 1$, **(c)** $y = -x + 3$, **(d)** $y = 2x + 1$,

(e) $y = -3x - 2$, **(f)** $y = \dfrac{2}{3}x + 1$, **(g)** $y = -\dfrac{3}{4}x + 1$, **(h)** $y = -4x$

25.

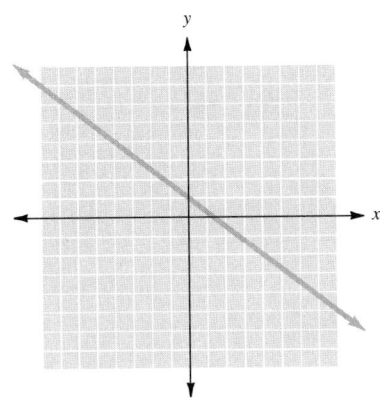

26.

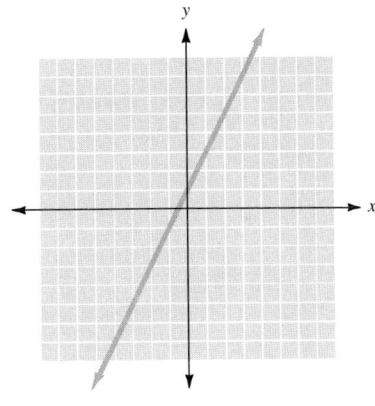

27.

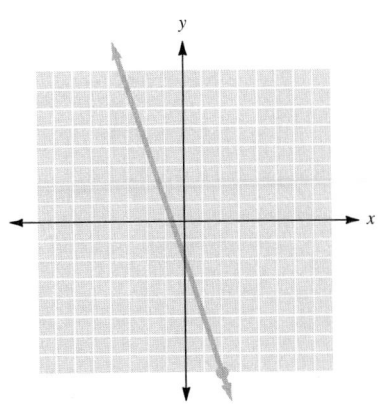

28.

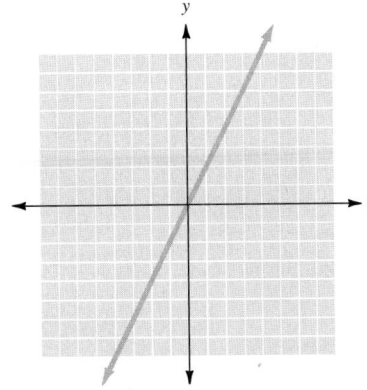

29. _____

30. _____

31. _____

32. _____

33. _____

34. _____

35. _____

36. _____

37. _____

38. _____

39. _____

40. _____

29.

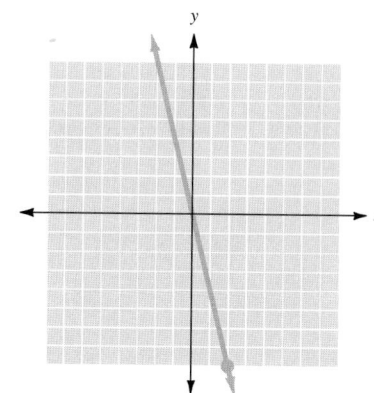

30.

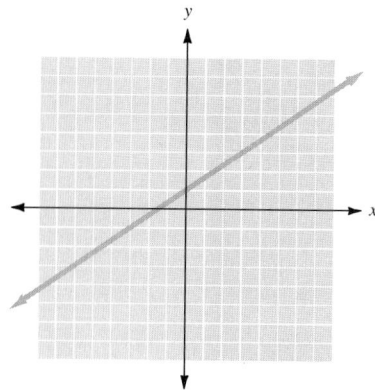

31.

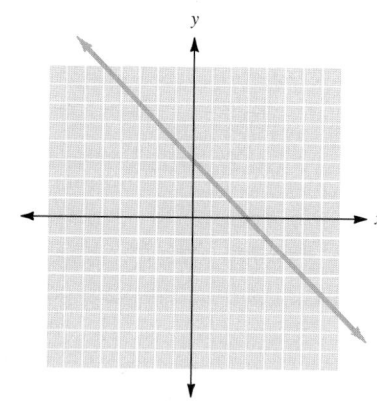

32.

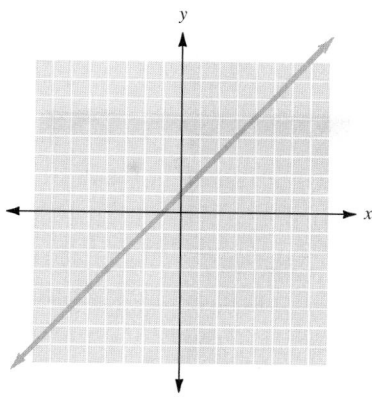

In which quadrant(s) are there no solutions for each line?

33. $y = 2x + 1$

34. $y = 3x + 2$

35. $y = -x + 1$

36. $y = -2x + 5$

37. $y = -2x - 5$

38. $y = -5x - 7$

39. $y = 3$

40. $x = -2$

41. Recycling. The equation $y = 0.10x + 200$ describes the award money in a recycling contest. What are the slope and the y intercept for this equation?

42. Fundraising. The equation $y = 15x - 100$ describes the amount of money a high school class might earn from a paper drive. What are the slope and y intercept for this equation?

43. Science. On a certain February day in Philadelphia, the temperature at 6:00 A.M. was 10°F. By 2:00 P.M. the temperature was up to 26°F. What was the hourly rate of temperature change?

44. Slope of a roof. A roof rises 8.75 feet (ft) in a horizontal distance of 15.09 ft. Find the slope of the roof to the nearest hundredth.

45. Slope of airplane descent. An airplane covered 15 miles (mi) of its route while decreasing its altitude by 24,000 ft. Find the slope of the line of descent that was followed. (1 mi = 5280 ft.) Round to the nearest hundredth.

46. Slope of road descent. Driving down a mountain, Tom finds that he has descended 1800 ft in elevation by the time he is 3.25 mi horizontally away from the top of the mountain. Find the slope of his descent to the nearest hundredth.

47. Complete the following statement: "The difference between undefined slope and zero slope is . . . ."

48. Complete the following: "The slope of a line tells you . . . ."

49. In a study on nutrition conducted in 1984, 18 normal adults aged 23 to 61 years old were measured for body fat, which is given as percentage of weight. The mean (average) body fat percentage for women 40 years old was 28.6 percent, and for women 53 years old was 38.4 percent. Work with a partner to decide how to show this information on a scatterplot. Try to find a linear equation that will tell you percentage of body fat based on a woman's age. What does your equation give for 20 years of age? For 60? Do you think a linear model works well for predicting body fat percentage in women as they age?

41.	
42.	
43.	
44.	
45.	
46.	
47.	
48.	
49.	

50.

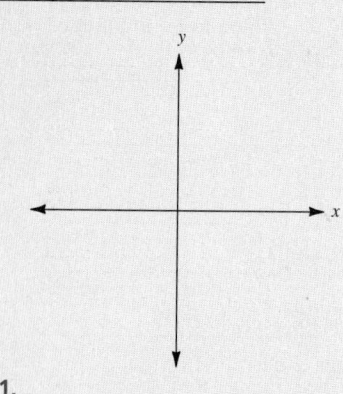

51.

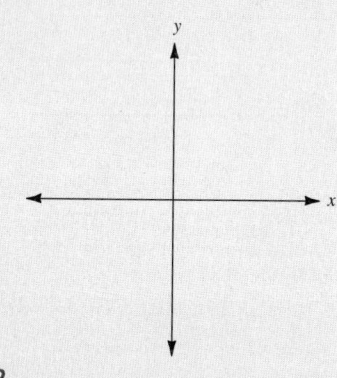

52.

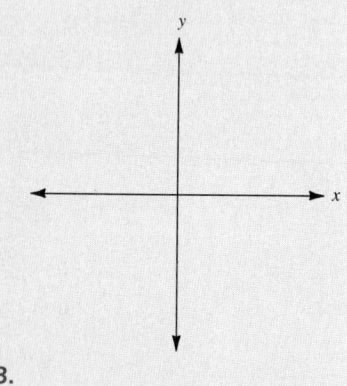

53.

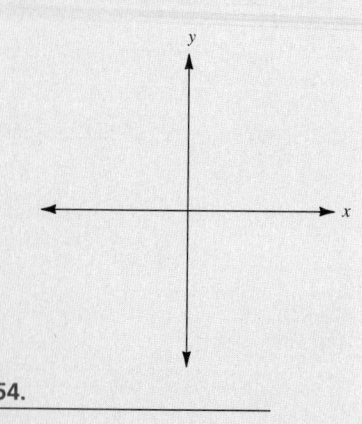

54.

50. On two occasions last month, Sam Johnson rented a car on a business trip. Both times it was the same model from the same company, and both times it was in San Francisco. Sam now has to fill out an expense account form and needs to know how much he was charged per mile and the base rate. On both occasions he dropped the car at the airport booth and just got the total charge, not the details. All Sam knows is that he was charged $210 for 625 miles on the first occasion and $133.50 for 370 miles on the second trip. Sam has called accounting to ask for help. Plot these two points on a graph, and draw the line that goes through them. What question does the slope of the line answer for Sam? How does the y intercept help? Write a memo to Sam explaining the answers to his question and how a knowledge of algebra and graphing has helped you find the answers.

51. On the same graph, sketch the following lines:

$$y = 2x - 1 \quad \text{and} \quad y = 2x + 3$$

What do you observe about these graphs? Will the lines intersect?

52. Repeat exercise 51 using

$$y = -2x + 4 \quad \text{and} \quad y = -2x + 1$$

53. On the same graph, sketch the following lines:

$$y = \frac{2}{3}x \quad \text{and} \quad y = -\frac{3}{2}x$$

What do you observe concerning these graphs? Find the product of the slopes of these two lines.

54. Repeat exercise 53 using

$$y = \frac{4}{3}x \quad \text{and} \quad y = -\frac{3}{4}x$$

55. Based on exercises 53 and 54, write the equation of a line that is perpendicular to

$$y = \frac{3}{5}x$$

 Getting Ready

Find the slope of the line connecting the given points.

(a) $(-4, 6)$ and $(3, 20)$ (b) $(2, 8)$ and $(-6, -8)$ (c) $(5, -7)$ and $(-5, 3)$

(d) $(2, 8)$ and $(2, 5)$ (e) $(6, 9)$ and $(3, 9)$ (f) $(4, 6)$ and $(-4, -2)$

Answers

1. Slope 3, y intercept $(0, 5)$ **3.** Slope -2, y intercept $(0, -5)$

5. Slope $\frac{3}{4}$, y intercept $(0, 1)$ **7.** Slope $\frac{2}{3}$, y intercept $(0, 0)$

9. Slope $-\frac{4}{3}$, y intercept $(0, 4)$ **11.** Slope 0, y intercept $(0, 9)$

13. Slope $\frac{3}{2}$, y intercept $(0, -4)$

15. $y = 3x + 5$ **17.** $y = -3x + 4$

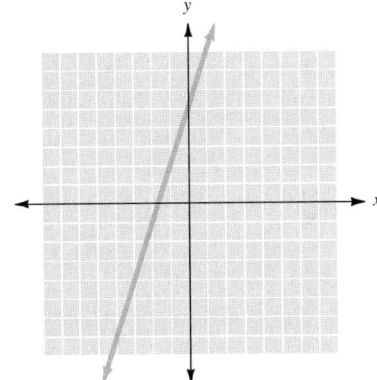 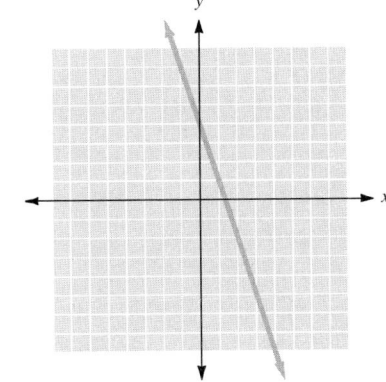

19. $y = \frac{1}{2}x - 2$ **21.** $y = -\frac{2}{3}x$

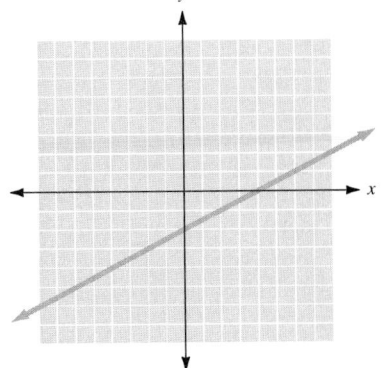 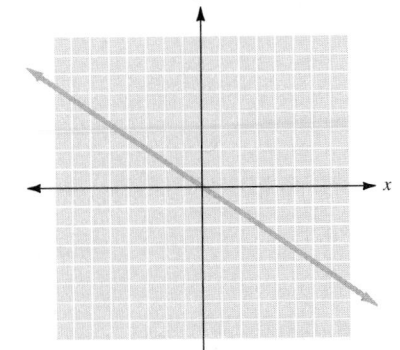

23. $y = \dfrac{3}{4}x + 3$

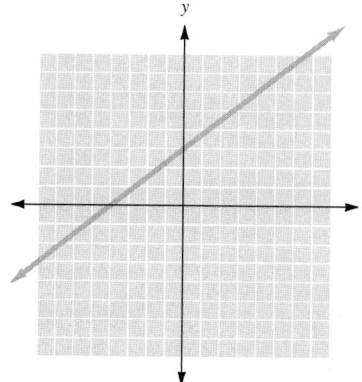

25. g **27.** e **29.** h **31.** c **33.** IV   **35.** III   **37.** I

39. III and IV   **41.** Slope $= 0.10$; y intercept $= (0, 200)$ **43.** $2°/\text{hr}$

45. -0.30 **47.** 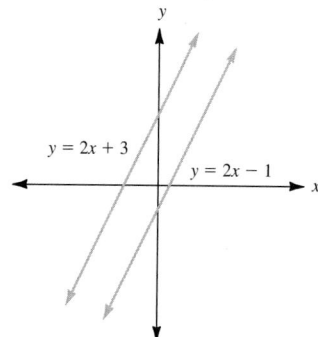   **49.**

51.   Parallel lines; no

53.   Perpendicular lines; -1

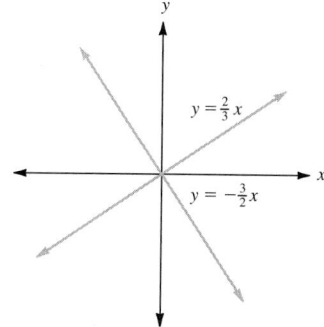

55. $y = -\dfrac{5}{3}x$ **a.** 2 **b.** 2 **c.** -1 **d.** Undefined   **e.** 0 **f.** 1

2.5 Graphing Linear Inequalities

2.5 OBJECTIVE

1. Graph a linear inequality in two variables

In Section 1.13 you learned to graph inequalities in one variable on a number line. We now want to extend our work with graphing to include linear inequalities in two variables. We begin with a definition.

Definitions: Linear Inequality in Two Variables

An inequality that can be written in the form

$$Ax + By < C$$

in which A and B are not both 0, is called a **linear inequality in two variables.**

NOTE The inequality symbols $\leq$, $>$, and $\geq$ can also be used.

Some examples of linear inequalities in two variables are

$$x + 3y > 6 \qquad y \leq 3x + 1 \qquad 2x - y \geq 3$$

The *graph* of a linear inequality is always a region (actually a half plane) of the plane whose boundary is a straight line. Let's look at an example of graphing such an inequality.

Example 1

Graphing a Linear Inequality

Graph $2x + y < 4$.

First, replace the inequality symbol ($<$) with an equals sign. We then have $2x + y = 4$. This equation forms the **boundary line** of the graph of the original inequality. You can graph the line by any of the methods discussed earlier.

The boundary line for our inequality is shown at left. We see that the boundary line separates the plane into two regions, each of which is called a **half plane.**

We now need to choose the correct half plane. Choose any convenient test point not on the boundary line. The origin $(0, 0)$ is a good choice because it makes for easy calculation.

Substitute $x = 0$ and $y = 0$ into the inequality.

$$2 \cdot 0 + 0 < 4$$
$$0 + 0 < 4$$
$$0 < 4 \qquad \text{A true statement}$$

Because the inequality is *true* for the test point, we shade the half plane containing that test point (here the origin). The origin and all other points *below* the boundary line then represent solutions for our original inequality.

NOTE The dotted line indicates that the points on the line $2x + y = 4$ are *not* part of the solution to the inequality $2x + y < 4$.

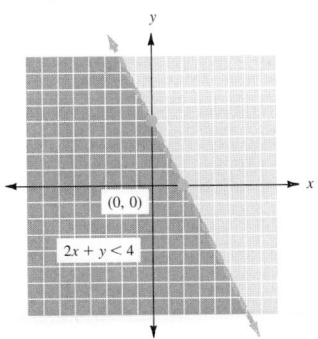

NOTE You can always use the origin for a test point unless the boundary line passes through the origin.

CHECK YOURSELF 1

Graph the inequality x + 3y < 3.

The process is similar when the boundary line is included in the solution.

Example 2

Graphing a Linear Inequality

Graph $4x - 3y \geq 12$.

First, graph the boundary line, $4x - 3y = 12$.

NOTE Again, we replace the inequality symbol ($\geq$) with an equals sign to write the equation for our boundary line.

Note: When equality *is included* ($\leq$ or $\geq$), use a *solid line* for the graph of the boundary line. This means the line is included in the graph of the linear inequality.

The graph of our boundary line (a solid line here) is shown on the figure.

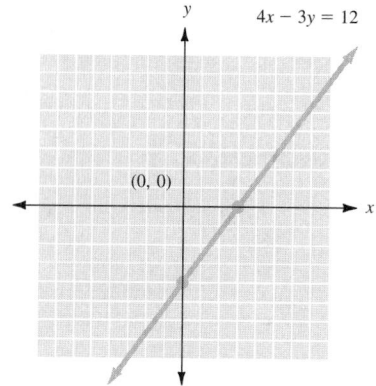

NOTE Although any of our graphing methods can be used here, the intercept method is probably the most efficient.

Again, we use (0, 0) as a convenient test point. Substituting 0 for *x* and for *y* in the original inequality, we have

$$4 \cdot 0 - 3 \cdot 0 \geq 12$$

$$0 \geq 12 \qquad \text{A false statement}$$

Because the inequality is *false* for the test point, we shade the half plane that does *not* contain that test point, here (0, 0).

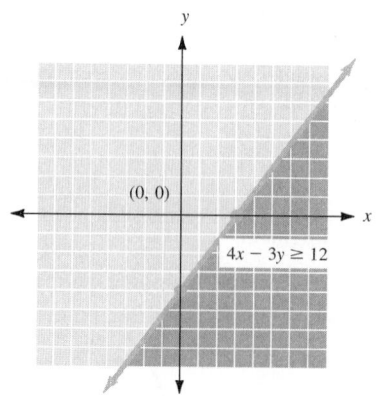

NOTE All points *on and below* the boundary line represent solutions for our original inequality.

CHECK YOURSELF 2

Graph the inequality 3x + 2y ≥ 6.

Example 3

Graphing a Linear Inequality

Graph $x \leq 5$.

The boundary line is $x = 5$. Its graph is a solid line because equality is included. Using $(0, 0)$ as a test point, we substitute 0 for x with the result

$0 \leq 5$ A true statement

Because the inequality is *true* for the test point, we shade the half plane containing the origin.

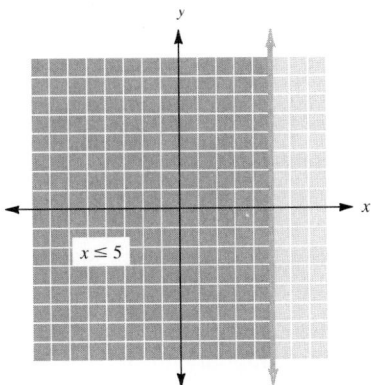

NOTE If the correct half plane is obvious, you may not need to use a test point. Did you know without testing which half plane to shade in this example?

 CHECK YOURSELF 3

Graph the inequality $y < 2$.

As we mentioned earlier, we may have to use a point other than the origin as our test point. Example 4 illustrates this approach.

Example 4

Graphing a Linear Inequality

Graph $2x + 3y < 0$.

The boundary line is $2x + 3y = 0$. Its graph is shown on the figure.

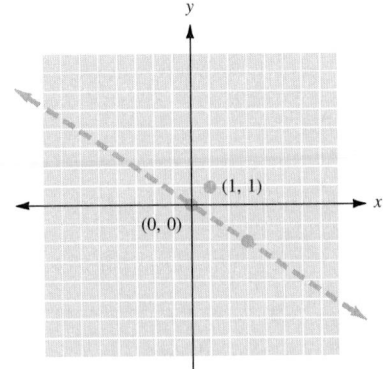

NOTE We use a dotted line for our boundary line because equality is not included.

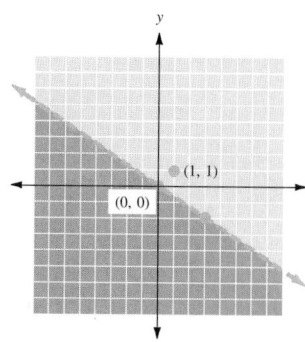

We cannot use (0, 0) as our test point in this case. Do you see why?

Choose any other point *not* on the line. For instance, we have picked (1, 1) as a test point. Substituting 1 for *x* and 1 for *y* gives

$$2 \cdot 1 + 3 \cdot 1 < 0$$
$$2 + 3 < 0$$
$$5 < 0 \quad \text{A false statement}$$

Because the inequality is *false* at our test point, we shade the half plane *not* containing (1, 1). This is shown in the graph in the margin.

✔ CHECK YOURSELF 4

Graph the inequality x − 2y < 0.

The following steps summarize our work in graphing linear inequalities in two variables.

Step by Step: To Graph a Linear Inequality

Step 1   Replace the inequality symbol with an equals sign to form the equation of the boundary line of the graph.
Step 2   Graph the boundary line. Use a dotted line if equality is not included (< or >). Use a solid line if equality is included (≤ or ≥).
Step 3   Choose any convenient test point *not* on the line.
Step 4   If the inequality is *true* at the checkpoint, shade the half plane including the test point. If the inequality is *false* at the checkpoint, shade the half plane not including the test point.

✔ CHECK YOURSELF ANSWERS

1.
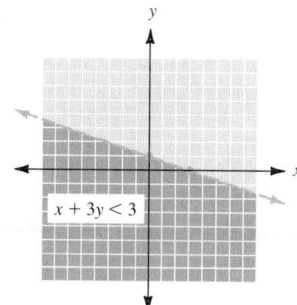

x + 3y < 3

2.
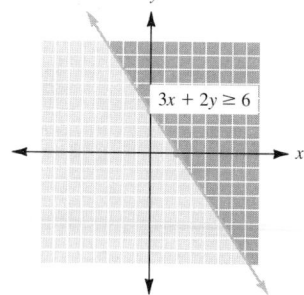

3x + 2y ≥ 6

3.
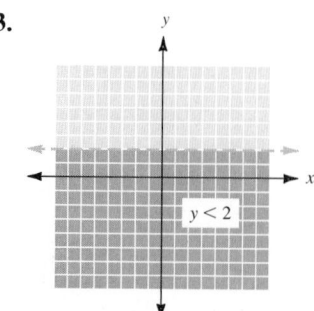

y < 2

4.
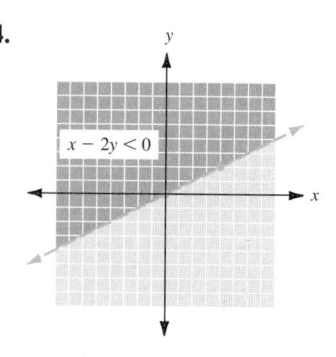

x − 2y < 0

2.5 Exercises

In exercises 1 to 8, we have graphed the boundary line for the linear inequality. Determine the correct half plane in each case, and complete the graph.

1. $x + y < 5$

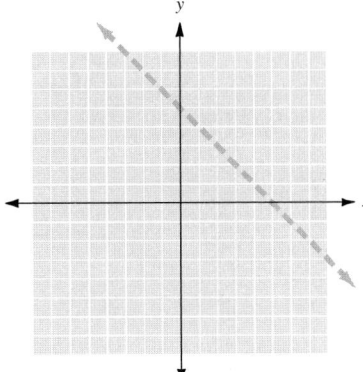

2. $x - y \geq 4$

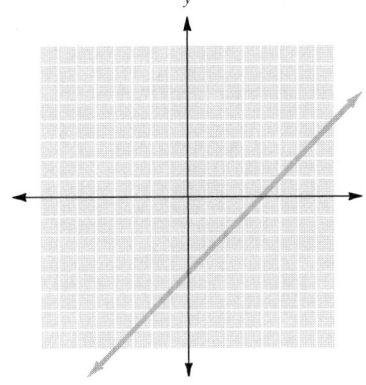

3. $x - 2y \geq 4$

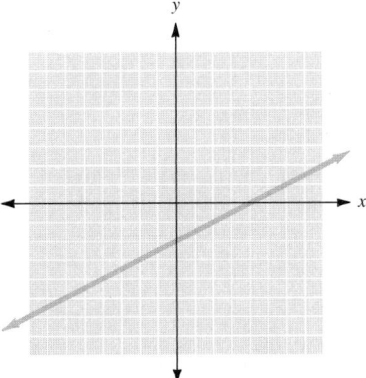

4. $2x + y < 6$

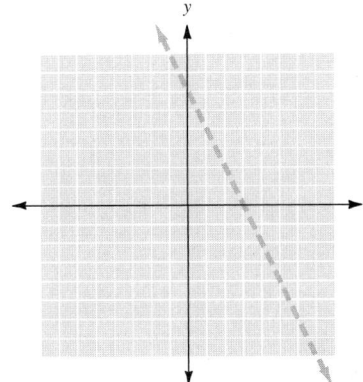

5. $x \leq -3$

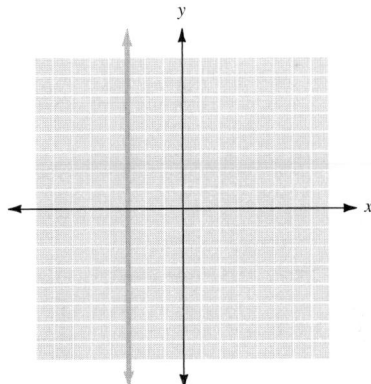

6. $y \geq 2x$

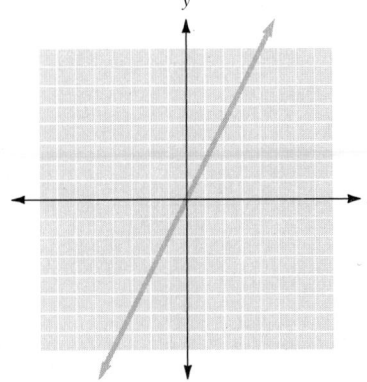

7. $y < 2x - 6$

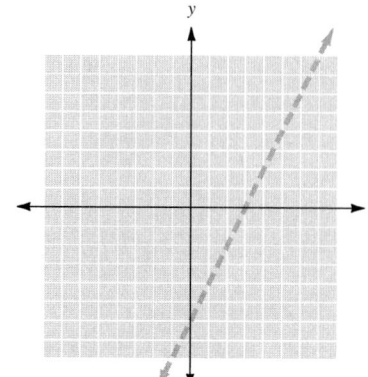

8. $y > 3$

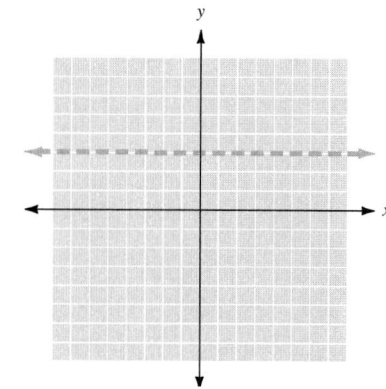

Graph each of the following inequalities.

9. $x + y < 3$

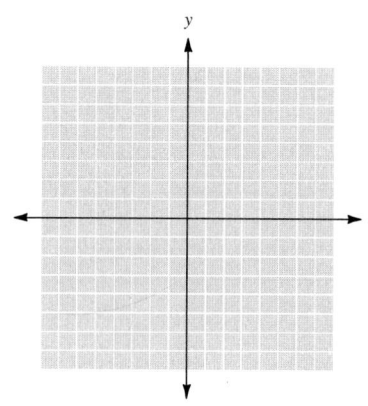

10. $x - y \geq 4$

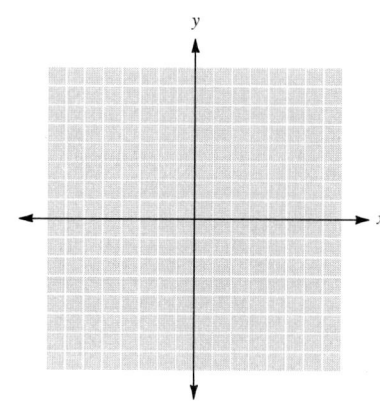

11. $x - y \leq 5$

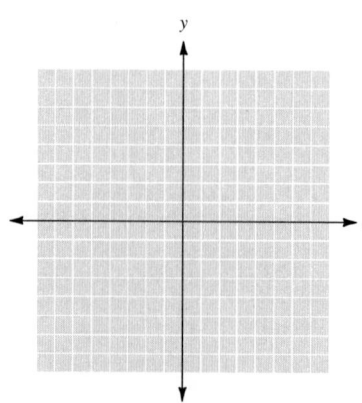

12. $x + y > 5$

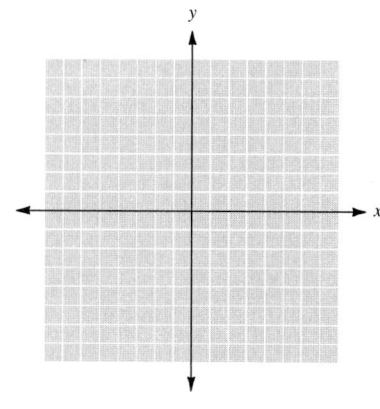

13. $2x + y < 6$

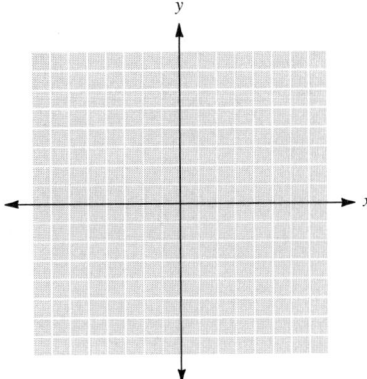

14. $3x + y \geq 6$

15. $x \leq 3$

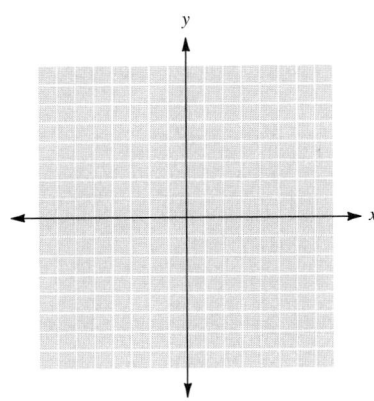

16. $4x + y \geq 4$

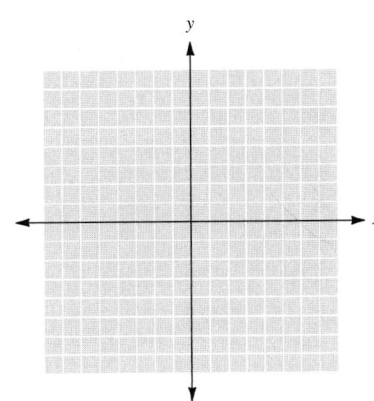

17. $x - 5y < 5$

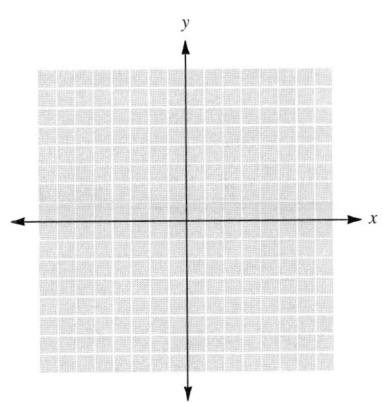

18. $y > 3$

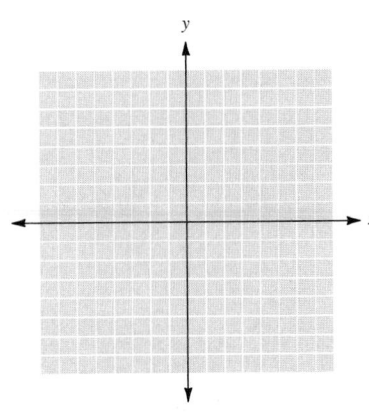

ANSWERS

13. _____

14. _____

15. _____

16. _____

17. _____

18. _____

ANSWERS

19. _____

20. _____

21. _____

22. _____

23. _____

24. _____

19. $y < -4$

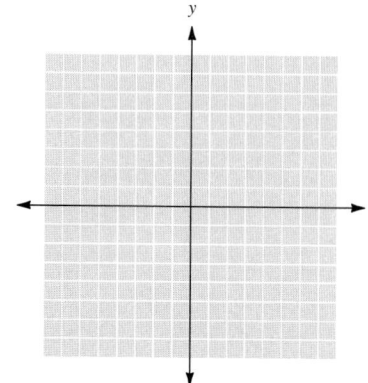

20. $4x + 3y > 12$

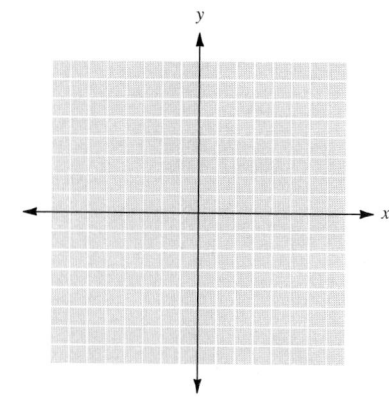

21. $2x - 3y \geq 6$

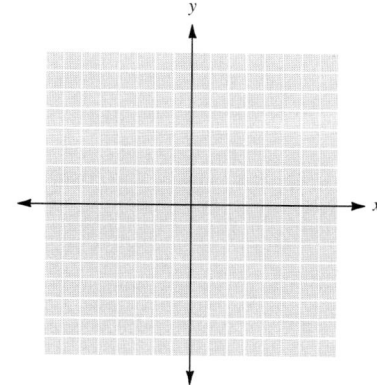

22. $x \geq -2$

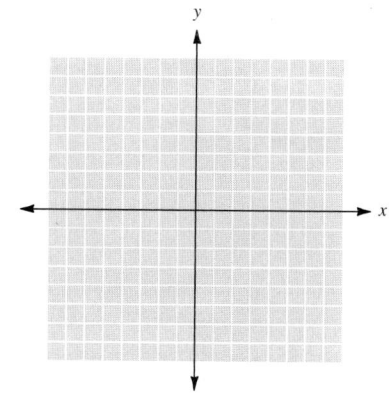

23. $3x + 2y \geq 0$

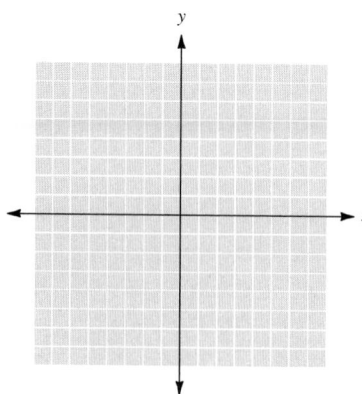

24. $3x + 5y < 15$

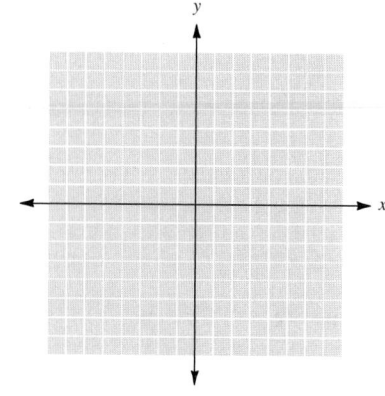

25. $5x + 2y > 10$

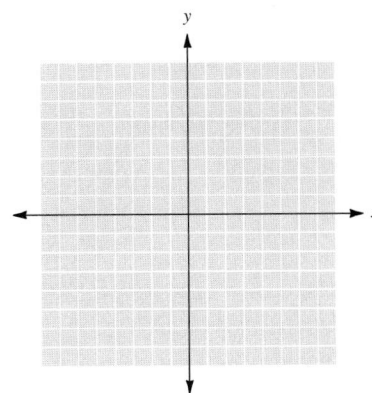

26. $x - 3y \geq 0$

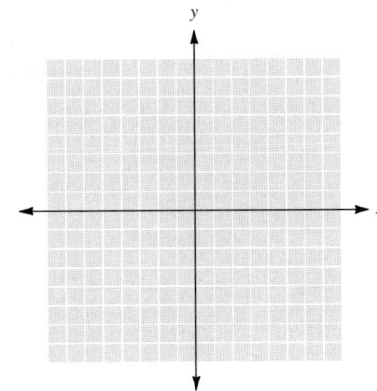

27. $y \leq 2x$

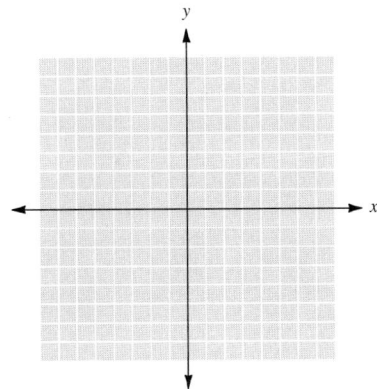

28. $3x - 4y < 12$

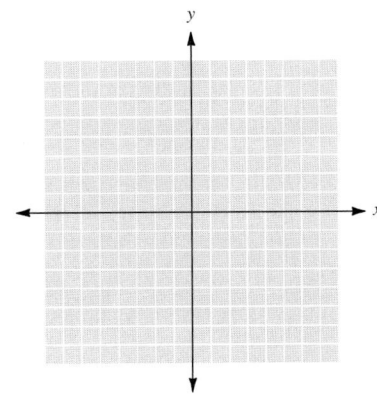

29. $y > 2x - 3$

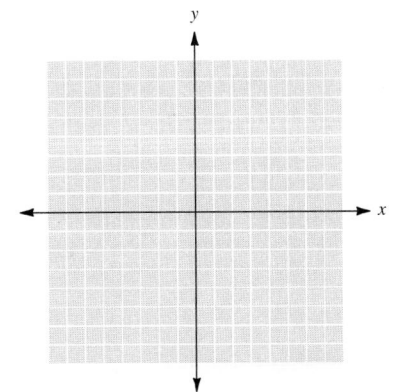

30. $y \geq -2x$

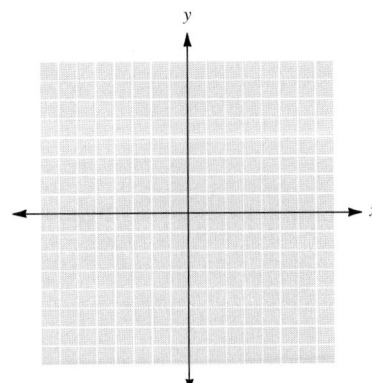

ANSWERS

25. _____

26. _____

27. _____

28. _____

29. _____

30. _____

ANSWERS

31. _____

32. _____

33. _____

34. _____

35. _____

36. _____

37. _____

31. $y < -2x - 3$

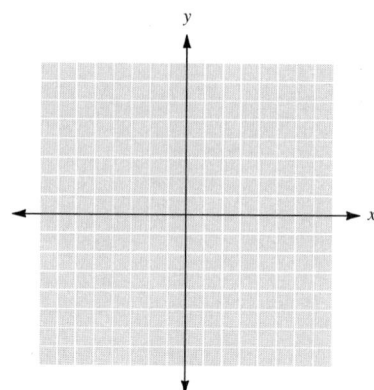

32. $y \leq 3x + 4$

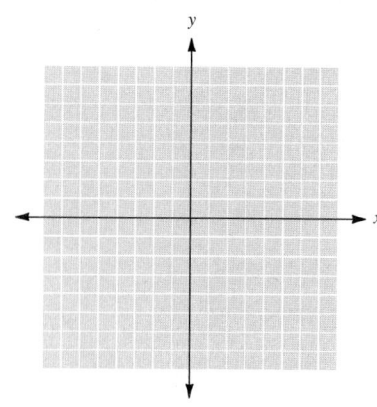

Graph each of the following inequalities.

33. $2(x + y) - x > 6$

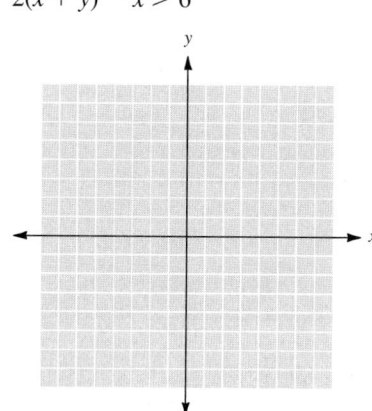

34. $3(x + y) - 2y < 3$

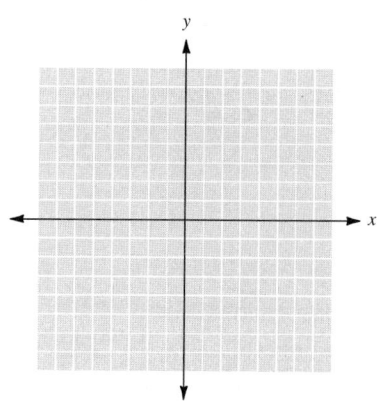

35. $4(x + y) - 3(x + y) \leq 5$

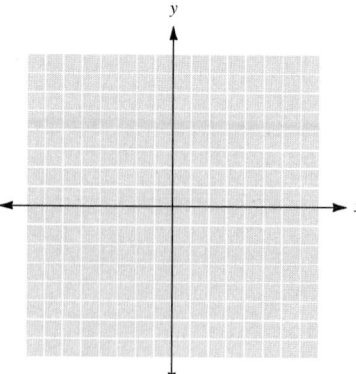

36. $5(2x + y) - 4(2x + y) \geq 4$

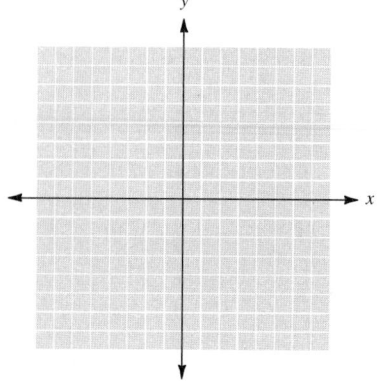

37. Hours worked. Suppose you have two part-time jobs. One is at a video store that pays $9 per hour and the other is at a convenience store that pays $8 per hour. Between the two jobs, you want to earn at least $240 per week. Write an inequality that shows the various number of hours you can work at each job.

38. Money problem. You have at least $30 in change in your drawer, consisting of dimes and quarters. Write an inequality that shows the different number of coins in your drawer.

39. Linda Williams has just begun a nursery business and seeks your advice. She has limited funds to spend and wants to stock two kinds of fruit-bearing plants. She lives in the northeastern part of Texas and thinks that blueberry bushes and peach trees would sell well there. Linda can buy blueberry bushes from a supplier for $2.50 each and young peach trees for $5.50 each. She wants to know what combination she should buy and keep her outlay to $500 or less. Write an equation and draw a graph to depict what combinations of blueberry bushes and peach trees she can buy for the amount of money she has. Explain the graph and her options.

40. After reading an article on the front page of *The New York Times* titled "You Have to be Good at Algebra to Figure Out the Best Deal for Long Distance," Rafaella De La Cruz decided to apply her skills in algebra to try to decide between two competing long-distance companies. It was difficult at first to get the companies to explain their charge policies. They both kept repeating that they were 25% cheaper than their competition. Finally, Rafaella found someone who explained that the charge depended on when she called, where she called, how long she talked, and how often she called. "Too many variables!" she exclaimed. So she decided to ask one company what they charged as a base amount, just for using the service.

Company A said that they charged $5 for the privilege of using their long-distance service whether or not she made any phone calls, and that because of this fee they were able to allow her to call anywhere in the United States after 6 P.M. for only $0.15 a minute. Complete this table of charges based on this company's plan:

Total Minutes Long Distance in 1 Month (After 6 P.M.)	Total Charge
0 minutes	
10 minutes	
30 minutes	
60 minutes	
120 minutes	

Use this table to make a whole-page graph of the monthly charges from Company A based on the number of minutes of long distance.

Rafaella wanted to compare this offer to Company B, which she was currently using. She looked at her phone bill and saw that one month she had been charged $7.50 for 30 minutes and another month she had been charged $11.25 for 45 minutes of long-distance calling. These calls were made after 6 P.M. to her relatives in Indiana and in Arizona. Draw a graph on the same set of axes you made for Company A's figures. Use your graph and what you know about linear inequalities to advise Rafaella about which company is best.

Getting Ready

Evaluate each expression for the given variable value.

(a) $2x + 1 \ (x = 2)$ (b) $2x + 1 \ (x = -2)$

(c) $3 - 2x \ (x = 1)$ (d) $3 - 2x \ (x = -1)$

(e) $x^2 - 2 \ (x = 2)$ (f) $x^2 - 2 \ (x = -2)$

(g) $x^2 + 5 \ (x = 1)$ (h) $x^2 + 5 \ (x = -1)$

Answers

1. $x + y < 5$

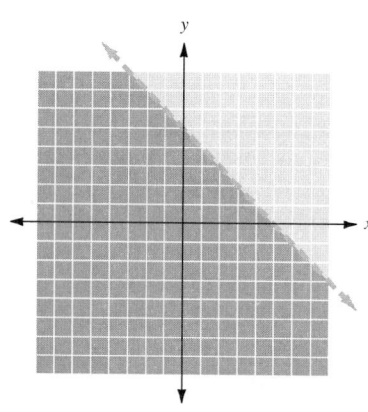

3. $x - 2y \geq 4$

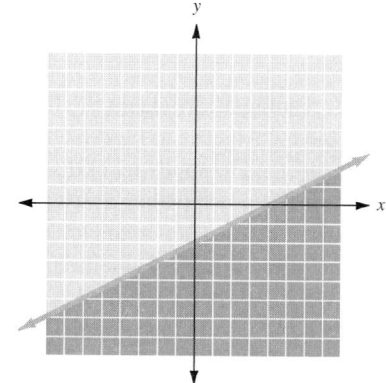

5. $x \leq -3$

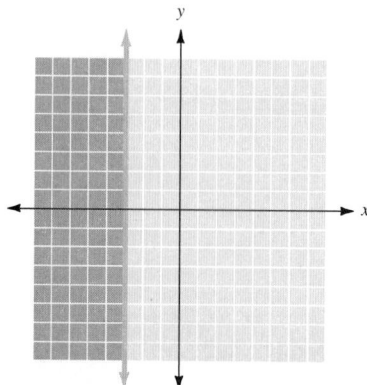

7. $y < 2x - 6$

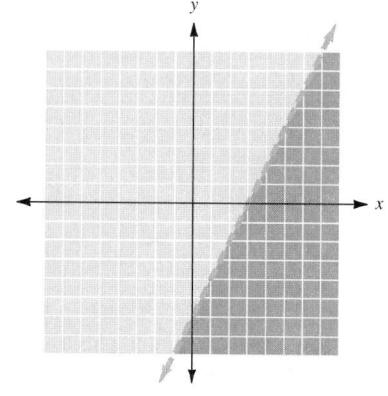

9. $x + y < 3$

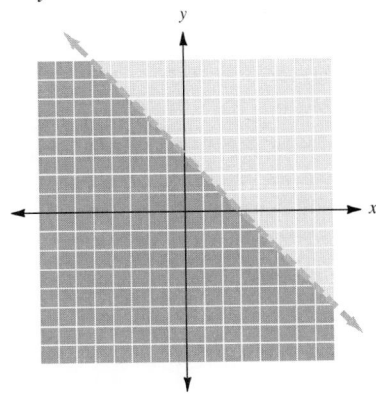

11. $x - y \leq 5$

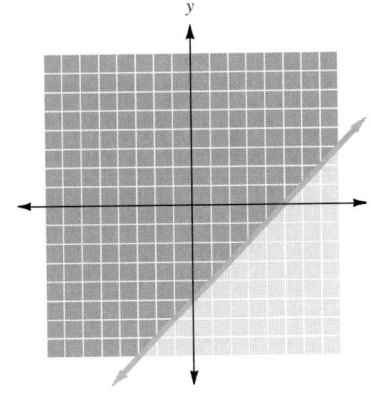

13. $2x + y < 6$

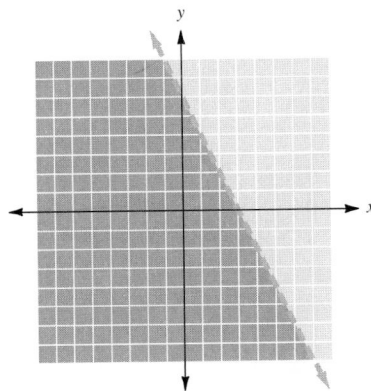

15. $x \leq 3$

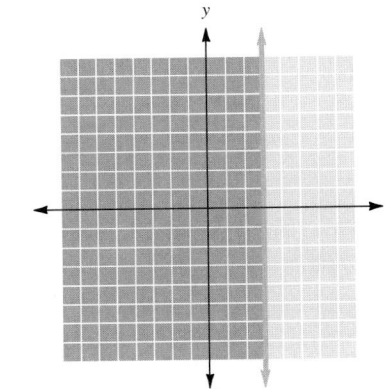

17. $x - 5y < 5$

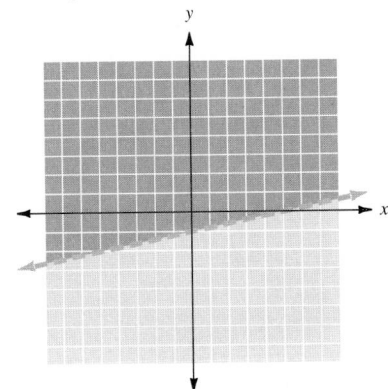

19. $y < -4$

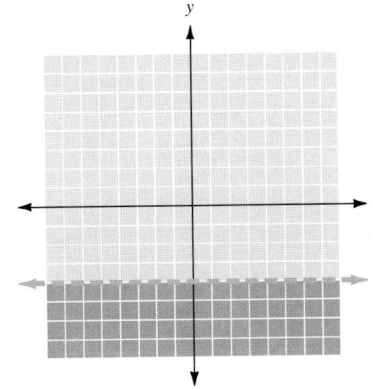

21. $2x - 3y \geq 6$

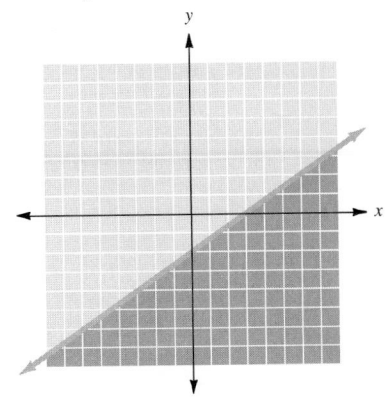

23. $3x + 2y \geq 0$

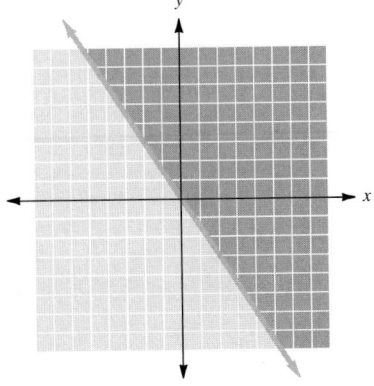

25. $5x + 2y > 10$

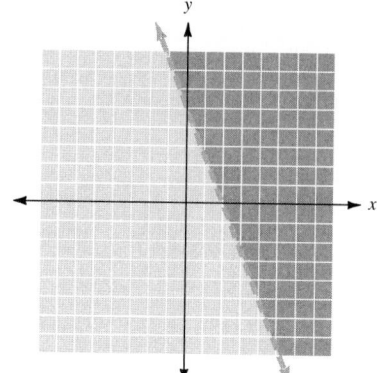

27. $y \le 2x$

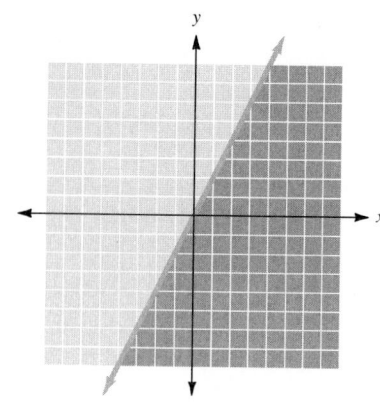

29. $y > 2x - 3$

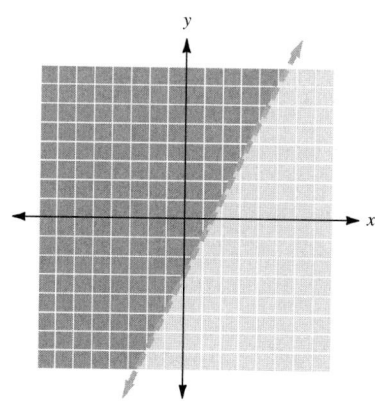

31. $y < -2x - 3$

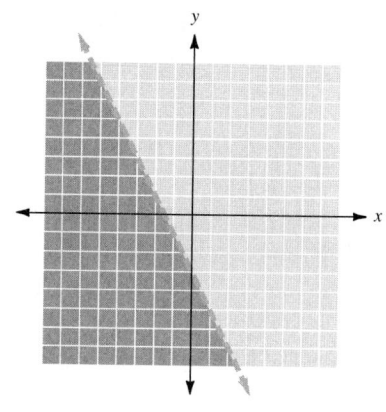

33. $x + 2y > 6$

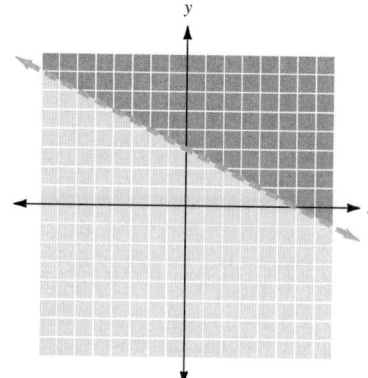

35. $x + y \le 5$

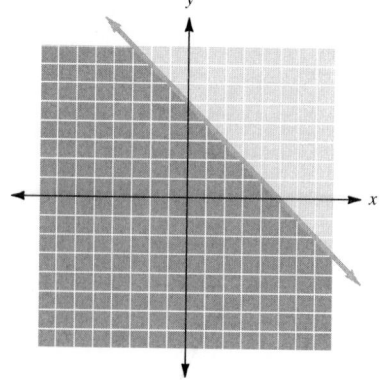

37. $9x + 8y \ge 240$　　**39.** 　　**a.** 5　　**b.** -3　　**c.** 1　　**d.** 5

e. 2　　**f.** 2　　**g.** 6　　**h.** 6

2.6 Ordered Pairs and Relations

2.6 **OBJECTIVES**

1. Identify ordered pairs
2. Identify a relation
3. Identify the domain and range of a function

In Chapter 1, we introduced the idea of a set of numbers. In this chapter, we will look at pairs of numbers.

Given the two related values x and y, we write the pair as (x, y). The set of all possible ordered pairs of real numbers is written as $\{(x, y) \mid x \in R, y \in R\}$.

The ordered pair $(2, -3)$ is different from the ordered pair $(-3, 2)$. By contrast, the set $\{2, -3\}$ is identical to the set $\{-3, 2\}$.

NOTE We read this as, "the set of ordered pairs, (x, y) in which x is a real number and y is a real number. Note that sets always use braces to enclose their contents.

Example 1

Identifying Ordered Pairs

Which of the following are ordered pairs?

(a) $(2, -\pi)$ **(b)** $\{2, -4\}$ **(c)** $(1, 3, -1)$

(d) $\{(1, -5), (9, 0)\}$ **(e)** $2, 5$

Only (a) is an ordered pair. (b) is a set (it uses braces instead of parentheses), (c) has three numbers instead of two, (d) is a set of ordered pairs, and (e) is simply a list of two numbers.

 CHECK YOURSELF 1

Which of the following are ordered pairs?

(a) $\left\{\dfrac{1}{2}, -3\right\}$ **(b)** $\left(-3, \dfrac{1}{3}\right)$ **(c)** $\{(5, 0)\}$

(d) $(1, -5)$ **(e)** $-3, 6$

Ordered pairs are not necessarily made up of two numbers. Given something like (John Doe, 123-45-6789), we have an ordered pair. In this case, it is a name paired with that person's Social Security number (SSN).

Definitions: Relation

A set of ordered pairs is called a **relation.**

We usually denote a relation with a capital letter.

Given

$R = \{(\text{John Doe, 123-45-6789}), (\text{Jacob Smith, 987-65-4321}), (\text{Julia Jones, 111-22-3333})\}$

we have a relation, which we call R. In this case, there are three ordered pairs in the relation R.

Within this relation, there are two interesting sets. The first is the set of names, which happens to be the set of first elements. The second is the set of SSNs, which is the set of second elements. Each of these sets has a name.

Definitions: Domain

The set of first elements in a relation is called the **domain** of the relation.

Example 2

Finding the Domain of a Relation

Find the domain of each relation.

(a) $A = \{(\text{Ben Bender, 58}), (\text{Carol Clairol, 32}), (\text{David Duval, 29})\}$

The domain of A is {Ben Bender, Carol Clairol, David Duval}.

(b) $B = \left\{ \left(5, \dfrac{1}{2}\right), (-4, -5), (-12, 10), (-16, \pi) \right\}$

The domain of B is $\{5, -4, -12, -16\}$.

 CHECK YOURSELF 2

Find the domain of each relation.

(a) $R = \{(\text{Secretariat, 10}), (\text{Seattle Slew, 8}), (\text{Charismatic, 5}), (\text{Gallant Man, 7})\}$

(b) $S = \left\{ \left(-\dfrac{1}{2}, \dfrac{3}{4}\right), (0, 0), (1, 5), (\pi, \pi) \right\}$

NOTE $X \rightarrow$ Domain
$Y \rightarrow$ Range
Many students find it helpful to remember that domain and range occur in alphabetical order.

Definitions: Range

The set of second elements in a relation is called the **range** of the relation.

Example 3

Finding the Range of a Relation

Find the range for each relation.

(a) $A = \{(\text{Ben Bender}, 58), (\text{Carol Clairol}, 32), (\text{David Duval } 29)\}$

The range of A is $\{58, 32, 29\}$

(b) $B = \left\{\left(5, \dfrac{1}{2}\right), (-4, -5), (-12, 10), (-16, \pi)\right\}$

The range of B is $\left\{\dfrac{1}{2}, -5, 10, \pi\right\}$

CHECK YOURSELF 3

Find the range of each relation.

(a) $R = \{(\text{Secretariat}, 10), (\text{Seattle Slew}, 8), (\text{Charismatic}, 5), (\text{Gallant Man}, 7)\}$

(b) $S = \left\{\left(-\dfrac{1}{2}, \dfrac{3}{4}\right), (0, 0), (1, 5), (\pi, \pi)\right\}$

CHECK YOURSELF ANSWERS

1. **(b)** and **(d)** are ordered pairs

2. **(a)** The domain of R is {Secretariat, Seattle Slew, Charismatic, Gallant Man};

   (b) The domain of S is $\left\{-\dfrac{1}{2}, 0, 1, \pi\right\}$

3. **(a)** The range of R is $\{10, 8, 5, 7\}$; **(b)** The range of S is $\left\{\dfrac{3}{4}, 0, 5, \pi\right\}$

2.6 Exercises

Name _____

Section _____ Date _____

In exercises 1 to 4, identify the ordered pairs.

1. (a) $(3, -5)$ **(b)** $\{7, 9\}$ **(c)** $(2, 5)$ **(d)** $5, 2$ **(e)** $((3, 1), 4)$

2. (a) $\{7, 23\}$ **(b)** $(1, 0, (5, 6))$ **(c)** $\left(\dfrac{1}{2}, -1\right)$ **(d)** $[5, 6]$ **(e)** $(23, 7)$

3. (a) $18, 67$ **(b)** $(-3, -9)$ **(c)** $\{3, 9\}$ **(d)** $(3, 7, -3)$ **(e)** $[12, 56]$

4. (a) $\{45, 67]$ **(b)** $(9, 3)$ **(c)** $5, 8$ **(d)** $(11, -3, 9)$ **(e)** $[5, 2]$

In exercises 5 to 20, find the domain and range of each relation.

5. $A = \{(\text{Colorado}, 21), (\text{Edmonton}, 5), (\text{Calgary}, 18), (\text{Vancouver}, 17)\}$

6. $B = \{(\text{Eric Lindros}, 88), (\text{Mark Recchi}, 8), (\text{John LeClair}, 10), (\text{Keith Primeau}, 25)\}$

7. $C = \{(\text{John Adams}, -16), (\text{John Kennedy}, -23), (\text{Richard Nixon}, -5),$
$(\text{Harry Truman}, -11)\}$

8. $E = \{(\text{Utah}, 27), (\text{San Antonio}, 28), (\text{Minnesota}, 24), (\text{Denver}, 19)\}$

9. $F = \left\{ \left(\text{St. Louis}, \dfrac{1}{2}\right), \left(\text{Denver}, -\dfrac{3}{4}\right), \left(\text{Green Bay}, \dfrac{7}{8}\right), \left(\text{Dallas}, -\dfrac{4}{5}\right) \right\}$

10. $G = \left\{ (\text{Chamber}, \pi), (\text{Testament}, 2\pi), \left(\text{Rainmaker}, \dfrac{1}{2}\right), (\text{Street Lawyer}, 6) \right\}$

11. $\{(1, 2), (3, 4), (5, 6), (7, 8), (9, 10)\}$

12. $\{(2, 3), (3, 5), (4, 7), (5, 9), (6, 11)\}$

13. $\{(1, 2), (4, 6), (3, 3), (5, 4), (6, 1)\}$

14. $\{(3, 4), (5, 7), (6, 1), (2, 2), (4, 3)\}$

15. $\{(1, 2), (1, 3), (1, 4), (1, 5), (1, 6)\}$

16. $\{(3, 4), (3, 6), (3, 8), (3, 9), (3, 10)\}$

17. $\{(1, 5), (2, 5), (3, 6), (2, 4), (4, 5)\}$

18. $\{(2, 8), (3, 9), (2, 9), (3, 8), (4, 7)\}$

19. $\{(-1, 3), (-2, 4), (-3, 5), (4, 4), (5, 6)\}$

20. $\{(-2, 4), (1, 4), (-3, 4), (5, 4), (7, 4)\}$

ANSWERS

1. _____ 2. _____

3. _____ 4. _____

5. _____

6. _____

7. _____

8. _____

9. _____

10. _____

11. _____

12. _____

13. _____

14. _____

15. _____

16. _____

17. _____

18. _____

19. _____

20. _____

21. _____

22. _____

23. _____

24. _____

25. _____

26. _____

21. The stock prices for a given stock over a week's time are displayed in a table. List this information as a set of ordered pairs using the day of the week as the domain.

Day	1	2	3	4	5
Price	$9\frac{1}{8}$	8	$8\frac{7}{8}$	$9\frac{1}{4}$	9

22. Food Purchases. In the snack department of the local supermarket, candy costs $1.58 per pound. For 1 to 5 pounds, write the cost of candy as a set of ordered pairs.

Bulk Candy
$1⁵⁸ per pound

In exercises 23 to 26, write a set of ordered pairs that describes each situation. Give the domain and range of each relation.

23. The first element is an integer between −3 and 3. The second coordinate is the cube of the first coordinate.

24. The first element is a positive integer less than 6. The second coordinate is the sum of the first coordinate and −2.

25. The first element is the number of hours worked 10, 20, 30, 40; the second coordinate is the salary at $6 per hour.

26. The first coordinate is the number of toppings on a pizza (up to 4); the second coordinate is the price of the pizza, which is $9 plus $1 per topping.

Answers

1. (a) and (c)   **3.** (b)
5. D: {Colorado, Edmonton, Calgary, Vancouver}; R: {21, 5, 18, 17}
7. D: {John Adams, John Kennedy, Richard Nixon, Harry Truman};
R: {−16, −23, −5, −11}

9. D: {St. Louis, Denver, Green Bay, Dallas}; R: $\left\{\frac{1}{2}, -\frac{3}{4}, \frac{7}{8}, -\frac{4}{5}\right\}$

11. D: {1, 3, 5, 7, 9}; R: {2, 4, 6, 8, 10}   **13.** D: {1, 3, 4, 5, 6}; R: {1, 2, 3, 4, 6}
15. D: {1}; R: {2, 3, 4, 5, 6}   **17.** D: {1, 2, 3, 4}; R: {4, 5, 6}
19. D: {−1, −2, −3, 4, 5}; R: {3, 4, 5, 6}

21. $\left\{\left(1, 9\frac{1}{8}\right), (2, 8), \left(3, 8\frac{7}{8}\right), \left(4, 9\frac{1}{4}\right), (5, 9)\right\}$

23. {(−2, −8), (−1, −1), (0, 0), (1, 1), (2, 8)}; D: {−2, −1, 0, 1, 2}; R: {−8, −1, 0, 1, 8}
25. {(10, 60), (20, 120), (30, 180), (40, 240)}; D: {10, 20, 30, 40}; R: {60, 120, 180, 240}

2.7 An Introduction to Functions

2.7 **OBJECTIVES**

1. Evaluate an expression
2. Determine whether a relation is a function
3. Use the vertical line test
4. Identify the domain and range of a function

Variables can be used to represent numbers whose value is unknown. Using addition, subtraction, multiplication, division, and exponentiation, these numbers and variables form expressions such as:

$$3 + 5 \qquad 7x - 4 \qquad x^2 - 3x - 4 \qquad x^4 - x^2 + 2$$

If a specific value is given for the variable, we **evaluate the expression.**

Example 1

Evaluating Expressions

Evaluate the expression $x^4 - 2x^2 + 3x + 4$ for the indicated value of x.

(a) $x = 0$

Substituting 0 for x in the expression yields:

$$(0)^4 - 2(0)^2 + 3(0) + 4 = 0 - 0 + 0 + 4$$
$$= 4$$

(b) $x = 2$

Substituting 2 for x in the expression yields:

$$(2)^4 - 2(2)^2 + 3(2) + 4 = 16 - 8 + 6 + 4$$
$$= 18$$

(c) $x = -1$

Substituting -1 for x in the expression yields:

$$(-1)^4 - 2(-1)^2 + 3(-1) + 4 = 1 - 2 - 3 + 4$$
$$= 0$$

 CHECK YOURSELF 1

Evaluate the expression $2x^3 - 3x^2 + 3x + 1$ for the indicated value of x.

(a) $x = 0$ **(b)** $x = 1$ **(c)** $x = -2$

We could design a machine whose purpose would be to crank out the value of an expression for each given value of x. We could call this machine something simple such as f, our **function machine.** Our machine might look like this.

For example, when we put -1 into the machine, the machine would substitute -1 for x in the expression, and 5 would come out the other end because

$$2(-1)^3 + 3(-1)^2 - 5(-1) - 1 = -2 + 3 + 5 - 1 = 5$$

Note that, with this function machine, an input of -1 will always result in an output of 5. One of the most important aspects of a function machine is that each input has a unique output.

In fact, the idea of the function machine is very useful in mathematics. Your graphing calculator can be used as a function machine. You can enter the expression into the calculator as Y_1 and then evaluate Y_1 for different values of x.

Generally, in mathematics, we do not write $Y_1 = 2x^3 + 3x^2 - 5x - 1$. Instead, we write $f(x) = 2x^3 + 3x^2 - 5x - 1$, which is read "$f$ of x is equal to . . . ." Instead of calling f a function machine, we say that f is a function of x. The greatest benefit of this notation is that it lets us easily note the input value of x along with the output of the function. Instead of "the value of Y_1 is 155 when $x = 4$," we can write $f(4) = 155$.

Example 2

Evaluating a Function

Given $f(x) = x^3 + 3x^2 - x + 5$, find the following.

(a) $f(0)$

Substituting 0 for x in the expression on the right, we get

$$(0)^3 + 3(0)^2 - (0) + 5 = 5$$

(b) $f(-3)$

Substituting -3 for x in the expression on the right, we get

$$(-3)^3 + 3(-3)^2 - (-3) + 5 = -27 + 27 + 3 + 5$$
$$= 8$$

(c) $f\left(\dfrac{1}{2}\right)$

Substituting $\dfrac{1}{2}$ for x in the expression on the right, we get

$$\left(\frac{1}{2}\right)^3 + 3\left(\frac{1}{2}\right)^2 - \left(\frac{1}{2}\right) + 5 = \frac{1}{8} + 3\left(\frac{1}{4}\right) - \frac{1}{2} + 5$$

$$= \frac{1}{8} + \frac{3}{4} - \frac{1}{2} + 5$$

$$= \frac{1}{8} + \frac{6}{8} - \frac{4}{8} + 5$$

$$= \frac{3}{8} + 5$$

$$= 5\frac{3}{8} \text{ or } \frac{43}{8}$$

CHECK YOURSELF 2

Given $f(x) = 2x^3 - x^2 + 3x - 2$, find the following.

(a) $f(0)$ **(b)** $f(3)$ **(c)** $f\left(-\dfrac{1}{2}\right)$

We can rewrite the relationship between x and $f(x)$ in Example 2 as a series of ordered pairs.

$$f(x) = x^3 + 3x^2 - x + 5$$

From this we found that

$$f(0) = 5, \qquad f(-3) = 8, \qquad \text{and} \qquad f\left(\frac{1}{2}\right) = \frac{43}{8}$$

NOTE Because $y = f(x)$, $(x, f(x))$ is another way of writing (x, y).

There is an ordered pair, which we could write as $(x, f(x))$, associated with each of these. Those three ordered pairs are

$$(0, 5), \qquad (-3, 8), \qquad \text{and} \qquad \left(\frac{1}{2}, \frac{43}{8}\right)$$

Example 3

Finding Ordered Pairs

Given the function $f(x) = 2x^2 - 3x + 5$, find the ordered pair $(x, f(x))$ associated with each given value for x.

(a) $x = 0$

$f(0) = 2(0)^2 - 3(0) + 5 = 5$, so the ordered pair is $(0, 5)$.

(b) $x = -1$

$f(-1) = 2(-1)^2 - 3(-1) + 5 = 10$. The ordered pair is $(-1, 10)$.

(c) $x = \dfrac{1}{4}$

$f\left(\dfrac{1}{4}\right) = 2\left(\dfrac{1}{4}\right)^2 - 3\left(\dfrac{1}{4}\right) + 5 = \dfrac{35}{8}$. The ordered pair is $\left(\dfrac{1}{4}, \dfrac{35}{8}\right)$.

CHECK YOURSELF 3

Given $f(x) = 2x^3 - x^2 + 3x - 2$, find the ordered pair associated with each given value of x.

(a) $x = 0$ **(b)** $x = 3$ **(c)** $x = -\dfrac{1}{2}$

In Section 2.6, we defined a relation as a set of ordered pairs. In the following example, we will determine which relations can be modeled by a function machine.

Example 4

Modeling with a Function Machine

Determine which relations can be modeled by a function machine.

(a) The set of all possible ordered pairs in which the first element is a U.S. state and the second element is a U.S. senator from that state.

New Jersey

We cannot model this relation with a function machine. Because there are two senators from each state, each input does not have a unique output. In the picture, New Jersey is the input, but New Jersey has two different senators.

(b) The set of all ordered pairs in which the input is the year and the output is the U.S. Open golf champion of that year.

Year 2000

Tiger Woods

This relation can be modeled with the function machine. Each input has a unique output. In the picture, an input of 2000 gives an output of Tiger Woods. Every time the input is 2000, the output will be Tiger Woods.

(c) The set of all ordered pair in the relation R, when

$R = \{(1, 3), (2, 5), (2, 7), (3 - 4)\}$

2

5

7

This relation cannot be modeled with a function machine. An input of 2 can result in two different outputs, either 5 or 7.

(d) The set of all ordered pairs in the relation S, when

$S = \{(-1, 3), (0, 3), (3, 5), (5, -2)\}$

0

3

This relation can be modeled with a function machine. Each input has a unique output.

✔ CHECK YOURSELF 4

Determine which relations can be modeled by a function machine.

(a) The set of all ordered pairs in which the first element is a U.S. city and the second element is the mayor of that city.
(b) The set of all ordered pairs in which the first element is a street name and the second element is a U.S. city in which a street of that name is found.
(c) The relation $R = \{(-2, 3), (-4, 9), (9, -4)\}$.
(d) The relation $S = \{(1, 2), (3, 4), (3, 5)\}$.

The idea of a function machine leads us to a more formal definition of a function.

Definitions: Function

A function is a set of distinct ordered pairs (a relation) in which no two first coordinates are equal.

In our next example, the set of ordered pairs will be represented by a table.

Example 5

Identifying a Function

For each table of values below, decide whether the relation is a function.

(a)

x	y
-2	1
-1	1
1	3
2	3

(b)

x	y
-5	-2
-1	3
-1	6
2	9

(c)

x	y
-3	1
-1	0
0	2
2	4

Part (a) represents a function. No two first coordinates are equal. Part (b) is not a function because -1 appears as a first coordinate with two different second coordinates. Part (c) is a function.

✔ CHECK YOURSELF 5

For each table of values below, decide whether the relation is a function.

(a)

x	y
-3	0
-1	1
1	2
3	3

(b)

x	y
-2	-2
-1	-2
1	3
2	3

(c)

x	y
-2	0
-1	1
0	2
0	3

We defined a function in terms of ordered pairs. A set of ordered pairs can be specified in several ways; here are the most common.

Rules and Properties: Ordered Pairs

1. We can present ordered pairs in a list or table, as in Example 5.
2. We can give a rule or equation that will generate ordered pairs.
3. We can use a graph to indicate ordered pairs. The graph can show distinct ordered pairs, or it can show all the ordered pairs on a line or curve.

Let's look at a graph of the ordered pairs from Example 5 to introduce the **vertical line test,** which is a graphic test for identifying a function.

(a)

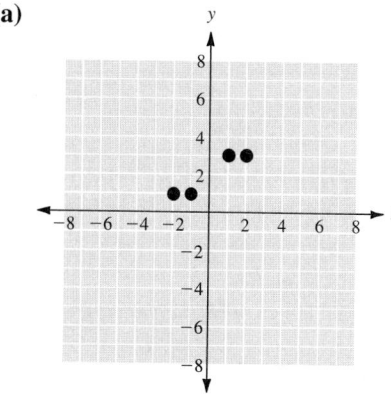

(b)

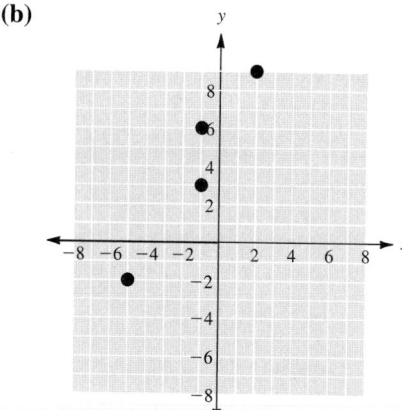

(c)

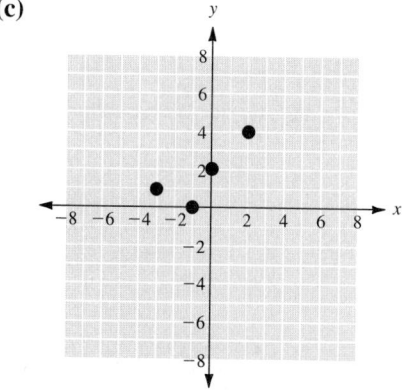

Notice that in the graphs of relations (a) and (c), there is no vertical line that can pass through two different points of the graph. In relation (b), a vertical line can pass through the two points that represent the ordered pairs $(-1, 3)$ and $(-1, 6)$. This leads to the following definition.

Definitions: Vertical Line Test

A relation is a function if no vertical line can pass through two or more points on its graph.

Example 6

Identifying a Function

For each set of ordered pairs, plot the related points on the provided axes. Then use the vertical line test to determine which of the sets is a function.

(a) $\{(0, -1), (2, 3), (2, 6), (4, 2), (6, 3)\}$

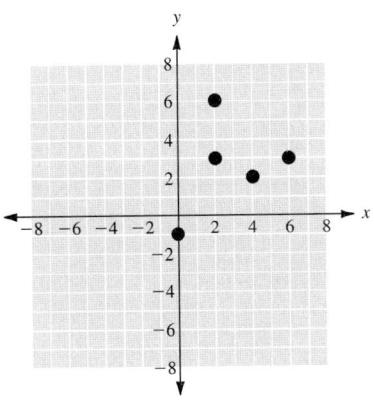

Because a vertical line can be drawn through the points $(2, 3)$ and $(2, 6)$, the relation does not pass the vertical line test. This is not a function.

(b) $\{(1, 1), (2, 0), (3, 3), (4, 3), (5, 3)\}$

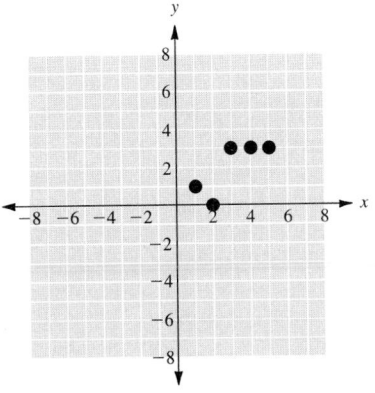

This is a function. Although a horizontal line can be drawn through several points, no vertical line passes through more than one point.

✔ CHECK YOURSELF 6

For each set of ordered pairs, plot the related points. Then use the vertical line test to determine which of the sets is a function.

(a) $\{(-2, 4), (-1, 4), (0, 4), (1, 3), (5, 5)\}$

(b) $\{(-3, -1), (-1, -3), (1, -3), (1, 3)\}$

The vertical line test can be used to determine whether a graph is the graph of a function.

Example 7

Identifying a Function

Which of the following graphs represents the graph of a function?

(a)

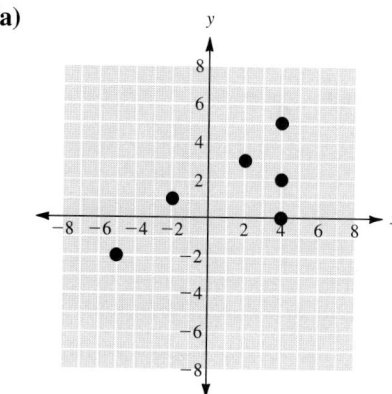

(b)

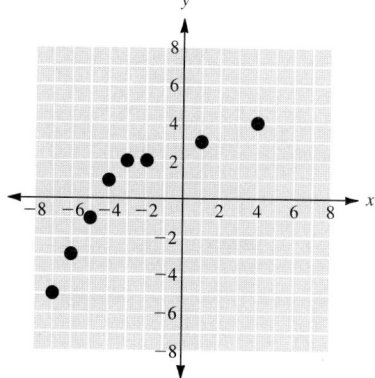

(c)

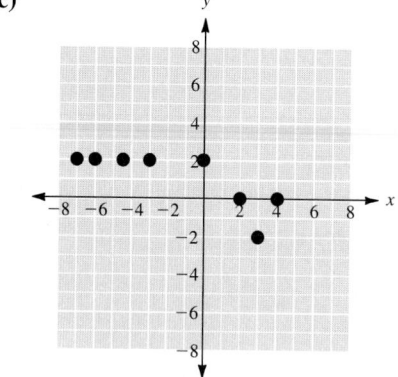

Part (a) is not a function, part (b) is a function, and part (c) is a function.

✓ CHECK YOURSELF 7

Which of the following graphs represents the graph of a function?

(a)

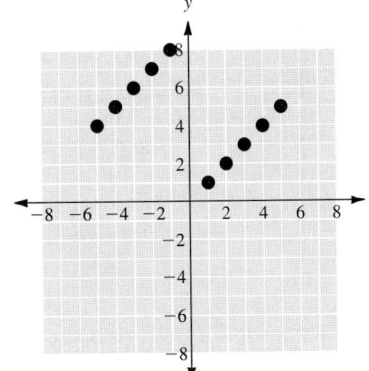

(b)

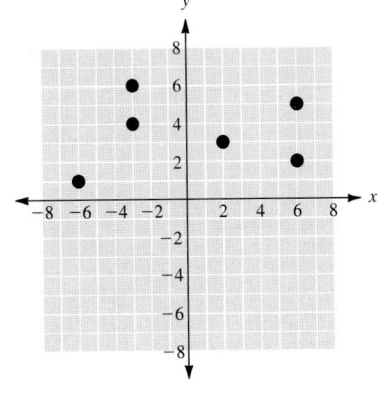

(c)

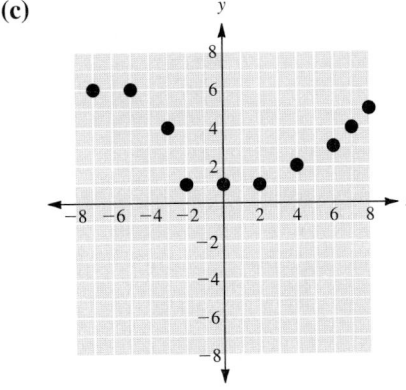

Example 8

Identifying a Function

Which of the following graphs represents the graph of a function?

(a)

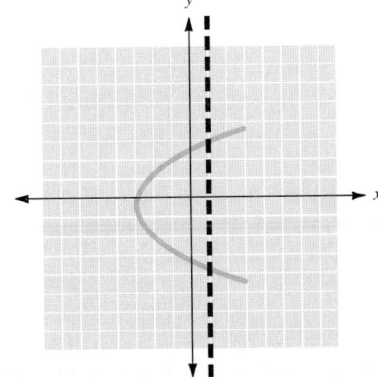

(b)

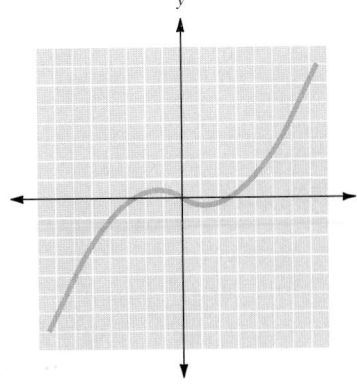

NOTE Curves, like the number line, are made up of a continuous set of points.

(c)

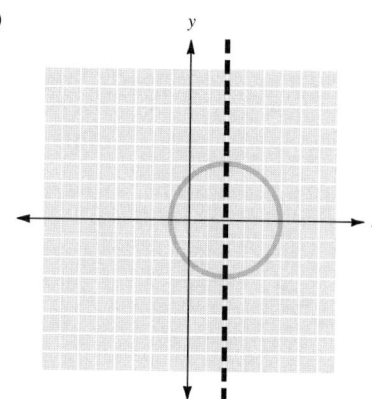

Part (a) is not a function; it does not pass the vertical line test. Part (b) is a function because it passes the vertical line test. Part (c) is not a function.

 CHECK YOURSELF 8

Which of the following graphs represents the graph of a function?

(a)

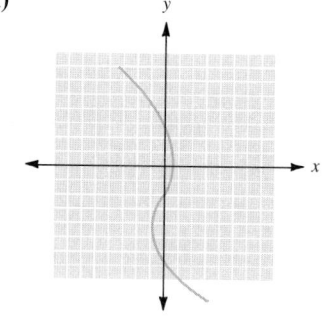

(b)

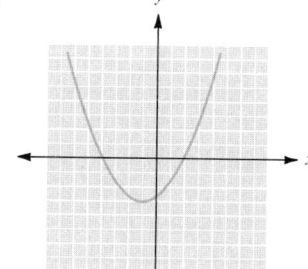

(c)

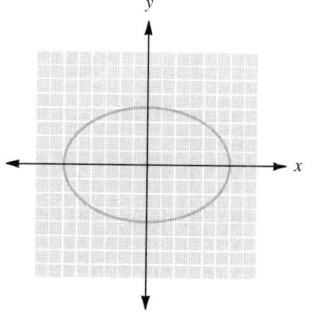

The graph of a relation can be used to determine the domain and range of the relation.

Example 9

Identifying Functions, Domain, and Range

For each of the following graphs, determine whether the relation is a function, find the domain of the relation, and find the range of the relation.

(a)

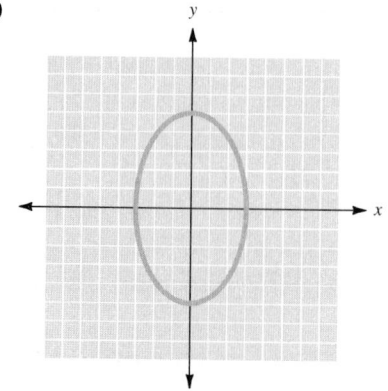

NOTE You might ask yourself "What values do we see used as x coordinates in the graph?" Answer: "All values between −3 and 3, inclusive."

This is not a function.

The domain is the set of x values from −3 to 3, inclusive. We write $D = \{x \mid -3 \leq x \leq 3\}$.

The range is the set of y values from −5 to 5, inclusive. We write $R = \{y \mid -5 \leq y \leq 5\}$.

(b)

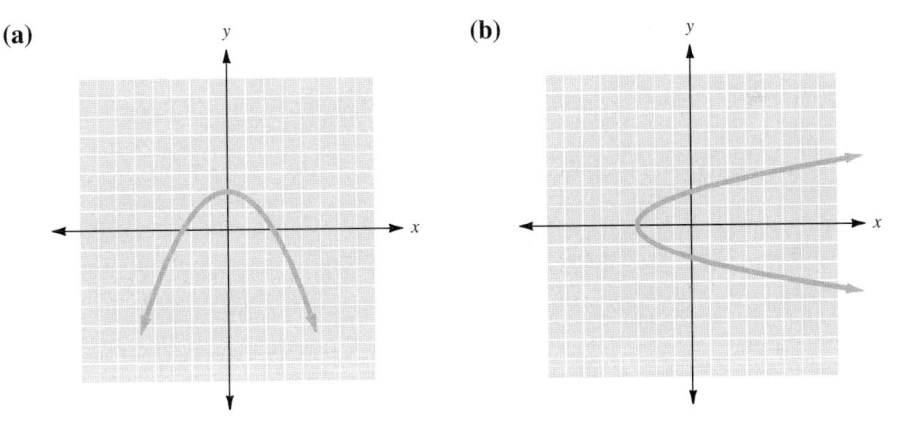

This is a function.

The graph continues forever in both the positive x direction and the negative x direction. Because there is a point on this graph related to every x value, the domain is the set of all real x values. We write

$$D = \{x \mid x \in R\}$$

The range is the set of y values greater than or equal to −5. We write $R = \{y \mid y \geq -5\}$.

 CHECK YOURSELF 9

For each of the following graphs, determine whether the relation is a function, find the domain of the relation, and find the range of the relation.

(a)

(b)

At this point, you may be wondering how the concept of function relates to anything outside the study of mathematics. A function is a relation that yields a single output (y value) each time a specific input (x value) is given. Any field in which predictions are made is building on the idea of functions. Here are a few examples:

• The physicist looks for the relationship that uses a planet's mass to predict its gravitational pull.

• The economist looks for the relationship that uses the tax rate to predict the employment rate.

• The business marketer looks for the relationship that uses an item's price to predict the number that will be sold.

- The college board looks for the relationship between tuition costs and the number of students enrolled at the college.
- The biologist looks for the relationship that uses temperature to predict a body of water's nutrient level.

CHECK YOURSELF ANSWERS

1. **(a)** 1; **(b)** 3; **(c)** -33 2. **(a)** -2; **(b)** 52; **(c)** -4
3. **(a)** $(0, -2)$; **(b)** $(3, 52)$; **(c)** $\left(-\dfrac{1}{2}, -4\right)$
4. **(a)** Is a function; **(b)** is not a function; **(c)** is a function; **(d)** is not a function
5. **(a)** Is a function; **(b)** is a function; **(c)** is not a function
6. **(a)** Is a function; **(b)** is not a function
7. **(a)** Is a function; **(b)** is not a function; **(c)** is a function
8. **(a)** Is not a function; **(b)** is a function; **(c)** is not a function
9. **(a)** This is a function; $D = \{x | x \in R\}$; $R = \{y | y \leq 2\}$
   (b) This is not a function; $D = \{x | x \geq -3\}$; $R = \{y | y \in R\}$

Exercises

Name _____

Section _____ Date _____

In exercises 1 to 10, evaluate each function for the value specified.

1. $f(x) = x^2 - x - 2$; find **(a)** $f(0)$, **(b)** $f(-2)$, and **(c)** $f(1)$.

1. _____

2. _____

2. $f(x) = x^2 - 7x + 10$; find **(a)** $f(0)$, **(b)** $f(5)$, and **(c)** $f(-2)$.

3. _____

4. _____

5. _____

3. $f(x) = 3x^2 + x - 1$; find **(a)** $f(-2)$, **(b)** $f(0)$, and **(c)** $f(1)$.

6. _____

7. _____

8. _____

4. $f(x) = -x^2 - x - 2$; find **(a)** $f(-1)$, **(b)** $f(0)$, and **(c)** $f(2)$.

9. _____

10. _____

5. $f(x) = x^3 - 2x^2 + 5x - 2$; find **(a)** $f(-3)$, **(b)** $f(0)$, and **(c)** $f(1)$.

6. $f(x) = -2x^3 + 5x^2 - x - 1$; find **(a)** $f(-1)$, **(b)** $f(0)$, and **(c)** $f(2)$.

7. $f(x) = -3x^3 + 2x^2 - 5x + 3$; find **(a)** $f(-2)$, **(b)** $f(0)$, and **(c)** $f(3)$.

8. $f(x) = -x^3 + 5x^2 - 7x - 8$; find **(a)** $f(-3)$, **(b)** $f(0)$, and **(c)** $f(2)$.

9. $f(x) = 2x^3 + 4x^2 + 5x + 2$; find **(a)** $f(-1)$, **(b)** $f(0)$, and **(c)** $f(1)$.

10. $f(x) = -x^3 + 2x^2 - 7x + 9$; find **(a)** $f(-2)$, **(b)** $f(0)$, and **(c)** $f(2)$.

11. _____

12. _____

13. _____

14. _____

15. _____

16. _____

17. _____

18. _____

19. _____

20. _____

21. _____

22. _____

23. _____

24. _____

25. _____

26. _____

In exercises 11 to 18, determine which of the relations are also functions.

11. $\{(1, 6), (2, 8), (3, 9)\}$

12. $\{(2, 3), (3, 4), (5, 9)\}$

13. $\{(-1, 4), (-2, 5), (-3, 7)\}$

14. $\{(-2, 1), (-3, 4), (-4, 6)\}$

15. $\{(1, 3), (1, 2), (1, 1)\}$

16. $\{(2, 4), (2, 5), (3, 6)\}$

17. $\{(-1, 1), (2, 1), (2, 3)\}$

18. $\{(2, -1), (3, 4), (3, -1)\}$

In exercises 19 to 24, decide whether the relation, shown as a table of values, is a function.

19.

x	y
3	1
-2	4
5	3
-7	4

20.

x	y
-2	3
1	4
5	6
2	-1

21.

x	y
2	3
4	2
2	-5
-6	-3

22.

x	y
1	5
3	-6
1	-5
-2	-9

23.

x	y
-1	2
3	6
6	2
-9	4

24.

x	y
4	-6
2	3
-7	1
-3	-6

In exercises 25 to 30, for each set of ordered pairs, plot the related points on the graph. Then use the vertical line test to determine which sets are functions.

25. $\{(-3, 1), (-1, 2), (-2, 3), (1, 4)\}$

26. $\{(2, 2), (1, 1), (3, 3), (4, 5)\}$

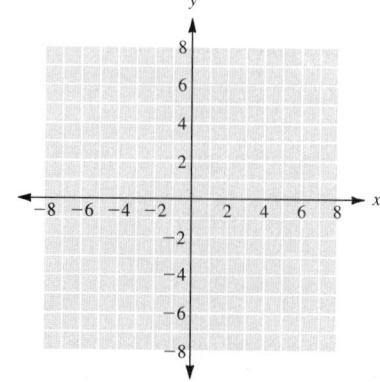

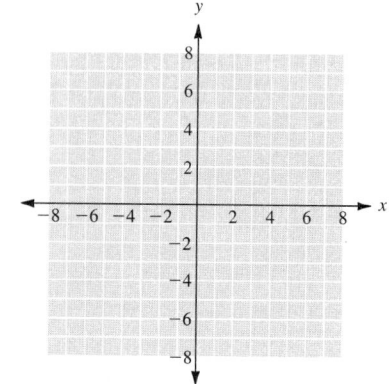

27. $\{(-1, 1), (2, 2), (3, 4), (5, 6)\}$

28. $\{(1, 4), (-1, 5), (0, 2), (2, 3)\}$

27. _____

28. _____

29. _____

30. _____

31. _____

32. _____

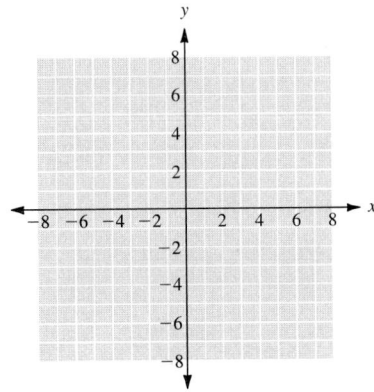

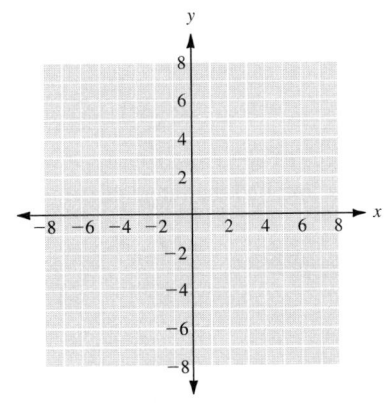

29. $\{(1, 2), (1, 3), (2, 1), (3, 1)\}$

30. $\{(-1, 1), (3, 4), (-1, 2), (5, 3)\}$

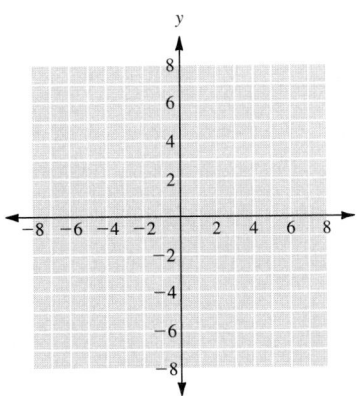

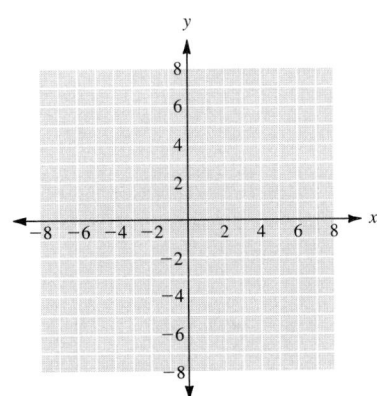

Your graphing calculator can be used to evaluate a function for a specific value of x. If $f(x) = 3x^2 - 7$, and you wish to find $f(-3)$,

1. Use the $\boxed{Y =}$ key to enter $Y_1 = 3x^2 - 7$.

2. Select $\boxed{\text{TABLE}}$ ($\boxed{2^{\text{nd}}}$ $\boxed{\text{GRAPH}}$), and choose -3 for x.

3. The table will give you a value of 20 for Y_1.

Use that technique to evaluate the functions in exercises 31 to 34.

31. $f(x) = 3x^2 - 5x + 7$; find **(a)** $f(-5)$, **(b)** $f(5)$, and **(c)** $f(12)$.

32. $f(x) = 4x^3 - 7x^2 + 9$; find **(a)** $f(-6)$, **(b)** $f(6)$, and **(c)** $f(10)$.

33. _____

34. _____

35. _____

36. _____

37. _____

38. _____

39. _____

40. _____

33. $f(x) = 3x^4 - 6x^3 + 2x^2 - 17$; find **(a)** $f(-3)$, **(b)** $f(4)$, and **(c)** $f(7)$.

34. $f(x) = 5x^7 + 8x^4 - 9x^2 - 13$; find **(a)** $f(-4)$, **(b)** $f(-3)$, and **(c)** $f(2)$.

For exercises 35 to 44, determine whether the relation is a function, find the domain of the relation, and find the range of the relation.

35.

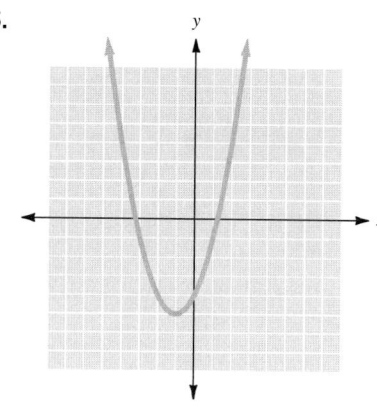

36.

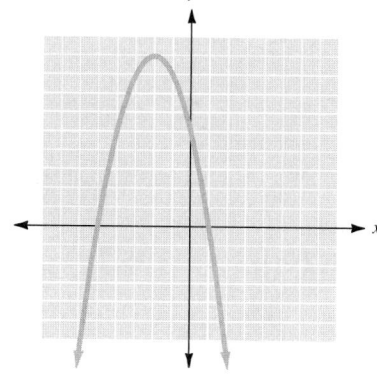

37.

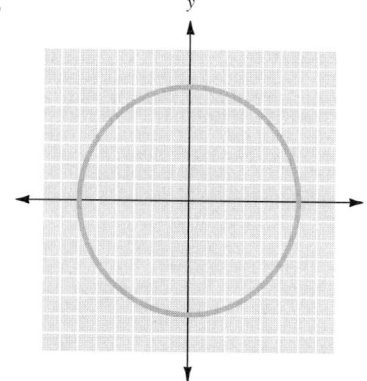

38.

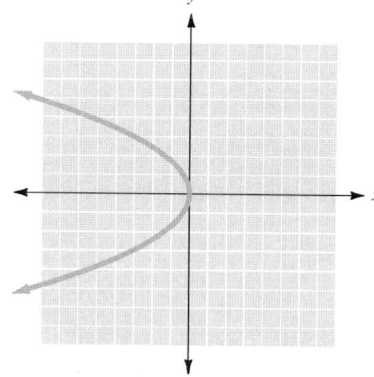

39.

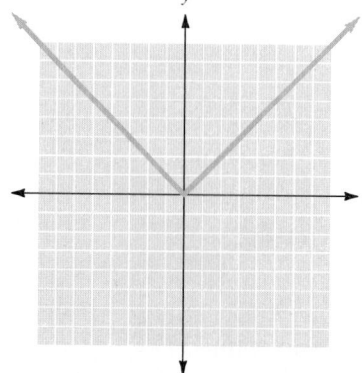

40.

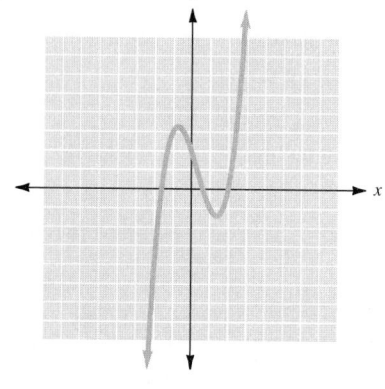

41.

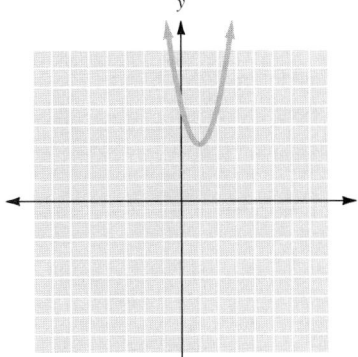

42.

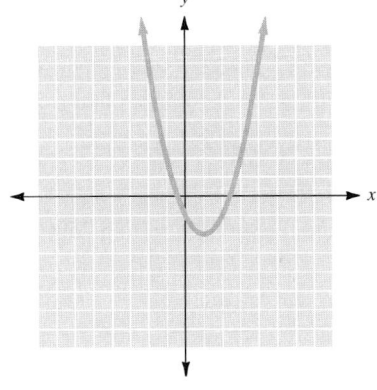

43.

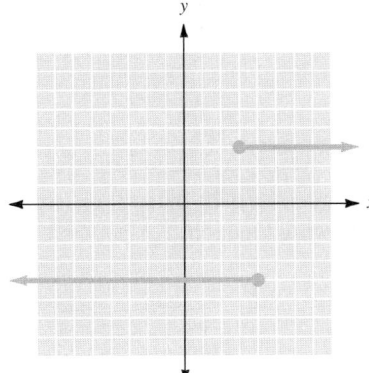

44.

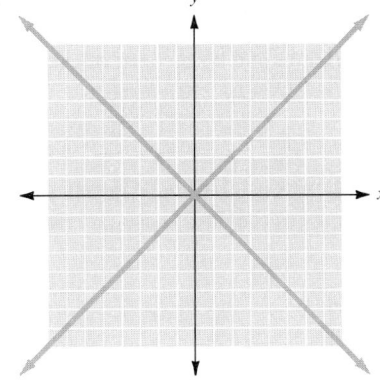

45. The following table shows the average hourly earnings for blue collar workers from 1947 to 1993. These figures are given in "real" wages, which means that the *purchasing power* of the money is given rather than the actual dollar amount. In other words, the amount earned for 1947 is not the actual amount listed here; in fact, it was much lower. The amount you see here is the amount in dollars that 1947 earnings could buy in 1947 compared to what 1993 wages could buy in 1993.

Year	Average Hourly Earnings (in 1993 dollars)
1947	$ 6.75
1967	10.67
1973	12.06
1979	12.03
1982	11.61
1989	11.26
1991	10.95
1993	10.83

Make a Cartesian coordinate graph of this data, using the year as the domain and the hourly earnings as the range. You will have to decide how to set up the axes so that the data all fit on the graph nicely. (*Hint:* Do not start the year at 0!) In complete sentences, answer the following questions: What are the trends that you notice from reading the table? What additional information does the graph show? Is this relation a function? Why or why not?

Solve the following application problems.

46. Profit. The marketing department of a company has determined that the profit for selling x units of a product is approximated by the function

$$f(x) = 50\sqrt{x} - 0.25x - 600$$

Find the profit in selling 2500 units.

47. Cost. The inventor of a new product believes that the cost of producing the product is given by the function

$$C(x) = 1.75x + 7000$$

What would be the cost of producing 2000 units of the product?

48. Phone cost. A phone company has two different rates for calls made at different times of the day. These rates are given by the following function

$$C(x) = \begin{cases} 24x + 33 & \text{between 5 P.M. and 11 P.M.} \\ 36x + 52 & \text{between 8 A.M. and 5 P.M.} \end{cases}$$

when x is the number of minutes of a call and C is the cost of a call in cents.

(a) What is the cost of a 10-minute call at 10:00 A.M.?

(b) What is the cost of a 10-minute call at 10:00 P.M.?

49. Accidents. The number of accidents in 1 month involving drivers x years of age can be approximated by the function

$$f(x) = 2x^2 - 125x + 3000$$

Find the number of accidents in 1 month that involved **(a)** 17-year-olds and **(b)** 25-year-olds.

50. **Stopping distance.** The distance x, (in feet) that a car will skid on a certain road surface after the brakes are applied is a function of the car's velocity v (in miles per hour). The function can be approximated by

$$x = f(v) = 0.017v^2$$

How far will the car skid if the brakes are applied at **(a)** 55 mph? **(b)** 70 mph?

51. **Science.** An object is thrown upward with an initial velocity of 128 ft/s. Its height h after t seconds is given by the function

$$h(t) = -16t^2 + 128t$$

What is the height of the object at **(a)** 2 s? **(b)** 4 s? **(c)** 6 s?

Answers

1. (a) -2; (b) 4; (c) -2 **3.** (a) 9; (b) -1; (c) 3   **5.** (a) -62; (b) -2; (c) 2
7. (a) 45; (b) 3; (c) -75 **9.** (a) -1; (b) 2; (c) 13   **11.** Function
13. Function   **15.** Not a function   **17.** Not a function
19. Function   **21.** Not a function   **23.** Function
25. Function   **27.** Function

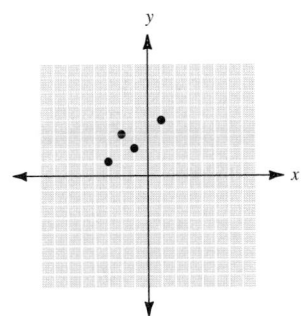

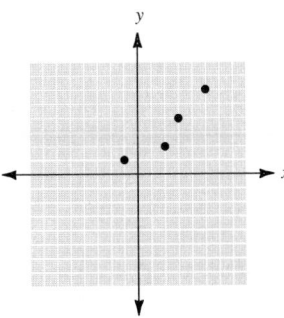

29. Not a function

31. $107, 57, 379$

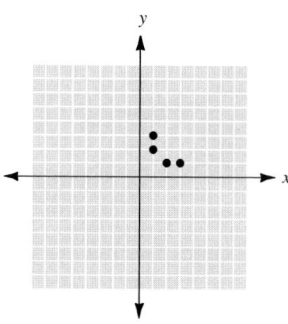

33. $406, 399, 5226$

35. Function; $D = \{x \mid x \in R\}$
$R = \{y \mid y \geq -5\}$

37. Not a function; $D = \{x \mid -6 \leq x \leq 6\}$
$R = \{y \mid -6 \leq y \leq 6\}$

39. Function; $D = \{x \mid x \in R\}$
$R = \{y \mid y \geq 0\}$

41. Function; $D = \{x \mid x \in R\}$
$R = \{y \mid y \geq 3\}$

43. Not a function; $D = \{x \mid x \in R\}$
$R = \{y \mid y = -4 \text{ or } 3\}$

45.

47. $10,500

49. **(a)** 1453; **(b)** 1125

51. **(a)** 192 ft; **(b)** 256 ft; **(c)** 192 ft

FACTORING

3

INTRODUCTION

Developing secret codes is big business because of the widespread use of computers and the Internet. Corporations all over the world sell encryption systems that are supposed to keep data secure and safe.

In 1977, three professors from the Massachusetts Institute of Technology developed an encryption system they call RSA, a name derived from the first letters of their last names. They offered a $100 reward to anyone who could break their security code, which was based on a number that has *129 digits*. They called the code RSA-129. For the code to be broken, the 129-digit number must be factored into two prime numbers; that is, two prime numbers must be found that when multiplied together give the 129-digit number. The three professors predicted that it would take *40 quadrillion* years to find the two numbers.

In April 1994, a research scientist, three computer hobbyists, and more than 600 volunteers from the Internet, using 1600 computers, found the two numbers after 8 months of work and won the $100.

A data security company says that people who are using their system are safe because as yet no truly efficient algorithm for finding prime factors of massive numbers has been found, although one may someday exist. This company, hoping to test its encrypting system, now sponsors contests challenging people to factor more very large numbers into two prime numbers. RSA-150 up to RSA-500 are being worked on now.

Software companies are waging a legal battle against the U.S. government because the government does not allow any codes to be used for which it does not have the key. The software firms claim that this prohibition is costing them about $60 billion in lost sales because many companies will not buy an encryption system knowing they can be monitored by the U.S. government.

(3) # Pre-Test Chapter 3

Factor each of the following polynomials.

1. $15c + 35$

2. $8q^4 - 20q^3$

3. $6x^2 - 12x + 24$

4. $7c^3d^2 - 21cd + 14cd^3$

Factor each of the following polynomials completely.

5. $b^2 + 2b - 15$

6. $x^2 + 10x + 24$

7. $x^2 - 14x + 45$

8. $a^2 + 7ab + 12b^2$

Factor each of the following polynomials completely.

9. $3y^2 + 5y - 12$

10. $5w^2 + 23w + 12$

11. $6x^2 + 5xy - 21y^2$

12. $2x^3 - 7x^2 - 15x$

Factor each of the following polynomials completely.

13. $b^2 - 49$

14. $36p^2 - q^2$

15. $9x^2 - 12xy + 4y^2$

16. $27xy^2 - 48x^3$

Solve each of the following equations for x.

17. $x^2 - 11x + 28 = 0$

18. $x^2 - 5x = 14$

19. $5x^2 + 7x - 6 = 0$

20. $9p^2 - 18p = 0$

Adding and Subtracting Polynomials

 OBJECTIVES

1. Add two polynomials
2. Subtract two polynomials

Addition is always a matter of combining like quantities (two apples plus three apples, four books plus five books, and so on). If you keep that basic idea in mind, adding polynomials will be easy. It is just a matter of combining like terms. Suppose that you want to add

$$5x^2 + 3x + 4 \qquad \text{and} \qquad 4x^2 + 5x - 6$$

Parentheses are sometimes used in adding, so for the sum of these polynomials, we can write

NOTE The plus sign between the parentheses indicates the addition.

$$(5x^2 + 3x + 4) + (4x^2 + 5x - 6)$$

Now what about the parentheses? You can use the following rule.

Rules and Properties: Removing Signs of Grouping Case 1

If a plus sign ($+$) or nothing at all appears in front of parentheses, just remove the parentheses. No other changes are necessary.

Now let's return to the addition.

NOTE Just remove the parentheses. No other changes are necessary.

$$(5x^2 + 3x + 4) + (4x^2 + 5x - 6)$$
$$= 5x^2 + 3x + 4 + 4x^2 + 5x - 6$$

Like terms   Like terms   Like terms
Like terms

NOTE Note the use of the associative and commutative properties in reordering and regrouping.

Collect like terms. (*Remember:* Like terms have the same variables raised to the same power).

$$= (5x^2 + 4x^2) + (3x + 5x) + (4 - 6)$$

Combine like terms for the result:

NOTE Here we use the distributive property. For example,
$$5x^2 + 4x^2 = (5 + 4)x^2$$
$$= 9x^2$$

$$= 9x^2 + 8x - 2$$

As should be clear, much of this work can be done mentally. You can then write the sum directly by locating like terms and combining. Example 1 illustrates this property.

Example 1

Combining Like Terms

NOTE We call this the "horizontal method" because the entire problem is written on one line.
$3 + 4 = 7$ is the horizontal method.

$$\begin{array}{r} 3 \\ + 4 \\ \hline 7 \end{array}$$

is the vertical method.

Add $3x - 5$ and $2x + 3$.

Write the sum.

$$(3x - 5) + (2x + 3)$$

$$= 3x - 5 + 2x + 3 = 5x - 2$$

Like terms   Like terms

419

Add $6x^2 + 2x$ and $4x^2 - 7x$.

The same technique is used to find the sum of two trinomials.

Example 2

Adding Polynomials Using the Horizontal Method

Add $4a^2 - 7a + 5$ and $3a^2 + 3a - 4$.

Write the sum.

$(4a^2 - 7a + 5) + (3a^2 + 3a - 4)$

REMEMBER Only the like terms are combined in the sum.

$= 4a^2 - 7a + 5 + 3a^2 + 3a - 4 = 7a^2 - 4a + 1$

Like terms

Like terms

Like terms

Add $5y^2 - 3y + 7$ and $3y^2 - 5y - 7$.

Example 3

Adding Polynomials Using the Horizontal Method

Add $2x^2 + 7x$ and $4x - 6$.

Write the sum.

$(2x^2 + 7x) + (4x - 6)$

$= 2x^2 + 7x + 4x - 6$

These are the only like terms; $2x^2$ and -6 cannot be combined.

$= 2x^2 + 11x - 6$

CHECK YOURSELF 3

Add $5m^2 + 8$ and $8m^2 - 3m$.

As we mentioned in Section 1.16 writing polynomials in descending-exponent form usually makes the work easier. Look at Example 4.

Example 4

Adding Polynomials Using the Horizontal Method

Add $3x - 2x^2 + 7$ and $5 + 4x^2 - 3x$.

Write the polynomials in descending-exponent form, then add.

$(-2x^2 + 3x + 7) + (4x^2 - 3x + 5)$

$= 2x^2 + 12$

CHECK YOURSELF 4

Add $8 - 5x^2 + 4x$ and $7x - 8 + 8x^2$.

Subtracting polynomials requires another rule for removing signs of grouping.

> **Rules and Properties:** Removing Signs of Grouping Case 2
>
> If a minus sign ($-$) appears in front of a set of parentheses, the parentheses can be removed by changing the sign of each term inside the parentheses.

The use of this rule is illustrated in Example 5.

Example 5

Removing Parentheses

In each of the following, remove the parentheses.

(a) $-(2x + 3y) = -2x - 3y$ Change each sign to remove the parentheses.

NOTE This uses the distributive property, because

$-(2x + 3y) = (-1)(2x + 3y)$

$\qquad\qquad = -2x - 3y$

(b) $m - (5n - 3p) = \underline{m - 5n + 3p}$

Sign changes.

(c) $2x - (-3y + z) = \underline{2x + 3y - z}$

Sign changes.

CHECK YOURSELF 5

(a) $-(3m + 5n)$ **(b)** $-(5w - 7z)$ **(c)** $3r - (2s - 5t)$ **(d)** $5a - (-3b - 2c)$

Subtracting polynomials is now a matter of using the previous rule to remove the parentheses and then combining the like terms. Consider Example 6.

Example 6

Subtracting Polynomials Using the Horizontal Method

(a) Subtract $5x - 3$ from $8x + 2$.

Write

NOTE The expression following "from" is written first in the problem.

$(8x + 2) - (5x - 3)$

$= 8x + 2 - 5x + 3$ Recall that subtracting $5x$ is the same as adding $-5x$.

Sign changes.

$= 3x + 5$

(b) Subtract $4x^2 - 8x + 3$ from $8x^2 + 5x - 3$.

Write

$(8x^2 + 5x - 3) - (4x^2 - 8x + 3)$

$= 8x^2 + 5x \underbrace{- 3 - 4x^2 + 8x - 3}$

Sign changes.

$= 4x^2 + 13x - 6$

 CHECK YOURSELF 6

(a) Subtract $7x + 3$ from $10x - 7$.

(b) Subtract $5x^2 - 3x + 2$ from $8x^2 - 3x - 6$.

Again, writing all polynomials in descending-exponent form will make locating and combining like terms much easier. Look at Example 7.

Example 7

Subtracting Polynomials Using the Horizontal Method

(a) Subtract $4x^2 - 3x^3 + 5x$ from $8x^3 - 7x + 2x^2$.

Write

$(8x^3 + 2x^2 - 7x) - (-3x^3 + 4x^2 + 5x)$

$= 8x^3 + 2x^2 \underbrace{- 7x + 3x^3 - 4x^2 - 5x}$

Sign changes.

$= 11x^3 - 2x^2 - 12x$

(b) Subtract $8x - 5$ from $-5x + 3x^2$.

Write

$(3x^2 - 5x) - (8x - 5)$

$= 3x^2 \underbrace{- 5x - 8x} + 5$

Only the like terms can be combined.

$= 3x^2 - 13x + 5$

 CHECK YOURSELF 7

(a) Subtract $7x - 3x^2 + 5$ from $5 - 3x + 4x^2$.

(b) Subtract $3a - 2$ from $5a + 4a^2$.

If you think back to addition and subtraction in arithmetic, you'll remember that the work was arranged vertically. That is, the numbers being added or subtracted were placed under one another so that each column represented the same place value. This meant that in adding or subtracting columns you were always dealing with "like quantities."

It is also possible to use a vertical method for adding or subtracting polynomials. First rewrite the polynomials in descending-exponent form, then arrange them one under another, so that each column contains like terms. Then add or subtract in each column.

Example 8

Adding Using the Vertical Method

Add $2x^2 - 5x$, $3x^2 + 2$, and $6x - 3$.

Like terms

$$
\begin{array}{r}
2x^2 - 5x \\
3x^2 + 2 \\
6x - 3 \\
\hline
5x^2 + x - 1
\end{array}
$$

 CHECK YOURSELF 8

Add $3x^2 + 5$, $x^2 - 4x$, and $6x + 7$.

The following example illustrates subtraction by the vertical method.

Example 9

Subtracting Using the Vertical Method

(a) Subtract $5x - 3$ from $8x - 7$.

Write

$$
\begin{array}{r}
8x - 7 \\
(-)\ 5x - 3 \\
\hline
3x - 4
\end{array}
$$

To subtract, change each sign of $5x - 3$ to get $-5x + 3$, then add.

$$
\begin{array}{r}
8x - 7 \\
= -5x + 3 \\
\hline
3x - 4
\end{array}
$$

(b) Subtract $5x^2 - 3x + 4$ from $8x^2 + 5x - 3$.

Write

$$
\begin{array}{r}
8x^2 + 5x - 3 \\
(-)\ 5x^2 - 3x + 4 \\
\hline
3x^2 + 8x - 7
\end{array}
$$

To subtract, change each sign of $5x^2 - 3x + 4$ to get $-5x^2 + 3x - 4$, then add.

$$
\begin{array}{r}
8x^2 + 5x - 3 \\
= -5x^2 + 3x - 4 \\
\hline
3x^2 + 8x - 7
\end{array}
$$

Subtracting using the vertical method takes some practice. Take time to study the method carefully. You'll be using it in long division in Section. 4.5.

✔ CHECK YOURSELF 9

Subtract, using the vertical method.

(a) $4x^2 - 3x$ from $8x^2 + 2x$ **(b)** $8x^2 + 4x - 3$ from $9x^2 - 5x + 7$

CHECK YOURSELF ANSWERS

1. $10x^2 - 5x$ **2.** $8y^2 - 8y$ **3.** $13m^2 - 3m + 8$ **3.** $3x^2 + 11x$
5. (a) $-3m - 5n$; **(b)** $-5w + 7z$; **(c)** $3r - 2s + 5t$; **(d)** $5a + 3b + 2c$
6. (a) $3x - 10$; **(b)** $3x^2 - 8$ **7. (a)** $7x^2 - 10x$; **(b)** $4a^2 + 2a + 2$
8. $4x^2 + 2x + 12$ **9. (a)** $4x^2 + 5x$; **(b)** $x^2 - 9x + 10$

Add.

1. $6a - 5$ and $3a + 9$

2. $9x + 3$ and $3x - 4$

3. $8b^2 - 11b$ and $5b^2 - 7b$

4. $2m^2 + 3m$ and $6m^2 - 8m$

5. $3x^2 - 2x$ and $-5x^2 + 2x$

6. $3p^2 + 5p$ and $-7p^2 - 5p$

7. $2x^2 + 5x - 3$ and $3x^2 - 7x + 4$

8. $4d^2 - 8d + 7$ and $5d^2 - 6d - 9$

9. $2b^2 + 8$ and $5b + 8$

10. $4x - 3$ and $3x^2 - 9x$

11. $8y^3 - 5y^2$ and $5y^2 - 2y$

12. $9x^4 - 2x^2$ and $2x^2 + 3$

13. $2a^2 - 4a^3$ and $3a^3 + 2a^2$

14. $9m^3 - 2m$ and $-6m - 4m^3$

15. $4x^2 - 2 + 7x$ and $5 - 8x - 6x^2$

16. $5b^3 - 8b + 2b^2$ and $3b^2 - 7b^3 + 5b$

Remove the parentheses in each of the following expressions, and simplify when possible.

17. $-(2a + 3b)$

18. $-(7x - 4y)$

19. $5a - (2b - 3c)$

20. $7x - (4y + 3z)$

21. $9r - (3r + 5s)$

22. $10m - (3m - 2n)$

23. $5p - (-3p + 2q)$

24. $8d - (-7c - 2d)$

ANSWERS

1. _____
2. _____
3. _____
4. _____
5. _____
6. _____
7. _____
8. _____
9. _____
10. _____
11. _____
12. _____
13. _____
14. _____
15. _____
16. _____
17. _____
18. _____
19. _____
20. _____
21. _____
22. _____
23. _____
24. _____

Subtract.

25. $x + 4$ from $2x - 3$

26. $x - 2$ from $3x + 5$

27. $3m^2 - 2m$ from $4m^2 - 5m$

28. $9a^2 - 5a$ from $11a^2 - 10a$

29. $6y^2 + 5y$ from $4y^2 + 5y$

30. $9n^2 - 4n$ from $7n^2 - 4n$

31. $x^2 - 4x - 3$ from $3x^2 - 5x - 2$

32. $3x^2 - 2x + 4$ from $5x^2 - 8x - 3$

33. $3a + 7$ from $8a^2 - 9a$

34. $3x^3 + x^2$ from $4x^3 - 5x$

35. $4b^2 - 3b$ from $5b - 2b^2$

36. $7y - 3y^2$ from $3y^2 - 2y$

37. $x^2 - 5 - 8x$ from
$3x^2 - 8x + 7$

38. $4x - 2x^2 + 4x^3$ from
$4x^3 + x - 3x^2$

Perform the indicated operations.

39. Subtract $3b + 2$ from the sum of $4b - 2$ and $5b + 3$.

40. Subtract $5m - 7$ from the sum of $2m - 8$ and $9m - 2$.

41. Subtract $3x^2 + 2x - 1$ from the sum of $x^2 + 5x - 2$ and $2x^2 + 7x - 8$.

42. Subtract $4x^2 - 5x - 3$ from the sum of $x^2 - 3x - 7$ and $2x^2 - 2x + 9$.

43. Subtract $2x^2 - 3x$ from the sum of $4x^2 - 5$ and $2x - 7$.

44. Subtract $5a^2 - 3a$ from the sum of $3a - 3$ and $5a^2 + 5$.

45. Subtract the sum of $3y^2 - 3y$ and $5y^2 + 3y$ from $2y^2 - 8y$.

46. Subtract the sum of $7r^3 - 4r^2$ and $-3r^3 + 4r^2$ from $2r^3 + 3r^2$.

Add, using the vertical method.

47. $2w^2 + 7$, $3w - 5$, and $4w^2 - 5w$

48. $3x^2 - 4x - 2$, $6x - 3$, and $2x^2 + 8$

49. $3x^2 + 3x - 4$, $4x^2 - 3x - 3$, and $2x^2 - x + 7$

50. $5x^2 + 2x - 4$, $x^2 - 2x - 3$, and $2x^2 - 4x - 3$

Subtract, using the vertical method.

51. $3a^2 - 2a$ from $5a^2 + 3a$

52. $6r^3 + 4r^2$ from $4r^3 - 2r^2$

53. $5x^2 - 6x + 7$ from $8x^2 - 5x + 7$

54. $8x^2 - 4x + 2$ from $9x^2 - 8x + 6$

55. $5x^2 - 3x$ from $8x^2 - 9$

56. $7x^2 + 6x$ from $9x^2 - 3$

Perform the indicated operations.

57. $[(9x^2 - 3x + 5) - (3x^2 + 2x - 1)] - (x^2 - 2x - 3)$

58. $[(5x^2 + 2x - 3) - (-2x^2 + x - 2)] - (2x^2 + 3x - 5)$

Find values for a, b, c, and d so that the following equations are true.

59. $3ax^4 - 5x^3 + x^2 - cx + 2 = 9x^4 - bx^3 + x^2 - 2d$

60. $(4ax^3 - 3bx^2 - 10) - 3(x^3 + 4x^2 - cx - d) = x^2 - 6x + 8$

61. Geometry. A rectangle has sides of $8x + 9$ and $6x - 7$. Find the polynomial that represents its perimeter.

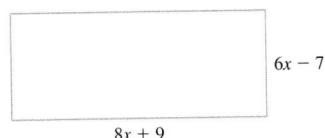

6x − 7

8x + 9

62. Geometry. A triangle has sides $3x + 7$, $4x - 9$, and $5x + 6$. Find the polynomial that represents its perimeter.

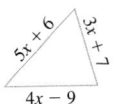

5x + 6

3x + 7

4x − 9

63. Business. The cost of producing x units of an item is $C = 150 + 25x$. The revenue for selling x units is $R = 90x - x^2$. The profit is given by the revenue minus the cost. Find the polynomial that represents profit.

64. Business. The revenue for selling y units is $R = 3y^2 - 2y + 5$ and the cost of producing y units is $C = y^2 + y - 3$. Find the polynomial that represents profit.

51. _____

52. _____

53. _____

54. _____

55. _____

56. _____

57. _____

58. _____

59. _____

60. _____

61. _____

62. _____

63. _____

64. _____

Getting Ready

Multiply.

(a) $x^5 \cdot x^7$

(b) $y^8 \cdot y^{12}$

(c) $2a^3 \cdot d^4$

(d) $3m^5 \cdot m^2$

(e) $4r^5 \cdot 3r$

(f) $6w^2 \cdot 5w^3$

(g) $(-2x^2)(8x^7)$

(h) $(-10a)(-3a^5)$

Answers for Pre-Test for Chapter 3

1. $5(3c + 7)$ **2.** $4q^3(2q - 5)$ **3.** $6(x^2 - 2x + 4)$
4. $7cd(c^2d - 3 + 2d^2)$ **5.** $(b - 3)(b + 5)$ **6.** $(x + 4)(x + 6)$
7. $(x - 9)(x - 5)$ **8.** $(a + 3b)(a + 4b)$ **9.** $(3y - 4)(y + 3)$
10. $(5w + 3)(w + 4)$ **11.** $(3x + 7y)(2x - 3y)$ **12.** $x(2x + 3)(x - 5)$
13. $(b + 7)(b - 7)$ **14.** $(6p + q)(6p - q)$ **15.** $(3x - 2y)^2$

16. $3x(3y - 4x)(3y + 4x)$ **17.** $4, 7$ **18.** $-2, 7$ **19.** $\frac{3}{5}, -2$ **20.** $0, 2$

Answers

1. $9a + 4$ **3.** $13b^2 - 18b$ **5.** $-2x^2$ **7.** $5x^2 - 2x + 1$
9. $2b^2 + 5b + 16$ **11.** $8y^3 - 2y$ **13.** $-a^3 + 4a^2$ **15.** $-2x^2 - x + 3$
17. $-2a - 3b$ **19.** $5a - 2b + 3c$ **21.** $6r - 5s$ **23.** $8p - 2q$
25. $x - 7$ **27.** $m^2 - 3m$ **29.** $-2y^2$ **31.** $2x^2 - x + 1$
33. $8a^2 - 12a - 7$ **35.** $-6b^2 + 8b$ **37.** $2x^2 + 12$ **39.** $6b - 1$
41. $10x - 9$ **43.** $2x^2 + 5x - 12$ **45.** $-6y^2 - 8y$ **47.** $6w^2 - 2w + 2$
49. $9x^2 - x$ **51.** $2a^2 + 5a$ **53.** $3x^2 + x$ **55.** $3x^2 + 3x - 9$
57. $5x^2 - 3x + 9$ **59.** $a = 3, b = 5, c = 0, d = -1$ **61.** $28x + 4$
63. $-x^2 + 65x - 150$ **a.** x^{12} **b.** y^{20} **c.** $2a^7$ **d.** $3m^7$ **e.** $12r^6$
f. $30w^5$ **g.** $-16x^9$ **h.** $30a^6$

An Introduction to Functions

 **OBJECTIVES**

1. Evaluate expressions
2. Evaluate functions
3. Express the equation of a line as a linear function
4. Write an equation as a function
5. Graph a linear function

Variables can be used to represent unknown real numbers. Together with the operations of addition, subtraction, multiplication, division, and exponentiation, these numbers and variables form expressions such as

$$3x + 5 \qquad 7x - 4 \qquad x^2 - 3x - 10 \qquad x^4 - 2x^2 + 3x + 4$$

Four different actions can be taken with expressions. We can

1. Substitute values for the variable(s) and **evaluate the expression.**
2. Rewrite an expression as some simpler equivalent expression. This rewriting is called **simplifying the expression.**
3. Set two expressions equal to each other and **solve for the stated variable.**
4. Set two expressions equal to each other and **graph the equation.**

Throughout this book, everything we do will involve one of these four actions. We now return our focus to the first item, evaluating expressions. As we saw in Section 1.7, expressions can be evaluated for an indicated value of the variable(s). Example 1 illustrates.

Example 1

Evaluating Expressions

Evaluate the expression $x^4 - 2x^2 + 3x + 4$ for the indicated value of x.

(a) $x = 0$

Substituting 0 for x in the expression yields

$$(0)^4 - 2(0)^2 + 3(0) + 4 = 0 - 0 + 0 + 4$$
$$= 4$$

(b) $x = 2$

Substituting 2 for x in the expression yields

$$(2)^4 - 2(2)^2 + 3(2) + 4 = 16 - 8 + 6 + 4$$
$$= 18$$

(c) $x = -1$

Substituting -1 for x in the expression yields

$$(-1)^4 - 2(-1)^2 + 3(-1) + 4 = 1 - 2 - 3 + 4$$
$$= 0$$

✔ **CHECK YOURSELF 1**

Evaluate the expression $2x^3 - 3x^2 + 3x + 1$ for the indicated value of x.

(a) $x = 0$ **(b)** $x = 1$ **(c)** $x = -2$

We could design a machine whose function would be to crank out the value of an expression for each given value of x. We could call this machine something simple such as f. Our *function* machine might look like this.

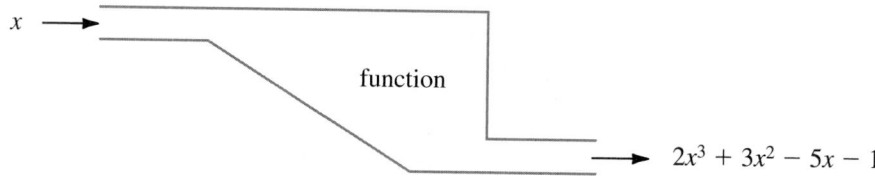

For example, when we put -1 into the machine, the machine would substitute -1 for x in the expression, and 5 would come out the other end because

$$2(-1)^3 + 3(-1)^2 - 5(-1) - 1 = -2 + 3 + 5 - 1 = 5$$

In fact, the idea of the function machine is very useful in mathematics. Your graphing calculator can be used as a function machine. You can enter the expression into the calculator as Y_1 and then evaluate Y_1 for different values of x.

Generally, in mathematics, we do not write $Y_1 = 2x^3 + 3x^2 - 5x - 1$. Instead, we write $f(x) = 2x^3 + 3x^2 - 5x - 1$, which is read as "$f$ of x is equal to . . . ." Instead of calling f a function machine, we say that f is a function of x. The greatest benefit of this notation is that it lets us easily note the input value of x along with the output of the function. Instead of "Evaluate Y_1 for $x = 4$" we say "Find $f(4)$."

Example 2

Evaluating Expressions with Function Notation

Given $f(x) = x^3 - 3x^2 + x + 5$, find the following:

(a) $f(0)$

Substituting 0 for x in the expression, we get

$$(0)^3 - 3(0)^2 + (0) + 5 = 5$$

(b) $f(-3)$

Substituting -3 for x in the expression, we get

$$(-3)^3 - 3(-3)^2 + (-3) + 5 = -27 - 27 - 3 + 5$$
$$= -52$$

(c) $f\left(\dfrac{1}{2}\right)$

Substituting $\frac{1}{2}$ for x in the expression, we get

$$\left(\frac{1}{2}\right)^3 - 3\left(\frac{1}{2}\right)^2 + \left(\frac{1}{2}\right) + 5 = \frac{1}{8} - 3\left(\frac{1}{4}\right) + \frac{1}{2} + 5$$

$$= \frac{1}{8} - \frac{3}{4} + \frac{1}{2} + 5$$

$$= \frac{1}{8} - \frac{6}{8} + \frac{4}{8} + 5$$

$$= -\frac{1}{8} + 5$$

$$= 4\frac{7}{8} \text{ or } \frac{39}{8}$$

CHECK YOURSELF 2

Given $f(x) = 2x^3 - x^2 + 3x - 2$, find the following.

(a) $f(0)$ **(b)** $f(3)$ **(c)** $f\left(-\frac{1}{2}\right)$

Given a function f, the pair of numbers $(x, f(x))$ is very significant. We always write them in that order, hence the name *ordered pairs*. In Example 2, part a, we saw that given $f(x) = x^3 - 3x^2 + x + 5$, $f(0) = 5$, which meant that the ordered pair $(0, 5)$ was associated with the function. The ordered pair consists of the x value first and the function value at that x (the $f(x)$) second.

Example 3

Finding Ordered Pairs

Given the function $f(x) = 2x^2 - 3x + 5$, find the ordered pair $(x, f(x))$ associated with each given value for x.

(a) $x = 0$

$f(0) = 5$

so the ordered pair is $(0, 5)$.

(b) $x = -1$

$f(-1) = 2(-1)^2 - 3(-1) + 5 = 10$

The ordered pair is $(-1, 10)$.

(c) $x = \frac{1}{4}$

$$f\left(\frac{1}{4}\right) = 2\left(\frac{1}{16}\right) - 3\left(\frac{1}{4}\right) + 5 = \frac{35}{8}$$

The ordered pair is $\left(\frac{1}{4}, \frac{35}{8}\right)$.

CHECK YOURSELF 3

Given $f(x) = 2x^3 - x^2 + 3x - 2$, *find the ordered pair associated with each given value of x.*

(a) $x = 0$ **(b)** $x = 3$ **(c)** $x = -\dfrac{1}{2}$

We have discussed the graph of a linear equation. We saw that the graph for a vertical line had the form $x = a$. The equation for such a line cannot be rewritten as a function, but the equation for any nonvertical line can be written as a function.

Example 4

Writing Equations as Functions

Rewrite each linear equation as a function of x.

(a) $y = 3x - 4$

This can be rewritten as

$f(x) = 3x - 4$

(b) $2x - 3y = 6$

We must first solve the equation for y (recall that this will give us the slope-intercept form).

$$-3y = -2x + 6$$

$$y = \frac{2}{3}x - 2$$

This can be rewritten as

$$f(x) = \frac{2}{3}x - 2$$

CHECK YOURSELF 4

Rewrite each equation as a function of x.

(a) $y = -2x + 5$ **(b)** $3x + 5y = 15$

The process of finding the graph of a linear function is identical to the process of finding the graph of a linear equation.

Example 5

Graphing a Linear Function

Graph the function

$f(x) = 3x - 5$

We could use the slope and y intercept to graph the line, or we can find three points (the third is a checkpoint) and draw the line through them. We will do the latter.

$$f(0) = -5 \qquad f(1) = -2 \qquad f(2) = 1$$

We will use the three points $(0, -5)$, $(1, -2)$, and $(2, 1)$ to graph the line.

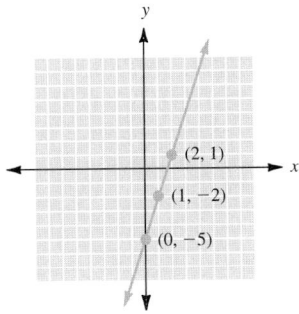

 CHECK YOURSELF 5

Graph the function

$$f(x) = 5x - 3$$

One benefit of having a function written in $f(x)$ form is that it makes it fairly easy to substitute values for x. In Example 5, we substituted the values 0, 1, and 2. Sometimes it is useful to substitute nonnumeric values for x.

Example 6

Substituting Nonnumeric Values for *x*

Let $f(x) = 2x + 3$. Evaluate f as indicated.

(a) $f(a)$

Substituting a for x in our equation, we see that

$$f(a) = 2a + 3$$

(b) $f(2 + h)$

Substituting $2 + h$ for x in our equation, we get

$$f(2 + h) = 2(2 + h) + 3$$

Distributing the 2, then simplifying, we have

$$f(2 + h) = 4 + 2h + 3$$
$$= 2h + 7$$

CHECK YOURSELF 6

Let f(x) = 4x − 2. Evaluate f as indicated.

(a) $f(b)$ **(b)** $f(4 + h)$

CHECK YOURSELF ANSWERS

1. (a) 1; **(b)** 3; **(c)** -33 **2. (a)** -2; **(b)** 52; **(c)** -4

3. (a) $(0, -2)$; **(b)** $(3, 52)$; **(c)** $\left(-\dfrac{1}{2}, -4\right)$ **4. (a)** $f(x) = -2x + 5$;

(b) $f(x) = -\dfrac{3}{5}x + 3$ **5.**

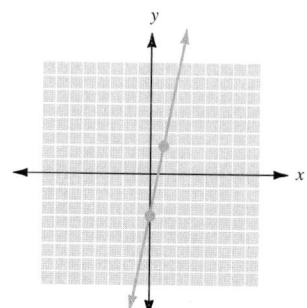

6. (a) $4b - 2$; **(b)** $4h + 14$

3.2 Exercises

In exercises 1 to 10, evaluate each function for the value specified.

1. $f(x) = x^2 - x - 2$; find (a) $f(0)$, (b) $f(-2)$, and (c) $f(1)$.

2. $f(x) = x^2 - 7x + 10$; find (a) $f(0)$, (b) $f(5)$, and (c) $f(-2)$.

3. $f(x) = 3x^2 + x - 1$; find (a) $f(-2)$, (b) $f(0)$, and (c) $f(1)$.

4. $f(x) = -x^2 - x - 2$; find (a) $f(-1)$, (b) $f(0)$, and (c) $f(2)$.

5. $f(x) = x^3 - 2x^2 + 5x - 2$; find (a) $f(-3)$, (b) $f(0)$, and (c) $f(1)$.

6. $f(x) = -2x^3 + 5x^2 - x - 1$; find (a) $f(-1)$, (b) $f(0)$, and (c) $f(2)$.

7. $f(x) = -3x^3 + 2x^2 - 5x + 3$; find (a) $f(-2)$, (b) $f(0)$, and (c) $f(3)$.

8. $f(x) = -x^3 + 5x^2 - 7x - 8$; find (a) $f(-3)$, (b) $f(0)$, and (c) $f(2)$.

9. $f(x) = 2x^3 + 4x^2 + 5x + 2$; find (a) $f(-1)$, (b) $f(0)$, and (c) $f(1)$.

10. $f(x) = -x^3 + 2x^2 - 7x + 9$; find (a) $f(-2)$, (b) $f(0)$, and (c) $f(2)$.

In exercises 11 to 20, rewrite each equation as a function of x.

11. $y = -3x + 2$ **12.** $y = 5x + 7$ **13.** $y = 4x - 8$

14. $y = -7x - 9$ **15.** $3x + 2y = 6$ **16.** $4x + 3y = 12$

17. $-2x + 6y = 9$ **18.** $-3x + 4y = 11$ **19.** $-5x - 8y = -9$

20. $4x - 7y = -10$

In exercises 21 to 26, graph the functions.

21. $f(x) = 3x + 7$

22. $f(x) = -2x - 5$

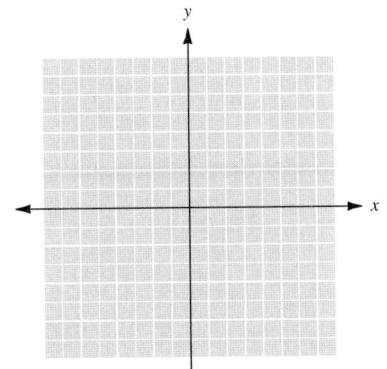

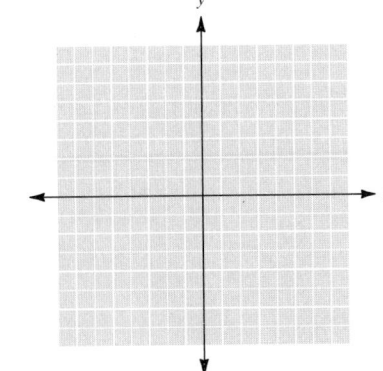

1. _____

2. _____

3. _____

4. _____

5. _____

6. _____

7. _____

8. _____

9. _____

10. _____

11. _____

12. _____

13. _____

14. _____

15. _____

16. _____

17. _____

18. _____

19. _____

20. _____

21. _____

22. _____

23. $f(x) = -2x + 7$

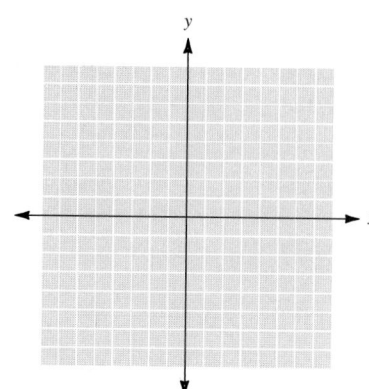

24. $f(x) = -3x + 8$

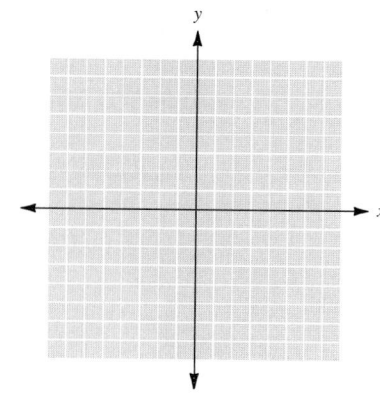

25. $f(x) = -x - 1$

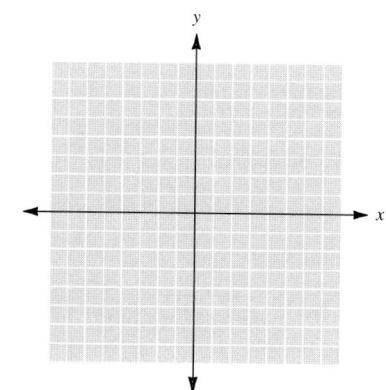

26. $f(x) = -2x - 5$

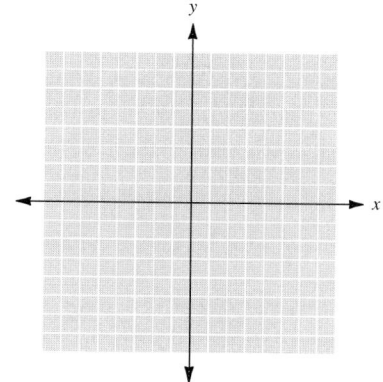

In exercises 27 to 32, if $f(x) = 4x - 3$, find the following:

27. $f(5)$

28. $f(0)$

29. $f(4)$

30. $f(-1)$

31. $f(-4)$

32. $f\left(\dfrac{1}{2}\right)$

In exercises 33 to 38, if $f(x) = 5x - 1$, find the following:

33. $f(a)$

34. $f(2r)$

35. $f(x + 1)$

36. $f(a - 2)$

37. $f(x + h)$

38. $\dfrac{f(x + h) - f(x)}{h}$

In exercises 39 to 42, if $g(x) = -3x + 2$, find the following:

39. $g(m)$ **40.** $g(5n)$ **41.** $g(x + 2)$ **42.** $g(s - 1)$

In exercises 43 to 46, let $f(x) = 2x + 3$.

43. Find $f(1)$.

44. Find $f(3)$.

45. Form the ordered pairs $(1, f(1))$ and $(3, f(3))$.

46. Write the equation of the line passing through the points determined by the ordered pairs in exercise 45.

47. Let $f(x) = 5x - 2$. Find (a) $f(4) - f(3)$; (b) $f(9) - f(8)$; (c) $f(12) - f(11)$. (d) How do the results of (a) through (c) compare to the slope of the line that is the graph of f?

48. Repeat exercise 47 with $f(x) = 7x + 1$.

49. Repeat exercise 47 with $f(x) = mx + b$.

ANSWERS

39. _____

40. _____

41. _____

42. _____

43. _____

44. _____

45. _____

46. _____

47. _____

48. _____

49. _____

Answers

1. (a) -2, (b) 4, (c) -2 **3.** (a) 9, (b) -1, (c) 3

5. (a) -62, (b) -2, (c) 2 **7.** (a) 45, (b) 3, (c) -75

9. (a) -1, (b) 2, (c) 13 **11.** $f(x) = -3x + 2$ **13.** $f(x) = 4x - 8$

15. $f(x) = -\dfrac{3}{2}x + 3$ **17.** $f(x) = \dfrac{1}{3}x + \dfrac{3}{2}$ **19.** $f(x) = -\dfrac{5}{8}x + \dfrac{9}{8}$

21. $f(x) = 3x + 7$ **23.** $f(x) = -2x + 7$

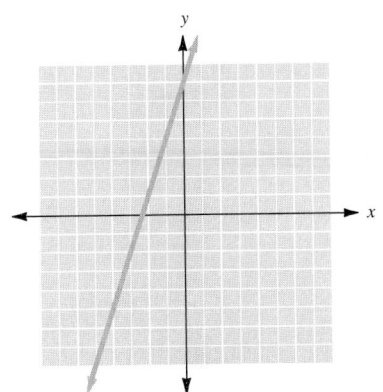 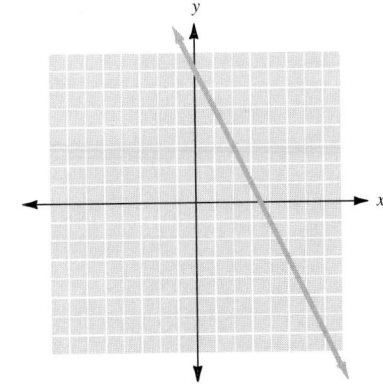

25. $f(x) = -x - 1$

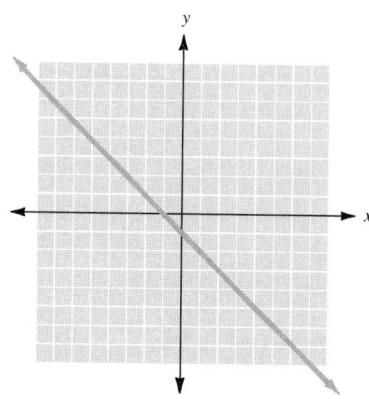

27. 17 **29.** 13 **31.** −19

33. $5a - 1$ **35.** $5x + 4$ **37.** $5x + 5h - 1$ **39.** $-3m + 2$

41. $-3x - 4$ **43.** 5 **45.** $(1, 5), (3, 9)$ **47.** (a) 5, (b) 5, (c) 5, (d) same

49. (a) m, (b) m, (c) m, (d) same

3.3 Multiplying Polynomials

3.3 OBJECTIVES

1. Find the product of a monomial and a polynomial
2. Find the product of two polynomials

You have already had some experience in multiplying polynomials. We stated the first property of exponents and used that property to find the product of two monomial terms. Let's review briefly.

> **Step by Step:** To Find the Product of Monomials
>
> **Step 1** Multiply the coefficients.
> **Step 2** Use the first property of exponents to combine the variables.

NOTE The first property of exponents:

$x^m \cdot x^n = x^{m+n}$

Example 1

Multiplying Monomials

Multiply $3x^2y$ and $2x^3y^5$.

NOTE Once again we have used the commutative and associative properties to rewrite the problem.

Write

$(3x^2y)(2x^3y^5)$

$= (3 \cdot 2)(x^2 \cdot x^3)(y \cdot y^5)$

Multiply   Add the exponents.
the coefficients.

$= 6x^5y^6$

 CHECK YOURSELF 1

Multiply.

(a) $(5a^2b)(3a^2b^4)$ **(b)** $(-3xy)(4x^3y^5)$

Our next task is to find the product of a monomial and a polynomial. Here we use the distributive property, which we introduced in Section 1.3. That property leads us to the following rule for multiplication.

> **Rules and Properties:** To Multiply a Polynomial by a Monomial
>
> Use the distributive property to multiply each term of the polynomial by the monomial.

NOTE Distributive property:

$a(b + c) = ab + ac$

Example 2

Multiplying a Monomial and a Binomial

(a) Multiply $2x + 3$ by x.

© 2001 McGraw-Hill Companies

439

© 2001 McGraw-Hill Companies

NOTE With practice you will do this step mentally.

Write

$x(2x + 3)$

$= x \cdot 2x + x \cdot 3$

$= 2x^2 + 3x$

Multiply x by $2x$ and then by 3, the terms of the polynomial. That is, "distribute" the multiplication over the sum.

(b) Multiply $2a^3 + 4a$ by $3a^2$.

Write

$3a^2(2a^3 + 4a)$

$= 3a^2 \cdot 2a^3 + 3a^2 \cdot 4a = 6a^5 + 12a^3$

 CHECK YOURSELF 2

Multiply.

(a) $2y(y^2 + 3y)$

(b) $3w^2(2w^3 + 5w)$

The patterns of Example 2 extend to *any* number of terms.

Example 3

Multiplying a Monomial and a Polynomial

Multiply the following.

(a) $3x(4x^3 + 5x^2 + 2)$

$= 3x \cdot 4x^3 + 3x \cdot 5x^2 + 3x \cdot 2 = 12x^4 + 15x^3 + 6x$

NOTE Again we have shown all the steps of the process. With practice you can write the product directly, and you should try to do so.

(b) $5y^2(2y^3 - 4)$

$= 5y^2 \cdot 2y^3 - 5y^2 \cdot 4 = 10y^5 - 20y^2$

(c) $-5c(4c^2 - 8c)$

$= (-5c)(4c^2) - (-5c)(8c) = -20c^3 + 40c^2$

(d) $3c^2d^2(7cd^2 - 5c^2d^3)$

$= 3c^2d^2 \cdot 7cd^2 - 3c^2d^2 \cdot 5c^2d^3 = 21c^3d^4 - 15c^4d^5$

 CHECK YOURSELF 3

Multiply.

(a) $3(5a^2 + 2a + 7)$

(b) $4x^2(8x^3 - 6)$

(c) $-5m(8m^2 - 5m)$

(d) $9a^2b(3a^3b - 6a^2b^4)$

Example 4

Multiplying Binomials

(a) Multiply $x + 2$ by $x + 3$.

NOTE Note that this ensures that each term, x and 2, of the first binomial is multiplied by each term, x and 3, of the second binomial.

We can think of $x + 2$ as a single quantity and apply the distributive property.

$\overline{(x + 2)}(x + 3)$ Multiply $x + 2$ by x and then by 3.

$= (x + 2)x + (x + 2)\, 3$

$= x \cdot x + 2 \cdot x + x \cdot 3 + 2 \cdot 3$

$= x^2 + 2x + 3x + 6$

$= x^2 + 5x + 6$

(b) Multiply $a - 3$ by $a - 4$. (Think of $a - 3$ as a single quantity and distribute.)

$(a - 3)(a - 4)$

$= (a - 3)a - (a - 3)(4)$

$= a \cdot a - 3 \cdot a - [(a \cdot 4) - (3 \cdot 4)]$

$= a^2 - 3a - (4a - 12)$ Note that the parentheses are needed here because a *minus sign* precedes the binomial.

$= a^2 - 3a - 4a + 12$

$= a^2 - 7a + 12$

 CHECK YOURSELF 4

Multiply.

(a) $(x + 4)(x + 5)$ **(b)** $(y + 5)(y - 6)$

Fortunately, there is a pattern to this kind of multiplication that allows you to write the product of the two binomials directly without going through all these steps. We call it the **FOIL method** of multiplying. The reason for this name will be clear as we look at the process in more detail.

To multiply $(x + 2)(x + 3)$:

NOTE Remember this by F!

1. $(x + 2)(x + 3)$ Find the product of the *first* terms of the factors.

$x \cdot x$

NOTE Remember this by O!

2. $(x + 2)(x + 3)$ Find the product of the *outer* terms.

$x \cdot 3$

NOTE Remember this by I!

3. $(x + 2)(x + 3)$ Find the product of the *inner* terms.

$2 \cdot x$

NOTE Remember this by L!

4. $(x + 2)(x + 3)$ Find the product of the *last* terms.

$2 \cdot 3$

Combining the four steps, we have

NOTE Of course these are the same four terms found in Example 4a.

$(x + 2)(x + 3)$

$= x^2 + 3x + 2x + 6$

$= x^2 + 5x + 6$

NOTE It's called FOIL to give you an easy way of remembering the steps: *First, Outer, Inner,* and *Last.*

With practice, the FOIL method will let you write the products quickly and easily. Consider Example 5, which illustrates this approach.

Example 5

Using the FOIL Method

Find the following products, using the FOIL method.

$$\begin{array}{cc} F & L \\ x \cdot x & 4 \cdot 5 \end{array}$$

(a) $(x + 4)(x + 5)$

$$\begin{array}{c} 4x \\ I \\ 5x \\ O \end{array}$$

NOTE When possible, you should combine the outer and inner products mentally and write just the final product.

$$= x^2 + 5x + 4x + 20$$
$$\quad\; F \quad O \quad\; I \quad\; L$$
$$= x^2 + 9x + 20$$

$$\begin{array}{cc} F & L \\ x \cdot x & (-7)(3) \end{array}$$

(b) $(x - 7)(x + 3)$

$$\begin{array}{c} -7x \\ I \\ 3x \\ O \end{array}$$

Combine the outer and inner products as $-4x$.

$$= x^2 - 4x - 21$$

✓ CHECK YOURSELF 5

Multiply.

(a) $(x + 6)(x + 7)$　　　**(b)** $(x + 3)(x - 5)$　　　**(c)** $(x - 2)(x - 8)$

Using the FOIL method, you can also find the product of binomials with coefficients other than 1 or with more than one variable.

Example 6

Using the FOIL Method

Find the following products, using the FOIL method.

$$\begin{array}{cc} F & L \\ 12x^2 & -6 \end{array}$$

(a) $(4x - 3)(3x + 2)$

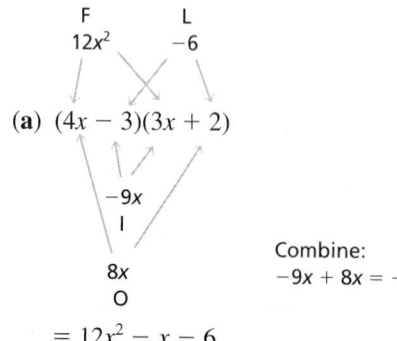

$$\begin{array}{c} -9x \\ I \\ 8x \\ O \end{array}$$

Combine:
$-9x + 8x = -x$

$$= 12x^2 - x - 6$$

$$6x^2 \qquad 35y^2$$

(b) $(3x - 5y)(2x - 7y)$

$$-10xy$$

$$-21xy$$

Combine:
$$-10xy - 21xy = -31xy$$

$$= 6x^2 - 31xy + 35y^2$$

The following rule summarizes our work in multiplying binomials.

Step by Step: To Multiply Two Binomials

Step 1 Find the first term of the product of the binomials by multiplying the first terms of the binomials (F).

Step 2 Find the middle term of the product as the sum of the outer and inner products (O + I).

Step 3 Find the last term of the product by multiplying the last terms of the binomials (L).

 CHECK YOURSELF 6

Multiply.

(a) $(5x + 2)(3x - 7)$ **(b)** $(4a - 3b)(5a - 4b)$ **(c)** $(3m + 5n)(2m + 3n)$

Sometimes, especially with larger polynomials, it is easier to use the vertical method to find their product. This is the same method you originally learned when multiplying two large integers.

Example 7

Multiplying Using the Vertical Method

Use the vertical method to find the product of $(3x + 2)(4x - 1)$.
First, we rewrite the multiplication in vertical form.

$$3x + 2$$
$$4x + (-1)$$

Multiplying the quantity $3x + 2$ by -1 yields

$$3x + 2$$
$$4x + (-1)$$
$$\overline{-3x + (-2)}$$

Note that we maintained the columns of the original binomial when we found the product. We will continue with those columns as we multiply by the $4x$ term.

$$3x + 2$$
$$4x + (-1)$$
$$\overline{-3x + (-2)}$$
$$12x^2 + 8x$$
$$\overline{12x^2 + 5x + (-2)}$$

We could write the product as $(3x + 2)(4x - 1) = 12x^2 + 5x - 2$.

CHECK YOURSELF 7

Use the vertical method to find the product of $(5x - 3)(2x + 1)$.

We'll use the vertical method again in our next example. This time, we will multiply a binomial and a trinomial. Note that the FOIL method can never work for anything but the product of two binomials.

Example 8

Using the Vertical Method

Multiply $x^2 - 5x + 8$ by $x + 3$.

Step 1
$$
\begin{array}{r}
x^2 - 5x + 8 \\
x + 3 \\
\hline
3x^2 - 15x + 24
\end{array}
$$
Multiply each term of $x^2 - 5x + 8$ by 3.

Step 2
$$
\begin{array}{r}
x^2 - 5x + 8 \\
x + 3 \\
\hline
3x^2 - 15x + 24 \\
x^3 - 5x^2 + 8x
\end{array}
$$
Now multiply each term by x.

Note that this line is shifted over so that like terms are in the same columns.

NOTE Using this vertical method ensures that each term of one factor multiplies each term of the other. That's why it works!

Step 3
$$
\begin{array}{r}
x^2 - 5x + 8 \\
x + 3 \\
\hline
3x^2 - 15x + 24 \\
x^3 - 5x^2 + 8x \\
\hline
x^3 - 2x^2 - 7x + 24
\end{array}
$$
Now add to combine like terms to write the product.

CHECK YOURSELF 8

Multiply $2x^2 - 5x + 3$ *by* $3x + 4$.

CHECK YOURSELF ANSWERS

1. **(a)** $15a^4b^5$; **(b)** $-12x^4y^6$ 2. **(a)** $2y^3 + 6y^2$; **(b)** $6w^5 + 15w^3$
3. **(a)** $15a^2 + 6a + 21$; **(b)** $32x^5 - 24x^2$; **(c)** $-40m^3 + 25m^2$; **(d)** $27a^5b^2 - 54a^4b^5$
4. **(a)** $x^2 + 9x + 20$; **(b)** $y^2 - y - 30$
5. **(a)** $x^2 + 13x + 42$; **(b)** $x^2 - 2x - 15$; **(c)** $x^2 - 10x + 16$
6. **(a)** $15x^2 - 29x - 14$; **(b)** $20a^2 - 31ab + 12b^2$; **(c)** $6m^2 + 19mn + 15n^2$
7. $10x^2 - x - 3$ 8. $6x^3 - 7x^2 - 11x + 12$

3.3 Exercises

Multiply.

1. $(5x^2)(3x^3)$

2. $(7a^5)(4a^6)$

3. $(-2b^2)(14b^8)$

4. $(14y^4)(-4y^6)$

5. $(-10p^6)(-4p^7)$

6. $(-6m^8)(9m^7)$

7. $(4m^5)(-3m)$

8. $(-5r^7)(-3r)$

9. $(4x^3y^2)(8x^2y)$

10. $(-3r^4s^2)(-7r^2s^5)$

11. $(-3m^5n^2)(2m^4n)$

12. $(7a^3b^5)(-6a^4b)$

13. $5(2x + 6)$

14. $4(7b - 5)$

15. $3a(4a + 5)$

16. $5x(2x - 7)$

17. $3s^2(4s^2 - 7s)$

18. $9a^2(3a^3 + 5a)$

19. $2x(4x^2 - 2x + 1)$

20. $5m(4m^3 - 3m^2 + 2)$

21. $3xy(2x^2y + xy^2 + 5xy)$

22. $5ab^2(ab - 3a + 5b)$

23. $6m^2n(3m^2n - 2mn + mn^2)$

24. $8pq^2(2pq - 3p + 5q)$

ANSWERS

1. _____
2. _____
3. _____
4. _____
5. _____
6. _____
7. _____
8. _____
9. _____
10. _____
11. _____
12. _____
13. _____
14. _____
15. _____
16. _____
17. _____
18. _____
19. _____
20. _____
21. _____
22. _____
23. _____
24. _____

25. _____

26. _____

27. _____

28. _____

29. _____

30. _____

31. _____

32. _____

33. _____

34. _____

35. _____

36. _____

37. _____

38. _____

39. _____

40. _____

41. _____

42. _____

43. _____

44. _____

45. _____

46. _____

47. _____

48. _____

49. _____

50. _____

51. _____

52. _____

Multiply.

25. $(x + 3)(x + 2)$ **26.** $(a - 3)(a - 7)$

27. $(m - 5)(m - 9)$ **28.** $(b + 7)(b + 5)$

29. $(p - 8)(p + 7)$ **30.** $(x - 10)(x + 9)$

31. $(w + 10)(w + 20)$ **32.** $(s - 12)(s - 8)$

33. $(3x - 5)(x - 8)$ **34.** $(w + 5)(4w - 7)$

35. $(2x - 3)(3x + 4)$ **36.** $(5a + 1)(3a + 7)$

37. $(3a - b)(4a - 9b)$ **38.** $(7s - 3t)(3s + 8t)$

39. $(3p - 4q)(7p + 5q)$ **40.** $(5x - 4y)(2x - y)$

41. $(2x + 5y)(3x + 4y)$ **42.** $(4x - 5y)(4x + 3y)$

43. $(x + 5)^2$ **44.** $(y + 8)^2$

45. $(y - 9)^2$ **46.** $(2a + 3)^2$

47. $(6m + n)^2$ **48.** $(7b - c)^2$

49. $(a - 5)(a + 5)$ **50.** $(x - 7)(x + 7)$

51. $(x - 2y)(x + 2y)$ **52.** $(7x + y)(7x - y)$

53. $(5s + 3t)(5s - 3t)$

54. $(9c - 4d)(9c + 4d)$

Multiply, using the vertical method.

55. $(x + 2)(3x + 5)$

56. $(a - 3)(2a + 7)$

57. $(2m - 5)(3m + 7)$

58. $(5p + 3)(4p + 1)$

59. $(3x + 4y)(5x - 2y)$

60. $(7a - 2b)(2a + 4b)$

61. $(a^2 + 3ab - b^2)(a^2 - 5ab + b^2)$

62. $(m^2 - 5mn + 3n^2)(m^2 + 4mn - 2n^2)$

63. $(x - 2y)(x^2 + 2xy + 4y^2)$

64. $(m + 3n)(m^2 - 3mn + 9n^2)$

65. $(3a + 4b)(9a^2 - 12ab + 16b^2)$

66. $(2r - 3s)(4r^2 + 6rs + 9s^2)$

Multiply.

67. $2x(3x - 2)(4x + 1)$

68. $3x(2x + 1)(2x - 1)$

69. $5a(4a - 3)(4a + 3)$

70. $6m(3m - 2)(3m - 7)$

71. $3s(5s - 2)(4s - 1)$

72. $7w(2w - 3)(2w + 3)$

73. $(x - 2)(x + 1)(x - 3)$

74. $(y + 3)(y - 2)(y - 4)$

75. $(a - 1)^3$

76. $(x + 1)^3$

53. _____

54. _____

55. _____

56. _____

57. _____

58. _____

59. _____

60. _____

61. _____

62. _____

63. _____

64. _____

65. _____

66. _____

67. _____

68. _____

69. _____

70. _____

71. _____

72. _____

73. _____

74. _____

75. _____

76. _____

77. _____

78. _____

79. _____

80. _____

81. _____

82. _____

83. _____

84. _____

85. _____

86. _____

87. _____

88. _____

Multiply the following.

77. $\left(\dfrac{x}{2} + \dfrac{2}{3}\right)\left(\dfrac{2x}{3} - \dfrac{2}{5}\right)$

78. $\left(\dfrac{x}{3} + \dfrac{3}{4}\right)\left(\dfrac{3x}{4} - \dfrac{3}{5}\right)$

79. $[x + (y - 2)][x - (y - 2)]$

80. $[x + (3 - y)][x - (3 - y)]$

Label the following as true or false.

81. $(x + y)^2 = x^2 + y^2$

82. $(x - y)^2 = x^2 - y^2$

83. $(x + y)^2 = x^2 + 2xy + y^2$

84. $(x - y)^2 = x^2 - 2xy + y^2$

85. Length. The length of a rectangle is given by $3x + 5$ centimeters (cm) and the width is given by $2x - 7$ cm. Express the area of the rectangle in terms of x.

86. Area. The base of a triangle measures $3y + 7$ inches (in.) and the height is $2y - 3$ in. Express the area of the triangle in terms of y.

87. Revenue. The price of an item is given by $p = 2x - 10$. If the revenue generated is found by multiplying the number of items (x) sold by the price of an item, find the polynomial which represents the revenue.

88. Revenue. The price of an item is given by $p = 2x^2 - 100$. Find the polynomial that represents the revenue generated from the sale of x items.

89. Work with another student to complete this table and write the polynomial. A paper box is to be made from a piece of cardboard 20 inches (in.) wide and 30 in. long. The box will be formed by cutting squares out of each of the four corners and folding up the sides to make a box.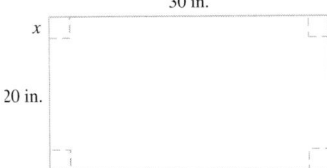

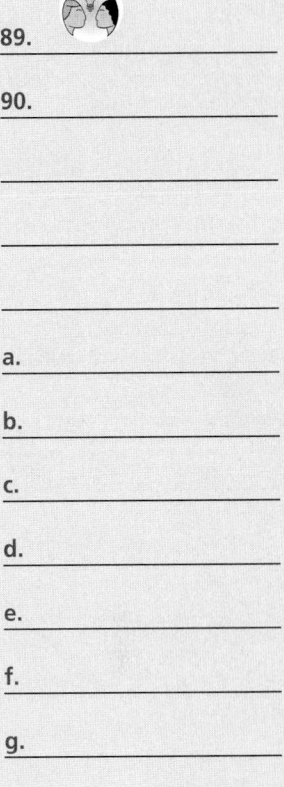

30 in.

x

20 in.

If x is the dimension of the side of the square cut out of the corner, when the sides are folded up, the box will be x inches tall. You should use a piece of paper to try this to see how the box will be made. Complete the following chart.

Length of Side of Corner Square	Length of Box	Width of Box	Depth of Box	Volume of Box
1 in.				
2 in.				
3 in.				
n in.				

Write a general formula for the width, length, and height of the box and a general formula for the *volume* of the box, and simplify it by multiplying. The variable will be the height, the side of the square cut out of the corners. What is the highest power of the variable in the polynomial you have written for the volume _____?

90. (a) Multiply $(x - 1)(x + 1)$
   (b) Multiply $(x - 1)(x^2 + x + 1)$
   (c) Multiply $(x - 1)(x^3 + x^2 + x + 1)$
   (d) Based on your results to (a), (b), and (c), find the product $(x - 1)(x^{29} + x^{28} + \cdots + x + 1)$.

 Getting Ready

Simplify.

(a) $(3a)(3a)$ (b) $(3a)^2$
(c) $(5x)(5x)$ (d) $(5x)^2$
(e) $(-2w)(-2w)$ (f) $(-2w)^2$
(g) $(-4r)(-4r)$ (h) $(-4r)^2$

Answers

1. $15x^5$ **3.** $-28b^{10}$ **5.** $40p^{13}$ **7.** $-12m^6$ **9.** $32x^5y^3$ **11.** $-6m^9n^3$

13. $10x + 30$ **15.** $12a^2 + 15a$ **17.** $12s^4 - 21s^3$ **19.** $8x^3 - 4x^2 + 2x$

21. $6x^3y^2 + 3x^2y^3 + 15x^2y^2$ **23.** $18m^4n^2 - 12m^3n^2 + 6m^3n^3$ **25.** $x^2 + 5x + 6$

27. $m^2 - 14m + 45$ **29.** $p^2 - p - 56$ **31.** $w^2 + 30w + 200$

33. $3x^2 - 29x + 40$ **35.** $6x^2 - x - 12$ **37.** $12a^2 - 31ab + 9b^2$

39. $21p^2 - 13pq - 20q^2$ **41.** $6x^2 + 23xy + 20y^2$ **43.** $x^2 + 10x + 25$

45. $y^2 - 18y + 81$ **47.** $36m^2 + 12mn + n^2$ **49.** $a^2 - 25$ **51.** $x^2 - 4y^2$

53. $25s^2 - 9t^2$ **55.** $3x^2 + 11x + 10$ **57.** $6m^2 - m - 35$

59. $15x^2 + 14xy - 8y^2$ **61.** $a^4 - 2a^3b - 15a^2b^2 + 8ab^3 - b^4$

63. $x^3 - 8y^3$ **65.** $27a^3 + 64b^3$ **67.** $24x^3 - 10x^2 - 4x$

69. $80a^3 - 45a$ **71.** $60s^3 - 39s^2 + 6s$ **73.** $x^3 - 4x^2 + x + 6$

75. $a^3 - 3a^2 + 3a - 1$ **77.** $\dfrac{x^2}{3} + \dfrac{11x}{45} - \dfrac{4}{15}$ **79.** $x^2 - y^2 + 4y - 4$

81. False **83.** True **85.** $6x^2 - 11x - 35\text{cm}^2$ **87.** $2x^2 - 10x$

89. **a.** $9a^2$ **b.** $9a^2$ **c.** $25x^2$ **d.** $25x^2$ **e.** $4w^2$ **f.** $4w^2$

g. $16r^2$ **h.** $16r^2$

Special Products

3.4 **OBJECTIVES**

1. Square a binomial
2. Find the product of two binomials that differ only in their sign

Certain products occur frequently enough in algebra that it is worth learning special formulas for dealing with them. First, let's look at the **square of a binomial,** which is the product of two equal binomial factors.

$$(x + y)^2 = (x + y)(x + y)$$
$$= x^2 + 2xy + y^2$$

$$(x - y)^2 = (x - y)(x - y)$$
$$= x^2 - 2xy + y^2$$

The patterns above lead us to the following rule.

Step by Step: To Square a Binomial

Step 1   Find the first term of the square by squaring the first term of the binomial.

Step 2   Find the middle term of the square as twice the product of the two terms of the binomial.

Step 3   Find the last term of the square by squaring the last term of the binomial.

Example 1

Squaring a Binomial

CAUTION

A very common mistake in squaring binomials is to forget the middle term.

(a) $(x + 3)^2 = x^2 + \underbrace{2 \cdot x \cdot 3} + 3^2$

   Square of first term   Twice the product of the two terms   Square of the last term

$$= x^2 + 6x + 9$$

(b) $(3a + 4b)^2 = (3a)^2 + 2(3a)(4b) + (4b)^2$
$$= 9a^2 + 24ab + 16b^2$$

(c) $(y - 5)^2 = y^2 + 2 \cdot y \cdot (-5) + (-5)^2$
$$= y^2 - 10y + 25$$

(d) $(5c - 3d)^2 = (5c)^2 + 2(5c)(-3d) + (-3d)^2$
$$= 25c^2 - 30cd + 9d^2$$

Again we have shown all the steps. With practice you can write just the square.

CHECK YOURSELF 1

Multiply.

(a) $(2x + 1)^2$

(b) $(4x - 3y)^2$

Example 2

Squaring a Binomial

Find $(y + 4)^2$.

NOTE You should see that $(2 + 3)^2 \neq 2^2 + 3^2$ because $5^2 \neq 4 + 9$

$(y + 4)^2$ is *not* equal to $y^2 + 4^2$ or $y^2 + 16$

The correct square is

$(y + 4)^2 = y^2 + 8y + 16$

The middle term is twice the product of *y* and 4.

 CHECK YOURSELF 2

Multiply.

(a) $(x + 5)^2$ **(b)** $(3a + 2)^2$ **(c)** $(y - 7)^2$ **(d)** $(5x - 2y)^2$

A second special product will be very important in the next chapter, which deals with factoring. Suppose the form of a product is

$(x + y)(x - y)$

The two terms differ
only in sign.

Let's see what happens when we multiply.

$(x + y)(x - y)$

$= x^2 - xy + xy - y^2$

$= 0$

$= x^2 - y^2$

Because the middle term becomes 0, we have the following rule.

Rules and Properties: **Special Product**

The product of two binomials that differ only in the sign between the terms is the square of the first term minus the square of the second term.

Let's look at the application of this rule in Example 3.

Example 3

Multiplying Polynomials

Multiply each pair of binomials.

(a) $(x + 5)(x - 5) = x^2 - 5^2$

Square of the first term   Square of the second term

$= x^2 - 25$

NOTE

$(2y)^2 = (2y)(2y)$
$= 4y^2$

(b) $(x + 2y)(x - 2y) = x^2 - (2y)^2$

Square of the first term   Square of the second term

$= x^2 - 4y^2$

(c) $(3m + n)(3m - n) = 9m^2 - n^2$

(d) $(4a - 3b)(4a + 3b) = 16a^2 - 9b^2$

CHECK YOURSELF 3

Find the products.

(a) $(a - 6)(a + 6)$ **(b)** $(x - 3y)(x + 3y)$

(c) $(5n + 2p)(5n - 2p)$ **(d)** $(7b - 3c)(7b + 3c)$

When finding the product of three or more factors, it is useful to first look for the pattern in which two binomials differ only in their sign. Finding this product first will make it easier to find the product of all the factors.

Example 4

Multiplying Polynomials

(a) $x(x - 3)(x + 3)$ These binomials differ only in the sign.

$= x(x^2 - 9)$

$= x^3 - 9x$

(b) $(x + 1)(x - 5)(x + 5)$ These binomials differ only in the sign.

$= (x + 1)(x^2 - 25)$ With two binomials, use the FOIL method.

$= x^3 + x^2 - 25x - 25$

(c) $(2x - 1)(x + 3)(2x + 1)$ These two binomials differ only in the sign of the second term. We can use the commutative property to rearrange the terms.

$= (x + 3)(2x - 1)(2x + 1)$

$= (x + 3)(4x^2 - 1)$

$= 4x^3 + 12x^2 - x - 3$

 CHECK YOURSELF 4

Multiply.

(a) $3x(x - 5)(x + 5)$

(b) $(x - 4)(2x + 3)(2x - 3)$

(c) $(x - 7)(3x - 1)(x + 7)$

CHECK YOURSELF ANSWERS

1. **(a)** $4x^2 + 4x + 1$; **(b)** $16x^2 - 24xy + 9y^2$

2. **(a)** $x^2 + 10x + 25$; **(b)** $9a^2 + 12a + 4$; **(c)** $y^2 - 14y + 49$; **(d)** $25x^2 - 20xy + 4y^2$

3. **(a)** $a^2 - 36$; **(b)** $x^2 - 9y^2$; **(c)** $25n^2 - 4p^2$; **(d)** $49b^2 - 9c^2$

4. **(a)** $3x^3 - 75x$; **(b)** $4x^3 - 16x^2 - 9x + 36$; **(c)** $3x^3 - x^2 - 147x + 49$

3.4 Exercises

Find each of the following squares.

1. $(x + 5)^2$

2. $(y + 9)^2$

3. $(w - 6)^2$

4. $(a - 8)^2$

5. $(z + 12)^2$

6. $(p - 20)^2$

7. $(2a - 1)^2$

8. $(3x - 2)^2$

9. $(6m + 1)^2$

10. $(7b - 2)^2$

11. $(3x - y)^2$

12. $(5m + n)^2$

13. $(2r + 5s)^2$

14. $(3a - 4b)^2$

15. $(8a - 9b)^2$

16. $(7p + 6q)^2$

17. $\left(x + \dfrac{1}{2}\right)^2$

18. $\left(w - \dfrac{1}{4}\right)^2$

Find each of the following products.

19. $(x - 6)(x + 6)$

20. $(y + 8)(y - 8)$

21. $(m + 12)(m - 12)$

22. $(w - 10)(w + 10)$

23. $\left(x - \dfrac{1}{2}\right)\left(x + \dfrac{1}{2}\right)$

24. $\left(x + \dfrac{2}{3}\right)\left(x - \dfrac{2}{3}\right)$

1. _____
2. _____
3. _____
4. _____
5. _____
6. _____
7. _____
8. _____
9. _____
10. _____
11. _____
12. _____
13. _____
14. _____
15. _____
16. _____
17. _____
18. _____
19. _____
20. _____
21. _____
22. _____
23. _____
24. _____

25. _____

26. _____

27. _____

28. _____

29. _____

30. _____

31. _____

32. _____

33. _____

34. _____

35. _____

36. _____

37. _____

38. _____

39. _____

40. _____

41. _____

42. _____

43. _____

44. _____

45. _____

46. _____

47. _____

48. _____

49. _____

50. _____

25. $(p - 0.4)(p + 0.4)$ **26.** $(m - 0.6)(m + 0.6)$

27. $(a - 3b)(a + 3b)$ **28.** $(p + 4q)(p - 4q)$

29. $(4r - s)(4r + s)$ **30.** $(7x - y)(7x + y)$

31. $(8w + 5z)(8w - 5z)$ **32.** $(7c + 2d)(7c - 2d)$

33. $(5x - 9y)(5x + 9y)$ **34.** $(6s - 5t)(6s + 5t)$

35. $x(x - 2)(x + 2)$ **36.** $a(a + 5)(a - 5)$

37. $2s(s - 3r)(s + 3r)$ **38.** $5w(2w - z)(2w + z)$

39. $5r(r + 3)^2$ **40.** $3x(x - 2)^2$

For each of the following problems, let x represent the number, then write an expression for the product.

41. The product of 6 more than a number and 6 less than that number

42. The square of 5 more than a number

43. The square of 4 less than a number

44. The product of 5 less than a number and 5 more than that number

Note that $(28)(32) = (30 - 2)(30 + 2) = 900 - 4 = 896$. Use this pattern to find each of the following products.

45. $(49)(51)$ **46.** $(27)(33)$

47. $(34)(26)$ **48.** $(98)(102)$

49. $(55)(65)$ **50.** $(64)(56)$

51. Tree planting. Suppose an orchard is planted with trees in straight rows. If there are $5x - 4$ rows with $5x - 4$ trees in each row, how many trees are there in the orchard?

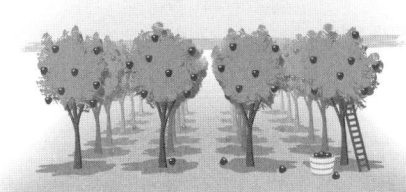

52. Area of a square. A square has sides of length $3x - 2$ centimeters (cm). Express the area of the square as a polynomial.

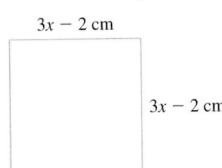

$3x - 2$ cm

$3x - 2$ cm

53. Complete the following statement: $(a + b)^2$ is not equal to $a^2 + b^2$ because. . . . But, wait! Isn't $(a + b)^2$ *sometimes* equal to $a^2 + b^2$? What do you think?

54. Is $(a + b)^3$ ever equal to $a^3 + b^3$? Explain.

55. In the following figures, identify the length, width, and area of the square:

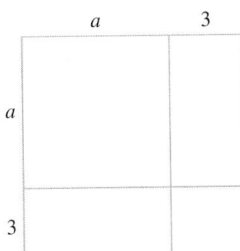

a b

a

b

Length = _____

Width = _____

Area = _____

a 3

a

3

Length = _____

Width = _____

Area = _____

x

x x^2 $2x$

$2x$

Length = _____

Width = _____

Area = _____

457

56. _____

a. _____

b. _____

c. _____

d. _____

e. _____

f. _____

g. _____

h. _____

56. The square below is x units on a side. The area is _____.

Draw a picture of what happens when the sides are doubled. The area is _____.

Continue the picture to show what happens when the sides are tripled. The area is _____.

If the sides are quadrupled, the area is _____.

In general, if the sides are multiplied by n, the area is _____.

If each side is increased by 3, the area is increased by _____.

If each side is decreased by 2, the area is decreased by _____.

In general, if each side is increased by n, the area is increased by _____, and if each side is decreased by n, the area is decreased by _____.

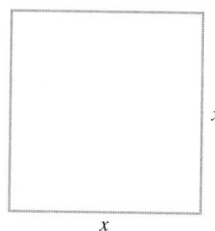

x

x

 Getting Ready

Divide.

(a) $\dfrac{2x^2}{2x}$

(b) $\dfrac{3a^3}{3a}$

(c) $\dfrac{6p^3}{2p^2}$

(d) $\dfrac{10m^4}{5m^2}$

(e) $\dfrac{20a^3}{5a^3}$

(f) $\dfrac{6x^2y}{3xy}$

(g) $\dfrac{12r^3s^2}{4rs}$

(h) $\dfrac{49c^4d^6}{7cd^3}$

Answers

1. $x^2 + 10x + 25$ **3.** $w^2 - 12w + 36$ **5.** $z^2 + 24z + 144$ **7.** $4a^2 - 4a + 1$
9. $36m^2 + 12m + 1$ **11.** $9x^2 - 6xy + y^2$ **13.** $4r^2 + 20rs + 25s^2$

15. $64a^2 - 144ab + 81b^2$ **17.** $x^2 + x + \dfrac{1}{4}$ **19.** $x^2 - 36$ **21.** $m^2 - 144$

23. $x^2 - \dfrac{1}{4}$ **25.** $p^2 - 0.16$ **27.** $a^2 - 9b^2$ **29.** $16r^2 - s^2$

31. $64w^2 - 25z^2$ **33.** $25x^2 - 81y^2$ **35.** $x^3 - 4x$ **37.** $2s^3 - 18r^2s$
39. $5r^3 + 30r^2 + 45r$ **41.** $x^2 - 36$ **43.** $x^2 - 8x + 16$ **45.** 2499
47. 884 **49.** 3575 **51.** $25x^2 - 40x + 16$
53.   **55.**   **a.** x **b.** a^2 **c.** $3p$ **d.** $2m^2$ **e.** 4

f. $2x$ **g.** $3r^2s$ **h.** $7c^3d^3$

3.5 An Introduction to Factoring

Overcoming Math Anxiety

Hint #6

Working Together

How many of your classmates do you know? Whether you are by nature gregarious or shy, you have much to gain by getting to know your classmates.

1. It is important to have someone to call when you have missed class or if you are unclear on an assignment.

2. Working with another person is almost always beneficial to both people. If you don't understand something, it helps to have someone to ask about it. If you do understand something, nothing will cement that understanding more than explaining the idea to another person.

3. Sometimes we need to commiserate. If an assignment is particularly frustrating, it is reassuring to find that it is also frustrating for other students.

4. Have you ever thought you had the right answer, but it doesn't match the answer in the text? Frequently the answers are equivalent, but that's not always easy to see. A different perspective can help you see that. Occasionally there is an error in a textbook (here we are talking about *other* textbooks). In such cases it is wonderfully reassuring to find that someone else has the same answer you do.

You were given factors and asked to find a product. We are now going to reverse the process. You will be given a polynomial and asked to find its factors. This is called **factoring.**

Let's start with an example from arithmetic. To *multiply* $5 \cdot 7$, you write

$$5 \cdot 7 = 35$$

To *factor* 35, you would write

$$35 = 5 \cdot 7$$

Factoring is the *reverse* of multiplication.

Now let's look at factoring in algebra. You have used the distributive property as

$$a(b + c) = ab + ac$$

For instance,

NOTE 3 and $x + 5$ are the factors of $3x + 15$.

$$3(x + 5) = 3x + 15$$

To use the distributive property in factoring, we apply that property in the opposite fashion, as

$$ab + ac = a(b + c)$$

The property lets us remove the common monomial factor a from the terms of $ab + ac$. To use this in factoring, the first step is to see whether each term of the polynomial has a common monomial factor. In our earlier example,

$$3x + 15 = 3 \cdot x + 3 \cdot 5$$

Common factor

So, by the distributive property,

$$3x + 15 = 3(x + 5)$$ The original terms are each divided by the greatest common factor to determine the terms in parentheses.

NOTE Again, factoring is the reverse of multiplication.

To check this, multiply $3(x + 5)$.

Multiplying

$$3(x + 5) = 3x + 15$$

NOTE This diagram relates the idea of multiplication and factoring.

Factoring

The first step in factoring is to identify the *greatest common factor* (GCF) of a set of terms. This is the monomial with the largest common numerical coefficient and the largest power common to any variables.

NOTE In fact, we will see that factoring out the GCF is the *first* method to try in any of the factoring problems we will discuss.

Definitions: Greatest Common Factor

The **greatest common factor (GCF)** of a polynomial is the monomial with the highest degree and the largest numerical coefficient that is a factor of each term of the polynomial.

Example 1

Finding the GCF

Find the GCF for each set of terms.

(a) 9 and 12   The largest number that is a factor of both is 3.
(b) 10, 25, 150   The GCF is 5.
(c) x^4 and x^7 The largest power that divides both terms is x^4.
(d) $12a^3$ and $18a^2$ The GCF is $6a^2$.

 CHECK YOURSELF 1

Find the GCF for each set of terms.

(a) 14, 24   **(b)** 9, 27, 81   **(c)** a^9, a^5 **(d)** $10x^5, 35x^4$

Step by Step: To Factor a Monomial from a Polynomial

NOTE Checking your answer is always important and perhaps is never easier than after you have factored.

Step 1   Find the *greatest common factor* (GCF) for all the terms.
Step 2   Factor the GCF from each term, then apply the distributive property.
Step 3   Mentally check your factoring by multiplication.

Example 2

Finding the GCF of a Binomial

(a) Factor $8x^2 + 12x$.

The largest common numerical factor of 8 and 12 is 4, and x is the variable factor with the largest power. So $4x$ is the GCF. Write

$$8x^2 + 12x = 4x \cdot 2x + 4x \cdot 3$$

GCF

NOTE It is always a good idea to check your answer by multiplying to make sure that you get the original polynomial. Try it here. Multiply $4x$ by $2x + 3$.

Now, by the distributive property, we have

$$8x^2 + 12x = 4x(2x + 3)$$

(b) Factor $6a^4 - 18a^2$.

The GCF in this case is $6a^2$. Write

$$6a^4 + (-18a^2) = 6a^2 \cdot a^2 + 6a^2 \cdot (-3)$$

GCF

NOTE It is also true that $6a^4 + (-18a^2) = 3a(2a^3 + (-6a))$. However, this is *not completely factored*. Do you see why? You want to find the common monomial factor with the *largest possible* coefficient and the *largest* exponent, in this case $6a^2$.

Again, using the distributive property yields

$$6a^4 - 18a^2 = 6a^2(a^2 - 3)$$

You should check this by multiplying.

✔ CHECK YOURSELF 2

Factor each of the following polynomials.

(a) $5x + 20$ **(b)** $6x^2 - 24x$ **(c)** $10a^3 - 15a^2$

The process is exactly the same for polynomials with more than two terms. Consider Example 3.

Example 3

Finding the GCF of a Polynomial

(a) Factor $5x^2 - 10x + 15$.

NOTE The GCF is 5.

$$5x^2 - 10x + 15 = 5 \cdot x^2 - 5 \cdot 2x + 5 \cdot 3$$

GCF

$$= 5(x^2 - 2x + 3)$$

(b) Factor $6ab + 9ab^2 - 15a^2$.

NOTE The GCF is $3a$.

$$6ab + 9ab^2 - 15a^2 = 3a \cdot 2b + 3a \cdot 3b^2 - 3a \cdot 5a$$

GCF

$$= 3a(2b + 3b^2 - 5a)$$

(c) Factor $4a^4 + 12a^3 - 20a^2$.

NOTE The GCF is $4a^2$.

$$4a^4 + 12a^3 - 20a^2 = 4a^2 \cdot a^2 + 4a^2 \cdot 3a - 4a^2 \cdot 5$$

GCF

$$= 4a^2(a^2 + 3a - 5)$$

NOTE In each of these examples, you will want to check the result by multiplying the factors.

(d) Factor $6a^2b + 9ab^2 + 3ab$.

Mentally note that 3, a, and b are factors of each term, so

$$6a^2b + 9ab^2 + 3ab = 3ab(2a + 3b + 1)$$

 CHECK YOURSELF 3

Factor each of the following polynomials.

(a) $8b^2 + 16b - 32$

(b) $4xy - 8x^2y + 12x^3$

(c) $7x^4 - 14x^3 + 21x^2$

(d) $5x^2y^2 - 10xy^2 + 15x^2y$

We can have two or more terms that have a binomial factor in common, as is the case in Example 4.

> **Example 4**

Finding a Common Factor

(a) Factor $3x(x + y) + 2(x + y)$.

We see that *the binomial $x + y$ is a common factor* and can be removed.

NOTE Because of the commutative property, the factors can be written in either order.

$$3x(x + y) + 2(x + y)$$
$$= (x + y) \cdot 3x + (x + y) \cdot 2$$
$$= (x + y)(3x + 2)$$

(b) Factor $3x^2(x - y) + 6x(x - y) + 9(x - y)$.

We note that here the GCF is $3(x - y)$. Factoring as before, we have

$$3(x - y)(x^2 + 2x + 3)$$

 CHECK YOURSELF 4

Completely factor each of the polynomials.

(a) $7a(a - 2b) + 3(a - 2b)$

(b) $4x^2(x + y) - 8x(x + y) - 16(x + y)$

CHECK YOURSELF ANSWERS

1. **(a)** 2; **(b)** 9; **(c)** a^5; **(d)** $5x^4$ **2.** **(a)** $5(x + 4)$; **(b)** $6x(x - 4)$; **(c)** $5a^2(2a - 3)$

3. **(a)** $8(b^2 + 2b - 4)$; **(b)** $4x(y - 2xy + 3x^2)$; **(c)** $7x^2(x^2 - 2x + 3)$;

(d) $5xy(xy - 2y + 3x)$ **4.** **(a)** $(a - 2b)(7a + 3)$; **(b)** $4(x + y)(x^2 - 2x - 4)$

Exercises

Find the greatest common factor for each of the following sets of terms.

1. 10, 12

2. 15, 35

3. 16, 32, 88

4. 55, 33, 132

5. x^2, x^5

6. y^7, y^9

7. a^3, a^6, a^9

8. b^4, b^6, b^8

9. $5x^4, 10x^5$

10. $8y^9, 24y^3$

11. $8a^4, 6a^6, 10a^{10}$

12. $9b^3, 6b^5, 12b^4$

13. $9x^2y, 12xy^2, 15x^2y^2$

14. $12a^3b^2, 18a^2b^3, 6a^4b^4$

15. $15ab^3, 10a^2bc, 25b^2c^3$

16. $9x^2, 3xy^3, 6y^3$

17. $15a^2bc^2, 9ab^2c^2, 6a^2b^2c^2$

18. $18x^3y^2z^3, 27x^4y^2z^3, 81xy^2z$

19. $(x + y)^2, (x + y)^3$

20. $12(a + b)^4, 4(a + b)^3$

Factor each of the following polynomials.

21. $8a + 4$

22. $5x - 15$

23. $24m - 32n$

24. $7p - 21q$

25. $12m^2 + 8m$

26. $24n^2 - 32n$

ANSWERS

1. _____ 2. _____

3. _____ 4. _____

5. _____

6. _____

7. _____

8. _____

9. _____

10. _____

11. _____

12. _____

13. _____

14. _____

15. _____

16. _____

17. _____

18. _____

19. _____

20. _____

21. _____

22. _____

23. _____

24. _____

25. _____

26. _____

27. _____

28. _____

29. _____

30. _____

31. _____

32. _____

33. _____

34. _____

35. _____

36. _____

37. _____

38. _____

39. _____

40. _____

41. _____

42. _____

43. _____

44. _____

45. _____

46. _____

47. _____

48. _____

49. _____

50. _____

51. _____

52. _____

27. $10s^2 + 5s$

28. $12y^2 - 6y$

29. $12x^2 + 24x$

30. $14b^2 - 28b$

31. $15a^3 - 25a^2$

32. $36b^4 + 24b^2$

33. $6pq + 18p^2q$

34. $8ab - 24ab^2$

35. $7m^3n - 21mn^3$

36. $36p^2q^2 - 9pq$

37. $6x^2 - 18x + 30$

38. $7a^2 + 21a - 42$

39. $3a^3 + 6a^2 - 12a$

40. $5x^3 - 15x^2 + 25x$

41. $6m + 9mn - 15mn^2$

42. $4s + 6st - 14st^2$

43. $10x^2y + 15xy - 5xy^2$

44. $3ab^2 + 6ab - 15a^2b$

45. $10r^3s^2 + 25r^2s^2 - 15r^2s^3$

46. $28x^2y^3 - 35x^2y^2 + 42x^3y$

47. $9a^5 - 15a^4 + 21a^3 - 27a$

48. $8p^6 - 40p^4 + 24p^3 - 16p^2$

49. $15m^3n^2 - 20m^2n + 35mn^3 - 10mn$

50. $14ab^4 + 21a^2b^3 - 35a^3b^2 + 28ab^2$

51. $x(x - 2) + 3(x - 2)$

52. $y(y + 5) - 3(y + 5)$

53. The GCF of $2x - 6$ is 2. The GCF of $5x + 10$ is 5. Find the greatest common factor of the product $(2x - 6)(5x + 10)$.

54. The GCF of $3z + 12$ is 3. The GCF of $4z + 8$ is 4. Find the GCF of the product $(3z + 12)(4z + 8)$.

55. The GCF of $2x^3 - 4x$ is $2x$. The GCF of $3x + 6$ is 3. Find the GCF of the product $(2x^3 - 4x)(3x + 6)$.

56. State, in a sentence, the rule that the previous three exercises illustrated.

Find the GCF for each product.

57. $(2a + 8)(3a - 6)$

58. $(5b - 10)(2b + 4)$

59. $(2x^2 + 5x)(7x - 14)$

60. $(6y^2 - 3y)(y + 7)$

61. Area of a rectangle. The area of a rectangle with width t is given by $33t - t^2$. Factor the expression and determine the length of the rectangle in terms of t.

62. Area of a rectangle. The area of a rectangle of length x is given by $3x^2 + 5x$. Find the width of the rectangle.

63. For centuries, mathematicians have found factoring numbers into prime factors a fascinating subject. A prime number is a number that cannot be written as a product of any numbers but 1 and itself. The list of primes begins with 2 because 1 is not considered a prime number and then goes on: 3, 5, 7, 11, . . . What are the first 10 primes? What are the primes less than 100? If you list the numbers from 1 to 100 and then cross out all numbers that are multiples of 2, 3, 5, and 7, what is left? Are all the numbers not crossed out prime? Write a paragraph to explain why this might be so. You might want to investigate the sieve of Eratosthenes, a system from 230 B.C.E. for finding prime numbers.

64. If we made a list of all the prime numbers, what number would be at the end of the list? Because there are an infinite number of prime numbers, there is no "largest prime number." But is there some formula that will give us all the primes? Here are some formulas proposed over the centuries:

$$n^2 + n + 17 \qquad 2n^2 + 29 \qquad n^2 - n + 11$$

In all these expressions, $n = +1, 2, 3, 4, \ldots$, that is, a positive integer beginning with 1. Investigate these expressions with a partner. Do the expressions give prime numbers when they are evaluated for these values of n? Do the expressions give *every* prime in the range of resulting numbers? Can you put in *any* positive number for n?

65. How are primes used in coding messages and for security? Work together to decode the messages. The messages are coded using this code: After the numbers are factored into prime factors, the power of 2 gives the number of the letter in the alphabet. This code would be easy for a code breaker to figure out, but you might make up code that would be more difficult to break.

a. 1310720, 229376, 1572864, 1760, 460, 2097152, 336

b. 786432, 143, 4608, 278528, 1344, 98304, 1835008, 352, 4718592, 5242880

c. Code a message using this rule. Exchange your message with a partner to decode it.

ANSWERS

53. _____

54. _____

55. _____

56. _____

57. _____

58. _____

59. _____

60. _____

61. _____

62. _____

63. _____

64. _____

65. _____

Getting Ready

Multiply.

(a) $(a - 1)(a + 4)$ (b) $(x - 1)(x + 3)$

(c) $(x - 3)(x - 3)$ (d) $(y - 11)(y + 3)$

(e) $(x + 5)(x + 7)$ (f) $(y + 1)(y - 13)$

Answers

1. 2   **3.** 8   **5.** x^2 **7.** a^3 **9.** $5x^4$ **11.** $2a^4$ **13.** $3xy$

15. $5b$ **17.** $3abc^2$ **19.** $(x + y)^2$ **21.** $4(2a + 1)$ **23.** $8(3m - 4n)$

25. $4m(3m + 2)$ **27.** $5s(2s + 1)$ **29.** $12x(x + 2)$ **31.** $5a^2(3a - 5)$

33. $6pq(1 + 3p)$ **35.** $7mn(m^2 - 3n^2)$ **37.** $6(x^2 - 3x + 5)$

39. $3a(a^2 + 2a - 4)$ **41.** $3m(2 + 5n)(1 - n)$ **43.** $5xy(2x + 3 - y)$

45. $5r^2s^2(2r + 5 - 3s)$ **47.** $3a(3a^4 - 5a^3 + 7a^2 - 9)$

49. $5mn(3m^2n - 4m + 7n^2 - 2)$ **51.** $(x - 2)(x + 3)$ **53.** 10   **55.** $6x$

57. 6   **59.** $7x$ **61.** $t(33 - t)$; $33 - t$ **63.**   **65.**

a. $a^2 + 3a - 4$ **b.** $x^2 + 2x - 3$ **c.** $x^2 - 6x + 9$ **d.** $y^2 - 8y - 33$

e. $x^2 + 12x + 35$ **f.** $y^2 - 12y - 13$

466

Factoring Trinomials of the Form $x^2 + bx + c$

1. Factor a trinomial of the form $x^2 + bx + c$
2. Factor a trinomial containing a common factor

NOTE The process used to factor here is frequently called the *trial-and-error method.* You'll see the reason for the name as you work through this section.

You learned how to find the product of any two binomials by using the FOIL method in Section 3.3. Because factoring is the reverse of multiplication, we now want to use that pattern to find the factors of certain trinomials.

Recall that to multiply two binomials, we have

$(x + 2)(x + 3) = x^2 + 5x + 6$

The product of the first terms $(x \cdot x)$.	The sum of the products of the outer and inner terms ($3x$ and $2x$).	The product of the last terms ($2 \cdot 3$).

 C A U T I O N

Not every trinomial can be written as the product of two binomials.

Suppose now that you are given $x^2 + 5x + 6$ and want to find its factors. First, you know that the factors of a trinomial may be two binomials. So write

$x^2 + 5x + 6 = (\qquad)(\qquad)$

Because the first term of the trinomial is x^2, the first terms of the binomial factors must be x and x. We now have

$x^2 + 5x + 6 = (x \qquad)(x \qquad)$

The product of the last terms must be 6. Because 6 is positive, the factors must have *like* signs. Here are the possibilities:

$$6 = 1 \cdot 6$$
$$= 2 \cdot 3$$
$$= (-1)(-6)$$
$$= (-2)(-3)$$

This means that the possible factors of the trinomial are

$(x + 1)(x + 6)$

$(x + 2)(x + 3)$

$(x - 1)(x - 6)$

$(x - 2)(x - 3)$

How do we tell which is the correct pair? From the FOIL pattern we know that the sum of the outer and inner products must equal the middle term of the trinomial, in this case $5x$. This is the crucial step!

Possible Factors	Middle Terms	
$(x + 1)(x + 6)$	$7x$	
$(x + 2)(x + 3)$	$5x$	The correct middle term!
$(x - 1)(x - 6)$	$-7x$	
$(x - 2)(x - 3)$	$-5x$	

467

So we know that the correct factorization is

$$x^2 + 5x + 6 = (x + 2)(x + 3)$$

Are there any clues so far that will make this process quicker? Yes, there is an important one that you may have spotted. We started with a trinomial that had a positive middle term and a positive last term. The negative pairs of factors for 6 led to negative middle terms. So you don't need to bother with the negative factors if the middle term and the last term of the trinomial are both positive.

Example 1

Factoring a Trinomial

(a) Factor $x^2 + 9x + 8$.

Because the middle term and the last term of the trinomial are both positive, consider only the positive factors of 8, that is, $8 = 1 \cdot 8$ or $8 = 2 \cdot 4$.

NOTE If you are wondering why we didn't list $(x + 8)(x + 1)$ as a possibility, remember that multiplication is commutative. The order doesn't matter!

Possible Factors	Middle Terms
$(x + 1)(x + 8)$	$9x$
$(x + 2)(x + 4)$	$6x$

Because the first pair gives the correct middle term,

$$x^2 + 9x + 8 = (x + 1)(x + 8)$$

(b) Factor $x^2 + 12x + 20$.

NOTE The factors for 20 are
$20 = 1 \cdot 20$
$ = 2 \cdot 10$
$ = 4 \cdot 5$

Possible Factors	Middle Terms
$(x + 1)(x + 20)$	$21x$
$(x + 2)(x + 10)$	$12x$
$(x + 4)(x + 5)$	$9x$

So

$$x^2 + 12x + 20 = (x + 2)(x + 10)$$

 CHECK YOURSELF 1

Factor.

(a) $x^2 + 6x + 5$ 　　　　　　　　　　　**(b)** $x^2 + 10x + 16$

Let's look at some examples in which the middle term of the trinomial is negative but the first and last terms are still positive. Consider

Positive   Positive

$$x^2 - 11x + 18$$

Negative

Because we want a negative middle term ($-11x$), we use *two negative factors* for 18. Recall that the product of two negative numbers is positive.

Example 2

Factoring a Trinomial

(a) Factor $x^2 - 11x + 18$.

NOTE The negative factors of 18 are

$18 = (-1)(-18)$
$\quad = (-2)(-9)$
$\quad = (-3)(-6)$

Possible Factors	Middle Terms
$(x - 1)(x - 18)$	$-19x$
$(x - 2)(x - 9)$	$-11x$
$(x - 3)(x - 6)$	$-9x$

So

$$x^2 - 11x + 18 = (x - 2)(x - 9)$$

(b) Factor $x^2 - 13x + 12$.

NOTE The negative factors of 12 are

$12 = (-1)(-12)$
$\quad = (-2)(-6)$
$\quad = (-3)(-4)$

Possible Factors	Middle Terms
$(x - 1)(x - 12)$	$-13x$
$(x - 2)(x - 6)$	$-8x$
$(x - 3)(x - 4)$	$-7x$

So

$$x^2 - 13x + 12 = (x - 1)(x - 12)$$

A few more clues: We have listed all the possible factors in the above examples. It really isn't necessary. Just work until you find the right pair. Also, with practice much of this work can be done mentally.

 CHECK YOURSELF 2

Factor.

(a) $x^2 - 10x + 9$ **(b)** $x^2 - 10x + 21$

Let's look now at the process of factoring a trinomial whose last term is negative. For instance, to factor $x^2 + 2x - 15$, we can start as before:

$$x^2 + 2x - 15 = (x \quad ?)(x \quad ?)$$

Note that the product of the last terms must be negative (-15 here). So we must choose factors that have different signs.

What are our choices for the factors of -15?

$$-15 = (1)(-15)$$
$$= (-1)(15)$$
$$= (3)(-5)$$
$$= (-3)(5)$$

This means that the possible factors and the resulting middle terms are

NOTE Another clue: Some students prefer to look at the list of numerical factors rather than looking at the actual algebraic factors. Here you want the pair whose sum is 2, the coefficient of the middle term of the trinomial. That pair is -3 and 5, which leads us to the correct factors.

Possible Factors	Middle Terms
$(x + 1)(x - 15)$	$-14x$
$(x - 1)(x + 15)$	$14x$
$(x + 3)(x - 5)$	$-2x$
$(x - 3)(x + 5)$	$2x$

So $x^2 + 2x - 15 = (x - 3)(x + 5)$.

Let's work through some examples in which the constant term is negative.

Example 3

Factoring a Trinomial

(a) Factor $x^2 - 5x - 6$.

First, list the factors of -6. Of course, one factor will be positive, and one will be negative.

NOTE You may be able to pick the factors directly from this list. You want the pair whose sum is -5 (the coefficient of the middle term).

$$-6 = (1)(-6)$$
$$= (-1)(6)$$
$$= (2)(-3)$$
$$= (-2)(3)$$

For the trinomial, then, we have

Possible Factors	Middle Terms
$(x + 1)(x - 6)$	$-5x$
$(x - 1)(x + 6)$	$5x$
$(x + 2)(x - 3)$	$-x$
$(x - 2)(x + 3)$	x

So $x^2 - 5x - 6 = (x + 1)(x - 6)$.

(b) Factor $x^2 + 8xy - 9y^2$.

The process is similar if two variables are involved in the trinomial you are to factor. Start with

$$x^2 + 8xy - 9y^2 = (x \quad ?)(x \quad ?).$$

The product of the last terms must be $-9y^2$.

$$-9y^2 = (-y)(9y)$$
$$= (y)(-9y)$$
$$= (3y)(-3y)$$

Possible Factors	Middle Terms
$(x - y)(x + 9y)$	$8xy$
$(x + y)(x - 9y)$	$-8xy$
$(x + 3y)(x - 3y)$	0

So $x^2 + 8xy - 9y^2 = (x - y)(x + 9y)$.

 CHECK YOURSELF 3

Factor.

(a) $x^2 + 7x - 30$ **(b)** $x^2 - 3xy - 10y^2$

As was pointed out in the last section, any time that we have a common factor, that factor should be removed *before* we try any other factoring technique. Consider the following example.

Example 4

Factoring a Trinomial

(a) Factor $3x^2 - 21x + 18$.

$3x^2 - 21x + 18 = 3(x^2 - 7x + 6)$ Remove the common factor of 3.

We now factor the remaining trinomial. For $x^2 - 7x + 6$:

Possible Factors	Middle Terms	
$(x - 2)(x - 3)$	$-5x$	
$(x - 1)(x - 6)$	$-7x$	The correct middle term

 CAUTION

A common mistake is to forget to write the 3 that was factored out as the first step.

So $3x^2 - 21x + 18 = 3(x - 1)(x - 6)$.

(b) Factor $2x^3 + 16x^2 - 40x$.

$2x^3 + 16x^2 - 40x = 2x(x^2 + 8x - 20)$ Remove the common factor of 2x.

To factor the remaining trinomial, which is $x^2 + 8x - 20$, we have

Possible Factors	Middle Terms
$(x - 4)(x + 5)$	x
$(x - 5)(x + 4)$	$-x$
$(x - 10)(x + 2)$	$-8x$
$(x - 2)(x + 10)$	$8x$

The correct middle term

NOTE Once we have found the desired middle term, there is no need to continue.

So $2x^3 + 16x^2 - 40x = 2x(x - 2)(x + 10)$.

CHECK YOURSELF 4

Factor.

(a) $3x^2 - 3x - 36$

(b) $4x^3 + 24x^2 + 32x$

One further comment: Have you wondered if all trinomials are factorable? Look at the trinomial

$x^2 + 2x + 6$

The only possible factors are $(x + 1)(x + 6)$ and $(x + 2)(x + 3)$. Neither pair is correct (you should check the middle terms), and so this trinomial does not have factors with integer coefficients. Of course, there are many others.

CHECK YOURSELF ANSWERS

1. **(a)** $(x + 1)(x + 5)$; **(b)** $(x + 2)(x + 8)$ **2.** **(a)** $(x - 9)(x - 1)$; **(b)** $(x - 3)(x - 7)$
3. **(a)** $(x + 10)(x - 3)$; **(b)** $(x + 2y)(x - 5y)$
4. **(a)** $3(x - 4)(x + 3)$; **(b)** $4x(x + 2)(x + 4)$

Name _____

Section _____ Date _____

Complete each of the following statements.

1. $x^2 - 8x + 15 = (x - 3)($ $)$

2. $y^2 - 3y - 18 = (y - 6)($ $)$

3. $m^2 + 8m + 12 = (m + 2)($ $)$

4. $x^2 - 10x + 24 = (x - 6)($ $)$

5. $p^2 - 8p - 20 = (p + 2)($ $)$

6. $a^2 + 9a - 36 = (a + 12)($ $)$

7. $x^2 - 16x + 64 = (x - 8)($ $)$

8. $w^2 - 12w - 45 = (w + 3)($ $)$

9. $x^2 - 7xy + 10y^2 = (x - 2y)($ $)$

10. $a^2 + 18ab + 81b^2 = (a + 9b)($ $)$

Factor each of the following trinomials.

11. $x^2 + 8x + 15$

12. $x^2 - 11x + 24$

13. $x^2 - 11x + 28$

14. $y^2 - y - 20$

15. $s^2 + 13s + 30$

16. $b^2 + 14b + 33$

17. $a^2 - 2a - 48$

18. $x^2 - 17x + 60$

19. $x^2 - 8x + 7$

20. $x^2 + 7x - 18$

21. $m^2 + 3m - 28$

22. $a^2 + 10a + 25$

ANSWERS

1. _____
2. _____
3. _____
4. _____
5. _____
6. _____
7. _____
8. _____
9. _____
10. _____
11. _____
12. _____
13. _____
14. _____
15. _____
16. _____
17. _____
18. _____
19. _____
20. _____
21. _____
22. _____

23. _____

24. _____

25. _____

26. _____

27. _____

28. _____

29. _____

30. _____

31. _____

32. _____

33. _____

34. _____

35. _____

36. _____

37. _____

38. _____

39. _____

40. _____

41. _____

42. _____

43. _____

44. _____

45. _____

46. _____

23. $x^2 - 6x - 40$

24. $x^2 - 11x + 10$

25. $x^2 - 14x + 49$

26. $s^2 - 4s - 32$

27. $p^2 - 10p - 24$

28. $x^2 - 11x - 60$

29. $x^2 + 5x - 66$

30. $a^2 + 2a - 80$

31. $c^2 + 19c + 60$

32. $t^2 - 4t - 60$

33. $n^2 + 5n - 50$

34. $x^2 - 16x + 63$

35. $x^2 + 7xy + 10y^2$

36. $x^2 - 8xy + 12y^2$

37. $a^2 - ab - 42b^2$

38. $m^2 - 8mn + 16n^2$

39. $x^2 - 13xy + 40y^2$

40. $r^2 - 9rs - 36s^2$

41. $b^2 + 6ab + 9a^2$

42. $x^2 + 3xy - 10y^2$

43. $x^2 - 2xy - 8y^2$

44. $u^2 + 6uv - 55v^2$

45. $25m^2 + 10mn + n^2$

46. $64m^2 - 16mn + n^2$

Factor each of the following trinomials completely. Factor out the greatest common factor first.

47. $3a^2 - 3a - 126$

48. $2c^2 + 2c - 60$

49. $r^3 + 7r^2 - 18r$

50. $m^3 + 5m^2 - 14m$

51. $2x^3 - 20x^2 - 48x$

52. $3p^3 + 48p^2 - 108p$

53. $x^2y - 9xy^2 - 36y^3$

54. $4s^4 - 20s^3t - 96s^2t^2$

55. $m^3 - 29m^2n + 120mn^2$

56. $2a^3 - 52a^2b + 96ab^2$

Find a positive value for k for which each of the following can be factored.

57. $x^2 + kx + 8$

58. $x^2 + kx + 9$

59. $x^2 - kx + 16$

60. $x^2 - kx + 17$

61. $x^2 - kx - 5$

62. $x^2 - kx - 7$

63. $x^2 + 3x + k$

64. $x^2 + 5x + k$

65. $x^2 + 2x - k$

66. $x^2 + x - k$

 Getting Ready

Multiply.

(a) $(2x - 1)(2x + 3)$

(b) $(3a - 1)(a + 4)$

(c) $(x - 4)(2x - 3)$

(d) $(2w - 11)(w + 2)$

(e) $(y + 5)(2y + 9)$

(f) $(2x + 1)(x - 12)$

(g) $(p + 9)(2p + 5)$

(h) $(3a - 5)(2a + 4)$

47. _____
48. _____
49. _____
50. _____
51. _____
52. _____
53. _____
54. _____
55. _____
56. _____
57. _____
58. _____
59. _____
60. _____
61. _____
62. _____
63. _____
64. _____
65. _____
66. _____
a. _____
b. _____
c. _____
d. _____
e. _____
f. _____
g. _____
h. _____

Answers

1. $x - 5$ **3.** $m + 6$ **5.** $p - 10$ **7.** $x - 8$ **9.** $x - 5y$

11. $(x + 3)(x + 5)$ **13.** $(x - 4)(x - 7)$ **15.** $(s + 10)(s + 3)$

17. $(a - 8)(a + 6)$ **19.** $(x - 1)(x - 7)$ **21.** $(m + 7)(m - 4)$

23. $(x - 10)(x + 4)$ **25.** $(x - 7)(x - 7)$ **27.** $(p - 12)(p + 2)$

29. $(x + 11)(x - 6)$ **31.** $(c + 4)(c + 15)$ **33.** $(n + 10)(n - 5)$

35. $(x + 2y)(x + 5y)$ **37.** $(a - 7b)(a + 6b)$ **39.** $(x - 5y)(x - 8y)$

41. $(b + 3a)(b + 3a)$ **43.** $(x - 4y)(x + 2y)$ **45.** $(5m + n)(5m + n)$

47. $3(a - 7)(a + 6)$ **49.** $r(r + 9)(r - 2)$ **51.** $2x(x - 12)(x + 2)$

53. $y(x - 12y)(x + 3y)$ **55.** $m(m - 5n)(m - 24n)$ **57.** 6 or 9

59. 8, 10, or 17   **61.** 4   **63.** 2   **65.** 3, 8, 15, 24, . . .   **a.** $4x^2 + 4x - 3$

b. $3a^2 + 11a - 4$ **c.** $2x^2 - 11x + 12$ **d.** $2w^2 - 7w - 22$

e. $2y^2 + 19y + 45$ **f.** $2x^2 - 23x - 12$ **g.** $2p^2 + 23p + 45$

h. $6a^2 + 2a - 20$

3.7 Difference of Squares and Perfect Square Trinomials

3.7 OBJECTIVES

1. Factor a binomial that is the difference of two squares
2. Factor a perfect square trinomial

In Section 3.3, we introduced some special products. Recall the following formula for the product of a sum and difference of two terms:

$$(a + b)(a - b) = a^2 - b^2 \qquad (1)$$

This also means that a binomial of the form $a^2 - b^2$, called a **difference of two squares,** has as its factors $a + b$ and $a - b$.

To use this idea for factoring, we can write

$$a^2 - b^2 = (a + b)(a - b) \qquad (2)$$

A **perfect square** term has a coefficient that is a square (1, 4, 9, 16, 25, 36, etc.), and any variables have exponents that are multiples of 2 (x^2, y^4, z^6, etc.).

Example 1

Identifying Perfect Square Terms

For each of the following, decide whether it is a perfect square term. If it is, find the expression that was squared (called the *root*).

(a) $36x$
(b) $24x^6$
(c) $9x^4$
(d) $64x^6$
(e) $16x^9$

Only parts c and d are perfect square terms.

$$9x^4 = (3x^2)^2$$

$$64x^6 = (8x^3)^2$$

 CHECK YOURSELF 1

For each of the following, decide whether it is a perfect square term. If it is, find the expression that was squared.

(a) $36x^{12}$ **(b)** $4x^6$
(c) $9x^7$ **(d)** $25x^8$
(e) $16x^{25}$

We will now use equation 2 above to factor the difference between two perfect square terms.

Example 2

Factoring the Difference of Two Squares

Factor $x^2 - 16$.

Think $x^2 - 4^2$

NOTE You could also write $(x - 4)(x + 4)$. The order doesn't matter because multiplication is commutative.

Because $x^2 - 16$ is a difference of squares, we have

$$x^2 - 16 = (x + 4)(x - 4)$$

 CHECK YOURSELF 2

Factor $m^2 - 49$.

Any time an expression is a difference of two squares, it can be factored.

Example 3

Factoring the Difference of Two Squares

Factor $4a^2 - 9$.

Think $(2a)^2 - 3^2$

So

$$4a^2 - 9 = (2a)^2 - (3)^2$$
$$= (2a + 3)(2a - 3)$$

 CHECK YOURSELF 3

Factor $9b^2 - 25$.

The process for factoring a difference of squares does not change when more than one variable is involved.

Example 4

Factoring the Difference of Two Squares

NOTE Think $(5a)^2 - (4b^2)^2$

Factor $25a^2 - 16b^4$.

$$25a^2 - 16b^4 = (5a + 4b^2)(5a - 4b^2)$$

 CHECK YOURSELF 4

Factor $49c^4 - 9d^2$.

We will now consider an example that combines common-term factoring with difference-of-squares factoring. Note that the common factor is always removed as the *first step.*

Example 5

Removing the GCF First

Factor $32x^2y - 18y^3$.

Note that $2y$ is a common factor, so

$$32x^2y - 18y^3 = 2y(\underbrace{16x^2 - 9y^2})$$

Difference of squares

$$= 2y(4x + 3y)(4x - 3y)$$

 CHECK YOURSELF 5

Factor $50a^3 - 8ab^2$.

Recall the following multiplication pattern.

 **CAUTION**

Note that this is different from
the sum of two squares (like
$x^2 + y^2$), which never has
integer factors.

$$(a + b)^2 = a^2 + 2ab + b^2$$

For example,

$$(x + 2)^2 = x^2 + 4x + 4$$

$$(x + 5)^2 = x^2 + 10x + 25$$

$$(2x + 1)^2 = 4x^2 + 4x + 1$$

Recognizing this pattern can simplify the process of factoring perfect square trinomials.

Example 6

Factoring a Perfect Square Trinomial

Factor the trinomial $4x^2 + 12xy + 9y^2$.

Note that this is a perfect square trinomial in which

$$a = 2x \quad \text{and} \quad b = 3y.$$

In factored form, we have

$$4x^2 + 12xy + 9y^2 = (2x + 3y)^2$$

 CHECK YOURSELF 6

Factor the trinomial $16u^2 + 24uv + 9v^2$.

Recognizing the same pattern can simplify the process of factoring perfect square trinomials in which the second term is negative.

Example 7

Factoring a Perfect Square Trinomial

Factor the trinomial $25x^2 - 10xy + y^2$.

This is also a perfect square trinomial, in which

$$a = 5x \quad \text{and} \quad b = -y.$$

In factored form, we have

$$25x^2 - 10xy + y^2 = (5x + (-y))^2 = (5x - y)^2$$

CHECK YOURSELF 7

Factor the trinomial $4u^2 - 12uv + 9v^2$.

CHECK YOURSELF ANSWERS

1. (a) $(6x^6)^2$; **(b)** $(2x^3)^2$; **(d)** $(5x^4)^2$ **2.** $(m + 7)(m - 7)$ **3.** $(3b + 5)(3b - 5)$
4. $(7c^2 + 3d)(7c^2 - 3d)$ **5.** $2a(5a + 2b)(5a - 2b)$ **6.** $(4u + 3v)^2$
7. $(2u - 3v)^2$

For each of the following binomials, state whether the binomial is a difference of squares.

1. $3x^2 + 2y^2$

2. $5x^2 - 7y^2$

3. $16a^2 - 25b^2$

4. $9n^2 - 16m^2$

5. $16r^2 + 4$

6. $p^2 - 45$

7. $16a^2 - 12b^3$

8. $9a^2b^2 - 16c^2d^2$

9. $a^2b^2 - 25$

10. $4a^3 - b^3$

Factor the following binomials.

11. $m^2 - n^2$

12. $r^2 - 9$

13. $x^2 - 49$

14. $c^2 - d^2$

15. $49 - y^2$

16. $81 - b^2$

17. $9b^2 - 16$

18. $36 - x^2$

19. $16w^2 - 49$

20. $4x^2 - 25$

21. $4s^2 - 9r^2$

22. $64y^2 - x^2$

23. $9w^2 - 49z^2$

24. $25x^2 - 81y^2$

ANSWERS

1. _____

2. _____

3. _____

4. _____

5. _____

6. _____

7. _____

8. _____

9. _____

10. _____

11. _____

12. _____

13. _____

14. _____

15. _____

16. _____

17. _____

18. _____

19. _____

20. _____

21. _____

22. _____

23. _____

24. _____

25. $16a^2 - 49b^2$

26. $64m^2 - 9n^2$

27. $x^4 - 36$

28. $y^6 - 49$

29. $x^2y^2 - 16$

30. $m^2n^2 - 64$

31. $25 - a^2b^2$

32. $49 - w^2z^2$

33. $r^4 - 4s^2$

34. $p^2 - 9q^4$

35. $81a^2 - 100b^6$

36. $64x^4 - 25y^4$

37. $18x^3 - 2xy^2$

38. $50a^2b - 2b^3$

39. $12m^3n - 75mn^3$

40. $63p^4 - 7p^2q^2$

41. $48a^2b^2 - 27b^4$

42. $20w^5 - 45w^3z^4$

Determine whether each of the following trinomials is a perfect square. If it is, factor the trinomial.

43. $x^2 - 14x + 49$

44. $x^2 + 9x + 16$

45. $x^2 - 18x - 81$

46. $x^2 + 10x + 25$

47. $x^2 - 18x + 81$

48. $x^2 - 24x + 48$

Factor the following trinomials.

49. $x^2 + 4x + 4$

50. $x^2 + 6x + 9$

51. $x^2 - 10x + 25$

52. $x^2 - 8x + 16$

53. $4x^2 + 12xy + 9y^2$

54. $16x^2 + 40xy + 25y^2$

55. $9x^2 - 24xy + 16y^2$

56. $9w^2 - 30wv + 25v^2$

57. $y^3 - 10y^2 + 25y$

58. $12b^3 - 12b^2 + 3b$

Factor each expression.

59. $x^2(x + y) - y^2(x + y)$

60. $a^2(b - c) - 16b^2(b - c)$

61. $2m^2(m - 2n) - 18n^2(m - 2n)$

62. $3a^3(2a + b) - 27ab^2(2a + b)$

63. Find a value for k so that $kx^2 - 25$ will have the factors $2x + 5$ and $2x - 5$.

64. Find a value for k so that $9m^2 - kn^2$ will have the factors $3m + 7n$ and $3m - 7n$.

65. Find a value for k so that $2x^3 - kxy^2$ will have the factors $2x$, $x - 3y$, and $x + 3y$.

66. Find a value for k so that $20a^3b - kab^3$ will have the factors $5ab$, $2a - 3b$, and $2a + 3b$.

67. Complete the following statement in complete sentences: "To factor a number you . . . ."

68. Complete this statement: To factor an algebraic expression into prime factors means . . . .

53. _____

54. _____

55. _____

56. _____

57. _____

58. _____

59. _____

60. _____

61. _____

62. _____

63. _____

64. _____

65. _____

66. _____

67. _____

68. _____

a. _____

b. _____

c. _____

d. _____

e. _____

Getting Ready

Factor.

(a) $2x(3x + 2) - 5(3x + 2)$

(b) $3y(y - 4) + 5(y - 4)$

(c) $3x(x + 2y) + y(x + 2y)$

(d) $5x(2x - y) - 3(2x - y)$

(e) $4x(2x - 5y) - 3y(2x - 5y)$

Answers

1. No   **3.** Yes   **5.** No   **7.** No   **9.** Yes   **11.** $(m + n)(m - n)$

13. $(x + 7)(x - 7)$ **15.** $(7 + y)(7 - y)$ **17.** $(3b + 4)(3b - 4)$

19. $(4w + 7)(4w - 7)$ **21.** $(2s + 3r)(2s - 3r)$ **23.** $(3w + 7z)(3w - 7z)$

25. $(4a + 7b)(4a - 7b)$ **27.** $(x^2 + 6)(x^2 - 6)$ **29.** $(xy + 4)(xy - 4)$

31. $(5 + ab)(5 - ab)$ **33.** $(r^2 + 2s)(r^2 - 2s)$ **35.** $(9a + 10b^3)(9a - 10b^3)$

37. $2x(3x + y)(3x - y)$ **39.** $3mn(2m + 5n)(2m - 5n)$

41. $3b^2(4a + 3b)(4a - 3b)$ **43.** Yes; $(x - 7)^2$ **45.** No   **47.** Yes; $(x - 9)^2$

49. $(x + 2)^2$ **51.** $(x - 5)^2$ **53.** $(2x + 3y)^2$ **55.** $(3x - 4y)^2$

57. $y(y - 5)^2$ **59.** $(x + y)^2(x - y)$ **61.** $2(m - 2n)(m + 3n)(m - 3n)$

63. 4   **65.** 18   **67.**   **a.** $(3x + 2)(2x - 5)$

b. $(y - 4)(3y + 5)$ **c.** $(x + 2y)(3x + y)$ **d.** $(2x - y)(5x - 3)$

e. $(2x - 5y)(4x - 3y)$

3.8 Factoring Trinomials of the Form $ax^2 + bx + c$

 OBJECTIVES

1. Factor a trinomial of the form $ax^2 + bx + c$
2. Completely factor a trinomial

Factoring trinomials is more time-consuming when the coefficient of the first term is not 1. Look at the following multiplication.

$(5x + 2)(2x + 3) = 10x^2 + 19x + 6$

Factors   Factors
of $10x^2$ of 6

Do you see the additional problem? We must consider all possible factors of the first coefficient (10 in the example) as well as those of the third term (6 in our example).

You need to form all possible combinations of factors and then check the middle term until the proper pair is found. Some call this process factoring by *trial and error.*

We can simplify the work a bit by reviewing the sign patterns.

Rules and Properties: Sign Patterns for Factoring Trinomials

NOTE Any time the leading coefficient is negative, factor out a negative one from the trinomial. This will leave one of these cases.

1. If all terms of a trinomial are positive, the signs between the terms in the binomial factors are both plus signs.
2. If the third term of the trinomial is positive and the middle term is negative, the signs between the terms in the binomial factors are both minus signs.
3. If the third term of the trinomial is negative, the signs between the terms in the binomial factors are opposite (one is + and one is −).

Example 1

Factoring a Trinomial

Factor $3x^2 + 14x + 15$.

First, list the possible factors of 3, the coefficient of the first term.

$3 = 1 \cdot 3$

Now list the factors of 15, the last term.

$15 = 1 \cdot 15$

$ = 3 \cdot 5$

Because the signs of the trinomial are all positive, we know any factors will have the form

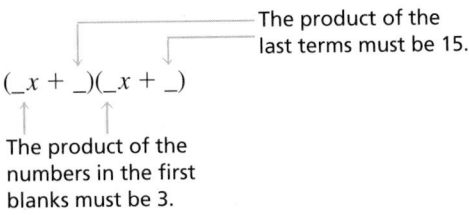

The product of the last terms must be 15.

$(\_x + \_)(\_x + \_)$

The product of the numbers in the first blanks must be 3.

© 2001 McGraw-Hill Companies

485

So the following are the possible factors and the corresponding middle terms:

Possible Factors	Middle Terms
$(x + 1)(3x + 15)$	$18x$
$(x + 15)(3x + 1)$	$46x$
$(3x + 3)(x + 5)$	$18x$
$(3x + 5)(x + 3)$	$14x$

The correct middle term

NOTE Take the time to multiply the binomial factors. This habit will ensure that you have an expression equivalent to the original problem.

So

$$3x^2 + 14x + 15 = (3x + 5)(x + 3)$$

 CHECK YOURSELF 1

Factor.

(a) $5x^2 + 14x + 8$ **(b)** $3x^2 + 20x + 12$

Example 2

Factoring a Trinomial

Factor $4x^2 - 11x + 6$.

Because only the middle term is negative, we know the factors have the form

$$(\_x - \_)(\_x - \_)$$

Both signs are negative.

Now look at the factors of the first coefficient and the last term.

$$4 = 1 \cdot 4 \qquad 6 = 1 \cdot 6$$
$$= 2 \cdot 2 \qquad = 2 \cdot 3$$

This gives us the possible factors:

Possible Factors	Middle Terms
$(x - 1)(4x - 6)$	$-10x$
$(x - 6)(4x - 1)$	$-25x$
$(x - 2)(4x - 3)$	$-11x$

The correct middle term

NOTE Again, at least mentally, check your work by multiplying the factors.

Note that, in this example, we *stopped* as soon as the correct pair of factors was found. So

$$4x^2 - 11x + 6 = (x - 2)(4x - 3)$$

 CHECK YOURSELF 2

Factor.

(a) $2x^2 - 9x + 9$ **(b)** $6x^2 - 17x + 10$

Let's factor a trinomial whose last term is negative.

Example 3

Factoring a Trinomial

Factor $5x^2 + 6x - 8$.

Because the last term is negative, the factors have the form

$$(\_x + \_)(\_x - \_)$$

Consider the factors of the first coefficient and the last term.

$$5 = 1 \cdot 5 \qquad 8 = 1 \cdot 8$$
$$= 2 \cdot 4$$

The possible factors are then

Possible Factors	Middle Terms
$(x + 1)(5x - 8)$	$-3x$
$(x + 8)(5x - 1)$	$39x$
$(5x + 1)(x - 8)$	$-39x$
$(5x + 8)(x - 1)$	$3x$
$(x + 2)(5x - 4)$	$6x$

Again we stop as soon as the correct pair of factors is found.

$$5x^2 + 6x - 8 = (x + 2)(5x - 4)$$

 CHECK YOURSELF 3

Factor $4x^2 + 5x - 6$.

The same process is used to factor a trinomial with more than one variable.

Example 4

Factoring a Trinomial

Factor $6x^2 + 7xy - 10y^2$.

The form of the factors must be

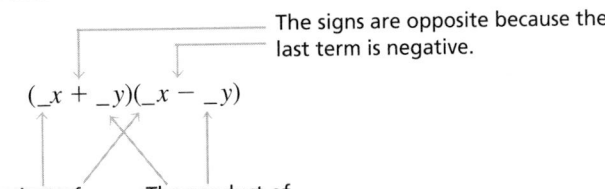

The signs are opposite because the last term is negative.

$$(\_x + \_y)(\_x - \_y)$$

The product of the first terms is an x^2 term.

The product of the second terms is a y^2 term.

Again look at the factors of the first and last coefficients.

$$6 = 1 \cdot 6 \qquad 10 = 1 \cdot 10$$
$$= 2 \cdot 3 \qquad\quad = 2 \cdot 5$$

NOTE Be certain that you have
a pattern that matches up every
possible pair of coefficients.

Possible Factors	Middle Terms
$(x + y)(6x - 10y)$	$-4xy$
$(x + 10y)(6x - y)$	$59xy$
$(6x + y)(x - 10y)$	$-59xy$
$(6x + 10y)(x - y)$	$4xy$
$(x + 2y)(6x - 5y)$	$7xy$

Once more, we stop as soon as the correct factors are found.

$$6x^2 + 7xy - 10y^2 = (x + 2y)(6x - 5y)$$

 CHECK YOURSELF 4

Factor $15x^2 - 4xy - 4y^2$.

The next example illustrates a special kind of trinomial called a *perfect square trinomial*.

Example 5

Factoring a Trinomial

Factor $9x^2 + 12xy + 4y^2$.

Because all terms are positive, the form of the factors must be

$$(\_x + \_y)(\_x + \_y)$$

Consider the factors of the first and last coefficients.

$$9 = 9 \cdot 1 \qquad 4 = 4 \cdot 1$$
$$= 3 \cdot 3 \qquad\quad = 2 \cdot 2$$

Possible Factors	Middle Terms
$(x + y)(9x + 4y)$	$13xy$
$(x + 4y)(9x + y)$	$37xy$
$(3x + 2y)(3x + 2y)$	$12xy$

So

NOTE Perfect square trinomials
can be factored by using
previous methods. Recognizing
the special pattern simply saves
time.

$$9x^2 + 12xy + 4y^2 = (3x + 2y)(3x + 2y)$$
$$= (3x + 2y)^2$$

Square $2(3x)(2y)$ Square
of $3x$ of $2y$

This trinomial is the result of squaring a binomial, thus the special name of perfect square trinomial.

 CHECK YOURSELF 5

Factor.

(a) $4x^2 + 28x + 49$

(b) $16x^2 - 40xy + 25y^2$

Before we look at our next example, let's review one important point. Recall that when you factor trinomials, you should not forget to look for a common factor as the first step. If there is a common factor, remove it and factor the remaining trinomial as before.

Example 6

Factoring a Trinomial

Factor $18x^2 - 18x + 4$.

First look for a common factor in all three terms. Here that factor is 2, so write

$$18x^2 - 18x + 4 = 2(9x^2 - 9x + 2)$$

By our earlier methods, we can factor the remaining trinomial as

NOTE If you don't see why this is true, you need to use your pencil to work it out before you move on!

$$9x^2 - 9x + 2 = (3x - 1)(3x - 2)$$

So

$$18x^2 - 18x + 4 = 2(3x - 1)(3x - 2)$$

Don't forget the 2 that was factored out!

 CHECK YOURSELF 6

Factor $16x^2 + 44x - 12$.

Let's look at an example in which the common factor includes a variable.

Example 7

Factoring a Trinomial

Factor

$$6x^3 + 10x^2 - 4x$$

The common factor is $2x$.

So

$$6x^3 + 10x^2 - 4x = 2x(3x^2 + 5x - 2)$$

Because

$$3x^2 + 5x - 2 = (3x - 1)(x + 2)$$

we have

NOTE Remember to include the monomial factor.

$$6x^3 + 10x^2 - 4x = 2x(3x - 1)(x + 2)$$

 CHECK YOURSELF 7

Factor $6x^3 - 27x^2 + 30x$.

You have now had a chance to work with a variety of factoring techniques. Your success in factoring polynomials depends on your ability to recognize when to use which technique. Here are some guidelines to help you apply the factoring methods you have studied in this chapter.

Step by Step: Factoring Polynomials

Step 1   Look for a greatest common factor other than 1. If such a factor exists, factor out the GCF.

Step 2   If the polynomial that remains is a *trinomial*, try to factor the trinomial by the trial-and-error methods.

The following example illustrates the use of this strategy.

Example 8

Factoring a Trinomial

(a) Factor $5m^2n + 20n$.

First, we see that the GCF is $5n$. Removing that factor gives

$$5m^2n + 20n = 5n(m^2 + 4)$$

(b) Factor $3x^3 - 24x^2 + 48x$.

First, we see that the GCF is $3x$. Factoring out $3x$ yields

$$3x^3 - 24x^2 + 48x = 3x(x^2 - 8x + 16)$$
$$= 3x(x - 4)(x - 4)$$

(c) Factor $8r^2s + 20rs^2 - 12s^3$.

First, the GCF is $4s$, and we can write the original polynomial as

$$8r^2s + 20rs^2 - 12s^3 = 4s(2r^2 + 5rs - 3s^2)$$

Because the remaining polynomial is a trinomial, we can use the trial-and-error method to complete the factoring as

$$8r^2s + 20rs^2 - 12s^3 = 4s(2r - s)(r + 3s)$$

 CHECK YOURSELF 8

Factor the following polynomials.

(a) $8a^3 + 32a^2b + 32ab^2$ **(b)** $7x^3 + 7x^2y - 42xy^2$ **(c)** $5m^4 + 15m^3 + 5m^2$

CHECK YOURSELF ANSWERS

1. (a) $(5x + 4)(x + 2)$; **(b)** $(3x + 2)(x + 6)$ **2. (a)** $(2x - 3)(x - 3)$;
(b) $(6x - 5)(x - 2)$ **3.** $(4x - 3)(x + 2)$ **4.** $(3x - 2y)(5x + 2y)$
5. (a) $(2x + 7)^2$; **(b)** $(4x - 5y)^2$ **6.** $4(4x - 1)(x + 3)$ **7.** $3x(2x - 5)(x - 2)$
8. (a) $8a(a + 2b)(a + 2b)$; **(b)** $7x(x + 3y)(x - 2y)$; **(c)** $5m^2(m^2 + 3m + 1)$

Exercises

Name _____

Section _____ Date _____

Complete each of the following statements.

1. $4x^2 - 4x - 3 = (2x + 1)(\quad)$

2. $3w^2 + 11w - 4 = (w + 4)(\quad)$

3. $6a^2 + 13a + 6 = (2a + 3)(\quad)$

4. $25y^2 - 10y + 1 = (5y - 1)(\quad)$

5. $15x^2 - 16x + 4 = (3x - 2)(\quad)$

6. $6m^2 + 5m - 4 = (3m + 4)(\quad)$

7. $16a^2 + 8ab + b^2 = (4a + b)(\quad)$

8. $6x^2 + 5xy - 4y^2 = (3x + 4y)(\quad)$

9. $4m^2 + 5mn - 6n^2 = (m + 2n)(\quad)$

10. $10p^2 - pq - 3q^2 = (5p - 3q)(\quad)$

Factor each of the following polynomials.

11. $3x^2 + 7x + 2$

12. $5y^2 + 8y + 3$

13. $2w^2 + 13w + 15$

14. $3x^2 - 16x + 21$

15. $5x^2 - 16x + 3$

16. $2a^2 + 7a + 5$

17. $4x^2 - 12x + 5$

18. $2x^2 + 11x + 12$

19. $3x^2 - 5x - 2$

20. $4m^2 - 23m + 15$

21. $4p^2 + 19p - 5$

22. $5x^2 - 36x + 7$

23. $6x^2 + 19x + 10$

24. $6x^2 - 7x - 3$

ANSWERS

1. _____
2. _____
3. _____
4. _____
5. _____
6. _____
7. _____
8. _____
9. _____
10. _____
11. _____
12. _____
13. _____
14. _____
15. _____
16. _____
17. _____
18. _____
19. _____
20. _____
21. _____
22. _____
23. _____
24. _____

25.

26.

27.

28.

29.

30.

31.

32.

33.

34.

35.

36.

37.

38.

39.

40.

41.

42.

43.

44.

45.

46.

47.

48.

25. $15x^2 + x - 6$

26. $12w^2 + 19w + 4$

27. $6m^2 + 25m - 25$

28. $8x^2 - 6x - 9$

29. $9x^2 - 12x + 4$

30. $20x^2 - 23x + 6$

31. $12x^2 - 8x - 15$

32. $16a^2 + 40a + 25$

33. $3y^2 + 7y - 6$

34. $12x^2 + 11x - 15$

35. $8x^2 - 27x - 20$

36. $24v^2 + 5v - 36$

37. $2x^2 + 3xy + y^2$

38. $3x^2 - 5xy + 2y^2$

39. $5a^2 - 8ab - 4b^2$

40. $5x^2 + 7xy - 6y^2$

41. $9x^2 + 4xy - 5y^2$

42. $16x^2 + 32xy + 15y^2$

43. $6m^2 - 17mn + 12n^2$

44. $15x^2 - xy - 6y^2$

45. $36a^2 - 3ab - 5b^2$

46. $3q^2 - 17qr - 6r^2$

47. $x^2 + 4xy + 4y^2$

48. $25b^2 - 80bc + 64c^2$

Factor each of the following polynomials completely.

49. $20x^2 - 20x - 15$

50. $24x^2 - 18x - 6$

51. $8m^2 + 12m + 4$

52. $14x^2 - 20x + 6$

53. $15r^2 - 21rs + 6s^2$

54. $10x^2 + 5xy - 30y^2$

55. $2x^3 - 2x^2 - 4x$

56. $2y^3 + y^2 - 3y$

57. $2y^4 + 5y^3 + 3y^2$

58. $4z^3 - 18z^2 - 10z$

59. $36a^3 - 66a^2 + 18a$

60. $20n^4 - 22n^3 - 12n^2$

61. $9p^2 + 30pq + 21q^2$

62. $12x^2 + 2xy - 24y^2$

Factor each of the following polynomials completely.

63. $10(x + y)^2 - 11(x + y) - 6$

64. $8(a - b)^2 + 14(a - b) - 15$

65. $5(x - 1)^2 - 15(x - 1) - 350$

66. $3(x + 1)^2 - 6(x + 1) - 45$

67. $15 + 29x - 48x^2$

68. $12 + 4a - 21a^2$

69. $-6x^2 + 19x - 15$

70. $-3s^2 - 10s + 8$

ANSWERS

49. _____
50. _____
51. _____
52. _____
53. _____
54. _____
55. _____
56. _____
57. _____
58. _____
59. _____
60. _____
61. _____
62. _____
63. _____
64. _____
65. _____
66. _____
67. _____
68. _____
69. _____
70. _____

Getting Ready

Multiply.

(a) $(x - 1)(x + 1)$

(b) $(a + 7)(a - 7)$

(c) $(x - y)(x + y)$

(d) $(2x - 5)(2x + 5)$

(e) $(3a - b)(3a + b)$

(f) $(5a - 4b)(5a + 4b)$

Answers

1. $2x - 3$　　**3.** $3a + 2$　　**5.** $5x - 2$　　**7.** $4a + b$　　**9.** $4m - 3n$

11. $(3x + 1)(x + 2)$　　**13.** $(2w + 3)(w + 5)$　　**15.** $(5x - 1)(x - 3)$

17. $(2x - 5)(2x - 1)$　　**19.** $(3x + 1)(x - 2)$　　**21.** $(4p - 1)(p + 5)$

23. $(3x + 2)(2x + 5)$　　**25.** $(5x - 3)(3x + 2)$　　**27.** $(6m - 5)(m + 5)$

29. $(3x - 2)(3x - 2)$　　**31.** $(6x + 5)(2x - 3)$　　**33.** $(3y - 2)(y + 3)$

35. $(8x + 5)(x - 4)$　　**37.** $(2x + y)(x + y)$　　**39.** $(5a + 2b)(a - 2b)$

41. $(9x - 5y)(x + y)$　　**43.** $(3m - 4n)(2m - 3n)$　　**45.** $(12a - 5b)(3a + b)$

47. $(x + 2y)^2$　　**49.** $5(2x - 3)(2x + 1)$　　**51.** $4(2m + 1)(m + 1)$

53. $3(5r - 2s)(r - s)$　　**55.** $2x(x - 2)(x + 1)$　　**57.** $y^2(2y + 3)(y + 1)$

59. $6a(3a - 1)(2a - 3)$　　**61.** $3(p + q)(3p + 7q)$

63. $(5x + 5y + 2)(2x + 2y - 3)$　　**65.** $5(x - 11)(x + 6)$

67. $(1 + 3x)(15 - 16x)$　　**69.** $(3x - 5)(-2x + 3)$　　**a.** $x^2 - 1$

b. $a^2 - 49$　　**c.** $x^2 - y^2$　　**d.** $4x^2 - 25$　　**e.** $9a^2 - b^2$　　**f.** $25a^2 - 16b^2$

3.9 **Using the *ac* Method to Factor**

1. Use the *ac* test to determine factorability
2. Use the results of the *ac* test
3. Completely factor a trinomial

We have used the trial-and-error method to factor trinomials. We also learned that not all trinomials can be factored. In this section we will look at the same kinds of trinomials, but in a slightly different context. We first determine whether a trinomial is factorable. We then use the results of that analysis to factor the trinomial.

   Some students prefer the trial-and-error method for factoring. Other students prefer the method of this section (called the *ac* method) because it yields the answer in a systematic way. We will let you determine which method you prefer.

   We will begin by looking at some factored trinomials.

Example 1

Matching Trinomials and Their Factors

Determine which of the following are true statements.

(a) $x^2 - 2x - 8 = (x - 4)(x + 2)$

This is a true statement. Using the FOIL method, we see that

$$(x - 4)(x + 2) = x^2 + 2x - 4x - 8$$
$$= x^2 - 2x - 8$$

(b) $x^2 + 6x + 5 = (x + 2)(x + 3)$

This is not a true statement.

$$(x + 2)(x + 3) = x^2 + 3x + 2x + 6 = x^2 + 5x + 6$$

(c) $x^2 + 5x - 14 = (x - 2)(x + 7)$

This is true: $(x - 2)(x + 7) = x^2 + 7x - 2x - 14 = x^2 + 5x - 14$

(d) $x^2 - 8x - 15 = (x - 5)(x - 3)$

This is false: $(x - 5)(x - 3) = x^2 - 3x - 5x + 15 = x^2 - 8x + 15$

 CHECK YOURSELF 1

Determine which of the following are true statements.

(a) $2x^2 - 2x - 3 = (2x - 3)(x + 1)$
(b) $3x^2 + 11x - 4 = (3x - 1)(x + 4)$
(c) $2x^2 - 7x + 3 = (x - 3)(2x - 1)$

The first step in learning to factor a trinomial is to identify its coefficients. So that we are consistent, we first write the trinomial in standard $ax^2 + bx + c$ form, then label the three coefficients as a, b, and c.

Example 2

Identifying the Coefficients of $ax^2 + bx + c$

First, when necessary, rewrite the trinomial in $ax^2 + bx + c$ form. Then give the values for a, b, and c, in which a is the coefficient of the x^2 term, b is the coefficient of the x term, and c is the constant.

(a) $x^2 - 3x - 18$

$a = 1 \qquad b = -3 \qquad c = -18$

NOTE Notice that the negative sign is attached to the coefficients.

(b) $x^2 - 24x + 23$

$a = 1 \qquad b = -24 \qquad c = 23$

(c) $x^2 + 8 - 11x$

First rewrite the trinomial in descending order:

$x^2 - 11x + 8$

$a = 1 \qquad b = -11 \qquad c = 8$

 CHECK YOURSELF 2

First, when necessary, rewrite the trinomials in $ax^2 + bx + c$ form. Then label a, b, and c, in which a is the coefficient of the x^2 term, b is the coefficient of the x term, and c is the constant.

(a) $x^2 + 5x - 14$ **(b)** $x^2 - 18x + 17$ **(c)** $x - 6 + 2x^2$

Not all trinomials can be factored. To discover if a trinomial is factorable, we try the *ac* **test.**

Definitions: The *ac* Test

A trinomial of the form $ax^2 + bx + c$ is factorable if (and only if) there are two integers, m and n, such that

$$ac = mn \qquad \text{and} \qquad b = m + n$$

In Example 3 we will look for m and n to determine whether each trinomial is factorable.

Example 3

Using the *ac* Test

Use the *ac* test to determine which of the following trinomials can be factored. Find the values of m and n for each trinomial that can be factored.

(a) $x^2 - 3x - 18$

First, we find the values of a, b, and c, so that we can find ac.

$$a = 1 \qquad b = -3 \qquad c = -18$$

$$ac = 1(-18) = -18 \qquad \text{and} \qquad b = -3$$

Then, we look for two numbers, m and n, such that $mn = ac$, and $m + n = b$. In this case, that means

$$mn = -18 \qquad \text{and} \qquad m + n = -3$$

We now look at all pairs of integers with a product of -18. We then look at the sum of each pair of integers, looking for a sum of -3.

mn	*m + n*	
$1(-18) = -18$	$1 + (-18) = -17$	
$2(-9) = -18$	$2 + (-9) \;\; = \;\; -7$	We need look no further
$3(-6) = -18$	$3 + (-6) \;\; = \;\; -3$	than 3 and -6.
$6(-3) = -18$		
$9(-2) = -18$		
$18(-1) = -18$		

3 and -6 are the two integers with a product of ac and a sum of b. We can say that

$$m = 3 \qquad \text{and} \qquad n = -6$$

NOTE We could have chosen $m = -6$ and $n = 3$ as well.

Because we found values for m and n, we know that $x^2 - 3x - 18$ is factorable.

(b) $x^2 - 24x + 23$

We find that

$$a = 1 \qquad b = -24 \qquad c = 23$$

$$ac = 1(23) = 23 \qquad \text{and} \qquad b = -24$$

So

$$mn = 23 \qquad \text{and} \qquad m + n = -24$$

We now calculate integer pairs, looking for two numbers with a product of 23 and a sum of -24.

mn	*m + n*
$1(23) = 23$	$1 + 23 = 24$
$-1(-23) = 23$	$-1 + (-23) = -24$

$$m = -1 \qquad \text{and} \qquad n = -23$$

So, $x^2 - 24x + 23$ is factorable.

(c) $x^2 - 11x + 8$

We find that $a = 1$, $b = -11$, and $c = 8$. Therefore, $ac = 8$ and $b = -11$. Thus $mn = 8$ and $m + n = -11$. We calculate integer pairs:

mn	$m + n$
$1(8) = 8$	$1 + 8 = 9$
$2(4) = 8$	$2 + 4 = 6$
$-1(-8) = 8$	$-1 + (-8) = -9$
$-2(-4) = 8$	$-2 + (-4) = -6$

There are no other pairs of integers with a product of 8, and none of these pairs has a sum of -11. The trinomial $x^2 - 11x + 8$ is not factorable.

(d) $2x^2 + 7x - 15$

We find that $a = 2$, $b = 7$, and $c = -15$. Therefore, $ac = 2(-15) = -30$ and $b = 7$. Thus $mn = -30$ and $m + n = 7$. We calculate integer pairs:

mn	$m + n$
$1(-30) = -30$	$1 + (-30) = -29$
$2(-15) = -30$	$2 + (-15) = -13$
$3(-10) = -30$	$3 + (-10) = -7$
$5(-6) = -30$	$5 + (-6) = -1$
$6(-5) = -30$	$6 + (-5) = 1$
$10(-3) = -30$	$10 + (-3) = 7$

There is no need to go any further. We see that 10 and -3 have a product of -30 and a sum of 7, so

$$m = 10 \quad \text{and} \quad n = -3$$

Therefore, $2x^2 + 7x - 15$ is factorable.

   It is not always necessary to evaluate all the products and sums to determine whether a trinomial is factorable. You may have noticed patterns and shortcuts that make it easier to find m and n. By all means, use them to help you find m and n. This is essential in mathematical thinking. You are taught a mathematical process that will always work for solving a problem. Such a process is called an **algorithm.** It is very easy to teach a computer to use an algorithm. It is very difficult (some would say impossible) for a computer to have insight. Shortcuts that you discover are *insights*. They may be the most important part of your mathematical education.

✔ CHECK YOURSELF 3

Use the ac test to determine which of the following trinomials can be factored. Find the values of m and n for each trinomial that can be factored.

(a) $x^2 - 7x + 12$ **(b)** $x^2 + 5x - 14$

(c) $3x^2 - 6x + 7$ **(d)** $2x^2 + x - 6$

So far we have used the results of the *ac* test only to determine whether a trinomial is factorable. The results can also be used to help factor the trinomial.

How to factor the quadratic $ax^2 + bx + c$

Step 1 Identify a, b, and c in the given quadratic

Step 2 Apply the ac test to find factors (call them m & n) of ac whose sum is b

Step 3 Use the factors m & n to rewrite the middle term

Step 4 Use "factoring by grouping" to find the GCF of each pair of terms

Step 5 Finally, factor out the common binomial factor

Not all possible product pairs need to be tried to find m and n. A look at the sign pattern of the trinomial will eliminate many of the possibilities. Assuming the leading coefficient is positive, there are four possible sign patterns.

Pattern	Example	Conclusion
1. b and c are both positive.	$2x^2 + 13x + 15$	m and n must both be positive.
2. b is negative and c is positive.	$x^2 - 7x + 12$	m and n must both be negative.
3. b is positive and c is negative.	$x^2 + 3x - 10$	m and n are of opposite signs. (The value with the larger absolute value is positive.)
4. b is negative and c is negative.	$x^2 - 3x - 10$	m and n are of opposite signs. (The value with the larger absolute value is negative.)

Example 4

Using the Results of the *ac* Test to Factor

Rewrite the middle term as the sum of two terms, then factor by grouping.

(a) $x^2 - 3x - 18$

We find that $a = 1$, $b = -3$, and $c = -18$, so $ac = -18$ and $b = -3$. We are looking for two numbers, m and n, where $mn = -18$ and $m + n = -3$. In Example 3, part a, we looked at every pair of integers whose product (mn) was -18, to find a pair that had a sum ($m + n$) of -3. We found the two integers to be 3 and -6, because $3(-6) = -18$ and $3 + (-6) = -3$, so $m = 3$ and $n = -6$. We now use that result to rewrite the middle term as the sum of $3x$ and $-6x$.

$x^2 + 3x - 6x - 18$

We then factor by grouping:

$x^2 + 3x - 6x - 18 = x(x + 3) - 6(x + 3)$

$$= (x + 3)(x - 6)$$

(b) $x^2 - 24x + 23$

We use the results from Example 3, part b, in which we found $m = -1$ and $n = -23$, to rewrite the middle term of the equation.

$x^2 - 24x + 23 = x^2 - x - 23x + 23$

Then we factor by grouping:

$$x^2 - x - 23x + 23 = (x^2 - x) - (23x - 23)$$

$$= x(x - 1) - 23(x - 1)$$

$$= (x - 1)(x - 23)$$

(c) $2x^2 + 7x - 15$

From Example 3, part d, we know that this trinomial is factorable, and $m = 10$ and $n = -3$. We use that result to rewrite the middle term of the trinomial.

$$2x^2 + 7x - 15 = 2x^2 + 10x - 3x - 15$$

$$= (2x^2 + 10x) - (3x + 15)$$

$$= 2x(x + 5) - 3(x + 5)$$

$$= (x + 5)(2x - 3)$$

Careful readers will note that we did not ask you to factor Example 3, part c, $x^2 - 11x + 8$. Recall that, by the *ac* method, we determined that this trinomial was not factorable.

 CHECK YOURSELF 4

Use the results of Check Yourself 3 to rewrite the middle term as the sum of two terms, then factor by grouping.

(a) $x^2 - 7x + 12$ **(b)** $x^2 + 5x - 14$ **(c)** $2x^2 + x - 6$

   Let's look at some examples that require us to first find m and n, then factor the trinomial.

Example 5

Rewriting Middle Terms to Factor

Rewrite the middle term as the sum of two terms, then factor by grouping.

(a) $2x^2 - 13x - 7$

We find that $a = 2$, $b = -13$, and $c = -7$, so $mn = ac = -14$ and $m + n = b = -13$. Therefore,

mn	*m + n*
$1(-14) = -14$	$1 + (-14) = -13$

So, $m = 1$ and $n = -14$. We rewrite the middle term of the trinomial as follows:

$$2x^2 - 13x - 7 = 2x^2 + x - 14x - 7$$

$$= (2x^2 + x) - (14x + 7)$$

$$= x(2x + 1) - 7(2x + 1)$$

$$= (2x + 1)(x - 7)$$

(b) $6x^2 - 5x - 6$

We find that $a = 6$, $b = -5$, and $c = -6$, so $mn = ac = -36$ and $m + n = b = -5$.

mn	m + n
$1(-36) = -36$	$1 + (-36) = -35$
$2(-18) = -36$	$2 + (-18) = -16$
$3(-12) = -36$	$3 + (-12) = -9$
$4(-9) = -36$	$4 + (-9) = -5$

So, $m = 4$ and $n = -9$. We rewrite the middle term of the trinomial:

$$6x^2 - 5x - 6 = 6x^2 + 4x - 9x - 6$$

$$= (6x^2 + 4x) - (9x + 6)$$

$$= 2x(3x + 2) - 3(3x + 2)$$

$$= (3x + 2)(2x - 3)$$

 CHECK YOURSELF 5

Rewrite the middle term as the sum of two terms, then factor by grouping.

(a) $2x^2 - 7x - 15$ **(b)** $6x^2 - 5x - 4$

Be certain to check trinomials and binomial factors for any common monomial factor. (There is no common factor in the binomial unless it is also a common factor in the original trinomial.) Example 6 shows the removal of monomial factors.

Example 6

Removing Common Factors

Completely factor the trinomial.

$3x^2 + 12x - 15$

We could first remove the common factor of 3:

$$3x^2 + 12x - 15 = 3(x^2 + 4x - 5)$$

Finding m and n for the trinomial $x^2 + 4x - 5$ yields $mn = -5$ and $m + n = 4$.

mn	m + n
$1(-5) = -5$	$1 + (-5) = -4$
$5(-1) = -5$	$-1 + (5) = 4$

So, $m = 5$ and $n = -1$. This gives us

$$3x^2 + 12x - 15 = 3(x^2 + 4x - 5)$$
$$= 3(x^2 + 5x - x - 5)$$
$$= 3[(x^2 + 5x) - (x + 5)]$$
$$= 3[x(x + 5) - (x + 5)]$$
$$= 3[(x + 5)(x - 1)]$$
$$= 3(x + 5)(x - 1)$$

✔ CHECK YOURSELF 6

Completely factor the trinomial.

$6x^3 + 3x^2 - 18x$

CHECK YOURSELF ANSWERS

1. (a) False; **(b)** true; **(c)** true   **2. (a)** $a = 1, b = 5, c = -14$;
(b) $a = 1, b = -18, c = 17$; **(c)** $a = 2, b = 1, c = -6$
3. (a) Factorable, $m = -3, n = -4$; **(b)** factorable, $m = 7, n = -2$;
(c) not factorable; **(d)** factorable, $m = 4, n = -3$
4. (a) $x^2 - 3x - 4x + 12 = (x - 3)(x - 4)$;
(b) $x^2 + 7x - 2x - 14 = (x + 7)(x - 2)$;
(c) $2x^2 + 4x - 3x - 6 = (2x - 3)(x + 2)$
5. (a) $2x^2 - 10x + 3x - 15 = (2x + 3)(x - 5)$;
(b) $6x^2 - 8x + 3x - 4 = (3x - 4)(2x + 1)$ **6.** $3x(2x - 3)(x + 2)$

3.9 Exercises

State whether each of the following is true or false.

1. $x^2 + 2x - 3 = (x + 3)(x - 1)$

2. $y^2 - 3y - 18 = (y - 6)(y + 3)$

3. $x^2 - 10x - 24 = (x - 6)(x + 4)$

4. $a^2 + 9a - 36 = (a - 12)(a + 4)$

5. $x^2 - 16x + 64 = (x - 8)(x - 8)$

6. $w^2 - 12w - 45 = (w - 9)(w - 5)$

7. $25y^2 - 10y + 1 = (5y - 1)(5y + 1)$

8. $6x^2 + 5xy - 4y^2 = (6x - 2y)(x + 2y)$

9. $10p^2 - pq - 3q^2 = (5p - 3q)(2p + q)$

10. $6a^2 + 13a + 6 = (2a + 3)(3a + 2)$

For each of the following trinomials, label a, b, and c.

11. $x^2 + 4x - 9$

12. $x^2 + 5x + 11$

13. $x^2 - 3x + 8$

14. $x^2 + 7x - 15$

15. $3x^2 + 5x - 8$

16. $2x^2 + 7x - 9$

17. $4x^2 + 8x + 11$

18. $5x^2 + 7x - 9$

19. $-3x^2 + 5x - 10$

20. $-7x^2 + 9x - 18$

21. _____

22. _____

23. _____

24. _____

25. _____

26. _____

27. _____

28. _____

29. _____

30. _____

31. _____

32. _____

33. _____

34. _____

35. _____

36. _____

37. _____

38. _____

39. _____

40. _____

41. _____

42. _____

43. _____

44. _____

Use the *ac* test to determine which of the following trinomials can be factored. Find the values of *m* and *n* for each trinomial that can be factored.

21. $x^2 + x - 6$

22. $x^2 + 2x - 15$

23. $x^2 + x + 2$

24. $x^2 - 3x + 7$

25. $x^2 - 5x + 6$

26. $x^2 - x + 2$

27. $2x^2 + 5x - 3$

28. $3x^2 - 14x - 5$

29. $6x^2 - 19x + 10$

30. $4x^2 + 5x + 6$

Rewrite the middle term as the sum of two terms and then factor by grouping.

31. $x^2 + 6x + 8$

32. $x^2 + 3x - 10$

33. $x^2 - 9x + 20$

34. $x^2 - 8x + 15$

35. $x^2 - 2x - 63$

36. $x^2 + 6x - 55$

Rewrite the middle term as the sum of two terms and then factor completely.

37. $x^2 + 8x + 15$

38. $x^2 - 11x + 24$

39. $x^2 - 11x + 28$

40. $y^2 - y - 20$

41. $s^2 + 13s + 30$

42. $b^2 + 14b + 33$

43. $a^2 - 2a - 48$

44. $x^2 - 17x + 60$

45. $x^2 - 8x + 7$

46. $x^2 + 7x - 18$

47. $x^2 - 6x - 40$

48. $x^2 - 11x + 10$

49. $x^2 - 14x + 49$

50. $s^2 - 4s - 32$

51. $p^2 - 10p - 24$

52. $x^2 - 11x - 60$

53. $x^2 + 5x - 66$

54. $a^2 + 2a - 80$

55. $c^2 + 19c + 60$

56. $t^2 - 4t - 60$

57. $n^2 + 5n - 50$

58. $x^2 - 16x + 63$

59. $x^2 + 7xy + 10y^2$

60. $x^2 - 8xy + 12y^2$

61. $a^2 - ab - 42b^2$

62. $m^2 - 8mn + 16n^2$

63. $x^2 - 13xy + 40y^2$

64. $r^2 - 9rs - 36s^2$

65. $6x^2 + 19x + 10$

66. $6x^2 - 7x - 3$

67. $15x^2 + x - 6$

68. $12w^2 + 19w + 4$

69. $6m^2 + 25m - 25$

70. $8x^2 - 6x - 9$

71. $9x^2 - 12x + 4$

72. $20x^2 - 23x + 6$

45. _____
46. _____
47. _____
48. _____
49. _____
50. _____
51. _____
52. _____
53. _____
54. _____
55. _____
56. _____
57. _____
58. _____
59. _____
60. _____
61. _____
62. _____
63. _____
64. _____
65. _____
66. _____
67. _____
68. _____
69. _____
70. _____
71. _____
72. _____

73. _____

74. _____

75. _____

76. _____

77. _____

78. _____

79. _____

80. _____

81. _____

82. _____

83. _____

84. _____

85. _____

86. _____

87. _____

88. _____

89. _____

90. _____

91. _____

92. _____

93. _____

94. _____

73. $12x^2 - 8x - 15$

74. $16a^2 + 40a + 25$

75. $3y^2 + 7y - 6$

76. $12x^2 + 11x - 15$

77. $8x^2 - 27x - 20$

78. $24v^2 + 5v - 36$

79. $2x^2 + 3xy + y^2$

80. $3x^2 - 5xy + 2y^2$

81. $5a^2 - 8ab - 4b^2$

82. $5x^2 + 7xy - 6y^2$

83. $9x^2 + 4xy - 5y^2$

84. $16x^2 + 32xy + 15y^2$

85. $6m^2 - 17mn + 12n^2$

86. $15x^2 - xy - 6y^2$

87. $36a^2 - 3ab - 5b^2$

88. $3q^2 - 17qr - 6r^2$

89. $x^2 + 4xy + 4y^2$

90. $25b^2 - 80bc + 64c^2$

91. $20x^2 - 20x - 15$

92. $24x^2 - 18x - 6$

93. $8m^2 + 12m + 4$

94. $14x^2 - 20x + 6$

95. $15r^2 - 21rs + 6s^2$

96. $10x^2 + 5xy - 30y^2$

97. $2x^3 - 2x^2 - 4x$

98. $2y^3 + y^2 - 3y$

99. $2y^4 + 5y^3 + 3y^2$

100. $4z^3 - 18z^2 - 10z$

101. $36a^3 - 66a^2 + 18a$

102. $20n^4 - 22n^3 - 12n^2$

103. $9p^2 + 30pq + 21q^2$

104. $12x^2 + 2xy - 24y^2$

Find a positive value for k for which each of the following can be factored.

105. $x^2 + kx + 8$

106. $x^2 + kx + 9$

107. $x^2 - kx + 16$

108. $x^2 - kx + 17$

109. $x^2 - kx - 5$

110. $x^2 - kx - 7$

111. $x^2 + 3x + k$

112. $x^2 + 5x + k$

113. $x^2 + 2x - k$

114. $x^2 + x - k$

Getting Ready

Solve.

  (a) $x - 5 = 0$ (b) $2x - 1 = 0$ (c) $3x + 2 = 0$

  (d) $x + 4 = 0$ (e) $7 - x = 0$ (f) $9 - 4x = 0$

ANSWERS

95.

96.

97.

98.

99.

100.

101.

102.

103.

104.

105.

106.

107.

108.

109.

110.

111.

112.

113.

114.

a.

b.

c.

d.

e.

f.

Answers

1. True **3.** False **5.** True **7.** False **9.** True

11. $a = 1, b = 4, c = -9$ **13.** $a = 1, b = -3, c = 8$

15. $a = 3, b = 5, c = -8$ **17.** $a = 4, b = 8, c = 11$

19. $a = -3, b = 5, c = -10$ **21.** Factorable; $3, -2$

23. Not factorable **25.** Factorable; $-3, -2$ **27.** Factorable; $6, -1$

29. Factorable; $-15, -4$ **31.** $x^2 + 2x + 4x + 8; (x + 2)(x + 4)$

33. $x^2 - 5x - 4x + 20; (x - 5)(x - 4)$ **35.** $x^2 - 9x + 7x - 63; (x - 9)(x + 7)$

37. $(x + 3)(x + 5)$ **39.** $(x - 4)(x - 7)$ **41.** $(s + 10)(s + 3)$

43. $(a - 8)(a + 6)$ **45.** $(x - 1)(x - 7)$ **47.** $(x - 10)(x + 4)$

49. $(x - 7)(x - 7)$ **51.** $(p - 12)(p + 2)$ **53.** $(x + 11)(x - 6)$

55. $(c + 4)(c + 15)$ **57.** $(n + 10)(n - 5)$ **59.** $(x + 2y)(x + 5y)$

61. $(a - 7b)(a + 6b)$ **63.** $(x - 5y)(x - 8y)$ **65.** $(3x + 2)(2x + 5)$

67. $(5x - 3)(3x + 2)$ **69.** $(6m - 5)(m + 5)$ **71.** $(3x - 2)(3x - 2)$

73. $(6x + 5)(2x - 3)$ **75.** $(3y - 2)(y + 3)$ **77.** $(8x + 5)(x - 4)$

79. $(2x + y)(x + y)$ **81.** $(5a + 2b)(a - 2b)$ **83.** $(9x - 5y)(x + y)$

85. $(3m - 4n)(2m - 3n)$ **87.** $(12a - 5b)(3a + b)$

89. $(x + 2y)^2$ **91.** $5(2x - 3)(2x + 1)$ **93.** $4(2m + 1)(m + 1)$

95. $3(5r - 2s)(r - s)$ **97.** $2x(x - 2)(x + 1)$ **99.** $y^2(2y + 3)(y + 1)$

101. $6a(3a - 1)(2a - 3)$ **103.** $3(p + q)(3p + 7q)$ **105.** 6 or 9

107. 8 or 10 or 17 **109.** 4 **111.** 2 **113.** 3, 8, 15, 24, . . .

a. $x = 5$ **b.** $x = \dfrac{1}{2}$ **c.** $x = -\dfrac{2}{3}$ **d.** $x = -4$ **e.** $x = 7$ **f.** $x = \dfrac{9}{4}$

 # Solving Quadratic Equations by Factoring

OBJECTIVE

1. Solve quadratic equations by factoring

The factoring techniques you have learned provide us with tools for solving equations that can be written in the form

$$ax^2 + bx + c = 0 \qquad a \neq 0$$

> This is a quadratic equation in one variable, here x. You can recognize such a quadratic equation by the fact that the highest power of the variable x is the second power.

in which a, b, and c are constants.

An equation written in the form $ax^2 + bx + c = 0$ is called a **quadratic equation in standard form.** Using factoring to solve quadratic equations requires the **zero-product principle,** which says that if the product of two factors is 0, then one or both of the factors must be equal to 0. In symbols:

> **Definitions: Zero-Product Principle**
>
> If $a \cdot b = 0$, then $a = 0$ or $b = 0$ or $a = b = 0$.

Let's see how the principle is applied to solving quadratic equations.

> **Example 1**

Solving Equations by Factoring

Solve.

$$x^2 - 3x - 18 = 0$$

NOTE To use the zero-product principle, 0 must be on one side of the equation.

Factoring on the left, we have

$$(x - 6)(x + 3) = 0$$

By the zero-product principle, we know that one or both of the factors must be zero. We can then write

$$x - 6 = 0 \qquad \text{or} \qquad x + 3 = 0$$

Solving each equation gives

$$x = 6 \qquad \text{or} \qquad x = -3$$

The two solutions are 6 and -3.

Quadratic equations can be checked in the same way as linear equations were checked: by substitution. For instance, if $x = 6$, we have

$$6^2 - 3 \cdot 6 - 18 \stackrel{?}{=} 0$$

$$36 - 18 - 18 \stackrel{?}{=} 0$$

$$0 = 0$$

which is a true statement. We leave it to you to check the solution -3.

CHECK YOURSELF 1

Solve $x^2 - 9x + 20 = 0$.

Other factoring techniques are also used in solving quadratic equations. Example 2 illustrates this concept.

Example 2

Solving Equations by Factoring

(a) Solve $x^2 - 5x = 0$.

Again, factor the left side of the equation and apply the zero-product principle.

$x(x - 5) = 0$

 CAUTION

A *common mistake* is to forget the statement $x = 0$ when you are solving equations of this type. Be sure to include the *two statements* obtained.

Now

$x = 0$ or $x - 5 = 0$

$x = 5$

The two solutions are 0 and 5.

(b) Solve $x^2 - 9 = 0$.

Factoring yields

$(x + 3)(x - 3) = 0$

$x + 3 = 0$ or $x - 3 = 0$

$x = -3$ $x = 3$

NOTE The symbol $\pm$ is read "plus or minus."

The solutions may be written as $x = \pm 3$.

 CHECK YOURSELF 2

Solve by factoring.

(a) $x^2 + 8x = 0$ **(b)** $x^2 - 16 = 0$

Example 3 illustrates a crucial point. Our solution technique depends on the zero-product principle, which means that the product of factors *must be equal to 0*. The importance of this is shown now.

CAUTION

Consider the equation

$x(2x - 1) = 3$

NOTE Students are sometimes tempted to write

$x = 3$ or $2x - 1 = 3$

This is *not correct*. Instead, subtract 3 from both sides of the equation *as the first step* to write

$x^2 - 2x - 3 = 0$

in standard form. Only *now* can you factor and proceed as before.

Example 3

Solving Equations by Factoring

Solve $2x^2 - x = 3$.

The first step in the solution is to write the equation in standard form (that is, when one side of the equation is 0). So start by adding -3 to both sides of the equation. Then,

$2x^2 - x - 3 = 0$ Make sure all terms are on one side of the equation. The other side will be 0.

You can now factor and solve by using the zero-product principle.

$(2x - 3)(x + 1) = 0$

$$2x - 3 = 0 \quad \text{or} \quad x + 1 = 0$$

$$2x = 3 \qquad\qquad x = -1$$

$$x = \frac{3}{2}$$

The solutions are $\frac{3}{2}$ and -1.

CHECK YOURSELF 3

Solve $3x^2 = 5x + 2$.

In all the previous examples, the quadratic equations had two distinct real number solutions. That may not always be the case, as we shall see.

Example 4

Solving Equations by Factoring

Solve $x^2 - 6x + 9 = 0$.

Factoring, we have

$(x - 3)(x - 3) = 0$

and

$$x - 3 = 0 \quad \text{or} \quad x - 3 = 0$$

$$x = 3 \qquad\qquad x = 3$$

The solution is 3.

A quadratic (or second-degree) equation always has *two* solutions. When an equation such as this one has two solutions that are the same number, we call 3 the **repeated** (or **double**) **solution** of the equation.

Although a quadratic equation will always have two solutions, they may not always be real numbers. You will learn more about this in a later course.

CHECK YOURSELF 4

Solve $x^2 + 6x + 9 = 0$.

Always examine the quadratic member of an equation for common factors. It will make your work much easier, as Example 5 illustrates.

Example 5

Solving Equations by Factoring

Solve $3x^2 - 3x - 60 = 0$.

First, note the common factor 3 in the quadratic member of the equation. Factoring out the 3, we have

$3(x^2 - x - 20) = 0$

Now divide both sides of the equation by 3.

NOTE Notice the advantage of dividing both members by 3. The coefficients in the quadratic member become smaller, and that member is much easier to factor.

$$\frac{3(x^2 - x - 20)}{3} = \frac{0}{3}$$

or

$x^2 - x - 20 = 0$

We can now factor and solve as before.

$(x - 5)(x + 4) = 0$

$x - 5 = 0 \qquad \text{or} \qquad x + 4 = 0$

$x = 5 \qquad\qquad\qquad x = -4$

CHECK YOURSELF 5

Solve $2x^2 - 10x - 48 = 0$.

CHECK YOURSELF ANSWERS

1. $4, 5$ **2.** (a) $0, -8$; (b) $4, -4$ **3.** $-\dfrac{1}{3}, 2$ **4.** -3 **5.** $-3, 8$

3.10 Exercises

Name _____

Section _____ Date _____

Solve each of the following quadratic equations.

1. $(x - 3)(x - 4) = 0$

2. $(x - 7)(x + 1) = 0$

3. $(3x + 1)(x - 6) = 0$

4. $(5x - 4)(x - 6) = 0$

5. $x^2 - 2x - 3 = 0$

6. $x^2 + 5x + 4 = 0$

7. $x^2 - 7x + 6 = 0$

8. $x^2 + 3x - 10 = 0$

9. $x^2 + 8x + 15 = 0$

10. $x^2 - 3x - 18 = 0$

11. $x^2 + 4x - 21 = 0$

12. $x^2 - 12x + 32 = 0$

13. $x^2 - 4x = 12$

14. $x^2 + 8x = -15$

15. $x^2 + 5x = 14$

16. $x^2 = 11x - 24$

17. $2x^2 + 5x - 3 = 0$

18. $3x^2 + 7x + 2 = 0$

19. $4x^2 - 24x + 35 = 0$

20. $6x^2 + 11x - 10 = 0$

21. $4x^2 + 11x = -6$

22. $5x^2 + 2x = 3$

ANSWERS

1. _____
2. _____
3. _____
4. _____
5. _____
6. _____
7. _____
8. _____
9. _____
10. _____
11. _____
12. _____
13. _____
14. _____
15. _____
16. _____
17. _____
18. _____
19. _____
20. _____
21. _____
22. _____

23. _____

24. _____

25. _____

26. _____

27. _____

28. _____

29. _____

30. _____

31. _____

32. _____

33. _____

34. _____

35. _____

36. _____

37. _____

38. _____

39. _____

40. _____

41. _____

42. _____

43. _____

23. $5x^2 + 13x = 6$

24. $4x^2 = 13x + 12$

25. $x^2 - 2x = 0$

26. $x^2 + 5x = 0$

27. $x^2 = -8x$

28. $x^2 = 7x$

29. $5x^2 - 15x = 0$

30. $4x^2 + 20x = 0$

31. $x^2 - 25 = 0$

32. $x^2 = 49$

33. $x^2 = 81$

34. $x^2 = 64$

35. $2x^2 - 18 = 0$

36. $3x^2 - 75 = 0$

37. $3x^2 + 24x + 45 = 0$

38. $4x^2 - 4x = 24$

39. $6x^2 + 28x = 10$

40. $15x^2 + 27x = 6$

41. $(x + 3)(x - 2) = 14$

42. $(x - 5)(x + 2) = 18$

Solve the following problems.

43. Consecutive integers. The product of two consecutive integers is 132. Find the two integers.

44. Consecutive integers. If the product of two consecutive positive even integers is 120, find the two integers.

44. _____

45. _____

46. _____

47. _____

48. _____

49. _____

50. _____

45. Integers. The sum of an integer and its square is 72. What is the integer?

46. Integers. The square of an integer is 56 more than the integer. Find the integer.

47. Geometry. If the sides of a square are increased by 3 in., the area is increased by 39 in.^{2}. What were the dimensions of the original square?

48. Geometry. If the sides of a square are decreased by 2 cm, the area is decreased by 36 cm^2. What were the dimensions of the original square?

49. Business. The profit on a small appliance is given by $P = x^2 - 3x - 60$, in which x is the number of appliances sold per day. How many appliances were sold on a day when there was a $20 loss?

50. Business. The relationship between the number x of calculators that a company can sell per month and the price of each calculator p is given by $x = 1700 - 100p$. Find the price at which a calculator should be sold to produce a monthly revenue of $7000. (*Hint:* Revenue $= xp$.)

51. Write a short comparison that explains the difference between $ax^2 + bx + c$ and $ax^2 + bx + c = 0$.

515

52.

52. When solving quadratic equations, some people try to solve an equation in the manner shown below, but this doesn't work! Write a paragraph to explain what is wrong with this approach.

$$2x^2 + 7x + 3 = 52$$

$$(2x + 1)(x + 3) = 52$$

$$2x + 1 = 52 \quad \text{or} \quad x + 3 = 52$$

$$x = \frac{51}{2} \quad \text{or} \quad x = 49$$

Answers

1. $3, 4$ **3.** $-\dfrac{1}{3}, 6$ **5.** $-1, 3$ **7.** $1, 6$ **9.** $-3, -5$ **11.** $-7, 3$

13. $-2, 6$ **15.** $-7, 2$ **17.** $-3, \dfrac{1}{2}$ **19.** $\dfrac{5}{2}, \dfrac{7}{2}$ **21.** $-\dfrac{3}{4}, -2$

23. $-3, \dfrac{2}{5}$ **25.** $0, 2$ **27.** $0, -8$ **29.** $0, 3$ **31.** $-5, 5$ **33.** $-9, 9$

35. $-3, 3$ **37.** $-5, -3$ **39.** $-5, \dfrac{1}{3}$ **41.** $4, -5$

43. $11, 12$ or $-12, -11$ **45.** -9 or 8 **47.** 5 in. by 5 in.   **49.** 8

51.

The Quadratic Formula

3.11 **OBJECTIVES**

1. Solve a quadratic equation by using the quadratic formula
2. Solve an application by using the quadratic formula

We are now ready to derive and use the **quadratic formula,** which will allow us to solve all quadratic equations. We derive the formula by using the method of completing the square.

To use the quadratic formula, the quadratic equation you want to solve must be in *standard form.* That form is

$$ax^2 + bx + c = 0 \qquad \text{in which } a \neq 0$$

Example 1

Writing Equations in Standard Form

Write each equation in standard form.

(a) $2x^2 - 5x + 3 = 0$

The equation is already in standard form.

$$a = 2 \qquad b = -5 \qquad \text{and} \qquad c = 3$$

(b) $5x^2 + 3x = 5$

The equation is *not* in standard form. Rewrite it by adding -5 to both sides.

$$5x^2 + 3x - 5 = 0 \qquad \text{Standard form}$$

$$a = 5 \qquad b = 3 \qquad \text{and} \qquad c = -5$$

 CHECK YOURSELF 1

Rewrite each quadratic equation in standard form.

(a) $x^2 - 3x = 5$ **(b)** $3x^2 = 7 - 2x$

Once a quadratic equation is written in standard form, we will be able to find both solutions to the equation. Remember that a solution is a value for x that will make the equation true.

What follows is the derivation of the quadratic formula, which can be used to solve quadratic equations.

Step by Step: Deriving the Quadratic Formula

Let $ax^2 + bx + c = 0$, in which $a \neq 0$.

$ax^2 + bx = -c$	Subtract c from both sides.
$x^2 + \dfrac{b}{a}x = -\dfrac{c}{a}$	Divide both sides by a.
$x^2 + \dfrac{b}{a}x + \dfrac{b^2}{4a^2} = \dfrac{b^2}{4a^2} - \dfrac{c}{a}$	Add $\dfrac{b^2}{4a^2}$ to both sides.
$\left(x + \dfrac{b}{2a}\right)^2 = \dfrac{b^2 - 4ac}{4a^2}$	Factor on the left, and add the fractions on the right.
$x + \dfrac{b}{2a} = \pm\sqrt{\dfrac{b^2 - 4ac}{4a^2}}$	Take the square root of both sides.
$x + \dfrac{b}{2a} = \pm\dfrac{\sqrt{b^2 - 4ac}}{2a}$	Simplify the radical on the right.
$x = -\dfrac{b}{2a} \pm \dfrac{\sqrt{b^2 - 4ac}}{2a}$	Add $-\dfrac{b}{2a}$ to both sides.
$x = \dfrac{-b \pm \sqrt{b^2 - 4ac}}{2a}$	Use the common denominator, $2a$

NOTE This is the completing-the-square step that makes the left-hand side a perfect square.

Definitions: The Quadratic Formula

$$x = \frac{-b \pm \sqrt{b^2 - 4ac}}{2a}$$

Let's use the quadratic formula to solve some equations.

Example 2

Using the Quadratic Formula to Solve an Equation

Solve $x^2 - 5x + 4 = 0$ by formula.

The equation is in standard form, so first identify a, b, and c.

NOTE The leading coefficient is 1, so $a = 1$.

$$x^2 - 5x + 4 = 0$$

$$a = 1 \quad b = -5 \quad c = 4$$

We now substitute the values for a, b, and c into the formula.

$$x = \frac{-b \pm \sqrt{b^2 - 4ac}}{2a}$$

$$= \frac{-(-5) \pm \sqrt{(-5)^2 - 4(1)(4)}}{2(1)}$$

NOTE Simplify the expression.

$$= \frac{5 \pm \sqrt{25 - 16}}{2}$$

$$= \frac{5 \pm \sqrt{9}}{2}$$

$$= \frac{5 \pm 3}{2}$$

NOTE These results could also have been found by factoring the original equation. You should check that for yourself.

Now,

$$x = \frac{5 + 3}{2} \quad \text{or} \quad x = \frac{5 - 3}{2}$$

$$= 4 \qquad\qquad = 1$$

The solutions are 4 and 1.

 CHECK YOURSELF 2

Solve $x^2 - 2x - 8 = 0$ by formula. Check your result by factoring.

The main use of the quadratic formula is to solve equations that *cannot* be factored.

Example 3

Using the Quadratic Formula to Solve an Equation

Solve $2x^2 = x + 4$ by formula.

First, the equation *must be written* in standard form to find a, b, and c.

$$2x^2 - x - 4 = 0$$

$a = 2 \qquad b = -1 \qquad c = -4$

NOTE Substitute the values for a, b, and c into the formula.

$$x = \frac{-b \pm \sqrt{b^2 - 4ac}}{2a}$$

$$= \frac{-(-1) \pm \sqrt{(-1)^2 - 4(2)(-4)}}{2(2)}$$

$$= \frac{1 \pm \sqrt{1 + 32}}{4}$$

$$= \frac{1 \pm \sqrt{33}}{4}$$

CHECK YOURSELF 3

Solve $3x^2 = 3x + 4$ by formula.

Example 4

Using the Quadratic Formula to Solve an Equation

Solve $x^2 - 2x = 4$ by formula.

In standard form, the equation is

$$x^2 - 2x - 4 = 0$$

$a = 1 \qquad b = -2 \qquad c = -4$

NOTE Again substitute the values into the quadratic formula.

$$x = \frac{-(-2) \pm \sqrt{(-2)^2 - 4(1)(-4)}}{2(1)}$$

$$= \frac{2 \pm \sqrt{20}}{2}$$

NOTE Because 20 has a perfect-square factor,
$$\sqrt{20} = \sqrt{4 \cdot 5}$$
$$= 2\sqrt{5}$$

You should always write your solution in simplest form.

$$x = \frac{2 \pm 2\sqrt{5}}{2}$$

$$= \frac{2(1 \pm \sqrt{5})}{2}$$

$$= 1 \pm \sqrt{5}$$

NOTE Now factor the numerator and divide by the common factor 2.

 CHECK YOURSELF 4

Solve $3x^2 = 2x + 4$ by formula.

Sometimes equations have common factors. Factoring first simplifies these equations, making them easier to solve. This is illustrated in Example 5.

Example 5

Using the Quadratic Formula to Solve an Equation

Solve $3x^2 - 6x - 3 = 0$ by formula.

Because the equation is in standard form, we could use

$$a = 3 \qquad b = -6 \qquad \text{and} \qquad c = -3$$

in the quadratic formula. There is, however, a better approach.

Note the common factor of 3 in the quadratic member of the original equation. Factoring, we have

$$3(x^2 - 2x - 1) = 0$$

and dividing both sides of the equation by 3 gives

$$x^2 - 2x - 1 = 0$$

NOTE The advantage to this approach is that these values will require much less simplification after we substitute into the quadratic formula.

Now let $a = 1$, $b = -2$, and $c = -1$. Then

$$x = \frac{-(-2) \pm \sqrt{(-2)^2 - 4(1)(-1)}}{2 \cdot 1}$$

$$= \frac{2 \pm \sqrt{8}}{2}$$

$$= \frac{2 \pm 2\sqrt{2}}{2}$$

$$= \frac{2(1 \pm \sqrt{2})}{2}$$

$$= 1 \pm \sqrt{2}$$

 CHECK YOURSELF 5

Solve $4x^2 - 20x = 12$ by formula.

In applications that lead to quadratic equations, you may want to find approximate values for the solutions.

Example 6

Using the Quadratic Formula to Solve an Equation

Solve $x^2 - 5x + 5 = 0$ by formula, and write your solutions in approximate decimal form.
Substituting $a = 1$, $b = -5$, and $c = 5$ gives

$$x = \frac{-(-5) \pm \sqrt{(-5)^2 - 4(1)(5)}}{2(1)}$$

$$= \frac{5 \pm \sqrt{5}}{2}$$

 Use your calculator to find $\sqrt{5} \approx 2.236$, so

$$x \approx \frac{5 + 2.236}{2} \qquad \text{or} \qquad x \approx \frac{5 - 2.236}{2}$$

$$= \frac{7.236}{2} \qquad\qquad\qquad = \frac{2.764}{2}$$

$$= 3.618 \qquad\qquad\qquad = 1.382$$

 CHECK YOURSELF 6

Solve $x^2 - 3x - 5 = 0$ by formula, and approximate the solutions in decimal form to the thousandth.

You may be wondering whether the quadratic formula can be used to solve all quadratic equations. It can, but not all quadratic equations will have real number solutions, as Example 7 shows.

Example 7

Using the Quadratic Formula to Solve an Equation

NOTE Make sure the quadratic equation is in standard form. $x^2 - 3x = -5$ is equivalent to $x^2 - 3x + 5 = 0$.

Solve $x^2 - 3x = -5$ by formula.
Substituting $a = 1$, $b = -3$, and $c = 5$, we have

$$x = \frac{-(-3) \pm \sqrt{(-3)^2 - 4(1)(5)}}{2(1)}$$

$$= \frac{3 \pm \sqrt{-11}}{2}$$

In this case, there are no real number solutions because of the negative number in the radical.

 CHECK YOURSELF 7

Solve $x^2 - 3x = -3$ by formula.

Let's review the steps used for solving equations by the use of the quadratic formula.

Step by Step: Solving Equations with the Quadratic Formula

Step 1   Rewrite the equation in standard form.

$$ax^2 + bx + c = 0$$

Step 2   If a common factor exists, divide both sides of the equation by that common factor.

Step 3   Identify the coefficients a, b, and c.

Step 4   Substitute values for a, b, and c into the formula

$$x = \frac{-b \pm \sqrt{b^2 - 4ac}}{2a}$$

Step 5   Simplify the right side of the expression formed in step 4 to write the solutions for the original equation.

Often, applied problems will lead to quadratic equations that must be solved by the methods of this or the previous section.

CHECK YOURSELF ANSWERS

1. (a) $x^2 - 3x - 5 = 0$; (b) $3x^2 + 2x - 7 = 0$

2. $x = 4, -2$ **3.** $x = \dfrac{3 \pm \sqrt{57}}{6}$ **4.** $x = \dfrac{1 \pm \sqrt{13}}{3}$

5. $x = \dfrac{5 \pm \sqrt{37}}{2}$ **6.** $x \approx 4.193$ or -1.193 **7.** $\dfrac{3 \pm \sqrt{-3}}{2}$, no real solutions

Name _____

Section _____ Date _____

Solve each of the following quadratic equations by formula.

1. $x^2 + 9x + 20 = 0$

2. $x^2 - 9x + 14 = 0$

3. $x^2 - 4x + 3 = 0$

4. $x^2 - 13x + 22 = 0$

5. $3x^2 + 2x - 1 = 0$

6. $x^2 - 8x + 16 = 0$

7. $x^2 + 5x = -4$

8. $4x^2 + 5x = 6$

9. $x^2 = 6x - 9$

10. $2x^2 - 5x = 3$

11. $2x^2 - 3x - 7 = 0$

12. $x^2 - 5x + 2 = 0$

13. $x^2 + 2x - 4 = 0$

14. $x^2 - 4x + 2 = 0$

15. $2x^2 - 3x = 3$

16. $3x^2 - 2x + 1 = 0$

17. $3x^2 - 2x = 6$

18. $4x^2 = 4x + 5$

19. $3x^2 + 3x + 2 = 0$

20. $2x^2 - 3x = 6$

21. $5x^2 = 8x - 2$

22. $5x^2 - 2 = 2x$

23. $2x^2 - 9 = 4x$

24. $3x^2 - 6x = 2$

ANSWERS

1. _____ 2. _____

3. _____ 4. _____

5. _____ 6. _____

7. _____ 8. _____

9. _____ 10. _____

11. _____

12. _____

13. _____

14. _____

15. _____

16. _____

17. _____

18. _____

19. _____

20. _____

21. _____

22. _____

23. _____

24. _____

25. $3x - 5 = \dfrac{1}{x}$

26. $x + 3 = \dfrac{1}{x}$

27. $(x - 2)(x + 1) = 3$

28. $(x - 3)(x + 2) = 5$

Solve the following quadratic equations by factoring or by any of the techniques of this chapter.

29. $(x - 1)^2 = 7$

30. $(2x + 3)^2 = 5$

31. $x^2 - 5x - 14 = 0$

32. $3x^2 + 2x - 1 = 0$

33. $6x^2 - 23x + 10 = 0$

34. $x^2 + 7x - 18 = 0$

35. $2x^2 - 8x + 3 = 0$

36. $x^2 + 2x - 1 = 0$

37. $x^2 - 9x - 4 = 6$

38. $5x^2 + 10x + 2 = 2$

39. $4x^2 - 8x + 3 = 5$

40. $x^2 + 4x = 21$

Solve the following equations.

41. $\dfrac{3}{x} + \dfrac{5}{x^2} = 9$

42. $\dfrac{8}{x} - \dfrac{3}{x^2} = -6$

43. $\dfrac{x}{x + 1} + \dfrac{10x}{x^2 + 4x + 3} = \dfrac{15}{x + 3}$

44. $x - \dfrac{9x}{x - 2} = \dfrac{-10}{x - 2}$

Use your calculator for the following exercises. Round your answer to the nearest thousandth.

45. Dimensions of a square. The perimeter of a square is numerically 3 less than its area. Find the length of one side.

46. Dimensions of a square. The perimeter of a square is numerically 1 more than its area. Find the length of one side.

47. Width of a picture frame. A picture frame is 15 inches (in.) by 12 in. The area of the picture that shows is 140 in^2. What is the width of the frame?

48. **Width of a garden path.** A garden area is 30 feet (ft) long by 20 ft wide. A path of uniform width is set around the edge. If the remaining garden area is 400 ft², what is the width of the path?

49. **Solar frames.** A solar collector is 2.5 meters (m) long by 2.0 m wide. It is held in place by a frame of uniform width around its outside edge. If the exposed collector area is 2.5 m², what is the width of the frame, to the nearest tenth of a centimeter?

50. **Solar frames.** A solar collector is 2.5 m long by 2.0 m wide. It is held in place by a frame of uniform width around its outside edge. If the exposed collector is 4 m², what is the width of the frame to the nearest tenth of a centimeter?

51. The part of the quadratic formula, $b^2 - 4ac$, that is under the radical is called the **discriminant.** Complete the following sentences to show how this value indicates whether there are *no* solutions, *one* solution, or *two* solutions for the quadratic equation.

   (a) When $b^2 - 4ac$ is _____, there are no real number solutions because. . . .
   (b) When $b^2 - 4ac$ is _____, there is one solution because. . . .
   (c) When $b^2 - 4ac$ is _____, there are two solutions because. . . .
   (d) When $b^2 - 4ac$ is _____, there are two *rational* solutions because. . . .
   (e) When $b^2 - 4ac$ is _____, there are two *irrational* solutions because. . . .

52. Work with a partner to decide all values of b in the following equations that will give one or more real number solutions.

   (a) $3x^2 + bx - 3 = 0$
   (b) $5x^2 + bx + 1 = 0$
   (c) $-3x^2 + bx - 3 = 0$
   (d) Write a rule for judging if an equation has solutions by looking at it in standard form.

53. _____

54. _____

a. _____

b. _____

c. _____

d. _____

e. _____

f. _____

53. Which method of solving a quadratic equation seems simplest to you? Which method do you try first?

54. Complete this statement: "You can tell an equation is quadratic and not linear by. . . ."

Getting Ready

Evaluate each of the given expressions for the value of the variable given.

(a) $x^2 + 3x - 5$; $x = 3$

(b) $x^2 - 3x - 5$; $x = -2$

(c) $3x^2 + 4x - 6$; $x = -2$

(d) $-2x^2 - 5x + 3$; $x = 4$

(e) $-5x^2 - 5x + 6$; $x = -1$

(f) $\frac{2}{3}x^2 - \frac{1}{3}x + 5$; $x = 6$

Answers

1. $-4, -5$ **3.** $3, 1$ **5.** $-1, \frac{1}{3}$ **7.** $-4, -1$ **9.** 3 **11.** $\dfrac{3 \pm \sqrt{65}}{4}$

13. $-1 \pm \sqrt{5}$ **15.** $\dfrac{3 \pm \sqrt{33}}{4}$ **17.** $\dfrac{1 \pm \sqrt{19}}{3}$

19. No real number solutions   **21.** $\dfrac{4 \pm \sqrt{6}}{5}$ **23.** $\dfrac{2 \pm \sqrt{22}}{2}$

25. $\dfrac{5 \pm \sqrt{37}}{6}$ **27.** $\dfrac{1 \pm \sqrt{21}}{2}$ **29.** $1 \pm \sqrt{7}$ **31.** $-2, 7$ **33.** $\dfrac{1}{2}, \dfrac{10}{3}$

35. $\dfrac{4 \pm \sqrt{10}}{2}$ **37.** $10, -1$ **39.** $\dfrac{2 \pm \sqrt{6}}{2}$ **41.** $\dfrac{1 \pm \sqrt{21}}{6}$ **43.** 5

45. 4.646 **47.** 0.787 in.   **49.** ≈ 32.5 cm   **51.**   **53.**

a. 13 **b.** 5 **c.** -2 **d.** -49 **e.** 6 **f.** 27

ALGEBRAIC FRACTIONS

INTRODUCTION

In the United States, disorders of the heart and circulatory system kill more people than all other causes combined. The major risk factors for heart disease are smoking, high blood pressure, obesity, cholesterol over 240 g/dL, and a family history of heart problems. Although nothing can be done about family history, everyone can affect the first four risk factors by diet and exercise.

One quick way to check your risk of heart problems is to compare your waist and hip measurements. Measure around your waist at the navel and around your hips at the largest point. These measures may be in inches or centimeters. Use the ratio w/h to assess your risk. For women, $w/h \geq 0.8$ indicates an increased health risk, and for men, $w/h \geq 0.95$ is the indicator of an increased risk.

The American Medical Association sponsored a study using Body Mass Index, or BMI, which used height and weight measurements:

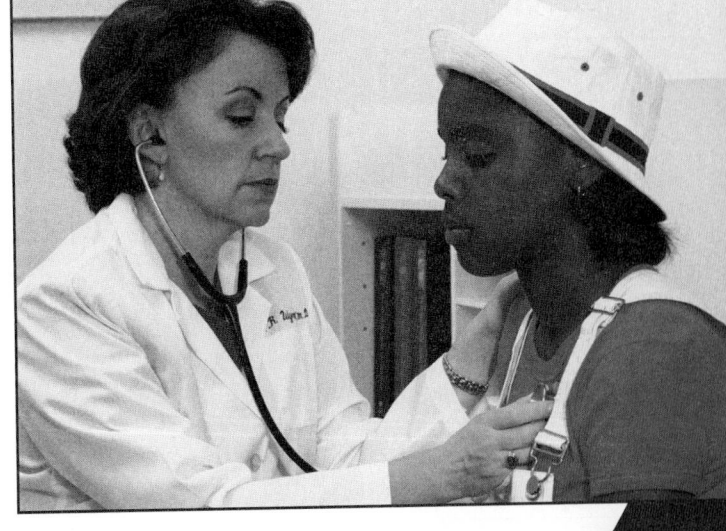

$$BMI = \frac{705w}{h^2}$$

in which w = weight in pounds
$\quad\quad h$ = height in inches

This study concluded that people with BMI ≤ 21 had the lowest rates of heart disease, and that an increase of only 2 points in the BMI dramatically raises the risk of heart problems.

Medical professionals and researchers continue to disagree about how accurate these indicators are because each is a statistical average. One issue is how well the measures relate to the percentage of total body fat. A person may have a relatively low percentage of body fat and be in excellent health but have a BMI over 21 because of a very muscular build or large bone structure.

4 **Pre-Test Chapter 4**

ANSWERS

1. _____ 2. _____

3. _____ 4. _____

5. _____ 6. _____

7. _____ 8. _____

9. _____ 10. _____

11. _____ 12. _____

13. _____ 14. _____

15. _____ 16. _____

17. _____

18. _____

19. _____

20. _____

21. _____

22. _____

23. _____

24. _____

25. _____

Write each fraction in simplest form.

1. $\dfrac{-15a^4b^7}{25a^6b}$

2. $\dfrac{x^2 - 16}{2x - 8}$

3. $\dfrac{3x^2 - 2x - 1}{6x^2 + 2x}$

Add or subtract as indicated.

4. $\dfrac{7a}{12} + \dfrac{19a}{12}$

5. $\dfrac{5x}{x + 1} + \dfrac{5}{x + 1}$

6. $\dfrac{x^2}{x - 6} - \dfrac{36}{x - 6}$

7. $\dfrac{5}{2w} - \dfrac{3}{w^2}$

8. $\dfrac{4}{b - 3} - \dfrac{1}{b}$

9. $\dfrac{2}{3x - 3} - \dfrac{5}{2x - 2}$

10. $\dfrac{4x}{x^2 - 8x + 15} + \dfrac{6}{x - 3}$

Multiply or divide as indicated.

11. $\dfrac{-4a^2}{6ab^3} \cdot \dfrac{3ab^2}{-4ab}$

12. $\dfrac{x^2 + 5x + 4}{2x^2 + 2x} \cdot \dfrac{x^2 - x - 12}{x^2 - 16}$

13. $\dfrac{8b^4}{5bc} \div \dfrac{12b^2c^2}{15bc^3}$

14. $\dfrac{x^2y + 2xy^2}{x^2 - 4y^2} \div \dfrac{4x^2y}{x^2 - xy - 2y^2}$

Simplify the complex fractions.

15. $\dfrac{\dfrac{x^3}{16}}{\dfrac{x^2}{24}}$

16. $\dfrac{2 - \dfrac{x}{y}}{4 - \dfrac{x^2}{y^2}}$

What values for x, if any, must be excluded in the following algebraic fractions?

17. $\dfrac{5}{x - 3}$

18. $\dfrac{4}{x^2 - 3x - 10}$

Solve the following equations for x.

19. $\dfrac{x}{4} - \dfrac{x}{5} = 2$

20. $\dfrac{x}{x - 2} + 1 = \dfrac{x + 4}{x - 2}$

21. $\dfrac{7}{x} - \dfrac{1}{x - 3} = \dfrac{9}{x^2 - 3x}$

22. $\dfrac{x - 3}{8} = \dfrac{x - 2}{10}$

Solve the following applications.

23. One number is 4 times another. If the sum of their reciprocals is $\dfrac{1}{4}$, find the two numbers.

24. Mark drove 240 mi to visit Sandra. Returning by a shorter route, he found that the trip was only 200 mi, but traffic slowed his speed by 8 mi/h. If the two trips took exactly the same time, what was his rate each way?

25. A 55-ft cable is to be cut into two pieces whose lengths have the ratio 3 to 8. Find the lengths of the two pieces.

Simplifying Algebraic Fractions

1. Find the GCF for two monomials and simplify a fraction
2. Find the GCF for two polynomials and simplify a fraction

Much of our work with algebraic fractions will be similar to your work in arithmetic. For instance, in algebra, as in arithmetic, many fractions name the same number. You will remember from Chapter 0 that

$$\frac{1}{4} = \frac{1 \cdot 2}{4 \cdot 2} = \frac{2}{8}$$

or

$$\frac{1}{4} = \frac{1 \cdot 3}{4 \cdot 3} = \frac{3}{12}$$

So $\frac{1}{4}, \frac{2}{8}$, and $\frac{3}{12}$ all name the same number. They are called **equivalent fractions.** These examples illustrate what is called the **Fundamental Principle of Fractions.** In algebra it becomes

---

Rules and Properties: Fundamental Principle of Algebraic Fractions

For polynomials P, Q, and R,

$$\frac{P}{Q} = \frac{PR}{QR} \qquad \text{when } Q \neq 0 \text{ and } R \neq 0$$

This principle allows us to multiply or divide the numerator and denominator of a fraction by the same nonzero polynomial. The result will be an expression that is equivalent to the original one.

Our objective in this section is to simplify algebraic fractions by using the fundamental principle. In algebra, as in arithmetic, to write a fraction in simplest form, you divide the numerator and denominator of the fraction by their greatest common factor (GCF). The numerator and denominator of the resulting fraction will have no common factors other than 1, and the fraction is then in **simplest form.** The following rule summarizes this procedure.

Step by Step: To Write Algebraic Fractions in Simplest Form

NOTE Notice that step 2 uses the Fundamental Principle of Fractions. The GCF is R in the rule above.

Step 1 Factor the numerator and denominator.
Step 2 Divide the numerator and denominator by the greatest common factor (GCF). The resulting fraction will be in lowest terms.

Example 1

Writing Fractions in Simplest Form

(a) Write $\dfrac{18}{30}$ in simplest form.

NOTE This is the same as dividing both the numerator and denominator of $\dfrac{18}{30}$ by 6.

$$\frac{18}{30} = \frac{2 \cdot 3 \cdot 3}{2 \cdot 3 \cdot 5} = \frac{\overset{1}{\cancel{2}} \cdot \overset{1}{\cancel{3}} \cdot 3}{\cancel{2} \cdot \cancel{3} \cdot 5} = \frac{3}{5}$$

Divide by the GCF. The slash lines indicate that we have divided the numerator and denominator by 2 and by 3.

(b) Write $\dfrac{4x^3}{6x}$ in simplest form.

$$\frac{4x^3}{6x} = \frac{2 \cdot 2 \cdot \overset{1}{\cancel{x}} \cdot x \cdot x}{\underset{1}{\cancel{2}} \cdot 3 \cdot \underset{1}{\cancel{x}}} = \frac{2x^2}{3}$$

(c) Write $\dfrac{15x^3y^2}{20xy^4}$ in simplest form.

$$\frac{15x^3y^2}{20xy^4} = \frac{3 \cdot \cancel{5} \cdot \cancel{x} \cdot x \cdot x \cdot \cancel{y} \cdot \cancel{y}}{2 \cdot 2 \cdot \cancel{5} \cdot \cancel{x} \cdot \cancel{y} \cdot \cancel{y} \cdot y \cdot y} = \frac{3x^2}{4y^2}$$

(d) Write $\dfrac{3a^2b}{9a^3b^2}$ in simplest form.

$$\frac{3a^2b}{9a^3b^2} = \frac{\cancel{3} \cdot \cancel{a} \cdot \cancel{a} \cdot \cancel{b}}{\cancel{3} \cdot 3 \cdot \cancel{a} \cdot \cancel{a} \cdot a \cdot \cancel{b} \cdot b} = \frac{1}{3ab}$$

(e) Write $\dfrac{10a^5b^4}{2a^2b^3}$ in simplest form.

$$\frac{10a^5b^4}{2a^2b^3} = \frac{5 \cdot \cancel{2} \cdot \cancel{a} \cdot \cancel{a} \cdot a \cdot a \cdot a \cdot \cancel{b} \cdot \cancel{b} \cdot \cancel{b} \cdot b}{\cancel{2} \cdot \cancel{a} \cdot \cancel{a} \cdot \cancel{b} \cdot \cancel{b} \cdot \cancel{b}} = \frac{5a^3b}{1} = 5a^3b$$

CHECK YOURSELF 1

NOTE Most of the methods of this chapter build on our factoring work of the last chapter.

Write each fraction in simplest form.

(a) $\dfrac{30}{66}$ **(b)** $\dfrac{5x^4}{15x}$ **(c)** $\dfrac{12xy^4}{18x^3y^2}$ **(d)** $\dfrac{5m^2n}{10m^3n^3}$ **(e)** $\dfrac{12a^4b^6}{2a^3b^4}$

In simplifying arithmetic fractions, common factors are generally easy to recognize. With algebraic fractions, the factoring techniques you studied in Chapter 3 will have to be used as the *first step* in determining those factors.

Example 2

Writing Fractions in Simplest Form

Write each fraction in simplest form.

(a) $\dfrac{2x - 4}{x^2 - 4} = \dfrac{2(x - 2)}{(x + 2)(x - 2)}$ Factor the numerator and denominator.

$= \dfrac{2(x - 2)}{(x + 2)(x - 2)}$ Divide by the GCF $x - 2$. The slash lines indicate that we have divided by that common factor.

$= \dfrac{2}{x + 2}$

(b) $\dfrac{3x^2 - 3}{x^2 - 2x - 3} = \dfrac{3(x - 1)(x + 1)}{(x - 3)(x + 1)}$

$= \dfrac{3(x - 1)}{x - 3}$

(c) $\dfrac{2x^2 + x - 6}{2x^2 - x - 3} = \dfrac{(x + 2)(2x - 3)}{(x + 1)(2x - 3)}$

$= \dfrac{x + 2}{x + 1}$

CAUTION

Pick any value, other than 0, for x and substitute. You will quickly see that

$\dfrac{x + 2}{x + 1} \neq \dfrac{2}{1}$

Be Careful! The expression $\dfrac{x + 2}{x + 1}$ is already in simplest form. Students are often tempted to divide as follows:

$\dfrac{\cancel{x} + 2}{\cancel{x} + 1}$ is *not equal* to $\dfrac{2}{1}$

The x's are *terms* in the numerator and denominator. They *cannot* be divided out. Only *factors* can be divided. The fraction

$\dfrac{x + 2}{x + 1}$

is in its simplest form.

✓ **CHECK YOURSELF 2**

Write each fraction in simplest form.

(a) $\dfrac{5x - 15}{x^2 - 9}$ (b) $\dfrac{a^2 - 5a + 6}{3a^2 - 6a}$

(c) $\dfrac{3x^2 + 14x - 5}{3x^2 + 2x - 1}$ (d) $\dfrac{5p - 15}{p^2 - 4}$

Remember the rules for signs in division. The quotient of a positive number and a negative number is always negative. Thus there are three equivalent ways to write such a quotient. For instance,

$$\frac{-2}{3} = \frac{2}{-3} = -\frac{2}{3}$$

NOTE $\frac{-2}{3}$, with the negative sign in the numerator, is the most common way to write the quotient.

The quotient of two positive numbers or two negative numbers is always positive. For example,

$$\frac{-2}{-3} = \frac{2}{3}$$

Example 3

Writing Fractions in Simplest Form

Write each fraction in simplest form.

NOTE In part (a), the final quotient is written in the most common way with the minus sign in the numerator.

(a) $\dfrac{6x^2}{-3xy} = \dfrac{2 \cdot \overset{1}{\cancel{3}} \cdot \overset{1}{\cancel{x}} \cdot x}{(-1) \cdot \underset{1}{\cancel{3}} \cdot \underset{1}{\cancel{x}} \cdot y} = \dfrac{2x}{-y} = \dfrac{-2x}{y}$

(b) $\dfrac{-5a^2b}{-10b^2} = \dfrac{\overset{1}{\cancel{(-1)}} \cdot \overset{1}{\cancel{5}} \cdot a \cdot a \cdot \overset{1}{\cancel{b}}}{\underset{1}{\cancel{(-1)}} \cdot 2 \cdot \underset{1}{\cancel{5}} \cdot \underset{1}{\cancel{b}} \cdot b} = \dfrac{a^2}{2b}$

CHECK YOURSELF 3

Write each fraction in simplest form.

(a) $\dfrac{8x^3y}{-4xy^2}$

(b) $\dfrac{-16a^4b^2}{-12a^2b^5}$

It is sometimes necessary to factor out a monomial before simplifying the fraction.

Example 4

Writing Fractions in Simplest Form

Write each fraction in simplest form.

(a) $\dfrac{6x^2 + 2x}{2x^2 + 12x} = \dfrac{2x(3x + 1)}{2x(x + 6)} = \dfrac{3x + 1}{x + 6}$

(b) $\dfrac{x^2 - 4}{x^2 + 6x + 8} = \dfrac{(x + 2)(x - 2)}{(x + 2)(x + 4)} = \dfrac{x - 2}{x + 4}$

✔ CHECK YOURSELF 4

Simplify each fraction.

(a) $\dfrac{3x^3 - 6x^2}{9x^4 - 3x^2}$

(b) $\dfrac{x^2 - 9}{x^2 - 12x + 27}$

Reducing certain algebraic fractions will be easier with the following result. First, verify for yourself that

$$5 - 8 = -(8 - 5)$$

In general, it is true that

$$a - b = -(b - a)$$

or, by dividing both sides of the equation by $b - a$,

$$\frac{a - b}{b - a} = \frac{-(b - a)}{b - a}$$

So dividing by $b - a$ on the right, we have

NOTE Remember that a and b cannot be divided out because they are not factors.

$$\frac{a - b}{b - a} = -1$$

Let's look at some applications of that result in Example 5.

Example 5

Writing Fractions in Simplest Form

Write each fraction in simplest form.

(a) $\dfrac{2x - 4}{4 - x^2} = \dfrac{2(x - 2)}{(2 + x)(2 - x)}$ This is equal to -1.

$$= \frac{2(-1)}{2 + x} = \frac{-2}{2 + x}$$

(b) $\dfrac{9 - x^2}{x^2 + 2x - 15} = \dfrac{(3 + x)(3 - x)}{(x + 5)(x - 3)}$ This is equal to -1.

$$= \frac{(3 + x)(-1)}{x + 5}$$

$$= \frac{-x - 3}{x + 5}$$

✔ **CHECK YOURSELF 5**_____

Write each fraction in simplest form.

(a) $\dfrac{3x - 9}{9 - x^2}$

(b) $\dfrac{x^2 - 6x - 27}{81 - x^2}$

CHECK YOURSELF ANSWERS_____

1. (a) $\dfrac{5}{11}$; (b) $\dfrac{x^3}{3}$; (c) $\dfrac{2y^2}{3x^2}$; (d) $\dfrac{1}{2mn^2}$; (e) $6ab^2$ 2. (a) $\dfrac{5}{x + 3}$; (b) $\dfrac{a - 3}{3a}$; (c) $\dfrac{x + 5}{x + 1}$;

(d) $\dfrac{5(p - 3)}{(p + 2)(p - 2)}$ 3. (a) $\dfrac{-2x^2}{y}$; (b) $\dfrac{4a^2}{3b^3}$ 4. (a) $\dfrac{x - 2}{3x^2 - 1}$; (b) $\dfrac{x + 3}{x - 9}$

5. (a) $\dfrac{-3}{x + 3}$; (b) $\dfrac{-x - 3}{x + 9}$

Name _____

Section _____ Date _____

Write each fraction in simplest form.

1. $\dfrac{16}{24}$

2. $\dfrac{56}{64}$

3. $\dfrac{80}{180}$

4. $\dfrac{18}{30}$

5. $\dfrac{4x^5}{6x^2}$

6. $\dfrac{10x^2}{15x^4}$

7. $\dfrac{9x^3}{27x^6}$

8. $\dfrac{25w^6}{20w^2}$

9. $\dfrac{10a^2b^5}{25ab^2}$

10. $\dfrac{18x^4y^3}{24x^2y^3}$

11. $\dfrac{42x^3y}{14xy^3}$

12. $\dfrac{18pq}{45p^2q^2}$

13. $\dfrac{2xyw^2}{6x^2y^3w^3}$

14. $\dfrac{3c^2d^2}{6bc^3d^3}$

15. $\dfrac{10x^5y^5}{2x^3y^4}$

16. $\dfrac{3bc^6d^3}{bc^3d}$

17. $\dfrac{-4m^3n}{6mn^2}$

18. $\dfrac{-15x^3y^3}{-20xy^4}$

19. $\dfrac{-8ab^3}{-16a^3b}$

20. $\dfrac{14x^2y}{-21xy^4}$

1. _____

2. _____

3. _____

4. _____

5. _____

6. _____

7. _____

8. _____

9. _____

10. _____

11. _____

12. _____

13. _____

14. _____

15. _____

16. _____

17. _____

18. _____

19. _____

20. _____

21. _____

22. _____

23. _____

24. _____

25. _____

26. _____

27. _____

28. _____

29. _____

30. _____

31. _____

32. _____

33. _____

34. _____

35. _____

36. _____

37. _____

38. _____

39. _____

40. _____

41. _____

42. _____

21. $\dfrac{8r^2s^3t}{-16rs^4t^3}$

22. $\dfrac{-10a^3b^2c^3}{15ab^4c}$

23. $\dfrac{3x + 18}{5x + 30}$

24. $\dfrac{4x - 28}{5x - 35}$

25. $\dfrac{3x - 6}{5x - 15}$

26. $\dfrac{x^2 - 25}{3x - 15}$

27. $\dfrac{6a - 24}{a^2 - 16}$

28. $\dfrac{5x - 5}{x^2 - 4}$

29. $\dfrac{x^2 + 3x + 2}{5x + 10}$

30. $\dfrac{4w^2 - 20w}{w^2 - 2w - 15}$

31. $\dfrac{x^2 - 6x - 16}{x^2 - 64}$

32. $\dfrac{y^2 - 25}{y^2 - y - 20}$

33. $\dfrac{2m^2 + 3m - 5}{2m^2 + 11m + 15}$

34. $\dfrac{6x^2 - x - 2}{3x^2 - 5x + 2}$

35. $\dfrac{p^2 + 2pq - 15q^2}{p^2 - 25q^2}$

36. $\dfrac{4r^2 - 25s^2}{2r^2 + 3rs - 20s^2}$

37. $\dfrac{2x - 10}{25 - x^2}$

38. $\dfrac{3a - 12}{16 - a^2}$

39. $\dfrac{25 - a^2}{a^2 + a - 30}$

40. $\dfrac{2x^2 - 7x + 3}{9 - x^2}$

41. $\dfrac{x^2 + xy - 6y^2}{4y^2 - x^2}$

42. $\dfrac{16z^2 - w^2}{2w^2 - 5wz - 12z^2}$

43. $\dfrac{x^2 + 4x + 4}{x + 2}$

44. $\dfrac{4x^2 + 12x + 9}{2x + 3}$

45. $\dfrac{xy - 2y + 4x - 8}{2y + 6 - xy - 3x}$

46. $\dfrac{ab - 3a + 5b - 15}{15 + 3a^2 - 5b - a^2 b}$

47. $\dfrac{y - 7}{7 - y}$

48. $\dfrac{5 - y}{y - 5}$

49. The area of the rectangle is represented by $6x^2 + 19x + 10$. What is the length?

3x + 2

50. The volume of the box is represented by $(x^2 + 5x + 6)(x + 5)$. Find the polynomial that represents the area of the bottom of the box.

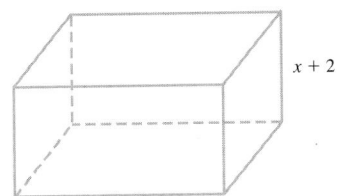

x + 2

51. To work with algebraic fractions correctly, it is important to understand the difference between a *factor* and a *term* of an expression. In your own words, write difinitions for both, explaining the difference between the two.

52. Give some examples of terms and factors in algebraic fractions, and explain how both are affected when a fraction is reduced.

53. Show how the following algebraic fraction can be reduced:

$$\dfrac{x^2 - 9}{4x + 12}$$

Note that your reduced fraction is equivalent to the given fraction. Are there other algebraic fractions equivalent to this one? Write another algebraic fraction that you think is equivalent to this one. Exchange papers with another student. Do you agree that their fraction is equivalent to yours? Why or why not?

54. Explain the reasoning involved in each step of reducing the fraction $\dfrac{42}{56}$.

55. Describe why $\dfrac{3}{5}$ and $\dfrac{27}{45}$ are *equivalent fractions*.

ANSWERS

43. _____

44. _____

45. _____

46. _____

47. _____

48. _____

49. _____

50. _____

51. _____

52. _____

53. _____

54. _____

55. _____

a. _____

b. _____

c. _____

d. _____

e. _____

f. _____

g. _____

h. _____

Getting Ready

Perform the indicated operations.

(a) $\dfrac{3}{10} + \dfrac{4}{10}$

(b) $\dfrac{5}{8} - \dfrac{4}{8}$

(c) $\dfrac{5}{12} - \dfrac{1}{12}$

(d) $\dfrac{7}{16} + \dfrac{3}{16}$

(e) $\dfrac{7}{20} + \dfrac{9}{20}$

(f) $\dfrac{13}{8} - \dfrac{5}{8}$

(g) $\dfrac{11}{6} - \dfrac{2}{6}$

(h) $\dfrac{5}{9} + \dfrac{7}{9}$

Answers for Pre-Test for Chapter 4

1. $\dfrac{-3b^6}{5a^2}$ **2.** $\dfrac{x+4}{2}$ **3.** $\dfrac{x-1}{2x}$ **4.** $\dfrac{13a}{6}$ **5.** 5 **6.** $x+6$

7. $\dfrac{5w-6}{2w^2}$ **8.** $\dfrac{3b+3}{b(b-3)}$ **9.** $\dfrac{-11}{6(x-1)}$ **10.** $\dfrac{10}{x-5}$ **11.** $\dfrac{a}{2b^2}$

12. $\dfrac{x+3}{2x}$ **13.** $2b^2$ **14.** $\dfrac{x+y}{4x}$ **15.** $\dfrac{3x}{2}$ **16.** $\dfrac{y}{2y+x}$ **17.** 3

18. $-2, 5$ **19.** 40 **20.** No solution **21.** 5 **22.** 7 **23.** $5, 20$
24. 48 mi/h going; 40 mi/h returning **25.** 15 ft, 40 ft

Answers

1. $\dfrac{2}{3}$ **3.** $\dfrac{4}{9}$ **5.** $\dfrac{2x^3}{3}$ **7.** $\dfrac{1}{3x^3}$ **9.** $\dfrac{2ab^3}{5}$ **11.** $\dfrac{3x^2}{y^2}$ **13.** $\dfrac{1}{3xy^2w}$

15. $5x^2y$ **17.** $\dfrac{-2m^2}{3n}$ **19.** $\dfrac{b^2}{2a^2}$ **21.** $\dfrac{-r}{2st^2}$ **23.** $\dfrac{3}{5}$ **25.** $\dfrac{3(x-2)}{5(x-3)}$

27. $\dfrac{6}{a+4}$ **29.** $\dfrac{x+1}{5}$ **31.** $\dfrac{x+2}{x+8}$ **33.** $\dfrac{m-1}{m+3}$ **35.** $\dfrac{p-3q}{p-5q}$

37. $\dfrac{-2}{x+5}$ **39.** $\dfrac{-a-5}{a+6}$ **41.** $\dfrac{-x-3y}{2y+x}$ **43.** $x+2$ **45.** $\dfrac{-(y+4)}{y+3}$

47. -1 **49.** $2x+5$ **51.** **53.** **55.**

a. $\dfrac{7}{10}$ b. $\dfrac{1}{8}$ c. $\dfrac{1}{3}$ d. $\dfrac{5}{8}$ e. $\dfrac{4}{5}$ f. 1 g. $\dfrac{3}{2}$ h. $\dfrac{4}{3}$

4.2 Adding and Subtracting Like Fractions

1. Write the sum of two like fractions in simplest form
2. Write the difference of two like fractions in simplest form

You probably remember from arithmetic that **like fractions** are fractions that have the same denominator. The same is true in algebra.

$\dfrac{2}{5}$, $\dfrac{12}{5}$, and $\dfrac{4}{5}$ are like fractions.

$\dfrac{x}{3}$, $\dfrac{y}{3}$, and $\dfrac{z-5}{3}$ are like fractions.

$\dfrac{3x}{2}$, $\dfrac{x}{4}$, and $\dfrac{3x}{8}$ are unlike fractions.

NOTE The fractions have different denominators.

$\dfrac{3}{x}$, $\dfrac{2}{x^2}$, and $\dfrac{x+1}{x^3}$ are unlike fractions.

In arithmetic, the sum or difference of like fractions was found by adding or subtracting the numerators and writing the result over the common denominator. For example,

$$\frac{3}{11} + \frac{5}{11} = \frac{3+5}{11} = \frac{8}{11}$$

In symbols, we have

Rules and Properties: To Add or Subtract Like Fractions

$$\frac{P}{R} + \frac{Q}{R} = \frac{P+Q}{R} \qquad R \neq 0$$

$$\frac{P}{R} - \frac{Q}{R} = \frac{P-Q}{R} \qquad R \neq 0$$

Adding or subtracting like fractions in algebra is just as straightforward. You can use the following steps.

Step by Step: To Add or Subtract Like Algebraic Fractions

Step 1 Add or subtract the numerators.
Step 2 Write the sum or difference over the common denominator.
Step 3 Write the resulting fraction in simplest form.

Example 1

Adding and Subtracting Algebraic Fractions

Add or subtract as indicated. Express your results in simplest form.

Add the numerators.

(a) $\dfrac{2x}{15} + \dfrac{x}{15} = \dfrac{2x + x}{15}$

$= \dfrac{3x}{15} = \dfrac{x}{5}$

Simplify.

Subtract the numerators.

(b) $\dfrac{5y}{6} - \dfrac{y}{6} = \dfrac{5y - y}{6}$

$= \dfrac{4y}{6} = \dfrac{2y}{3}$

Simplify.

(c) $\dfrac{3}{x} + \dfrac{5}{x} = \dfrac{3 + 5}{x} = \dfrac{8}{x}$

(d) $\dfrac{9}{a^2} - \dfrac{7}{a^2} = \dfrac{9 - 7}{a^2} = \dfrac{2}{a^2}$

(e) $\dfrac{7}{2ab} - \dfrac{5}{2ab} = \dfrac{7 - 5}{2ab}$

$= \dfrac{2}{2ab}$

$= \dfrac{1}{ab}$

 CHECK YOURSELF 1

Add or subtract as indicated.

(a) $\dfrac{3a}{10} + \dfrac{2a}{10}$ (b) $\dfrac{7b}{8} - \dfrac{3b}{8}$ (c) $\dfrac{4}{x} + \dfrac{3}{x}$ (d) $\dfrac{5}{3xy} - \dfrac{2}{3xy}$

If polynomials are involved in the numerators or denominators, the process is exactly the same.

Example 2

Adding and Subtracting Algebraic Fractions

Add or subtract as indicated. Express your results in simplest form.

(a) $\dfrac{5}{x + 3} + \dfrac{2}{x + 3} = \dfrac{5 + 2}{x + 3} = \dfrac{7}{x + 3}$

(b) $\dfrac{4x}{x-4} - \dfrac{16}{x-4} = \dfrac{4x-16}{x-4}$

Factor and simplify.

$$= \dfrac{4(x-4)}{x-4} = 4$$

NOTE The final answer is always written in simplest form.

(c) $\dfrac{a-b}{3} + \dfrac{2a+b}{3} = \dfrac{(a-b)+(2a+b)}{3}$

$$= \dfrac{a-b+2a+b}{3}$$

$$= \dfrac{3a}{3} = a$$

Be sure to enclose the second numerator in parentheses!

(d) $\dfrac{3x+y}{2x} - \dfrac{x-3y}{2x} = \dfrac{(3x+y)-(x-3y)}{2x}$

Change both signs.

$$= \dfrac{3x+y-x+3y}{2x}$$

$$= \dfrac{2x+4y}{2x}$$

$$= \dfrac{2(x+2y)}{2x}$$ Factor and divide by the common factor of 2.

$$= \dfrac{x+2y}{x}$$

(e) $\dfrac{3x-5}{x^2+x-2} - \dfrac{2x-4}{x^2+x-2} = \dfrac{(3x-5)-(2x-4)}{x^2+x-2}$ Put the second numerator in parentheses.

Change both signs.

$$= \dfrac{3x-5-2x+4}{x^2+x-2}$$

$$= \dfrac{x-1}{x^2+x-2}$$

$$= \dfrac{(x-1)}{(x+2)(x-1)}$$ Factor and divide by the common factor of $x-1$.

$$= \dfrac{1}{x+2}$$

(f) $\dfrac{2x + 7y}{x + 3y} - \dfrac{x + 4y}{x + 3y} = \dfrac{(2x + 7y) - (x + 4y)}{x + 3y}$

Change both signs.

$= \dfrac{2x + 7y - x - 4y}{x + 3y}$

$= \dfrac{x + 3y}{x + 3y} = 1$

CHECK YOURSELF 2

Add or subtract as indicated.

(a) $\dfrac{4}{x - 5} - \dfrac{2}{x - 5}$

(b) $\dfrac{3x}{x + 3} + \dfrac{9}{x + 3}$

(c) $\dfrac{5x - y}{3y} - \dfrac{2x - 4y}{3y}$

(d) $\dfrac{5x + 8}{x^2 - 2x - 15} - \dfrac{4x + 5}{x^2 - 2x - 15}$

CHECK YOURSELF ANSWERS

1. (a) $\dfrac{a}{2}$; (b) $\dfrac{b}{2}$; (c) $\dfrac{7}{x}$; (d) $\dfrac{1}{xy}$ 2. (a) $\dfrac{2}{x - 5}$; (b) 3; (c) $\dfrac{x + y}{y}$; (d) $\dfrac{1}{x - 5}$

Name _____

Section _____ Date _____

Add or subtract as indicated. Express your results in simplest form.

1. $\dfrac{7}{18} + \dfrac{5}{18}$

2. $\dfrac{5}{18} - \dfrac{2}{18}$

3. $\dfrac{13}{16} - \dfrac{9}{16}$

4. $\dfrac{5}{12} + \dfrac{11}{12}$

5. $\dfrac{x}{8} + \dfrac{3x}{8}$

6. $\dfrac{5y}{16} + \dfrac{7y}{16}$

7. $\dfrac{7a}{10} - \dfrac{3a}{10}$

8. $\dfrac{5x}{12} - \dfrac{x}{12}$

9. $\dfrac{5}{x} + \dfrac{3}{x}$

10. $\dfrac{9}{y} - \dfrac{3}{y}$

11. $\dfrac{8}{w} - \dfrac{2}{w}$

12. $\dfrac{7}{z} + \dfrac{9}{z}$

13. $\dfrac{2}{xy} + \dfrac{3}{xy}$

14. $\dfrac{8}{ab} + \dfrac{4}{ab}$

15. $\dfrac{2}{3cd} + \dfrac{4}{3cd}$

16. $\dfrac{5}{4cd} + \dfrac{11}{4cd}$

17. $\dfrac{7}{x-5} + \dfrac{9}{x-5}$

18. $\dfrac{11}{x+7} - \dfrac{4}{x+7}$

19. $\dfrac{2x}{x-2} - \dfrac{4}{x-2}$

20. $\dfrac{7w}{w+3} + \dfrac{21}{w+3}$

21. $\dfrac{8p}{p+4} + \dfrac{32}{p+4}$

22. $\dfrac{5a}{a-3} - \dfrac{15}{a-3}$

23. $\dfrac{x^2}{x+4} + \dfrac{3x-4}{x+4}$

24. $\dfrac{x^2}{x-3} - \dfrac{9}{x-3}$

25. $\dfrac{m^2}{m-5} - \dfrac{25}{m-5}$

26. $\dfrac{s^2}{s+3} + \dfrac{2s-3}{s+3}$

27. $\dfrac{a-1}{3} + \dfrac{2a-5}{3}$

28. $\dfrac{y+2}{5} + \dfrac{4y+8}{5}$

29. $\dfrac{3x-1}{4} - \dfrac{x+7}{4}$

30. $\dfrac{4x+2}{3} - \dfrac{x-1}{3}$

31. $\dfrac{4m+7}{6m} + \dfrac{2m+5}{6m}$

32. $\dfrac{6x-y}{4y} - \dfrac{2x+3y}{4y}$

33. $\dfrac{4w-7}{w-5} - \dfrac{2w+3}{w-5}$

34. $\dfrac{3b-8}{b-6} + \dfrac{b-16}{b-6}$

35. $\dfrac{x-7}{x^2-x-6} + \dfrac{2x-2}{x^2-x-6}$

36. $\dfrac{5a-12}{a^2-8a+15} - \dfrac{3a-2}{a^2-8a+15}$

37. $\dfrac{y^2}{2y+8} + \dfrac{3y-4}{2y+8}$

38. $\dfrac{x^2}{4x-12} - \dfrac{9}{4x-12}$

39. $\dfrac{7w}{w+3} + \dfrac{21}{w+3}$

40. $\dfrac{2x}{x-3} - \dfrac{6}{x-3}$

ANSWERS

1. _____ 2. _____

3. _____ 4. _____

5. _____ 6. _____

7. _____ 8. _____

9. _____ 10. _____

11. _____ 12. _____

13. _____ 14. _____

15. _____ 16. _____

17. _____ 18. _____

19. _____ 20. _____

21. _____ 22. _____

23. _____ 24. _____

25. _____ 26. _____

27. _____ 28. _____

29. _____ 30. _____

31. _____ 32. _____

33. _____ 34. _____

35. _____ 36. _____

37. _____ 38. _____

39. _____ 40. _____

41. $\dfrac{x^2}{x^2 + x - 6} - \dfrac{6}{(x + 3)(x - 2)} + \dfrac{x}{(x^2 + x - 6)}$

42. $\dfrac{-12}{x^2 + x - 12} + \dfrac{x^2}{(x + 4)(x - 3)} + \dfrac{x}{x^2 + x - 12}$

43. Find the perimeter of the given figure.

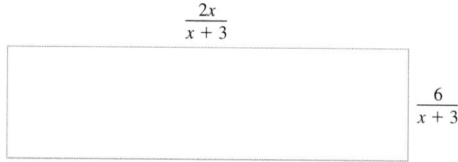

44. Find the perimeter of the following figure.

Getting Ready

(a) $\dfrac{3}{4} + \dfrac{1}{2}$ (b) $\dfrac{5}{6} - \dfrac{2}{3}$

(c) $\dfrac{7}{10} - \dfrac{3}{5}$ (d) $\dfrac{5}{8} + \dfrac{3}{4}$

(e) $\dfrac{5}{6} + \dfrac{3}{8}$ (f) $\dfrac{7}{8} - \dfrac{3}{5}$

(g) $\dfrac{9}{10} - \dfrac{2}{15}$ (h) $\dfrac{5}{12} + \dfrac{7}{18}$

Answers

1. $\dfrac{2}{3}$ **3.** $\dfrac{1}{4}$ **5.** $\dfrac{x}{2}$ **7.** $\dfrac{2a}{5}$ **9.** $\dfrac{8}{x}$ **11.** $\dfrac{6}{w}$ **13.** $\dfrac{5}{xy}$

15. $\dfrac{2}{cd}$ **17.** $\dfrac{16}{x - 5}$ **19.** 2 **21.** 8 **23.** $x - 1$ **25.** $m + 5$

27. $a - 2$ **29.** $\dfrac{x - 4}{2}$ **31.** $\dfrac{m + 2}{m}$ **33.** 2 **35.** $\dfrac{3}{x + 2}$

37. $\dfrac{y - 1}{2}$ **39.** 7 **41.** 1 **43.** 4 **a.** $\dfrac{5}{4}$ **b.** $\dfrac{1}{6}$ **c.** $\dfrac{1}{10}$

d. $\dfrac{11}{8}$ **e.** $\dfrac{29}{24}$ **f.** $\dfrac{11}{40}$ **g.** $\dfrac{23}{30}$ **h.** $\dfrac{29}{36}$

Multiplying and Dividing Algebraic Fractions

4.3 OBJECTIVES

1. Write the product of two algebraic fractions in simplest form
2. Write the quotient of two algebraic fractions in simplest form
3. Simplify a complex fraction by the method of common denominators

In arithmetic, you found the product of two fractions by multiplying the numerators and the denominators. For example,

$$\frac{2}{5} \cdot \frac{3}{7} = \frac{2 \cdot 3}{5 \cdot 7} = \frac{6}{35}$$

In symbols, we have

Rules and Properties: Multiplying Algebraic Fractions

NOTE P, Q, R, and S again represent polynomials.

$$\frac{P}{Q} \cdot \frac{R}{S} = \frac{PR}{QS} \qquad \text{when } Q \neq 0 \text{ and } S \neq 0$$

It is easier to divide the numerator and denominator by any common factors *before* multiplying. Consider the following.

NOTE Divide by the common factors of 3 and 4. The alternative is to multiply *first:*

$$\frac{3}{8} \cdot \frac{4}{9} = \frac{12}{72}$$

and then use the GCF to reduce to lowest terms

$$\frac{12}{72} = \frac{1}{6}$$

$$\frac{3}{8} \cdot \frac{4}{9} = \frac{\overset{1}{\cancel{3}} \cdot \overset{1}{\cancel{4}}}{\underset{2}{\cancel{8}} \cdot \underset{3}{\cancel{9}}} = \frac{1}{6}$$

In algebra, we multiply fractions in exactly the same way.

Step by Step: To Multiply Algebraic Fractions

Step 1 Factor the numerators and denominators.
Step 2 Divide the numerator and denominator by any common factors.
Step 3 Write the product of the remaining factors in the numerator over the product of the remaining factors in the denominator.

Example 1 illustrates this property.

Example 1

Multiplying Algebraic Fractions

Multiply the following fractions.

NOTE Divide by the common factors of 5, x^2, and y.

(a) $\dfrac{2x^3}{5y^2} \cdot \dfrac{10y}{3x^2} = \dfrac{2x^3 \cdot 10y}{5y^2 \cdot 3x^2} = \dfrac{4x}{3y}$

(b) $\dfrac{x}{x^2 - 3x} \cdot \dfrac{6x - 18}{9x} = \dfrac{x}{x(x - 3)} \cdot \dfrac{6(x - 3)}{9x}$

Factor

NOTE Divide by the common factors of 3, x, and $x - 3$.

$$= \dfrac{\overset{1}{\cancel{x}} \cdot \overset{2}{\cancel{6}}\cancel{(x - 3)}}{\underset{1}{\cancel{x}}\underset{1}{\cancel{(x - 3)}} \cdot \underset{3}{\cancel{9}x}}$$

$$= \dfrac{2}{3x}$$

(c) $\dfrac{4}{x^2 - 2x} \cdot \dfrac{10 - 5x}{8} = \dfrac{4}{x(x - 2)} \cdot \dfrac{5(2 - x)}{8}$

NOTE

$\dfrac{2 - x}{x - 2} = \dfrac{-(x - 2)}{x - 2} = -1$

$$= \dfrac{\overset{1}{\cancel{4}} \cdot 5\overset{-1}{\cancel{(2 - x)}}}{x\underset{1}{\cancel{(x - 2)}} \cdot \underset{2}{\cancel{8}}} = \dfrac{-5}{2x}$$

NOTE Divide by the common factors of $x - 4$, x, and 3.

(d) $\dfrac{x^2 - 2x - 8}{3x^2} \cdot \dfrac{6x}{3x - 12} = \dfrac{\overset{1}{\cancel{(x - 4)}}(x + 2)}{\underset{x}{3x^2}} \cdot \dfrac{\overset{2}{\cancel{6x}}}{3\underset{1}{\cancel{(x - 4)}}}$

$$= \dfrac{2(x + 2)}{3x}$$

(e) $\dfrac{x^2 - y^2}{5x - 5y} \cdot \dfrac{10xy}{x^2 + 2xy + y^2} = \dfrac{\overset{1}{\cancel{(x - y)}}\overset{1}{\cancel{(x + y)}}}{5\underset{1}{\cancel{(x - y)}}} \cdot \dfrac{\overset{2}{\cancel{10}}xy}{\underset{1}{\cancel{(x + y)}}(x + y)}$

$$= \dfrac{2xy}{x + y}$$

✔ CHECK YOURSELF 1

Multiply.

(a) $\dfrac{3x^2}{5y^2} \cdot \dfrac{10y^5}{15x^3}$ **(b)** $\dfrac{5x + 15}{x} \cdot \dfrac{2x^2}{x^2 + 3x}$ **(c)** $\dfrac{x}{2x - 6} \cdot \dfrac{3x - x^2}{2}$

(d) $\dfrac{3x - 15}{6x^2} \cdot \dfrac{2x}{x^2 - 25}$ **(e)** $\dfrac{x^2 - 5x - 14}{4x^2} \cdot \dfrac{8x}{x^2 - 49}$

You can also use your experience from arithmetic in dividing fractions. Recall that, to divide fractions, we *invert the divisor* (the *second* fraction) and multiply. For example,

NOTE Recall, $\dfrac{6}{5}$ is the reciprocal of $\dfrac{5}{6}$.

$$\dfrac{2}{3} \div \dfrac{5}{6} = \dfrac{2}{3} \cdot \dfrac{6}{5} = \dfrac{2 \cdot 6}{3 \cdot 5} = \dfrac{4}{5}$$

In symbols, we have

Rules and Properties: Dividing Algebraic Fractions

NOTE Once more P, Q, R, and S are polynomials.

$$\dfrac{P}{Q} \div \dfrac{R}{S} = \dfrac{P}{Q} \cdot \dfrac{S}{R} = \dfrac{PS}{QR}$$

when $Q \neq 0$, $R \neq 0$, and $S \neq 0$.

Division of algebraic fractions is done in exactly the same way.

Step 1 Invert the divisor and change the operation to multiplication.
Step 2 Proceed, using the steps for multiplying algebraic fractions.

Example 2 illustrates this approach.

Example 2

Dividing Algebraic Fractions

Divide the following.

(a) $\dfrac{6}{x^2} \div \dfrac{9}{x^3} = \dfrac{6}{x^2} \cdot \dfrac{x^3}{9}$ Invert the divisor and multiply.

$$= \dfrac{\overset{2}{\cancel{6}}\,\overset{x}{\cancel{x^3}}}{\underset{3}{\cancel{9}}\,\underset{1}{\cancel{x^2}}}$$ No simplification can be done until the divisor is inverted. Then divide by the common factors of 3 and x^2.

$$= \dfrac{2x}{3}$$

(b) $\dfrac{3x^2y}{8xy^3} \div \dfrac{9x^3}{4y^4} = \dfrac{3x^2y}{8xy^3} \cdot \dfrac{4y^4}{9x^3}$

$$= \dfrac{y^2}{6x^2}$$

(c) $\dfrac{2x + 4y}{9x - 18y} \div \dfrac{4x + 8y}{3x - 6y} = \dfrac{2x + 4y}{9x - 18y} \cdot \dfrac{3x - 6y}{4x + 8y}$

NOTE Factor all numerators and denominators *before* dividing out any common factors.

$$= \dfrac{\overset{1}{\cancel{2}}\overset{1}{\cancel{(x + 2y)}} \cdot \overset{1}{\cancel{3}}\overset{1}{\cancel{(x - 2y)}}}{\underset{3}{\cancel{9}}\underset{1}{\cancel{(x - 2y)}} \cdot \underset{2}{\cancel{4}}\underset{1}{\cancel{(x + 2y)}}}$$

$$= \dfrac{1}{6}$$

(d) $\dfrac{x^2 - x - 6}{2x - 6} \div \dfrac{x^2 - 4}{4x^2} = \dfrac{x^2 - x - 6}{2x - 6} \cdot \dfrac{4x^2}{x^2 - 4}$

$$= \dfrac{\overset{1}{\cancel{(x - 3)}}\overset{1}{\cancel{(x + 2)}} \cdot \overset{2}{\cancel{4}}x^2}{\underset{1}{\cancel{2}}\underset{1}{\cancel{(x - 3)}} \cdot \underset{1}{\cancel{(x + 2)}}(x - 2)}$$

$$= \dfrac{2x^2}{x - 2}$$

✔ CHECK YOURSELF 2

Divide.

(a) $\dfrac{4}{x^5} \div \dfrac{12}{x^3}$ **(b)** $\dfrac{5xy^2}{7x^3y} \div \dfrac{10y^2}{14x^3}$

(c) $\dfrac{3x - 9y}{2x + 10y} \div \dfrac{x^2 - 3xy}{4x + 20y}$ **(d)** $\dfrac{x^2 - 9}{4x} \div \dfrac{x^2 - 2x - 15}{2x - 10}$

Before we continue, let's review why the invert-and-multiply rule works for dividing fractions. We will use an example from arithmetic for the explanation. Suppose that we want to divide as follows:

$$\frac{3}{5} \div \frac{2}{3} \tag{1}$$

We can write

$$\underbrace{\frac{3}{5} \div \frac{2}{3}}_{(1)} = \frac{\dfrac{3}{5}}{\dfrac{2}{3}} = \frac{\dfrac{3}{5} \cdot \dfrac{3}{2}}{\dfrac{2}{3} \cdot \dfrac{3}{2}} \qquad \text{We are multiplying by 1.}$$

Interpret the division as a fraction. $= \dfrac{\dfrac{3}{5} \cdot \dfrac{3}{2}}{1}$

$$\frac{2}{3} \cdot \frac{3}{2} = 1$$

$$= \frac{3}{5} \cdot \frac{3}{2} \tag{2}$$

We then have

$$\frac{3}{5} \div \frac{2}{3} = \overset{1}{\frac{3}{5}} \cdot \overset{2}{\frac{3}{2}}$$

Comparing expressions (1) and (2), you should see the rule for dividing fractions. Invert the fraction that follows the division symbol and multiply.

A fraction that has a fraction in its numerator, in its denominator, or in both is called a **complex fraction.** For example, the following are complex fractions

$$\frac{\dfrac{5}{6}}{\dfrac{3}{4}} \qquad \frac{\dfrac{4}{x}}{\dfrac{3}{x^2}} \qquad \text{and} \qquad \frac{\dfrac{a+2}{3}}{\dfrac{a-2}{5}}$$

Remember that we can always multiply the numerator and the denominator of a fraction by the same nonzero term.

NOTE This is the Fundamental Principle of Fractions.

$$\frac{P}{Q} = \frac{P \cdot R}{Q \cdot R} \qquad \text{in which } Q \neq 0 \text{ and } R \neq 0$$

To simplify a complex fraction, multiply the numerator and denominator by the LCD of all fractions that appear within the complex fraction.

Example 3

Simplifying Complex Fractions

Simplify $\dfrac{\dfrac{3}{4}}{\dfrac{5}{8}}$.

The LCD of $\dfrac{3}{4}$ and $\dfrac{5}{8}$ is 8. So multiply the numerator and denominator by 8.

$$\dfrac{\dfrac{3}{4}}{\dfrac{5}{8}} = \dfrac{\dfrac{3}{4} \cdot 8}{\dfrac{5}{8} \cdot 8} = \dfrac{3 \cdot 2}{5 \cdot 1} = \dfrac{6}{5}$$

 CHECK YOURSELF 3

Simplify.

(a) $\dfrac{\dfrac{4}{7}}{\dfrac{3}{7}}$

(b) $\dfrac{\dfrac{3}{8}}{\dfrac{5}{6}}$

The same method can be used to simplify a complex fraction when variables are involved in the expression. Consider Example 4.

Example 4

Simplifying Complex Algebraic Fractions

Simplify $\dfrac{\dfrac{5}{x}}{\dfrac{10}{x^2}}$.

The LCD of $\dfrac{5}{x}$ and $\dfrac{10}{x^2}$ is x^2, so multiply the numerator and denominator by x^2.

NOTE Be sure to write the result in simplest form.

$$\dfrac{\dfrac{5}{x}}{\dfrac{10}{x^2}} = \dfrac{\left(\dfrac{5}{x}\right)x^2}{\left(\dfrac{10}{x^2}\right)x^2} = \dfrac{5x}{10} = \dfrac{x}{2}$$

 CHECK YOURSELF 4

Simplify.

(a) $\dfrac{\dfrac{6}{x^3}}{\dfrac{9}{x^2}}$

(b) $\dfrac{\dfrac{m^4}{15}}{\dfrac{m^3}{20}}$

We may also have a sum or a difference in the numerator or denominator of a complex fraction. The simplification steps are exactly the same. Consider Example 5.

Example 5

Simplifying Complex Algebraic Fractions

Simplify $\dfrac{1 + \dfrac{x}{y}}{1 - \dfrac{x}{y}}$.

The LCD of $1, \dfrac{x}{y}, 1,$ and $\dfrac{x}{y}$ is y, so multiply the numerator and denominator by y.

NOTE Notice the use of the distributive property to multiply *each term* in the numerator and in the denominator by *y*.

$$\frac{1 + \dfrac{x}{y}}{1 - \dfrac{x}{y}} = \frac{\left(1 + \dfrac{x}{y}\right)y}{\left(1 - \dfrac{x}{y}\right)y} = \frac{1 \cdot y + \dfrac{x}{y} \cdot y}{1 \cdot y - \dfrac{x}{y} \cdot y}$$

$$= \frac{y + x}{y - x}$$

 CHECK YOURSELF 5

Simplify.

$$\frac{\dfrac{x}{y} - 2}{\dfrac{x}{y} + 2}$$

A second method for simplifying complex fractions uses the fact that

NOTE To divide by a fraction, we invert the divisor (it *follows* the division sign) and multiply.

$$\frac{\dfrac{P}{Q}}{\dfrac{R}{S}} = \frac{P}{Q} \div \frac{R}{S} = \frac{P}{Q} \cdot \frac{S}{R}$$

To use this method, we must write the numerator and denominator of the complex fraction as single fractions. We can then divide the numerator by the denominator as before.

The following algorithm summarizes our work with simplifying complex fractions.

Step by Step: To Simplify Complex Fractions

Step 1   Multiply the numerator and denominator of the complex fraction by the LCD of all the fractions that appear within the complex fraction.

Step 2   Write the resulting fraction in simplest form.

CHECK YOURSELF ANSWERS

1. (a) $\dfrac{2y^3}{5x}$; (b) 10; (c) $\dfrac{-x^2}{4}$; (d) $\dfrac{1}{x(x + 5)}$; (e) $\dfrac{2(x + 2)}{x(x + 7)}$

2. (a) $\dfrac{1}{3x^2}$; (b) $\dfrac{x}{y}$; (c) $\dfrac{6}{x}$; (d) $\dfrac{x - 3}{2x}$

3. (a) $\dfrac{4}{3}$; (b) $\dfrac{9}{20}$ 4. (a) $\dfrac{2}{3x}$; (b) $\dfrac{4m}{3}$ 5. $\dfrac{x - 2y}{x + 2y}$

Name _____

Section _____ Date _____

Multiply.

ANSWERS

1. $\dfrac{3}{7} \cdot \dfrac{14}{27}$

2. $\dfrac{9}{20} \cdot \dfrac{5}{36}$

3. $\dfrac{x}{2} \cdot \dfrac{y}{6}$

4. $\dfrac{w}{2} \cdot \dfrac{5}{14}$

5. $\dfrac{3a}{2} \cdot \dfrac{4}{a^2}$

6. $\dfrac{5x^3}{3x} \cdot \dfrac{9}{20x}$

7. $\dfrac{3x^3y}{10xy^3} \cdot \dfrac{5xy^2}{9xy^2}$

8. $\dfrac{8xy^5}{5x^3y^2} \cdot \dfrac{15y^2}{16xy^3}$

9. $\dfrac{-4ab^2}{15a^3} \cdot \dfrac{25ab}{-16b^3}$

10. $\dfrac{-7xy^2}{12x^2y} \cdot \dfrac{24x^3y^5}{-21x^2y^7}$

11. $\dfrac{-3m^3n}{10mn^3} \cdot \dfrac{5mn^2}{-9mn^3}$

12. $\dfrac{3x}{2x-6} \cdot \dfrac{x^2-3x}{6}$

13. $\dfrac{x^2+5x}{3x^2} \cdot \dfrac{10x}{5x+25}$

14. $\dfrac{x^2-3x-10}{5x} \cdot \dfrac{15x^2}{3x-15}$

15. $\dfrac{p^2-8p}{4p} \cdot \dfrac{12p^2}{p^2-64}$

16. $\dfrac{a^2-81}{a^2+9a} \cdot \dfrac{5a^2}{a^2-7a-18}$

17. $\dfrac{m^2-4m-21}{3m^2} \cdot \dfrac{m^2+7m}{m^2-49}$

18. $\dfrac{2x^2-x-3}{3x^2+7x+4} \cdot \dfrac{3x^2-11x-20}{4x^2-9}$

19. $\dfrac{4r^2-1}{2r^2-9r-5} \cdot \dfrac{3r^2-13r-10}{9r^2-4}$

20. $\dfrac{a^2+ab}{2a^2-ab-3b^2} \cdot \dfrac{4a^2-9b^2}{5a^2-4ab}$

1. _____

2. _____

3. _____

4. _____

5. _____

6. _____

7. _____

8. _____

9. _____

10. _____

11. _____

12. _____

13. _____

14. _____

15. _____

16. _____

17. _____

18. _____

19. _____

20. _____

21. _____

22. _____

23. _____

24. _____

25. _____

26. _____

27. _____

28. _____

29. _____

30. _____

31. _____

32. _____

33. _____

34. _____

35. _____

36. _____

37. _____

38. _____

39. _____

40. _____

21. $\dfrac{x^2 - 4y^2}{x^2 - xy - 6y^2} \cdot \dfrac{7x^2 - 21xy}{5x - 10y}$

22. $\dfrac{a^2 - 9b^2}{a^2 + ab - 6b^2} \cdot \dfrac{6a^2 - 12ab}{7a - 21b}$

23. $\dfrac{2x - 6}{x^2 + 2x} \cdot \dfrac{3x}{3 - x}$

24. $\dfrac{3x - 15}{x^2 + 3x} \cdot \dfrac{4x}{5 - x}$

Divide.

25. $\dfrac{5}{8} \div \dfrac{15}{16}$

26. $\dfrac{4}{9} \div \dfrac{12}{18}$

27. $\dfrac{5}{x^2} \div \dfrac{10}{x}$

28. $\dfrac{w^2}{3} \div \dfrac{w}{9}$

29. $\dfrac{4x^2y^2}{9x^3} \div \dfrac{8y^2}{27xy}$

30. $\dfrac{8x^3y}{27xy^3} \div \dfrac{16x^3y}{45y}$

31. $\dfrac{3x + 6}{8} \div \dfrac{5x + 10}{6}$

32. $\dfrac{x^2 - 2x}{4x} \div \dfrac{6x - 12}{8}$

33. $\dfrac{4a - 12}{5a + 15} \div \dfrac{8a^2}{a^2 + 3a}$

34. $\dfrac{6p - 18}{9p} \div \dfrac{3p - 9}{p^2 + 2p}$

35. $\dfrac{x^2 + 2x - 8}{9x^2} \div \dfrac{x^2 - 16}{3x - 12}$

36. $\dfrac{16x}{4x^2 - 16} \div \dfrac{4x - 24}{x^2 - 4x - 12}$

37. $\dfrac{x^2 - 9}{2x^2 - 6x} \div \dfrac{2x^2 + 5x - 3}{4x^2 - 1}$

38. $\dfrac{2m^2 - 5m - 7}{4m^2 - 9} \div \dfrac{5m^2 + 5m}{2m^2 + 3m}$

39. $\dfrac{a^2 - 9b^2}{4a^2 + 12ab} \div \dfrac{a^2 - ab - 6b^2}{12ab}$

40. $\dfrac{r^2 + 2rs - 15s^2}{r^3 + 5r^2s} \div \dfrac{r^2 - 9s^2}{5r^3}$

41. $\dfrac{x^2 - 16y^2}{3x^2 - 12xy} \div (x^2 + 4xy)$

42. $\dfrac{p^2 - 4pq - 21q^2}{4p - 28q} \div (2p^2 + 6pq)$

43. $\dfrac{x - 7}{2x + 6} \div \dfrac{21 - 3x}{x^2 + 3x}$

44. $\dfrac{x - 4}{x^2 + 2x} \div \dfrac{16 - 4x}{3x + 6}$

Perform the indicated operations.

45. $\dfrac{x^2 - 2x - 8}{2x - 8} \cdot \dfrac{x^2 + 5x}{x^2 + 5x + 6} \div \dfrac{x^2 + 2x - 15}{x^2 - 9}$

46. $\dfrac{14x - 7}{x^2 + 3x - 4} \cdot \dfrac{x^2 + 6x + 8}{2x^2 + 5x - 3} \div \dfrac{x^2 + 2x}{x^2 + 2x - 3}$

47. $\dfrac{x^2 + 5x}{3x - 6} \cdot \dfrac{x^2 - 4}{3x^2 + 15x} \cdot \dfrac{6x}{x^2 + 6x + 8}$

48. $\dfrac{m^2 - n^2}{m^2 - mn} \cdot \dfrac{6m}{2m^2 + mn - n^2} \cdot \dfrac{8m - 4n}{12m^2 + 12mn}$

Simplify each complex fraction.

49. $\dfrac{\dfrac{2}{3}}{\dfrac{6}{8}}$

50. $\dfrac{\dfrac{5}{6}}{\dfrac{10}{15}}$

51. $\dfrac{1 + \dfrac{1}{2}}{2 + \dfrac{1}{4}}$

52. $\dfrac{1 + \dfrac{3}{4}}{2 - \dfrac{1}{8}}$

53. $\dfrac{\dfrac{x}{8}}{\dfrac{x^2}{4}}$

54. $\dfrac{\dfrac{m^2}{10}}{\dfrac{m^3}{15}}$

55. $\dfrac{\dfrac{3}{a}}{\dfrac{2}{a^2}}$

56. $\dfrac{\dfrac{6}{x^2}}{\dfrac{9}{x^3}}$

57. $\dfrac{\dfrac{y + 1}{y}}{\dfrac{y - 1}{2y}}$

58. $\dfrac{\dfrac{w + 3}{4w}}{\dfrac{w - 3}{2w}}$

41. _____

42. _____

43. _____

44. _____

45. _____

46. _____

47. _____

48. _____

49. _____

50. _____

51. _____

52. _____

53. _____

54. _____

55. _____

56. _____

57. _____

58. _____

59. _____

60. _____

61. _____

62. _____

63. _____

64. _____

65. _____

66. _____

67. _____

68. _____

69. _____

70. _____

71. _____

72. _____

73. _____

74. _____

75. _____

76. _____

59. $\dfrac{2 - \dfrac{1}{x}}{2 + \dfrac{1}{x}}$

60. $\dfrac{3 + \dfrac{1}{a}}{3 - \dfrac{1}{a}}$

61. $\dfrac{3 - \dfrac{x}{y}}{\dfrac{6}{y}}$

62. $\dfrac{2 + \dfrac{x}{y}}{\dfrac{4}{y}}$

63. $\dfrac{\dfrac{x^2}{y^2} - 1}{\dfrac{x}{y} + 1}$

64. $\dfrac{\dfrac{a}{b} + 2}{\dfrac{a^2}{b^2} - 4}$

65. $\dfrac{1 + \dfrac{3}{x} - \dfrac{4}{x^2}}{1 + \dfrac{2}{x} - \dfrac{3}{x^2}}$

66. $\dfrac{1 - \dfrac{2}{r} - \dfrac{8}{r^2}}{1 - \dfrac{1}{r} - \dfrac{6}{r^2}}$

67. $\dfrac{\dfrac{2}{x} - \dfrac{1}{xy}}{\dfrac{1}{xy} + \dfrac{2}{y}}$

68. $\dfrac{\dfrac{1}{xy} + \dfrac{2}{x}}{\dfrac{3}{y} - \dfrac{1}{xy}}$

69. $\dfrac{\dfrac{2}{x - 1} + 1}{1 - \dfrac{3}{x - 1}}$

70. $\dfrac{\dfrac{3}{a + 2} - 1}{1 + \dfrac{2}{a + 2}}$

71. $\dfrac{1 - \dfrac{1}{y - 1}}{y - \dfrac{8}{y + 2}}$

72. $\dfrac{1 + \dfrac{1}{x + 2}}{x - \dfrac{18}{x - 3}}$

73. $1 + \dfrac{1}{1 + \dfrac{1}{x}}$

74. $1 + \dfrac{1}{1 - \dfrac{1}{y}}$

75. Ecology. Herbicides constitute $\dfrac{2}{3}$ of all pesticides used in the United States. Insecticides are $\dfrac{1}{4}$ of all pesticides used in the United States. The ratio of herbicides to insecticides used in the United States can be written $\dfrac{2}{3} \div \dfrac{1}{4}$. Write this ratio in simplest form.

76. Ecology. Fungicides account for $\dfrac{1}{10}$ of the pesticides used in the United States. Insecticides account for $\dfrac{1}{4}$ of all the pesticides used in the United States. The ratio of fungicides to insecticides used in the United States can be written $\dfrac{1}{10} \div \dfrac{1}{4}$. Write this ratio in simplest form.

77. Ecology. The ratio of insecticides to herbicides applied to wheat, soybeans, corn, and cotton can be expressed as $\dfrac{7}{10} \div \dfrac{4}{5}$. Simplify this ratio.

78. Find the area of the rectangle shown.

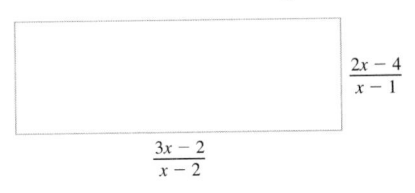

$\dfrac{2x-4}{x-1}$

$\dfrac{3x-2}{x-2}$

79. Find the area of the rectangle shown.

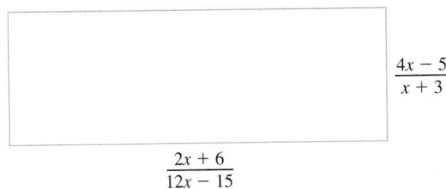

$\dfrac{4x-5}{x+3}$

$\dfrac{2x+6}{12x-15}$

80. Electricity. The combined resistance of two resistors R_1 and R_2 in parallel is given by the formula

$$R_T = \dfrac{1}{\dfrac{1}{R_1} + \dfrac{1}{R_2}}$$

Simplify the formula.

81. Complex fractions have some interesting patterns. Work with a partner to evaluate each complex fraction in the sequence below. This is an interesting sequence of fractions because the numerators and denominators are a famous sequence of whole numbers, and the fractions get closer and closer to a number called "the golden mean."

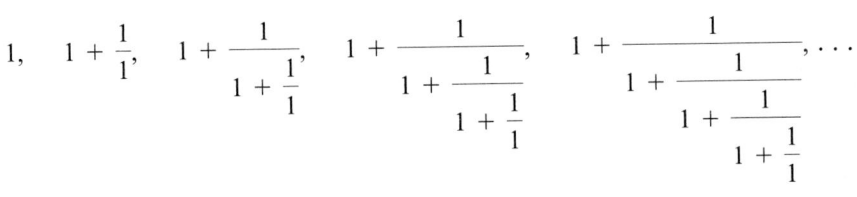

$$1, \quad 1 + \frac{1}{1}, \quad 1 + \frac{1}{1 + \dfrac{1}{1}}, \quad 1 + \frac{1}{1 + \dfrac{1}{1 + \dfrac{1}{1}}}, \quad 1 + \frac{1}{1 + \dfrac{1}{1 + \dfrac{1}{1 + \dfrac{1}{1}}}}, \ldots$$

____, \quad ____, \quad ____, \quad ____, \quad ____, \quad ____, \quad ____, \quad ____

After you have evaluated these first five, you no doubt will see a pattern in the resulting fractions that allows you to go on indefinitely without having to evaluate more complex fractions. Write each of these fractions as decimals. Write your observations about the sequence of fractions and about the sequence of decimal fractions.

77. _____

78. _____

79. _____

80. _____

81. _____

Getting Ready

Solve each of the following equations.

(a) $x + 8 = 10$ (b) $5x - 4 = 2$

(c) $3x + 8 = 4$ (d) $3(x - 2) - 4 = 5$

(e) $4(2x + 1) - 3 = -23$ (f) $4(2x - 5) - 3(3x + 1) = -8$

Answers

1. $\dfrac{2}{9}$ 3. $\dfrac{xy}{12}$ 5. $\dfrac{6}{a}$ 7. $\dfrac{x^2}{6y^2}$ 9. $\dfrac{5}{12a}$ 11. $\dfrac{m^2}{6n^3}$ 13. $\dfrac{2}{3}$

15. $\dfrac{3p^2}{p + 8}$ 17. $\dfrac{m + 3}{3m}$ 19. $\dfrac{2r - 1}{3r - 2}$ 21. $\dfrac{7x}{5}$ 23. $\dfrac{-6}{x + 2}$ 25. $\dfrac{2}{3}$

27. $\dfrac{1}{2x}$ 29. $\dfrac{3y}{2}$ 31. $\dfrac{9}{20}$ 33. $\dfrac{a - 3}{10a}$ 35. $\dfrac{x - 2}{3x^2}$ 37. $\dfrac{2x + 1}{2x}$

39. $\dfrac{3b}{a + 2b}$ 41. $\dfrac{1}{3x^2}$ 43. $\dfrac{-x}{6}$ 45. $\dfrac{x}{2}$ 47. $\dfrac{2x}{3(x + 4)}$ 49. $\dfrac{8}{9}$

51. $\dfrac{2}{3}$ 53. $\dfrac{1}{2x}$ 55. $\dfrac{3a}{2}$ 57. $\dfrac{2(y + 1)}{y - 1}$ 59. $\dfrac{2x - 1}{2x + 1}$ 61. $\dfrac{3y - x}{6}$

63. $\dfrac{x - y}{y}$ 65. $\dfrac{x + 4}{x + 3}$ 67. $\dfrac{2y - 1}{1 + 2x}$ 69. $\dfrac{x + 1}{x - 4}$ 71. $\dfrac{y + 2}{(y - 1)(y + 4)}$

73. $\dfrac{2x + 1}{x + 1}$ 75. $\dfrac{8}{3}$ 77. $\dfrac{7}{8}$ 79. $\dfrac{2}{3}$ 81. a. 2 b. $\dfrac{6}{5}$

c. $-\dfrac{4}{3}$ d. 5 e. -3 f. -15

4.4 Equations Involving Fractions

4.4 OBJECTIVES

1. Determine the excluded values for the variables of an algebraic fraction
2. Solve a fractional equation
3. Solve a proportion for an unknown

You learned how to solve a variety of equations. We now want to extend that work to the solution of **fractional equations,** which are equations that involve algebraic fractions as one or more of their terms.

To solve a fractional equation, we multiply each term of the equation by the LCD of any fractions. The resulting equation should be equivalent to the original equation and be cleared of all fractions.

NOTE The resulting equation *will* be equivalent unless a solution results that makes a denominator in the original equation 0. More about this later!

Example 1

Solving Fractional Equations

Solve

$$\frac{x}{2} - \frac{1}{3} = \frac{2x + 3}{6} \tag{1}$$

NOTE This equation has three terms: $\frac{x}{2}$, $-\frac{1}{3}$, and $\frac{2x + 3}{6}$. The sign of the term is not used to find the LCD.

The LCD for $\frac{x}{2}$, $\frac{1}{3}$, and $\frac{2x + 3}{6}$ is 6. Multiply both sides of the equation by 6. Using the distributive property, we multiply *each* term by 6.

NOTE By the multiplication property of equality, this equation is equivalent to the original equation, labeled (1).

$$6 \cdot \frac{x}{2} - 6 \cdot \frac{1}{3} = 6\left(\frac{2x + 3}{6}\right) \qquad \text{or} \qquad 3x - 2 = 2x + 3 \tag{2}$$

Solving as before, we have

$$3x - 2x = 3 + 2 \qquad \text{or} \qquad x = 5$$

To check, substitute 5 for x in the *original* equation.

$$\frac{5}{2} - \frac{1}{3} \stackrel{?}{=} \frac{2 \cdot 5 + 3}{6}$$

$$\frac{13}{6} = \frac{13}{6} \qquad \text{(True)}$$

 C A U T I O N

Be Careful! Many students have difficulty because they don't distinguish between adding or subtracting *expressions* (as we did in Section 1.8) and solving equations (illustrated in the above example). In the **expression**

$$\frac{x + 1}{2} + \frac{x}{3}$$

we want to add the two fractions to form a single fraction. In the **equation**

$$\frac{x + 1}{2} = \frac{x}{3} + 1$$

we want to solve for x.

CHECK YOURSELF 1

Solve and check.

$$\frac{x}{4} - \frac{1}{6} = \frac{4x - 5}{12}$$

Recall that, for any fraction, the denominator must not be equal to zero. When a fraction has a variable in the denominator, we must exclude any value for the variable that would result in division by zero.

Example 2

Finding Excluded Values for *x*

In the following algebraic fractions, what values for x must be excluded?

(a) $\frac{x}{5}$. Here x can have any value, so none need to be excluded.

(b) $\frac{3}{x}$. If $x = 0$, then $\frac{3}{x}$ is undefined; 0 is the excluded value.

(c) $\frac{5}{x - 2}$. If $x = 2$, then $\frac{5}{x - 2} = \frac{5}{2 - 2} = \frac{5}{0}$, which is undefined, so 2 is the excluded value.

CHECK YOURSELF 2

What values for x, if any, must be excluded?

(a) $\frac{x}{7}$ **(b)** $\frac{5}{x}$ **(c)** $\frac{7}{x - 5}$

If the denominator of an algebraic fraction contains a product of two or more variable factors, the zero-product principle must be used to determine the excluded values for the variable.

In some cases, you will have to factor the denominator to see the restrictions on the values for the variable.

Example 3

Finding Excluded Values for *x*

What values for x must be excluded in each fraction?

(a) $\frac{3}{x^2 - 6x - 16}$

Factoring the denominator, we have

$$\frac{3}{x^2 - 6x - 16} = \frac{3}{(x - 8)(x + 2)}$$

Letting $x - 8 = 0$ or $x + 2 = 0$, we see that 8 and -2 make the denominator 0 so both 8 and -2 must be excluded.

(b) $\dfrac{3}{x^2 + 2x - 48}$

The denominator is zero when

$x^2 + 2x - 48 = 0$

Factoring, we find

$(x - 6)(x + 8) = 0$

The denominator is zero when

$x = 6$ or $x = -8$

 CHECK YOURSELF 3

What values for x must be excluded in the following fractions?

(a) $\dfrac{5}{x^2 - 3x - 10}$

(b) $\dfrac{7}{x^2 + 5x - 14}$

The steps for solving an equation involving fractions are summarized in the following rule.

Step by Step: To Solve a Fractional Equation

Step 1 Remove the fractions in the equation by multiplying each term by the LCD of all the fractions.

Step 2 Solve the equation resulting from step 1 as before.

Step 3 Check your solution in the *original equation.*

We can also solve fractional equations with variables in the denominator by using the above algorithm. Example 4 illustrates this approach.

Example 4

Solving Fractional Equations

Solve

$$\frac{7}{4x} - \frac{3}{x^2} = \frac{1}{2x^2}$$

NOTE The factor *x* appears twice in the LCD.

The LCD of the three terms in the equation is $4x^2$, and so we multiply both sides of the equation by $4x^2$.

$$4x^2 \cdot \frac{7}{4x} - 4x^2 \cdot \frac{3}{x^2} = 4x^2 \cdot \frac{1}{2x^2}$$

Simplifying, we have

$$7x - 12 = 2$$
$$7x = 14$$
$$x = 2$$

We'll leave the check to you. Be sure to return to the original equation.

✔ CHECK YOURSELF 4

Solve and check.

$$\frac{5}{2x} - \frac{4}{x^2} = \frac{7}{2x^2}$$

The process of solving fractional equations is exactly the same when binomials are involved in the denominators.

Example 5

Solving Fractional Equations

(a) Solve

NOTE There are three terms.

$$\frac{x}{x - 3} - 2 = \frac{1}{x - 3}$$

The LCD is $x - 3$, and so we multiply each side (every term) by $x - 3$.

NOTE Each of the terms is multiplied by $x - 3$.

$$(x - 3) \cdot \left(\frac{x}{x - 3}\right) - 2(x - 3) = (x - 3) \cdot \left(\frac{1}{x - 3}\right)$$

 **CAUTION**

Be careful of the signs!

Simplifying, we have

$$x - 2(x - 3) = 1$$
$$x - 2x + 6 = 1$$
$$-x = -5$$
$$x = 5$$

To check, substitute 5 for x in the original equation.

(b) Solve

NOTE Recall that
$x^2 - 9 = (x - 3)(x + 3)$

$$\frac{3}{x - 3} - \frac{7}{x + 3} = \frac{2}{x^2 - 9}$$

In factored form, the three denominators are $x - 3$, $x + 3$, and $(x + 3)(x - 3)$. This means that the LCD is $(x + 3)(x - 3)$, and so we multiply:

$$(x - 3)(x + 3)\left(\frac{3}{x - 3}\right) - (x + 3)(x - 3)\left(\frac{7}{x + 3}\right) = (x + 3)(x - 3)\left(\frac{2}{x^2 - 9}\right)$$

Simplifying, we have

$$3(x + 3) - 7(x - 3) = 2$$
$$3x + 9 - 7x + 21 = 2$$
$$-4x + 30 = 2$$
$$-4x = -28$$
$$x = 7$$

CHECK YOURSELF 5

Solve and check.

(a) $\dfrac{x}{x-5} - 2 = \dfrac{2}{x-5}$

(b) $\dfrac{4}{x-4} - \dfrac{3}{x+1} = \dfrac{5}{x^2 - 3x - 4}$

You should be aware that some fractional equations have no solutions. Example 6 shows that possibility.

Example 6

Solving Fractional Equations

Solve

$$\frac{x}{x-2} - 7 = \frac{2}{x-2}$$

The LCD is $x - 2$, and so we multiply each side (every term) by $x - 2$.

$$(x-2)\left(\frac{x}{x-2}\right) - 7(x-2) = (x-2)\left(\frac{2}{x-2}\right)$$

Simplifying, we have

$$x - 7x + 14 = 2$$
$$-6x = -12$$
$$x = 2$$

Now, when we try to check our result, we have

NOTE 2 is substituted for *x* in the original equation.

$$\frac{2}{2-2} - 7 \overset{?}{=} \frac{2}{2-2} \qquad \text{or} \qquad \frac{2}{0} - 7 \overset{?}{=} \frac{2}{0}$$

These terms are undefined.

What went wrong? Remember that two of the terms in our original equation were $\dfrac{x}{x-2}$ and $\dfrac{2}{x-2}$. The variable x cannot have the value 2 because 2 is an excluded value (it makes the denominator 0). So our original equation has *no solution*.

CHECK YOURSELF 6

Solve, if possible.

$$\frac{x}{x+3} - 6 = \frac{-3}{x+3}$$

Equations involving fractions may also lead to quadratic equations, as Example 7 illustrates.

> **Example 7**

Solving Fractional Equations

Solve

$$\frac{x}{x - 4} = \frac{15}{x - 3} - \frac{2x}{x^2 - 7x + 12}$$

The LCD is $(x - 4)(x - 3)$. Multiply each side (every term) by $(x - 4)(x - 3)$.

$$\frac{x}{(x-4)}\cancel{(x-4)}(x - 3) = \frac{15}{(x-3)}(x - 4)\cancel{(x-3)} - \frac{2x}{(x-4)(x-3)}\cancel{(x-4)}\cancel{(x-3)}$$

Simplifying, we have

$$x(x - 3) = 15(x - 4) - 2x$$

Multiply to clear of parentheses:

$$x^2 - 3x = 15x - 60 - 2x$$

NOTE Notice that this equation is *quadratic*. It can be solved by the methods of Section 3.7.

In standard form, the equation is

$$x^2 - 16x + 60 = 0 \qquad \text{or} \qquad (x - 6)(x - 10) = 0$$

Setting the factors to 0, we have

$$x - 6 = 0 \qquad \text{or} \qquad x - 10 = 0$$
$$x = 6 \qquad\qquad\qquad x = 10$$

So $x = 6$ and $x = 10$ are possible solutions. We will leave the check of *each* solution to you.

CHECK YOURSELF 7

Solve and check.

$$\frac{3x}{x + 2} - \frac{2}{x + 3} = \frac{36}{x^2 + 5x + 6}$$

As the examples of this section illustrated, *whenever* an equation involves algebraic fractions, the *first step* of the solution is to clear the equation of fractions by multiplication.

The following algorithm summarizes our work in solving equations that involve algebraic fractions.

> **Step by Step:** To Solve an Equation Involving Fractions

Step 1	Remove the fractions appearing in the equation by multiplying each side (every term) by the LCD of all the fractions.
Step 2	Solve the equation resulting from step 1. If the equation is linear, use the methods of Chapter 1 for the solution. If the equation is quadratic, use the methods of Chapter 3.
Step 3	Check all solutions by substitution in the *original equation*. Be sure to discard any *extraneous* solutions, that is, solutions that would result in a zero denominator in the original equation.

 **4.4** **Exercises**

What values for x, if any, must be excluded in each of the following algebraic fractions?

ANSWERS

1. $\dfrac{x}{15}$

2. $\dfrac{8}{x}$

3. $\dfrac{17}{x}$

4. $\dfrac{x}{8}$

5. $\dfrac{3}{x-2}$

6. $\dfrac{x-1}{5}$

7. $\dfrac{-5}{x+4}$

8. $\dfrac{4}{x+3}$

9. $\dfrac{x-5}{2}$

10. $\dfrac{x-1}{x-5}$

11. $\dfrac{3x}{(x+1)(x-2)}$

12. $\dfrac{5x}{(x-3)(x+7)}$

13. $\dfrac{x-1}{(2x-1)(x+3)}$

14. $\dfrac{x+3}{(3x+1)(x-2)}$

15. $\dfrac{7}{x^2-9}$

16. $\dfrac{5x}{x^2+x-2}$

17. $\dfrac{x+3}{x^2-7x+12}$

18. $\dfrac{3x-4}{x^2-49}$

19. $\dfrac{2x-1}{3x^2+x-2}$

20. $\dfrac{3x+1}{4x^2-11x+6}$

Solve each of the following equations for x.

21. $\dfrac{x}{2}+3=6$

22. $\dfrac{x}{3}-2=1$

ANSWERS
1. _____
2. _____
3. _____
4. _____
5. _____
6. _____
7. _____
8. _____
9. _____
10. _____
11. _____
12. _____
13. _____
14. _____
15. _____
16. _____
17. _____
18. _____
19. _____
20. _____
21. _____
22. _____

23. _____

24. _____

25. _____

26. _____

27. _____

28. _____

29. _____

30. _____

31. _____

32. _____

33. _____

34. _____

35. _____

36. _____

37. _____

38. _____

39. _____

40. _____

41. _____

42. _____

43. _____

44. _____

45. _____

46. _____

47. _____

48. _____

23. $\dfrac{3x}{4} - 6 = -3$

24. $\dfrac{3x}{8} + 5 = 2$

25. $\dfrac{2x}{3} - 5 = -3$

26. $\dfrac{x}{5} - 6 = -1$

27. $\dfrac{x}{2} - \dfrac{x}{3} = 2$

28. $\dfrac{x}{6} - \dfrac{x}{8} = 1$

29. $\dfrac{x}{4} - \dfrac{x}{5} = 2$

30. $\dfrac{x}{3} - \dfrac{x}{4} = 3$

31. $\dfrac{2x}{5} - \dfrac{x}{3} = \dfrac{7}{15}$

32. $\dfrac{2x}{7} - \dfrac{3x}{5} = \dfrac{6}{35}$

33. $\dfrac{2x}{3} - \dfrac{4x}{5} = 2$

34. $\dfrac{3x}{2} - \dfrac{5x}{3} = 2$

35. $\dfrac{x}{5} - \dfrac{1}{3} = \dfrac{x - 7}{3}$

36. $\dfrac{x}{6} + \dfrac{3}{4} = \dfrac{x - 1}{4}$

37. $\dfrac{x}{4} - \dfrac{1}{5} = \dfrac{4x + 3}{20}$

38. $\dfrac{x}{12} - \dfrac{1}{6} = \dfrac{2x - 7}{12}$

39. $\dfrac{3}{x} + 2 = \dfrac{7}{x}$

40. $\dfrac{4}{x} - 3 = \dfrac{16}{x}$

41. $\dfrac{4}{x} + \dfrac{3}{4} = \dfrac{10}{x}$

42. $\dfrac{3}{x} = \dfrac{5}{3} - \dfrac{7}{x}$

43. $\dfrac{5}{2x} - \dfrac{1}{x} = \dfrac{9}{2x^2}$

44. $\dfrac{4}{3x} + \dfrac{1}{x} = \dfrac{14}{3x^2}$

45. $\dfrac{2}{x - 3} + 1 = \dfrac{7}{x - 3}$

46. $\dfrac{x}{x + 1} + 2 = \dfrac{14}{x + 1}$

47. $\dfrac{12}{x + 3} = \dfrac{x}{x + 3} + 2$

48. $\dfrac{5}{x - 3} + 3 = \dfrac{x}{x - 3}$

49. $\dfrac{3}{x-5} + 4 = \dfrac{2x+5}{x-5}$

50. $\dfrac{24}{x+5} - 2 = \dfrac{x+2}{x+5}$

51. $\dfrac{2}{x+3} + \dfrac{1}{2} = \dfrac{x+6}{x+3}$

52. $\dfrac{6}{x-5} - \dfrac{2}{3} = \dfrac{x-9}{x-5}$

53. $\dfrac{x}{3x+12} + \dfrac{x-1}{x+4} = \dfrac{5}{3}$

54. $\dfrac{x}{4x-12} - \dfrac{x-4}{x-3} = \dfrac{1}{8}$

55. $\dfrac{x}{x-3} - 2 = \dfrac{3}{x-3}$

56. $\dfrac{x}{x-5} + 2 = \dfrac{5}{x-5}$

57. $\dfrac{x-1}{x+3} - \dfrac{x-3}{x} = \dfrac{3}{x^2+3x}$

58. $\dfrac{x}{x-2} - \dfrac{x+1}{x} = \dfrac{8}{x^2-2x}$

59. $\dfrac{1}{x-2} - \dfrac{2}{x+2} = \dfrac{2}{x^2-4}$

60. $\dfrac{1}{x+4} + \dfrac{1}{x-4} = \dfrac{12}{x^2-16}$

61. $\dfrac{3}{x-1} - \dfrac{1}{x+9} = \dfrac{18}{x^2+8x-9}$

62. $\dfrac{2}{x+2} = \dfrac{3}{x+6} + \dfrac{9}{x^2+8x+12}$

63. $\dfrac{3}{x+3} + \dfrac{25}{x^2+x-6} = \dfrac{5}{x-2}$

64. $\dfrac{5}{x+6} + \dfrac{2}{x^2+7x+6} = \dfrac{3}{x+1}$

65. $\dfrac{7}{x-5} - \dfrac{3}{x+5} = \dfrac{40}{x^2-25}$

66. $\dfrac{3}{x-3} - \dfrac{18}{x^2-9} = \dfrac{5}{x+3}$

67. $\dfrac{2x}{x-3} + \dfrac{2}{x-5} = \dfrac{3x}{x^2-8x+15}$

68. $\dfrac{x}{x-4} = \dfrac{5x}{x^2-x-12} - \dfrac{3}{x+3}$

69. $\dfrac{2x}{x+2} = \dfrac{5}{x^2-x-6} - \dfrac{1}{x-3}$

70. $\dfrac{3x}{x-1} = \dfrac{2}{x-2} - \dfrac{2}{x^2-3x+2}$

71. $\dfrac{7}{x-2} + \dfrac{16}{x+3} = 3$

72. $\dfrac{5}{x-2} + \dfrac{6}{x+2} = 2$

73. $\dfrac{11}{x-3} - 1 = \dfrac{10}{x+3}$

74. $\dfrac{17}{x-4} - 2 = \dfrac{10}{x+2}$

49. _____

50. _____

51. _____

52. _____

53. _____

54. _____

55. _____

56. _____

57. _____

58. _____

59. _____

60. _____

61. _____

62. _____

63. _____

64. _____

65. _____

66. _____

67. _____

68. _____

69. _____

70. _____

71. _____

72. _____

73. _____

74. _____

75. _____

76. _____

77. _____

78. _____

79. _____

80. _____

81. _____

82. _____

a. _____

b. _____

c. _____

d. _____

e. _____

f. _____

Solve each of the following equations for x.

75. $\dfrac{x + 1}{5} = \dfrac{20}{25}$

76. $\dfrac{2}{5} = \dfrac{x - 2}{20}$

77. $\dfrac{3}{5} = \dfrac{x - 1}{20}$

78. $\dfrac{5}{x - 3} = \dfrac{15}{21}$

79. $\dfrac{3x + 4}{5} = \dfrac{x}{2}$

80. $\dfrac{2x - 1}{7} = \dfrac{x}{4}$

81. $\dfrac{x}{6} = \dfrac{x + 5}{16}$

82. $\dfrac{x - 2}{x + 2} = \dfrac{12}{20}$

83. $\dfrac{x - 3}{8} = \dfrac{x - 2}{10}$

84. $\dfrac{x - 1}{5} = \dfrac{x + 2}{8}$

85. $\dfrac{x}{x + 7} = \dfrac{10}{17}$

86. $\dfrac{x}{10} = \dfrac{x + 6}{30}$

87. $\dfrac{2}{x - 1} = \dfrac{6}{x + 9}$

88. $\dfrac{3}{x - 3} = \dfrac{4}{x - 5}$

89. $\dfrac{1}{x + 3} = \dfrac{7}{x^2 - 9}$

90. $\dfrac{1}{x + 5} = \dfrac{4}{x^2 + 3x - 10}$

Write each of the following phrases using symbols. Use the variable *x* to represent the number in each case.

(a) One-fourth of a number added to four-fifths of the same number

(b) 6 times a number, decreased by 12

(c) The quotient when 5 more than a number is divided by 6

(d) Three times the length of a side of a rectangle decreased by 4

(e) A distance traveled divided by 5

(f) The speed of a truck that is 5 mi/h slower than a car

Answers

1. None   **3.** 0   **5.** 2   **7.** -4 **9.** None   **11.** $-1, 2$ **13.** $-3, \dfrac{1}{2}$

15. $-3, 3$ **17.** $3, 4$ **19.** $-1, \dfrac{2}{3}$ **21.** 6   **23.** -3 **25.** -3 **27.** 12

29. $x = 40$ **31.** $x = 7$ **33.** 2   **35.** 15   **37.** 7   **39.** 2   **41.** 8

43. 3   **45.** 8   **47.** 2   **49.** 11   **51.** -5 **53.** -23

55. No solution   **57.** 6   **59.** 4   **61.** -5 **63.** No solution

65. $-\dfrac{5}{2}$ **67.** $-\dfrac{1}{2}, 6$ **69.** $-\dfrac{1}{2}$ **71.** $-\dfrac{1}{3}, 7$ **73.** $-8, 9$ **75.** 3

77. 13   **79.** -8 **81.** 3   **83.** 7   **85.** 10   **87.** 6   **89.** $x = 10$

4.5 Dividing Polynomials

OBJECTIVES

1. Find the quotient when a polynomial is divided by a monomial
2. Find the quotient of two polynomials

In Section 1.16, we introduced the second property of exponents, which was used to divide one monomial by another monomial. Let's review that process.

Step by Step: To Divide a Monomial by a Monomial

Step 1 Divide the coefficients.
Step 2 Use the second property of exponents to combine the variables.

NOTE The second property says: If x is not zero,

$$\frac{x^m}{x^n} = x^{m-n}$$

Example 1

Dividing Monomials

Divide: $\frac{8}{2} = 4$

(a) $\dfrac{8x^4}{2x^2} = 4x^{4-2}$

Subtract the exponents.

$= 4x^2$

(b) $\dfrac{45a^5b^3}{9a^2b} = 5a^3b^2$

 CHECK YOURSELF 1

Divide.

(a) $\dfrac{16a^5}{8a^3}$

(b) $\dfrac{28m^4n^3}{7m^3n}$

Now let's look at how this can be extended to divide any polynomial by a monomial. For example, to divide $12a^3 + 8a^2$ by $4a$, proceed as follows:

NOTE Technically, this step depends on the distributive property and the definition of division.

$$\frac{12a^3 + 8a^2}{4a} = \frac{12a^3}{4a} + \frac{8a^2}{4a}$$

Divide each term in the numerator by the denominator, $4a$.

Now do each division.

$= 3a^2 + 2a$

The work above leads us to the following rule.

Step by Step: To Divide a Polynomial by a Monomial

1. Divide each term of the polynomial by the monomial.
2. Simplify the results.

Example 2

Dividing by Monomials

Divide each term by 2.

(a) $\dfrac{4a^2 + 8}{2} = \dfrac{4a^2}{2} + \dfrac{8}{2}$

$= 2a^2 + 4$

Divide each term by $6y$.

(b) $\dfrac{24y^3 + (-18y^2)}{6y} = \dfrac{24y^3}{6y} + \dfrac{-18y^2}{6y}$

$= 4y^2 - 3y$

Remember the rules for signs in division.

(c) $\dfrac{15x^2 + 10x}{-5x} = \dfrac{15x^2}{-5x} + \dfrac{10x}{-5x}$

$= -3x - 2$

NOTE With practice you can write just the quotient.

(d) $\dfrac{14x^4 + 28x^3 - 21x^2}{7x^2} = \dfrac{14x^4}{7x^2} + \dfrac{28x^3}{7x^2} - \dfrac{21x^2}{7x^2}$

$= 2x^2 + 4x - 3$

(e) $\dfrac{9a^3b^4 - 6a^2b^3 + 12ab^4}{3ab} = \dfrac{9a^3b^4}{3ab} - \dfrac{6a^2b^3}{3ab} + \dfrac{12ab^4}{3ab}$

$= 3a^2b^3 - 2ab^2 + 4b^3$

✔ **CHECK YOURSELF 2**

Divide.

(a) $\dfrac{20y^3 - 15y^2}{5y}$

(b) $\dfrac{8a^3 - 12a^2 + 4a}{-4a}$

(c) $\dfrac{16m^4n^3 - 12m^3n^2 + 8mn}{4mn}$

We are now ready to look at dividing one polynomial by another polynomial (with more than one term). The process is very much like long division in arithmetic, as Example 3 illustrates.

Example 3

Dividing by Binomials

Divide $x^2 + 7x + 10$ by $x + 2$.

NOTE The first term in the dividend, x^2, is divided by the first term in the divisor, x.

Step 1
$$x + 2 \overline{) x^2 + 7x + 10 }^{x}$$

Divide x^2 by x to get x.

Step 2
$$x + 2 \overline{) x^2 + 7x + 10 }^{x}$$
$$x^2 + 2x$$

Multiply the divisor, $x + 2$, by x.

REMEMBER To subtract $x^2 + 2x$, mentally change each sign to $-x^2 - 2x$, and add. Take your time and be careful here. It's where most errors are made.

Step 3
$$x + 2 \overline{) x^2 + 7x + 10 }^{x}$$
$$x^2 + 2x$$
$$\overline{5x + 10}$$

Subtract and bring down 10.

Step 4
$$x + 2 \overline{) x^2 + 7x + 10 }^{x + 5}$$
$$x^2 + 2x$$
$$\overline{5x + 10}$$

Divide $5x$ by x to get 5.

NOTE Notice that we repeat the process until the degree of the remainder is less than that of the divisor or until there is no remainder.

Step 5
$$x + 2 \overline{) x^2 + 7x + 10 }^{x + 5}$$
$$x^2 + 2x$$
$$\overline{5x + 10}$$
$$5x + 10$$
$$\overline{0}$$

Multiply $x + 2$ by 5 and then subtract.

The quotient is $x + 5$.

 CHECK YOURSELF 3

Divide $x^2 + 9x + 20$ by $x + 4$.

In Example 3, we showed all the steps separately to help you see the process. In practice, the work can be shortened.

Example 4

Dividing by Binomials

Divide $x^2 + x - 12$ by $x - 3$.

NOTE You might want to write out a problem like $408 \div 17$, to compare the steps.

$$
\begin{array}{r}
x + 4 \\
x - 3 \overline{) x^2 + x - 12} \\
\underline{x^2 - 3x} \\
4x - 12 \\
\underline{4x - 12} \\
0
\end{array}
$$

Step 1 Divide x^2 by x to get x, the first term of the quotient.
Step 2 Multiply $x - 3$ by x.
Step 3 Subtract and bring down -12. Remember to mentally change the signs to $-x^2 + 3x$ and add.
Step 4 Divide $4x$ by x to get 4, the second term of the quotient.
Step 5 Multiply $x - 3$ by 4 and subtract.

The quotient is $x + 4$.

CHECK YOURSELF 4

Divide.

$(x^2 + 2x - 24) \div (x - 4)$

You may have a remainder in algebraic long division just as in arithmetic. Consider Example 5.

Example 5

Dividing by Binomials

Divide $4x^2 - 8x + 11$ by $2x - 3$.

$$
\begin{array}{r}
2x - 1 \quad \text{Quotient} \\
2x - 3 \overline{) 4x^2 - 8x + 11} \\
\underline{4x^2 - 6x} \\
-2x + 11 \\
\underline{-2x + 3} \\
8
\end{array}
$$

Divisor

Remainder

This result can be written as

$$
\frac{4x^2 - 8x + 11}{2x - 3}
$$

$$
= 2x - 1 + \frac{8}{2x - 3}
$$

Remainder

Divisor

Quotient

CHECK YOURSELF 5

Divide.

$(6x^2 - 7x + 15) \div (3x - 5)$

The division process shown in our previous examples can be extended to dividends of a higher degree. The steps involved in the division process are exactly the same, as Example 6 illustrates.

Example 6

Dividing by Binomials

Divide $6x^3 + x^2 - 4x - 5$ by $3x - 1$.

$$
\require{enclose}
\begin{array}{r}
2x^2 + x - 1 \\[-2pt]
3x - 1 \enclose{longdiv}{6x^3 + x^2 - 4x - 5} \\
\underline{6x^3 - 2x^2} \\
3x^2 - 4x \\
\underline{3x^2 - x} \\
-3x - 5 \\
\underline{-3x + 1} \\
-6
\end{array}
$$

The result can be written as

$$
\frac{6x^3 + x^2 - 4x - 5}{3x - 1} = 2x^2 + x - 1 + \frac{-6}{3x - 1}
$$

 CHECK YOURSELF 6

Divide $4x^3 - 2x^2 + 2x + 15$ by $2x + 3$.

Suppose that the dividend is "missing" a term in some power of the variable. You can use 0 as the coefficient for the missing term. Consider Example 7.

Example 7

Dividing by Binomials

Divide $x^3 - 2x^2 + 5$ by $x + 3$.

$$
\require{enclose}
\begin{array}{r}
x^2 - 5x + 15 \\[-2pt]
x + 3 \enclose{longdiv}{x^3 - 2x^2 + 0x + 5} \\
\underline{x^3 + 3x^2} \\
-5x^2 + 0x \\
\underline{-5x^2 - 15x} \\
15x + 5 \\
\underline{15x + 45} \\
-40
\end{array}
$$

Write 0x for the "missing" term in x.

This result can be written as

$$
\frac{x^3 - 2x^2 + 5}{x + 3} = x^2 - 5x + 15 + \frac{-40}{x + 3}
$$

CHECK YOURSELF 7

Divide.

$$(4x^3 + x + 10) \div (2x - 1)$$

You should always arrange the terms of the divisor and dividend in descending-exponent form before starting the long division process, as illustrated in Example 8.

Example 8

Dividing by Binomials

Divide $5x^2 - x + x^3 - 5$ by $-1 + x^2$.

Write the divisor as $x^2 - 1$ and the dividend as $x^3 + 5x^2 - x - 5$.

$$
\begin{array}{r}
x + 5 \\
x^2 - 1 \overline{\smash{)}\,x^3 + 5x^2 - x - 5} \\
\underline{x^3 \qquad\; - x} \\
5x^2 \qquad - 5 \\
\underline{5x^2 \qquad - 5} \\
0
\end{array}
$$

Write $x^3 - x$, the product of x and $x^2 - 1$, so that like terms fall in the same columns.

CHECK YOURSELF 8

Divide:

$$(5x^2 + 10 + 2x^3 + 4x) \div (2 + x^2)$$

CHECK YOURSELF ANSWERS

1. (a) $2a^2$; (b) $4mn^2$ **2.** (a) $4y^2 - 3y$; (b) $-2a^2 + 3a - 1$; (c) $4m^3n^2 - 3m^2n + 2$

3. $x + 5$ **4.** $x + 6$ **5.** $2x + 1 + \dfrac{20}{3x - 5}$ **6.** $2x^2 - 4x + 7 + \dfrac{-6}{2x + 3}$

7. $2x^2 + x + 1 + \dfrac{11}{2x - 1}$ **8.** $2x + 5$

4.5 Exercises

Name _____

Section _____ Date _____

Divide.

1. $\dfrac{18x^6}{9x^2}$

2. $\dfrac{20a^7}{5a^5}$

3. $\dfrac{35m^3n^2}{7mn^2}$

4. $\dfrac{42x^5y^2}{6x^3y}$

5. $\dfrac{3a + 6}{3}$

6. $\dfrac{4x - 8}{4}$

7. $\dfrac{9b^2 - 12}{3}$

8. $\dfrac{10m^2 + 5m}{5}$

9. $\dfrac{16a^3 - 24a^2}{4a}$

10. $\dfrac{9x^3 + 12x^2}{3x}$

11. $\dfrac{12m^2 + 6m}{-3m}$

12. $\dfrac{20b^3 - 25b^2}{-5b}$

13. $\dfrac{18a^4 + 12a^3 - 6a^2}{6a}$

14. $\dfrac{21x^5 - 28x^4 + 14x^3}{7x}$

15. $\dfrac{20x^4y^2 - 15x^2y^3 + 10x^3y}{5x^2y}$

16. $\dfrac{16m^3n^3 + 24m^2n^2 - 40mn^3}{8mn^2}$

Perform the indicated divisions.

17. $\dfrac{x^2 + 5x + 6}{x + 2}$

18. $\dfrac{x^2 + 8x + 15}{x + 3}$

19. $\dfrac{x^2 - x - 20}{x + 4}$

20. $\dfrac{x^2 - 2x - 35}{x + 5}$

21. $\dfrac{2x^2 + 5x - 3}{2x - 1}$

22. $\dfrac{3x^2 + 20x - 32}{3x - 4}$

23. $\dfrac{2x^2 - 3x - 5}{x - 3}$

24. $\dfrac{3x^2 + 17x - 12}{x + 6}$

ANSWERS

1. _____
2. _____
3. _____
4. _____
5. _____
6. _____
7. _____
8. _____
9. _____
10. _____
11. _____
12. _____
13. _____
14. _____
15. _____
16. _____
17. _____
18. _____
19. _____
20. _____
21. _____
22. _____
23. _____
24. _____

25. _____

26. _____

27. _____

28. _____

29. _____

30. _____

31. _____

32. _____

33. _____

34. _____

35. _____

36. _____

37. _____

38. _____

39. _____

40. _____

41. _____

42. _____

43. _____

44. _____

45. _____

46. _____

47. _____

48. _____

25. $\dfrac{4x^2 - 18x - 15}{x - 5}$

26. $\dfrac{3x^2 - 18x - 32}{x - 8}$

27. $\dfrac{6x^2 - x - 10}{3x - 5}$

28. $\dfrac{4x^2 + 6x - 25}{2x + 7}$

29. $\dfrac{x^3 + x^2 - 4x - 4}{x + 2}$

30. $\dfrac{x^3 - 2x^2 + 4x - 21}{x - 3}$

31. $\dfrac{4x^3 + 7x^2 + 10x + 5}{4x - 1}$

32. $\dfrac{2x^3 - 3x^2 + 4x + 4}{2x + 1}$

33. $\dfrac{x^3 - x^2 + 5}{x - 2}$

34. $\dfrac{x^3 + 4x - 3}{x + 3}$

35. $\dfrac{25x^3 + x}{5x - 2}$

36. $\dfrac{8x^3 - 6x^2 + 2x}{4x + 1}$

37. $\dfrac{2x^2 - 8 - 3x + x^3}{x - 2}$

38. $\dfrac{x^2 - 18x + 2x^3 + 32}{x + 4}$

39. $\dfrac{x^4 - 1}{x - 1}$

40. $\dfrac{x^4 + x^2 - 16}{x + 2}$

41. $\dfrac{x^3 - 3x^2 - x + 3}{x^2 - 1}$

42. $\dfrac{x^3 + 2x^2 + 3x + 6}{x^2 + 3}$

43. $\dfrac{x^4 + 2x^2 - 2}{x^2 + 3}$

44. $\dfrac{x^4 + x^2 - 5}{x^2 - 2}$

45. $\dfrac{y^3 + 1}{y + 1}$

46. $\dfrac{y^3 - 8}{y - 2}$

47. $\dfrac{x^4 - 1}{x^2 - 1}$

48. $\dfrac{x^6 - 1}{x^3 - 1}$

49. Find the value of c so that $\dfrac{y^2 - y + c}{y + 1} = y - 2$

50. Find the value of c so that $\dfrac{x^3 + x^2 + x + c}{x^2 + 1} = x + 1$

51. Write a summary of your work with polynomials. Explain how a polynomial is recognized, and explain the rules for the arithmetic of polynomials—how to add, subtract, multiply, and divide. What parts of this chapter do you feel you understand very well, and what part(s) do you still have questions about, or feel unsure of? Exchange papers with another student and compare your questions.

52. A funny (and useful) thing about division of polynomials: To find out about this funny thing, do this division. Compare your answer with another student's.

$(x - 2)\overline{)2x^2 + 3x - 5}$ Is there a remainder?

Now, evaluate the polynomial $2x^2 + 3x - 5$ when $x = 2$. Is this value the same as the remainder?

Try $(x + 3)\overline{)5x^2 - 2x + 1}$ Is there a remainder?

Evaluate the polynomial $5x^2 - 2x + 1$ when $x = -3$. Is this value the same as the remainder?
    What happens when there is no remainder?

Try $(x - 6)\overline{)3x^3 + 14x^2 - 23x + 6}$ Is the remainder zero?

Evaluate the polynomial $3x^3 + 14x - 23x + 6$ when $x = 6$. Is this value zero? Write a description of the patterns you see. When does the pattern hold? Make up several more examples, and test your conjecture.

53. (a) Divide $\dfrac{x^2 - 1}{x - 1}$ (b) Divide $\dfrac{x^3 - 1}{x - 1}$ (c) Divide $\dfrac{x^4 - 1}{x - 1}$

    (d) Based on your results to (a), (b), and (c), predict $\dfrac{x^{50} - 1}{x - 1}$

54. (a) Divide $\dfrac{x^2 + x + 1}{x - 1}$ (b) Divide $\dfrac{x^3 + x^2 + x + 1}{x - 1}$

    (c) Divide $\dfrac{x^4 + x^3 + x^2 + x + 1}{x - 1}$

    (d) Based on your results to (a), (b), and (c), predict $\dfrac{x^{10} + x^9 + x^8 + \cdots + x + 1}{x - 1}$

ANSWERS

49. _____

50. _____

51. _____

52. _____

53. (a) _____

    (b) _____

    (c) _____

    (d) _____

54. (a) _____

    (b) _____

    (c) _____

    (d) _____

Answers

1. $2x^4$ **3.** $5m^2$ **5.** $a + 2$ **7.** $3b^2 - 4$ **9.** $4a^2 - 6a$ **11.** $-4m - 2$

13. $3a^3 + 2a^2 - a$ **15.** $4x^2y - 3y^2 + 2x$ **17.** $x + 3$ **19.** $x - 5$

21. $x + 3$ **23.** $2x + 3 + \dfrac{4}{x - 3}$ **25.** $4x + 2 + \dfrac{-5}{x - 5}$

27. $2x + 3 + \dfrac{5}{3x - 5}$ **29.** $x^2 - x - 2$ **31.** $x^2 + 2x + 3 + \dfrac{8}{4x - 1}$

33. $x^2 + x + 2 + \dfrac{9}{x - 2}$ **35.** $5x^2 + 2x + 1 + \dfrac{2}{5x - 2}$

37. $x^2 + 4x + 5 + \dfrac{2}{x - 2}$ **39.** $x^3 + x^2 + x + 1$ **41.** $x - 3$

43. $x^2 - 1 + \dfrac{1}{x^2 + 3}$ **45.** $y^2 - y + 1$ **47.** $x^2 + 1$ **49.** $c = -2$

51.   **53.** (a) $x + 1$; (b) $x^2 + x + 1$; (c) $x^3 + x^2 + x + 1$;

(d) $x^{49} + x^{48} + \cdots + x + 1$

4.6 Roots and Radicals

4.6 OBJECTIVES

1. Use the radical notation to represent roots
2. Distinguish between rational and irrational numbers

In Chapter 3, we discussed the properties of exponents. Over the next four sections, we will work with a new notation that "reverses" the process of raising to a power.

We know that when we have a statement such as

$$x^2 = 9$$

it is read as "x squared equals 9."

Here we are concerned with the relationship between the variable x and the number 9. We call that relationship the **square root** and say, equivalently, that "x is the square root of 9."

We know from experience that x must be 3 (because $3^2 = 9$) or -3 [because $(-3)^2 = 9$]. We see that 9 has two square roots, 3 and -3. In fact, every positive number will have *two* square roots. In general, if $x^2 = a$, we call x a *square root of a*.

We are now ready for our new notation. The symbol $\sqrt{}$ is called a **radical sign.** We saw above that 3 was the positive square root of 9. We also call 3 the **principal square root** of 9 and can write

$$\sqrt{9} = 3$$

to indicate that 3 is the principal square root of 9.

NOTE The symbol $\sqrt{}$ first appeared in print in 1525. In Latin, "radix" means **root,** and this was contracted to a small *r*. The present symbol may have evolved from the manuscript form of that small *r*.

Definitions: Square Root

$\sqrt{a}$ is the *positive* (or *principal*) square root of *a*. It is the positive number whose square is *a*.

Example 1

Finding Principal Square Roots

Find the following square roots.

(a) $\sqrt{49} = 7$ Because 7 is the positive number we must square to get 49.

(b) $\sqrt{\dfrac{4}{9}} = \dfrac{2}{3}$ Because $\dfrac{2}{3}$ is the positive number we must square to get $\dfrac{4}{9}$.

 CHECK YOURSELF 1

Find the following square roots.

(a) $\sqrt{64}$ **(b)** $\sqrt{144}$ **(c)** $\sqrt{\dfrac{16}{25}}$

NOTE When you use the radical sign, you are referring to the *positive square root:*
$\sqrt{25} = 5$

Each positive number has two square roots. For instance, 25 has square roots of 5 and -5 because

$$5^2 = 25 \qquad \text{and} \qquad (-5)^2 = 25$$

If you want to indicate the negative square root, you must use a minus sign in front of the radical.

$$-\sqrt{25} = -5$$

Example 2

Finding Square Roots

Find the following square roots.

(a) $\sqrt{100} = 10$ The principal root

(b) $-\sqrt{100} = -10$ The negative square root

(c) $-\sqrt{\dfrac{9}{16}} = -\dfrac{3}{4}$

 CHECK YOURSELF 2

Find the following square roots.

(a) $\sqrt{16}$ **(b)** $-\sqrt{16}$ **(c)** $-\sqrt{\dfrac{16}{25}}$

 C A U T I O N

Be Careful! Do not confuse
$-\sqrt{9}$ with $\sqrt{-9}$
The expression $-\sqrt{9}$ is −3,
whereas $\sqrt{-9}$ is not a real
number.

Every number that we have encountered in this text is a **real number.** The square roots of negative numbers are *not* real numbers. For instance, $\sqrt{-9}$ is *not* a real number because there is *no* real number x such that

$$x^2 = -9$$

Example 3 summarizes our discussion thus far.

Example 3

Finding Square Roots

Evaluate each of the following square roots.

(a) $\sqrt{36} = 6$ **(b)** $\sqrt{121} = 11$

(c) $-\sqrt{64} = -8$ **(d)** $\sqrt{-64}$ is not a real number.

(e) $\sqrt{0} = 0$ (Because $0 \cdot 0 = 0$)

 CHECK YOURSELF 3

Evaluate, if possible.

(a) $\sqrt{81}$ **(b)** $\sqrt{49}$ **(c)** $-\sqrt{49}$ **(d)** $\sqrt{-49}$

All calculators have square root keys, but the only integers for which the calculator gives the exact value of the square root are perfect square integers. For all other positive integers, *a calculator gives only an approximation of the correct answer.* In Example 4 you will use your calculator to approximate square roots.

Example 4

Approximating Square Roots

Use your calculator to approximate each square root to the nearest hundredth.

NOTE The $\approx$ sign means "is approximately equal to."

(a) $\sqrt{45} \approx 6.708203932 \approx 6.71$ **(b)** $\sqrt{8} \approx 2.83$

(c) $\sqrt{20} \approx 4.47$ **(d)** $\sqrt{273} \approx 16.52$

CHECK YOURSELF 4

Use your calculator to approximate each square root to the nearest hundredth.

(a) $\sqrt{3}$ **(b)** $\sqrt{14}$ **(c)** $\sqrt{91}$ **(d)** $\sqrt{756}$

As we mentioned earlier, finding the square root of a number is the reverse of squaring a number. We can extend that idea to work with other roots of numbers. For instance, the *cube root* of a number is the number we must cube (or raise to the third power) to get that number. For example, the cube root of 8 is 2 because $2^3 = 8$, and we write

NOTE $\sqrt[3]{8}$ is read "the cube root of 8."

$$\sqrt[3]{8} = 2$$

The parts of a radical expression are summarized as follows.

Definitions: Parts of a Radical Expression

Every radical expression contains three parts as shown below. The principal *n*th root of *a* is written as

NOTE The index for $\sqrt[3]{a}$ is 3.

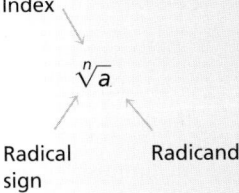

Index

$\sqrt[n]{a}$

Radical   Radicand
sign

NOTE The index of 2 for square roots is generally not written. We understand that $\sqrt{a}$ is the principal square root of *a*.

To illustrate, the *cube root* of 64 is written

$\text{Index} \longrightarrow \sqrt[3]{64} = 4$
of 3

because $4^3 = 64$. And

$\text{Index} \longrightarrow \sqrt[4]{81} = 3$
of 4

is the *fourth root* of 81 because $3^4 = 81$.

We can find roots of negative numbers as long as the index is *odd* (3, 5, etc.). For example,

$$\sqrt[3]{-64} = -4$$

because $(-4)^3 = -64$.

If the index is *even* (2, 4, etc.), roots of negative numbers are *not* real numbers. For example,

$$\sqrt[4]{-16}$$

NOTE The *even power* of a real number is always *positive* or *zero*.

NOTE It would be helpful for your work here and in future mathematics classes to memorize these roots.

is not a real number because there is no real number x such that $x^4 = -16$.

The following table shows the most common roots.

Square Roots		Cube Roots	Fourth Roots
$\sqrt{1} = 1$	$\sqrt{49} = 7$	$\sqrt[3]{1} = 1$	$\sqrt[4]{1} = 1$
$\sqrt{4} = 2$	$\sqrt{64} = 8$	$\sqrt[3]{8} = 2$	$\sqrt[4]{16} = 2$
$\sqrt{9} = 3$	$\sqrt{81} = 9$	$\sqrt[3]{27} = 3$	$\sqrt[4]{81} = 3$
$\sqrt{16} = 4$	$\sqrt{100} = 10$	$\sqrt[3]{64} = 4$	$\sqrt[4]{256} = 4$
$\sqrt{25} = 5$	$\sqrt{121} = 11$	$\sqrt[3]{125} = 5$	$\sqrt[4]{625} = 5$
$\sqrt{36} = 6$	$\sqrt{144} = 12$		

You can use the table in Example 5, which summarizes the discussion so far.

Example 5

Evaluating Cube Roots and Fourth Roots

Evaluate each of the following.

NOTE The cube root of a negative number will be negative.

NOTE The fourth root of a negative number is not a real number.

(a) $\sqrt[5]{32} = 2$ because $2^5 = 32$.

(b) $\sqrt[3]{-125} = -5$ because $(-5)^3 = -125$.

(c) $\sqrt[4]{-81}$ is not a real number.

CHECK YOURSELF 5

Evaluate, if possible.

(a) $\sqrt[3]{64}$ **(b)** $\sqrt[4]{16}$ **(c)** $\sqrt[4]{-256}$ **(d)** $\sqrt[3]{-8}$

The radical notation helps us to distinguish between two important types of numbers: rational numbers and irrational numbers.

A **rational number** can be represented by a fraction whose numerator and denominator are integers and whose denominator is nonzero. The form of a rational number is

$$\frac{a}{b} \quad a \text{ and } b \text{ are integers, } b \neq 0$$

Certain square roots are rational numbers also. For example,

NOTE Notice that each radicand is a **perfect-square integer** (that is, an integer that is the square of another integer).

$$\sqrt{4} \quad \sqrt{25} \quad \text{and} \quad \sqrt{64}$$

represent the rational numbers 2, 5, and 8, respectively.

NOTE The fact that the square root of 2 is irrational will be proved in later mathematics courses and was known to Greek mathematicians over 2000 years ago.

An **irrational number** is a number that *cannot* be written as the ratio of two integers. For example, the square root of any positive number that is not itself a perfect square is an irrational number. Because the radicands are *not* perfect squares, the expressions $\sqrt{2}$, $\sqrt{3}$, and $\sqrt{5}$ represent irrational numbers.

Example 6

Identifying Rational Numbers

Which of the following numbers are rational and which are irrational?

$$\sqrt{\frac{2}{3}} \qquad \sqrt{\frac{4}{9}} \qquad \sqrt{7} \qquad \sqrt{16} \qquad \sqrt{25}$$

Here $\sqrt{7}$ and $\sqrt{\frac{2}{3}}$ are irrational numbers. And $\sqrt{16}$ and $\sqrt{25}$ are rational numbers because 16 and 25 are perfect squares. Also $\sqrt{\frac{4}{9}}$ is rational because $\sqrt{\frac{4}{9}} = \frac{2}{3}$.

 CHECK YOURSELF 6

Which of the following numbers are rational and which are irrational?

(a) $\sqrt{26}$ **(b)** $\sqrt{49}$ **(c)** $\sqrt{\frac{6}{7}}$ **(d)** $\sqrt{105}$ **(e)** $\sqrt{\frac{16}{9}}$

NOTE The decimal representation of a rational number always terminates or repeats. For instance,

$$\frac{3}{8} = 0.375$$

$$\frac{5}{11} = 0.454545\ldots$$

An important fact about the irrational numbers is that their decimal representations are always *nonterminating* and *nonrepeating*. We can therefore only approximate irrational numbers with a decimal that has been rounded off. A calculator can be used to find roots. However, note that the values found for the irrational roots are only approximations. For instance, $\sqrt{2}$ is approximately 1.414 (to three decimal places), and we can write

$$\sqrt{2} \approx 1.414$$

With a calculator we find that

$$(1.414)^2 = 1.999396$$

NOTE 1.414 is an approximation to the number whose square is 2.

The set of all rational numbers and the set of all irrational numbers together form the set of *real numbers*. The real numbers will represent every point that can be pictured on the number line. Some examples are shown below.

NOTE For this reason we refer to the number line as the **real number line.**

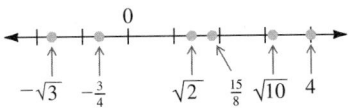

The following diagram summarizes the relationships among the various numeric sets.

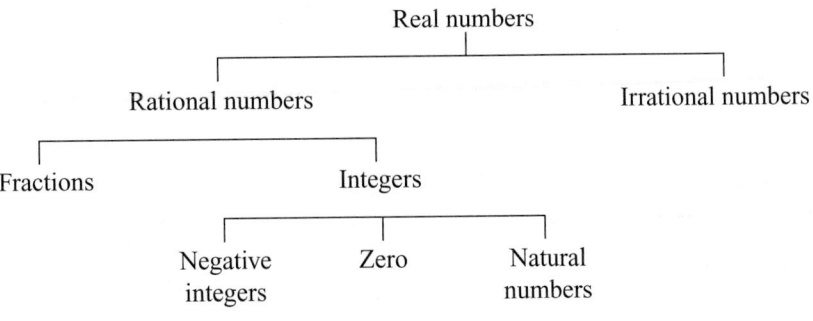

We conclude our work in this section by developing a general result that we will need later. Let's start by looking at two numerical examples.

$$\sqrt{2^2} = \sqrt{4} = 2 \tag{1}$$
$$\sqrt{(-2)^2} = \sqrt{4} = 2 \qquad \text{because } (-2)^2 = 4 \tag{2}$$

Consider the value of $\sqrt{x^2}$ when x is positive or negative.

NOTE This is because the principal square root of a number is always positive or zero.

In (1) when $x = 2$:

$$\sqrt{2^2} = 2$$

In (2) when $x = -2$:

$$\sqrt{(-2)^2} \neq -2$$
$$\sqrt{(-2)^2} = -(-2) = 2$$

Comparing the results of (1) and (2), we see that $\sqrt{x^2}$ is x if x is positive (or 0) and $\sqrt{x^2}$ is $-x$ if x is negative. We can write

$$\sqrt{x^2} = \begin{cases} x & \text{when } x \geq 0 \\ -x & \text{when } x < 0 \end{cases}$$

From your earlier work with absolute values you will remember that

$$|x| = \begin{cases} x & \text{when } x \geq 0 \\ -x & \text{when } x < 0 \end{cases}$$

and we can summarize the discussion by writing

$$\sqrt{x^2} = |x| \qquad \text{for any real number } x$$

Example 7

Evaluating Radical Expressions

NOTE Alternatively in (b), we could write
$$\sqrt{(-4)^2} = \sqrt{16} = 4$$

Evaluate each of the following.

(a) $\sqrt{5^2} = 5$

(b) $\sqrt{(-4)^2} = |-4| = 4$

CHECK YOURSELF 7

Evaluate.

(a) $\sqrt{6^2}$

(b) $\sqrt{(-6)^2}$

CHECK YOURSELF ANSWERS

1. **(a)** 8; **(b)** 12; **(c)** $\dfrac{4}{5}$ 2. **(a)** 4; **(b)** -4; **(c)** $-\dfrac{4}{5}$ 3. **(a)** 9; **(b)** 7; **(c)** -7;

(d) not a real number   4. **(a)** 1.73; **(b)** 3.74; **(c)** 9.54; **(d)** 27.50

5. **(a)** 4; **(b)** 2; **(c)** not a real number; **(d)** -2 6. **(a)** Irrational;

(b) rational (because $\sqrt{49} = 7$); **(c)** irrational; **(d)** irrational

(e) $\left(\text{because } \sqrt{\dfrac{16}{9}} = \dfrac{4}{3}\right)$ 7. **(a)** 6; **(b)** 6

© 2001 McGraw-Hill Companies

4.6 Exercises

Evaluate, if possible.

1. $\sqrt{16}$

2. $\sqrt{121}$

3. $\sqrt{400}$

4. $\sqrt{64}$

5. $-\sqrt{100}$

6. $\sqrt{-100}$

7. $\sqrt{-81}$

8. $-\sqrt{81}$

9. $\sqrt{\dfrac{16}{9}}$

10. $-\sqrt{\dfrac{1}{25}}$

11. $\sqrt{-\dfrac{4}{5}}$

12. $\sqrt{\dfrac{4}{25}}$

13. $\sqrt[3]{27}$

14. $\sqrt[4]{81}$

15. $\sqrt[3]{-27}$

16. $\sqrt[4]{-16}$

17. $\sqrt[4]{-81}$

18. $-\sqrt[3]{64}$

19. $-\sqrt[3]{27}$

20. $-\sqrt[3]{-8}$

21. $\sqrt[4]{625}$

22. $\sqrt[3]{1000}$

23. $\sqrt[3]{\dfrac{1}{27}}$

24. $\sqrt[3]{-\dfrac{8}{27}}$

ANSWERS

1. _____

2. _____

3. _____

4. _____

5. _____

6. _____

7. _____

8. _____

9. _____

10. _____

11. _____

12. _____

13. _____

14. _____

15. _____

16. _____

17. _____

18. _____

19. _____

20. _____

21. _____

22. _____

23. _____ 24. _____

25.
_____

26.
_____

27.
_____

28.
_____

29.
_____

30.
_____

31.
_____

32.
_____

33.
_____

34.
_____

35.
_____

36.
_____

37.
_____

38.
_____

39.
_____

40.
_____

41.
_____

42.
_____

43.
_____

44.
_____

45.
_____

46.
_____

Which of the following roots are rational numbers and which are irrational numbers?

25. $\sqrt{19}$ **26.** $\sqrt{36}$

27. $\sqrt{100}$ **28.** $\sqrt{7}$

29. $\sqrt[3]{9}$ **30.** $\sqrt[3]{8}$

31. $\sqrt[4]{16}$ **32.** $\sqrt{\dfrac{4}{9}}$

33. $\sqrt{\dfrac{4}{7}}$ **34.** $\sqrt[3]{5}$

35. $\sqrt[3]{-27}$ **36.** $-\sqrt[4]{81}$

Use your calculator to approximate the square root to the nearest hundredth.

37. $\sqrt{11}$ **38.** $\sqrt{14}$

39. $\sqrt{7}$ **40.** $\sqrt{23}$

41. $\sqrt{46}$ **42.** $\sqrt{78}$

43. $\sqrt{\dfrac{2}{5}}$ **44.** $\sqrt{\dfrac{3}{4}}$

45. $\sqrt{\dfrac{8}{9}}$ **46.** $\sqrt{\dfrac{7}{15}}$

47. $-\sqrt{18}$

48. $-\sqrt{31}$

49. $-\sqrt{27}$

50. $-\sqrt{65}$

For exercises 51 to 56, find the two expressions that are equivalent.

51. $\sqrt{-16}, -\sqrt{16}, -4$

52. $-\sqrt{25}, -5, \sqrt{-25}$

53. $\sqrt[3]{-125}, -\sqrt[3]{125}, |-5|$

54. $\sqrt[5]{-32}, -\sqrt[5]{32}, |-2|$

55. $\sqrt[4]{10,000}, 100, \sqrt[3]{1000}$

56. $10^2, \sqrt{10,000}, \sqrt[3]{100,000}$

In exercises 57 to 62, label the statement as true or false.

57. $\sqrt{16x^{16}} = 4x^4$

58. $\sqrt{(x-4)^2} = x - 4$

59. $\sqrt{16x^{-4}y^{-4}}$ is a real number

60. $\sqrt{x^2 + y^2} = x + y$

61. $\dfrac{\sqrt{x^2 - 25}}{x - 5} = \sqrt{x + 5}$

62. $\sqrt{2} + \sqrt{6} = \sqrt{8}$

63. Dimensions of a square. The area of a square is 32 square feet (ft^2). Find the length of a side to the nearest hundredth.

64. Dimensions of a square. The area of a square is 83 ft^2. Find the length of the side to the nearest hundredth.

65. Radius of a circle. The area of a circle is 147 ft^2. Find the radius to the nearest hundredth.

66. Radius of a circle. If the area of a circle is 72 square centimeters (cm^2), find the radius to the nearest hundredth.

ANSWERS

47.

48.

49.

50.

51.

52.

53.

54.

55.

56.

57.

58.

59.

60.

61.

62.

63.

64.

65.

66.

ANSWERS

67. _____

68. _____

69. _____

70. _____

71. _____

72. _____

73. _____

74. _____

75. _____

67. Freely falling objects. The time in seconds (s) that it takes for an object to fall from rest is given by $t = \dfrac{1}{4}\sqrt{s}$, in which s is the distance fallen. Find the time required for an object to fall to the ground from a building that is 800 ft high.

68. Freely falling objects. Find the time required for an object to fall to the ground from a building that is 1400 ft high. (Use the formula in exercise 67.)

In exercises 69 to 71, the area is given in square feet. Find the length of a side of the square. Round your answer to the nearest hundredth of a foot.

69. **70.** **71.**

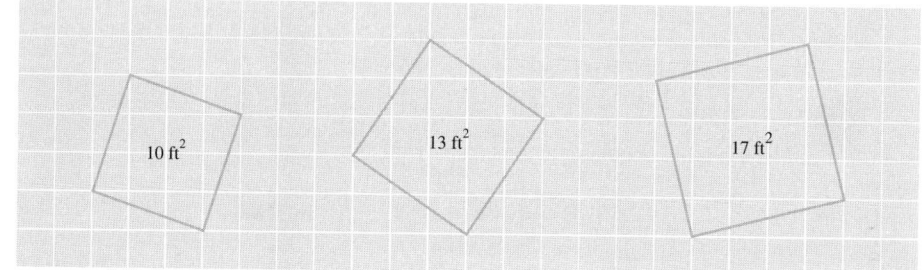

$10\ \text{ft}^2$ $13\ \text{ft}^2$ $17\ \text{ft}^2$

72. Is there any prime number whose square root is an integer? Explain your answer.

73. Explain the difference between the conjugate, in which the middle sign is changed, of a binomial and the opposite of a binomial. To illustrate, use $4 - \sqrt{7}$.

74. Determine two consecutive integers whose square roots are also consecutive integers.

75. Determine the missing binomial in the following: $(\sqrt{3} - 2)(\quad) = -1$.

76. Try the following using your calculator.

   (a) Choose a number greater than 1 and find its square root. Then find the square root of the result and continue in this manner, observing the successive square roots. Do these numbers seem to be approaching a certain value? If so, what?

   (b) Choose a number greater than 0 but less than 1 and find its square root. Then find the square root of the result, and continue in this manner, observing successive square roots. Do these numbers seem to be approaching a certain value? If so, what?

77. (a) Can a number be equal to its own square root?

   (b) Other than the number(s) found in part a, is a number always greater than its square root? Investigate.

78. Let a and b be positive numbers. If a is greater than b, is it always true that the square root of a is greater than the square root of b? Investigate.

79. Suppose that a weight is attached to a string of length L, and the other end of the string is held fixed. If we pull the weight and then release it, allowing the weight to swing back and forth, we can observe the behavior of a simple pendulum. The period, T, is the time required for the weight to complete a full cycle, swinging forward and then back. The following formula may be used to describe the relationship between T and L.

$$T = 2\pi\sqrt{\frac{L}{g}}$$

If L is expressed in centimeters, then $g = 980$ cm/s^2. For each of the following string lengths, calculate the corresponding period. Round to the nearest tenth of a second.

   (a) 30 cm   (b) 50 cm   (c) 70 cm   (d) 90 cm   (e) 110 cm

 Getting Ready

Find each of the following products.

   (a) $(4x^2)(2x)$ (b) $(9a^4)(5a)$ (c) $(16m^2)(3m)$ (d) $(8b^3)(2b)$

   (e) $(27p^6)(3p)$ (f) $(81s^4)(s^3)$ (g) $(100y^4)(2y)$ (h) $(49m^6)(2m)$

76. _____

77. _____

78. _____
   (a)
   (b)
   (c)
   (d)
79. (e) _____

a. _____

b. _____

c. _____

d. _____

e. _____

f. _____

g. _____

h. _____

Answers

1. 4   **3.** 20   **5.** -10 **7.** Not a real number   **9.** $\dfrac{4}{3}$

11. Not a real number   **13.** 3   **15.** -3 **17.** Not a real number

19. -3 **21.** 5   **23.** $\dfrac{1}{3}$ **25.** Irrational   **27.** Rational   **29.** Irrational

31. Rational   **33.** Irrational   **35.** Rational   **37.** 3.32   **39.** 2.65

41. 6.78   **43.** 0.63   **45.** 0.94   **47.** -4.24 **49.** -5.20

51. $-\sqrt{16}, -4$ **53.** $\sqrt[3]{-125}, -\sqrt[3]{125}$ **55.** $\sqrt[4]{10{,}000}, \sqrt[3]{1000}$

57. False   **59.** True   **61.** False   **63.** 5.66 ft   **65.** 6.84 ft

67. 7.07 s   **69.** 3.16 ft   **71.** 4.12 ft

73. Conjugate: $4 + \sqrt{7}$; opposite: $-4 + \sqrt{7}$ **75.** $\sqrt{3} + 2$ **77.**

79. (a) 1.1 s; **(b)** 1.4 s; **(c)** 1.7 s; **(d)** 1.9 s; **(e)** 2.1 s   **a.** $8x^3$ **b.** $45a^5$

c. $48m^3$ **d.** $16b^4$ **e.** $81p^7$ **f.** $81s^7$ **g.** $200y^5$ **h.** $98m^7$

Simplifying Radical Expressions

1. Simplify expressions involving numeric radicals
2. Simplify expressions involving algebraic radicals

In Section 4.6, we introduced the radical notation. For most applications, we will want to make sure that all radical expressions are in *simplest form*. To accomplish this, the following three conditions must be satisfied.

> **Rules and Properties:** Square Root Expressions in Simplest Form
>
> An expression involving square roots is in *simplest form* if
>
> **1.** There are no perfect-square factors in a radical.
> **2.** No fraction appears inside a radical.
> **3.** No radical appears in the denominator.

For instance, considering condition 1,

$\sqrt{17}$ is in simplest form because 17 has *no* perfect-square factors

whereas

$\sqrt{12}$ is *not* in simplest form

because it does contain a perfect-square factor.

$$\sqrt{12} = \sqrt{4 \cdot 3}$$

A perfect square

To simplify radical expressions, we'll need to develop two important properties. First, look at the following expressions:

$$\sqrt{4 \cdot 9} = \sqrt{36} = 6$$
$$\sqrt{4} \cdot \sqrt{9} = 2 \cdot 3 = 6$$

Because this tells us that $\sqrt{4 \cdot 9} = \sqrt{4} \cdot \sqrt{9}$, the following general rule for radicals is suggested.

> **Rules and Properties:** Property 1 of Radicals
>
> For any positive real numbers a and b,
>
> $$\sqrt{ab} = \sqrt{a} \cdot \sqrt{b}$$
>
> In words, the square root of a product is the product of the square roots.

Let's see how this property is applied in simplifying expressions when radicals are involved.

> ## Example 1

Simplifying Radical Expressions

NOTE Perfect-square factors are 1, 4, 9, 16, 25, 36, 49, 64, 81, 100, and so on.

Simplify each expression.

(a) $\sqrt{12} = \sqrt{4 \cdot 3}$

A perfect square

NOTE Apply Property 1.

$= \sqrt{4} \cdot \sqrt{3}$

NOTE Notice that we have removed the perfect-square factor from inside the radical, so the expression is in simplest form.

$= 2\sqrt{3}$

NOTE It would not have helped to write
$\sqrt{45} = \sqrt{15 \cdot 3}$
because neither factor is a perfect square.

(b) $\sqrt{45} = \sqrt{9 \cdot 5}$

A perfect square

$= \sqrt{9} \cdot \sqrt{5}$

$= 3\sqrt{5}$

NOTE We look for the *largest* perfect-square factor, here 36.

(c) $\sqrt{72} = \sqrt{36 \cdot 2}$

A perfect square

NOTE Then apply Property 1.

$= \sqrt{36} \cdot \sqrt{2}$

$= 6\sqrt{2}$

(d) $5\sqrt{18} = 5\sqrt{9 \cdot 2}$

A perfect square

$= 5 \cdot \sqrt{9} \cdot \sqrt{2} = 5 \cdot 3 \cdot \sqrt{2} = 15\sqrt{2}$

 CAUTION

Be Careful!   Even though

$\sqrt{a \cdot b} = \sqrt{a} \cdot \sqrt{b}$

$\sqrt{a + b}$ is *not the same* as $\sqrt{a} + \sqrt{b}$

Let $a = 4$ and $b = 9$, and substitute.

$\sqrt{a + b} = \sqrt{4 + 9} = \sqrt{13}$

$\sqrt{a} + \sqrt{b} = \sqrt{4} + \sqrt{9} = 2 + 3 = 5$

Because $\sqrt{13} \neq 5$, we see that the expressions $\sqrt{a + b}$ and $\sqrt{a} + \sqrt{b}$ are not in general the same.

✔ **CHECK YOURSELF 1**

Simplify.

(a) $\sqrt{20}$ **(b)** $\sqrt{75}$ **(c)** $\sqrt{98}$ **(d)** $\sqrt{48}$

The process is the same if variables are involved in a radical expression. In our remaining work with radicals, we will assume that all variables represent positive real numbers.

Example 2

Simplifying Radical Expressions

Simplify each of the following radicals.

(a) $\sqrt{x^3} = \sqrt{x^2 \cdot x}$

      A perfect square

NOTE By our first rule for radicals.
NOTE $\sqrt{x^2} = x$ (as long as x is positive).

$= \sqrt{x^2} \cdot \sqrt{x}$

$= x\sqrt{x}$

(b) $\sqrt{4b^3} = \sqrt{4 \cdot b^2 \cdot b}$

      Perfect squares

$= \sqrt{4b^2} \cdot \sqrt{b}$

$= 2b\sqrt{b}$

NOTE Notice that we want the perfect-square factor to have the largest possible even exponent, here 4. Keep in mind that
$a^2 \cdot a^2 = a^4$

(c) $\sqrt{18a^5} = \sqrt{9 \cdot a^4 \cdot 2a}$

      Perfect squares

$= \sqrt{9a^4} \cdot \sqrt{2a}$

$= 3a^2\sqrt{2a}$

CHECK YOURSELF 2

Simplify.

(a) $\sqrt{9x^3}$ **(b)** $\sqrt{27m^3}$ **(c)** $\sqrt{50b^5}$

To develop a second property for radicals, look at the following expressions:

$$\sqrt{\frac{16}{4}} = \sqrt{4} = 2$$

$$\frac{\sqrt{16}}{\sqrt{4}} = \frac{4}{2} = 2$$

Because $\sqrt{\dfrac{16}{4}} = \dfrac{\sqrt{16}}{\sqrt{4}}$, a second general rule for radicals is suggested.

> **Rules and Properties:** Property 2 of Radicals
>
> For any positive real numbers a and b,
>
> $$\sqrt{\frac{a}{b}} = \frac{\sqrt{a}}{\sqrt{b}}$$
>
> In words, the square root of a quotient is the quotient of the square roots.

This property is used in a fashion similar to Property 1 in simplifying radical expressions. Remember that our second condition for a radical expression to be in simplest form states that no fraction should appear inside a radical. Example 3 illustrates how expressions that violate that condition are simplified.

> **Example 3**
>
> **Simplifying Radical Expressions**

Write each expression in simplest form.

NOTE Apply Property 2 to write the numerator and denominator as separate radicals.

(a) $\sqrt{\dfrac{9}{4}} = \dfrac{\sqrt{9}}{\sqrt{4}}$ ⎰ Remove any perfect squares from the radical.

$= \dfrac{3}{2}$

NOTE Apply Property 2.

(b) $\sqrt{\dfrac{2}{25}} = \dfrac{\sqrt{2}}{\sqrt{25}}$

$= \dfrac{\sqrt{2}}{5}$

NOTE Apply Property 2.

(c) $\sqrt{\dfrac{8x^2}{9}} = \dfrac{\sqrt{8x^2}}{\sqrt{9}}$

NOTE Factor $8x^2$ as $4x^2 \cdot 2$.

$= \dfrac{\sqrt{4x^2 \cdot 2}}{3}$

NOTE Apply Property 1 in the numerator.

$= \dfrac{\sqrt{4x^2} \cdot \sqrt{2}}{3}$

$= \dfrac{2x\sqrt{2}}{3}$

✔ **CHECK YOURSELF 3**

Simplify.

(a) $\sqrt{\dfrac{25}{16}}$ **(b)** $\sqrt{\dfrac{7}{9}}$ **(c)** $\sqrt{\dfrac{12x^2}{49}}$

In our previous examples, the denominator of the fraction appearing in the radical was a perfect square, and we were able to write each expression in simplest radical form by removing that perfect square from the denominator.

If the denominator of the fraction in the radical is *not* a perfect square, we can still apply Property 2 of radicals. As we will see in Example 4, the third condition for a radical to be in simplest form is then violated, and a new technique is necessary.

Example 4

Simplifying Radical Expressions

Write each expression in simplest form.

NOTE We begin by applying Property 2.

(a) $\sqrt{\dfrac{1}{3}} = \dfrac{\sqrt{1}}{\sqrt{3}} = \dfrac{1}{\sqrt{3}}$

Do you see that $\dfrac{1}{\sqrt{3}}$ is still not in simplest form because of the radical in the denominator? To solve this problem, we multiply the numerator and denominator by $\sqrt{3}$. Note that the denominator will become

$$\sqrt{3} \cdot \sqrt{3} = \sqrt{9} = 3$$

We then have

NOTE We can do this because we are multiplying the fraction by $\dfrac{\sqrt{3}}{\sqrt{3}}$ or 1, which does not change its value.

$$\dfrac{1}{\sqrt{3}} = \dfrac{1 \cdot \sqrt{3}}{\sqrt{3} \cdot \sqrt{3}} = \dfrac{\sqrt{3}}{3}$$

The expression $\dfrac{\sqrt{3}}{3}$ is now in simplest form because all three of our conditions are satisfied.

(b) $\sqrt{\dfrac{2}{5}} = \dfrac{\sqrt{2}}{\sqrt{5}}$

NOTE
$\sqrt{2} \cdot \sqrt{5} = \sqrt{2 \cdot 5} = \sqrt{10}$
$\sqrt{5} \cdot \sqrt{5} = 5$

$$= \dfrac{\sqrt{2} \cdot \sqrt{5}}{\sqrt{5} \cdot \sqrt{5}}$$

$$= \dfrac{\sqrt{10}}{5}$$

and the expression is in simplest form because again our three conditions are satisfied.

(c) $\sqrt{\dfrac{3x}{7}} = \dfrac{\sqrt{3x}}{\sqrt{7}}$

NOTE We multiply numerator and denominator by $\sqrt{7}$ to "clear" the denominator of the radical. This is also known as "rationalizing" the denominator.

$$= \dfrac{\sqrt{3x} \cdot \sqrt{7}}{\sqrt{7} \cdot \sqrt{7}}$$

$$= \dfrac{\sqrt{21x}}{7}$$

The expression is in simplest form.

CHECK YOURSELF 4

Simplify.

(a) $\sqrt{\dfrac{1}{2}}$ **(b)** $\sqrt{\dfrac{2}{3}}$ **(c)** $\sqrt{\dfrac{2y}{5}}$

Both of the properties of radicals given in this section are true for cube roots, fourth roots, and so on. Here we have limited ourselves to simplifying expressions involving square roots.

CHECK YOURSELF ANSWERS

1. (a) $2\sqrt{5}$; **(b)** $5\sqrt{3}$; **(c)** $7\sqrt{2}$; **(d)** $4\sqrt{3}$ **2. (a)** $3x\sqrt{x}$; **(b)** $3m\sqrt{3m}$;

(c) $5b^2\sqrt{2b}$ **3. (a)** $\dfrac{5}{4}$; **(b)** $\dfrac{\sqrt{7}}{3}$; **(c)** $\dfrac{2x\sqrt{3}}{7}$ **4. (a)** $\dfrac{\sqrt{2}}{2}$; **(b)** $\dfrac{\sqrt{6}}{3}$; **(c)** $\dfrac{\sqrt{10y}}{5}$

Use Property 1 to simplify each of the following radical expressions. Assume that all variables represent positive real numbers.

1. $\sqrt{18}$ 2. $\sqrt{50}$

3. $\sqrt{28}$ 4. $\sqrt{108}$

5. $\sqrt{45}$ 6. $\sqrt{80}$

7. $\sqrt{48}$ 8. $\sqrt{125}$

9. $\sqrt{200}$ 10. $\sqrt{96}$

11. $\sqrt{147}$ 12. $\sqrt{300}$

13. $3\sqrt{12}$ 14. $5\sqrt{24}$

15. $\sqrt{5x^2}$ 16. $\sqrt{7a^2}$

17. $\sqrt{3y^4}$ 18. $\sqrt{10x^6}$

19. $\sqrt{2r^3}$ 20. $\sqrt{5a^5}$

21. $\sqrt{27b^2}$ 22. $\sqrt{98m^4}$

23. $\sqrt{24x^4}$ 24. $\sqrt{72x^3}$

ANSWERS

1. _____
2. _____
3. _____
4. _____
5. _____
6. _____
7. _____
8. _____
9. _____
10. _____
11. _____
12. _____
13. _____
14 _____
15. _____
16. _____
17. _____
18. _____
19. _____
20. _____
21. _____
22. _____
23. _____
24. _____

25. _____

26. _____

27. _____

28. _____

29. _____

30. _____

31. _____

32. _____

33. _____

34. _____

35. _____

36. _____

37. _____

38. _____

39. _____

40. _____

41. _____

42. _____

43. _____

44. _____

45. _____

46. _____

47. _____ 48. _____

25. $\sqrt{54a^5}$

26. $\sqrt{200y^6}$

27. $\sqrt{x^3y^2}$

28. $\sqrt{a^2b^5}$

Use Property 2 to simplify each of the following radical expressions.

29. $\sqrt{\dfrac{4}{25}}$

30. $\sqrt{\dfrac{64}{9}}$

31. $\sqrt{\dfrac{9}{16}}$

32. $\sqrt{\dfrac{49}{25}}$

33. $\sqrt{\dfrac{3}{4}}$

34. $\sqrt{\dfrac{5}{9}}$

35. $\sqrt{\dfrac{5}{36}}$

36. $\sqrt{\dfrac{10}{49}}$

Use the properties for radicals to simplify each of the following expressions. Assume that all variables represent positive real numbers.

37. $\sqrt{\dfrac{8a^2}{25}}$

38. $\sqrt{\dfrac{12y^2}{49}}$

39. $\sqrt{\dfrac{1}{5}}$

40. $\sqrt{\dfrac{1}{7}}$

41. $\sqrt{\dfrac{3}{2}}$

42. $\sqrt{\dfrac{5}{3}}$

43. $\sqrt{\dfrac{3a}{5}}$

44. $\sqrt{\dfrac{2x}{7}}$

45. $\sqrt{\dfrac{2x^2}{3}}$

46. $\sqrt{\dfrac{5m^2}{2}}$

47. $\sqrt{\dfrac{8s^3}{7}}$

48. $\sqrt{\dfrac{12x^3}{5}}$

Decide whether each of the following is already written in simplest form. If it is not, explain what needs to be done.

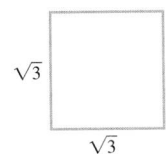

49. $\sqrt{10mn}$

50. $\sqrt{18ab}$

51. $\sqrt{\dfrac{98x^2y}{7x}}$

52. $\dfrac{\sqrt{6xy}}{3x}$

53. Find the area and perimeter of this square:

$\sqrt{3}$ [square with sides labeled $\sqrt{3}$]

$\sqrt{3}$

One of these measures, the area, is a rational number, and the other, the perimeter, is an irrational number. Explain how this happened. Will the area always be a rational number? Explain.

54. **(a)** Evaluate the three expressions $\dfrac{n^2 - 1}{2}$, n, $\dfrac{n^2 + 1}{2}$ using odd values of n: 1, 3, 5, 7, etc. Make a chart like the one below and complete it.

n	$a = \dfrac{n^2 - 1}{2}$	$b = n$	$c = \dfrac{n^2 + 1}{2}$	a^2	b^2	c^2
1						
3						
5						
7						
9						
11						
13						
15						

(b) Check for each of these sets of three numbers to see if this statement is true: $\sqrt{a^2 + b^2} = \sqrt{c^2}$. For how many of your sets of three did this work? Sets of three numbers for which this statement is true are called "Pythagorean triples" because $a^2 + b^2 = c^2$. Can the radical equation be written in this way: $\sqrt{a^2 + b^2} = a + b$? Explain your answer.

ANSWERS

49. _____

50. _____

51. _____

52. _____

53. _____

54. _____

Getting Ready

Use the distributive property to combine the like terms in each of the following expressions.

(a) $5x + 6x$ (b) $8a - 3a$

(c) $10y - 12y$ (d) $7m + 10m$

(e) $9a + 7a - 12a$ (f) $5s - 8s + 4s$

(g) $12m + 3n - 6m$ (h) $8x + 5y - 4x$

Answers

1. $3\sqrt{2}$ **3.** $2\sqrt{7}$ **5.** $3\sqrt{5}$ **7.** $4\sqrt{3}$ **9.** $10\sqrt{2}$ **11.** $7\sqrt{3}$

13. $6\sqrt{3}$ **15.** $x\sqrt{5}$ **17.** $y^2\sqrt{3}$ **19.** $r\sqrt{2r}$ **21.** $3b\sqrt{3}$

23. $2x^2\sqrt{6}$ **25.** $3a^2\sqrt{6a}$ **27.** $xy\sqrt{x}$ **29.** $\dfrac{2}{5}$ **31.** $\dfrac{3}{4}$ **33.** $\dfrac{\sqrt{3}}{2}$

35. $\dfrac{\sqrt{5}}{6}$ **37.** $\dfrac{2a\sqrt{2}}{5}$ **39.** $\dfrac{\sqrt{5}}{5}$ **41.** $\dfrac{\sqrt{6}}{2}$ **43.** $\dfrac{\sqrt{15a}}{5}$ **45.** $\dfrac{x\sqrt{6}}{3}$

47. $\dfrac{2s\sqrt{14s}}{7}$ **49.** Simplest form

51. Remove the perfect-square factors from the radical and simplify. **53.**

a. $11x$ **b.** $5a$ **c.** $-2y$ **d.** $17m$ **e.** $4a$ **f.** s **g.** $6m + 3n$

h. $4x + 5y$

4.8 Adding and Subtracting Radicals

4.8 OBJECTIVES

1. Add and subtract expressions involving numeric radicals
2. Add and subtract expressions involving algebraic radicals

Two radicals that have the same index and the same radicand (the expression inside the radical) are called **like radicals.** For example,

$2\sqrt{3}$ and $5\sqrt{3}$ are like radicals.

$\sqrt{2}$ and $\sqrt{5}$ are not like radicals—they have different radicands.

NOTE "Indices" is the plural of "index."

$\sqrt{2}$ and $\sqrt[3]{2}$ are not like radicals—they have different indices (2 and 3, representing a square root and a cube root).

Like radicals can be added (or subtracted) in the same way as like terms. We apply the distributive property and then combine the coefficients:

$$2\sqrt{5} + 3\sqrt{5} = (2 + 3)\sqrt{5} = 5\sqrt{5}$$

Example 1

Adding and Subtracting Like Radicals

Simplify each expression.

NOTE Apply the distributive property, then combine the coefficients.

(a) $5\sqrt{2} + 3\sqrt{2} = (5 + 3)\sqrt{2} = 8\sqrt{2}$

(b) $7\sqrt{5} - 2\sqrt{5} = (7 - 2)\sqrt{5} = 5\sqrt{5}$

(c) $8\sqrt{7} - \sqrt{7} + 2\sqrt{7} = (8 - 1 + 2)\sqrt{7} = 9\sqrt{7}$

 CHECK YOURSELF 1

Simplify.

(a) $2\sqrt{5} + 7\sqrt{5}$ **(b)** $9\sqrt{7} - \sqrt{7}$
(c) $5\sqrt{3} - 2\sqrt{3} + \sqrt{3}$

If a sum or difference involves terms that are *not* like radicals, we may be able to combine terms after simplifying the radicals according to our earlier methods.

Example 2

Adding and Subtracting Radicals

Simplify each expression.

(a) $3\sqrt{2} + \sqrt{8}$

We do not have like radicals, but we can simplify $\sqrt{8}$. Remember that

$$\sqrt{8} = \sqrt{4 \cdot 2} = 2\sqrt{2}$$

so

$$3\sqrt{2} + \sqrt{8} = 3\sqrt{2} + \overset{\sqrt{8}}{2\sqrt{2}}$$

$$= (3 + 2)\sqrt{2} = 5\sqrt{2}$$

NOTE Simplify $\sqrt{12}$.

(b) $5\sqrt{3} - \sqrt{12} = 5\sqrt{3} - \sqrt{4 \cdot 3}$

NOTE The radicals can now be combined. Do you see why?

$$= 5\sqrt{3} - \sqrt{4} \cdot \sqrt{3}$$

$$= 5\sqrt{3} - 2\sqrt{3}$$

$$= (5 - 2)\sqrt{3} = 3\sqrt{3}$$

 CHECK YOURSELF 2

Simplify.

(a) $\sqrt{2} + \sqrt{18}$

(b) $5\sqrt{3} - \sqrt{27}$

If variables are involved in radical expressions, the process of combining terms proceeds in a fashion similar to that shown in previous examples. Consider Example 3. We again assume that all variables represent positive real numbers.

Example 3

Simplifying Expressions Involving Variables

Simplify each expression.

NOTE Because like radicals are involved, we apply the distributive property and combine terms as before.

(a) $5\sqrt{3x} - 2\sqrt{3x} = (5 - 2)\sqrt{3x} = 3\sqrt{3x}$

(b) $2\sqrt{3a^3} + 5a\sqrt{3a}$

NOTE Simplify the first term.

$$= 2\sqrt{a^2 \cdot 3a} + 5a\sqrt{3a}$$

$$= 2\sqrt{a^2} \cdot \sqrt{3a} + 5a\sqrt{3a}$$

$$= 2a\sqrt{3a} + 5a\sqrt{3a}$$

NOTE The radicals can now be combined.

$$= (2a + 5a)\sqrt{3a} = 7a\sqrt{3a}$$

 CHECK YOURSELF 3

Simplify each expression.

(a) $2\sqrt{7y} + 3\sqrt{7y}$

(b) $\sqrt{20a^2} - a\sqrt{45}$

CHECK YOURSELF ANSWERS

1. (a) $9\sqrt{5}$; **(b)** $8\sqrt{7}$; **(c)** $4\sqrt{3}$ **2. (a)** $4\sqrt{2}$; **(b)** $2\sqrt{3}$

3. (a) $5\sqrt{7y}$; **(b)** $-a\sqrt{5}$

Name _____

Section _____ Date _____

Simplify by combining like terms.

ANSWERS

1. $2\sqrt{2} + 4\sqrt{2}$

2. $\sqrt{3} + 5\sqrt{3}$

3. $11\sqrt{7} - 4\sqrt{7}$

4. $5\sqrt{3} - 3\sqrt{2}$

5. $5\sqrt{7} + 3\sqrt{6}$

6. $3\sqrt{5} - 5\sqrt{5}$

7. $2\sqrt{3} - 5\sqrt{3}$

8. $2\sqrt{11} + 5\sqrt{11}$

9. $2\sqrt{3x} + 5\sqrt{3x}$

10. $7\sqrt{2a} - 3\sqrt{2a}$

11. $2\sqrt{3} + \sqrt{3} + 3\sqrt{3}$

12. $3\sqrt{5} + 2\sqrt{5} + \sqrt{5}$

13. $5\sqrt{7} - 2\sqrt{7} + \sqrt{7}$

14. $3\sqrt{10} - 2\sqrt{10} + \sqrt{10}$

15. $2\sqrt{5x} + 5\sqrt{5x} - 2\sqrt{5x}$

16. $5\sqrt{3b} - 2\sqrt{3b} + 4\sqrt{3b}$

17. $2\sqrt{3} + \sqrt{12}$

18. $5\sqrt{2} + \sqrt{18}$

19. $\sqrt{20} - \sqrt{5}$

20. $\sqrt{98} - 3\sqrt{2}$

21. $2\sqrt{6} - \sqrt{54}$

22. $2\sqrt{3} - \sqrt{27}$

23. $\sqrt{72} + \sqrt{50}$

24. $\sqrt{27} - \sqrt{12}$

1. _____
2. _____
3. _____
4. _____
5. _____
6. _____
7. _____
8. _____
9. _____
10. _____
11. _____
12. _____
13. _____
14. _____
15. _____
16. _____
17. _____
18. _____
19. _____
20. _____
21. _____
22. _____
23. _____
24. _____

25. _____

26. _____

27. _____

28. _____

29. _____

30. _____

31. _____

32. _____

33. _____

34. _____

35. _____

36. _____

37. _____

38. _____

39. _____

40. _____

41. _____

42. _____

43. _____

44. _____

45. _____

46. _____

25. $3\sqrt{12} - \sqrt{48}$

26. $5\sqrt{8} + 2\sqrt{18}$

27. $2\sqrt{45} - 2\sqrt{20}$

28. $2\sqrt{98} - 4\sqrt{18}$

29. $\sqrt{12} + \sqrt{27} - \sqrt{3}$

30. $\sqrt{50} + \sqrt{32} - \sqrt{8}$

31. $3\sqrt{24} - \sqrt{54} + \sqrt{6}$

32. $\sqrt{63} - 2\sqrt{28} + 5\sqrt{7}$

33. $2\sqrt{50} + 3\sqrt{18} - \sqrt{32}$

34. $3\sqrt{27} + 4\sqrt{12} - \sqrt{300}$

Simplify by combining like terms.

35. $a\sqrt{27} - 2\sqrt{3a^2}$

36. $5\sqrt{2y^2} - 3y\sqrt{8}$

37. $5\sqrt{3x^3} + 2\sqrt{27x}$

38. $7\sqrt{2a^3} - \sqrt{8a}$

Use a calculator to find a decimal approximation for each of the following. Round your answer to the nearest hundredth.

39. $\sqrt{3} - \sqrt{2}$

40. $\sqrt{7} + \sqrt{11}$

41. $\sqrt{5} + \sqrt{3}$

42. $\sqrt{17} - \sqrt{13}$

43. $4\sqrt{3} - 7\sqrt{5}$

44. $8\sqrt{2} + 3\sqrt{7}$

45. $5\sqrt{7} + 8\sqrt{13}$

46. $7\sqrt{2} - 4\sqrt{11}$

47.	
48.	
49.	
50.	
a.	
b.	
c.	
d.	
e.	
f.	
g.	
h.	

47. Perimeter of a rectangle. Find the perimeter of the rectangle shown in the figure.

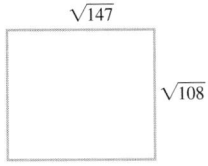

48. Perimeter of a rectangle. Find the perimeter of the rectangle shown in the figure. Write your answer in radical form.

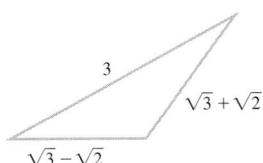

49. Perimeter of a triangle. Find the perimeter of the triangle shown in the figure.

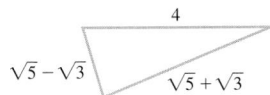

50. Perimeter of a triangle. Find the perimeter of the triangle shown in the figure.

Getting Ready

Perform the indicated multiplication.

(a) $2(x + 5)$ (b) $3(a - 3)$

(c) $m(m - 8)$ (d) $y(y + 7)$

(e) $(w + 2)(w - 2)$ (f) $(x - 3)(x + 3)$

(g) $(x + y)(x + y)$ (h) $(b - 7)(b - 7)$

Answers

1. $6\sqrt{2}$ **3.** $7\sqrt{7}$ **5.** Cannot be simplified **7.** $-3\sqrt{3}$ **9.** $7\sqrt{3x}$
11. $6\sqrt{3}$ **13.** $4\sqrt{7}$ **15.** $5\sqrt{5x}$ **17.** $4\sqrt{3}$ **19.** $\sqrt{5}$ **21.** $-\sqrt{6}$
23. $11\sqrt{2}$ **25.** $2\sqrt{3}$ **27.** $2\sqrt{5}$ **29.** $4\sqrt{3}$ **31.** $4\sqrt{6}$ **33.** $15\sqrt{2}$
35. $a\sqrt{3}$ **37.** $(5x+6)\sqrt{3x}$ **39.** 0.32 **41.** 3.97 **43.** -8.72
45. 42.07 **47.** 26 **49.** $2\sqrt{3}+3$ **a.** $2x+10$ **b.** $3a-9$
c. m^2-8m **d.** y^2+7y **e.** w^2-4 **f.** x^2-9 **g.** $x^2+2xy+y^2$
h. $b^2-14b+49$

4.9 Solving Radical Equations

4.9 OBJECTIVES

1. Solve an equation containing a radical expression
2. Solve an equation containing two radical expressions
3. Solve an application that involves a radical equation

In this section, we wish to establish procedures for solving equations involving radicals. The basic technique we will use involves raising both sides of an equation to some power. However, doing so requires some caution.

For example, let's begin with the equation $x = 1$. Squaring both sides gives us $x^2 = 1$, which has two solutions, 1 and -1. Clearly -1 is not a solution to the original equation. We refer to -1 as an *extraneous solution*.

We must be aware of the possibility of extraneous solutions any time we raise both sides of an equation to any *even power*. Having said that, we are now prepared to introduce the power property of equality.

NOTE

$$x^2 = 1$$
$$x^2 - 1 = 0$$
$$(x + 1)(x - 1) = 0$$

so the solutions are 1 and -1.

Rules and Properties: The Power Property of Equality

Given any two expressions a and b and any positive integer n,

If $a = b$, then $a^n = b^n$.

Note that although in applying the power property you will never lose a solution, you will often find an extraneous one as a result of raising both sides of an equation to some power. Because of this, it is very important that you *check all solutions*.

Example 1

Solving a Radical Equation

Solve $\sqrt{x + 2} = 3$.

Squaring each side, we have

$$(\sqrt{x + 2})^2 = 3^2$$
$$x + 2 = 9$$
$$x = 7$$

Substituting 7 into the original equation, we find

$$\sqrt{7 + 2} \stackrel{?}{=} 3$$
$$\sqrt{9} \stackrel{?}{=} 3$$
$$3 = 3$$

Because this is a true statement, we have found the solution for the equation, $x = 7$.

NOTE Notice that

$$(\sqrt{x + 2})^2 = x + 2$$

That is why squaring both sides of the equation removes the radical.

 CHECK YOURSELF 1

Solve the equation $\sqrt{x - 5} = 4$.

Example 2

Solving a Radical Equation

NOTE Applying the power property will only remove the radical if that radical is isolated on one side of the equation.

Solve $\sqrt{4x + 5} + 1 = 0$.

We must *first isolate the radical* on the left side:

$$\sqrt{4x + 5} = -1$$

NOTE Notice that on the right $(-1)^2 = 1$.

Then, squaring both sides, we have

$$(\sqrt{4x + 5})^2 = (-1)^2$$
$$4x + 5 = 1$$

and solving for x, we find that

$$x = -1$$

Now we will check the solution by substituting -1 for x in the original equation:

NOTE $\sqrt{1} = 1$, the principal root.

$$\sqrt{4(-1) + 5} + 1 \stackrel{?}{=} 0$$
$$\sqrt{1} + 1 \stackrel{?}{=} 0$$

NOTE This is clearly a false statement, so -1 is *not* a solution for the original equation.

and $\qquad 2 \neq 0$

Because -1 is an extraneous solution, there are *no solutions* to the original equation.

CHECK YOURSELF 2

Solve $\sqrt{3x - 2} + 2 = 0$.

Let's consider an example in which the procedure we have described will involve squaring a binomial.

Example 3

Solving a Radical Equation

NOTE These problems can also be solved graphically. With a graphing utility, plot the two graphs $Y_1 = \sqrt{x + 3}$ and $Y_2 = x + 1$. Note that the graphs have one point of intersection, where $x = 1$.

Solve $\sqrt{x + 3} = x + 1$.

We can square each side, as before.

$$(\sqrt{x + 3})^2 = (x + 1)^2$$
$$x + 3 = x^2 + 2x + 1$$

Simplifying this gives us the quadratic equation

$$x^2 + x - 2 = 0$$

Factoring, we have

$$(x - 1)(x + 2) = 0$$

which gives us the possible solutions

NOTE Verify this for yourself by substituting 1 and then −2 for *x* in the original equation.

$$x = 1 \qquad \text{or} \qquad x = -2$$

Now we check for extraneous solutions and find that $x = 1$ is a valid solution, but that $x = -2$ does not yield a true statement.

 CAUTION

Be Careful! Sometimes (as in this example), one side of the equation contains a binomial. In that case, we must remember the middle term when we square the binomial. The square of a binomial *is always a trinomial.*

✔ **CHECK YOURSELF 3**

Solve $\sqrt{x - 5} = x - 7$.

It is not always the case that one of the solutions is extraneous. We may have zero, one, or two valid solutions when we generate a quadratic from a radical equation.

In the following example we see a case in which both of the solutions derived will satisfy the equation.

Example 4

Solving a Radical Equation

Solve $\sqrt{7x + 1} - 1 = 2x$.

First, *we must isolate the term involving the radical.*

NOTE Again, with a graphing utility plot $Y_1 = \sqrt{7x + 1}$ and $Y_2 = 2x + 1$. Where do they intersect?

$$\sqrt{7x + 1} = 2x + 1$$

We can now square both sides of the equation.

$$7x + 1 = 4x^2 + 4x + 1$$

Now we write the quadratic equation in standard form.

$$4x^2 - 3x = 0$$

Factoring, we have

$$x(4x - 3) = 0$$

which yields two possible solutions

$$x = 0 \qquad \text{or} \qquad x = \frac{3}{4}$$

Checking the solutions by substitution, we find that both values for *x* give true statements, as follows.

Letting *x* be 0, we have

$$\sqrt{7(0) + 1} - 1 \stackrel{?}{=} 2(0)$$

$$\sqrt{1} - 1 \stackrel{?}{=} 0$$

or $\qquad\qquad 0 = 0 \qquad$ A true statement.

Letting x be $\dfrac{3}{4}$, we have

$$\sqrt{7\left(\frac{3}{4}\right) + 1} - 1 \stackrel{?}{=} 2\left(\frac{3}{4}\right)$$

$$\sqrt{\frac{25}{4}} - 1 \stackrel{?}{=} \frac{3}{2}$$

$$\frac{5}{2} - 1 \stackrel{?}{=} \frac{3}{2}$$

$$\frac{3}{2} = \frac{3}{2} \qquad \text{Again a true statement.}$$

 CHECK YOURSELF 4

Solve $\sqrt{5x + 1} - 1 = 3x$.

Sometimes when an equation involves more than one radical, we must apply the power property more than once. In such a case, it is generally best to avoid having to work with two radicals on the same side of the equation. The following example illustrates one approach to the solution of such equations.

Example 5

Solving an Equation Containing Two Radicals

Solve $\sqrt{x - 2} - \sqrt{2x - 6} = 1$.

First we isolate $\sqrt{x - 2}$ by adding $\sqrt{2x - 6}$ to both sides of the equation. This gives

NOTE $1 + \sqrt{2x - 6}$ is a binomial of the form $a + b$, in which a is 1 and b is $\sqrt{2x - 6}$. The square on the right then has the form $a^2 + 2ab + b^2$.

$$\sqrt{x - 2} = 1 + \sqrt{2x - 6}$$

Then squaring each side, we have

$$x - 2 = 1 + 2\sqrt{2x - 6} + 2x - 6$$

We now isolate the radical that remains on the right side.

$$-x + 3 = 2\sqrt{2x - 6}$$

We must square again to remove that radical.

$$x^2 - 6x + 9 = 4(2x - 6)$$

Now solve the quadratic equation that results.

$$x^2 - 14x + 33 = 0$$

$$(x - 3)(x - 11) = 0$$

So

$$x = 3 \qquad \text{or} \qquad x = 11 \text{ are the possible solutions.}$$

Checking the possible solutions, you will find that $x = 3$ yields the only valid solution. You should verify that for yourself.

CHECK YOURSELF 5

Solve $\sqrt{x + 3} - \sqrt{2x + 4} + 1 = 0$.

Earlier in this section, we noted that extraneous roots were possible whenever we raised both sides of the equation to an *even power*. In the following example, we will raise both sides of the equation to an odd power. We will still check the solutions, but in this case it will simply be a check of our work and not a search for extraneous solutions.

Example 6

Solving a Radical Equation

NOTE Because a *cube root* is involved, we *cube* both sides to remove the radical.

Solve $\sqrt[3]{x^2 + 23} = 3$.

Cubing each side, we have

$$x^2 + 23 = 27$$

which results in the quadratic equation

$$x^2 - 4 = 0$$

This has two solutions

$$x = 2 \qquad \text{or} \qquad x = -2$$

Checking the solutions, we find that both result in true statements. Again you should verify this result.

CHECK YOURSELF 6

Solve $\sqrt[3]{x^2 - 8} - 2 = 0$.

We summarize our work in this section in the following algorithm for solving equations involving radicals.

Step by Step: Solving Equations Involving Radicals

Step 1 Isolate a radical on one side of the equation.
Step 2 Raise each side of the equation to the smallest power that will eliminate the isolated radical.
Step 3 If any radicals remain in the equation derived in step 2, return to step 1 and continue the solution process.
Step 4 Solve the resulting equation to determine any possible solutions.
Step 5 Check all solutions to determine whether extraneous solutions may have resulted from step 2.

Did you ever stand on a beach and wonder how far out into the ocean you could see? Or have you wondered how close a ship has to be to spot land? In either case, the function

$$d(h) = \sqrt{2h}$$

can be used to estimate the distance to the horizon (in miles) from a given height (in feet).

Example 7

Estimating a Distance

Cordelia stood on a cliff gazing out at the ocean. Her eyes were 100 ft above the ocean. She saw a ship on the horizon. Approximately how far was she from that ship?

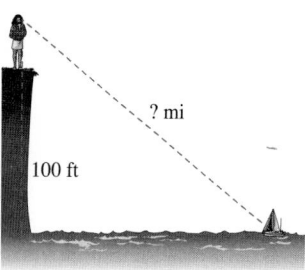

Substituting 100 for h in the equation, we get

$$d(h) = \sqrt{2(100)}$$

$$d(h) = \sqrt{200}$$

$$d(h) \approx 14 \text{ mi}$$

 CHECK YOURSELF 7

From a plane flying at 35,000 ft, how far away is the horizon?

CHECK YOURSELF ANSWERS

1. {21}   **2.** No solution   **3.** {9}   **4.** $\left\{0, -\dfrac{1}{9}\right\}$ **5.** {6}   **6.** {4, −4}

7. $d(h) \approx 265$ mi

4.9 Exercises

Solve each of the following equations. Be sure to check your solutions.

© 2001 McGraw-Hill Companies

1. $\sqrt{x} = 2$

2. $\sqrt{x} - 3 = 0$

3. $\sqrt{x} = 6$

4. $\sqrt{x} = 5$

5. $2\sqrt{y} - 1 = 0$

6. $3\sqrt{2z} = 9$

7. $\sqrt{5x} + 1 = 6$

8. $\sqrt{7x} + 1 = 6$

9. $\sqrt{m + 5} = 3$

10. $\sqrt{y + 7} = 5$

11. $\sqrt{2x + 4} - 4 = 0$

12. $\sqrt{3x + 3} - 6 = 0$

13. $\sqrt{3x - 2} + 2 = 0$

14. $\sqrt{4x + 1} + 3 = 0$

15. $\sqrt{x - 1} = \sqrt{1 - x}$

16. $\sqrt{x + 1} = \sqrt{1 + x}$

17. $\sqrt{w + 3} = \sqrt{3 + w}$

18. $\sqrt{w - 3} = \sqrt{3 - w}$

19. $\sqrt{2x - 3} + 1 = 3$

20. $\sqrt{3x + 1} - 2 = -1$

21. $2\sqrt{3z + 2} - 1 = 5$

22. $3\sqrt{4q - 1} - 2 = 7$

23. $\sqrt{15 - 2x} = x$

24. $\sqrt{48 - 2y} = y$

ANSWERS

1. _____

2. _____

3. _____

4. _____

5. _____

6. _____

7. _____

8. _____

9. _____

10. _____

11. _____

12. _____

13. _____

14. _____

15. _____

16. _____

17. _____

18. _____

19. _____

20. _____

21. _____

22. _____

23. _____

24. _____

25. _____

26. _____

27. _____

28. _____

29. _____

30. _____

31. _____

32. _____

33. _____

34. _____

35. _____

36. _____

37. _____

38. _____

39. _____

40. _____

41. _____

42. _____

43. _____

44. _____

45. _____

46. _____

47. _____

48. _____

25. $\sqrt{x + 5} = x - 1$

26. $\sqrt{2x - 1} = x - 8$

27. $\sqrt{3m - 2} + m = 10$

28. $\sqrt{2x + 1} + x = 7$

29. $\sqrt{t + 9} + 3 = t$

30. $\sqrt{2y + 7} + 4 = y$

31. $\sqrt{6x + 1} - 1 = 2x$

32. $\sqrt{7x + 1} - 1 = 3x$

33. $\sqrt[3]{x - 5} = 3$

34. $\sqrt[3]{x + 6} = 2$

35. $\sqrt[3]{x^2 - 1} = 2$

36. $\sqrt[3]{x^2 + 11} = 3$

Solve each of the following equations. Be sure to check your solutions.

37. $\sqrt{2x} = \sqrt{x + 1}$

38. $\sqrt{3x} = \sqrt{5x - 1}$

39. $2\sqrt{3r} = \sqrt{r + 11}$

40. $5\sqrt{2q - 7} = \sqrt{15q}$

41. $\sqrt{x + 2} + 1 = \sqrt{x + 4}$

42. $\sqrt{x + 5} - 1 = \sqrt{x + 3}$

43. $\sqrt{4m - 3} - 2 = \sqrt{2m - 5}$

44. $\sqrt{2c - 1} = \sqrt{3c + 1} - 1$

45. $\sqrt{x + 1} + \sqrt{x} = 1$

46. $\sqrt{z - 1} - \sqrt{6 - z} = 1$

47. $\sqrt{5x + 6} - \sqrt{x + 3} = 3$

48. $\sqrt{5y + 6} - \sqrt{3y + 4} = 2$

49. $\sqrt{y^2 + 12y} - 3\sqrt{5} = 0$

50. $\sqrt{x^2 + 2x} - 2\sqrt{6} = 0$

51. $\sqrt{\dfrac{x - 3}{x + 2}} = \dfrac{2}{3}$

52. $\dfrac{\sqrt{x - 2}}{x - 2} = \dfrac{x - 5}{\sqrt{x - 2}}$

53. $\sqrt{\sqrt{t + 5}} = 3$

54. $\sqrt{\sqrt{s - 1}} = \sqrt{s - 7}$

55. For what values of x is $\sqrt{(x - 1)^2} = x - 1$ a true statement?

56. For what values of x is $\sqrt[3]{(x - 1)^3} = x - 1$ a true statement?

Solve for the indicated variable.

57. $h = \sqrt{pq}$ for q

58. $c = \sqrt{a^2 + b^2}$ for a

59. $v = \sqrt{2gR}$ for R

60. $v = \sqrt{2gR}$ for g

61. $r = \sqrt{\dfrac{S}{2\pi}}$ for S

62. $r = \sqrt{\dfrac{3V}{4\pi}}$ for V

63. $r = \sqrt{\dfrac{2V}{\pi h}}$ for V

64. $r = \sqrt{\dfrac{2V}{\pi h}}$ for h

65. $d = \sqrt{(x - 1)^2 + (y - 2)^2}$ for x

66. $d = \sqrt{(x - 1)^2 + (y - 2)^2}$ for y

49. _____
50. _____
51. _____
52. _____
53. _____
54. _____
55. _____
56. _____
57. _____
58. _____
59. _____
60. _____
61. _____
62. _____
63. _____
64. _____
65. _____
66. _____

67. _____

68. _____

69. _____

70. _____

71. _____

72. _____

73. _____

74. _____

A weight suspended on the end of a string is a *pendulum.* The most common example of a pendulum (this side of Edgar Allen Poe) is the kind found in many clocks.

The regular back-and-forth motion of the pendulum is *periodic,* and one such cycle of motion is called a *period.* The time, in seconds, that it takes for one period is given by the radical equation

$$t = 2\pi\sqrt{\frac{l}{g}}$$

in which g is the force of gravity (10 m/s^2) and l is the length of the pendulum.

67. Find the period (to the nearest hundredth of a second) if the pendulum is 0.9 m long.

68. Find the period if the pendulum is 0.049 m long.

69. Solve the equation for length l.

70. How long would the pendulum be if the period were exactly 1 s?

Solve each of the following applications.

71. The sum of an integer and its square root is 12. Find the integer.

72. The difference between an integer and its square root is 12. What is the integer?

73. The sum of an integer and twice its square root is 24. What is the integer?

74. The sum of an integer and 3 times its square root is 40. Find the integer.

75. If a plane flies at 30,000 ft, how far away is the horizon?

76. Janine was looking out across the ocean from her hotel room on the beach. Her eyes were 250 ft above the ground. She saw a ship on the horizon. Approximately how far was the ship from her?

77. Given a distance, d, to the horizon, what altitude would allow you to see that far?

When a car comes to a sudden stop, you can determine the skidding distance (in feet) for a given speed (in miles per hour) using the formula $s(x) = 2\sqrt{5x}$, in which s is skidding distance and x is speed. Calculate the skidding distance for the following speeds.

78. 55 mi/h

79. 65 mi/h

80. 75 mi/h

81. 40 mi/h

82. Given the skidding distance s, what formula would allow you to calculate the speed in miles per hour?

83. Use the formula obtained in exercise 78 to determine the speed of a car in miles per hour if the skid marks were 35 ft long.

For each given equation, use a graphing calculator to solve. Express solutions to the nearest hundredth. (*Hint:* Define Y_1 by the expression on the left side of the equation and define Y_2 by the expression on the right side. Graph these functions and locate any intersection points. For each such point, the x value represents a solution.)

84. $\sqrt{x + 4} = x - 3$

85. $\sqrt{2 - x} = x + 4$

86. $3 - 2\sqrt{x + 4} = 2x - 5$

87. $5 - 3\sqrt{2 - x} = 3 - 4x$

ANSWERS

75. _____

76. _____

77. _____

78. _____

79. _____

80. _____

81. _____

82. _____

83. _____

84. _____

85. _____

86. _____

87. _____

Answers

1. 4   **3.** $x = 36$ **5.** $\dfrac{1}{4}$ **7.** $x = 7$ **9.** 4   **11.** 6   **13.** No solution

15. 1   **17.** All real numbers   **19.** $\dfrac{7}{2}$ **21.** $\dfrac{7}{3}$ **23.** 3   **25.** 4

27. 6   **29.** 7   **31.** $0, \dfrac{1}{2}$ **33.** 32   **35.** ± 3 **37.** 1   **39.** 1

41. $-\dfrac{7}{4}$ **43.** 3, 7   **45.** 0   **47.** 6   **49.** $-15, 3$ **51.** 7   **53.** 16

55. $x \geq 1$ **57.** $q = \dfrac{h^2}{p}$ **59.** $R = \dfrac{v^2}{2g}$ **61.** $S = 2\pi r^2$ **63.** $V = \dfrac{\pi h r^2}{2}$

65. $x = 1 \pm \sqrt{d^2 - (y - 2)^2}$ **67.** 1.88 s   **69.** $l = \dfrac{t^2 g}{4\pi^2}$ **71.** 9

73. 16   **75.** ≈ 245 mi   **77.** $\dfrac{d^2}{2}$ **79.** ≈ 36 ft   **81.** ≈ 28 ft

83. ≈ 60 mi/h   **85.** $\{-2\}$ **87.** $\{0.44\}$

4.10 Complex Numbers

4.10 OBJECTIVES

1. Define a complex number
2. Add and subtract complex numbers
3. Multiply and divide complex numbers

Radicals such as

$$\sqrt{-4} \quad \text{and} \quad \sqrt{-49}$$

are *not* real numbers because no real number squared produces a negative number. Our work in this section will extend our number system to include these **imaginary numbers,** which will allow us to consider radicals such as $\sqrt{-4}$.

First we offer a definition.

Definitions: The Imaginary Number *i*

The number *i* is defined as

$$i = \sqrt{-1}$$

Note that this means that

$$i^2 = -1$$

This definition of the number *i* gives us an alternate means of indicating the square root of a negative number.

Definitions: Rules and Procedures: Writing an Imaginary Number

When *a* is a positive real number,

$$\sqrt{-a} = \sqrt{a}\,i \quad \text{or} \quad i\sqrt{a}$$

Example 1

Using the Number *i*

Write each expression as a multiple of *i*.

(a) $\sqrt{-4} = \sqrt{4}\,i = 2i$

(b) $-\sqrt{-9} = -\sqrt{9}\,i = -3i$

NOTE We simplify $\sqrt{8}$ as $2\sqrt{2}$. Note that we write the *i* in front of the radical to make it clear that *i* is *not part of* the radicand.

(c) $\sqrt{-8} = \sqrt{8}\,i = 2\sqrt{2}\,i$ or $2i\sqrt{2}$

(d) $\sqrt{-7} = \sqrt{7}\,i$ or $i\sqrt{7}$

 CHECK YOURSELF 1

Write each radical as a multiple of i.

(a) $\sqrt{-25}$ **(b)** $\sqrt{-24}$

We are now ready to define complex numbers in terms of the number i.

NOTE The term "imaginary number" was introduced by René Descartes in 1637. Euler used i to indicate $\sqrt{-1}$ in 1748, but it was not until 1832 that Gauss used the term "complex number."

NOTE The first application of these numbers was made by Charles Steinmetz (1865–1923) in explaining the behavior of electric circuits.

NOTE Also, $5i$ is called a **pure imaginary** number.

NOTE The real numbers can be considered a subset of the set of complex numbers.

> ### Definitions: Complex Number
>
> A **complex number** is any number that can be written in the form
>
> $a + bi$
>
> in which a and b are real numbers and
>
> $i = \sqrt{-1}$

The form $a + bi$ is called the **standard form** of a complex number. We call a the **real part** of the complex number and b the **imaginary part.** Some examples follow.

$3 + 7i$ is an example of a complex number with real part 3 and imaginary part 7.

$5i$ is also a complex number because it can be written as $0 + 5i$.

-3 is a complex number because it can be written as $-3 + 0i$.

The basic operations of addition and subtraction on complex numbers are defined here.

> ### Rules and Properties: Adding and Subtracting Complex Numbers
>
> For the complex numbers $a + bi$ and $c + di$,
>
> $(a + bi) + (c + di) = (a + c) + (b + d)i$
>
> $(a + bi) - (c + di) = (a - c) + (b - d)i$
>
> In words, we add or subtract the real parts and the imaginary parts of the complex numbers.

Example 2 illustrates the use of these definitions.

Example 2

Adding and Subtracting Complex Numbers

Perform the indicated operations.

NOTE The regrouping is essentially a matter of combining like terms.

(a) $(5 + 3i) + (6 - 7i) = (5 + 6) + (3 - 7)i$

$\qquad\qquad\qquad\qquad = 11 - 4i$

(b) $5 + (7 - 5i) = (5 + 7) + (-5i)$

$\qquad\qquad\qquad = 12 - 5i$

(c) $(8 - 2i) - (3 - 4i) = (8 - 3) + [-2 - (-4)]i$

$\qquad\qquad\qquad\qquad = 5 + 2i$

CHECK YOURSELF 2

Perform the indicated operations.

(a) $(4 - 7i) + (3 - 2i)$ **(b)** $-7 + (-2 + 3i)$ **(c)** $(-4 + 3i) - (-2 - i)$

Because complex numbers are binomial in form, the product of two complex numbers is found by applying our earlier multiplication pattern for binomials, as Example 3 illustrates.

Example 3

Multiplying Complex Numbers

Multiply.

(a) $(2 + 3i)(3 - 4i)$

$= 2 \cdot 3 + 2(-4i) + (3i)3 + (3i)(-4i)$

$= 6 + (-8i) + 9i + (-12i^2)$

NOTE We can replace i^2 with -1 because of the definition of i, and we usually do so because of the resulting simplification.

$= 6 - 8i + 9i + (-12)(-1)$

$= 6 + i + 12$

$= 18 + i$

(b) $(1 - 2i)(3 - 4i)$

$= 1 \cdot 3 + 1(-4i) + (-2i)3 + (-2i)(-4i)$

$= 3 + (-4i) + (-6i) + 8i^2$

$= 3 - 10i + 8(-1)$

$= 3 + 10i - 8$

$= -5 - 10i$

 CHECK YOURSELF 3

Multiply $(2 - 5i)(3 - 2i)$.

Example 3 suggests the following pattern for multiplication on complex numbers.

Rules and Properties: Multiplying Complex Numbers

For the complex numbers $a + bi$ and $c + di$,

$(a + bi)(c + di) = ac + adi + bci + bdi^2$

$= ac + adi + bci - bd$

$= (ac - bd) + (ad + bc)i$

This formula for the general product of two complex numbers can be memorized. However, you will find it much easier to get used to the multiplication pattern as it is applied to complex numbers than to memorize this formula.

There is one particular product form that will seem very familiar. We call $a + bi$ and $a - bi$ **complex conjugates.** For instance,

$$3 + 2i \quad \text{and} \quad 3 - 2i$$

are complex conjugates.

Consider the product

$$(3 + 2i)(3 - 2i) = 3^2 - (2i)^2$$
$$= 9 - 4i^2 = 9 - 4(-1)$$
$$= 9 + 4 = 13$$

The product of $3 + 2i$ and $3 - 2i$ is a real number. In general, we can write the product of two complex conjugates as

$$(a + bi)(a - bi) = a^2 + b^2$$

The fact that this product is always a real number will be very useful when we consider the division of complex numbers later in this section.

Example 4

Multiplying Complex Numbers

Multiply.

NOTE We could get the same result by applying the formula above with $a = 7$ and $b = 4$.

$$(7 - 4i)(7 + 4i) = 7^2 - (4i)^2$$
$$= 7^2 - 4^2(-1)$$
$$= 7^2 + 4^2$$
$$= 49 + 16 = 65$$

 CHECK YOURSELF 4

Multiply $(5 + 3i)(5 - 3i)$.

We are now ready to discuss the division of complex numbers. Generally, we find the quotient by multiplying the numerator and denominator by the conjugate of the denominator, as Example 5 illustrates.

Example 5

Dividing Complex Numbers

Divide.

NOTE Think of $3i$ as $0 + 3i$ and of its conjugate as $0 - 3i$, or $-3i$.

(a) $\dfrac{6 + 9i}{3i}$

$\dfrac{6 + 9i}{3i} = \dfrac{(6 + 9i)(-3i)}{(3i)(-3i)}$ The conjugate of $3i$ is $-3i$, and so we multiply the numerator and denominator by $-3i$.

NOTE Multiplying the numerator and denominator in the original expression by i would yield the same result. Try it yourself.

$= \dfrac{-18i - 27i^2}{-9i^2}$

$= \dfrac{-18i - 27(-1)}{(-9)(-1)}$

$= \dfrac{27 - 18i}{9} = 3 - 2i$

NOTE We multiply by $\dfrac{3 - 2i}{3 - 2i}$, which equals 1.

(b) $\dfrac{3 - i}{3 + 2i} = \dfrac{(3 - i)(3 - 2i)}{(3 + 2i)(3 - 2i)}$

$= \dfrac{9 - 6i - 3i + 2i^2}{9 - 4i^2}$

$= \dfrac{9 - 9i - 2}{9 + 4}$

NOTE To write a complex number in standard form, we separate the real component from the imaginary.

$= \dfrac{7 - 9i}{13} = \dfrac{7}{13} - \dfrac{9}{13}i$

(c) $\dfrac{2 + i}{4 - 5i} = \dfrac{(2 + i)(4 + 5i)}{(4 - 5i)(4 + 5i)}$

$= \dfrac{8 + 4i + 10i + 5i^2}{16 - 25i^2}$

$= \dfrac{8 + 14i - 5}{16 + 25}$

$= \dfrac{3 + 14i}{41} = \dfrac{3}{41} + \dfrac{14}{41}i$

✔ **CHECK YOURSELF 5**

Divide.

(a) $\dfrac{5 + i}{5 - 3i}$

(b) $\dfrac{4 + 10i}{2i}$

We conclude this section with the following diagram, which summarizes the structure of the system of complex numbers.

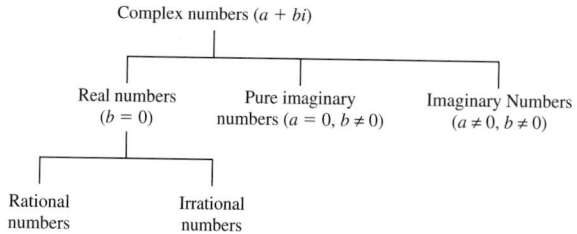

CHECK YOURSELF ANSWERS

1. **(a)** $5i$; **(b)** $2i\sqrt{6}$ **2.** **(a)** $7 - 9i$; **(b)** $-9 + 3i$; **(c)** $-2 + 4i$ **3.** $-4 - 19i$

4. 34 **5.** **(a)** $\dfrac{11}{17} + \dfrac{10}{17}i$; **(b)** $5 - 2i$

In exercises 1 to 10, write each root as a multiple of i. Simplify your results when necessary.

Name _____

Section _____ Date _____

ANSWERS

1. $\sqrt{-16}$ **2.** $\sqrt{-36}$

3. $-\sqrt{-64}$ **4.** $-\sqrt{-25}$

5. $\sqrt{-21}$ **6.** $\sqrt{-19}$

7. $\sqrt{-12}$ **8.** $\sqrt{-24}$

9. $-\sqrt{-108}$ **10.** $-\sqrt{-192}$

In exercises 11 to 26, perform the indicated operations.

11. $(3 + i) + (5 + 2i)$ **12.** $(2 + 3i) + (4 + 5i)$

13. $(3 - 2i) + (-2 + 7i)$ **14.** $(-5 + 3i) + (-2 + 7i)$

15. $(5 + 4i) - (3 + 2i)$ **16.** $(7 + 6i) - (3 + 5i)$

17. $(8 - 5i) - (3 + 2i)$ **18.** $(7 - 3i) - (-2 - 5i)$

19. $(5 + i) + (2 + 3i) + 7i$ **20.** $(3 - 2i) + (2 + 3i) + 7i$

21. $(2 + 3i) - (3 - 5i) + (4 + 3i)$ **22.** $(5 - 7i) + (7 + 3i) - (2 - 7i)$

23. $(7 + 3i) - [(3 + i) - (2 - 5i)]$ **24.** $(8 - 2i) - [(4 + 3i) - (-2 + i)]$

25. $(5 + 3i) + (-5 - 3i)$ **26.** $(8 - 7i) + (-8 + 7i)$

In exercises 27 to 42, find each product. Write your answer in standard form.

27. $3i(3 + 5i)$ **28.** $2i(7 + 3i)$

29. $4i(3 - 7i)$ **30.** $2i(6 + 3i)$

1. _____	2. _____
3. _____	4. _____
5. _____	6. _____
7. _____	8. _____
9. _____	10. _____

11. _____

12. _____

13. _____

14. _____

15. _____

16. _____

17. _____

18. _____

19. _____

20. _____

21. _____

22. _____

23. _____

24. _____

25. _____

26. _____

27. _____

28. _____

29. _____

30. _____

31. _____

32. _____

33. _____

34. _____

35. _____

36. _____

37. _____

38. _____

39. _____

40. _____

41. _____

42. _____

43. _____

44. _____

45. _____

46. _____

47. _____

48. _____

49. _____

50. _____

51. _____

52. _____

53. _____

54. _____

55. _____

56. _____

31. $-2i(4 - 3i)$

32. $-5i(2 - 7i)$

33. $6i\left(\dfrac{2}{3} + \dfrac{5}{6}i\right)$

34. $4i\left(\dfrac{1}{2} + \dfrac{3}{4}i\right)$

35. $(3 + 2i)(2 + 3i)$

36. $(5 - 2i)(3 - i)$

37. $(4 - 3i)(2 + 5i)$

38. $(7 + 2i)(3 - 2i)$

39. $(-2 - 3i)(-3 + 4i)$

40. $(-5 - i)(-3 - 4i)$

41. $(5 - 2i)^2$

42. $(3 + 7i)^2$

In exercises 43 to 50, write the conjugate of each complex number. Then find the product of the given number and the conjugate.

43. $3 - 2i$

44. $5 + 2i$

45. $2 + 3i$

46. $7 - i$

47. $-3 - 2i$

48. $-5 - 7i$

49. $5i$

50. $-3i$

In exercises 51 to 62, find each quotient, and write your answer in standard form.

51. $\dfrac{3 + 2i}{i}$

52. $\dfrac{5 - 3i}{-i}$

53. $\dfrac{6 - 4i}{2i}$

54. $\dfrac{8 + 12i}{-4i}$

55. $\dfrac{3}{2 + 5i}$

56. $\dfrac{5}{2 - 3i}$

57. $\dfrac{13}{2 + 3i}$

58. $\dfrac{-17}{3 + 5i}$

59. $\dfrac{2 + 3i}{4 + 3i}$

60. $\dfrac{4 - 2i}{5 - 3i}$

61. $\dfrac{3 - 4i}{3 + 4i}$

62. $\dfrac{7 + 2i}{7 - 2i}$

63. The first application of complex numbers was suggested by the Norwegian surveyor Caspar Wessel in 1797. He found that complex numbers could be used to represent distance and direction on a two-dimensional grid. Why would a surveyor care about such a thing?

64. To what sets of numbers does 1 belong?

In this section, we defined $\sqrt{-4} = \sqrt{4}\,i = 2i$ in the process of expressing the square root of a negative number as a multiple of i.

Particular care must be taken with products in which two negative radicands are involved. For instance,

$$\sqrt{-3} \cdot \sqrt{-12} = (i\sqrt{3})(i\sqrt{12})$$
$$= i^2\sqrt{36} = (-1)\sqrt{36} = -6$$

is correct. However, if we try to apply the product property for radicals, we have

$$\sqrt{-3} \cdot \sqrt{-12} \stackrel{?}{=} \sqrt{(-3)(-12)} = \sqrt{36} = 6$$

which is *not* correct. The property $\sqrt{a} \cdot \sqrt{b} = \sqrt{ab}$ is not applicable in the case in which a and b are both negative. Radicals such as $\sqrt{-a}$ must be written in the standard form $i\sqrt{a}$ *before* multiplying, to use the rules for real-valued radicals.

In exercises 65 to 72, find each product.

65. $\sqrt{-5} \cdot \sqrt{-7}$

66. $\sqrt{-3} \cdot \sqrt{-10}$

67. $\sqrt{-2} \cdot \sqrt{-18}$

68. $\sqrt{-4} \cdot \sqrt{-25}$

69. $\sqrt{-6} \cdot \sqrt{-15}$

70. $\sqrt{-5} \cdot \sqrt{-30}$

71. $\sqrt{-10} \cdot \sqrt{-10}$

72. $\sqrt{-11} \cdot \sqrt{-11}$

ANSWERS

57. _____

58. _____

59. _____

60. _____

61. _____

62. _____

63. _____

64. _____

65. _____

66. _____

67. _____

68. _____

69. _____

70. _____

71. _____

72. _____

73. _____

74. _____

75. _____

76. _____

77. _____

78. _____

79. _____

80. _____

81. _____

Because $i^2 = -1$, the positive integral powers of i form an interesting pattern. Consider the following.

$i = i$ $\qquad\qquad i^5 = i^4 \cdot i = 1 \cdot i = i$

$i^2 = -1$ $\qquad\qquad i^6 = i^4 \cdot i^2 = 1(-1) = -1$

$i^3 = i^2 \cdot i = (-1)i = -i$ $\qquad i^7 = i^4 \cdot i^3 = 1(-i) = -i$

$i^4 = i^2 \cdot i^2 = (-1)(-1) = 1$ $\qquad i^8 = i^4 \cdot i^4 = 1 \cdot 1 = 1$

Given the pattern above, do you see that any power of i will simplify to i, -1, $-i$, or 1? The easiest approach to simplifying higher powers of i is to write that power in terms of i^4 (because $1^4 = 1$). As an example,

$i^{18} = i^{16} \cdot i^2 = (i^4)^4 \cdot i^2 = 1^4(-1) = -1$

In exercises 73 to 80, use these comments to simplify each power of i.

73. i^{10} $\qquad\qquad\qquad\qquad\qquad$ **74.** i^9

75. i^{20} $\qquad\qquad\qquad\qquad\qquad$ **76.** i^{15}

77. i^{38} $\qquad\qquad\qquad\qquad\qquad$ **78.** i^{40}

79. i^{51} $\qquad\qquad\qquad\qquad\qquad$ **80.** i^{61}

81. Show that a square root of i is $\dfrac{\sqrt{2}}{2} + \dfrac{\sqrt{2}}{2}i$. That is, $\left(\dfrac{\sqrt{2}}{2} + \dfrac{\sqrt{2}}{2}i\right)^2 = i$.

Answers

1. $4i$ $\quad$ **3.** $-8i$ $\quad$ **5.** $i\sqrt{21}$ $\quad$ **7.** $2i\sqrt{3}$ $\quad$ **9.** $-6i\sqrt{3}$ $\quad$ **11.** $8 + 3i$
13. $1 + 5i$ $\quad$ **15.** $2 + 2i$ $\quad$ **17.** $5 - 7i$ $\quad$ **19.** $7 + 11i$ $\quad$ **21.** $3 + 11i$
23. $6 - 3i$ $\quad$ **25.** $0 + 0i$ $\quad$ **27.** $-15 + 9i$ $\quad$ **29.** $28 + 12i$ $\quad$ **31.** $-6 - 8i$
33. $-5 + 4i$ $\quad$ **35.** $13i$ $\quad$ **37.** $23 + 14i$ $\quad$ **39.** $18 + i$ $\quad$ **41.** $21 - 20i$
43. $3 + 2i, 13$ $\quad$ **45.** $2 - 3i, 13$ $\quad$ **47.** $-3 + 2i, 13$ $\quad$ **49.** $-5i, 25$

51. $2 - 3i$ $\quad$ **53.** $-2 - 3i$ $\quad$ **55.** $\dfrac{6}{29} - \dfrac{15}{29}i$ $\quad$ **57.** $2 - 3i$ $\quad$ **59.** $\dfrac{17}{25} + \dfrac{6}{25}i$

61. $-\dfrac{7}{25} - \dfrac{24}{25}i$ $\quad$ **63.** $\qquad$ **65.** $-\sqrt{35}$ $\quad$ **67.** -6 $\quad$ **69.** $-3\sqrt{10}$

71. -10 $\quad$ **73.** -1 $\quad$ **75.** 1 $\quad$ **77.** -1 $\quad$ **79.** $-i$ $\quad$ **81.**

Index

Contents

Chapter 0 An Arithmetic Review

Exercises 0.1

1. In $5 + 4 = 9$, 5 is the *addend,* 4 is the *addend,* and 9 is the *sum.*

3. The order of the addends, 5 and 8, was changed. The sum remains the same by the commutative property of addition.

5. The grouping of the addends was changed. The sum remains the same by the associative property of addition.

7. The order of the addends, 7 and 6, was changed. The sum remains the same by the commutative property of addition.

9. The order of the addends, 5 and (2 + 3), was changed. The sum remains the same by the commutative property of addition.

11.
$$\begin{array}{r} 2792 \\ + \ 205 \\ \hline 2997 \end{array}$$

13.
$$\begin{array}{r} 2345 \\ + 6053 \\ \hline 8398 \end{array}$$

15.
$$\begin{array}{r} 2531 \\ + 5354 \\ \hline 7885 \end{array}$$

17.
$$\begin{array}{r} 21,314 \\ + 43,042 \\ \hline 64,356 \end{array}$$

19.
$$\begin{array}{r} {\scriptstyle 1\ 1\ 1} \\ 3490 \\ 548 \\ + \ \ 25 \\ \hline 4063 \end{array}$$

21.
$$\begin{array}{r} {\scriptstyle 1\ 2\ 3} \\ 2289 \\ 38 \\ 578 \\ + 3489 \\ \hline 6394 \end{array}$$

23.
$$\begin{array}{r} {\scriptstyle 1\ \ 1} \\ 23,458 \\ + 32,623 \\ \hline 56,081 \end{array}$$

25.
$$\begin{array}{r} {\scriptstyle 11\ 22} \\ 26,735 \\ 259 \\ 3,056 \\ + 35,489 \\ \hline 65,539 \end{array}$$

27. $2 + 7 + 9 = 9 + 9 = 18$

29. $2 + 3 + 4 + 9 = 5 + 4 + 9 = 9 + 9 = 18$

31. 356 more than 1213 is written $1213 + 356 = 1569$.

33.
$$\begin{array}{r} {\scriptstyle 1\ 1\ 2} \\ 23 \\ 2845 \\ 5 \\ + \ 589 \\ \hline 3462 \end{array}$$

35.
$$\begin{array}{r} {\scriptstyle 2\ 32} \\ 2,195 \\ 348 \\ 640 \\ 59 \\ + 23,785 \\ \hline 27,027 \end{array}$$

37. 34 more than 125 is written $125 + 34 = 159$.

39.
$$\begin{array}{r} 23 \\ 122 \\ + \ 451 \\ \hline 596 \end{array}$$

41. Since we want a total, use addition.
Write $42 + 46 = 88$.
Her total score for the round was 88.

43. Since we want a total, use addition.
Write $325 + 273 = 598$.
In those two days, they drove 598 mi.

45. Since we want a total, use addition.
Write $230 + 312 + 244 + 213 = 999$.
During this period, 999 people saw the play.

47. Since we want a total, use addition.
Write $5200 + 7100 + 7450 = 19,750$.
He invested $19,750 in the three cars.

49. Since we want a total, use addition.
Write $4200 + 5970 + 4850 = 15,020$.
15,020 lb were shipped.

51.

Category of film	Jan.	Feb.	Mar.	Category Totals
Comedy	4568	3269	2189	10,026
Drama	5612	4129	3879	13,620
Action/Adventure	2654	3178	1984	7,816
Musical	897	623	528	2,048
Monthly Totals	13,731	11,199	8580	35,510

53. Number of firms in Washington   193,600
Number of firms in Philadelphia   144,600
Number of firms in New York   282,000
Since we want a total, use addition.
Write $193,600 + 144,600 + 282,000 = 620,200$.
There are 620,200 firms in total.

55. Total sales for firms in Houston $78,180,300
Total sales for firms in Dallas   63,114,900
Since we want a total, use addition.
Write $78,180,300 + 63,114,900 = 141,295,200$.
Total sales for firms in Houston and Dallas is $141,295,200.

57. Each number after the first is 7 more than the previous number. The next four numbers in the sequence are 33, 40, 47, 54.

59. Each number after the first is 6 more than the previous number. The next four numbers are 31, 37, 43, 49.

61. The next number in the sequence is $34 + 55 = 89$.
The number after 89 will be $55 + 89 = 144$. The number after 144 will be $89 + 144 = 233$. The number after 233 will be $144 + 233 = 377$.
So, the next four numbers in the sequence are 89, 144, 233, 377.

63. Answers may vary. One example is shown.

8	3	4
1	5	9
6	7	2

65. writing exercise

67. a. The associative property of addition states that the sum of numbers is not affected when the order in which the numbers are grouped is changed. Changing the grouping of the addends of $5 + (8 + 0)$ gives $(5 + 8) + 0$. So the associative property of addition tells us $5 + (8 + 0) = (5 + 8) + 0$.

   b. The commutative property of addition states that the sum of numbers is not affected when the order of two numbers around an addition sign is changed. Changing the order of 8 and 0 around the addition sign inside the parentheses of $5 + (8 + 0)$ gives $5 + (0 + 8)$. So the commutative property of addition tells us $5 + (8 + 0) = 5 + (0 + 8)$. Changing the order of 5 and $(8 + 0)$ around the addition sign outside the parentheses gives $(8 + 0) + 5$. So the commutative property of addition tells us $5 + (8 + 0) = (8 + 0) + 5$.

   c. The additive identity property states that the sum of zero and any number is that number. This means that $8 + 0 = 8$. So the additive identity property tells us $5 + (8 + 0) = 5 + 8$.

Exercises 0.2

1. In $9 - 6 = 3$, 9 is the *minuend,* 6 is the *subtrahend,* and 3 is the *difference.* $3 + 6 = 9$ is the related addition statement.

3.
$$\begin{array}{r} 347 \\ -\ 201 \\ \hline 146 \end{array}$$
check:
$$\begin{array}{r} 146 \\ +\ 201 \\ \hline 347 \end{array}$$

5.
$$\begin{array}{r} 689 \\ -\ 245 \\ \hline 444 \end{array}$$
check:
$$\begin{array}{r} 444 \\ +\ 245 \\ \hline 689 \end{array}$$

7.
$$\begin{array}{r} 3446 \\ -\ 2326 \\ \hline 1120 \end{array}$$
check:
$$\begin{array}{r} 1120 \\ +\ 2326 \\ \hline 3446 \end{array}$$

9.
$$\begin{array}{r} \overset{5}{\cancel{6}}4 \\ -\ 27 \\ \hline 37 \end{array}$$
check:
$$\begin{array}{r} 37 \\ +\ 27 \\ \hline 64 \end{array}$$

11.
$$\begin{array}{r} 6\overset{1}{2}7 \\ -\ 358 \\ \hline 9 \end{array}$$

$$\begin{array}{r} \overset{511}{\cancel{6}}\overset{}{2}7 \\ -\ 358 \\ \hline 269 \end{array}$$
check:
$$\begin{array}{r} 269 \\ +\ 358 \\ \hline 627 \end{array}$$

13.
$$\begin{array}{r} 642\overset{1}{2}3 \\ -\ 3678 \\ \hline 5 \end{array}$$

$$\begin{array}{r} 6\overset{3}{\cancel{4}}\overset{11}{2}3 \\ -\ \ 3678 \\ \hline 45 \end{array}$$

$$\begin{array}{r} \overset{5\ 13\ 11}{\cancel{6}\cancel{4}\cancel{2}3} \\ -\ \ 3678 \\ \hline 2745 \end{array}$$
check:
$$\begin{array}{r} 2745 \\ +\ 3678 \\ \hline 6423 \end{array}$$

15.
$$
\begin{array}{r}
\overset{2}{6}\overset{1}{0}\,3\,4 \\
-\ 2569 \\
\hline
5
\end{array}
$$

$$
\begin{array}{r}
\overset{5}{\cancel{6}}\,\overset{1}{0}\,\overset{2}{3}\,\overset{1}{4} \\
-\ 2569 \\
\hline
5
\end{array}
$$

$$
\begin{array}{r}
\overset{9}{5}\,\overset{10}{\cancel{0}}\,\overset{12}{3}\,\overset{1}{4} \\
\cancel{6}\ 0\ 3\ 4 \\
-\ 2569 \\
\hline
3465
\end{array}
$$
check:
$$
\begin{array}{r}
3465 \\
+\ 2569 \\
\hline
6034
\end{array}
$$

17.
$$
\begin{array}{r}
\overset{3}{\cancel{4}}\overset{1}{0}\,00 \\
-\ 2345
\end{array}
$$

$$
\begin{array}{r}
\overset{3}{\cancel{4}}\,\overset{9}{\cancel{0}}\,\overset{1}{0}\,0 \\
-\ 2345
\end{array}
$$

$$
\begin{array}{r}
\overset{3}{\cancel{4}}\,\overset{9}{\cancel{0}}\,\overset{9}{\cancel{0}}\,\overset{1}{0} \\
-\ 2345 \\
\hline
1655
\end{array}
$$
check:
$$
\begin{array}{r}
1655 \\
+\ 2345 \\
\hline
4000
\end{array}
$$

19.
$$
\begin{array}{r}
33{,}4\overset{7}{\cancel{8}}\overset{1}{6} \\
-\ 14{,}047 \\
\hline
439
\end{array}
$$

$$
\begin{array}{r}
\overset{2}{\cancel{3}}3{,}\overset{7}{\cancel{4}}\overset{1}{8}6 \\
-\ 14{,}047 \\
\hline
19{,}439
\end{array}
$$
check:
$$
\begin{array}{r}
19{,}439 \\
+\ 14{,}047 \\
\hline
33{,}486
\end{array}
$$

21.
$$
\begin{array}{r}
2\overset{8}{\cancel{9}}{,}\overset{1}{4}00 \\
-\ 17{,}900 \\
\hline
11{,}500
\end{array}
$$
check:
$$
\begin{array}{r}
11{,}500 \\
+\ 17{,}900 \\
\hline
29{,}400
\end{array}
$$

23.
$$
\begin{array}{r}
5\overset{8}{\cancel{9}}{,}\overset{1}{0}00 \\
-\ 23{,}458
\end{array}
$$

$$
\begin{array}{r}
5\overset{8}{\cancel{9}}{,}\overset{9}{\cancel{0}}\overset{10}{0}0 \\
-\ 23{,}458
\end{array}
$$

$$
\begin{array}{r}
8\,\overset{9}{10}\,10 \\
5\overset{}{\cancel{9}}{,}\overset{}{\cancel{0}}\,0\,0 \\
-\ 23{,}458 \\
\hline
35{,}542
\end{array}
$$
check:
$$
\begin{array}{r}
35{,}542 \\
+\ 23{,}458 \\
\hline
59{,}000
\end{array}
$$

25.
$$
\begin{array}{r}
3\overset{4}{\cancel{5}}\overset{1}{3}7 \\
-\ 2675 \\
\hline
62
\end{array}
$$

$$
\begin{array}{r}
\overset{2}{\cancel{3}}\,\overset{14}{\cancel{5}}\overset{1}{3}7 \\
-\ 2675 \\
\hline
862
\end{array}
$$
check:
$$
\begin{array}{r}
862 \\
+\ 2675 \\
\hline
3537
\end{array}
$$

27. 25 less than 76 is written $76 - 25 = 51$.

29. The difference between 97 and 43 is written $97 - 43 = 54$.

31. 298 decreased by 47 is written $298 - 47 = 251$.

33. Yes, the difference 8 mi – 4 mi produces a meaningful result since the units, miles, are identical.

35. No, the sum 7 ft + 11 in. does not produce a meaningful result since the units, feet and inches, are not identical.

37. Yes, the difference 17 yd – 10 yd produces a meaningful result since the units, yards, are identical.

39.
starting elevation	1053
increase of 123 ft	+ 123
	1176
decrease of 98 ft	− 98
	1078
increase of 63 ft	+ 63
	1141

The final elevation of the hiker is 1141 ft.

41.
starting elevation	7302
decrease of 623 ft	− 623
	6679
decrease of 123 ft	− 123
	6556
increase of 307 ft	+ 307
	6863

The final elevation of the hiker is 6863 ft.

43. Tony's score was 23 points less than Shaka's score of 87. 23 less than 87 is written $87 - 23 = 64$. Tony's score on the test was 64.

45. The smaller number is 134 less than the larger number, 655. 134 less than 655 is written $655 - 134 = 521$. The smaller number is 521.

47. Inez needs $228 less than $449. 228 less than 449 is written $449 - 228 = 221$. Inez needs $221 more.

49. We want the difference between the enrollments. The difference between 2653 and 2479 is written $2653 - 2479 = 174$. The college's enrollment increased by 174 students.

51. First, find the total amount deposited.
$85 + 272 = 357$
Next, find the total amount for which checks were written.
$35 + 27 + 89 + 178 = 329$
The balance is the difference between these totals, written $357 - 329 = 28$. Rafael's balance at the end of the month was $28.

53. First, find the total number of points scored by the professional basketball team.
$98 + 136 + 113 = 347$
Next, find the total number of points scored by the opponents.
$102 + 109 + 93 = 304$
The difference between the totals is written $347 - 304 = 43$.
The professional basketball team outscored its opponents by 43 points.

55.

Monthly income	$1620
House payment	$343
Balance	$1277
Car payment	$183
Balance	$1094
Food	$312
Balance	$782
Clothing	$89
Amount remaining	$693

57. First, find the total number of miles accumulated.
$13,850 + 2800 + 1475 + 4280 = 22,405$
Carmen must fly the difference between 30,000 and the total number of miles accumulated, written $30,000 - 22,405 = 7595$. Carmen must fly an additional 7595 mi for her free trip.

59. a. First, find the combined value of both types of lettuce.
$360 + 210 = 570$
The difference between this total and the value of broccoli is written
$570 - 246 = 324$.
The combined value of both types of lettuce is $324 million, or $324,000,000, greater than the value of broccoli.

b. First, find the value of lettuce and broccoli combined.
$360 + 210 + 246 = 816$
The difference between this total and the value of strawberries is written
$816 - 198 = 618$.
The value of lettuce and broccoli combined is $618 million, or $618,000,000, greater than the value of strawberries.

61.

4	3	a
b	5	c
d	e	6

Adding the diagonal from top left to bottom right gives $4+5+6=15$. Each row, each column, and each diagonal must add up to 15. a must be 8 since $4+3+8=15$. c must be 1 since $8+1+6=15$. b must be 9 since $9+5+1=15$. d must be 2 since $4+9+2=15$. e must be 7 since $3+5+7=15$. As a check, note that all rows, columns, and diagonals add to 15.

4	3	8
9	5	1
2	7	6

63.

7	a	b	14
2	13	8	11
16	c	d	e
f	6	15	g

Adding along the second row gives $2+13+8+11=34$. Each row, each column, and each diagonal must add up to 34. f must be 9 since $7+2+16+9=34$.
g must be 4 since $9+6+15+4=34$.
e must be 5 since $14+11+5+4=34$. c must be 3 since $9+3+8+14=34$.
a must be 12 since $12+13+3+6=34$. b must be 1 since $7+12+1+14=34$.
d must be 10 since $16+3+10+5=34$. As a check, note that all rows, columns, and diagonals add to 34.

7	12	1	14
2	13	8	11
16	3	10	5
9	6	15	4

65. writing exercise

67. writing exercise

Exercises 0.3

1. $3 \times 7 = 7+7+7 = 21$
$7 \times 3 = 3+3+3+3+3+3+3 = 21$

3. If $6 \times 7 = 42$, we call 6 and 7 factors of 42. And 42 is the product of 6 and 7.

5. If there are 9 rows, each with 12 tiles, then the total number of tiles using repeated addition is
$12+12+12+12+12+12+12+12+12$.
This is better written, using multiplication, as 9×12.

$$\begin{array}{r} \overset{1}{12} \\ \times 9 \\ \hline 108 \end{array}$$

There are 108 one-foot-square tiles.

7. The denominate number, 3 yd, is being multiplied by the abstract number, 8. The product will have the same unit as the denominate number, yards. Since $8 \times 3 = 24$, 8×3 yd $= 24$ yd.

9. The denominate number, 4°C, is being multiplied by the abstract number, 6. The product will have the same unit as the denominate number, degrees Celsius. Since $6 \times 4 = 24$, 6×4°C $= 24$°C.

11. False; The product of a denominate number and an abstract number has the same unit as the denominate number, so this product should be 24 mi.

13. True; Since $8 \times 22 = 176$ and the product has the same unit, hours, and the denominate number, 22 h, the product is correct.

15.
$$\begin{array}{r} 5 \\ \times\,3 \\ \hline 15 \end{array}$$

17.
$$\begin{array}{r} 8 \\ \times\,1 \\ \hline 8 \end{array}$$

19.
$$\begin{array}{r} 6 \\ \times\,0 \\ \hline 0 \end{array}$$

21.
$$\begin{array}{r} 2 \\ \times\,9 \\ \hline 18 \end{array}$$

23.
$$\begin{array}{r} 23 \\ \times\;\,2 \\ \hline 46 \end{array}$$

25.
$$\begin{array}{r} {}^{3}\;\;\; \\ 48 \\ \times\;\;4 \\ \hline 192 \end{array}$$

27.
$$\begin{array}{r} {}^{4}\;\;\;\; \\ 508 \\ \times\;\;\;\;6 \\ \hline 3048 \end{array}$$

29.
$$\begin{array}{r} {}^{1\,2}\;\;\; \\ 523 \\ \times\;\;\;\;8 \\ \hline 4184 \end{array}$$

31.
$$\begin{array}{r} {}^{3\,4}\;\;\;\; \\ 2035 \\ \times\;\;\;\;\;9 \\ \hline 18{,}315 \end{array}$$

33.
$$\begin{array}{r} {}^{3}\;\;\;\; \\ {}^{4}\;\;\;\; \\ 75 \\ \times\;68 \\ \hline 600 \\ 4500 \\ \hline 5100 \end{array}$$

35.
$$\begin{array}{r} {}^{1\,3}\;\;\; \\ {}^{2\,6}\;\;\; \\ 327 \\ \times\;\;\;59 \\ \hline 2943 \\ 16350 \\ \hline 19{,}293 \end{array}$$

37.
$$\begin{array}{r} {}^{6\,4}\;\;\;\; \\ {}^{3\,2}\;\;\;\; \\ 4075 \\ \times\;\;\;\;84 \\ \hline 16300 \\ 326000 \\ \hline 342{,}300 \end{array}$$

39.
$$\begin{array}{r} {}^{1\,2}\;\;\;\; \\ 124 \\ \times\;225 \\ \hline 620 \\ 2480 \\ 24800 \\ \hline 27{,}900 \end{array}$$

41.
$$\begin{array}{r} {}^{1\,2}\;\;\;\; \\ {}^{1\,4}\;\;\;\; \\ {}^{3\,7}\;\;\;\; \\ 639 \\ \times\;358 \\ \hline 5112 \\ 31950 \\ 191700 \\ \hline 228{,}762 \end{array}$$

43.
$$\begin{array}{r} {}^{2\,2}\;\;\;\; \\ {}^{3\,4}\;\;\;\; \\ 668 \\ \times\;305 \\ \hline 3340 \\ 200400 \\ \hline 203{,}740 \end{array}$$

45.
$$\begin{array}{r} {}^{1}\;\;\;\; \\ {}^{1\,1\,6}\;\;\;\; \\ 3219 \\ \times\;\;\;207 \\ \hline 22533 \\ 643800 \\ \hline 666{,}333 \end{array}$$

47.
$$\begin{array}{r} {}^{3}\;\;\; \\ {}^{2}\;{}^{1}\;\;\;\; \\ 2407 \\ \times\;\;\;521 \\ \hline 2407 \\ 48140 \\ 1203500 \\ \hline 1{,}254{,}047 \end{array}$$

49.
$$
\begin{array}{r}
\overset{1\,1}{} \\
\overset{1\,2}{} \\
\overset{2\,3}{} \\
3158 \\
\times\ 2034 \\
\hline
12632 \\
94740 \\
6316000 \\
\hline
6{,}423{,}372
\end{array}
$$

51.
$$
\begin{array}{r}
\overset{3}{} \\
58 \\
\times\,40 \\
\hline
2320
\end{array}
$$

53.
$$
\begin{array}{r}
\overset{6}{} \\
9\,0\,7 \\
\times\ \ \ 900 \\
\hline
816{,}300
\end{array}
$$

55.
$$
\begin{array}{r}
\overset{1}{} \\
362 \\
\times\ 310 \\
\hline
3620 \\
10860 \\
\hline
112{,}220
\end{array}
$$

57.
$$
\begin{array}{r}
\overset{2}{} \\
3\,0\,4 \\
\times\ \ \ 7 \\
\hline
2128
\end{array}
$$

59.
$$
\begin{array}{r}
\overset{5\,6\,7}{} \\
5679 \\
\times\ \ \ \ 8 \\
\hline
45{,}432
\end{array}
$$

61.
$$
\begin{array}{r}
\overset{1}{} \\
551 \\
\times\ \ 21 \\
\hline
551 \\
11020 \\
\hline
11{,}571
\end{array}
$$

63.
$$
\begin{array}{r}
\overset{2}{} \\
\overset{3}{} \\
5\,0\,7 \\
\times\ \ 135 \\
\hline
2535 \\
15210 \\
50700 \\
\hline
68{,}445
\end{array}
$$

65. The order of the factors, 5 and 8, was changed. The product remains the same by the commutative property of multiplication.

67. The factor, 3, was multiplied by each number inside the parentheses; then these products were added. The result is the same by the distributive property of multiplication over addition.

69. The grouping of the factors was changed. The product remains the same by the associative property of multiplication.

71. The order of the addends, 6 and 2, was changed. The result is the same by the commutative property of addition.

73. The commutative property of multiplication states that we can multiply two numbers in either order and get the same result. Changing the order of the factors of 3×8 gives 8×3. So the commutative property of multiplication tells us $7 + (3 \times 8) = 7 + (8 \times 3)$.

75. The distributive property states that, to multiply a factor by a sum of numbers, we can multiply the factor by each number inside the parentheses and then add the products. So the distributive property tells us $3 \times (2 \times 7) = (3 \times 2) + (3 \times 7)$.

77. There were 34 truck shipments carrying 8 cars each. Write $34 \times 8 = 272$. Thus, 272 cars were shipped.

79. There are 14 rows with 24 spaces in each row. Write $14 \times 24 = 336$. Thus, 336 cars can be parked in the lot.

Exercises 0.4

1. In $48 \div 8 = 6$, 8 is the *divisor*, 48 is the *dividend*, and 6 is the *quotient*.

3.
$$\begin{array}{cccc} 36 & 27 & 18 & 9 \\ -9 & -9 & -9 & -9 \\ \hline 27 & 18 & 9 & 0 \end{array}$$ because 9 can be subtracted from 36 four times, $36 \div 9 = 4$.

5. Since there are 63 plants with 9 plants per row, write $63 \div 9 = 7$. Stepahnie will have 7 rows.

7. Since $36 \div 7 = 9$, 36 pages $\div 4 = 9$ pages.

9. Since $4900 \div 7 = 700$, 4900 km $\div 7 = 700$ km.

11. Since $160 \div 4 = 40$, 160 mi $\div 4$ h $= 40$ mi/h.

13. Since $3720 \div 5 = 744$,
3720 h $\div 5$ mo $= 744$ h/mo.

15. $9\overline{)54}$ quotient 6   check: $9 \times 6 = 54$

17. $6\overline{)42}$ quotient 7   check: $6 \times 7 = 42$

19. $4\overline{)32}$ quotient 8   check: $4 \times 8 = 32$

21.
$$\begin{array}{r} 8 \\ 5\overline{)43} \\ \underline{40} \\ 3 \end{array}$$
We have $43 \div 5 = 8$ r3.
check: $43 = 5 \times 8 + 3$

23.
$$\begin{array}{r} 7 \\ 9\overline{)65} \\ \underline{63} \\ 2 \end{array}$$
We have $65 \div 9 = 7$ r2.
check: $65 = 9 \times 7 + 2$

25.
$$\begin{array}{r} 7 \\ 8\overline{)57} \\ \underline{56} \\ 1 \end{array}$$
We have $57 \div 8 = 7$ r1.
check: $57 = 8 \times 7 + 1$

27.
$$\begin{array}{r} 0 \\ 5\overline{)0} \\ \underline{0} \\ 0 \end{array}$$
$0 \div 5 = 0$ because $0 = 5 \times 0$.

29. $0\overline{)4}$ $4 \div 0$ is undefined since there is no number that can be multiplied by 0 to give a product of 4.

31.
$$\begin{array}{r} 0 \\ 6\overline{)0} \\ \underline{0} \\ 0 \end{array}$$
$0 \div 6 = 0$ because $0 = 6 \times 0$.

33.
$$\begin{array}{r} 1 \\ 5\overline{)83} \\ \underline{5} \\ 3 \end{array}$$

$$\begin{array}{r} 1 \\ 5\overline{)83} \\ \underline{5}| \\ 33 \end{array}$$

$$\begin{array}{r} 16 \\ 5\overline{)83} \\ \underline{5} \\ 33 \\ \underline{30} \\ 3 \end{array}$$
We have $83 \div 5 = 16$ r3.
check: $83 = 5 \times 16 + 3$

35.
$$\begin{array}{r} 5 \\ 3\overline{)162} \\ \underline{15} \\ 1 \end{array}$$

$$\begin{array}{r} 5 \\ 3\overline{)162} \\ \underline{15}| \\ 12 \end{array}$$

$$\begin{array}{r} 54 \\ 3\overline{)162} \\ \underline{15} \\ 12 \\ \underline{12} \\ 0 \end{array}$$
We have $162 \div 3 = 54$.
check: $162 = 3 \times 54$

37.

$$\begin{array}{r} 3 \\ 8\overline{)293} \\ \underline{24} \\ 5 \end{array}$$

$$\begin{array}{r} 3 \\ 8\overline{)293} \\ \underline{24}| \\ 53 \end{array}$$

$$\begin{array}{r} 36 \\ 8\overline{)293} \\ \underline{24} \\ 53 \\ \underline{48} \\ 5 \end{array}$$
We have $293 \div 8 = 36$ r5.
check: $293 = 8 \times 36 + 5$

39.

$$\begin{array}{r} 3 \\ 8\overline{)3136} \\ \underline{24} \\ 7 \end{array}$$

$$\begin{array}{r} 4 \\ 7\overline{)3136} \\ \underline{24}| \\ 73 \end{array}$$

$$\begin{array}{r} 39 \\ 8\overline{)3136} \\ \underline{24} \\ 73 \\ \underline{72} \\ 1 \end{array}$$

$$\begin{array}{r} 39 \\ 8\overline{)3136} \\ \underline{24}| \\ 73| \\ \underline{72}| \\ 16 \end{array}$$

$$\begin{array}{r} 392 \\ 8\overline{)3136} \\ \underline{24} \\ 73 \\ \underline{72} \\ 16 \\ \underline{16} \\ 0 \end{array}$$
We have $3136 \div 8 = 392$.
check: $3136 = 8 \times 392$

41.

$$\begin{array}{r} 6 \\ 8\overline{)5438} \\ \underline{48} \\ 6 \end{array}$$

$$\begin{array}{r} 6 \\ 8\overline{)5438} \\ \underline{48}| \\ 63 \end{array}$$

$$\begin{array}{r} 67 \\ 8\overline{)5438} \\ \underline{48} \\ 63 \\ \underline{56} \\ 7 \end{array}$$

$$\begin{array}{r} 67 \\ 8\overline{)5438} \\ \underline{48}| \\ 63| \\ \underline{56}\downarrow \\ 78 \end{array}$$

$$\begin{array}{r} 679 \\ 8\overline{)5438} \\ \underline{48} \\ 63 \\ \underline{56} \\ 78 \\ \underline{72} \\ 6 \end{array}$$
We have $5438 \div 8 = 679$ r6.
check: $5438 = 8 \times 679 + 6$

43.

$$\begin{array}{r} 2 \\ 8\overline{)22153} \\ \underline{16} \\ 6 \end{array}$$

$$\begin{array}{r} 2 \\ 8\overline{)22153} \\ \underline{16}| \\ 61 \end{array}$$

$$\begin{array}{r} 27 \\ 8\overline{)22153} \\ \underline{16} \\ 61 \\ \underline{56} \\ 5 \end{array}$$

$$\begin{array}{r} 27 \\ 8\overline{)22153} \\ 16 \\ \hline 61 \\ 56\downarrow \\ \hline 55 \end{array}$$

$$\begin{array}{r} 276 \\ 8\overline{)22153} \\ 16 \\ \hline 61 \\ 56 \\ \hline 55 \\ 48 \\ \hline 7 \end{array}$$

$$\begin{array}{r} 276 \\ 8\overline{)22153} \\ 16 \\ \hline 61 \\ 56 \\ \hline 55 \\ 48\downarrow \\ \hline 73 \end{array}$$

$$\begin{array}{r} 2769 \\ 8\overline{)22153} \\ 16 \\ \hline 61 \\ 56 \\ \hline 55 \\ 48 \\ \hline 73 \\ 72 \\ \hline 1 \end{array}$$

We have $22,153 \div 8 = 2769$ r1.
check: $22,153 = 8 \times 2769 + 1$

$$\begin{array}{r} 10 \\ 4\overline{)4351} \\ 4 \\ \hline 3 \\ 0\downarrow \\ \hline 35 \end{array}$$

$$\begin{array}{r} 108 \\ 4\overline{)4351} \\ 4 \\ \hline 3 \\ 0 \\ \hline 35 \\ 32 \\ \hline 3 \end{array}$$

$$\begin{array}{r} 108 \\ 4\overline{)4351} \\ 4 \\ \hline 3 \\ 0 \\ \hline 35\downarrow \\ 32\downarrow \\ \hline 31 \end{array}$$

$$\begin{array}{r} 1087 \\ 4\overline{)4351} \\ 4 \\ \hline 3 \\ 0 \\ \hline 35 \\ 32 \\ \hline 31 \\ 28 \\ \hline 3 \end{array}$$

We have $4351 \div 4 = 1087$ r3.
check: $4351 = 4 \times 1087 + 3$

45.

$$\begin{array}{r} 1 \\ 4\overline{)4351} \\ 4 \\ \hline 0 \end{array}$$

$$\begin{array}{r} 1 \\ 4\overline{)4351} \\ 4 \\ \hline 03 \end{array}$$

$$\begin{array}{r} 10 \\ 4\overline{)4351} \\ 4 \\ \hline 3 \\ 0 \\ \hline 3 \end{array}$$

47.

$$\begin{array}{r} 1 \\ 4\overline{)7321} \\ 4 \\ \hline 3 \end{array}$$

$$\begin{array}{r} 1 \\ 4\overline{)7321} \\ 4 \\ \hline 33 \end{array}$$

$$\begin{array}{r} 18 \\ 4\overline{)7321} \\ 4 \\ \hline 33 \\ 32 \\ \hline 1 \end{array}$$

$$\begin{array}{r} 18 \\ 4\overline{)7321} \\ 4 \\ \hline 33 \\ 32\!\downarrow \\ \hline 12 \end{array}$$

$$\begin{array}{r} 183 \\ 4\overline{)7321} \\ 4 \\ \hline 33 \\ 32 \\ \hline 12 \\ 12 \\ \hline 0 \end{array}$$

$$\begin{array}{r} 183 \\ 4\overline{)7321} \\ 4 \\ \hline 33 \\ 32 \\ \hline 12 \\ 12\!\downarrow \\ \hline 01 \end{array}$$

$$\begin{array}{r} 1830 \\ 4\overline{)7321} \\ 4 \\ \hline 33 \\ 32 \\ \hline 12 \\ 12 \\ \hline 1 \\ 0 \\ \hline 1 \end{array}$$

We have $7321 \div 4 = 1830$ r1.

check: $7321 = 4 \times 1830 + 1$

49. $\begin{array}{r} 4 \\ 3\overline{)13421} \\ 12 \\ \hline 1 \end{array}$

$$\begin{array}{r} 4 \\ 3\overline{)13421} \\ 12 \\ \hline 14 \end{array}$$

$$\begin{array}{r} 44 \\ 3\overline{)13421} \\ 12 \\ \hline 14 \\ 12 \\ \hline 2 \end{array}$$

$$\begin{array}{r} 44 \\ 7\overline{)13421} \\ 12 \\ \hline 14 \\ 12\!\downarrow \\ \hline 22 \end{array}$$

$$\begin{array}{r} 447 \\ 3\overline{)13421} \\ 12 \\ \hline 14 \\ 12 \\ \hline 22 \\ 21 \\ \hline 1 \end{array}$$

$$\begin{array}{r} 447 \\ 3\overline{)13421} \\ 12 \\ \hline 14 \\ 12 \\ \hline 22 \\ 21\!\downarrow \\ \hline 11 \end{array}$$

$$\begin{array}{r} 4473 \\ 3\overline{)13421} \\ 12 \\ \hline 14 \\ 12 \\ \hline 22 \\ 21 \\ \hline 11 \\ 9 \\ \hline 2 \end{array}$$

We have $13{,}421 \div 3 = 4473$ r2.

check: $13{,}421 = 3 \times 4473 + 2$

51. $\begin{array}{r} 1 \\ 48\overline{)892} \\ 48 \\ \hline 41 \end{array}$

$$\begin{array}{r} 8 \\ 48\overline{)892} \\ 48\!\downarrow \\ \hline 412 \end{array}$$

$$\begin{array}{r} 18 \\ 48\overline{)892} \\ 48 \\ \hline 412 \\ 384 \\ \hline 28 \end{array}$$

We have $892 \div 48 = 18$ r28.

check: $892 = 48 \times 18 + 28$

53.

$$
\begin{array}{r}
2 \\
23\overline{)534} \\
46 \\
\hline
7
\end{array}
$$

$$
\begin{array}{r}
2 \\
23\overline{)534} \\
46 \\
\hline
74
\end{array}
$$

$$
\begin{array}{r}
23 \\
23\overline{)534} \\
46 \\
\hline
74 \\
69 \\
\hline
5
\end{array}
$$

We have $534 \div 23 = 23$ r5.

check: $534 = 23 \times 23 + 5$

55.

$$
\begin{array}{r}
5 \\
45\overline{)2367} \\
225 \\
\hline
11
\end{array}
$$

$$
\begin{array}{r}
5 \\
45\overline{)2367} \\
225 \\
\hline
117
\end{array}
$$

$$
\begin{array}{r}
52 \\
45\overline{)2367} \\
225 \\
\hline
117 \\
90 \\
\hline
27
\end{array}
$$

We have $2367 \div 45 = 52$ r27.

check: $2367 = 45 \times 52 + 27$

57.

$$
\begin{array}{r}
2 \\
34\overline{)8748} \\
68 \\
\hline
19
\end{array}
$$

$$
\begin{array}{r}
2 \\
34\overline{)8748} \\
68 \\
\hline
194
\end{array}
$$

$$
\begin{array}{r}
25 \\
34\overline{)8748} \\
68 \\
\hline
194 \\
170 \\
\hline
24
\end{array}
$$

$$
\begin{array}{r}
25 \\
34\overline{)8748} \\
68 \\
\hline
194 \\
170 \\
\hline
248
\end{array}
$$

$$
\begin{array}{r}
257 \\
34\overline{)8748} \\
68 \\
\hline
194 \\
170 \\
\hline
248 \\
238 \\
\hline
10
\end{array}
$$

We have $8748 \div 34 = 257$ r10.

check: $8748 = 34 \times 257 + 10$

59.

$$
\begin{array}{r}
1 \\
42\overline{)7902} \\
42 \\
\hline
37
\end{array}
$$

$$
\begin{array}{r}
1 \\
42\overline{)7902} \\
42 \\
\hline
370
\end{array}
$$

$$
\begin{array}{r}
18 \\
42\overline{)7902} \\
42 \\
\hline
370 \\
336 \\
\hline
34
\end{array}
$$

$$
\begin{array}{r}
18 \\
42\overline{)7902} \\
42 \\
\hline
370 \\
336 \\
\hline
342
\end{array}
$$

$$
\begin{array}{r}
188 \\
42\overline{)7902} \\
42 \\
\hline
370 \\
336 \\
\hline
342 \\
336 \\
\hline
6
\end{array}
$$

We have $7902 \div 42 = 188$ r6.

check: $7902 = 42 \times 188 + 6$

61.

$$28\overline{)8547} \atop {\underset{1}{\underline{84}}}^{3}$$

$$28\overline{)8547} \atop \underset{14}{\underline{84}}^{3}$$

$$28\overline{)8547} \atop \underset{\underset{14}{\underline{0}}}{\underline{84}}^{30} \atop 14$$

$$28\overline{)8547} \atop \underset{\underset{\underset{147}{0}}{14}}{\underline{84}}^{30}$$

$$28\overline{)8547} \atop \underset{\underset{\underset{\underset{7}{\underline{140}}}{147}}{\underline{0}}}{\underline{84}}^{305} \atop 14$$

We have $8547 \div 28 = 305$ r7.
check: $8547 = 28 \times 305 + 7$

63.

$$763\overline{)3071} \atop \underset{19}{\underline{3052}}^{4}$$

We have $3071 \div 763 = 4$ r19.
check: $3071 = 763 \times 4 + 19$

65. There are 56 bags with 8 bags per box. Write $56 \div 8 = 7$. There are 7 boxes.

67. There are 63 candy bars in 7 boxes. Write $63 \div 7 = 9$. Thus, there are 9 candy bars per box.

69. There are 77 pictures with 8 pictures per page. Write $77 \div 8 = 9$ r5. Joaquin will fill 9 full pages with 5 pictures left over.

71. There is $552 with a $4 charge per ticket. Write $552 \div 4 = 138$. Thus, 138 tickets were purchased.

73. There is $2030 to be shared by 14 homeowners. Write $2030 \div 14 = 145$. Each owner will pay $145.

75. There are 1702 calls from 37 phones. Write $1702 \div 37 = 46$. There were 46 calls placed per phone.

77. There are 10,880 lines with 340 lines per minute. Write $10,880 \div 340 = 32$. It will take 32 min.

79. There are $16,488 for 36 employees. Write $16,488 \div 36 = 458$. Each employee will receive a $458 bonus.

81. estimate: 800 divided by 40 $40\overline{)800}^{20}$

83. estimate: 5000 divided by 100 $100\overline{)5000}^{50}$

85. estimate: 9000 divided by 90 $90\overline{)9000}^{100}$

87. estimate: 3900 divided by 130 $130\overline{)3900}^{30}$

89. estimate: 3800 divided by 190 $190\overline{)3800}^{20}$

91. estimate: 300 mi divided by 20 gal $20\overline{)300}^{15}$

José got about 15 mi/gal.

93. estimate: $27,000 divided by 10 people $10\overline{)27000}^{2700}$

Each person will receive about $2700.

95. estimate: $1900 minus $300
$1900 - 300 = 1600$

After the down payment, Tara will have about $1600 left to pay in monthly installments.

estimate: $1600 divided by 20 mo. $20\overline{)1600}^{80}$

Tara's monthly payments will be about $80.

97. writing exercise

99. writing exercise

101. challenge exercise

103. challenge exercise

Exercises 0.5

1. $\dfrac{3}{4} = 0.75$

$$
\begin{array}{r}
.75 \\
4\overline{)3.00} \\
\underline{-28} \\
20 \\
\underline{-20} \\
0
\end{array}
$$

3. $\dfrac{9}{20} = 0.45$

$$
\begin{array}{r}
.45 \\
20\overline{)9.00} \\
\underline{-80} \\
100 \\
\underline{-100} \\
0
\end{array}
$$

5. $\dfrac{1}{5} = 0.2$

$$
\begin{array}{r}
.2 \\
5\overline{)1.0} \\
\underline{-10} \\
0
\end{array}
$$

7. $\dfrac{5}{16} = 0.3125$

$$
\begin{array}{r}
.3125 \\
16\overline{)5.0000} \\
\underline{-48} \\
20 \\
\underline{-16} \\
40 \\
\underline{-32} \\
80 \\
\underline{-80} \\
0
\end{array}
$$

9. $\dfrac{7}{10} = 0.7$

$$
\begin{array}{r}
.7 \\
10\overline{)7.0} \\
\underline{-70} \\
0
\end{array}
$$

11. $\dfrac{27}{40} = 0.675$

$$
\begin{array}{r}
.675 \\
40\overline{)27.000} \\
\underline{-240} \\
300 \\
\underline{-280} \\
200 \\
\underline{-200} \\
0
\end{array}
$$

13. $\dfrac{5}{6} \approx 0.833$

$$
\begin{array}{r}
.833 \\
6\overline{)5.000} \\
\underline{-48} \\
20 \\
\underline{-18} \\
20 \\
\underline{-18} \\
2
\end{array}
$$

15. $\dfrac{4}{15} \approx 0.267$

$$
\begin{array}{r}
.2666 \\
15\overline{)4.0000} \\
\underline{-30} \\
100 \\
\underline{-90} \\
100 \\
\underline{-90} \\
100 \\
\underline{-90} \\
10
\end{array}
$$

17. $\frac{4}{9} = 0.\overline{4}$

$$9\overline{)4.00}^{.44}$$

$$\underline{-36}$$
$$40$$
$$\underline{-36}$$
$$4$$

19. $0.9 = \frac{9}{10}$

21. $0.8 = \frac{8}{10} = \frac{4}{5}$

23. $0.37 = \frac{37}{100}$

25. $0.587 = \frac{587}{1000}$

27. $0.48 = \frac{48}{100} = \frac{12}{25}$

29. $0.58 = \frac{58}{100} = \frac{29}{50}$

31.
$$7.1562$$
$$\underline{+14.78}$$
$$21.9362$$

33.
$$11.12$$
$$\underline{+8.3792}$$
$$19.4992$$

35.
$$9.20$$
$$\underline{-2.85}$$
$$6.35$$

37.
$$18.234$$
$$\underline{-13.64}$$
$$4.594$$

39.
$$3.21$$
$$\underline{\times 2.1}$$
$$321$$
$$\underline{6420}$$
$$6.741$$

41.
$$6.29$$
$$\underline{\times 9.13}$$
$$1887$$
$$6290$$
$$\underline{566100}$$
$$57.4277$$

43. $6\overline{)16.68}^{\,2.78}$

$$\underline{-12}$$
$$46$$
$$\underline{-42}$$
$$48$$
$$\underline{-48}$$
$$0$$

45. $4\overline{)1.92}^{\,0.48}$

$$\underline{-16}$$
$$32$$
$$\underline{-32}$$
$$0$$

47. $8\overline{)5.480}^{\,0.685}$

$$\underline{-48}$$
$$68$$
$$\underline{-64}$$
$$40$$
$$\underline{-40}$$
$$0$$

49. $6\overline{)13.890}^{\,2.315}$

$$\underline{-12}$$
$$18$$
$$\underline{-18}$$
$$09$$
$$\underline{-6}$$
$$30$$
$$\underline{-30}$$
$$0$$

51.
$$32\overline{)185.6}$$
with quotient 5.8
$$\begin{array}{r} 5.8 \\ 32\overline{)185.6} \\ \underline{-160} \\ 256 \\ \underline{-256} \\ 0 \end{array}$$

53.
$$\begin{array}{r} 2.35 \\ 34\overline{)79.90} \\ \underline{-68} \\ 119 \\ \underline{-102} \\ 170 \\ \underline{-170} \\ 0 \end{array}$$

55.
$$\begin{array}{r} 0.265 \\ 52\overline{)13.780} \\ \underline{-104} \\ 338 \\ \underline{-312} \\ 260 \\ \underline{-260} \\ 0 \end{array}$$

57. $0.6\overline{)11.07} = 6\overline{)110.70}$
$$\begin{array}{r} 18.45 \\ 6\overline{)110.70} \\ \underline{-6} \\ 50 \\ \underline{-48} \\ 27 \\ \underline{-24} \\ 30 \\ \underline{-30} \\ 0 \end{array}$$

59. $3.8\overline{)7.22} = 38\overline{)72.2}$
$$\begin{array}{r} 1.9 \\ 38\overline{)72.2} \\ \underline{-38} \\ 342 \\ \underline{-342} \\ 0 \end{array}$$

61. $5.2\overline{)11.622} = 52\overline{)116.220}$
$$\begin{array}{r} 2.235 \\ 52\overline{)116.220} \\ \underline{-104} \\ 122 \\ \underline{-104} \\ 182 \\ \underline{-156} \\ 260 \\ \underline{-260} \\ 0 \end{array}$$

63. $6\left(\dfrac{1}{100}\right) = \dfrac{6}{100} = \dfrac{3}{50}$

65. $75\left(\dfrac{1}{100}\right) = \dfrac{75}{100} = \dfrac{3}{4}$

67. $65\left(\dfrac{1}{100}\right) = \dfrac{65}{100} = \dfrac{13}{20}$

69. $50\left(\dfrac{1}{100}\right) = \dfrac{50}{100} = \dfrac{1}{2}$

71. $46\left(\dfrac{1}{100}\right) = \dfrac{46}{100} = \dfrac{23}{50}$

73. $66\left(\dfrac{1}{100}\right) = \dfrac{66}{100} = \dfrac{33}{50}$

75. $20\% = 0.20$

77. $35\% = 0.35$

79. $39\% = 0.39$

81. $5\% = 0.05$

83. $135\% = 1.35$

85. $240\% = 2.40$

87. $4.40 = 440\%$

89. $0.065 = 6.5\%$

91. $0.025 = 2.5\%$

93. $0.002 = 0.2\%$

95. $\dfrac{1}{4} = 0.25 = 25\%$

97. $\dfrac{2}{5} = 0.40 = 40\%$

99. $\dfrac{1}{5} = 0.20 = 20\%$

101. $\dfrac{5}{8} = 0.625 = 62.5\%$

103. $\dfrac{18}{20} = 0.90$

105. $\dfrac{39.90}{50} \approx \$0.80$

107. $\dfrac{284}{18} \approx \$15.78$

109. $\$490.64 - \$50 = \$440.64$

$\dfrac{440.64}{12} = \$36.72$

Exercises 0.6

1. $1 \cdot 4 = 4$
$2 \cdot 2 = 4$
Factors of 4: 1, 2, 4

3. $1 \cdot 10 = 10$
$2 \cdot 5 = 10$
Factors of 10: 1, 2, 5, 10

5. $1 \cdot 15 = 15$
$3 \cdot 5 = 15$
Factors of 15: 1, 3, 5, 15

7. $1 \cdot 24 = 24$
$2 \cdot 12 = 24$
$3 \cdot 8 = 24$
$4 \cdot 6 = 24$
Factors of 24: 1, 2, 3, 4, 6, 8, 12, 24

9. $1 \cdot 64 = 64$
$2 \cdot 32 = 64$
$4 \cdot 16 = 64$
$8 \cdot 8 = 64$
Factors of 64: 1, 2, 4, 8, 16, 32, 64

11. $1 \cdot 11 = 11$
Factors of 11: 1, 11

For exercises 13–15, a *sieve of Eratosthenes* may be helpful

	2	3	4	5	6	7	8	9	10
11	12	13	14	15	16	17	18	19	20
21	22	23	24	25	26	27	28	29	30
31	32	33	34	35	36	37	38	39	40
41	42	43	44	45	46	47	48	49	50
51	52	53	54	55	56	57	58	59	60
61	62	63	64	65	66	67	68	69	70
71	72	73	74	75	76	77	78	79	80
81	82	83	84	85	86	87	88	89	90
91	92	93	94	95	96	97	98	99	100
101	102	103	104	105	106	107	108	109	110

13. 19, 23, 31, 59, 97, 103

15. 31, 37, 41, 43, 47

17. $18 = 3 \cdot 6 = 3 \cdot 2 \cdot 3 = 2 \cdot 3 \cdot 3$

19. $30 = 5 \cdot 6 = 5 \cdot 2 \cdot 3 = 2 \cdot 3 \cdot 5$

21. $51 = 3 \cdot 17$

23. $63 = 7 \cdot 9 = 7 \cdot 3 \cdot 3 = 3 \cdot 3 \cdot 7$

25. $70 = 7 \cdot 10 = 7 \cdot 2 \cdot 5 = 2 \cdot 5 \cdot 7$

27. $66 = 6 \cdot 11 = 2 \cdot 3 \cdot 11$

29. $130 = 10 \cdot 13 = 2 \cdot 5 \cdot 13$

31. $315 = 9 \cdot 35 = 3 \cdot 3 \cdot 5 \cdot 7$

33. $225 = 9 \cdot 25 = 3 \cdot 3 \cdot 5 \cdot 5$

35. $189 = 9 \cdot 21 = 3 \cdot 3 \cdot 3 \cdot 7$

37. $1 \cdot 24 = 24$
$2 \cdot 12 = 24$
$3 \cdot 8 = 24$
$\mathbf{4} \cdot \mathbf{6} = 24$
$4 + 6 = 10; \, 4, \, 6$

39. $1 \cdot 30 = 30$
$2 \cdot 15 = 30$
$3 \cdot 10 = 30$
$\mathbf{5} \cdot \mathbf{6} = 30$
$\mathbf{6} - \mathbf{5} = 1; \, 5, \, 6$

41. Factor of 4: **1**, **2**, 4
Factors of 6: **1**, **2**, 3, 6
GCF: 2

43. Factors of 10: **1**, 2, **5**, 10
Factors of 15: **1**, 3, **5**, 15
GCF: 5

45. Factors of 21: **1**, **3**, 7, 21
Factors of 24: **1**, 2, **3**, 4, 6, 8, 12, 24
GCF: 3

47. Factors of 20: **1**, 2, 4, 5, 10, 20
Factors of 21: **1**, 3, 7, 21
GCF: 1

49. Factors of 18: **1**, **2**, **3**, **6**, 9, 18
Factors of 24: **1**, **2**, **3**, 4, **6**, 8, 12, 24
GCF: 6

51. Factors of 18: **1**, **2**, **3**, **6**, **9**, **18**
Factors of 54: **1**, **2**, **3**, **6**, **9**, **18**, 27, 54
GCF: 18

53. Factors of 36: **1**, **2**, **3**, **4**, **6**, 9, **12**, 18, 36
Factors of 48: **1**, **2**, **3**, **4**, **6**, 8, **12**, 16, 24, 48
GCF: 12

55. $84 = 4 \cdot 21 = 2 \cdot 2 \cdot \mathbf{3} \cdot \mathbf{7}$
$105 = 15 \cdot 7 = \mathbf{3} \cdot 5 \cdot \mathbf{7}$
$GCF = 3 \cdot 7 = 21$

57. $45 = 9 \cdot 5 = \mathbf{3} \cdot 3 \cdot \mathbf{5}$
$60 = 6 \cdot 10 = 2 \cdot 3 \cdot 2 \cdot 5 = 2 \cdot 2 \cdot \mathbf{3} \cdot \mathbf{5}$
$75 = 3 \cdot 25 = \mathbf{3} \cdot \mathbf{5} \cdot 5$
$GCF = 3 \cdot 5 = 15$

59. $12 = 4 \cdot 3 = \mathbf{2} \cdot \mathbf{2} \cdot \mathbf{3}$
$36 = 4 \cdot 9 = \mathbf{2} \cdot \mathbf{2} \cdot \mathbf{3} \cdot 3$
$60 = 6 \cdot 10 = 2 \cdot 3 \cdot 2 \cdot 5 = \mathbf{2} \cdot \mathbf{2} \cdot \mathbf{3} \cdot 5$
$GCF = 2 \cdot 2 \cdot 3 = 12$

61. $105 = 5 \cdot 21 = 5 \cdot 3 \cdot 7 = 3 \cdot \mathbf{5} \cdot \mathbf{7}$
$140 = 10 \cdot 14 = 2 \cdot 5 \cdot 2 \cdot 7 = 2 \cdot 2 \cdot \mathbf{5} \cdot \mathbf{7}$
$175 = 7 \cdot 25 = 7 \cdot 5 \cdot 5 = \mathbf{5} \cdot 5 \cdot \mathbf{7}$
$GCF = 5 \cdot 7 = 35$

63. $25 = \mathbf{5} \cdot \mathbf{5}$
$75 = 3 \cdot 25 = 3 \cdot \mathbf{5} \cdot \mathbf{5}$
$150 = 10 \cdot 15 = 2 \cdot 5 \cdot 3 \cdot 5 = 2 \cdot 3 \cdot \mathbf{5} \cdot \mathbf{5}$
$GCF = 5 \cdot 5 = 25$

65. Challenge exercise

67. Challenge exercise

69. Writing exercise

71. Group exercise

Exercises 0.7

1. $\dfrac{3}{7} \cdot \dfrac{2}{2} = \dfrac{6}{14}; \dfrac{3}{7} \cdot \dfrac{3}{3} = \dfrac{9}{21}; \dfrac{3}{7} \cdot \dfrac{4}{4} = \dfrac{12}{28};$
$\dfrac{6}{14}, \dfrac{9}{21}, \dfrac{12}{28}$

3. $\dfrac{4}{9} \cdot \dfrac{2}{2} = \dfrac{8}{18}; \dfrac{4}{9} \cdot \dfrac{4}{4} = \dfrac{16}{36}; \dfrac{4}{9} \cdot \dfrac{10}{10} = \dfrac{40}{90};$
$\dfrac{8}{18}, \dfrac{16}{36}, \dfrac{40}{90}$

5. $\dfrac{5}{6} \cdot \dfrac{2}{2} = \dfrac{10}{12}; \dfrac{5}{6} \cdot \dfrac{3}{3} = \dfrac{15}{18}; \dfrac{5}{6} \cdot \dfrac{10}{10} = \dfrac{50}{60};$
$\dfrac{10}{12}, \dfrac{15}{18}, \dfrac{50}{60}$

7. $\dfrac{10}{17} \cdot \dfrac{2}{2} = \dfrac{20}{34}; \dfrac{10}{17} \cdot \dfrac{3}{3} = \dfrac{30}{51}; \dfrac{10}{17} \cdot \dfrac{10}{10} = \dfrac{100}{170};$
$\dfrac{20}{34}, \dfrac{30}{51}, \dfrac{100}{170}$

9. $\dfrac{9}{16} \cdot \dfrac{2}{2} = \dfrac{18}{32}; \dfrac{9}{16} \cdot \dfrac{3}{3} = \dfrac{27}{48}; \dfrac{9}{16} \cdot \dfrac{10}{10} = \dfrac{90}{160};$
$\dfrac{18}{32}, \dfrac{27}{48}, \dfrac{90}{160}$

11. $\dfrac{7}{9} \cdot \dfrac{2}{2} = \dfrac{14}{18}; \dfrac{7}{9} \cdot \dfrac{5}{5} = \dfrac{35}{45}; \dfrac{7}{9} \cdot \dfrac{20}{20} = \dfrac{140}{180};$
$\dfrac{14}{18}, \dfrac{35}{45}, \dfrac{140}{180}$

13. $\dfrac{8}{12} = \dfrac{2 \cdot 2 \cdot 2}{2 \cdot 2 \cdot 3} = \dfrac{2}{3}$

15. $\dfrac{10}{14} = \dfrac{2 \cdot 5}{2 \cdot 7} = \dfrac{5}{7}$

17. $\dfrac{12}{18} = \dfrac{2 \cdot 2 \cdot 3}{2 \cdot 3 \cdot 3} = \dfrac{2}{3}$

19. $\dfrac{35}{40} = \dfrac{5 \cdot 7}{2 \cdot 2 \cdot 2 \cdot 5} = \dfrac{7}{8}$

21. $\dfrac{11}{44} = \dfrac{1 \cdot 11}{2 \cdot 2 \cdot 11} = \dfrac{1}{4}$

23. $\dfrac{12}{36} = \dfrac{2 \cdot 2 \cdot 3}{2 \cdot 2 \cdot 3 \cdot 3} = \dfrac{1}{3}$

25. $\dfrac{24}{27} = \dfrac{2 \cdot 2 \cdot 2 \cdot 3}{3 \cdot 3 \cdot 3} = \dfrac{8}{9}$

27. $\dfrac{32}{40} = \dfrac{2 \cdot 2 \cdot 2 \cdot 2 \cdot 2}{2 \cdot 2 \cdot 2 \cdot 5} = \dfrac{4}{5}$

29. $\dfrac{75}{105} = \dfrac{3 \cdot 5 \cdot 5}{3 \cdot 5 \cdot 7} = \dfrac{5}{7}$

31. $\dfrac{48}{60} = \dfrac{2 \cdot 2 \cdot 2 \cdot 2 \cdot 3}{2 \cdot 2 \cdot 3 \cdot 5} = \dfrac{4}{5}$

33. $\dfrac{105}{135} = \dfrac{3 \cdot 5 \cdot 7}{3 \cdot 3 \cdot 3 \cdot 5} = \dfrac{7}{9}$

35. $\dfrac{15}{44} = \dfrac{3 \cdot 5}{2 \cdot 2 \cdot 11} = \dfrac{15}{44}$

37. $\dfrac{3}{4} \cdot \dfrac{7}{5} = \dfrac{3 \cdot 7}{2 \cdot 2 \cdot 5} = \dfrac{21}{20}$

39. $\dfrac{3}{5} \cdot \dfrac{5}{7} = \dfrac{3 \cdot 5}{5 \cdot 7} = \dfrac{3}{7}$

41. $\dfrac{6}{13} \cdot \dfrac{4}{9} = \dfrac{2 \cdot 3 \cdot 2 \cdot 2}{13 \cdot 3 \cdot 3} = \dfrac{2 \cdot 2 \cdot 2}{13 \cdot 3} = \dfrac{8}{39}$

43. $\dfrac{3}{11} \cdot \dfrac{7}{9} = \dfrac{3 \cdot 7}{11 \cdot 3 \cdot 3} = \dfrac{7}{11 \cdot 3} = \dfrac{7}{33}$

45. $\dfrac{3}{10} \cdot \dfrac{5}{9} = \dfrac{3 \cdot 5}{2 \cdot 5 \cdot 3 \cdot 3} = \dfrac{1}{2 \cdot 3} = \dfrac{1}{6}$

47. $\dfrac{1}{5} \div \dfrac{3}{4} = \dfrac{1}{5} \cdot \dfrac{4}{3} = \dfrac{2 \cdot 2}{3 \cdot 5} = \dfrac{4}{15}$

49. $\dfrac{2}{5} \div \dfrac{3}{4} = \dfrac{2}{5} \cdot \dfrac{4}{3} = \dfrac{2 \cdot 2 \cdot 2}{3 \cdot 5} = \dfrac{8}{15}$

51. $\dfrac{8}{9} \div \dfrac{4}{3} = \dfrac{8}{9} \cdot \dfrac{3}{4} = \dfrac{2 \cdot 2 \cdot 2 \cdot 3}{3 \cdot 3 \cdot 2 \cdot 2} = \dfrac{2}{3}$

53. $\dfrac{7}{10} \div \dfrac{5}{9} = \dfrac{7}{10} \cdot \dfrac{9}{5} = \dfrac{7 \cdot 3 \cdot 3}{2 \cdot 5 \cdot 5} = \dfrac{63}{50}$

55. $\dfrac{8}{15} \div \dfrac{2}{5} = \dfrac{8}{15} \cdot \dfrac{5}{2} = \dfrac{2 \cdot 2 \cdot 2 \cdot 5}{3 \cdot 5 \cdot 2} = \dfrac{2 \cdot 2}{3} = \dfrac{4}{3}$

57. $\dfrac{5}{27} \div \dfrac{25}{36} = \dfrac{5}{27} \cdot \dfrac{36}{25}$
$= \dfrac{5 \cdot 2 \cdot 2 \cdot 3 \cdot 3}{3 \cdot 3 \cdot 3 \cdot 5 \cdot 5}$
$= \dfrac{2 \cdot 2}{3 \cdot 5}$
$= \dfrac{4}{15}$

59. $\dfrac{2}{5} + \dfrac{1}{4} = \dfrac{8}{20} + \dfrac{5}{20} = \dfrac{13}{20}$

61. $\dfrac{2}{5} + \dfrac{7}{15} = \dfrac{6}{15} + \dfrac{7}{15} = \dfrac{13}{15}$

63. $\dfrac{3}{8} + \dfrac{5}{12} = \dfrac{9}{24} + \dfrac{10}{24} = \dfrac{19}{24}$

65. $\dfrac{2}{15}+\dfrac{9}{20}=\dfrac{8}{60}+\dfrac{27}{60}=\dfrac{35}{60}=\dfrac{5\cdot7}{2\cdot2\cdot3\cdot5}=\dfrac{7}{12}$

67. $\dfrac{7}{15}+\dfrac{13}{18}=\dfrac{42}{90}+\dfrac{65}{90}=\dfrac{107}{90}$

69. $\dfrac{1}{2}+\dfrac{1}{4}+\dfrac{1}{8}=\dfrac{4}{8}+\dfrac{2}{8}+\dfrac{1}{8}=\dfrac{7}{8}$

71. $\dfrac{8}{9}-\dfrac{3}{9}=\dfrac{5}{9}$

73. $\dfrac{5}{8}-\dfrac{1}{8}=\dfrac{4}{8}=\dfrac{1}{2}$

75. $\dfrac{7}{8}-\dfrac{2}{3}=\dfrac{21}{24}-\dfrac{16}{24}=\dfrac{5}{24}$

77. $\dfrac{11}{18}-\dfrac{2}{9}=\dfrac{11}{18}-\dfrac{4}{18}=\dfrac{7}{18}$

79. $\dfrac{17}{4}=4\dfrac{1}{4}$

$$\begin{array}{r}4\\4\overline{)17}\\-16\\\hline 1\end{array}$$

81. $3\dfrac{1}{4}=\dfrac{(3\cdot4)+1}{4}=\dfrac{13}{4}$

83. $\dfrac{1}{2}+\dfrac{1}{3}+\dfrac{1}{4}=\dfrac{6}{12}+\dfrac{4}{12}+\dfrac{3}{12}=\dfrac{13}{12}$ yd

85. $\dfrac{2}{3}\cdot240=\dfrac{2\cdot3\cdot80}{3}=\$160$

87. $\dfrac{3}{8}\cdot\dfrac{200}{1}=\dfrac{3\cdot8\cdot25}{8}=75$ mi

89. $\dfrac{3}{4}\cdot80=\dfrac{240}{4}=60$ in.

91. $\dfrac{3}{4}\cdot\dfrac{5}{9}=\dfrac{3\cdot5}{2\cdot2\cdot3\cdot3}=\dfrac{5}{2\cdot2\cdot3}=\dfrac{5}{12}$

93. $3\dfrac{1}{3}\cdot3\dfrac{3}{4}=\dfrac{10}{3}\cdot\dfrac{15}{4}=\dfrac{2\cdot5\cdot3\cdot5}{3\cdot2\cdot2}=\dfrac{5\cdot5}{2}=\dfrac{25}{2}$

95. $540\cdot4\dfrac{2}{3}=\dfrac{540}{1}\cdot\dfrac{14}{3}=\dfrac{3\cdot180\cdot14}{3}$
$=180\cdot14=2520$ mi

97. $21\cdot\dfrac{22}{7}=\dfrac{3\cdot7\cdot2\cdot11}{7}=3\cdot2\cdot11=66$ in.

99. $2\dfrac{1}{4}\cdot3\dfrac{7}{8}\cdot4\dfrac{5}{6}=\dfrac{9}{4}\cdot\dfrac{31}{8}\cdot\dfrac{29}{6}$

$\qquad=\dfrac{3\cdot3\cdot31\cdot29}{2\cdot2\cdot2\cdot2\cdot2\cdot2\cdot3}$

$\qquad=\dfrac{3\cdot31\cdot29}{2\cdot2\cdot2\cdot2\cdot2\cdot2}$

$\qquad=\dfrac{2697}{64}$

$\qquad=42\dfrac{9}{64}$ in.^{3}

101. Challenge exercise

Exercises 0.8

1. $7\cdot7\cdot7\cdot7=7^4$

3. $6\cdot6\cdot6\cdot6\cdot6=6^5$

5. $8\cdot8\cdot8\cdot8\cdot8\cdot8\cdot8\cdot8\cdot8\cdot8=8^{10}$

7. $15\cdot15\cdot15\cdot15\cdot15\cdot15=15^6$

9. $7+2\cdot6=7+12=19$

11. $(7+2)\cdot6=9\cdot6=54$

13. $12-8\div4=12-2=10$

15. $(12-8)\div4=4\div4=1$

17. $8\cdot7+2\cdot2=56+4=60$

19. $8\cdot(7+2)\cdot2=8\cdot9\cdot2=144$

21. $3\cdot5^2=3\cdot25=75$

23. $(3\cdot5)^2=15^2=225$

25. $4\cdot3^2-2=4\cdot9-2=36-2=34$

27. $7\cdot(2^3-5)=7\cdot(8-5)=7\cdot3=21$

29. $3\cdot2^4-6\cdot2=3\cdot16-12=48-12=36$

31. $(2\cdot4)^2-8\cdot3=8^2-8\cdot3=64-24=40$

33. $4\cdot(2+6)^2=4\cdot8^2=4\cdot64=256$

35. $(4 \cdot 2 + 6)^2 = (8 + 6)^2 = 14^2 = 196$

37. $3 \cdot (4 + 3)^2 = 3 \cdot 7^2 = 3 \cdot 49 = 147$

39. $3 \cdot 4 + 3^2 = 12 + 9 = 21$

41. $\begin{aligned} 4 \cdot (2 + 3)^2 - 25 &= 4 \cdot 5^2 - 25 \\ &= 4 \cdot 25 - 25 \\ &= 100 - 25 \\ &= 75 \end{aligned}$

43. $\begin{aligned} (4 \cdot 2 + 3)^2 - 25 &= (8 + 3)^2 - 25 \\ &= 11^2 - 25 \\ &= 121 - 25 \\ &= 96 \end{aligned}$

45. 1.2

47. 7.8

49. 2^5

51. $36 \div (4 + 2) - 4 = 36 \div 6 - 4 = 6 - 4 = 2$

53. $\begin{aligned} (6 + 9) \div 3 + (16 - 4) \cdot 2 &= 15 \div 3 + 12 \cdot 2 \\ &= 5 + 24 \\ &= 29 \end{aligned}$

Chapter 1 The Language of Algebra

Exercises 1.1

1. The sum of c and d is written as $c + d$.

3. w plus z is written as $w + z$.

5. x increased by 2 is written as $x + 2$.

7. 10 more than y is written as $y + 10$.

9. a minus b is written as $a - b$.

11. b decreased by 7 is written as $b - 7$.

13. 6 less than r is written as $r - 6$.

15. w times z is written as wz.

17. The product of 5 and t is written as $5t$.

19. The product of 8, m, and n is written as $8mn$.

21. The product of 3 and the quantity p plus q is written as $3(p + q)$.

23. Twice the sum of x and y is written as $2(x + y)$.

25. The sum of twice x and y is written as $2x + y$.

27. Twice the difference of x and y is written as $2(x - y)$.

29. The quantity a plus b times the quantity a minus b is written as $(a + b)(a - b)$.

31. The product of m and 3 less than m is written as $m(m - 3)$.

33. x divided by 5 is written as $\dfrac{x}{5}$.

35. The quotient of a plus b, divided by 7 is written as $\dfrac{a + b}{7}$.

37. The difference of p and q, divided by 4 is written as $\dfrac{p - q}{4}$.

39. The sum of a and 3, divided by the difference of a and 3 is written as $\dfrac{a + 3}{a - 3}$.

41. 5 more than a number is written as $x + 5$.

43. 7 less than a number is written as $x - 7$.

45. 9 times a number is written as $9x$.

47. 6 more than 3 times a number is written as $3x + 6$.

49. Twice the sum of a number and 5 is written as $2(x + 5)$.

51. The product of 2 more than a number and 2 less than that same number is written as $(x + 2)(x - 2)$.

53. The quotient of a number and 7 is written as $\dfrac{x}{7}$.

55. The sum of a number and 5, divided by 8 is written as $\dfrac{x + 5}{8}$.

57. 6 more than a number divided by 6 less than that same number is written as $\dfrac{x + 6}{x - 6}$.

59. Four times the length of a side (s) is written as $4s$.

61. The radius (r) squared times the height (h) times π is written as $r^2 h\pi$ or $\pi r^2 h$.

63. One-half the product of the height (h) and the sum of two unequal sides (b_1 and b_2) is written as $\dfrac{1}{2}h(b_1 + b_2)$.

65. $2(x + 5)$ is an expression. It means we multiply 2 by the sum of x and 5.

67. $4 + \div m$ is not an expression. The two operations in a row have no meaning.

69. $2b = 6$ is not an expression. The equals sign is not an operation sign.

71. $2a + 5b$ is an expression. It means we add 5 times b to 2 times a.

73. Let x be Earth's population 40 years ago. Then $2x$ represents Earth's population today.

75. The interest (I) equals the principal (P) times the rate (r) times the time (t) is written as $I = Prt$.

77. Writing exercise

Section 1.2

1. +400

3. −200

5. −25,000

7.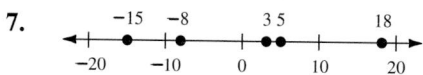

9. 5, 175, −234

11. −7, −5, −1, 0, 2, 3, 8

13. −11, −6, −2, 1, 4, 5, 9

15. −7, −6, −3, 3, 6, 7

17. Maximum: 15
Minimum: −6

19. Maximum: 21
Minimum: −15

21. Maximum: 5
Minimum: −2

23. −15

25. −11

27. 19

29. 7

31. $|17| = 17$

33. $|-10| = 10$

35. $-|3| = -3$

37. $-|-8| = -8$

39. $|-2| + |3| = 2 + 3 = 5$

41. $|-9| + |9| = 9 + 9 = 18$

43. $|4| - |-4| = 4 - 4 = 0$

45. $|15| - |8| = 7$

47. $|15 - 8| = |7| = 7$

49. $|-9| + |2| = 9 + 2 = 11$

51. $|-8| - |-7| = 8 - 7 = 1$

53. True

55. False; −6 is an integer that is not a whole number.

57. False; −4 is a negative integer that is not a whole number.

59. $|6 + (-2)| = |6 - 2| = |4| = 4$

61. $|6| + |-2| = 6 + 2 = 8$

63. −5 cm

65. −$50

67. −10°F

69. −8

71. +$90,000,000

73. **a.** −6

    b. 8

    c. 8

    d. −2

75. **a.** −2

    b. 6

    c. 6

    d. 0

77. Writing exercise

Exercises 1.3

1. $5 + 9 = 9 + 5$ demonstrates the commutative property of addition.

3. $2 \cdot (3 \cdot 5) = (2 \cdot 3) \cdot 5$ demonstrates the associative property of multiplication.

5. $10 \cdot 5 = 5 \cdot 10$ demonstrates the commutative property of multiplication.

7. $8 + 12 = 12 + 8$ demonstrates the commutative property of addition.

9. $(5 \cdot 7) \cdot 2 = 5 \cdot (7 \cdot 2)$ demonstrates the associative property of multiplication.

11. $9 \cdot 8 = 8 \cdot 9$ demonstrates the commutative property of multiplication.

13. $2(3 + 5) = 2 \cdot 3 + 2 \cdot 5$ demonstrates the distributive property.

15. $5 + (7 + 8) = (5 + 7) + 8$ demonstrates the associative property of addition.

17. $(10 + 5) + 9 = 10 + (5 + 9)$ demonstrates the associative property of addition.

19. $7 \cdot (3 + 8) = 7 \cdot 3 + 7 \cdot 8$ demonstrates the distributive property.

21. $7 \cdot (3 + 4) = 7 \cdot 7 = 49$
$7 \cdot 3 + 7 \cdot 4 = 21 + 28 = 49$
Since $49 = 49$,
$7 \cdot (3 + 4) = 7 \cdot 3 + 7 \cdot 4$

23. $2 + (9 + 8) = 2 + 17 = 19$
$(2 + 9) + 8 = 11 + 8 = 19$
Since $19 = 19$,
$2 + (9 + 8) = (2 + 9) + 8$

25. $5 \cdot (6 \cdot 3) = 5 \cdot 18 = 90$
$(5 \cdot 6) \cdot 3 = 30 \cdot 3 = 90$
Since $90 = 90$,
$5 \cdot (6 \cdot 3) = (5 \cdot 6) \cdot 3$

27. $5 \cdot (2 + 8) = 5 \cdot 10 = 50$
$5 \cdot 2 + 5 \cdot 8 = 10 + 40 = 50$
Since $50 = 50$,
$5 \cdot (2 + 8) = 5 \cdot 2 + 5 \cdot 8$

29. $(3 + 12) + 8 = 15 + 8 = 23$
$3 + (12 + 8) = 3 + 20 = 23$
Since $23 = 23$,
$(3 + 12) + 8 = 3 + (12 + 8)$

31. $(4 \cdot 7) \cdot 2 = 28 \cdot 2 = 56$
$4 \cdot (7 \cdot 2) = 4 \cdot 14 = 56$
Since $56 = 56$,
$(4 \cdot 7) \cdot 2 = 4 \cdot (7 \cdot 2)$

33. $\dfrac{1}{2} \cdot (2 + 6) = \dfrac{1}{2} \cdot 8 = 4$

$\dfrac{1}{2} \cdot 2 + \dfrac{1}{2} \cdot 6 = 1 + 3 = 4$

Since $4 = 4$,

$\dfrac{1}{2} \cdot (2 + 6) = \dfrac{1}{2} \cdot 2 + \dfrac{1}{2} \cdot 6$

35. $\left(\dfrac{2}{3} + \dfrac{1}{6}\right) + \dfrac{1}{3} = \dfrac{5}{6} + \dfrac{1}{3} = \dfrac{7}{6}$

$\dfrac{2}{3} + \left(\dfrac{1}{6} + \dfrac{1}{3}\right) = \dfrac{2}{3} + \dfrac{3}{6} = \dfrac{7}{6}$

37. $(2.3 + 3.9) + 4.1 = 6.2 + 4.1 = 10.3$
$2.3 + (3.9 + 4.1) = 2.3 + 8.0 = 10.3$
Since $10.3 = 10.3$,
$(2.3 + 3.9) + 4.1 = 2.3 + (3.9 + 4.1)$

39. $\dfrac{1}{2} \cdot (2 \cdot 8) = \dfrac{1}{2} \cdot 16 = 8$

$\left(\dfrac{1}{2} \cdot 2\right) \cdot 8 = 1 \cdot 8 = 8$

Since $8 = 8$,

$\dfrac{1}{2} \cdot (2 \cdot 8) = \left(\dfrac{1}{2} \cdot 2\right) \cdot 8$

41. $\left(\dfrac{3}{5} \cdot \dfrac{5}{6}\right) \cdot \dfrac{4}{3} = \dfrac{1}{2} \cdot \dfrac{4}{3} = \dfrac{2}{3}$

$\dfrac{3}{5} \cdot \left(\dfrac{5}{6} \cdot \dfrac{4}{3}\right) = \dfrac{3}{5} \cdot \dfrac{10}{9} = \dfrac{2}{3}$

Since $\dfrac{2}{3} = \dfrac{2}{3}$,

$\left(\dfrac{3}{5} \cdot \dfrac{5}{6}\right) \cdot \dfrac{4}{3} = \dfrac{3}{5} \cdot \left(\dfrac{5}{6} \cdot \dfrac{4}{3}\right)$

43. $2.5 \cdot (4 \cdot 5) = 2.5 \cdot 20 = 50$
$(2.5 \cdot 4) \cdot 5 = 10 \cdot 5 = 50$
Since $50 = 50$,
$2.5 \cdot (4.5) = (2.5 \cdot 4) \cdot 5$

45. $2(3 + 5) = 2 \cdot 3 + 2 \cdot 5$
$= 6 + 10$
$= 16$

47. $3(x + 5) = 3 \cdot x + 3 \cdot 5$
$= 3x + 15$

49. $4(w + v) = 4 \cdot w + 4 \cdot v$
$= 4w + 4v$

51. $2(3x + 5) = 2 \cdot 3x + 2 \cdot 5$
$= 6x + 10$

53. $\frac{1}{3} \cdot (15 + 9) = \frac{1}{3} \cdot 15 + \frac{1}{3} \cdot 9$
$= 5 + 3$
$= 8$

55. $5 + 7 = 7 + 5$ by the commutative property of addition.

57. $(8)(3) = (3)(8)$ by the commutative property of multiplication.

59. $7(2 + 5) = 7 \cdot 2 + 7 \cdot 5$ by the distributive property.

61. $3 + 7 = 7 + 3$ by the commutative property of addition.

63. $5 \cdot (3 \cdot 2) = (5 \cdot 3) \cdot 2$ by the associative property of multiplication.

65. $2 \cdot 4 + 2 \cdot 5 = 2 \cdot (4 + 5)$ by the distributive property.

67. $8 - 5 = 3$
$5 - 8 = -3$
Since 3 is not equal to –3,
subtraction is not commutative.

69. $(12 - 8) - 4 = 4 - 4 = 0$
$12 - (8 - 4) = 12 - 4 = 8$
Since 0 is not equal to 8, subtraction is not associative.

71. $3(6 - 2) = 3(4) = 12$
$3 \cdot 6 - 3 \cdot 2 = 18 - 6 = 12$
Since 12 = 12, multiplication is distributive over subtraction.

73. a. $5 \cdot (3 + 4) = 5 \cdot 3 + 5 \cdot 4$ by the distributive property.

b. $5 \cdot (3 + 4) = 5 \cdot (4 + 3)$ by the commutative property of addition.

c. $5 \cdot (3 + 5) = (3 + 4) \cdot 5$ by the commutative property of multiplication.

75. $5 + (6 + 7) = (5 + 6) + 7$ demonstrates the associative property of addition.

77. $4 \cdot (3 + 2) = 4 \cdot (2 + 3)$ demonstrates the commutative property of addition.

Exercises 1.4

1. $3 + 6 = 9$

3. $11 + 5 = 16$

5. $\frac{3}{4} + \frac{5}{4} = \frac{8}{4} = 2$

7. $\frac{1}{2} + \frac{4}{5} = \frac{5}{10} + \frac{8}{10} = \frac{13}{10}$

9. $(-2) + (-3) = -5$

11. $\left(-\frac{3}{5}\right) + \left(-\frac{7}{5}\right) = -\frac{10}{5} = -2$

13. $\left(-\frac{1}{2}\right) + \left(-\frac{3}{8}\right) = \left(-\frac{4}{8}\right) + \left(-\frac{3}{8}\right) = -\frac{7}{8}$

15. $(-1.6) + (-2.3) = -3.9$

17. $9 + (-3) = 6$

19. $\frac{3}{4} + \left(-\frac{1}{2}\right) = \frac{3}{4} + \left(-\frac{2}{4}\right) = \frac{1}{4}$

21. $\left(-\frac{4}{5}\right) + \frac{9}{20} = \left(-\frac{16}{20}\right) + \frac{9}{20} = -\frac{7}{20}$

23. $-11.4 + 13.4 = 2$

25. $-3.6 + 7.6 = 4$

27. $-9 + 0 = -9$

29. $7 + (-7) = 0$

31. $-4.5 + 4.5 = 0$

33. $7 + (-9) + (-5) + 6 = 13 + (-14) = -1$

35. $7 + (-3) + 5 + (-11) = 12 + (-14) = -2$

37. $-\dfrac{3}{2} + \left(-\dfrac{7}{4}\right) + \dfrac{1}{4} = -\dfrac{6}{4} + \left(-\dfrac{7}{4}\right) + \dfrac{1}{4} = -\dfrac{12}{4} = -3$

39. $2.3 + (-5.4) + (-2.9) = -6$

41. $21 - 13 = 21 + (-13) = 8$

43. $82 - 45 = 82 + (-45) = 37$

45. $\dfrac{15}{7} - \dfrac{8}{7} = \dfrac{15}{7} + \left(-\dfrac{8}{7}\right) = \dfrac{7}{7} = 1$

47. $7.9 - 5.4 = 7.9 + (-5.4) = 2.5$

49. $8 - 10 = 8 + (-10) = -2$

51. $24 - 45 = 24 + (-45) = -21$

53. $\dfrac{7}{6} - \dfrac{19}{6} = \dfrac{7}{6} + \left(-\dfrac{19}{6}\right) = -\dfrac{12}{6} = -2$

55. $7.8 - 11.6 = 7.8 + (-11.6) = -3.8$

57. $-5 - 3 = -5 + (-3) = -8$

59. $-9 - 14 = -9 + (-14) = -23$

61. $-\dfrac{2}{5} - \dfrac{7}{10} = -\dfrac{4}{10} + \left(-\dfrac{7}{10}\right) = -\dfrac{11}{10}$

63. $-3.4 - 4.7 = -3.4 + (-4.7) = -8.1$

65. $5 - (-11) = 5 + 11 = 16$

67. $7 - (-12) = 7 + 12 = 19$

69. $\dfrac{3}{4} - \left(-\dfrac{3}{2}\right) = \dfrac{3}{4} + \dfrac{3}{2} = \dfrac{3}{4} + \dfrac{6}{4} = \dfrac{9}{4}$

71. $\dfrac{6}{7} - \left(-\dfrac{5}{14}\right) = \dfrac{6}{7} + \dfrac{5}{14} = \dfrac{12}{14} + \dfrac{5}{14} = \dfrac{17}{14}$

73. $8.3 - (-5.7) = 8.3 + 5.7 = 14$

75. $8.9 - (-11.7) = 8.9 + 11.7 = 20.6$

77. $-36 - (-24) = -36 + 24 = -12$

79. $-19 - (-27) = -19 + 27 = 8$

81. $\left(-\dfrac{3}{4}\right) - \left(-\dfrac{11}{4}\right) = -\dfrac{3}{4} + \dfrac{11}{4} = \dfrac{8}{4} = 2$

83. $-12.7 - (-5.7) = -12.7 + 5.7 = -7$

85. $-6.9 - (-10.1) = -6.9 + 10.1 = 3.2$

87. $-4.1967 - 5.2943 = -9.491$

89. $-4.1623 - (-3.1468) = -1.0155$

91. $-6.3267 + 8.6789 = 2.3522$

93. $1, 3, 5, 7, 9$
The median is the element that is exactly in the middle of the set written in ascending order. The median for this set is 5.

95. $8, 7, 2, 25, 5, 13, 3$
First, rewrite the set in ascending order.
$2, 3, 5, 7, 8, 13, 25$
The median is the element that is exactly in the middle. The median for this set is 7.

97. $2, 7, 9, 15, 24$
The set is already written in ascending order. The range is the difference between the maximum, 24, and the minimum, 2.
$24 - 2 = 22$
The range is 22.

99. $-4, -3, 2, 7, 9$
The set is already written in ascending order. The range is the difference between the maximum, 9, and the minimum, -4.
$9 - (-4) = 9 + 4 = 13$
The range is 13.

101. $\dfrac{7}{8}, 2, -\dfrac{1}{2}, -8, \dfrac{3}{4}$
First, rewrite the set in ascending order.
$-8, -\dfrac{1}{2}, \dfrac{3}{4}, \dfrac{7}{8}, 2$
The maximum is 2. The minimum is -8.
The range is $2 - (-8) = 2 + 8 = 10$.

103. $3, 2, -5, 6, -3$
First, rewrite the set in ascending order.
$-5, -3, 2, 3, 6$
The maximum is 6. The minimum is -5.
The range is $6 - (-5) = 6 + 5 = 11$.

105. $100 + (-23) + 51 = 128$
His new balance is $128.

107. $23 + (-5) + 15 + (-10) = 23$
His net yardage change is 23 yards gained.

109. $82 + (-12) = 70$
The temperature was $70°$ at 4:00 P.M.

111. $-72 + (-23.50) = -95.5$
His checking account was overdrawn by $95.50.

113. $-750 + (-425) = -1175$
The total decrease in enrollment was 1175 students.

115. 87, 71, 95, 81, 90
First, rewrite the set in ascending order.
71, 81, 87, 90, 95
The maximum is 95. The minimum is 71.
The range is $95 - 71 = 24$.

Exercises 1.5

1. $10 + x$

3. $p + 12$

5. $n + 1$

7. $m - 14$

9. $x - 1$

11. mn

13. $\dfrac{s}{4}$

15. $2(c - d)$

17. $rs - 4$

19. $\dfrac{c + 4}{d}$

21. $5 + 4 \cdot 6 = 5 + 24 = 29$

23. $7(8 - 2) = 7 \cdot 6 = 42$

25. $6(8 - 4)^2 = 6(4)^2 = 6 \cdot 16 = 96$

27. $(4 + 3)(5 + 3) = 7 \cdot 8 = 56$

29. $4 + 3 \cdot 5 + 2 = 4 + 15 + 2 = 19 + 2 = 21$

31. $(7 + 5)(7 - 5) = 12 \cdot 2 = 24$

33. $7 + 5 \cdot 7 - 5 = 7 + 35 - 5 = 42 - 5 = 37$

35. $9^2 - 5^2 = 81 - 25 = 56$

37. $(9 - 5)^2 = 4^2 = 16$

39. $16 \div 2^3 \cdot 2 - 3 + 11 = 16 \div 8 \cdot 2 - 3 + 11$
$= 2 \cdot 2 - 3 + 11$
$= 4 - 3 + 11$
$= 1 + 11$
$= 12$

41. $-12 - 8 \div 4 = -12 - 2 = -14$

43. $\left(2^3 + 3\right)^2 + 12 \div 3 \cdot 2 = (8 + 3)^2 + 12 \div 3 \cdot 2$
$= 11^2 + 12 \div 3 \cdot 2$
$= 121 + 12 \div 3 \cdot 2$
$= 121 + 4 \cdot 2$
$= 121 + 8$
$= 129$

45. $3\left[35 - 3(6 - 2)^2\right] = 3\left[35 - 3(4)^2\right]$
$= 3(35 - 3 \cdot 16)$
$= 3(35 - 48)$
$= 3(-13)$
$= -39$

47. $\dfrac{5 - 15}{2 + 3} = \dfrac{-10}{5} = -2$

49. $\dfrac{-6 + 18}{-2 - 4} = \dfrac{12}{-6} = -2$

51. $\dfrac{(5)(-12)}{(-3)(5)} = \dfrac{-60}{-15} = 4$

53. $(b + 5) + 3 = b + (5 + 3) = b + 8$

55. $8 + (6 + a) = (8 + 6) + a = 14 + a$

57. $(2x + 5) + 12 = 2x + (5 + 12) = 2x + 17$

59. $8+(p+6) = 8+(6+p)$
$ = (8+6)+p$
$ = 14+p$
$ = p+14$

61. $(8+a)+(-8) = (a+8)+(-8)$
$ = a+[8+(-8)]$
$ = a+0$
$ = a$

63. $2(8x) = (2\cdot 8)x = 16x$

65. $\dfrac{1}{4}(4w) = \left(\dfrac{1}{4}\cdot 4\right)w = 1\cdot w = w$

67. $\left(\dfrac{2}{7}\right)\left(\dfrac{7}{2}\right)\left(\dfrac{1}{m}\right)m = 1\left(\dfrac{1}{m}\right)m = \left(\dfrac{1}{m}\right)m = 1$

69. $5(2m+3) = 5(2m)+5(3) = 10m+15$

71. $4a(a+4) = 4a(a)+4a(4) = 4a^2+16a$

73. $\dfrac{1}{2}(4a+10) = \dfrac{1}{2}(4a)+\dfrac{1}{2}(10) = 2a+5$

75. $5(3a+2b+4) = 5(3a)+5(2b)+5(4)$
$ = 15a+10b+20$

77. $\dfrac{1}{2}(4a+6b+2c) = \dfrac{1}{2}(4a)+\dfrac{1}{2}(6b)+\dfrac{1}{2}(2c)$
$\phantom{\dfrac{1}{2}(4a+6b+2c)} = 2a+3b+c$

79. $8b+2b = (8+2)b = 10b$

81. $3m+4m+m = (3+4+1)m = 8m$

83. $\dfrac{2}{3}a+\dfrac{4}{3}a = \left(\dfrac{2}{3}+\dfrac{4}{3}\right)a = \dfrac{6}{3}a = 2a$

85. $\dfrac{1}{2}a+\dfrac{1}{3}a = \left(\dfrac{1}{2}+\dfrac{1}{3}\right)a = \left(\dfrac{3}{6}+\dfrac{2}{6}\right)a = \dfrac{5}{6}a$

87. $6x+(2+3x) = 6x+(3x+2)$
$ = (6x+3x)+2$
$ = (6+3)x+2$
$ = 9x+2$

89. $8y+(2y+5) = (8y+2y)+5$
$ = (8+2)y+5$
$ = 10y+5$

91. $2x+9+4x+6 = 2x+4x+9+6$
$ = (2+4)x+(9+6)$
$ = 6x+15$

93. $3b+2b+5+4b = 3b+2b+4b+5$
$ = (3+2+4)b+5$
$ = 9b+5$

95. $3+7y+(-3)+y = 3+(-3)+7y+y$
$ = [3+(-3)]+(7+1)y$
$ = 0+8y$
$ = 8y$

97. $2+3(2y+1)+3y = 2+3(2y)+3(1)+3y$
$ = 2+6y+3+3y$
$ = 2+3+6y+3y$
$ = (2+3)+(6+3)y$
$ = 5+9y$
$ = 9y+5$

99. $2y^2+3y(2+y)+3y = 2y^2+3y(2)+3y(y)+3y$
$ = 2y^2+6y+3y^2+3y$
$ = 2y^2+3y^2+6y+3y$
$ = (2+3)y^2+(6+3)y$
$ = 5y^2+9y$

101. Commutative property of addition

103. Distributive property

105. Associative property of addition

107. Commutative property of addition

109. Distributive property

111. Additive inverse

113. False
$3+5(y+4) = 3+5(y)+5(4)$
$ = 3+5y+20$

115. True

117. False
$4(3w+3) = 4(3w)+4(3) = 12w+12$

119. True

121. True

123. False

$$2n + 6n = (2 + 6)n = 8n$$

125. Let x represent the baker's sales in April. Then the sales in May are represented by $2(x)$ or $2x$ and the sales in June are represented by $\frac{3}{4}(x)$ or $\frac{3}{4}x$.

127. challenge exercise

Exercises 1.6

1. $4 \cdot 10 = 40$

3. $(5)(-12) = -60$

5. $(-8)(9) = -72$

7. $(4)\left(-\frac{3}{2}\right) = -6$

9. $\left(-\frac{1}{4}\right)(8) = -2$

11. $(3.25)(-4) = -13$

13. $(-8)(-7) = 56$

15. $(-5)(-12) = 60$

17. $(-9)\left(-\frac{2}{3}\right) = 6$

19. $(-1.25)(-12) = 15$

21. $(0)(-18) = 0$

23. $(15)(0) = 0$

25. $\left(-\frac{11}{12}\right)(0) = 0$

27. $(-3.57)(0) = 0$

29. $\left(-\frac{3}{2}\right)\left(-\frac{2}{3}\right) = 1$

31. $\left(\frac{4}{7}\right)\left(-\frac{7}{4}\right) = -1$

33. $\frac{-20}{-4} = 5$

35. $\frac{48}{6} = 8$

37. $\frac{50}{-5} = -10$

39. $\frac{-52}{4} = -13$

41. $\frac{-75}{-3} = 25$

43. $\frac{0}{-8} = 0$

45. $\frac{-9}{-1} = 9$

47. $\frac{-96}{-8} = 12$

49. $\frac{18}{0}$ is undefined.

51. $\frac{-17}{1} = -17$

53. $\frac{-144}{-16} = 9$

55. $\frac{-29.4}{4.9} = -6$

57. $\frac{-8}{32} = -\frac{1}{4}$

59. $\frac{24}{-16} = -\frac{3}{2}$

61. $\frac{-28}{-42} = \frac{2}{3}$

63. $\frac{(-6)(-3)}{2} = \frac{18}{2} = 9$

65. $\frac{(-8)(2)}{-4} = \frac{-16}{-4} = 4$

67. $\frac{24}{-4-8} = \frac{24}{-12} = -2$

69. $\frac{-12-12}{-3} = \frac{-24}{-3} = 8$

71. $\dfrac{55-19}{-12-6} = \dfrac{36}{-18} = -2$

73. $\dfrac{7-5}{2-2} = \dfrac{2}{0}$ is undefined.

75. $5(7-2) = 5(5) = 25$

77. $2(5-8) = 2(-3) = -6$

79. $-3(9-7) = -3(2) = -6$

81. $-3(-2-5) = -3(-7) = 21$

83. $(-2)(3) - 5 = -6 - 5 = -11$

85. $4(-7) - 5 = -28 - 5 = -33$

87. $(-5)(-2) - 12 = 10 - 12 = -2$

89. $(3)(-7) + 20 = -21 + 20 = -1$

91. $-4 + (-3)(6) = -4 + (-18) = -22$

93. $7 - (-4)(-2) = 7 - 8 = -1$

95. $(-7)^2 - 17 = 49 - 17 = 32$

97. $(-5)^2 + 18 = 25 + 18 = 43$

99. $-6^2 - 4 = -36 - 4 = -40$

101. $(-4)^2 - (-2)(-5) = 16 - (-2)(-5)$
$\qquad\qquad\qquad\quad = 16 - 10$
$\qquad\qquad\qquad\quad = 6$

103. $(-8)^2 - 5^2 = 64 - 25$
$\qquad\qquad\qquad = 39$

105. $(-6)^2 - (-3)^2 = 36 - 9 = 27$

107. $-8^2 - 5^2 = -64 - 25 = -89$

109. $-8^2 - (-5)^2 = -64 - 25 = -89$

111. $23 \cdot 11 = 253$
I scored a total of 253 points.

113. $335 \cdot 1.25 = 43.75$
I made $43.75.

115. $-6 - (2 \cdot 8) = -22$
The temperature is $-22°$F.

117. $125 - (9 \cdot 9) = 44$
He had $44.

119. $\dfrac{16,232 - 20,000}{3} = \dfrac{-3768}{3} = -1256$
Each person lost $1256.

121. $84 \div \dfrac{2}{3} = 126$
He can fill 126 test tubes.

123. $\dfrac{-8}{-4+2} = 4$

125. $\dfrac{-10+4}{-7+10} = -2$

Exercises 1.7

For exercises 1–41, $a = -2$, $b = 5$ and $c = -4$, and $d = 6$.

1. $3c - 2b = 3(-4) - 2(5)$
$\qquad\qquad = -12 - 10$
$\qquad\qquad = -22$

3. $8b + 2c = 8(5) + 2(-4)$
$\qquad\qquad = 40 + (-8)$
$\qquad\qquad = 32$

5. $-b^2 + b = -5^2 + 5$
$\qquad\qquad = -25 + 5$
$\qquad\qquad = -20$

7. $3a^2 = 3(-2)^2$
$\qquad = 3(4)$
$\qquad = 12$

9. $c^2 - 2d = (-4)^2 - 2(6)$
$\qquad\qquad = 16 - 12$
$\qquad\qquad = 4$

11. $2a^2 + 3b^2 = 2(-2)^2 + 3(5)^2$
$\qquad\qquad\quad = 2(4) + 3(25)$
$\qquad\qquad\quad = 8 + 75$
$\qquad\qquad\quad = 83$

13. $2(a+b) = 2(-2+5)$
$\qquad\qquad = 2(3)$
$\qquad\qquad = 6$

15. $4(2a - d) = 4[2(-2) - 6]$
$$= 4(-4 - 6)$$
$$= 4(-10)$$
$$= -40$$

17. $a(b + 3c) = -2[5 + 3(-4)]$
$$= -2(5 - 12)$$
$$= -2(-7)$$
$$= 14$$

19. $\dfrac{6d}{c} = \dfrac{6 \cdot 6}{-4}$
$$= \dfrac{36}{-4}$$
$$= -9$$

21. $\dfrac{3d + 2c}{b} = \dfrac{3(6) + 2(-4)}{5}$
$$= \dfrac{18 + (-8)}{5}$$
$$= \dfrac{10}{5}$$
$$= 2$$

23. $\dfrac{2b - 3a}{c + 2d} = \dfrac{2(5) - 3(-2)}{-4 + 2(6)}$
$$= \dfrac{10 + 6}{-4 + 12}$$
$$= \dfrac{16}{8}$$
$$= 2$$

25. $d^2 - b^2 = 6^2 - 5^2$
$$= 36 - 25$$
$$= 11$$

27. $(d - b)^2 = (6 - 5)^2$
$$= 1^2$$
$$= 1$$

29. $(d - b)(d + b) = (6 - 5)(6 + 5) = (1)(11) = 11$

31. $d^3 - b^3 = (6)^3 - (5)^3 = 216 - 125 = 91$

33. $(d - b)^3 = (6 - 5)^3 = 1^3 = 1$

35. $(d - b)(d^2 + db + b^2) = (6 - 5)[6^2 + (6)(5) + 5^2]$
$$= (1)(36 + 30 + 25)$$
$$= (1)(91)$$
$$= 91$$

37. $b^2 + a^2 = (5)^2 + (-2)^2 = 25 + 4 = 29$

39. $(b + a)^2 = [5 + (-2)]^2 = 3^2 = 9$

41. $a^2 + 2ad + d^2 = (-2)^2 + 2(-2)(6) + (6)^2$
$$= 4 - 24 + 36$$
$$= 16$$

For exercises 43–49, $x = -2.34$, $y = -3.14$, and $z = 4.12$.

43. $x + yz = -2.34 + (-3.14)(4.12) = -15.3$

45. $x^2 - z^2 = (-2.34)^2 - (4.12)^2 = -11.5$

47. $\dfrac{xy}{z - x} = \dfrac{(-2.34)(-3.14)}{4.12 - (-2.34)} = 1.1$

49. $\dfrac{2x + y}{2x + z} = \dfrac{2(-2.34) + (-3.14)}{2(-2.34) + 4.12} = 14.0$

51. $\sum x = 1 + 2 + 3 + 7 + 8 + 9 + 11 = 41$

53. $\sum x = -5 + (-3) + (-1) + 2 + 3 + 4 + 8 = 8$

55. $\sum x = 3 + 2 + (-1) + (-4) + (-3) + 8 + 6 = 11$

57. $\sum x = -\dfrac{1}{2} + \left(-\dfrac{3}{4}\right) + 2 + 3 + \dfrac{1}{4} + \dfrac{3}{2} + (-1) = \dfrac{9}{2}$

59. $\sum x = -2.5 + (-3.2) + 2.6 + (-1) + 2 + 4 + (-3)$
$$= -1.1$$

61. $x - 7 = 22 - 7 = 15$
$2y + 5 = 2(5) + 5 = 15$
The statement is true.

63. $2(x + y) = 2[-4 + (-2)] = 2(-6) = -12$
$2x + y = 2(-4) + (-2) = -10$
The statement is false.

65. $R_T = \dfrac{R_1 R_2}{(R_1 + R_2)}$
$$= \dfrac{(6 \cdot 10)}{(6 + 10)} = 3.75$$
The total resistance is 3.75 ohms.

67. $P = 2L + 2W = 2(10) + 2(5) = 30$
The perimeter is 30 inches.

69. $P = \dfrac{I}{RT} = \dfrac{150}{(0.04)(2)} = 1875$

The principal is $1875.

71. $F = \dfrac{9}{5}C + 32 = \dfrac{9}{5}(-10) + 32 = 14$

The temperature is $14°$ F.

73. Writing exercise

75. Writing exercise

Exercises 1.8

1. $5a + 2$ has two terms: $5a$ and 2.

3. $4x^3$ has one term: $4x^3$.

5. $3x^2 + 3x - 7$ or $3x^2 + 3x + (-7)$ has three terms: $3x^2$, $3x$, and -7.

7. In the group of terms $5ab$, $3b$, $3a$, $4ab$, the like terms are $5ab$ and $4ab$.

9. In the group of terms
$4xy^2$, $2x^2y$, $5x^2$, $-3x^2y$, $5y$, $6x^2y$, the like terms are $2x^2y$, $-3x^2y$, and $6x^2y$.

11. $3m + 7m = (3 + 7)m = 10m$

13. $7b^3 + 10b^3 = (7 + 10)b^3 = 17b^3$

15. $21xyz + 7xyz = (21 + 7)xyz = 28xyz$

17. $9z^2 - 3z^2 = 9z^2 + (-3z^2) = 6z^2$

19. $5a^3 - 5a^3 = 5a^3 + (-5a^3) = 0$

21. $19n^2 - 18n^2 = 19n^2 + (-18n^2) = 1n^2 = n^2$

23. $21p^2q - 6p^2q = 21p^2q + (-6p^2q) = 15p^2q$

25. $10x^2 - 7x^2 + 3x^2 = 10x^2 + (-7x^2) + 3x^2$
$= (10 + (-7) + 3)x^2$
$= 6x^2$

27. $9a - 7a + 4b = 9a + (-7a) + 4b$
$= (9 + (-7))a + 4b$
$= 2a + 4b$

29. $7x + 5y - 4x - 4y = 7x + (-4x) + 5y + (-4y)$
$= (7 + (-4))x + (5 + (-4))y$
$= 3x + 1y$
$= 3x + y$

31. $4a + 7b + 3 - 2a + 3b - 2$
$= 4a + (-2a) + 7b + 3b + 3 + (-2)$
$= (4 + (-2))a + (7 + 3)b + 3 + (-2)$
$= 2a + 10b + 1$

33. $\dfrac{2}{3}m + 3 + \dfrac{4}{3}m = \left(\dfrac{2}{3} + \dfrac{4}{3}\right)m + 3$
$= \dfrac{6}{3}m + 3$
$= 2m + 3$

35. $\dfrac{13}{5}x + 2 - \dfrac{3}{5}x + 5 = \left(\dfrac{13}{5} - \dfrac{3}{5}\right)x + 2 + 5$
$= \dfrac{10}{5}x + 7$
$= 2x + 7$

37. $2.3a + 7 + 4.7a + 3 = (2.3 + 4.7)a + 7 + 3$
$= 7a + 10$

39. $5a^4 + 8a^4 = (5 + 8)a^4$
$= 13a^4$

41. $15a^3 - 12a^3 = 15a^3 + (-12a^3)$
$= 3a^3$

43. $(8x + 3x) - 4x = 11x - 4x$
$= 7x$

45. $(9mn^2 + 5mn^2) - 3mn^2 = 14mn^2 - 3mn^2$
$= 11mn^2$

47. $2(3x + 2) + 4 = 6x + 4 + 4$
$= 6x + 8$

49. $5(6a - 2) + 12a = 30a - 10 + 12a$
$= 42a - 10$

51. $4s + 2(s + 4) + 4 = 4s + 2s + 8 + 4$
$= 6s + 12$

53. Writing exercise

55. Writing exercise

57. Group exercise

Exercises 1.9

1. $x + 4 = 9$

$5 + 4 \overset{?}{=} 9$

$9 = 9$

5 is a solution.

3. $x - 15 = 6$

$-21 - 15 \overset{?}{=} 6$

$-36 \neq 6$

-21 is not a solution.

5. $5 - x = 2$

$5 - 4 \overset{?}{=} 2$

$1 \neq 2$

4 is not a solution.

7. $4 - x = 6$

$4 - (-2) \overset{?}{=} 6$

$4 + 2 \overset{?}{=} 6$

$6 = 6$

-2 is a solution.

9. $3x + 4 = 13$

$3(8) + 4 \overset{?}{=} 13$

$24 + 4 \overset{?}{=} 13$

$28 \neq 13$

8 is not a solution.

11. $4x - 5 = 7$

$4(2) - 5 \overset{?}{=} 7$

$8 - 5 \overset{?}{=} 7$

$3 \neq 7$

2 is not a solution.

13. $5 - 2x = 7$

$5 - 2(-1) \overset{?}{=} 7$

$5 + 2 \overset{?}{=} 7$

$7 = 7$

-1 is a solution.

15. $4x - 5 = 2x + 3$

$4(4) - 5 \overset{?}{=} 2(4) + 3$

$16 - 5 \overset{?}{=} 8 + 3$

$11 = 11$

4 is a solution.

17. $x + 3 + 2x = 5 + x + 8$

$3x + 3 = x + 13$

$3(5) + 3 \overset{?}{=} 5 + 13$

$15 + 3 \overset{?}{=} 5 + 13$

$18 = 18$

5 is a solution.

19. $\dfrac{3}{4}x = 20$

$\dfrac{3}{4}(18) \overset{?}{=} 20$

$\dfrac{54}{4} \neq 20$

18 is not a solution.

21. $\dfrac{3}{5}x + 5 = 11$

$\dfrac{3}{5}(10) + 5 \overset{?}{=} 11$

$6 + 5 \overset{?}{=} 11$

$11 = 11$

10 is a solution.

23. $2x + 1 = 9$ is a linear equation.

25. $2x - 8$ is an expression.

27. $7x + 2x + 9 - 3$ is an expression.

29. $2x - 8 = 3$ is a linear equation.

31. $x + 9 = 11$

$\underline{ -9 \quad -9}$

$x \quad = 2$

Check:

$2 + 9 \overset{?}{=} 11$

$11 = 11$

33. $x - 8 = \quad 3$

$\underline{ +8 \quad +8}$

$x \quad = \quad 11$

Check:

$11 - 8 \overset{?}{=} 3$

$3 = 3$

35. $x - 8 = -10$

$\underline{ +8 \quad +8}$

$x \quad = -2$

Check:

$-2 - 8 \overset{?}{=} -10$

$-10 = -10$

37. $x + 4 = -3$

$\underline{ -4 \quad -4}$

$x \quad = -7$

Check:

$-7 + 4 \overset{?}{=} -3$

$-3 = -3$

39.
$$11 = x + 5$$
$$\underline{-5 \qquad -5}$$
$$6 = x$$

Check:
$$11 \overset{?}{=} 6 + 5$$
$$11 = 11$$

41.
$$4x = 3x + 4$$
$$\underline{-3x \quad -3x}$$
$$x = \qquad 4$$

Check:
$$4(4) \overset{?}{=} 3(4) + 4$$
$$16 \overset{?}{=} 12 + 4$$
$$16 = 16$$

43.
$$11x = 10x - 10$$
$$\underline{-10x \quad -10x}$$
$$x = -10$$

Check:
$$11(-10) \overset{?}{=} 10(-10) - 10$$
$$-110 \overset{?}{=} -100 - 10$$
$$-110 = -110$$

45.
$$6x + 3 = 5x$$
$$\underline{-5x \qquad -5x}$$
$$x + 3 = 0$$
$$\underline{-3 \quad -3}$$
$$x \quad = -3$$

Check:
$$6(-3) + 3 \overset{?}{=} 5(-3)$$
$$-18 + 3 \overset{?}{=} -15$$
$$-15 = -15$$

47.
$$8x - 4 = 7x$$
$$\underline{-7x \qquad -7x}$$
$$x - 4 = 0$$
$$\underline{+4 \quad +4}$$
$$x \quad = 4$$

Check:
$$8(4) - 4 \overset{?}{=} 7(4)$$
$$32 - 4 \overset{?}{=} 28$$
$$28 = 28$$

49.
$$2x + 3 = x + 5$$
$$\underline{-x \qquad -x}$$
$$x + 3 = 5$$
$$\underline{-3 \quad -3}$$
$$x \quad = 2$$

Check:
$$2(2) + 3 \overset{?}{=} 2 + 5$$
$$4 + 3 \overset{?}{=} 2 + 5$$
$$7 = 7$$

51.
$$4x - \frac{3}{5} = 3x + \frac{1}{10}$$
$$\underline{-3x \qquad -3x}$$
$$x - \frac{3}{5} = \qquad \frac{1}{10}$$
$$\underline{+\frac{3}{5} \qquad +\frac{3}{5}}$$
$$x \quad = \qquad \frac{7}{10}$$

Check:
$$4\left(\frac{7}{10}\right) - \frac{3}{5} \overset{?}{=} 3\left(\frac{7}{10}\right) + \frac{1}{10}$$
$$\frac{28}{10} - \frac{6}{10} \overset{?}{=} \frac{21}{10} + \frac{1}{10}$$
$$\frac{22}{10} = \frac{22}{10}$$

53.
$$\frac{7}{8}(x - 2) = \frac{3}{4} - \frac{1}{8}x$$
$$\frac{7}{8}x - \frac{14}{8} = \frac{3}{4} - \frac{1}{8}x$$
$$\underline{+\frac{1}{8}x \qquad +\frac{1}{8}x}$$
$$x - \frac{14}{8} = \frac{3}{4}$$
$$\underline{+\frac{14}{8} \quad +\frac{14}{8}}$$
$$x \quad = \frac{20}{8}$$
$$x \quad = \frac{5}{2}$$

Check:
$$\frac{7}{8}\left(\frac{5}{2} - 2\right) \overset{?}{=} \frac{3}{4} - \frac{1}{8}\left(\frac{5}{2}\right)$$
$$\frac{7}{8}\left(\frac{1}{2}\right) \overset{?}{=} \frac{3}{4} - \frac{5}{16}$$
$$\frac{7}{16} = \frac{7}{16}$$

55.

$$3x - 0.54 = 2(x - 0.15)$$
$$3x - 0.54 = 2x - 0.30$$

$$\begin{array}{rcr} -2x & & -2x \\ \hline x - 0.54 = & & -0.30 \\ +0.54 & & +0.54 \\ \hline x & = & 0.24 \end{array}$$

Check:
$$3(0.24) - 0.54 \stackrel{?}{=} 2(0.24 - 0.15)$$
$$0.72 - 0.54 \stackrel{?}{=} 2(0.09)$$
$$0.18 = 0.18$$

57.

$$6x + 3(x - 0.2789) = 4(2x + 0.3912)$$
$$6x + 3x - 0.8367 = 8x + 1.5648$$
$$9x - 0.8367 = 8x + 1.5648$$

$$\begin{array}{rcr} -8x & & -8x \\ \hline x - 0.8367 & = & 1.5648 \\ +0.8367 & & +0.8367 \\ \hline x & = & 2.4015 \end{array}$$

Check:
$$6(2.4015) + 3(2.4015 - 0.2789) \stackrel{?}{=} 4(2 \cdot 2.4015 + 0.3912)$$
$$14.409 + 3(2.1226) \stackrel{?}{=} 4(4.803 + 0.3912)$$
$$14.409 + 3(2.1226) \stackrel{?}{=} 4(5.1942)$$
$$20.7768 = 20.7768$$

59.

$$3x - 5 + 2x - 7 + x = 5x + 2$$
$$6x - 12 = 5x + 2$$

$$\begin{array}{rcr} -5x & & -5x \\ \hline x - 12 = & & 2 \\ +12 & & +12 \\ \hline x & = & 14 \end{array}$$

Check:
$$3(14) - 5 + 2(14) - 7 + 14 \stackrel{?}{=} 5(14) + 2$$
$$42 - 5 + 28 - 7 + 14 \stackrel{?}{=} 70 + 2$$
$$72 = 72$$

61.

$$5x - (0.345 - x) = 5x + 0.8713$$
$$5x - 0.345 + x = 5x + 0.8713$$
$$6x - 0.345 = 5x + 0.8713$$

$$\begin{array}{rcr} -5x & & -5x \\ \hline x - 0.345 & = & 0.8713 \\ +0.345 & & +0.345 \\ \hline x & = & 1.2163 \end{array}$$

Check:
$$5(1.2163) - (0.345 - 1.2163) \stackrel{?}{=} 5(1.2163) + 0.8713$$
$$6.0815 - (-0.8713) \stackrel{?}{=} 6.0815 + 0.8713$$
$$6.0815 + 0.8713 \stackrel{?}{=} 6.8015 + 0.8713$$
$$6.9528 = 6.9258$$

63.

$$3(7x + 2) = 5(4x + 1) + 17$$
$$21x + 6 = 20x + 5 + 17$$
$$21x + 6 = 20x + 22$$

$$\begin{array}{rcr} -20x & & -20x \\ \hline x + 6 = & & 22 \\ -6 & & -6 \\ \hline x & = & 16 \end{array}$$

Check:
$$3(7 \cdot 16 + 2) \stackrel{?}{=} 5(4 \cdot 16 + 1) + 17$$
$$3(112 + 2) \stackrel{?}{=} 5(64 + 1) + 17$$
$$3(114) \stackrel{?}{=} 5(65) + 17$$
$$342 \stackrel{?}{=} 325 + 17$$
$$342 = 342$$

65.

$$\frac{5}{4}x - 1 = \frac{1}{4}x + 7$$

$$\begin{array}{rcr} -\frac{1}{4}x & & -\frac{1}{4}x \\ \hline x - 1 = & & 7 \\ +1 & & +1 \\ \hline x & = & 8 \end{array}$$

Check:
$$\frac{5}{4}(8) - 1 \stackrel{?}{=} \frac{1}{4}(8) + 7$$
$$10 - 1 \stackrel{?}{=} 2 + 7$$
$$9 = 9$$

67.

$$\frac{9}{2}x - \frac{3}{4} = \frac{7}{2}x + \frac{5}{4}$$

$$\begin{array}{rcr} -\frac{7}{2}x & & -\frac{7}{2}x \\ \hline x - \frac{3}{4} = & & \frac{5}{4} \\ +\frac{3}{4} & & +\frac{3}{4} \\ \hline x & = & \frac{8}{4} \\ x & = & 2 \end{array}$$

Check:
$$\frac{9}{2}(2) - \frac{3}{4} \stackrel{?}{=} \frac{7}{2}(2) + \frac{5}{4}$$
$$9 - \frac{3}{4} \stackrel{?}{=} 7 + \frac{5}{4}$$
$$\frac{36}{4} - \frac{3}{4} \stackrel{?}{=} \frac{28}{4} + \frac{5}{4}$$
$$\frac{33}{4} = \frac{33}{4}$$

69. $5x - 7 = 4x - 12$

$\quad \underline{-4x \qquad -4x}$

$\quad x - 7 = -12$

(d) is equivalent to the equation.

71. $7x + 5 = 12x - 10$

$\quad \underline{+10 \qquad +10}$

$\quad 7x + 15 = 12x$

(d) is equivalent to the equation.

73. It is false that isolating the variable on the right side of the equation will result in a negative solution.

75. Writing exercise

Exercises 1.10

1. $5x = 20$

$\quad \dfrac{5x}{5} = \dfrac{20}{5}$

$\quad x = 4$

Check:

$\quad 5(4) \stackrel{?}{=} 20$

$\quad 20 = 20$

3. $9x = 54$

$\quad \dfrac{9x}{9} = \dfrac{54}{9}$

$\quad x = 6$

Check:

$\quad 9(6) \stackrel{?}{=} 54$

$\quad 54 = 54$

5. $63 = 9x$

$\quad \dfrac{63}{9} = \dfrac{9x}{9}$

$\quad 7 = x$

Check:

$\quad 63 \stackrel{?}{=} 9(7)$

$\quad 63 = 63$

7. $4x = -16$

$\quad \dfrac{4x}{4} = \dfrac{-16}{4}$

$\quad x = -4$

Check:

$\quad 4(-4) \stackrel{?}{=} -16$

$\quad -16 = -16$

9. $-9x = 72$

$\quad \dfrac{-9x}{-9} = \dfrac{72}{-9}$

$\quad x = -8$

Check:

$\quad -9(-8) \stackrel{?}{=} 72$

$\quad 72 = 72$

11. $6x = -54$

$\quad \dfrac{6x}{6} = \dfrac{-54}{6}$

$\quad x = -9$

Check:

$\quad 6(-9) \stackrel{?}{=} -54$

$\quad -54 = -54$

13. $-4x = -12$

$\quad \dfrac{-4x}{-4} = \dfrac{-12}{-4}$

$\quad x = 3$

Check:

$\quad -4(3) \stackrel{?}{=} -12$

$\quad -12 = -12$

15. $-42 = 6x$

$\quad \dfrac{-42}{6} = \dfrac{6x}{6}$

$\quad -7 = x$

Check:

$\quad -42 \stackrel{?}{=} 6(-7)$

$\quad -42 = -42$

17. $-6x = -54$

$\quad \dfrac{-6x}{-6} = \dfrac{-54}{-6}$

$\quad x = 9$

Check:

$\quad -6(9) \stackrel{?}{=} -54$

$\quad -54 = -54$

19. $\dfrac{x}{2} = 4$

$\quad 2\left(\dfrac{x}{2}\right) = 2 \cdot 4$

$\quad x = 8$

Check:

$\quad \dfrac{8}{2} \stackrel{?}{=} 4$

$\quad 4 = 4$

21. $\dfrac{x}{5} = 3$

$5\left(\dfrac{x}{5}\right) = 5 \cdot 3$

$x = 15$

Check:

$\dfrac{15}{3} \overset{?}{=} 3$

$3 = 3$

23. $6 = \dfrac{x}{7}$

$7 \cdot 6 = 7\left(\dfrac{x}{7}\right)$

$42 = x$

Check:

$6 \overset{?}{=} \dfrac{42}{7}$

$6 = 6$

25. $\dfrac{x}{5} = -4$

$5\left(\dfrac{x}{5}\right) = 5(-4)$

$x = -20$

Check:

$\dfrac{-20}{5} \overset{?}{=} -4$

$-4 = -4$

27. $-\dfrac{x}{3} = 8$

$-3\left(-\dfrac{x}{3}\right) = -3(8)$

$x = -24$

Check:

$-\dfrac{-24}{3} \overset{?}{=} 8$

$8 = 8$

29. $\dfrac{2}{3}x = 0.9$

$\dfrac{3}{2}\left(\dfrac{2}{3}x\right) = \dfrac{3}{2}(0.9)$

$x = 1.35$

Check:

$\dfrac{2}{3}(1.35) \overset{?}{=} 0.9$

$0.9 = 0.9$

31. $\dfrac{3}{4}x = -15$

$\dfrac{4}{3}\left(\dfrac{3}{4}x\right) = \dfrac{4}{3}(-15)$

$x = -20$

Check:

$\dfrac{3}{4}(-20) \overset{?}{=} -15$

$-15 = -15$

33. $-\dfrac{5}{6}x = -15$

$-\dfrac{6}{5}\left(-\dfrac{5}{6}x\right) = -\dfrac{6}{5}(-15)$

$x = 18$

Check:

$-\dfrac{5}{6}(18) \overset{?}{=} -15$

$-15 = -15$

35. $16x - 9x = -16.1$

$7x = -16.1$

$\dfrac{7x}{7} = \dfrac{-16.1}{7}$

$x = -2.3$

Check:

$16(-2.3) - 9(-2.3) \overset{?}{=} -16.1$

$-36.8 + 20.7 \overset{?}{=} -16.1$

$-16.1 = -16.1$

37. $3.2x = 12.8$

$\dfrac{3.2x}{3.2} = \dfrac{12.8}{3.2}$

$x = 4$

Check:

$3.2(4) \overset{?}{=} 12.8$

$12.8 = 12.8$

39. $-4.5x = 3.51$

$\dfrac{-4.5x}{-4.5} = \dfrac{3.51}{-4.5}$

$x = -0.78$

Check:

$-4.5(-0.78) \overset{?}{=} 3.51$

$3.51 = 3.51$

41. $1.3x + 2.8x = 12.3$

$$4.1x = 12.3$$

$$\frac{4.1x}{4.1} = \frac{12.3}{4.1}$$

$$x = 3$$

Check:

$$1.3(3) + 2.8(3) \overset{?}{=} 12.3$$

$$3.9 + 8.4 \overset{?}{=} 12.3$$

$$12.3 = 12.3$$

43. The numbers are already in ascending order.

2, 3, 4, 5, 6

The median is the middle value, 4.

To find the mean, first find $\sum x$.

$$\sum x = 2 + 3 + 4 + 5 + 6 = 20$$

$$\bar{x} = \frac{\sum x}{n} = \frac{20}{5} = 4$$

45. The numbers are already in ascending order.

−3, −1, 2, 4, 6, 10

The median is $\dfrac{2+4}{2} = \dfrac{6}{2} = 3$.

To find the mean, first find $\sum x$.

$$\sum x = -3 + (-1) + 2 + 4 + 6 + 10 = 18$$

$$\bar{x} = \frac{\sum x}{n} = \frac{18}{6} = 3$$

47. The numbers are already in ascending order.

$$-\frac{3}{2}, -1, 2, \frac{5}{2}, 3, 7$$

The median is $\dfrac{2 + \frac{5}{2}}{2} = \dfrac{\frac{9}{2}}{2} = \dfrac{9}{4}$.

To find the mean, first find $\sum x$.

$$\sum x = -\frac{3}{2} + (-1) + 2 + \frac{5}{2} + 3 + 7 = 12$$

$$\bar{x} = \frac{\sum x}{n} = \frac{12}{6} = 2$$

49. To find the median, first put the numbers in ascending order. 15, 16, 18, 21

The median is $\dfrac{16 + 18}{2} = 17$ oz.

To find the mean, first find $\sum x$.

$$\sum x = 15 + 16 + 18 + 21 = 70$$

$$\bar{x} = \frac{\sum x}{n} = \frac{70}{4} = 17.5 \text{ oz.}$$

Exercises 1.11

1. $3x + 2 = 14$

$$\underline{ -2 \quad -2}$$

$$3x \quad = 12$$

$$\frac{3x}{3} = \frac{12}{3}$$

$$x = 4$$

Check:

$$3(4) + 2 = 14?$$

$$12 + 2 = 14?$$

$$14 = 14$$

3. $3x - 2 = 7$

$$\underline{ +2 \quad +2}$$

$$3x = 9$$

$$\frac{3x}{3} = \frac{9}{3}$$

$$x = 3$$

Check:

$$3(3) - 2 = 7?$$

$$9 - 2 = 7?$$

$$7 = 7$$

5. $4x + 7 = 35$

$$\underline{ -7 \quad -7}$$

$$4x \quad = 28$$

$$\frac{4x}{4} = \frac{28}{4}$$

$$x = 7$$

Check:

$$4(7) + 7 = 35?$$

$$28 + 7 = 35?$$

$$35 = 35$$

7. $2x + 9 = 5$

$$\underline{ -9 \quad -9}$$

$$2x \quad = -4$$

$$\frac{2x}{2} = \frac{-4}{2}$$

$$x = -2$$

Check:

$$2(-2) + 9 = 5?$$

$$-4 + 9 = 5?$$

$$5 = 5$$

9.

$$4 - 7x = 18$$
$$\underline{-4 \qquad -4}$$
$$-7x = 14$$
$$\frac{-7x}{-7} = \frac{14}{-7}$$
$$x = -2$$

Check:
$$4 - 7(-2) = 18\,?$$
$$4 + 14 = 18\,?$$
$$18 = 18$$

11. $5 - 3x = 11$

$$\underline{-5 \qquad -5}$$
$$-3x = 6$$
$$\frac{-3x}{-3} = \frac{6}{-3}$$
$$x = -2$$

Check:
$$5 - 3(-2) = 11\,?$$
$$5 + 6 = 11\,?$$
$$11 = 11$$

13. $\dfrac{x}{2} + 1 = 5$

$$\underline{-1 \quad -1}$$
$$\frac{x}{2} = 4$$
$$2\left(\frac{x}{2}\right) = (2)4$$
$$x = 8$$

Check:
$$\frac{8}{2} + 1 = 5\,?$$
$$4 + 1 = 5\,?$$
$$5 = 5$$

15. $\dfrac{x}{5} - 3 = 4$

$$\underline{+3 \quad +3}$$
$$\frac{x}{5} \quad = 7$$
$$5\left(\frac{x}{5}\right) = 5(7)$$
$$x = 35$$

Check:
$$\frac{35}{5} - 3 = 4\,?$$
$$7 - 3 = 4\,?$$
$$4 = 4$$

17. $\dfrac{2}{3}x + 5 = 17$

$$\underline{-5 \quad -5}$$
$$\frac{2}{3}x = 12$$
$$\frac{3}{2}\left(\frac{2}{3}x\right) = \frac{3}{2}(12)$$
$$x = 18$$

Check:
$$\frac{2}{3}(18) + 5 = 17\,?$$
$$12 + 5 = 17\,?$$
$$17 = 17$$

19. $\dfrac{3}{4}x - 2 = 16$

$$\underline{+2 \quad +2}$$
$$\frac{3}{4}x \quad = 18$$
$$\frac{4}{3}\left(\frac{3}{4}x\right) = \frac{4}{3}(18)$$
$$x = 24$$

Check:
$$\frac{3}{4}(24) - 2 = 16\,?$$
$$18 - 2 = 16\,?$$
$$16 = 16$$

21.

$$5x = 2x + 9$$
$$\underline{-2x \quad -2x}$$
$$3x = \qquad 9$$
$$\frac{3x}{3} = \frac{9}{3}$$
$$x = 3$$

Check:
$$5(3) = 2(3) + 9\,?$$
$$15 = 6 + 9\,?$$
$$15 = 15$$

23.

$$3x = 10 - 2x$$
$$\underline{+2x \qquad +2x}$$
$$5x = 10$$
$$\frac{5x}{5} = \frac{10}{5}$$
$$x = 2$$

Check:
$$3(2) = 10 - 2(2)\,?$$
$$6 = 10 - 4\,?$$
$$6 = 6$$

25.
$$9x + 2 = 3x + 38$$
$$\underline{-3x \qquad -3x}$$
$$6x + 2 = \quad 38$$
$$\underline{\quad -2 \qquad -2}$$
$$6x \quad = \quad 36$$
$$\frac{6x}{6} = \frac{36}{6}$$
$$x = 6$$

Check:
$$9(6) + 2 = 3(6) + 38?$$
$$54 + 2 = 18 + 38?$$
$$56 = 56$$

27.
$$4x - 8 = x - 14$$
$$\underline{-x \qquad -x}$$
$$3x - 8 = \quad -14$$
$$\underline{\quad +8 \qquad +8}$$
$$3x \quad = \quad -6$$
$$\frac{3x}{3} = \frac{-6}{3}$$
$$x = -2$$

Check:
$$4(-2) - 8 = -2 - 14?$$
$$-8 - 8 = -2 - 14?$$
$$-16 = -16$$

29.
$$5x + 7 = 2x - 3$$
$$\underline{-2x \qquad -2x}$$
$$3x + 7 = \quad -3$$
$$\underline{\quad -7 \qquad -7}$$
$$3x \quad = \quad -10$$
$$\frac{3x}{3} = \frac{-10}{3}$$
$$x = -\frac{10}{3}$$

Check:
$$5\left(-\frac{10}{3}\right) + 7 = 2\left(-\frac{10}{3}\right) - 3?$$
$$-\frac{50}{3} + \frac{21}{3} = -\frac{20}{3} - \frac{9}{3}?$$
$$-\frac{29}{3} = -\frac{29}{3}$$

31.
$$7x - 3 = 9x + 5$$
$$\underline{-7x \qquad -7x}$$
$$-3 = 2x + 5$$
$$\underline{\quad -5 \qquad -5}$$
$$-8 = 2x$$
$$\frac{-8}{2} = \frac{2x}{2}$$
$$-4 = x$$

Check:
$$7(-4) - 3 = 9(-4) + 5?$$
$$-28 - 3 = -36 + 5?$$
$$-31 = -31$$

33.
$$5x + 4 = 7x - 8$$
$$\underline{-5x \qquad -5x}$$
$$4 = 2x - 8$$
$$\underline{\quad +8 \qquad +8}$$
$$12 = 2x$$
$$\frac{12}{2} = \frac{2x}{2}$$
$$x = 6$$

Check:
$$5(6) + 4 = 7(6) - 8?$$
$$30 + 4 = 42 - 8?$$
$$34 = 34$$

35.
$$2x - 3 + 5x = 7 + 4x + 2$$
$$7x - 3 = 9 + 4x$$
$$\underline{-4x \qquad -4x}$$
$$3x - 3 = 9$$
$$\underline{\quad +3 \quad +3}$$
$$3x \quad = 12$$
$$\frac{3x}{3} = \frac{12}{3}$$
$$x = 4$$

Check:
$$2(4) - 3 + 5(4) = 7 + 4(4) + 2?$$
$$8 - 3 + 20 = 7 + 16 + 2?$$
$$25 = 25$$

37.
$$6x + 7 - 4x = 8 + 7x - 26$$
$$2x + 7 = 7x - 18$$
$$\underline{-2x \qquad -2x}$$
$$7 = 5x - 18$$
$$\underline{+18 \qquad +18}$$
$$25 = 5x$$
$$\frac{25}{5} = \frac{5x}{5}$$
$$x = 5$$

Check:
$$6(5) + 7 - 4(5) = 8 + 7(5) - 26?$$
$$30 + 7 - 20 = 8 + 35 - 26?$$
$$17 = 17$$

39.
$$9x - 2 + 7x + 13 = 10x - 13$$
$$16x + 11 = 10x - 13$$
$$\underline{-10x \qquad -10x}$$
$$6x + 11 = -13$$
$$\underline{-11 \quad -11}$$
$$6x = -24$$
$$\frac{6x}{6} = \frac{-24}{6}$$
$$x = -4$$

Check:
$$9(-4) - 2 + 7(-4) + 13 = 10(-4) - 13?$$
$$-36 - 2 - 28 + 13 = -40 - 13?$$
$$-53 = -53$$

41.
$$2(x + 3) = 8$$
$$2x + 6 = 8$$
$$\underline{-6 \quad -6}$$
$$\frac{2x}{2} = \frac{2}{2}$$
$$x = 1$$

Check:
$$2 \; 1 + 6 = 8?$$
$$2 + 6 = 8?$$
$$8 = 8$$

43.
$$7(2x - 1) - 5x = x + 25$$
$$14x - 7 - 5x = x + 25$$
$$9x - 7 = x + 25$$
$$\underline{-x \qquad -x}$$
$$8x - 7 = 25$$
$$\underline{+7 \quad +7}$$
$$8x = 32$$
$$\frac{8x}{8} = \frac{32}{8}$$
$$x = 4$$

Check:
$$7(2 \cdot 4 - 1) - 5 \cdot 4 = 4 + 25?$$
$$49 - 20 = 29?$$
$$29 = 29$$

45.
$$3x + 2(4x - 3) = 6x - 9$$
$$3x + 8x - 6 = 6x - 9$$
$$11x - 6 = 6x - 9$$
$$\underline{-6x \qquad -6x}$$
$$5x - 6 = -9$$
$$\underline{+6 \qquad +6}$$
$$5x = -3$$
$$\frac{5x}{5} = \frac{-3}{5}$$
$$x = -\frac{3}{5}$$

Check:
$$3\left(-\frac{3}{5}\right) + 2\left[4\left(-\frac{3}{5}\right) - 3\right] = 6\left(-\frac{3}{5}\right) - 9?$$
$$-\frac{9}{5} + 2\left(-\frac{27}{5}\right) = -\frac{18}{5} - \frac{45}{5}?$$
$$-\frac{63}{5} = -\frac{63}{5}$$

47.
$$\frac{8}{3}x - 3 = \frac{2}{3}x + 15$$
$$\underline{+3 \qquad +3}$$
$$\frac{8}{3}x = \frac{2}{3}x + 18$$
$$\underline{-\frac{2}{3}x \qquad -\frac{2}{3}x}$$
$$\frac{6}{3}x = 18$$
$$2x = 18$$
$$\frac{2x}{2} = \frac{18}{2}$$
$$x = 9$$

Check:
$$\frac{8}{3}(9) - 3 = \frac{2}{3}(9) + 15?$$
$$24 - 3 = 6 + 15?$$
$$21 = 21$$

49.

$$\frac{2x}{5} - \frac{x}{3} = \frac{7}{15}$$

$$\frac{6x}{15} - \frac{5x}{15} = \frac{7}{15}$$

$$15\left(\frac{x}{15}\right) = (15)\frac{7}{15}$$

$$x = 7$$

Check:

$$\frac{2 \cdot 7}{5} - \frac{7}{3} = \frac{7}{15}?$$

$$\frac{14}{5} - \frac{7}{3} = \frac{7}{15}?$$

$$\frac{42}{15} - \frac{35}{15} = \frac{7}{15}?$$

$$\frac{7}{15} = \frac{7}{15}$$

51.

$$5.3x - 7 = 2.3x + 5$$
$$\underline{-2.3x \qquad -2.3x}$$
$$3x - 7 = \qquad 5$$
$$\underline{+7 \qquad\quad +7}$$
$$3x = \qquad 12$$
$$\frac{3x}{3} = \frac{12}{3}$$
$$x = 4$$

Check:

$$5.3(4) - 7 = 2.3(4) + 5?$$
$$21.2 - 7 = 9.2 + 5?$$
$$14.2 = 14.2$$

53.

$$\frac{5x - 3}{4} - 2 = \frac{x}{3}$$

$$12\left[\frac{5x - 3}{4} - 2 = \frac{x}{3}\right]$$

$$15x - 9 - 24 = 4x$$
$$15x - 33 = 4x$$
$$\underline{-4x \qquad\quad -4x}$$
$$11x - 33 = 0$$
$$\underline{+33 \quad +33}$$
$$\frac{11x}{11} = \frac{33}{11}$$
$$x = 3$$

Check:

$$\frac{5 \cdot 3 - 3}{4} - 2 = \frac{3}{3}?$$

$$\frac{12}{4} - 2 = 1?$$

$$3 - 2 = 1?$$

$$1 = 1$$

55.

$$5(x + 1) - 4x = x - 5$$
$$5x + 5 - 4x = x - 5$$
$$x + 5 = x - 5$$
$$\underline{-x \qquad\quad -x}$$
$$5 = \quad -5$$

The original equation has no solution.

57.

$$6x - 4x + 1 = 12 + 2x - 11$$
$$2x + 1 = \quad 2x + 1$$
$$\underline{-2x \qquad\quad -2x}$$
$$1 = \quad 1$$

The original equation is an identity.

59.

$$-4(x + 2) - 11 = 2(-2x - 3) - 13$$
$$-4x - 8 - 11 = -4x - 6 - 13$$
$$-4x - 19 = -4x - 19$$
$$\underline{+4x \qquad\qquad +4x}$$
$$-19 = \qquad -19$$

The original equation is an identity.

61. Answers may vary.
Possible answer:

$$x = 2$$
$$6x = 6 \cdot 2$$
$$6x = 12$$
$$6x + 5 = 12 + 5$$
$$6x + 5 = 17$$

63. Writing exercise

65.

$$x + 2x - 2 + x + 2 = 24$$
$$4x = 24$$
$$\frac{4x}{4} = \frac{24}{4}$$
$$x = 6$$
$$2x - 2 = 10$$
$$x + 2 = 8$$

The sides are 6 in., 8 in., and 10 in.

67.

$$3x - 1 + 3x + 2x - 1 + x + 2 = 90$$
$$9x = 90$$
$$\frac{9x}{9} = \frac{90}{9}$$
$$x = 10$$
$$3x - 1 = 29$$
$$3x = 30$$
$$2x - 1 = 19$$
$$x + 2 = 12$$

The sides are 29 in., 30 in., 19 in., and 12 in.

1. $\dfrac{x}{11} = \dfrac{12}{33}$

$33x = 132$

$x = 4$

3. $\dfrac{5}{8} = \dfrac{20}{x}$

$5x = 160$

$x = 32$

5. $\dfrac{4x}{5} = 8$

$\dfrac{4x}{5} = \dfrac{8}{1}$

$\dfrac{4x}{4} = \dfrac{40}{4}$

$x = 10$

7. $\dfrac{x}{5} = \dfrac{3}{15}$

$15x = 15$

$\dfrac{15x}{15} = \dfrac{15}{15}$

$x = 1$

9. $\dfrac{3}{x} = \dfrac{9}{12}$

$36 = 9x$

$9x = 36$

$\dfrac{9x}{9} = \dfrac{36}{9}$

$x = 4$

11. $\dfrac{3x}{4} = -6$

$3x = -24$

$\dfrac{3x}{3} = \dfrac{-24}{3}$

$x = -8$

13. $\dfrac{Dose\,1}{Dose\,2} = \dfrac{(Distance\,2)^2}{(Distance\,1)^2}$

$\dfrac{100\,mAs}{Dose\,2} = \dfrac{(10\,ft)^2}{(5\,ft)^2}$

$\dfrac{100\,mAs}{Dose\,2} = \dfrac{100\,ft^2}{25\,ft^2}$

$100 \cdot 25\,mAs\,ft^2 = 100\,ft^2 \cdot Dose\,2$

$2500\,mAs\,ft^2 = 100\,ft^2 \cdot Dose\,2$

$\dfrac{2500\,mAs\,ft^2}{100\,ft^2} = Dose\,2$

$25\,mAs = Dose\,2$

$Dose\,2 = 25\,mAs$

15. $\dfrac{Dosage\,ordered}{Units\,given} = \dfrac{known\,dosage}{known\,units}$

$\dfrac{200\,mg}{Units\,given} = \dfrac{1000\,mg}{5cc}$

$200\,mg \cdot 5cc = 1000\,mg \cdot Units\,given$

$1000\,mg\,cc = 1000\,mg \cdot Units\,given$

$\dfrac{1000\,mg\,cc}{1000\,mg} = Units\,given$

$1cc = Units\,given$

17. $\dfrac{Dosage\,ordered}{Units\,given} = \dfrac{known\,dosage}{known\,units}$

$\dfrac{5\,mg}{Units\,given} = \dfrac{2\,mg}{1\,ml}$ (2 mg/ml means 2 mg per 1 ml)

$5\,mg \cdot 1\,ml = 2mg \cdot Units\,given$

$5\,mg\,ml = 2mg \cdot Units\,given$

$\dfrac{5\,mg\,ml}{2\,mg} = Units\,given$

$2.5\,mg = Units\,given$

19. $\dfrac{Percentage\,increase}{100} = \dfrac{Grip\,strength\,increase}{Beginning\,grip\,strength}$

$\dfrac{Percentage\,increase}{100} = \dfrac{78\,pounds - 60\,pounds}{60\,pounds}$

$\dfrac{Percentage\,increase}{100} = \dfrac{18\,pounds}{60\,pounds}$

$60\,pounds \cdot Percentage\,increase = 100 \cdot 18\,pounds$

$60\,pounds \cdot Percentage\,increase = 1800\,pounds$

$Percentage\,increase = \dfrac{1800\,pounds}{60\,pounds}$

$Percentage\,increase = 30$ Since 30% is bigger than 20%, yes, you met your goal.

21. $\dfrac{18 \text{ tea bags}}{90 \text{ ¢}} = \dfrac{48 \text{ tea bags}}{x \text{ ¢}}$

$$18x = 432.0$$

$$x = 240$$

48 tea bags should cost 240¢ or $2.40.

24 cans will cost 1116¢ or $11.16.

23. $\dfrac{15 \text{ tape players}}{6 \text{ h}} = \dfrac{x \text{ tape players}}{40 \text{ h}}$

$$6x = 600$$

$$x = 100$$

Workers can complete 100 tape players in 40 h.

25. $\dfrac{3 \text{ yes votes}}{2 \text{ no votes}} = \dfrac{2880 \text{ yes votes}}{x \text{ no votes}}$

$$3x = 5760$$

$$x = 1920$$

1920 no votes were cast.

27. $\dfrac{5 \text{ in. wide}}{6 \text{ in. high}} = \dfrac{15 \text{ in. wide}}{x \text{ in. high}}$

$$5x = 90$$

$$x = 18$$

The height of enlargement will be 18 in. high.

29. $\dfrac{110 \text{ mi}}{5 \text{ gal}} = \dfrac{x \text{ mi}}{12 \text{ gal}}$

$$5x = 1320$$

$$x = 264$$

Christy can go 264 mi on 12 gal.

31. $\dfrac{165 \text{ mi}}{3 \text{ h}} = \dfrac{x \text{ mi}}{8 \text{ h}}$

$$3x = 1320$$

$$x = 440$$

The car will travel 440 mi in 8 h.

33. $\dfrac{3 \text{ teeth (sm gear)}}{7 \text{ teeth (lg gear)}} = \dfrac{15 \text{ teeth (sm gear)}}{x \text{ teeth (lg gear)}}$

$$3x = 105$$

$$x = 35$$

The larger gear has 35 teeth.

35. The scale on the map given is $\dfrac{1}{2}$ in. $= 40$ mi.

The measured distance from Harrisburg to Philadelphia is $1\dfrac{3}{8}$ in. $= \dfrac{11}{8}$ in. Use the fact that the ratio of inches (on the map) to miles remains the same.

$$\dfrac{\dfrac{1}{2} \text{ in.}}{40 \text{ mi}} = \dfrac{\dfrac{11}{8} \text{ in.}}{x \text{ mi}}$$

$$\dfrac{1}{2}x = 55$$

$$x = 110$$

The actual distance from Harrisburg to Philadelphia is approximately 110 mi.

37. The scale on the map given is $\dfrac{1}{2}$ in. $= 40$ mi.

The measured distance from Gettysburg to Meadville is $2\dfrac{11}{16}$ in. $= \dfrac{43}{16}$ in. Use the fact that the ratio of inches (on the map) to miles remains the same.

$$\dfrac{\dfrac{1}{2} \text{ in.}}{40 \text{ mi.}} = \dfrac{\dfrac{43}{16} \text{ in.}}{x \text{ mi}}$$

$$\dfrac{1}{2}x = \dfrac{1720}{12}$$

$$x = 215$$

The actual distance from Gettysburg to Meadville is 215 mi.

39. $\dfrac{30 \text{ defective}}{500 \text{ total}} = \dfrac{x \text{ defective}}{1200 \text{ total}}$

$$500x = 36,000$$

$$x = 72$$

Expect 72 defective parts in the shipment.

41. $\dfrac{212 \text{ yd}}{2 \text{ games}} = \dfrac{x \text{ yd}}{11 \text{ games}}$

$$2x = 2332$$

$$x = 1166$$

The football back should gain 1166 yards in the 11 game season.

43. $\dfrac{2 \text{ lb}}{2500 \text{ ft}^2} = \dfrac{x \text{ lb}}{8750 \text{ ft}^2}$

$$2500x = 17,500$$

$$x = 7$$

A 7-lb box of seed is needed for 8750 ft^2.

45. $\dfrac{9}{15} = \dfrac{x}{40}$

$$15x = 360$$

$$x = 24$$

The tree is 24 ft tall.

47. $\dfrac{\frac{1}{2} \text{ in.}}{50 \text{ mi}} = \dfrac{6 \text{ in.}}{x \text{ mi}}$

$$\frac{1}{2}x = 300$$

$$x = 600$$

The towns are 600 miles apart.

49. $\dfrac{\frac{5}{2} \text{ qt}}{5000 \text{ mi}} = \dfrac{x \text{ qt}}{7200 \text{ mi}}$

$$5000x = 18,000$$

$$x = 3.6$$

Expect 3.6 qt when driving 7200 mi.

51. $\dfrac{10.5 \text{ cm}}{35 \text{ g}} = \dfrac{15 \text{ cm}}{x \text{ g}}$

$$10.5x = 525$$

$$x = 50$$

The weight of the same piece of tubing that is 15 cm long is 50g.

53. $\dfrac{80}{5.20} = \dfrac{150}{x}$

$$80x = 780$$

$$x = 9.75$$

The sales tax on an item costing $150 will be $9.75.

$$3 \text{ days } = 72 \text{ h}$$

55. $\dfrac{2 \text{ min}}{6 \text{ h}} = \dfrac{x \text{ min}}{72 \text{ h}}$

$$6x = 144$$

$$x = 24$$

Your watch will gain 24 min in 3 days.

$$5 \text{ qt} = 160 \text{ oz}$$

57. $\dfrac{4 \text{ qt}}{160 \text{ oz}} = \dfrac{1 \text{ qt}}{x \text{ oz}}$

$$4x = 160$$

$$x = 40$$

To mix 1 cup of paste, 40 oz of water should be used.

59. $\dfrac{7}{10} = \dfrac{x}{115,000}$

$$10x = 805,000$$

$$x = 80,500$$

80,500 cars will have one person in them.

61. $\dfrac{x}{2} = \dfrac{6}{4}$

$$4x = 12$$

$$x = 3$$

63. $\dfrac{12}{8} = \dfrac{x}{4}$

$$8x = 48$$

$$x = 6$$

65. challenge exercise

Exercises 1.13

1. $|x| = 5$
$x = 5 \quad \text{or} \quad x = -5$
$\{-5, 5\}$

3. $|x| = 10$
$x = 10 \quad \text{or} \quad x = -10$
$\{-10, 10\}$

5. $|x| = -8$
No solution

7. $|x - 2| = 3$
$x - 2 = 3 \quad \text{or} \quad x - 2 = -3$
$x = 5 \qquad\qquad x = -1$
$\{-1, 5\}$

9. $|x + 6| = 0$
$x + 6 = 0$
$x = -6 \text{ or } \{-6\}$

11. $|3 - x| = 7$
$3 - x = 7 \quad \text{or} \quad 3 - x = -7$
$-x = 4 \qquad\qquad -x = -10$
$x = -4 \qquad\qquad x = 10$
$\{-4, 10\}$

13. $|2x - 3| = 9$
$2x - 3 = 9 \quad \text{or} \quad 2x - 3 = -9$
$2x = 12 \qquad\qquad 2x = -6$
$x = 6 \qquad\qquad x = -3$
$\{-3, 6\}$

15. $|5 - 4x| = 1$
$5 - 4x = 1 \quad \text{or} \quad 5 - 4x = -1$
$-4x = -4 \qquad\qquad -4x = -6$
$x = 1 \qquad\qquad x = \dfrac{3}{2}$
$\left\{1, \dfrac{3}{2}\right\}$

17. $\left|\dfrac{1}{2}x + 5\right| = 7$
$\dfrac{1}{2}x + 5 = 7 \quad \text{or} \quad \dfrac{1}{2}x + 5 = -7$
$x + 10 = 14 \qquad\qquad x + 10 = -14$
$x = 4 \qquad\qquad x = -24$
$\{-24, 4\}$

19. $\left|4 - \dfrac{3}{4}x\right| = 8$
$4 - \dfrac{3}{4}x = 8 \quad \text{or} \quad 4 - \dfrac{3}{4}x = -8$
$16 - 3x = 32 \qquad\qquad 16 - 3x = -32$
$-3x = 16 \qquad\qquad -3x = -48$
$x = -\dfrac{16}{3} \qquad\qquad x = 16$
$\left\{-\dfrac{16}{3}, 16\right\}$

21. $|3x + 1| = -2$
No solution

23. $|x| - 3 = 2$
$|x| = 5 \quad \text{or}$
$x = 5 \qquad\qquad x = -5$
$\{-5, 5\}$

25. $|x| + 4 = 12$
$\underline{-4 \quad -4}$
$|x| = 8$
$x = 8 \quad \text{or} \quad x = -8$
$\{-8, 8\}$

27. $|x| + 7 = -3$
$\underline{-7 \quad -7}$
$|x| = -10$
No solution

29. $|x - 2| + 3 = 5$
$|x - 2| = 2$
$x - 2 = 2 \quad \text{or} \quad x - 2 = -2$
$x = 4 \qquad\qquad x = 0$
$\{0, 4\}$

31. $|2x - 3| - 1 = 6$
$|2x - 3| = 7$
$2x - 3 = 7 \quad \text{or} \quad 2x - 3 = -7$
$2x = 10 \qquad\qquad 2x = -4$
$x = 5 \qquad\qquad x = -2$
$\{-2, 5\}$

33. $\left|\dfrac{1}{2}x + 2\right| - 3 = 5$

$\left|\dfrac{1}{2}x + 2\right| = 8$

$\dfrac{1}{2}x + 2 = 8$ or $\dfrac{1}{2}x + 2 = -8$

$x + 4 = 16$ $\qquad$ $x + 4 = -16$

$x = 12$ $\qquad\quad$ $x = -20$

$\{-20, 12\}$

35. $8 - |x - 4| = 5$

$-|x - 4| = -3$

$|x - 4| = 3$

$x - 4 = 3$ or $x - 4 = -3$

$x = 7$ $\qquad\quad$ $x = 1$

$\{1, 7\}$

37. $|3x - 2| + 4 = 3$

$|3x - 2| = -1$

No solution

39. $|2x - 1| = |x + 3|$

$2x - 1 = x + 3$ or $2x - 1 = -(x + 3)$

$x - 1 = 3$ $\qquad\qquad$ $3x - 1 = -3$

$x = 4$ $\qquad\qquad\quad$ $3x = -2$

$\qquad\qquad\qquad\qquad$ $x = -\dfrac{2}{3}$

$\left\{-\dfrac{2}{3}, 4\right\}$

41. $|5x - 2| = |2x + 4|$

$5x - 2 = 2x + 4$ or $5x - 2 = -(2x + 4)$

$5x = 2x + 6$ $\qquad\quad$ $5x - 2 = -2x - 4$

$3x = 6$ $\qquad\qquad\quad$ $5x = -2x - 2$

$x = 2$ $\qquad\qquad\quad$ $7x = -2$

$\qquad\qquad\qquad\qquad$ $x = -\dfrac{2}{7}$

$\left\{-\dfrac{2}{7}, 2\right\}$

43. $|x - 2| = |x + 1|$

$x - 2 = x + 1$ or $x - 2 = -(x + 1)$

$x = x + 3$ $\qquad\quad$ $x - 2 = -x - 1$

No solution $\qquad\quad$ $x = -x + 1$

$\qquad\qquad\qquad\qquad$ $2x = 1$

$\qquad\qquad\qquad\qquad$ $x = \dfrac{1}{2}$

$\left\{\dfrac{1}{2}\right\}$

45. $|2x - 5| = |2x - 3|$

$2x - 5 = 2x - 3$ or $2x - 5 = -(2x - 3)$

$2x = 2x + 2$ $\qquad\quad$ $2x - 5 = -2x + 3$

No solution $\qquad\qquad$ $2x = -2x + 8$

$\qquad\qquad\qquad\qquad$ $4x = 8$

$\qquad\qquad\qquad\qquad$ $x = 2$

$\{2\}$

47. $|x - 2| = |2 - x|$

$x - 2 = 2 - x$ or $x - 2 = -(2 - x)$

$x = 4 - x$ $\qquad\quad$ $x - 2 = -2 + x$

$2x = 4$ $\qquad\qquad\quad$ $0 = 0$

$x = 2$ $\qquad\qquad$ All real numbers

All real

numbers

49. $|x| < 5$

$-5 < x < 5$

$\{x | -5 < x < 5\}$

51. $|x| \geq 7$

$x \leq -7$ or $x \geq 7$

$\{x | x \leq -7 \text{ or } x \geq 7\}$

53. $|x - 4| > 2$

$x - 4 < -2$ or $x - 4 > 2$

$x < 2$ $\qquad\qquad$ $x > 6$

$\{x | x < 2 \text{ or } x > 6\}$

55. $|x+6| \leq 4$

$-4 \leq x+6 \leq 4$

$-10 \leq x \leq -2$

$\{x \mid -10 \leq x \leq -2\}$

57. $|3-x| > 5$

$3-x < -5 \ \text{ or } \ 3-x > 5$

$-x < -8 \qquad -x > 2$

$x > 8 \qquad x < -2$

$\{x \mid x < -2 \ \text{ or } \ x > 8\}$

59. $|x-7| < 0$

No solution

61. $|2x-5| < 3$

$-3 < 2x-5 < 3$

$2 < 2x < 8$

$1 < x < 4$

$\{x \mid 1 < x < 4\}$

63. $|3x+4| \geq 5$

$3x+4 \leq -5 \ \text{ or } \ 3x+4 \geq 5$

$3x \leq -9 \qquad 3x \geq 1$

$x \leq -3 \qquad x \geq \dfrac{1}{3}$

$\left\{x \mid x \leq -3 \ \text{ or } \ x \geq \dfrac{1}{3}\right\}$

65. $|5x-3| > 7$

$5x-3 < -7 \ \text{ or } \ 5x-3 > 7$

$5x < -4 \qquad 5x > 10$

$x < -\dfrac{4}{5} \qquad x > 2$

$\left\{x \mid x < -\dfrac{4}{5} \ \text{ or } \ x > 2\right\}$

67. $|2-3x| < 11$

$-11 < 2-3x < 11$

$-13 < -3x < 9$

$\dfrac{13}{3} > x > -3$

$-3 < x < \dfrac{13}{3}$

$\left\{x \mid -3 < x < \dfrac{13}{3}\right\}$

69. $|3-5x| \geq 7$

$3-5x \leq -7 \ \text{ or } \ 3-5x \geq 7$

$-5x \leq -10 \qquad -5x \geq 4$

$x \geq 2 \qquad x \leq -\dfrac{4}{5}$

$\left\{x \mid x \leq -\dfrac{4}{5} \ \text{ or } \ x \geq 2\right\}$

71. $\left|\dfrac{3}{4}x-5\right| < 7$

$-7 < \dfrac{3}{4}x-5 < 7$

$-28 < 3x-20 < 28$

$-8 < 3x < 48$

$-\dfrac{8}{3} < x < 16$

$\left\{x \mid -\dfrac{8}{3} < x < 16\right\}$

73. abs $(x+2)$

75. abs $(2*x-3)$

77. abs $(3*x+2)-4$

79. $2*$abs $(3*x-1)$

Exercises 1.14

1. $5 < 10$

3. $7 > -2$

5. $0 < 4$

7. $-2 > -5$

9. $x < 3$: x is less than 3

11. $x \geq -4$: x is greater than or equal to -4

13. $-5 \leq x$: -5 is less than or equal to x

15. $x > 2$

17. $x < 9$

19. $x > 1$

21. $x < 8$

23. $x > -5$

25. $x \ 9$

27. $x < 0$

29. $\begin{array}{rl} x - 7 & < 6 \\ +7 & +7 \\ \hline x & < 13 \end{array}$

31. $\begin{array}{rl} x + 8 & \geq 10 \\ -8 & -8 \\ \hline x & \geq 2 \end{array}$

33. $\begin{array}{rl} 5x & < 4x + 7 \\ -4x & -4x \\ \hline x & < \quad 7 \end{array}$

35. $\begin{array}{rl} 6x - 8 & \leq 5x \\ -5x & -5x \\ \hline x - 8 & \leq 0 \\ +8 & +8 \\ \hline x & \leq 8 \end{array}$

37. $\begin{array}{rl} 4x - 3 & \geq 3x + 5 \\ -3x & -3x \\ \hline x - 3 & \geq \quad 5 \\ +3 & +3 \\ \hline x & \geq \quad 8 \end{array}$

39. $\begin{array}{rl} 7x + 5 & < 6x - 4 \\ -6x & -6x \\ \hline x + 5 & < \quad -4 \\ -5 & -5 \\ \hline x & < \quad -9 \end{array}$

41. $3x \leq 9$

$\dfrac{3x}{3} \leq \dfrac{9}{3}$

$x \leq 3$

43. $5x > -35$

$\dfrac{5x}{5} > \dfrac{-35}{5}$

$x > -7$

45. $-6x \geq 18$

$\dfrac{-6x}{-6} \leq \dfrac{18}{-6}$

$x \leq -3$

47. $-10x < -60$

$\dfrac{-10x}{-10} > \dfrac{-60}{-10}$

$x > +6$

49.
$$\frac{x}{4} > 5$$
$$4\left(\frac{x}{4}\right) > 4(5)$$
$$x > 20$$

51.
$$-\frac{x}{2} \geq -3$$
$$-2\left(-\frac{x}{2}\right) \leq -2(-3)$$
$$x \leq 6$$

53.
$$\frac{2x}{3} < 6$$
$$\frac{3}{2}\left(\frac{2x}{3}\right) < \frac{3}{2}(6)$$
$$x < 9$$

55.
$$5x > 3x + 8$$
$$\underline{-3x \quad -3x}$$
$$2x > 8$$
$$\frac{2x}{2} > \frac{8}{2}$$
$$x > 4$$

57.
$$5x - 2 > 3x$$
$$\underline{-3x \qquad -3x}$$
$$2x - 2 > 0$$
$$\underline{+2 \quad +2}$$
$$2x \quad > 2$$
$$\frac{2x}{2} \quad > \frac{2}{2}$$
$$x \quad > 1$$

59.
$$3 - 2x > 5$$
$$\underline{-3 \qquad -3}$$
$$-2x > 2$$
$$\frac{-2x}{-2} < \frac{2}{-2}$$
$$x < -1$$

61.
$$2x \geq 5x + 18$$
$$\underline{-5x \quad -5x}$$
$$-3x \geq 18$$
$$\frac{-3x}{-3} \leq \frac{18}{-3}$$
$$x \leq -6$$

63.
$$5x - 3 \leq 3x + 15$$
$$\underline{-3x \qquad -3x}$$
$$2x - 3 \leq 15$$
$$\underline{+3 \qquad +3}$$
$$2x \quad \leq 18$$
$$\frac{2x}{2} \quad \leq \frac{18}{2}$$
$$x \quad \leq 9$$

65.
$$9x + 7 > 2x - 28$$
$$\underline{-2x \qquad -2x}$$
$$7x + 7 > -28$$
$$\underline{-7 \qquad -7}$$
$$7x \quad > -35$$
$$\frac{7x}{7} \quad > \frac{-35}{7}$$
$$x \quad > -5$$

67.
$$7x - 5 < 3x + 2$$
$$\underline{-3x \qquad -3x}$$
$$4x - 5 < 2$$
$$\underline{+5 \qquad +5}$$
$$4x \quad < 7$$
$$\frac{4x}{4} \quad < \frac{7}{4}$$
$$x \quad < \frac{7}{4}$$

69.
$$5x + 7 > 8x - 17$$
$$\underline{-8x \qquad -8x}$$
$$-3x + 7 > -17$$
$$\underline{-7 \qquad -7}$$
$$-3x \quad > -24$$
$$\frac{-3x}{-3} \quad < \frac{-24}{-3}$$
$$x \quad < 8$$

71.

$$3x - 2 \leq 5x + 3$$
$$\underline{-5x \qquad -5x}$$
$$-2x - 2 \leq \qquad 3$$
$$\underline{+2 \qquad +2}$$
$$-2x \quad \leq \qquad 5$$
$$\frac{-2x}{-2} \quad \geq \quad \frac{5}{-2}$$
$$x \quad \geq \quad -\frac{5}{2}$$

73.

$$4(x + 7) \leq 2x + 31$$
$$4x + 28 \leq 2x + 31$$
$$\underline{-2x \qquad -2x}$$
$$2x + 28 \leq \qquad 31$$
$$\underline{-28 \qquad -28}$$
$$2x \quad \leq \qquad 3$$
$$\frac{2x}{2} \quad \leq \quad \frac{3}{2}$$
$$x \quad \leq \quad \frac{3}{2}$$

75.

$$2(x - 7) > 5x - 12$$
$$2x - 14 > 5x - 12$$
$$\underline{-5x \qquad -5x}$$
$$-3x - 14 > \qquad -12$$
$$\underline{+14 \qquad +14}$$
$$-3x \quad > \qquad 2$$
$$\frac{-3x}{-3} \quad < \quad \frac{2}{-3}$$
$$x \quad < \quad -\frac{2}{3}$$

77. $x + 5 > 3$

79. $2x - 4 \leq 7$

81. $4x - 15 > x$

83. x is nonnegative: $x \geq 0$; choice a

85. x is no more than 5: $x \leq 5$; choice c

87. x is at least 5: $x \geq 5$; choice b

89. P = panda population
$P < 1000$

91. Let x be grade on fourth test.
$$\frac{72 + 81 + 79 + x}{4} \geq 80$$
$$232 + x \geq 320$$
$$x \geq 88$$
Liza must earn a grade of at least 88 on the last test.

93. Let x be amount of sales needed.
$$0.05x > 500$$
$$x > 10,000$$
She needs to sell more than $10,000 to make the 5% offer a better deal.

95. Let x be width.
$$2(105 + x) \leq 250$$
$$210 + 2x \leq 250$$
$$2x \leq 40$$
$$x \leq 20$$
The width is to be no greater than 20 cm.

97. Writing exercise

Section 1.15

1. An inequality is a sentence that expresses inequality between two algebraic expressions.

3. If a is less than b, then a lies to the left of b on the number line.

5. When you multiply or divide by a negative number, the inequality symbol is reversed.

7. False, $-3 > -9$.

9. True, because $0 < 8$.

11. True, because $-60 > -120$.

13. True, because $9 - (-3) = 12$.

15. Yes, because $2(-3) - 4 < 8$ simplifies to $-10 < 8$.

17. No, because $2(5) - 3 \leq 3(5) - 9$ simplifies to $7 \leq 6$.

19. No, because $5 - (-1) < 4 - 2(-1)$ simplifies to $6 < 6$.

21. Shade the numbers to the left of –1, including –1.

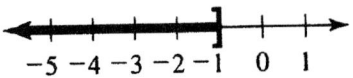

23. Shade numbers to the right of 20.

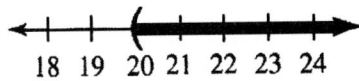

25. Since $3 \leq x$ is equivalent to $x \geq 3$, we shade the numbers to the right of 3, including 3.

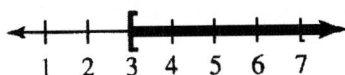

27. Shade to the left of 2.3.

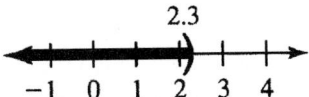

29. The set of all real numbers greater than 1 is expressed as $(1, \infty)$.

31. The set of all real numbers less than or equal to –3 is expressed as $(-\infty, -3]$.

33. The set of all real numbers less than 5 is expressed as $(-\infty, 5)$.

35. The set of all real numbers greater than or equal to –4 is expressed as $[-4, \infty)$.

37. $x + 5 > 12$ is equivalent to $x > 7$.

39. $-x < 6$ is equivalent to $x > -6$.

41. $-2x \geq 8$ is equivalent to $x \leq -4$.

43. $4 < x$ is equivalent to $x > 4$.

45. $7x > -14$
$\quad x > -2$
Solution set is $(-2, \infty)$.

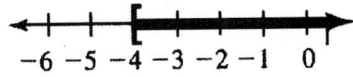

47. $-3x \leq 12$
$\quad x \geq -4$
Solution set is $[-4, \infty)$.

49. $2x - 3 > 7$
$\quad 2x > 10$
$\quad\quad x > 5$
Solution set is $(5, \infty)$.

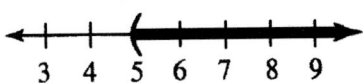

51. $3 - 5x \leq 18$
$\quad -5x \leq 15$
$\quad\quad x \geq -3$
Solution set is $[-3, \infty)$.

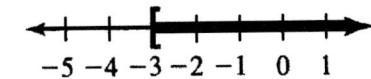

53. $\dfrac{x-3}{-5} < -2$
$\quad x - 3 > 10$
$\quad\quad x > 13$
Solution set is $(13, \infty)$.

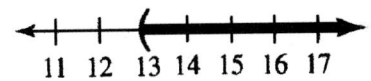

55. $\dfrac{5-3x}{4} \leq 2$
$\quad 5 - 3x \leq 8$
$\quad\quad -3x \leq 3$
$\quad\quad\quad x \geq -1$
Solution set is $[-1, \infty)$.

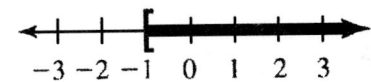

57. $4\left(3 - \dfrac{1}{4}x\right) \geq 4(2)$
$\quad 12 - x \geq 8$
$\quad\quad -x \geq -4$
$\quad\quad\quad x \leq 4$
Solution set is $(-\infty, 4]$.

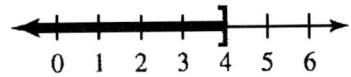

59. $12\left(\dfrac{1}{4}x - \dfrac{1}{2}\right) < 12\left(\dfrac{1}{2}x - \dfrac{2}{3}\right)$
$\quad 3x - 6 < 6x - 8$
$\quad\quad -3x < -2$
$\quad\quad\quad x > \dfrac{2}{3}$
Solution set is $(2/3, \infty)$.

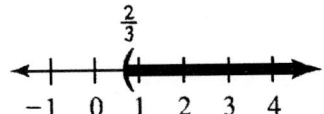

61. $4 \cdot \dfrac{y-3}{2} > 4 \cdot \dfrac{1}{2} - 4 \cdot \dfrac{y-5}{4}$

$\qquad 2y - 6 > 2 - y + 5$

$\qquad\qquad 3y > 14$

$\qquad\qquad\ \ y > \dfrac{13}{3}$

Solution set is $(13/3, \infty)$.

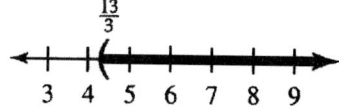

63. $2x + 3 > 2x - 8$

$\qquad\ \ 3 > -8$

Solution set is $(-\infty, \infty)$.

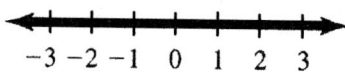

65. $-8x + 20 \le 12 - 8x$

$\qquad\quad 20 < 12$

Solution set is $\varnothing$.

67. $-\dfrac{1}{2}x + 3 < \dfrac{1}{2}x + 2$

$\qquad\quad -x < -1$

$\qquad\quad\ \ x > 1$

Solution set is $(1, \infty)$.

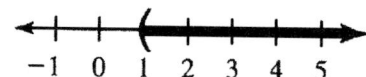

69. $4.273 + 2.8x \le 10.985$

$\qquad\quad\ 2.8x \le 6.712$

$\qquad\qquad x \le 2.397$

Solution set is $(-\infty, 2.397)$.

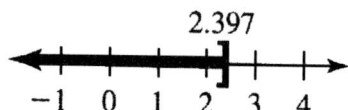

71. $3.25x - 27.39 > 4.06 + 5.1x$

$\qquad\quad -1.85x > 31.45$

$\qquad\qquad\ x < -17$

Solution set is $(-\infty, -17)$.

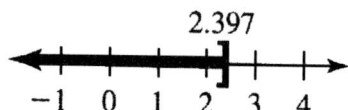

73. If x = Tony's height, then $x > 6$.

75. If s = Wilma's salary, then $s < 80{,}000$.

77. If v = speed of the Concorde, then $v \le 1450$.

79. If a = amount Julie can afford, then $a \le 400$.

81. If b = Burt's height, then $b \le 5$.

83. If t = Tina's hourly wage, then $t \le 8.20$.

85. Let x = the price of the car and $0.08x$ = the amount of tax. To spend less than \$10,000 we must satisfy the inequality

$\qquad x + 0.08x + 172 < 10{,}000$

$\qquad\qquad 1.08x < 9828$

$\qquad\qquad\quad x < 9100$

The price range for the car is $x < \$9{,}100$.

87. Let x = the price of the truck and $0.09x$ = the amount of sales tax. The total cost is at least \$10,000 and is expressed as

$\qquad x + 0.09x + 80 \ge 10{,}000$

$\qquad\qquad 1.09x \ge 9920$

$\qquad\qquad\quad x \ge 9100.9174$

The price range for the truck is $x \ge \$9{,}100.92$.

89. Let x = the number of daily miles. The daily cost at Beta is $35 + 0.25x$. For Beta to be cheaper we must have

$\qquad 35 + 0.25x < 45$

$\qquad\quad\ 0.25x < 10$

$\qquad\qquad\ \ x < 40.$

Beta is cheaper when x is in the interval $[0, 40)$.

91. a) Increasing

b) $16.45n + 980.20 > 1{,}300$

$\qquad\ 16.45n > 319.8$

$\qquad\qquad\ n > 19.44$

Since n is a whole number, the first value of n greater than 19.44 is 20. Bachelor's degrees will exceed 1.3 million in the year $1985 + 20$, or 2005.

93. Let x = the final exam score. One-third of the midterm plus two-thirds of the final must be at least 70:

$$\dfrac{1}{3}(56) + \dfrac{2}{3}x \ge 70$$

$$3\left(\dfrac{1}{3}(56) + \dfrac{2}{3}x\right) \ge 3(70)$$

$$56 + 2x \ge 210$$

$$2x \ge 154$$

$$x \ge 77$$

The final exam score must satisfy $x \ge 77$.

Exercises 1.16

1. $x^5 \cdot x^7 = x^{5+7} = x^{12}$

3. $5 \cdot 5^5 = 5^1 \cdot 5^5 = 5^{1+5} = 5^6$

5. $a^9 \cdot a = a^9 \cdot a^1 = a^{9+1} = a^{10}$

7. $z^{10} \cdot z^3 = z^{10+3} = z^{13}$

9. $p^5 \cdot p^7 = p^{5+7} = p^{12}$

11. $x^3 y \cdot x^2 y^4 = x^{3+2} y^{1+4} = x^5 y^5$

13. $w^5 \cdot w^2 \cdot w = w^{5+2+1} = w^8$

15. $m^3 \cdot m^2 \cdot m^4 = m^{3+2+4} = m^9$

17. $a^3 b \cdot a^2 b^2 \cdot ab^3 = a^{3+2+1} b^{1+2+3} = a^6 b^6$

19. $p^2 q \cdot p^3 q^5 \cdot pq^4 = p^{2+3+1} q^{1+5+4}$
$\qquad = p^6 q^{10}$

21. $3a^6 \cdot 2a^3 = (3 \cdot 2)(a^6 \cdot a^3)$
$\qquad = 6a^9$

23. $x^2 \cdot 3x^5 = (1 \cdot 3)(x^2 \cdot x^5)$
$\qquad = 3x^7$

25. $5m^3 n^2 \cdot 4mn^3 = (5 \cdot 4)(m^3 \cdot m)(n^2 \cdot n^3)$
$\qquad = 20m^4 n^5$

27. $6x^3 y \cdot 9xy^5 = (6 \cdot 9)(x^3 \cdot x)(y \cdot y^5)$
$\qquad = 54x^4 y^6$

29. $2a^2 \cdot a^3 \cdot 3a^7 = (2 \cdot 1 \cdot 3)(a^2 \cdot a^3 \cdot a^7)$
$\qquad = 6a^{12}$

31. $3c^2 d \cdot 4cd^3 \cdot 2c^5 d = (3 \cdot 4 \cdot 2)(c^2 \cdot c \cdot c^5)(d \cdot d^3 \cdot d)$
$\qquad = 24c^8 d^5$

33. $5m^2 \cdot m^3 \cdot 2m \cdot 3m^4$
$\qquad = (5 \cdot 1 \cdot 2 \cdot 3)(m^2 \cdot m^3 \cdot m \cdot m^4)$
$\qquad = 30m^{10}$

35. $2r^3 s \cdot rs^2 \cdot 3r^2 s \cdot 5rs$
$\qquad = (2 \cdot 1 \cdot 3 \cdot 5)(r^3 \cdot r \cdot r^2 \cdot r)(s \cdot s^2 \cdot s \cdot s)$
$\qquad = 30r^7 s^5$

37. $\dfrac{a^9}{a^6} = a^{9-6} = a^3$

39. $\dfrac{y^{10}}{y^4} = y^{10-4} = y^6$

41. $\dfrac{p^{15}}{p^{10}} = p^{15-10} = p^5$

43. $\dfrac{x^5 y^3}{x^2 y^2} = x^{5-2} \cdot y^{3-2} = x^3 y$

45. $\dfrac{6m^3}{3m} = 2m^{3-1} = 2m^2$

47. $\dfrac{24a^7}{6a^4} = 4a^{7-4} = 4a^3$

49. $\dfrac{26m^8 n}{13m^6} = 2m^{8-6} \cdot n = 2m^2 n$

51. $\dfrac{28w^3 z^5}{7wz} = 4w^{3-1} \cdot z^{5-1}$
$\qquad = 4w^2 z^4$

53. $\dfrac{18x^3 y^4 z^5}{9xy^2 z^2} = 2x^{3-1} \cdot y^{4-2} \cdot z^{5-2}$
$\qquad = 2x^2 y^2 z^3$

55. $2a^3 b \cdot 3a^2 b = (2 \cdot 3)(a^3 \cdot a^2)(b \cdot b)$
$\qquad = 6a^5 b^2$

57. $2a^3 b + 3a^2 b$ cannot be simplified.
The bases are not the same.

59. $2x^2 y^3 \cdot 3x^2 y^3 = (2 \cdot 3)(x^2 \cdot x^2)(y^3 \cdot y^3)$
$\qquad = 6x^4 y^6$

61. $2x^2 y^3 + 3x^2 y^3 = (2+3)x^2 y^3$
$\qquad = 5x^2 y^3$

63. $\dfrac{8a^2 b \cdot 6a^2 b}{2ab} = \dfrac{(8 \cdot 6)a^{2+2} b^{1+1}}{2ab}$
$\qquad = \dfrac{48a^4 b^2}{2ab}$
$\qquad = 24a^{4-1} \cdot b^{2-1}$
$\qquad = 24a^3 b$

65. $\dfrac{8a^2b+6a^2b}{2ab} = \dfrac{(8+6)a^2b}{2ab}$

$\qquad = \dfrac{14a^2b}{2ab}$

$\qquad = 7a^{2-1}b^{1-1}$

$\qquad = 7a^1b^0$

$\qquad = 7a$

67. Writing exercise

69. Writing exercise

Section 1.17

1. $(x^2)^3 = x^{2\cdot3} = x^6$

3. $(m^4)^4 = m^{4\cdot4} = m^{16}$

5. $(2^4)^2 = 2^{4\cdot2} = 2^8$

7. $(5^3)^5 = 5^{3\cdot5} = 5^{15}$

9. $(3x)^3 = 3^3 \cdot x^3 = 27x^3$

11. $(2xy)^4 = 2^4 \cdot x^4 \cdot y^4 = 16x^4y^4$

13. $5(3ab)^3 = 5\cdot3^3\cdot(ab)^3 = 135a^3b^3$

15. $\left(\dfrac{3}{4}\right)^2 = \dfrac{3^2}{4^2} = \dfrac{9}{16}$

17. $\left(\dfrac{x}{5}\right)^3 = \dfrac{x^3}{5^3} = \dfrac{x^3}{125}$

19. $(2x^2)^4 = 2^4 \cdot (x^2)^4 = 16x^8$

21. $(a^8b^6)^2 = (a^8)^2 \cdot (b^6)^2 = a^{16}b^{12}$

23. $(4x^2y)^3 = 4^3 \cdot (x^2)^3 y^3 = 64x^6y^3$

25. $(3m^2)^4(m^3)^2 = 81m^8 \cdot m^6 = 81m^{14}$

27. $\dfrac{(x^4)^3}{x^2} = \dfrac{x^{12}}{x^2} = x^{10}$

29. $\dfrac{(s^3)^2(s^2)^3}{(s^5)^2} = \dfrac{s^6\cdot s^6}{s^{10}} = \dfrac{s^{12}}{s^{10}} = s^2$

31. $\left(\dfrac{m^3}{n^2}\right)^3 = \dfrac{(m^3)^3}{(n^2)^3} = \dfrac{m^9}{n^6}$

33. $\left(\dfrac{a^3b^2}{c^4}\right)^2 = \dfrac{(a^3)^2(b^2)^2}{(c^4)^2} = \dfrac{a^6b^4}{c^8}$

35. Polynomial (with a single term)

37. Polynomial

39. Polynomial (with a single term)

41. Not a polynomial because $\dfrac{3+x}{x^2}$ is not a term.

43. Terms: $2x^2$, $-3x$
Coefficients: 2, –3

45. Terms: $4x^3$, $-3x$, 2
Coefficients: 4, –3, 2

47. Binomial because there are two terms

49. Trinomial because there are three terms

51. Not classified

53. Monomial because there is one term

55. Not a polynomial because $\dfrac{3}{x^2}$ is not a term

57. $4x^5 - 3x^2$: 5th degree

59. $-5x^9 + 7x^7 + 4x^3$: 9th degree

61. $4x$: 1st degree

63. $x^6 - 3x^5 + 5x^2 - 7$: 6th degree

65. $x = 1$: $6x + 1 = 6(1) + 1 = 7$
$x = -1$: $6x + 1 = 6(-1) + 1 = -5$

67. $x = 2$: $x^3 - 2x = (2)^3 - 2(2) = 4$
$x = -2$: $x^3 - 2x = (-2)^3 - 2(-2) = -4$

69. $x = 4$: $3x^2 + 4x - 2 = 3(4)^2 + 4(4) - 2$
$$= 48 + 16 - 2$$
$$= 62$$
$x = -4$: $3x^2 + 4x - 2 = 3(-4)^2 + 4(-4) - 2$
$$= 48 - 16 - 2$$
$$= 30$$

71. $x = 1$: $-x^2 - 2x + 3 = -(1)^2 - 2(1) + 3$
$$= -1 - 2 + 3$$
$$= 0$$
$x = -3$: $-x^2 - 2x + 3 = -(-3)^2 - 2(-3) + 3$
$$= -9 + 6 + 3$$
$$= 0$$

73. Always true

75. Sometimes true; The degree of $x^2 + 2x + 1$ is 2 but the degree of $x^3 + x + 1$ is 3.

77. Sometimes true; A polynomial can have any number of terms.

79. $x^{12} = (x^2)^6$

81. $a^{16} = (a^2)^8$

83. $2^{12} = (2^3)^4 = 8^4$
$2^{18} = (2^3)^6 = 8^6$
$(2^5)^3 = (2^3)^5 = 8^5$
$(2^7)^6 = (2^6)^7 = [(2^3)^2]^7 = (8^2)^7 = 8^{14}$

85. $-8x^6 y^9 z^{15} = (-2x^2 y^3 x^5)^3$

87. a. $105 = 35 \cdot 3$ so there are three doublings and $[(1.02)^{35}]^3 = (1.02)^{105} \approx 8$. The population will be 8 times as large.

  b. $3.8 \cdot 8 = 30.4$. Their population will be 30.4 billion.

89. Writing exercise

91. $P(1) = (1)^3 - 2(1)^2 + 5 = 4$

93. $Q(2) = 2(2)^2 + 3 = 11$

95. $P(3) = (3)^3 - 2(3)^2 + 5 = 14$

97. $P(0) = (0)^3 - 2(0)^2 + 5 = 5$

99. $P(2) + Q(-1) = [(2)^3 - 2(2)^2 + 5] + [2(-1)^2 + 3]$
$$= 5 + 5$$
$$= 10$$

101. $P(3) - Q(-3) \div Q(0)$
$$= [(3)^3 - 2(3)^2 + 5] - \{[2(-3)^2 + 3] \div [2(0)^2 + 3]\}$$
$$= 14 - (21 \div 3)$$
$$= 7$$

103. $|Q(4)| - |P(4)| = |2(4)^2 + 3| - |(4)^3 - 2(4)^2 + 5|$
$$= |35| - |37|$$
$$= -2$$

105. Cost $= 3y + 20$; $3(50) + 20 = 170$. The cost of typing 50 pages is \$170.

107. Revenue $= 3(12)^2 - 95 = 337$. The revenue is \$337. The average revenue per pair of shoes is $\frac{337}{12} = \$28.08$.

109. Writing exercise

Section 1.18

1. $4^0 = 1$

3. $(-29)^0 = 1$

5. $(x^3 y^2)^0 = 1$

7. $11x^0 = 11 \cdot 1 = 11$

9. $(-3p^6 q^8)^0 = 1$

11. $b^{-8} = \frac{1}{b^8}$

13. $3^{-4} = \frac{1}{3^4} = \frac{1}{81}$

15. $5^{-2} = \frac{1}{5^2} = \frac{1}{25}$

17. $10^{-4} = \frac{1}{10^4} = \frac{1}{10,000}$

19. $5x^{-1} = \frac{5}{x}$

21. $(5x)^{-1} = \dfrac{1}{5x}$

23. $-2x^{-5} = -2 \cdot \dfrac{1}{x^5} = -\dfrac{2}{x^5}$

25. $(-2x)^{-5} = \dfrac{1}{(-2x)^5} = -\dfrac{1}{32x^5}$

27. $a^5 a^3 = a^{5+3} = a^8$

29. $x^8 x^{-2} = x^{8+(-2)} = x^6$

31. $b^7 b^{-11} = b^{-4} = \dfrac{1}{b^4}$

33. $x^0 x^5 = 1 \cdot x^5 = x^5$

35. $\dfrac{a^8}{a^5} = a^{8-5} = a^3$

37. $\dfrac{x^7}{x^9} = x^{7-9} = x^{-2} = \dfrac{1}{x^2}$

39. $\dfrac{r^{-3}}{r^5} = r^{-3} r^{-5} = r^{-8} = \dfrac{1}{r^8}$

41. $\dfrac{x^{-4}}{x^{-5}} = x^{-4} x^5 = x$

43. $\dfrac{m^5 n^{-3}}{m^{-4} n^5} = m^{5-(-4)} n^{(-3-5)} = m^9 n^{-8} = \dfrac{m^9}{n^8}$

45. $(2a^{-3})^4 = 16a^{-12} = \dfrac{16}{a^{12}}$

47. $(x^{-2} y^3)^{-2} = x^4 y^{-6} = \dfrac{x^4}{y^6}$

49. $\dfrac{(r^{-2})^3}{r^{-4}} = \dfrac{r^{-6}}{r^{-4}} = r^{-6-(-4)} = r^{-2} = \dfrac{1}{r^2}$

51. $\dfrac{(x^{-3})^3}{(x^4)^{-2}} = \dfrac{x^{-9}}{x^{-8}} = x^{-9-(-8)} = x^{-1} = \dfrac{1}{x}$

53. $\dfrac{(a^{-3})^2 (a^4)}{(a^{-3})^{-3}} = \dfrac{a^{-2}}{a^9} = a^{-2-9} = a^{-11} = \dfrac{1}{a^{11}}$

55. $93{,}000{,}000 = 9.3 \times 10^7 \, \text{mi}$

57. $130{,}000{,}000{,}000 = 1.3 \times 10^{11} \text{cm}$

59. $30 - 2 = 28$ zeros

61. $8 \times 10^{-3} = 0.008$

63. $2.8 \times 10^{-5} = 0.000028$

65. $0.0005 = 5 \times 10^{-4}$

67. $0.00037 = 3.7 \times 10^{-4}$

69. $(4 \times 10^{-3})(2 \times 10^{-5}) = 4 \times 2 \times 10^{-3} \times 10^{-5}$
$\qquad\qquad = 8 \times 10^{-8}$

71. $\dfrac{9 \times 10^3}{3 \times 10^{-2}} = \dfrac{9}{3} \times 10^3 \times 10^2 = 3 \times 10^5$

73. $(2 \times 10^5)(4 \times 10^4) = 2 \times 4 \times 10^5 \times 10^4$
$\qquad\qquad = 8 \times 10^9$

75. $\dfrac{6 \times 10^9}{3 \times 10^7} = \left(\dfrac{6}{3}\right) \times 10^9 \times 10^{-7} = 2 \times 10^2$

77. $\dfrac{(3.3 \times 10^{15})(6 \times 10^{15})}{(1.1 \times 10^8)(3 \times 10^6)}$
$= \left(\dfrac{3.3}{1.1}\right) \times 10^{15} \times 10^{-8} \cdot \left(\dfrac{6}{3}\right) \times 10^{15} \times 10^{-6}$
$= 3 \times 10^7 \cdot 2 \times 10^9$
$= 6 \times 10^{16}$

79. $P = 4 \times 2^{(1960-1975)/35} \approx 2.97$. Earth's population in 1960 was approximately 2.97 billion.

81. $P = 250 \times 2^{(1960-1990)/66} \approx 182.44$. The U.S. population in 1960 was approximately 182 million.

83. $\left(6.6 \times 10^{17} \text{m}\right)\left(\dfrac{1 \text{ year}}{1 \times 10^{16} \text{m}}\right) = 6.6 \times 10^{17} \times 10^{-16}$
$\qquad\qquad\qquad\qquad = 6.6 \times 10^1$
$\qquad\qquad\qquad\qquad = 66 \text{ years}$

85. $15{,}500 \times 10^{19} = 1.55 \times 10^{23}$ L of water on Earth
$\dfrac{1.55 \times 10^{23}}{6 \times 10^9} \approx (0.2583) \times 10^{23} \times 10^{-9}$
$\qquad\qquad \approx 0.258 \times 10^{14}$
$\qquad\qquad = 2.58 \times 10^{13}$ L per person

87. $\left(\dfrac{2.6 \times 10^6 \, \text{L}}{\text{person}}\right)(3.2 \times 10^8 \text{ people}) = 8.32 \times 10^{14}$ L

Chapter 2 An Introduction to Graphing

Exercises 2.1

In exercises 1–9, count left or right for the
x coordinate, up or down for the *y* coordinate.

  1. *A*(5, 6)

  3. *C*(2, 0)

  5. *E*(–4, –5)

  7. *S*(–5, –3)

  9. *U*(–3, 5)

11–15.

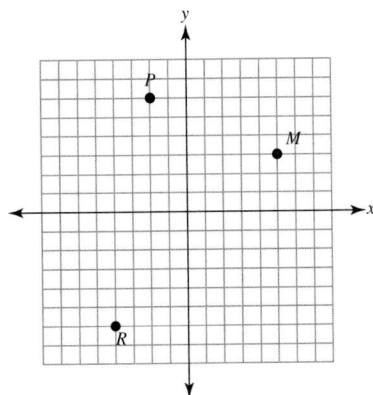

17–21.

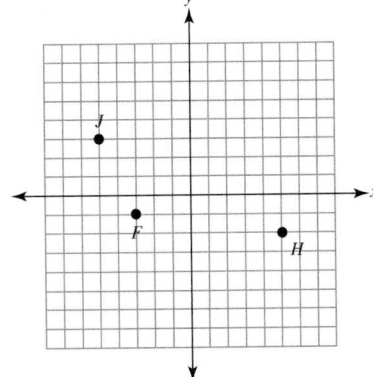

23. The points lie on a line; another point on the line
is the point (1, 2).

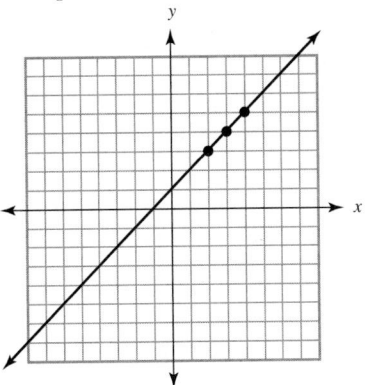

25. The points lie on a line; another point on the line
is the point (2, –6).

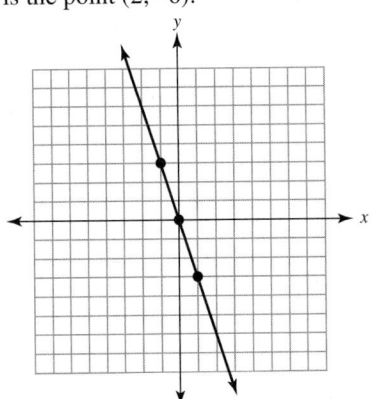

27. **(a)–(c)**
    The ordered pairs are *A*(1500, 350), *B*(2300,
    430), and *C*(1200, 320).

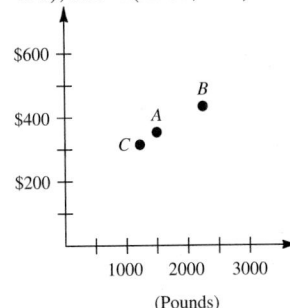

29. The ordered pairs are (1, 4), (2, 14), (3, 26), (4, 33), (5, 42), and (6, 51).

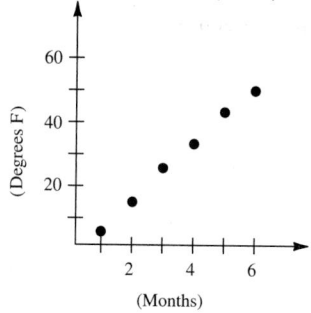

31. The ordered pairs are (1, 4), (2, 7), (3, 6), and (4, 4).

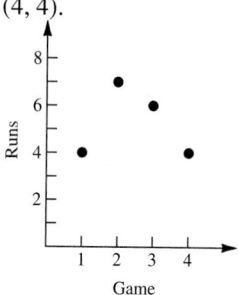

33. Writing exercise

35. **(a)** White Swan: A7; Newport: F2; Wheeler: C2
   (b) A2: Oysterville; F4: Sweet Home; A5: Mineral

Exercises 2.2

1. $x + y = 6$
   Two solutions are (0, 6) and (6, 0). The graph is the line through both points.

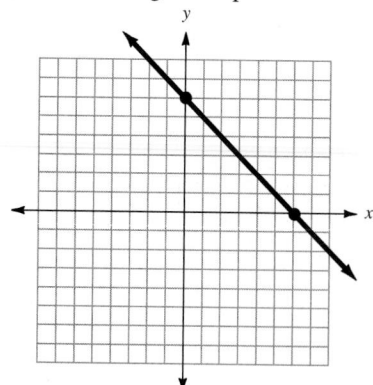

3. $x - y = -3$
   Two solutions are (−3, 0) and (0, 3). The graph is the line through both points.

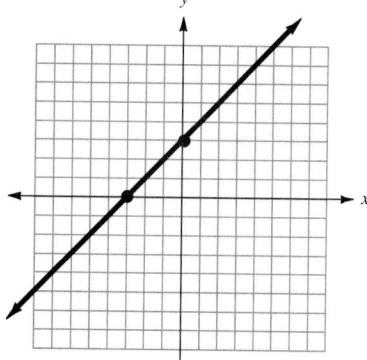

5. $2x + y = 2$
   Two solutions are (0, 2) and (1, 0). The graph is the line through both points.

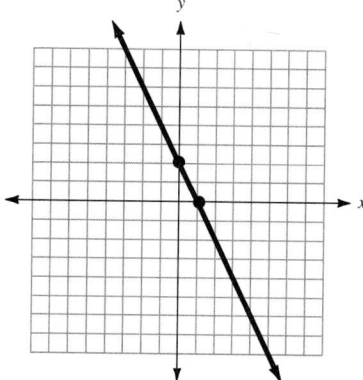

7. $3x + y = 0$
   Two solutions are (0, 0) and (1, −3). The graph is the line through both points.

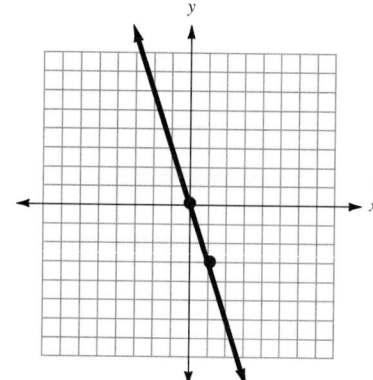

9. $x + 4y = 8$

Two solutions are $(0, 2)$ and $(4, 1)$. The graph is the line through both points.

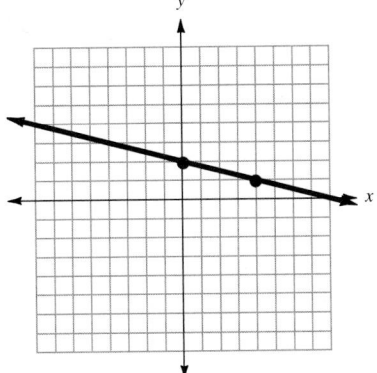

11. $y = 5x$

Two solutions are $(0, 0)$ and $(1, 5)$. The graph is the line through both points.

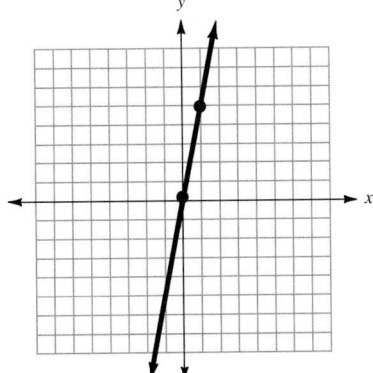

13. $y = 2x - 1$

Two solutions are $(0, -1)$ and $(3, 5)$. The graph is the line through both points.

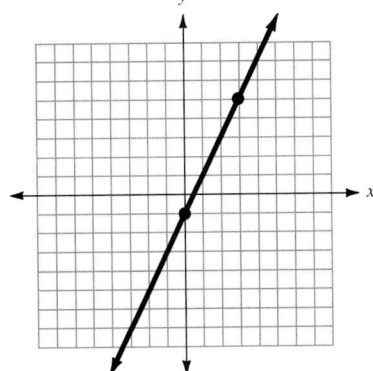

15. $y = -3x + 1$

Two solutions are $(0, 1)$ and $(2, -5)$. The graph is the line through both points.

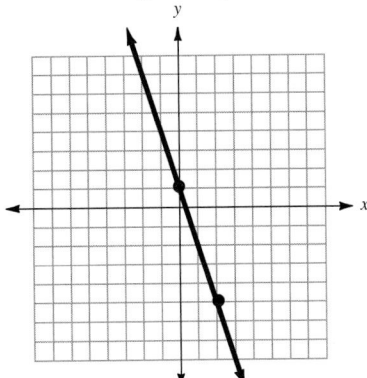

17. $y = \dfrac{1}{3}x$

Two solutions are $(0, 0)$ and $(3, 1)$. The graph is the line through both points.

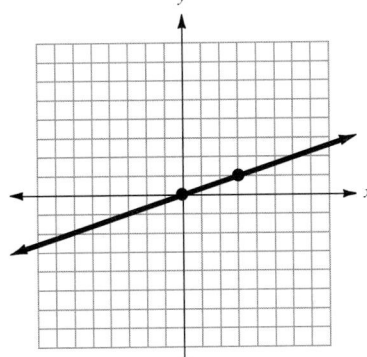

19. $y = \dfrac{2}{3}x - 3$

Two solutions are $(0, -3)$ and $(6, 1)$. The graph is the line through both points.

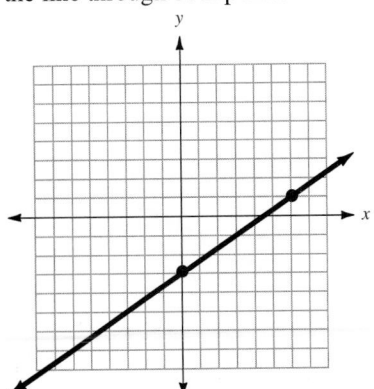

21. $x = 5$

Two solutions are (5, 0) and (5, 6). The graph is the line through both points.

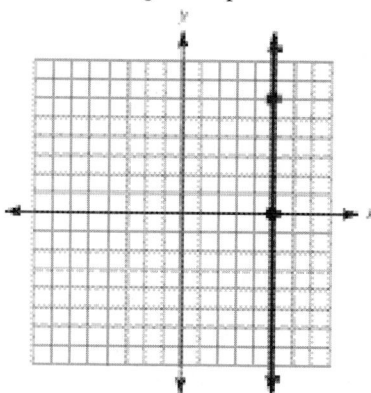

23. $y = 1$

Two solutions are (0, 1) and (4, 1). The graph is the line through both points.

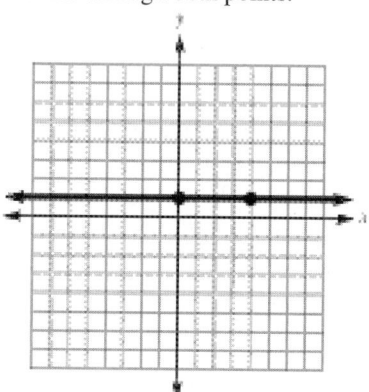

25. $x - 2y = 4$

$0 - 2y = 4 \qquad x - 2(0) = 4$

$-2y = 4 \qquad\quad x - 0 = 4$

$y = -2 \qquad\qquad x = 4$

$(0, -2) \qquad\quad (4, 0)$

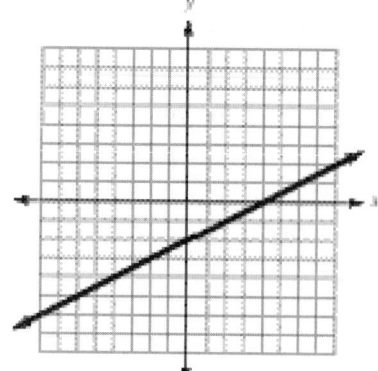

27. $5x + 2y = 10$

$5(0) + 2y = 10 \qquad 5x + 2(0) = 10$

$2y = 10 \qquad\qquad 5x = 10$

$y = 5 \qquad\qquad\quad x = 2$

$(0, 5) \qquad\qquad (2, 0)$

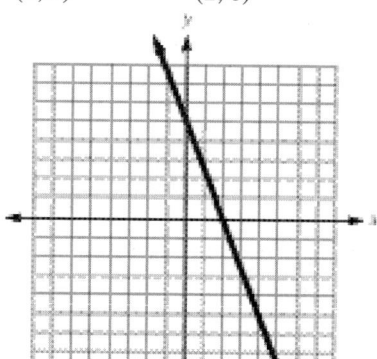

29. $3x + 5y = 15$

$3(0) + 5y = 15 \qquad 3x + 5(0) = 15$

$5y = 15 \qquad\qquad 3x = 15$

$y = 3 \qquad\qquad\quad x = 5$

$(0, 3) \qquad\qquad (5, 0)$

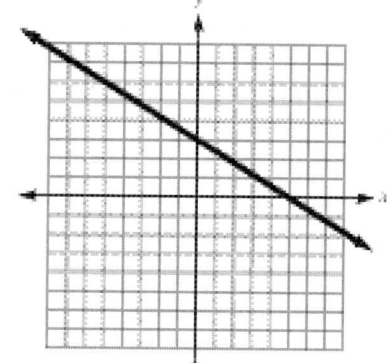

31. $x + 3y = 6$

$ 3y = 6 - x$

$ y = 2 - \dfrac{1}{3}x$

Two solutions are (0, 2) and (6, 0). The graph is the line through both points.

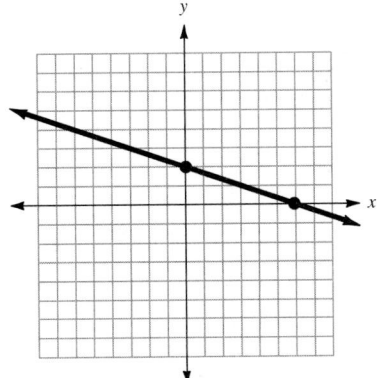

33. $3x + 4y = 12$

$ 4y = 12 - 3x$

$ y = 3 - \dfrac{3}{4}x$

Two solutions are (0, 3) and (4, 0). The graph is the line through both points.

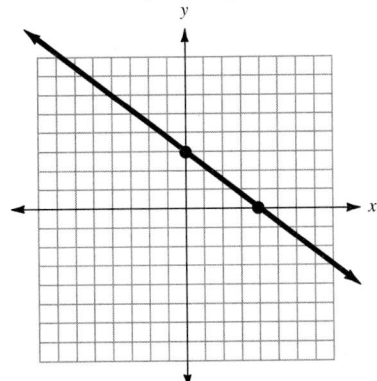

35. $5x - 4y = 20$

$ -4y = 20 - 5x$

$ y = -5 + \dfrac{5}{4}x$

Two solutions are (4, 0) and (0, –5). The graph is the line through both points.

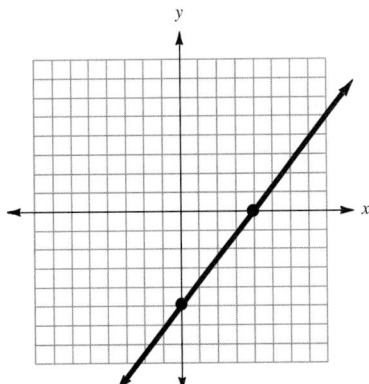

37. $y = 2x$

Two solutions are (0, 0) and (3, 6). The graph is the line through both points.

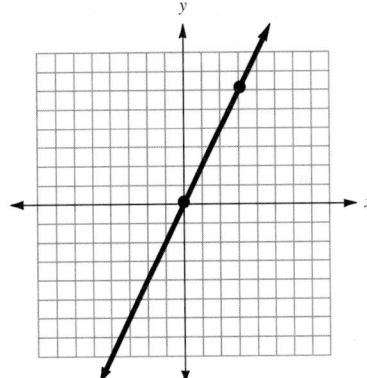

39. $y = x + 3$

Two solutions are (–3, 0) and (0, 3). The graph is the line through both points.

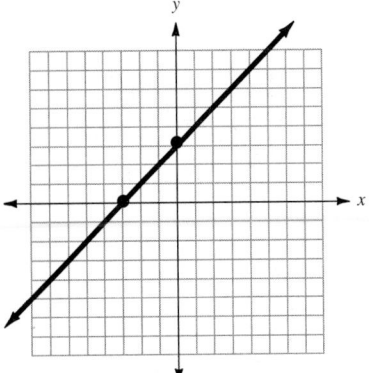

41. $y = 3x - 3$

Two solutions are $(0, -3)$ and $(1, 0)$. The graph is the line through both points.

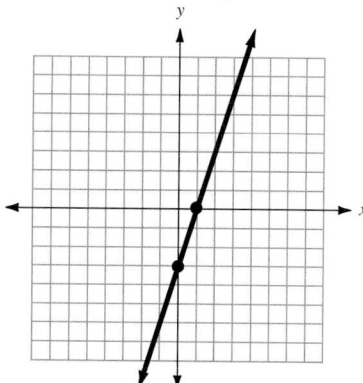

43. $x - 4y = 12$

Two solutions are $(0, -3)$ and $(4, -2)$. The graph is the line through both points.

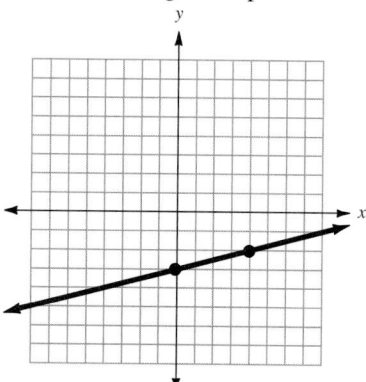

45. $x + y = 4$ $x - y = 2$
     $y = -x + 4$ $y = x - 2$

$(3, 1)$ is the point of intersection.

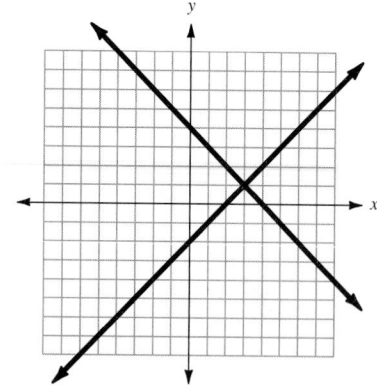

47. Two solutions are $(0, 200)$ and $(2000, 400)$. The graph is the line through both points.

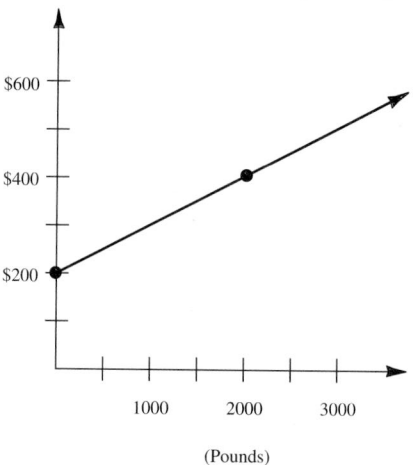

(Pounds)

49. **(a)** Two solutions to the equation $y = 11x - 100$ are $(0, -100)$ and $(10, 10)$. The graph is the line through both points.

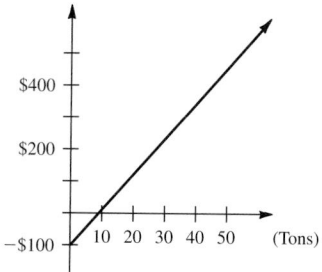

(b) Solve $0 = 11x - 100$.

$$x = \frac{100}{11} \approx 9 \text{ tons}$$

(c) $y = 11(16) - 100 = 76$
The class will make \$76.

(d) $y = 17x - 125$

51.

$y = 3x$	$y = 3x + 4$	$y = 3x - 5$
$y = 3(0)$	$y = 3(0) + 4$	$y = 3(0) - 5$
$y = 0$	$y = 4$	$y = -5$

The lines do not intersect. The y intercepts are $(0, 0)$, $(0, 4)$, and $(0, -5)$.

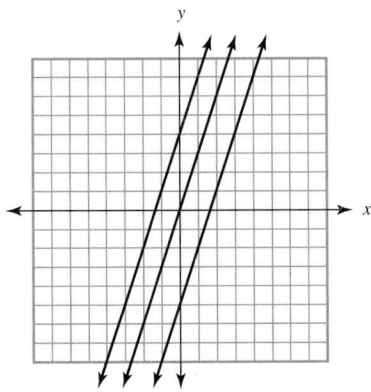

Exercises 2.3

1. $(5, 7)$ and $(9, 11)$
$$m = \frac{11 - 7}{9 - 5} = \frac{4}{4} = 1$$

3. $(-2, -5)$ and $(2, 15)$
$$m = \frac{15 - (-5)}{2 - (-2)} = \frac{20}{4} = 5$$

5. $(-2, 3)$ and $(3, 7)$
$$m = \frac{7 - 3}{3 - (-2)} = \frac{4}{5}$$

7. $(-3, 2)$ and $(2, -8)$
$$m = \frac{-8 - 2}{2 - (-3)} = \frac{-10}{5} = -2$$

9. $(3, 3)$ and $(5, 0)$
$$m = \frac{0 - 3}{5 - 3} = -\frac{3}{2}$$

11. $(5, -4)$ and $(5, 2)$
$$m = \frac{2 - (-4)}{5 - 5} = \frac{6}{0}; \text{ undefined}$$

13. $(-4, -2)$ and $(3, 3)$
$$m = \frac{3 - (-2)}{3 - (-4)} = \frac{5}{7}$$

15. $(-3, -4)$ and $(2, -4)$
$$m = \frac{-4 - (-4)}{2 - (-3)} = \frac{0}{5} = 0$$

17. $(-1, 7)$ and $(2, 3)$
$$m = \frac{3 - 7}{2 - (-1)} = -\frac{4}{3}$$

19. $(1, 3)$ and $(2, 5)$
$$m = \frac{5 - 3}{2 - 1} = \frac{2}{1} = 2$$

21. $(3, -1)$ and $(6, -7)$
$$m = \frac{-7 - (-1)}{6 - 3} = \frac{-6}{3} = -2$$

23. $(4, 5)$ and $(-6, 5)$
$$m = \frac{5 - 5}{-6 - 4} = \frac{0}{-10} = 0$$

25. The line passes through $(0, -3)$ and $(1, 1)$.
$$m = \frac{1 - (-3)}{1 - 0} = \frac{4}{1} = 4$$

27. The line passes through $(0, 2)$ and $(1, -3)$.
$$m = \frac{-3 - 2}{1 - 0} = \frac{-5}{1} = -5$$

29. The line passes through $(-6, 0)$ and $(0, 2)$.
$$m = \frac{2 - 0}{0 - (-6)} = \frac{2}{6} = \frac{1}{3}$$

31. $y = -4x$

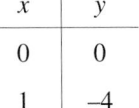

x	y
0	0
1	−4

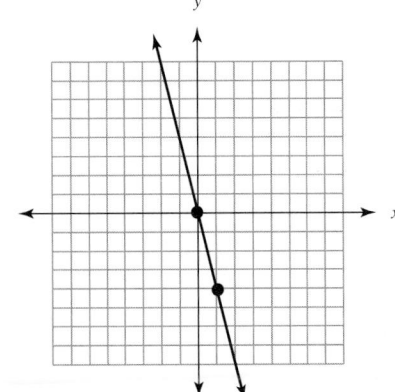

33. $y = \dfrac{2}{3}x$

x	y
0	0
3	2

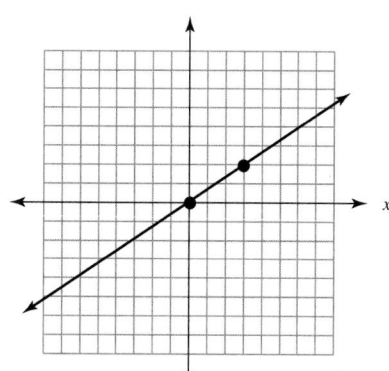

35. $y = \dfrac{5}{4}x$

x	y
0	0
4	5

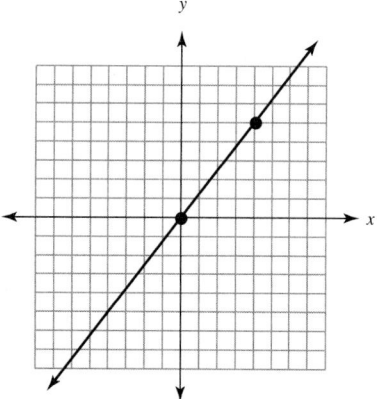

37. $y = 2x - 5$

(a)

x	y	
3	1	$y = 2(3) - 5 = 6 - 5 = 1$
4	3	$y = 2(4) - 5 = 8 - 5 = 3$

(b) $m = \dfrac{3-1}{4-3} = \dfrac{2}{1} = 2$

(c) The slope equals the coefficient of x.

39. $y = -\dfrac{1}{3}x + 2$

(a)

x	y	
3	1	$y = -\dfrac{1}{3}(3) + 2 = -1 + 2 = 1$
6	0	$y = -\dfrac{1}{3}(6) + 2 = -2 + 2 = 0$

(b) $m = \dfrac{0-1}{6-3} = -\dfrac{1}{3}$

(c) The slope equals the coefficient of x.

41. $y = 2x + 3$

(a)

Point	x	y	
A	5	13	$y = 2(5) + 3 = 13$
B	6	15	$y = 2(6) + 3 = 15$
C	7	17	$y = 2(7) + 3 = 17$
D	8	19	$y = 2(8) + 3 = 19$
E	9	21	$y = 2(9) + 3 = 21$

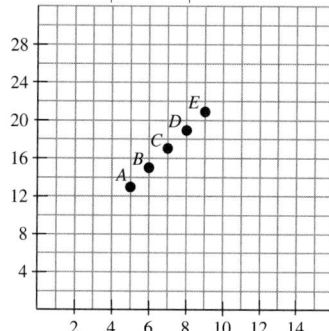

(b) It changes by 2.

(c) Yes

(d) Increases by 2

43. $y = -4x + 50$

(a)

Point	x	y	
A	5	30	$y = -4(5) + 50 = 30$
B	6	26	$y = -4(6) + 50 = 26$
C	7	22	$y = -4(7) + 50 = 22$
D	8	18	$y = -4(8) + 50 = 18$
E	9	14	$y = -4(9) + 50 = 14$

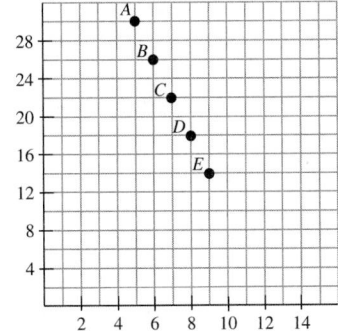

(b) It changes by –4.

(c) Yes

(d) Decreases by 4

45. $(3, 1), m = 2$

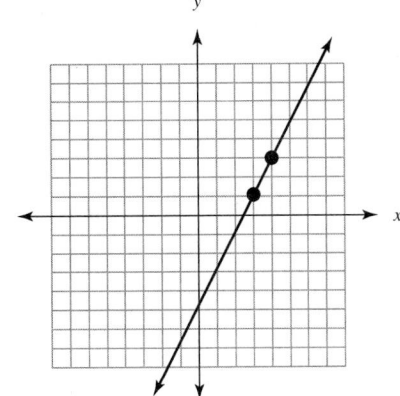

47. $(-2, -1), m = -4$

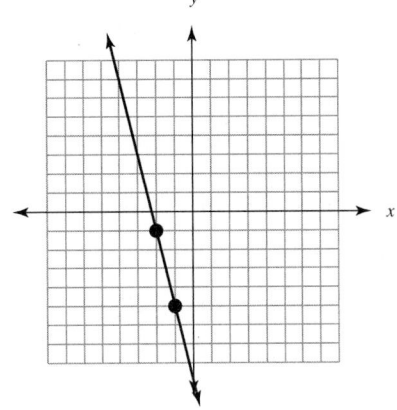

Exercises 2.4

1. $y = 3x + 5$
$m = 3, b = 5$
The slope is 3 and the y intercept is $(0, 5)$.

3. $y = -2x - 5$
$m = -2, b = -5$
The slope is –2 and the y intercept is $(0, -5)$.

5. $y = \dfrac{3}{4}x + 1$
$m = \dfrac{3}{4}, b = 1$
The slope is $\dfrac{3}{4}$ and the y intercept is $(0, 1)$.

7. $y = \dfrac{2}{3}x$
$m = \dfrac{2}{3}, b = 0$
The slope is $\dfrac{2}{3}$ and the y intercept is $(0, 0)$.

9. $4x + 3y = 12$
$\qquad 3y = -4x + 12$
$\qquad y = -\dfrac{4}{3}x + 4$
$m = -\dfrac{4}{3}, b = 4$
The slope is $-\dfrac{4}{3}$ and the y intercept is $(0, 4)$.

11. $y = 9$

$m = 0$, $b = 9$

The slope is 0 and the y intercept is (0, 9).

13. $3x - 2y = 8$

$-2y = -3x + 8$

$y = \dfrac{3}{2}x - 4$

$m = \dfrac{3}{2}$, $b = -4$

The slope is $\dfrac{3}{2}$ and the y intercept is (0, −4).

15. $m = 3$, $b = 5$

$y = mx + b$

$y = 3x + 5$

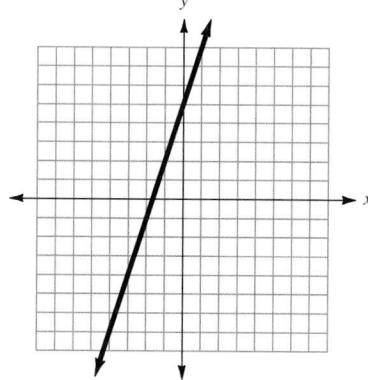

17. $m = -3$, $b = 4$

$y = mx + b$

$y = -3x + 4$

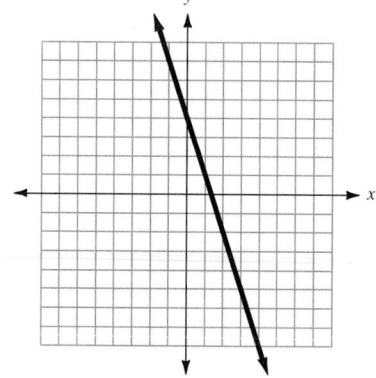

19. $m = \dfrac{1}{2}$, $b = -2$

$y = mx + b$

$y = \dfrac{1}{2}x - 2$

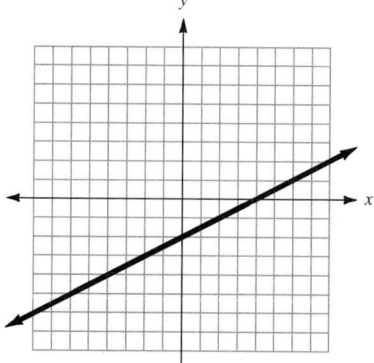

21. $m = -\dfrac{2}{3}$, $b = 0$

$y = mx + b$

$y = -\dfrac{2}{3}x$

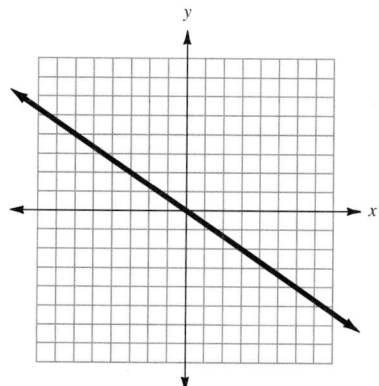

23. $m = \dfrac{3}{4}$, $b = 3$

$y = mx + b$

$y = \dfrac{3}{4}x + 3$

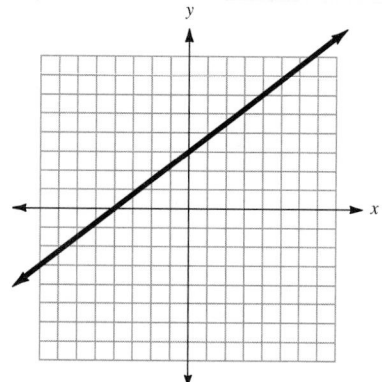

25. slope $= -\dfrac{3}{4}$

y intercept $= (0, 1)$

$y = -\dfrac{3}{4}x + 1$

(g)

27. slope $= -3$
y intercept $= (0, -2)$
$y = -3x - 2$
(e)

29. slope $= -4$
y intercept $= (0, 0)$
$y = -4x$
(h)

31. slope $= -1$
y intercept $= (0, 3)$
$y = -x + 3$
(c)

33. $y = 2x + 1$
Graph the line:

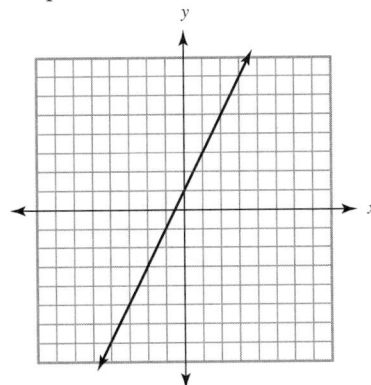

There are no solutions in quadrant IV.

35. $y = -x + 1$
Graph the line:

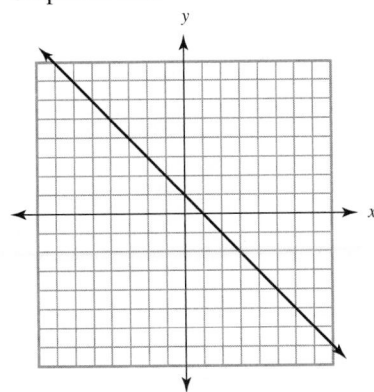

There are no solutions in quadrant III.

37. $y = -2x - 5$
Graph the line:

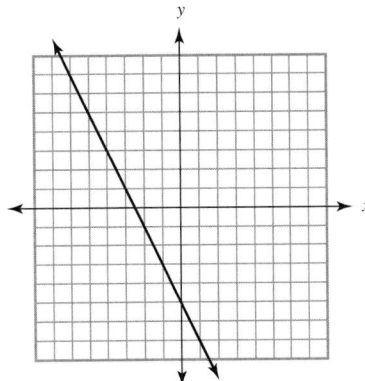

There are no solutions in quadrant I.

39. $y = 3$
Graph the line:

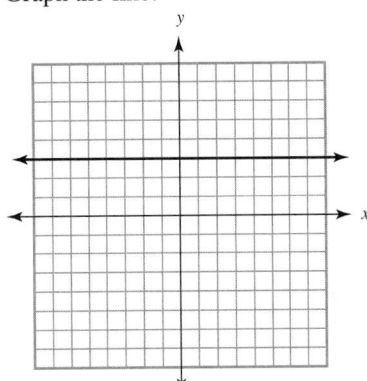

There are no solutions in quadrants III and IV.

41. $y = 0.10x + 200$
slope $= 0.10$
y intercept $= (0, 200)$

43. Hourly rate of change $= \dfrac{\text{change in temperature}}{\text{change in hours}}$

$= \dfrac{16°\,\text{F}}{8\,\text{h}}$

$= \dfrac{2°\,\text{F}}{\text{h}}$

45. slope $= \dfrac{\text{vertical change}}{\text{horizontal change}}$

$= \dfrac{-24{,}000\,\text{ft}}{15\,\text{mi}} \cdot \dfrac{1\,\text{mi}}{5280\,\text{ft}}$

≈ -0.30

47. Writing exercise

49. Group exercise

51.

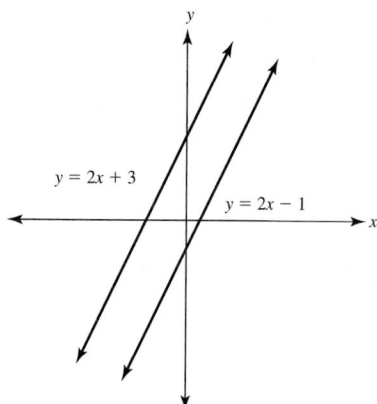

$y = 2x + 3$
$y = 2x - 1$

The lines are parallel. They will never intersect.

53.

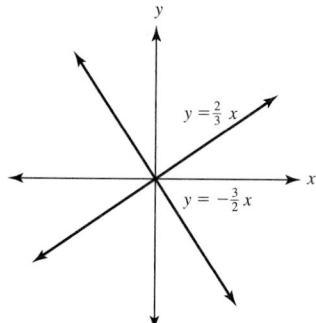

$y = \frac{2}{3}x$
$y = -\frac{3}{2}x$

The lines are perpendicular.
$$\frac{2}{3} \cdot \left(-\frac{3}{2}\right) = -1$$

55. Find a line perpendicular to $y = \frac{3}{5}x$.

$$\frac{3}{5} \cdot \left(-\frac{5}{3}\right) = -1$$
$$y = -\frac{5}{3}x$$

Exercises 2.5

1. $x + y < 5$
Test $(0, 0)$.
$0 + 0 < 5$
$\qquad 0 < 5$ A true statement
Shade the half plane containing $(0, 0)$.

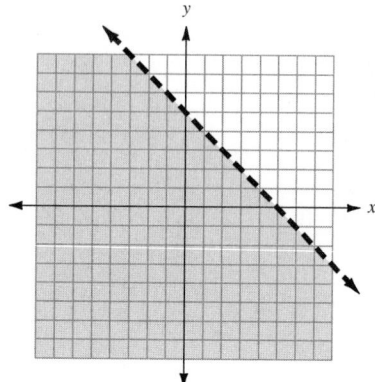

3. $x - 2y \geq 4$
Test $(0, 0)$.
$0 - 2(0) \geq 4$
$\qquad 0 \geq 4$ A false statement
Shade the half plane that does not contain $(0, 0)$.

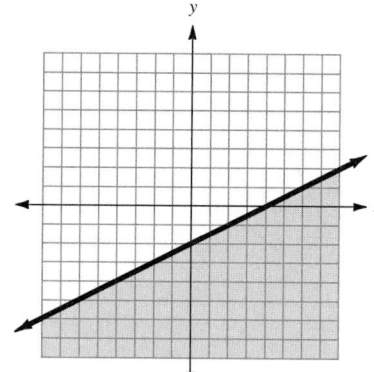

5. $x \le -3$

Test $(0, 0)$.

$0 \le -3$ A false statement

Shade the half plane that does not contain $(0, 0)$.

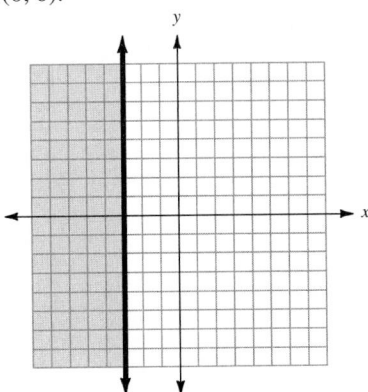

7. $y < 2x - 6$

Test $(0, 0)$

$0 < 2(0) - 6$

$0 < -6$ A false statement

Shade the half plane that does not contain $(0, 0)$.

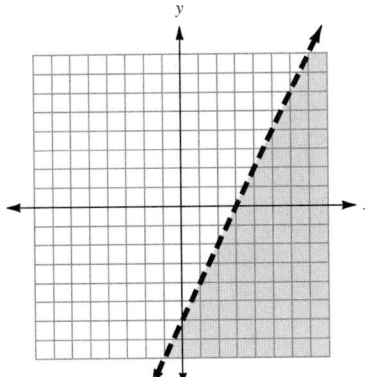

9. $x + y < 3$

$x + y = 3$

$y = -x + 3$

Graph a dashed line with slope -1 and y intercept $(0, 3)$.

Test $(0, 0)$.

$0 + 0 < 3$

    $0 < 3$ A true statement

Shade the half plane that contains $(0, 0)$.

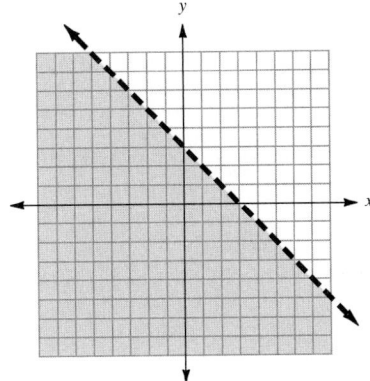

11. $x - y \le 5$

$x - y = 5$

$-y = -x + 5$

$y = x - 5$

Graph a solid line with slope 1 and y intercept $(0, -5)$.

Test $(0, 0)$.

$0 - 0 \le 5$

    $0 \le 5$ A true statement

Shade the half plane that contains $(0, 0)$.

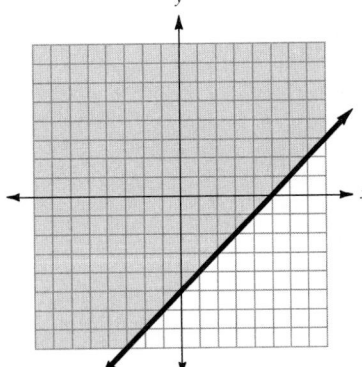

Chapter 2

13. $2x + y < 6$

$2x + y = 6$

$y = -2x + 6$

Graph a dashed line with slope -2 and y intercept $(0, 6)$.

Test $(0, 0)$.

$2(0) + 0 < 6$

$0 < 6$ A true statement

Shade the half plane that contains $(0, 0)$.

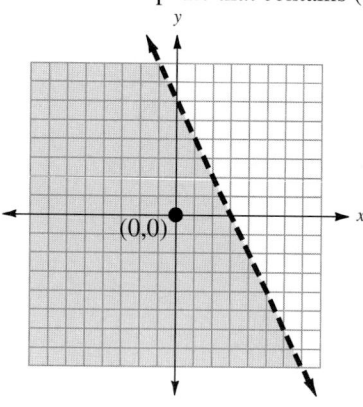

15. $x \leq 3$

Graph a solid vertical line at $x = 3$.

Test $(0, 0)$.

$0 \leq 3$ A true statement

Shade the half plane that contains $(0, 0)$.

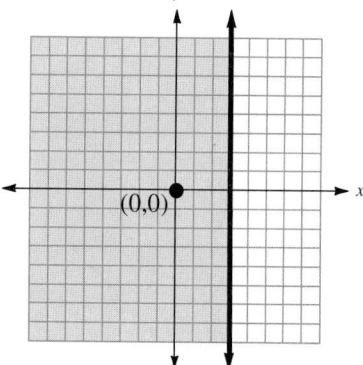

17. $x - 5y < 5$

$x - 5y = 5$

$-5y = -x + 5$

$y = \dfrac{1}{5}x - 1$

Graph a dashed line with slope $\dfrac{1}{5}$ and

y intercept $(0, -1)$.

Test $(0, 0)$.

$0 - 5(0) < 5$

$0 < 5$ A true statement

Shade the half plane that contains $(0, 0)$.

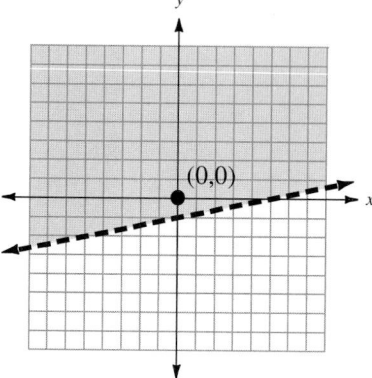

19. $y < -4$

Graph a dashed horizontal line at $y = -4$.

Test $(0, 0)$.

$0 < -4$ A false statement

Shade the half plane that does not contain $(0, 0)$.

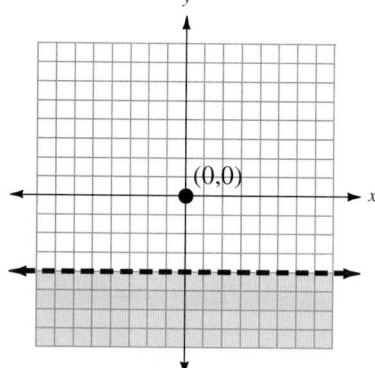

21. $2x - 3y \geq 6$

$2x - 3y = 6$

$-3y = -2x + 6$

$y = \dfrac{2}{3}x - 2$

Graph a solid line with slope $\dfrac{2}{3}$ and

y intercept $(0, -2)$.

Test $(0, 0)$.

$2(0) - 3(0) \geq 6$

$0 \geq 6$ A false statement

Shade the half plane that does not contain $(0, 0)$.

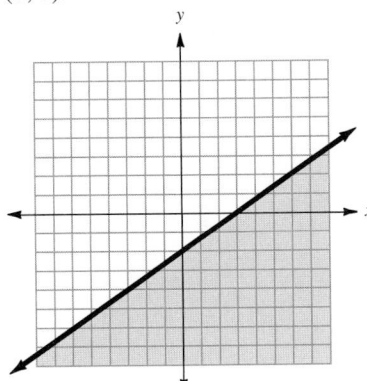

23. $3x + 2y \geq 0$

$3x + 2y = 0$

$2y = -3x$

$y = -\dfrac{3}{2}x$

Graph a solid line with slope $-\dfrac{3}{2}$ and y intercept

$(0, 0)$.

Test $(1, 1)$.

$3(1) + 2(1) \geq 0$

$3 + 2 \geq 0$

$5 \geq 0$ A true statement

Shade the half plane that contains $(1, 1)$.

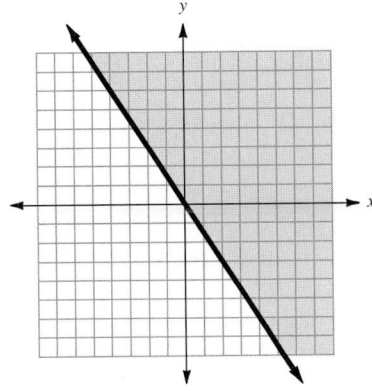

25. $5x + 2y > 10$

$5x + 2y = 10$

$2y = -5x + 10$

$y = -\dfrac{5}{2}x + 5$

Graph a dashed line with slope $-\dfrac{5}{2}$ and

y intercept $(0, 5)$.

Test $(0, 0)$.

$5(0) + 2(0) > 10$

$0 > 10$ A false statement

Shade the half plane that does not contain $(0, 0)$.

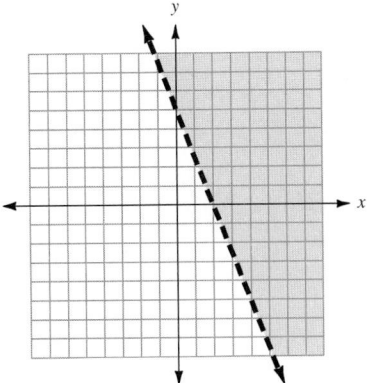

27. $y \leq 2x$

$y = 2x$

Graph a solid line with slope 2 and y intercept $(0, 0)$.

Test $(1, 1)$.

$1 \leq 2(1)$

$1 \leq 2$ A true statement

Shade the half plane that contains $(1, 1)$.

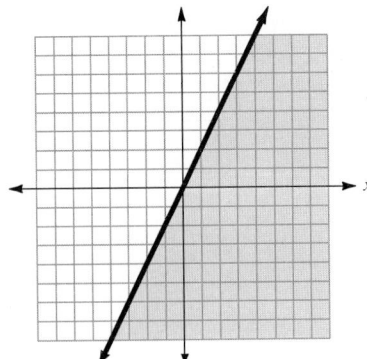

29. $y > 2x - 3$

$y = 2x - 3$

Graph a dashed line with slope 2 and
y intercept $(0, -3)$.
Test $(0, 0)$.
$0 > 2(0) - 3$
$0 > 0 - 3$
$0 > -3$ 　　 A true statement
Shade the half plane that contains $(0, 0)$.

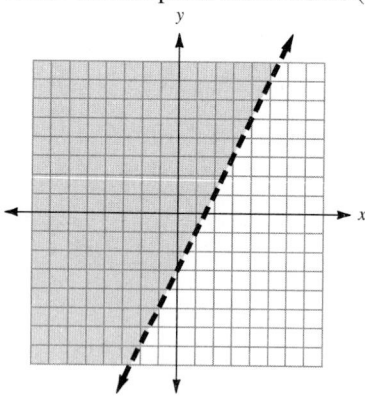

31. $y < -2x - 3$

$y = -2x - 3$

Graph a dashed line with slope -2 and
y intercept $(0, -3)$.
Test $(0, 0)$.
$0 < -2(0) - 3$
$0 < 0 - 3$
$0 < -3$ 　　 A false statement
Shade the half plane that does not contain
$(0, 0)$.

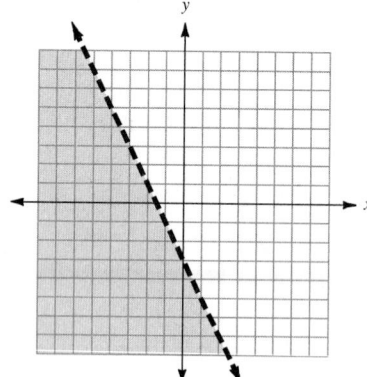

33. $2(x + y) - x > 6$

$2x + 2y - x > 6$

$x + 2y > 6$

$x + 2y = 6$

$2y = -x + 6$

$y = -\dfrac{1}{2}x + 3$

Graph a dashed line with slope $-\dfrac{1}{2}$ and

y intercept $(0, 3)$.
Test $(0, 0)$.
$0 + 2(0) > 6$
　　 $0 > 6$ A false statement
Shade the half plane that does not contain
$(0, 0)$.

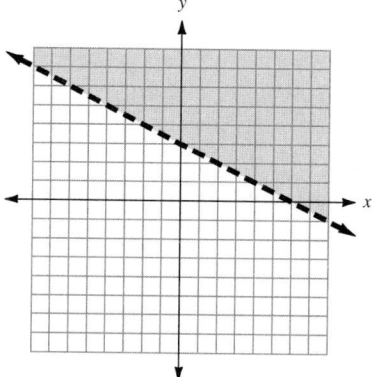

35. $4(x + y) - 3(x + y) \leq 5$

$x + y \leq 5$

$x + y = 5$

$y = -x + 5$

Graph a solid line with slope -1 and
y intercept $(0, 5)$.
Test $(0, 0)$.
$0 + 0 \leq 5$
　　 $0 \leq 5$ A true statement
Shade the half plane that contains $(0, 0)$.

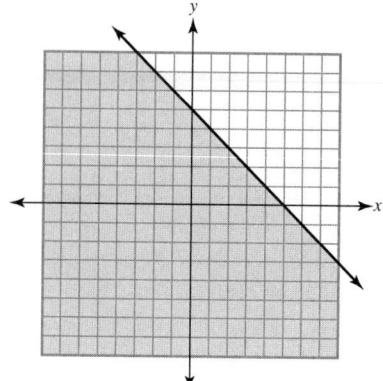

37. Let x be the number of hours worked at the video store, and let y be the number of hours worked at the convenience store.
$$9x + 8y \geq 240$$

39. Writing exercise

Exercises 2.6

1. (a) and (c) are ordered pairs of real numbers, since they are members of $\{(x,y) \mid x \in R, y \in R\}$.

   (b) is a set (it uses braces instead of parentheses), (d) is simply a list of two numbers, and (e) is not an ordered pair of real numbers since its first element is an ordered pair and its second element is a real number.

3. Only (b) is an ordered pair of real numbers, since it is a member of $\{(x,y) \mid x \in R, y \in R\}$. (a) is simply a list of two numbers, (c) is a set (it uses braces instead of parentheses), (d) has three numbers instead of two, and (e) uses brackets instead of parentheses.

5. The set of first elements is called the domain, therefore, the domain of A is {Colorado, Edmonton, Calgary, Vancouver}. The set of second elements is called the range, therefore, the range of A is $\{21, 5, 18, 17\}$.

7. The set of first elements is called the domain, therefore, the domain of C is {John Adams, John Kennedy, Richard Nixon, Harry Truman}. The set of second elements is called the range, therefore, the range of C is $\{-16, -23, -5, -11\}$.

9. The set of first elements is called the domain, therefore, the domain of F is {St. Louis, Denver, Green Bay, Dallas}. The set of second elements is called the range, therefore, the range of F is $\left\{\dfrac{1}{2}, -\dfrac{3}{4}, \dfrac{7}{8}, -\dfrac{4}{5}\right\}$.

11. The set of first elements is called the domain, therefore, the domain is $\{1, 3, 5, 7, 9\}$. The set of second elements is called the range, therefore, the range is $\{2, 4, 6, 8, 10\}$.

13. The set of first elements is called the domain, therefore, the domain is $\{1, 3, 4, 5, 6\}$. The set of second elements is called the range, therefore, the range is $\{1, 2, 3, 4, 6\}$.

15. The set of first elements is called the domain, therefore, the domain is $\{1\}$. The set of second elements is called the range, therefore, the range is $\{2, 3, 4, 5, 6\}$.

17. The set of first elements is called the domain, therefore, the domain is $\{1, 2, 3, 4\}$. The set of second elements is called the range, therefore, the range is $\{4, 5, 6\}$.

19. The set of first elements is called the domain, therefore, the domain is $\{-3, -2, -1, 4, 5\}$. The set of second elements is called the range, therefore, the range is $\{3, 4, 5, 6\}$.

21. Since the set of first elements is called the domain, we use the day of the week as the first element in an ordered pair, and the price as the second element of an ordered pair.
$$\left\{\left(1, 9\tfrac{1}{8}\right), (2, 8), \left(3, 8\tfrac{7}{8}\right), \left(4, 9\tfrac{1}{4}\right), (5, 9)\right\}$$

23. Since the first coordinate is an integer between -3 and 3, and the second coordinate is the cube of the first coordinate, we have
$$\left\{\left(-2, (-2)^3\right), \left(-1, (-1)^3\right), \left(0, 0^3\right), \left(1, 1^3\right), \left(2, 2^3\right)\right\}$$
$$= \{(-2, -8), (-1, -1), (0, 0), (1, 1), (2, 8)\}.$$
The domain is $\{-2, -1, 0, 1, 2\}$ and the range is $\{-8, -1, 0, 1, 8\}$.

25. Since the first coordinate is the number of hours worked, and the second coordinate is the salary at \$6 per hour, we have
$\{(10, 10(6)), (20, 20(6)), (30, 30(6)), (40, 40(6))\} = \{(10, 60), (20, 120), (30, 180), (40, 240)\}$. The domain is $\{10, 20, 30, 40\}$ and the range is $\{60, 120, 180, 240\}$.

Exercises 2.7

1. a. Substituting 0 for x in the expression on the right, we get
$$(0)^2 - (0) - 2 = -2.$$

   b. Substituting -2 for x in the expression on the right, we get
$$(-2)^2 - (-2) - 2 = 4 + 2 - 2 = 4.$$

   c. Substituting 1 for x in the expression on the right, we get
$$(1)^2 - (1) - 2 = 1 - 1 - 2 = -2.$$

3. a. Substituting –2 for x in the expression on the right, we get
$$3(-2)^2 + (-2) - 1 = 12 - 2 - 1 = 9.$$

b. Substituting 0 for x in the expression on the right, we get
$$3(0)^2 + (0) - 1 = -1.$$

c. Substituting 1 for x in the expression on the right, we get
$$3(1)^2 + (1) - 1 = 3 + 1 - 1 = 3.$$

5. a. Substituting –3 for x in the expression on the right, we get
$$(-3)^3 - 2(-3)^2 + 5(-3) - 2$$
$$= -27 - 18 - 15 - 2$$
$$= -62.$$

b. Substituting 0 for x in the expression on the right, we get
$$(0)^3 - 2(0)^2 + 5(0) - 2 = 0 - 0 + 0 - 2 = -2.$$

c. Substituting 1 for x in the expression on the right, we get
$$(1)^3 - 2(1)^2 + 5(1) - 2 = 1 - 2 + 5 - 2 = 2.$$

7. a. Substituting –2 for x in the expression on the right, we get
$$-3(-2)^3 + 2(-2)^2 - 5(-2) + 3$$
$$= 24 + 8 + 10 + 3$$
$$= 45.$$

b. Substituting 0 for x in the expression on the right, we get
$$-3(0)^3 + 2(0)^2 - 5(0) + 3 = 3.$$

c. Substituting 3 for x in the expression on the right, we get
$$-3(3)^3 + 2(3)^2 - 5(3) + 3$$
$$= -81 + 18 - 15 + 3$$
$$= -75.$$

9. a. Substituting –1 for x in the expression on the right, we get
$$2(-1)^3 + 4(-1)^2 + 5(-1) + 2$$
$$= -2 + 4 - 5 + 2$$
$$= -1.$$

b. Substituting 0 for x in the expression on the right, we get
$$2(0)^3 + 4(0)^2 + 5(0) + 2 = 2.$$

c. Substituting 1 for x in the expression on the right, we get
$$2(1)^3 + 4(1)^2 + 5(1) + 2$$
$$= 2 + 4 + 5 + 2$$
$$= 13.$$

11. This relation is a function since no two first coordinates are equal.

13. This relation is a function since no two first coordinates are equal.

15. This relation is not a function since 1 appears as a first coordinate three times with different second coordinates.

17. This relation is not a function since 2 appears as a first coordinate twice with different second coordinates.

19. This relation is a function since no two first coordinates are equal.

21. This relation is not a function since 2 appears as a first coordinate twice with different second coordinates.

23. This relation is a function since no two first coordinates are equal.

25.

This is a function. No vertical line passes through more than one point.

27.

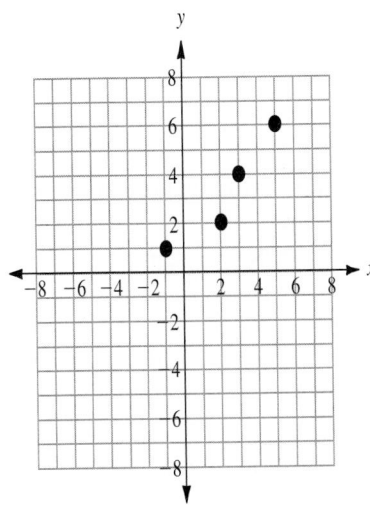

This is a function. No vertical line passes through more than one point.

29.

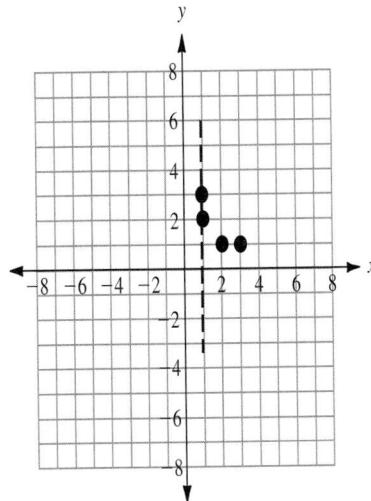

Because a vertical line can be drawn through the points $(1, 2)$ and $(1, 3)$, the relation does not pass the vertical line test. This is not a function.

31. a. Use the $\boxed{Y=}$ key to enter $Y_1 = 3x^2 - 5x + 7$. Select $\boxed{TABLE}$ ($\boxed{2^{nd}}$ $\boxed{GRAPH}$), and choose -5 for x. The table will give you a value of 107 for Y_1.

b. Now, choose 5 for x. The table will give you a value of 57 for Y_1.

c. Now, choose 12 for x. The table will give you a value of 379 for x.

33. a. Use the $\boxed{Y=}$ key to enter $Y_1 = 3x^4 - 6x^3 + 2x^2 - 17$. Select $\boxed{TABLE}$ ($\boxed{2^{nd}}$ $\boxed{GRAPH}$), and choose -3 for x. The table will give you a value of 406 for Y_1.

b. Now, choose 4 for x. The table will give you a value of 399 for Y_1.

c. Now, choose 7 for x. The table will give you a value of 5226 for Y_1.

35. This is a function because it passes the vertical line test. The graph continues forever in both the positive x direction and the negative x direction. Because there is a point on this graph related to every x-value, the domain is the set of all real x-values. We write $D = \{x \mid x \in R\}$. The range is the set of y-values greater than or equal to -5. We write $R = \{y \mid y \geq -5\}$.

37. This is not a function because it does not pass the vertical line test. The domain is the set of x-values from -6 to 6, inclusive. We write $D = \{x \mid -6 \leq x \leq 6\}$. The range is the set of y-values from -6 to 6, inclusive. We write $R = \{y \mid -6 \leq y \leq 6\}$.

39. This is a function because it passes the vertical line test. The graph continues forever in both the positive x direction and the negative x direction. Because there is a point on this graph related to every x-value, the domain is the set of all real x-values. We write $D = \{x \mid x \in R\}$. The range is the set of y-values greater than or equal to 0. We write $R = \{y \mid y \geq 0\}$.

41. This is a function because it passes the vertical line test. The graph continues forever in both the positive x direction and the negative x direction. Because there is a point on this graph related to every x-value, the domain is the set of all real x-values. We write $D = \{x \mid x \in R\}$. The range is the set of y-values greater than or equal to 3. We write $R = \{y \mid y \geq 3\}$.

43. This is not a function because it does not pass the vertical line test. The graph continues forever in both the positive x direction and the negative x direction. Because there is a point on this graph related to every x-value, the domain is the set of all real x-values. We write $D = \{x \mid x \in R\}$. The range is the set of y-values containing -4 and 3. We write $R = \{y \mid y = -4 \text{ or } 3\}$.

45. writing exercise

47. Substituting 2000 for x in the expression on the right, we get
$1.75(2000) + 7000 = 3500 + 7000 = 10{,}500$.
The cost of producing 2000 units will be $10,500.

49. a. Substituting 17 for x in the expression on the right, we get
$2(17)^2 - 125(17) + 3000$
$= 578 - 2125 + 3000$
$= 1453$.
The number of accidents in 1 month that involved 17-year-olds was 1453.

b. Substituting 25 for x in the expression on the right, we get
$2(25)^2 - 125(25) + 3000$
$= 1250 - 3125 + 3000$
$= 1125$.
The number of accidents in 1 month that involved 25-year-olds was 1125.

51. a. Substituting 2 for t in the expression on the right, we get
$-16(2)^2 + 128(2) = -64 + 256 = 192$.
The height of the object at 2 s is 192 ft.

b. Substituting 4 for t in the expression on the right, we get
$-16(4)^2 + 128(4) = -256 + 512 = 256$.
The height of the object at 4 s is 256 ft.

c. Substituting 6 for t in the expression on the right, we get
$-16(6)^2 + 128(6) = -576 + 768 = 192$.
The height of the object at 6 s is 192 ft.

Chapter 3 Factoring

Section 3.1

1. $(6a - 5) + (3a + 9) = 9a + 4$

3. $(8b^2 - 11b) + (5b^2 - 7b) = 13b^2 - 18b$

5. $(3x^2 - 2x) + (-5x^2 + 2x) = -2x^2$

7. $(2x^2 + 5x - 3) + (3x^2 - 7x + 4) = 5x^2 - 2x + 1$

9. $(2b^2 + 8) + (5b + 8) = 2b^2 + 5b + 16$

11. $(8y^3 - 5y^2) + (5y^2 - 2y) = 8y^3 - 2y$

13. $(2a^2 - 4a^3) + (3a^3 + 2a^2) = -a^3 + 4a^2$

15. $(4x^2 - 2 + 7x) + (5 - 8x - 6x^2) = -2x^2 - x + 3$

17. $-(2a + 3b) = -2a - 3b$

19. $5a - (2b - 3c) = 5a - 2b + 3c$

21. $9r - (3r + 5s) = 6r - 5s$

23. $5p - (-3p + 2q) = 8p - 2q$

25. $(2x - 3) - (x + 4) = x - 7$

27. $(4m^2 - 5m) - (3m^2 - 2m) = m^2 - 3m$

29. $(4y^2 + 5y) - (6y^2 + 5y) = -2y^2$

31. $(3x^2 - 5x - 2) - (x^2 - 4x - 3) = 2x^2 - x + 1$

33. $(8a^2 - 9a) - (3a + 7) = 8a^2 - 12a - 7$

35. $(5b - 2b^2) - (4b^2 - 3b) = -6b^2 + 8b$

37. $(3x^2 - 8x + 7) - (x^2 - 5 - 8x) = 2x^2 + 12$

39. $[(4b - 2) + (5b + 3)] - (3b + 2) = 9b + 1 - 3b - 2$
$= 6b - 1$

41. $[(x^2 + 5x - 2) + (2x^2 + 7x - 8)] - (3x^2 + 2x - 1)$
$= (3x^2 + 12x - 10) - 3x^2 - 2x + 1$
$= 10x - 9$

43. $[(4x^2 - 5) + (2x - 7)] - (2x^2 - 3x)$
$= (4x^2 + 2x - 12) - 2x^2 + 3x$
$= 2x^2 + 5x - 12$

45. $(2y^2 - 8y) - [(3y^2 - 3y) + (5y^2 + 3y)]$
$= (2y^2 - 8y) - 8y^2$
$= -6y^2 - 8y$

47. $\begin{array}{r} 2w^2 \qquad + 7 \\ 3w - 5 \\ \underline{4w^2 - 5w} \\ 6w^2 - 2w + 2 \end{array}$

49. $\begin{array}{r} 3x^2 + 3x - 4 \\ 4x^2 - 3x - 3 \\ \underline{2x^2 - x + 7} \\ 9x^2 - x \end{array}$

51. $\begin{array}{ll} 5a^2 + 3a & 5a^2 + 3a \\ \underline{(-)3a^2 - 2a} & \underline{-3a^2 + 2a} \\ & 2a^2 + 5a \end{array}$

53. $\begin{array}{ll} 8x^2 - 5x + 7 & 8x^2 - 5x + 7 \\ \underline{(-)5x^2 - 6x + 7} & \underline{-5x^2 + 6x - 7} \\ & 3x^2 + x \end{array}$

55. $\begin{array}{ll} 8x^2 \qquad - 9 & 8x^2 \qquad - 9 \\ \underline{(-)5x^2 - 3x} & \underline{-5x^2 + 3x} \\ & 3x^2 + 3x - 9 \end{array}$

57. $[(9x^2 - 3x + 5) - (3x^2 + 2x - 1)] - (x^2 - 2x - 3)$
$= (6x^2 - 5x + 6) - x^2 + 2x + 3$
$= 5x^2 - 3x + 9$

59. $3ax^4 - 5x^3 + x^2 - cx + 2 = 9x^4 - bx^3 + x^2 - 2d$
$3a = 9 \quad -5 = -b \quad -c = 0 \quad 2 = -2d$
$a = 3 \quad b = 5 \quad c = 0 \quad d = -1$

61. Perimeter $= 2l + 2w$
$= 2(8x + 9) + 2(6x - 7) = 28x + 4$

63. Profit $= R - C$
$= (90x - x^2) - (150 + 25x)$
$= -x^2 + 65x - 150$

Exercises 3.2

1. $f(x) = x^2 - x - 2$

(a) $f(0) = 0^2 - 0 - 2 = -2$

(b) $f(-2) = (-2)^2 - (-2) - 2$
$\qquad = 4 + 2 - 2$
$\qquad = 4$

(c) $f(1) = 1^2 - 1 - 2$
$\qquad = 1 - 1 - 2$
$\qquad = -2$

3. $f(x) = 3x^2 + x - 1$

(a) $f(-2) = 3(-2)^2 + (-2) - 1$
$\qquad = 3(4) - 2 - 1$
$\qquad = 12 - 2 - 1$
$\qquad = 9$

(b) $f(0) = 3(0)^2 + 0 - 1$
$\qquad = -1$

(c) $f(1) = 3(1)^2 + 1 - 1$
$\qquad = 3 + 1 - 1$
$\qquad = 3$

5. $f(x) = x^3 - 2x^2 + 5x - 2$

(a) $f(-3) = (-3)^3 - 2(-3)^2 + 5(-3) - 2$
$\qquad = -27 - 18 - 15 - 2$
$\qquad = -62$

(b) $f(0) = 0^3 - 2(0)^2 + 5(0) - 2$
$\qquad = -2$

(c) $f(1) = 1^3 - 2(1)^2 + 5(1) - 2$
$\qquad = 1 - 2 + 5 - 2$
$\qquad = 2$

7. $f(x) = -3x^3 + 2x^2 - 5x + 3$

(a) $f(-2) = -3(-2)^3 + 2(-2)^2 - 5(-2) + 3$
$\qquad = 24 + 8 + 10 + 3$
$\qquad = 45$

(b) $f(0) = -3(0)^3 + 2(0)^2 - 5(0) + 3$
$\qquad = 3$

(c) $f(3) = -3(3)^3 + 2(3)^2 - 5(3) + 3$
$\qquad = -81 + 18 - 15 + 3$
$\qquad = -75$

9. $f(x) = 2x^3 + 4x^2 + 5x + 2$

(a) $f(-1) = 2(-1)^3 + 4(-1)^2 + 5(-1) + 2$
$\qquad = -2 + 4 - 5 + 2$
$\qquad = -1$

(b) $f(0) = 2(0)^3 + 4(0)^2 + 5(0) + 2$
$\qquad = 2$

(c) $f(1) = 2(1)^3 + 4(1)^2 + 5(1) + 2$
$\qquad = 2 + 4 + 5 + 2$
$\qquad = 13$

11. $y = -3x + 2$
$f(x) = -3x + 2$

13. $y = 4x - 8$
$f(x) = 4x - 8$

15. $3x + 2y = 6$
$\qquad 2y = -3x + 6$
$\qquad y = -\dfrac{3}{2}x + 3$
$\qquad f(x) = -\dfrac{3}{2}x + 3$

17. $-2x + 6y = 9$
$\qquad 6y = 2x + 9$
$\qquad y = \dfrac{1}{3}x + \dfrac{3}{2}$
$\qquad f(x) = \dfrac{1}{3}x + \dfrac{3}{2}$

19. $-5x - 8y = -9$
$\qquad -8y = 5x - 9$
$\qquad y = -\dfrac{5}{8}x + \dfrac{9}{8}$
$\qquad f(x) = -\dfrac{5}{8}x + \dfrac{9}{8}$

21. $f(x) = 3x + 7$

Find three points:
$f(0) = 3(0) + 7 = 7$
$f(-1) = 3(-1) + 7 = 4$
$f(-2) = 3(-2) + 7 = 1$

Or use the slope and y intercept to graph the line:

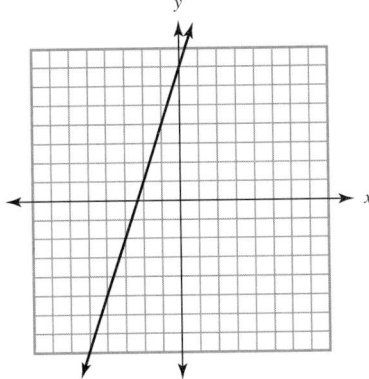

23. $f(x) = -2x + 7$

Find three points:
$f(0) = -2(0) + 7 = 7$
$f(2) = -2(2) + 7 = 3$
$f(4) = -2(4) + 7 = -1$

Or use the slope and y intercept to graph the line:

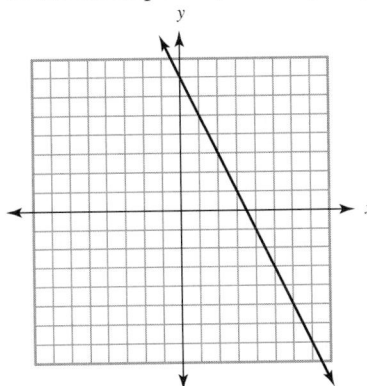

25. $f(x) = -x - 1$

Find three points:
$f(-3) = -(-3) - 1 = 2$
$f(0) = -(0) - 1 = -1$
$f(3) = -3 - 1 = -4$

Or use the slope and y intercept to graph the line:

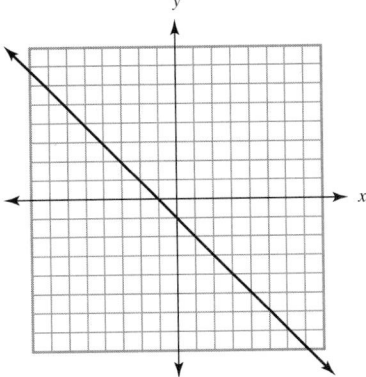

In exercises 27 to 31, $f(x) = 4x - 3$.

27. $f(5) = 4(5) - 3 = 20 - 3 = 17$

29. $f(4) = 4(4) - 3 = 16 - 3 = 13$

31. $f(-4) = 4(-4) - 3 = -16 - 3 = -19$

In exercises 33 to 37, $f(x) = 5x - 1$.

33. $f(a) = 5a - 1$

35. $f(x + 1) = 5(x + 1) - 1$
$\qquad\quad = 5x + 5 - 1$
$\qquad\quad = 5x + 4$

37. $f(x + h) = 5(x + h) - 1$
$\qquad\quad = 5x + 5h - 1$

In exercises 39 to 41, $g(x) = -3x + 2$.

39. $g(m) = -3m + 2$

41. $g(x + 2) = -3(x + 2) + 2$
$\qquad\quad = -3x - 6 + 2$
$\qquad\quad = -3x - 4$

In exercises 43 to 45, $f(x) = 2x + 3$.

43. $f(1) = 2(1) + 3 = 5$

45. From exercises 43 and 44, $f(1) = 5$ and
$f(3) = 9$.
$(1, f(1)) = (1, 5)$
$(3, f(3)) = (3, 9)$

47. $f(x) = 5x - 2$

    (a) $f(4) - f(3) = 5(4) - 2 - (5(3) - 2)$
$$= 20 - 2 - 15 + 2$$
$$= 5$$

    (b) $f(9) - f(8) = 5(9) - 2 - (5(8) - 2)$
$$= 45 - 2 - 40 + 2$$
$$= 5$$

    (c) $f(12) - f(11) = 5(12) - 2 - (5(11) - 2)$
$$= 60 - 2 - 55 + 2$$
$$= 5$$

    (d) The results of (a) through (c) are all 5, which is the same as the slope of the line that is the graph of f.

49. $f(x) = mx + b$

    (a) $f(4) - f(3) = m(4) + b - (m(3) + b)$
$$= 4m + b - 3m - b$$
$$= m$$

    (b) $f(9) - f(8) = m(9) + b - (m(8) + b)$
$$= 9m + b - 8m - b$$
$$= m$$

    (c) $f(12) - f(11) = m(12) + b - (m(11) + b)$
$$= 12m + b - 11m - b$$
$$= m$$

    (d) The results of (a) through (c) are m, which is the slope of the line that is the graph of f.

Section 3.3

1. $(5x^2)(3x^3) = (5 \cdot 3)(x^2 \cdot x^3)$
$$= 15x^5$$

3. $(-2b^2)(14b^8) = (-2 \cdot 14)(b^2 \cdot b^8)$
$$= -28b^{10}$$

5. $(-10p^6)(-4p^7) = (-10)(-4)(p^6 \cdot p^7)$
$$= 40p^{13}$$

7. $(4m^5)(-3m) = (4)(-3)(m^5 \cdot m)$
$$= -12m^6$$

9. $(4x^3y^2)(8x^2y) = (4 \cdot 8)(x^3 \cdot x^2)(y^2 \cdot y)$
$$= 32x^5y^3$$

11. $(-3m^5n^2)(2m^4n) = (-3)(2)(m^5 \cdot m^4)(n^2 \cdot n)$
$$= -6m^9n^3$$

13. $5(2x + 6) = 5(2x) + 5(6)$
$$= 10x + 30$$

15. $3a(4a + 5) = 3a(4a) + 3a(5)$
$$= 12a^2 + 15a$$

17. $3s^2(4s^2 - 7s) = 3s^2(4s^2) - 3s^2(7s)$
$$= 12s^4 - 21s^3$$

19. $2x(4x^2 - 2x + 1) = 2x(4x^2) - 2x(2x) + 2x(1)$
$$= 8x^3 - 4x^2 + 2x$$

21. $3xy(2x^2y + xy^2 + 5xy)$
$$= 3xy(2x^2y) + 3xy(xy^2) + 3xy(5xy)$$
$$= 6x^3y^2 + 3x^2y^3 + 15x^2y^2$$

23. $6m^2n(3m^2n - 2mn + mn^2)$
$$= 6m^2n(3m^2n) - 6m^2n(2mn) + 6m^2n(mn^2)$$
$$= 18m^4n^2 - 12m^3n^2 + 6m^3n^3$$

25. $(x + 3)(x + 2) = x^2 + 2x + 3x + 6$
$$= x^2 + 5x + 6$$

27. $(m - 5)(m - 9) = m^2 - 9m - 5m + 45$
$$= m^2 - 14m + 45$$

29. $(p - 8)(p + 7) = p^2 + 7p - 8p - 56$
$$= p^2 - p - 56$$

31. $(w + 10)(w + 20) = w^2 + 20w + 10w + 200$
$$= w^2 + 30w + 200$$

33. $(3x-5)(x-8) = 3x^2 - 24x - 5x + 40$
$$= 3x^2 - 29x + 40$$

35. $(2x-3)(3x+4) = 6x^2 + 8x - 9x - 12$
$$= 6x^2 - x - 12$$

37. $(3a-b)(4a-9b) = 12a^2 - 27ab - 4ab + 9b^2$
$$= 12a^2 - 31ab + 9b^2$$

39. $(3p-4q)(7p+5q) = 21p^2 + 15pq - 28pq - 20q^2$
$$= 21p^2 - 13pq - 20q^2$$

41. $(2x+5y)(3x+4y) = 6x^2 + 8xy + 15xy + 20y^2$
$$= 6x^2 + 23xy + 20y^2$$

43. $(x+5)^2 = (x+5)(x+5)$
$$= x^2 + 5x + 5x + 25$$
$$= x^2 + 10x + 25$$

45. $(y-9)^2 = (y-9)(y-9)$
$$= y^2 - 9y - 9y + 81$$
$$= y^2 - 18y + 81$$

47. $(6m+n)^2 = (6m+n)(6m+n)$
$$= 36m^2 + 6mn + 6mn + n^2$$
$$= 36m^2 + 12mn + n^2$$

49. $(a-5)(a+5) = a^2 + 5a - 5a - 25 = a^2 - 25$

51. $(x-2y)(x+2y) = x^2 + 2xy - 2xy - 4y^2$
$$= x^2 - 4y^2$$

53. $(5s+3t)(5s-3t) = 25s^2 - 15st + 15st - 9t^2$
$$= 25s^2 - 9t^2$$

55.
$$\begin{array}{r} x+2 \\ 3x+5 \\ \hline 5x+10 \\ 3x^2+6x \\ \hline 3x^2+11x+10 \end{array}$$

57.
$$\begin{array}{r} 2m+(-5) \\ 3m+7 \\ \hline 14m-35 \\ 6m^2+(-15m) \\ \hline 6m^2-\ \ m-35 \end{array}$$

59.
$$\begin{array}{r} 3x\ +\ 4y \\ 5x\ +(-2y) \\ \hline -6xy+(-8y^2) \\ 15x^2+20xy \\ \hline 15x^2+14xy-\ 8y^2 \end{array}$$

61.
$$\begin{array}{r} a^2+3ab-b^2 \\ a^2-5ab+b^2 \\ \hline a^2b^2+3ab^3-b^4 \\ -5a^3b-15a^2b^2+5ab^3 \\ a^4+3a^3b-\ \ a^2b^2 \\ \hline a^4-2a^3b-15a^2b^2+8ab^3-b^4 \end{array}$$

63.
$$\begin{array}{r} x^2\ +\ 2xy\ +\ 4y^2 \\ x\ \ +(-2y) \\ \hline -2x^2y+(-4xy^2)+(-8y^3) \\ x^3+2x^2y+\ 4xy^2 \\ \hline x^3\qquad\qquad\ -8y^3 \end{array}$$

65.
$$\begin{array}{r} 9a^2-12ab+16b^2 \\ 3a+\ 4b \\ \hline 36a^2b-48ab^2+64b^3 \\ 27a^3+(-36a^2b)+48ab^2 \\ \hline 27a^3\qquad\qquad\ +64b^3 \end{array}$$

67. $2x(3x-2)(4x+1) = 2x(12x^2 + 3x - 8x - 2)$
$$= 2x(12x^2 - 5x - 2)$$
$$= 24x^3 - 10x^2 - 4x$$

69. $5a(4a-3)(4a+3) = 5a(16a^2 + 12a - 12a - 9)$
$$= 5a(16a^2 - 9)$$
$$= 80a^3 - 45a$$

71. $3s(5s-2)(4s-1) = 3s(20s^2 - 13s + 2)$
$$= 60s^3 - 39s^2 + 6s$$

73. $(x-2)(x+1)(x-3)$
$$= (x-2)(x^2 - 2x - 3)$$
$$= x^3 - 2x^2 - 3x - 2x^2 + 4x + 6$$
$$= x^3 - 4x^2 + x + 6$$

75. $(a-1)^3 = (a-1)(a-1)(a-1)$
$$= (a-1)(a^2 - 2a + 1)$$
$$= a^3 - 2a^2 + a - a^2 + 2a - 1$$
$$= a^3 - 3a^2 + 3a - 1$$

77. $\left(\dfrac{x}{2}+\dfrac{2}{3}\right)\left(\dfrac{2x}{3}-\dfrac{2}{5}\right)=\dfrac{x^2}{3}-\dfrac{x}{5}+\dfrac{4x}{9}-\dfrac{4}{15}$

$\qquad = \dfrac{1}{3}x^2 + \dfrac{11}{45}x - \dfrac{4}{15}$

79. $[x+(y-2)][x-(y-2)]=x^2-(y-2)^2$

$\qquad = x^2-(y^2-4y+4)$

$\qquad = x^2-y^2+4y-4$

81. $(x+y)^2=x^2+2xy+y^2$

$\qquad \pi x^2+y^2$: False

83. $(x+y)^2=x^2+2xy+y^2$: True

85. Area $=(3x+5)(2x-7)$

$\qquad = 6x^2-11x-35$ cm^2

87. Revenue $=x(2x-10)=2x^2-10x$

89. Group exercise

Section 3.4

1. $(x+5)^2=x^2+2(5x)+5^2=x^2+10x+25$

3. $(w-6)^2=w^2-2(6w)+6^2=w^2-12w+36$

5. $(z+12)^2=z^2+2(12z)+12^2=z^2+24z+144$

7. $(2a-1)^2=(2a)^2-2(2a)+1^2=4a^2-4a+1$

9. $(6m+1)^2=(6m)^2+2(6m)+1^2$

$\qquad = 36m^2+12m+1$

11. $(3x-y)^2=(3x)^2-2(3xy)+y^2$

$\qquad = 9x^2-6xy+y^2$

13. $(2r+5s)^2=(2r)^2+2(2r)(5s)+(5s)^2$

$\qquad = 4r^2+20rs+25s^2$

15. $(8a-9b)^2=(8a)^2-2(8a)(9b)+(9b)^2$

$\qquad = 64a^2-144ab+81b^2$

17. $\left(x+\dfrac{1}{2}\right)^2=x^2+2\left(\dfrac{1}{2}x\right)+\left(\dfrac{1}{2}\right)^2$

$\qquad = x^2+x+\dfrac{1}{4}$

19. $(x-6)(x+6)=x^2-6^2=x^2-36$

21. $(m+12)(m-12)=m^2-12^2=m^2-144$

23. $\left(x-\dfrac{1}{2}\right)\left(x+\dfrac{1}{2}\right)=x^2-\left(\dfrac{1}{2}\right)^2=x^2-\dfrac{1}{4}$

25. $(p-0.4)(p+0.4)=p^2-(0.4)^2=p^2-0.16$

27. $(a-3b)(a+3b)=a^2-(3b)^2=a^2-9b^2$

29. $(4r-s)(4r+s)=(4r)^2-s^2=16r^2-s^2$

31. $(8w+5z)(8w-5z)=(8w)^2-(5z)^2$

$\qquad = 64w^2-25z^2$

33. $(5x-9y)(5x+9y)=(5x)^2-(9y)^2$

$\qquad = 25x^2-81y^2$

35. $x(x-2)(x+2)=x(x^2-4)=x^3-4x$

37. $2s(s-3r)(s+3r)=2s(s^2-9r^2)=2s^3-18sr^2$

39. $5r(r+3)^2=5r(r^2+6r+9)$

$\qquad = 5r^3+30r^2+45r$

41. The product of 6 more than a number and 6 less than that number $=(x+6)(x-6)$

$\qquad = x^2-36.$

43. The square of 4 less than a number

$\qquad = (x-4)^2$

$\qquad = x^2-8x+16$

45. $(49)(51)=(50-1)(50+1)=2500-1=2499$

47. $(34)(26)=(30+4)(30-4)=900-16=884$

49. $(55)(65)=(60-5)(60+5)=3600-25=3575$

51. $(5x-4)^2=25x^2-40x+16$ trees

53. Writing exercise

55. Challenge exercise

Exercises 3.5

1. 10, 12
The largest number that is a factor of both is 2.
The GCF is 2.

3. $16, 32, 88$
The GCF is 8.

5. $x^2, \ x^5$
The largest power that divides both terms is x^2.
The GCF is x^2.

7. $a^3, \ a^6, \ a^9$
The GCF is a^3.

9. $5x^4, \ 10x^5$
The GCF is $5x^4$.

11. $8a^4, \ 6a^6, \ 10a^{10}$
The GCF is $2a^4$.

13. $9x^2y, \ 12xy^2, \ 15x^2y^2$
The GCF is $3xy$.

15. $15ab^3, \ 10a^2bc, \ 25b^2c^3$
The GCF is $5b$.

17. $15a^2bc^2, \ 9ab^2c^2, \ 6a^2b^2c^2$
The GCF is $3abc^2$.

19. $(x+y)^2, \ (x+y)^3$
$x + y$ is a binomial used as a factor.
The GCF is $(x+y)^2$.

21. $8a + 4 = 4 \cdot 2a + 4 \cdot 1$
$ = 4(2a+1)$

23. $24m - 32n = 8 \cdot 3m + 8(-4n)$
$ = 8(3m - 4n)$

25. $12m^2 + 8m = 4m \cdot 3m + 4m \cdot 2$
$ = 4m(3m + 2)$

27. $10s^2 + 5s = 5s \cdot 2s + 5s \cdot 1$
$ = 5s(2s + 1)$

29. $12x^2 + 24x = 12x \cdot x + 12x \cdot 2$
$ = 12x(x + 2)$

31. $15a^3 - 25a^2 = 5a^2 \cdot 3a - 5a^2 \cdot 5$
$ = 5a^2(3a - 5)$

33. $6pq + 18p^2q = 6pq \cdot 1 + 6pq \cdot 3p$
$ = 6pq(1 + 3p)$

35. $7m^3n - 21mn^3 = 7mn \cdot m^2 - 7mn \cdot 3n^2$
$ = 7mn(m^2 - 3n^2)$

37. $6x^2 - 18x + 30 = 6 \cdot x^2 - 6 \cdot 3x + 6 \cdot 5$
$ = 6(x^2 - 3x + 5)$

39. $3a^3 + 6a^2 - 12a = 3a \cdot a^2 + 3a \cdot 2a - 3a \cdot 4$
$ = 3a(a^2 + 2a - 4)$

41. $6m + 9mn - 15mn^2$
$= 3m \cdot 2 + 3m \cdot 3n - 3m \cdot 5n^2$
$= 3m(2 + 3n - 5n^2)$
$= 3m(2 + 5n)(1 - n)$

43. $10x^2y + 15xy - 5xy^2$
$= 5xy \cdot 2x + 5xy \cdot 3 - 5xy \cdot y$
$= 5xy(2x + 3 - y)$

45. $10r^3s^2 + 25r^2s^2 - 15r^2s^3$
$= 5r^2s^2 \cdot 2r + 5r^2s^2 \cdot 5 - 5r^2s^2 \cdot 3s$
$= 5r^2s^2(2r + 5 - 3s)$

47. $9a^5 - 15a^4 + 21a^3 - 27a$
$= 3a \cdot 3a^4 - 3a \cdot 5a^3 + 3a \cdot 7a^2 - 3a \cdot 9$
$= 3a(3a^4 - 5a^3 + 7a^2 - 9)$

49. $15m^3n^2 - 20m^2n + 35mn^3 - 10mn$
$= 5mn \cdot 3m^2n - 5mn \cdot 4m + 5mn \cdot 7n^2 - 5mn \cdot 2$
$= 5mn(3m^2n - 4m + 7n^2 - 2)$

51. $x(x - 2) + 3(x - 2)$
Notice that the binomial $x - 2$ is a common factor.
$x(x - 2) + 3(x - 2) = (x - 2) \cdot x + (x - 2) \cdot 3$
$ = (x - 2)(x + 3)$

53. To find the GCF of the product
$(2x - 6)(5x + 10)$, first multiply the factors to get a polynomial.
$(2x - 6)(5x + 10) = 10x^2 - 10x - 60$
$ = 10 \cdot x^2 - 10 \cdot x - 10 \cdot 6$
The GCF is 10, or $5 \cdot 2$.

55. To find the GCF of the product
$(2x^3 - 4x)(3x + 6)$, multiply the factors to get a polynomial.
$(2x^3 - 4x)(3x + 6)$
$\quad = 6x^4 + 12x^3 - 12x^2 - 24x$
$\quad = 6x \cdot x^3 + 6x \cdot 2x^2 - 6x \cdot 2x - 6x \cdot 4$
The GCF is $6x$, or $2x \cdot 3$.

57. The GCF of $2a + 8$ is 2.
The GCF of $3a - 6$ is 3.
The GCF for the product is $2 \cdot 3 = 6$.

59. The GCF of $2x^2 + 5x$ is x.
The GCF of $7x - 14$ is 7.
The GCF for the product is $x \cdot 7 = 7x$.

61. $33t - t^2 = t \cdot 33 - t \cdot t = t(33 - t)$
The length of the rectangle is $33 - t$.

63. Writing exercise

65. Group exercise

Exercises 3.6

1. $x^2 - 8x + 15 = (x - 3)(x - 5)$

3. $m^2 + 8m + 12 = (m + 2)(m + 6)$

5. $p^2 - 8p - 20 = (p + 2)(p - 10)$

7. $x^2 - 16x + 64 = (x - 8)(x - 8)$

9. $x^2 - 7xy + 10y^2 = (x - 2y)(x - 5y)$

11. $x^2 + 8x + 15$
Consider only the positive factors of 15 because
the last two terms are positive.
$15 = (1)(15)$
$\quad = (3)(5)$

Possible Factors	Middle Terms
$(x + 1)(x + 15)$	$16x$
$(x + 3)(x + 5)$	$8x$

$x^2 + 8x + 15 = (x + 3)(x + 5)$

13. $x^2 - 11x + 28$
Consider only the negative factors of 28 because
the middle term is negative.
$28 = (-1)(-28)$
$\quad = (-2)(-14)$
$\quad = (-4)(-7)$

Possible Factors	Middle Terms
$(x - 1)(x - 28)$	$-29x$
$(x - 2)(x - 14)$	$-16x$
$(x - 4)(x - 7)$	$-11x$

$x^2 - 11x + 28 = (x - 4)(x - 7)$

15. $s^2 + 13s + 30$
Consider only the positive factors of 30 because
the last two terms are positive.
$30 = (1)(30)$
$\quad = (2)(15)$
$\quad = (3)(10)$
$\quad = (5)(6)$

Possible Factors	Middle Terms
$(s + 1)(s + 30)$	$31s$
$(s + 2)(s + 15)$	$17s$
$(s + 3)(s + 10)$	$13s$
$(s + 5)(s + 6)$	$11s$

$s^2 + 13s + 30 = (s + 3)(s + 10)$

17. $a^2 - 2a - 48$ Middle Terms

The factors of −48 will have different signs.

$$-48 = (1)(-48)$$
$$= (-1)(48)$$
$$= (2)(-24)$$
$$= (-2)(24)$$
$$= (3)(-16)$$
$$= (-3)(16)$$
$$= (4)(-12)$$
$$= (-4)(12)$$
$$= (6)(-8)$$
$$= (-6)(8)$$

Possible Factors	Middle Terms
$(a + 1)(a - 48)$	$-47a$
$(a - 1)(a + 48)$	$47a$
$(a + 2)(a - 24)$	$-22a$
$(a - 2)(a + 24)$	$22a$
$(a + 3)(a - 16)$	$-13a$
$(a - 3)(a + 16)$	$13a$
$(a + 4)(a - 12)$	$-8a$
$(a - 4)(a + 12)$	$8a$
$(a + 6)(a - 8)$	$-2a$
$(a - 6)(a + 8)$	$2a$

$$a^2 - 2a - 48 = (a + 6)(a - 8)$$

19. $x^2 - 8x + 7$

Consider only the negative factors of 7 because the middle term is negative.

$$7 = (-1)(-7)$$

Possible Factors	Middle Terms
$(x - 1)(x - 7)$	$-8x$

$$x^2 - 8x + 7 = (x - 1)(x - 7)$$

21. $m^2 + 3m - 28$

The factors of −28 will have different signs.

$$-28 = (1)(-28)$$
$$= (-1)(28)$$
$$= (2)(-14)$$
$$= (-2)(14)$$
$$= (4)(-7)$$
$$= (-4)(7)$$

Possible Factors	Middle Terms
$(m + 1)(m - 28)$	$-27m$
$(m - 1)(m + 28)$	$27m$
$(m + 2)(m - 14)$	$-12m$
$(m - 2)(m + 14)$	$12m$
$(m + 4)(m - 7)$	$-3m$
$(m - 4)(m + 7)$	$3m$

$$m^2 + 3m - 28 = (m - 4)(m + 7)$$

23. $x^2 - 6x - 40$

The factors of –40 will have different signs.

$$\begin{aligned} -40 &= (1)(-40) \\ &= (-1)(40) \\ &= (2)(-20) \\ &= (-2)(20) \\ &= (4)(-10) \\ &= (-4)(10) \\ &= (5)(-8) \\ &= (-5)(8) \end{aligned}$$

Possible Factors	Middle Terms
$(x + 1)(x - 40)$	$-39x$
$(x - 1)(x + 40)$	$39x$
$(x + 2)(x - 20)$	$-18x$
$(x - 2)(x + 20)$	$18x$
$(x + 4)(x - 10)$	$-6x$
$(x - 4)(x + 10)$	$6x$
$(x + 5)(x - 8)$	$-3x$
$(x - 5)(x + 8)$	$3x$

$x^2 - 6x - 40 = (x + 4)(x - 10)$

25. $x^2 - 14x + 49$

Consider only the negative factors of 49 because the middle term is negative.

$$\begin{aligned} 49 &= (-1)(-49) \\ &= (-7)(-7) \end{aligned}$$

Possible Factors	Middle Terms
$(x - 1)(x - 49)$	$-50x$
$(x - 7)(x - 7)$	$-14x$

$x^2 - 14x + 49 = (x - 7)(x - 7)$

27. $p^2 - 10p - 24$

The factors of –24 will have different signs.

$$\begin{aligned} -24 &= (1)(-24) \\ &= (-1)(24) \\ &= (2)(-12) \\ &= (-2)(12) \\ &= (3)(-8) \\ &= (-3)(8) \\ &= (4)(-6) \\ &= (-4)(6) \end{aligned}$$

Possible Factors	Middle Terms
$(p + 1)(p - 24)$	$-23p$
$(p - 1)(p + 24)$	$23p$
$(p + 2)(p - 12)$	$-10p$
$(p - 2)(p + 12)$	$10p$
$(p + 3)(p - 8)$	$-5p$
$(p - 3)(p + 8)$	$5p$
$(p + 4)(p - 6)$	$-2p$
$(p - 4)(p + 6)$	$2p$

$p^2 - 10p - 24 = (p + 2)(p - 12)$

29. $x^2 + 5x - 66$

The factors of –66 will have different signs.

$$\begin{aligned} -66 &= (1)(-66) \\ &= (-1)(66) \\ &= (2)(-33) \\ &= (-2)(33) \\ &= (3)(-22) \\ &= (-3)(22) \\ &= (6)(-11) \\ &= (-6)(11) \end{aligned}$$

Possible Factors	Middle Terms
$(x + 1)(x - 66)$	$-65x$
$(x - 1)(x + 66)$	$65x$
$(x + 2)(x - 33)$	$-31x$
$(x - 2)(x + 33)$	$31x$
$(x + 3)(x - 22)$	$-19x$
$(x - 3)(x + 22)$	$19x$
$(x + 6)(x - 11)$	$-5x$
$(x - 6)(x + 11)$	$5x$

$x^2 + 5x - 66 = (x - 6)(x + 11)$

31. $c^2 + 19c + 60$

Consider only the positive factors of 60 because the last two terms are both positive.

$$60 = (1)(60)$$
$$= (2)(30)$$
$$= (3)(20)$$
$$= (4)(15)$$
$$= (5)(12)$$
$$= (6)(10)$$

Possible Factors	Middle Terms
$(c + 1)(c + 60)$	$61c$
$(c + 2)(c + 30)$	$32c$
$(c + 3)(c + 20)$	$23c$
$(c + 4)(c + 15)$	$19c$

Stop when the right pair is found.
$$c^2 + 19c + 60 = (c + 4)(c + 15)$$

33. $n^2 + 5n - 50$

The factors of –50 will have different signs.

$$-50 = (1)(-50)$$
$$= (-1)(50)$$
$$= (2)(-25)$$
$$= (-2)(25)$$
$$= (5)(-10)$$
$$= (-5)(10)$$

Possible Factors	Middle Terms
$(n + 1)(n - 50)$	$-49n$
$(n - 1)(n + 50)$	$49n$
$(n + 2)(n - 25)$	$-23n$
$(n - 2)(n + 25)$	$23n$
$(n + 5)(n - 10)$	$-5n$
$(n - 5)(n + 10)$	$5n$

$$n^2 + 5n - 50 = (n - 5)(n + 10)$$

35. $x^2 + 7xy + 10y^2$

Consider only the positive factors of $10y^2$ because the last two terms are positive.

$$10y^2 = (y)(10y)$$
$$= (2y)(5y)$$

Possible Factors	Middle Terms
$(x + y)(x + 10y)$	$11xy$
$(x + 2y)(x + 5y)$	$7xy$

$$x^2 + 7xy + 10y^2 = (x + 2y)(x + 5y)$$

37. $a^2 - ab - 42b^2$

The factors of –42 will have different signs.

$$-42 = (1)(-42)$$
$$= (-1)(42)$$
$$= (2)(-21)$$
$$= (-2)(21)$$
$$= (3)(-14)$$
$$= (-3)(14)$$
$$= (6)(-7)$$
$$= (-6)(7)$$

Possible Factors	Middle Terms
$(a + b)(a - 42b)$	$-41ab$
$(a - b)(a + 42b)$	$41ab$
$(a + 2b)(a - 21b)$	$-19ab$
$(a - 2b)(a + 21b)$	$19ab$
$(a + 3b)(a - 14b)$	$-11ab$
$(a - 3b)(a + 14b)$	$11ab$
$(a + 6b)(a - 7b)$	$-ab$

Stop when the right pair is found.
$$a^2 - ab - 42b^2 = (a + 6b)(a - 7b)$$

39. $x^2 - 13xy + 40y^2$

Consider only the negative factors of 40 because the middle term is negative.

$$40 = (-1)(-40)$$
$$= (-2)(-20)$$
$$= (-4)(-10)$$
$$= (-5)(-8)$$

Possible Factors	Middle Terms
$(x - y)(x - 40y)$	$-41xy$
$(x - 2y)(x - 20y)$	$-22xy$
$(x - 4y)(x - 10y)$	$-14xy$
$(x - 5y)(x - 8y)$	$-13xy$

$$x^2 - 13xy + 40y^2 = (x - 5y)(x - 8y)$$

41. $b^2 + 6ab + 9a^2$

Consider only the positive factors of 9 because the last two terms are positive.
$$9 = (1)(9)$$
$$= (3)(3)$$

Possible Factors	Middle Terms
$(b + a)(b + 9a)$	$10ab$
$(b + 3a)(b + 3a)$	$6ab$

$$b^2 + 6ab + 9a^2 = (b + 3a)(b + 3a)$$

43. $x^2 - 2xy - 8y^2$

The factors of -8 will have different signs.
$$-8 = (1)(-8)$$
$$= (-1)(8)$$
$$= (2)(-4)$$
$$= (-2)(4)$$

Possible Factors	Middle Terms
$(x + y)(x - 8y)$	$-7xy$
$(x - y)(x + 8y)$	$7xy$
$(x + 2y)(x - 4y)$	$-2xy$
$(x - 2y)(x + 4y)$	$2xy$

$$x^2 - 2xy - 8y^2 = (x + 2y)(x - 4y)$$

45. $25m^2 + 10mn + n^2 = n^2 + 10mn + 25m^2$

Consider only the positive factors of 25 because the last two terms are positive.
$$25 = (1)(25)$$
$$= (5)(5)$$

Possible Factors	Middle Terms
$(n + m)(n + 25m)$	$26mn$
$(n + 5m)(n + 5m)$	$10mn$

$$25m^2 + 10mn + n^2 = (n + 5m)(n + 5m)$$

47. $3a^2 - 3a - 126 = 3(a^2 - a - 42)$
$$= 3(a + 6)(a - 7)$$

49. $r^3 + 7r^2 - 18r = r(r^2 + 7r - 18)$
$$= r(r - 2)(r + 9)$$

51. $2x^3 - 20x^2 - 48x = 2x(x^2 - 10x - 24)$
$$= 2x(x - 12)(x + 2)$$

53. $x^2y - 9xy^2 - 36y^3 = y(x^2 - 9xy - 36y^2)$
$$= y(x + 3y)(x - 12y)$$

55. $m^3 - 29m^2n + 120mn^2 = m(m^2 - 29mn + 120n^2)$
$$= m(m - 5n)(m - 24n)$$

57. $x^2 + kx + 8$

Consider the positive factors of 8.
$$8 = (1)(8)$$
$$= (2)(4)$$

Possible Factors	Middle Terms
$(x + 1)(x + 8)$	$9x$
$(x + 2)(x + 4)$	$6x$

$k = 6$ or 9

59. $x^2 - kx + 16$

Consider the negative factors of 16.
$$16 = (-1)(-16)$$
$$= (-2)(-8)$$
$$= (-4)(-4)$$

Possible Factors	Middle Terms
$(x - 1)(x - 16)$	$-17x$
$(x - 2)(x - 8)$	$-10x$
$(x - 4)(x - 4)$	$-8x$

$k = 8$, 10, or 17

61. $x^2 - kx - 5$

The factors of -5 will have different signs.
$$-5 = (1)(-5)$$
$$= (-1)(5)$$

Possible Factors	Middle Terms
$(x + 1)(x - 5)$	$-4x$
$(x - 1)(x + 5)$	$4x$

$k = 4$

63. $x^2 + 3x + k$

Since the sign of the last two terms is positive, then we need to find all pairs of positive integers whose sum is 3. $1 + 2 = 3$, and since $2 = (1)(2)$ and $(x + 1)(x + 2) = x^2 + 3x + 2$, then $k = 2$.

65. $x^2 + 2x - k$

Since the last term is negative, then we need to find pairs of integers of opposite sign whose sum is 2. $-1 + 3 = 2$, $-2 + 4 = 2$, $-3 + 5 = 2$, etc. So, since

$-3 = (-1)(3)$ and $(x - 1)(x + 3) = x^2 + 2x - 3$

$-8 = (-2)(4)$ and $(x - 2)(x + 4) = x^2 + 2x - 8$

$-15 = (-3)(5)$ and $(x - 3)(x + 5) = x^2 + 2x - 15$

$-24 = (-4)(6)$ and $(x - 4)(x + 6) = x^2 + 2x - 24$

etc.,

then $k = 3, 8, 15, 24, \ldots$

Exercises 3.7

1. The binomial $3x^2 + 2y^2$ is not the difference of squares.

3. Since $16a^2 - 25b^2 = (4a)^2 - (5b)^2$, it is the difference of squares.

5. The binomial $16r^2 + 4$ is not the difference of squares.

7. The binomial $16a^2 - 12b^2$ is not the difference of squares.

9. Since $a^2b^2 - 25 = (ab)^2 - (5)^2$, it is the difference of squares.

11. $m^2 - n^2 = (m + n)(m - n)$

13. $x^2 - 49 = (x + 7)(x - 7)$

15. $49 - y^2 = (7 + y)(7 - y)$

17. $9b^2 - 16 = (3b + 4)(3b - 4)$

19. $16w^2 - 49 = (4w + 7)(4w - 7)$

21. $4s^2 - 9r^2 = (2s + 3r)(2s - 3r)$

23. $9w^2 - 49z^2 = (3w + 7z)(3w - 7z)$

25. $16a^2 - 49b^2 = (4a + 7b)(4a - 7b)$

27. $x^4 - 36 = (x^2 + 6)(x^2 - 6)$

29. $x^2y^2 - 16 = (xy + 4)(xy - 4)$

31. $25 - a^2b^2 = (5 + ab)(5 - ab)$

33. $r^4 - 4s^2 = (r^2 + 2s)(r^2 - 2s)$

35. $81a^2 - 100b^6 = (9a + 10b^3)(9a - 10b^3)$

37. $18x^3 - 2xy^2 = 2x(9x^2 - y^2)$
$= 2x(3x + y)(3x - y)$

39. $12m^3n - 75mn^3 = 3mn(4m^2 - 25n^2)$
$= 3mn(2m + 5n)(2m - 5n)$

41. $48a^2b^2 - 27b^4 = 3b^2(16a^2 - 9b^2)$
$= 3b^2(4a + 3b)(4a - 3b)$

43. $x^2 - 14x + 49$ is a perfect square trinomial in which $a = x$ and $b = -7$.
$x^2 - 14x + 49 = (x - 7)^2$

45. $x^2 - 18x - 81$ is not a perfect square trinomial.

47. $x^2 - 18x + 81$ is a perfect square trinomial in which $a = x$ and $b = -9$.
$x^2 - 18x + 81 = (x - 9)^2$

49. $a = x, b = 2$
$x^2 + 4x + 4 = (x + 2)^2$

51. $a = x, b = -5$
$x^2 - 10x + 25 = (x - 5)^2$

53. $a = 2x, b = 3y$
$4x^2 + 12xy + 9y^2 = (2x + 3y)^2$

55. $a = 3x, b = -4y$
$9x^2 - 24xy + 16y^2 = (3x - 4y)^2$

57. $y^3 - 10y^2 + 25y = y(y^2 - 10y + 25) = y(y - 5)^2$
$a = y, b = -5$

59. $x^2(x + y) - y^2(x + y) = (x + y)(x^2 - y^2)$
$= (x + y)(x + y)(x - y)$
$= (x + y)^2(x - y)$

61. $2m^2(m - 2n) - 18n^2(m - 2n)$
$= 2(m - 2n)(m^2 - 9n^2)$
$= 2(m - 2n)(m + 3n)(m - 3n)$

63. $kx^2 - 25 = (2x + 5)(2x - 5)$
$kx^2 - 25 = 4x^2 - 25$ so $k = 4$

65. $2x^3 - kxy^2 = 2x(x - 3y)(x + 3y)$
$$= 2x(x^2 - 9y^2)$$
$$= 2x^3 - 18xy^2 \text{ so } k = 18$$

67. Writing exercise

Exercises 3.8

1. $4x^2 - 4x - 3 = (2x + 1)(2x - 3)$

3. $6a^2 + 13a + 6 = (2a + 3)(3a + 2)$

5. $15x^2 - 16x + 4 = (3x - 2)(5x - 2)$

7. $16a^2 + 8ab + b^2 = (4a + b)(4a + b)$

9. $4m^2 + 5mn - 6n^2 = (m + 2n)(4m - 3n)$

11. $3x^2 + 7x + 2$
$3 = 3 \cdot 1 \qquad 2 = 2 \cdot 1$
Notice all the signs of the trinomial are positive.

Possible Factors	Middle Terms
$(3x + 2)(x + 1)$	$5x$
$(3x + 1)(x + 2)$	$7x$

$3x^2 + 7x + 2 = (3x + 1)(x + 2)$

13. $2w^2 + 13w + 15$
$2 = 2 \cdot 1 \qquad 15 = 15 \cdot 1$
$\qquad\qquad\qquad\quad = 5 \cdot 3$
Notice all the signs of the trinomial are positive.

Possible Factors	Middle Terms
$(2w + 15)(w + 1)$	$17w$
$(2w + 1)(w + 15)$	$31w$
$(2w + 5)(w + 3)$	$11w$
$(2w + 3)(w + 5)$	$13w$

$2w^2 + 13w + 15 = (2w + 3)(w + 5)$

15. $5x^2 - 16x + 3$
$5 = 5 \cdot 1 \qquad 3 = 3 \cdot 1$
Notice only the middle term is negative.

Possible Factors	Middle Terms
$(5x - 3)(x - 1)$	$-8x$
$(5x - 1)(x - 3)$	$-16x$

17. $5x^2 - 16x + 3 = (5x - 1)(x - 3)$
$4x^2 - 12x + 5$
$4 = 4 \cdot 1 \qquad 5 = 5 \cdot 1$
$\quad = 2 \cdot 2$
Notice only the middle term is negative.

Possible Factors	Middle Terms
$(4x - 5)(x - 1)$	$-9x$
$(4x - 1)(x - 5)$	$-21x$
$(2x - 5)(2x - 1)$	$-12x$

$4x^2 - 12x + 5 = (2x - 5)(2x - 1)$

19. $3x^2 - 5x - 2$
$3 = 3 \cdot 1 \qquad 2 = 2 \cdot 1$
Notice two of the signs are negative.

Possible Factors	Middle Terms
$(3x + 2)(x - 1)$	$-x$
$(3x - 2)(x + 1)$	x
$(3x + 1)(x - 2)$	$-5x$
$(3x - 1)(x + 2)$	$5x$

$3x^2 - 5x - 2 = (3x + 1)(x - 2)$

21. $4p^2 + 19p - 5$
$4 = 4 \cdot 1 \qquad 5 = 5 \cdot 1$
$\quad = 2 \cdot 2$
Notice only the last term is negative.

Possible Factors	Middle Terms
$(4p + 5)(p - 1)$	p
$(4p - 5)(p + 1)$	$-p$
$(4p + 1)(p - 5)$	$-19p$
$(4p - 1)(p + 5)$	$19p$

Stop as soon as the correct pair is found.
$4p^2 + 19p - 5 = (4p - 1)(p + 5)$

23. $6x^2 + 19x + 10$

$6 = 6 \cdot 1 \qquad 10 = 10 \cdot 1$

$ = 3 \cdot 2 \qquad = 5 \cdot 2$

Notice all the signs of the trinomial are positive.

Possible Factors	Middle Terms
$(6x + 10)(x + 1)$	$16x$
$(6x + 1)(x + 10)$	$61x$
$(6x + 5)(x + 2)$	$17x$
$(6x + 2)(x + 5)$	$32x$
$(3x + 10)(2x + 1)$	$23x$
$(3x + 1)(2x + 10)$	$32x$
$(3x + 5)(2x + 2)$	$16x$
$(3x + 2)(2x + 5)$	$19x$

$6x^2 + 19x + 10 = (3x + 2)(2x + 5)$

25. $15x^2 + x - 6$

$15 = 15 \cdot 1 \qquad 6 = 6 \cdot 1$

$ = 5 \cdot 3 \qquad = 3 \cdot 2$

Notice only the last term is negative.

Possible Factors	Middle Terms
$(15x + 6)(x - 1)$	$-9x$
$(15x - 6)(x + 1)$	$9x$
$(15x + 1)(x - 6)$	$-89x$
$(15x - 1)(x + 6)$	$89x$
$(5x + 3)(3x - 2)$	$-x$
$(5x - 3)(3x + 2)$	x

Stop as soon as the correct pair is found.

$15x^2 + x - 6 = (5x - 3)(3x + 2)$

27. $6m^2 + 25m - 25$

$6 = 6 \cdot 1 \qquad 25 = 25 \cdot 1$

$ = 3 \cdot 2 \qquad = 5 \cdot 5$

Notice only the last term is negative.

Possible Factors	Middle Terms
$(6m + 25)(m - 1)$	$19m$
$(6m - 25)(m + 1)$	$-19m$
$(6m + 5)(m - 5)$	$-25m$
$(6m - 5)(m + 5)$	$25m$

Stop as soon as the correct pair is found.

$6m^2 + 25m - 25 = (6m - 5)(m + 5)$

29. $9x^2 - 12x + 4$

$9 = 3 \cdot 3 \qquad 4 = 2 \cdot 2$

$ = 9 \cdot 1 \qquad = 4 \cdot 1$

Consider only the negative factors of 4.

Possible Factors	Middle Terms
$(3x - 2)(3x - 2)$	$-12x$

Stop as soon as the correct pair is found.

$9x^2 - 12x + 4 = (3x - 2)(3x - 2)$

31. $12x^2 - 8x - 15$

$12 = 4 \cdot 3 \qquad 15 = 5 \cdot 3$

$ = 6 \cdot 2 \qquad = 15 \cdot 1$

$ = 12 \cdot 1$

Notice there are two negative signs.

Possible Factors	Middle Terms
$(4x - 5)(3x + 3)$	$-3x$
$(4x + 5)(3x - 3)$	$3x$
$(4x - 3)(3x + 5)$	$11x$
$(4x + 3)(3x - 5)$	$-11x$
$(6x - 5)(2x + 3)$	$8x$
$(6x + 5)(2x - 3)$	$-8x$

Stop as soon as the correct pair is found.

$12x^2 - 8x - 15 = (6x + 5)(2x - 3)$

33. $3y^2 + 7y - 6$

$3 = 3 \cdot 1 \qquad 6 = 6 \cdot 1$

$ \qquad = 3 \cdot 2$

Notice only one sign is negative.

Possible Factors	Middle Terms
$(3y + 6)(y - 1)$	$3y$
$(3y - 6)(y + 1)$	$-3y$
$(3y + 3)(y - 2)$	$-3y$
$(3y - 3)(y + 2)$	$3y$
$(3y + 2)(y - 3)$	$-7y$
$(3y - 2)(y + 3)$	$7y$

Stop as soon as the correct pair is found.

$3y^2 + 7y - 6 = (3y - 2)(y + 3)$

35. $8x^2 - 27x - 20$

$$8 = 8 \cdot 1 \qquad 20 = 20 \cdot 1$$
$$ = 4 \cdot 2 \qquad = 5 \cdot 4$$
$$ = 10 \cdot 2$$

Notice two of the signs are negative.

Possible Factors	Middle Terms
$(8x + 20)(x - 1)$	$12x$
$(8x - 20)(x + 1)$	$-12x$
$(8x + 1)(x - 20)$	$-159x$
$(8x - 1)(x + 20)$	$159x$
$(8x + 5)(x - 4)$	$-27x$

Stop as soon as the correct pair is found.
$$8x^2 - 27x - 20 = (8x + 5)(x - 4)$$

37. $2x^2 + 3xy + y^2$

$$2 = 2 \cdot 1 \qquad 1 = 1 \cdot 1$$

Notice all of the signs of the trinomial are positive.

Possible Factors	Middle Terms
$(2x + y)(x + y)$	$3xy$

$$2x^2 + 3xy + y^2 = (2xy + y)(x + y)$$

39. $5a^2 - 8ab - 4b^2$

$$5 = 5 \cdot 1 \qquad 4 = 4 \cdot 1$$
$$ = 2 \cdot 2$$

Notice two of the signs are negative.

Possible Factors	Middle Terms
$(5a + 4b)(a - b)$	$-ab$
$(5a - 4b)(a + b)$	ab
$(5a + b)(a - 4b)$	$-19ab$
$(5a - b)(a + 4b)$	$19ab$
$(5a + 2b)(a - 2b)$	$-8ab$

$$5a^2 - 8ab - 4b^2 = (5a + 2b)(a - 2b)$$

41. $9x^2 + 4xy - 5y^2$

$$9 = 9 \cdot 1 \qquad 5 = 5 \cdot 1$$
$$ = 3 \cdot 3$$

Notice only one of the signs is negative.

Possible Factors	Middle Terms
$(9x + 5y)(x - y)$	$-4xy$
$(9x - 5y)(x + y)$	$4xy$

Stop as soon as the correct pair is found.
$$9x^2 + 4xy - 5y^2 = (9x - 5y)(x + y)$$

43. $6m^2 - 17mn + 12n^2$

$$6 = 6 \cdot 1 \qquad 12 = 12 \cdot 1$$
$$ = 3 \cdot 2 \qquad = 4 \cdot 3$$

Consider only the negative factors of 12.

Possible Factors	Middle Terms
$(6m - 12n)(m - n)$	$-18mn$
$(6m - n)(m - 12n)$	$-73mn$
$(6m - 4n)(m - 3n)$	$-22mn$
$(6m - 3n)(m - 4n)$	$-27mn$
$(3m - 4n)(2m - 3n)$	$-17mn$

Stop as soon as the correct pair is found.
$$6m^2 - 17mn + 12n^2 = (3m - 4n)(2m - 3n)$$

45. $36a^2 - 3ab - 5b^2$

$$36 = 36 \cdot 1 \qquad 5 = 5 \cdot 1$$
$$ = 18 \cdot 2$$
$$ = 12 \cdot 3$$
$$ = 9 \cdot 4$$
$$ = 6 \cdot 6$$

Notice two of the signs are negative.

Possible Factors	Middle Terms
$(36a + 5b)(a - b)$	$-31ab$
$(36a - 5b)(a + b)$	$31ab$
$(36a + b)(a - 5b)$	$-179ab$
$(36a - b)(a + 5b)$	$179ab$
$(18a + 5b)(2a - b)$	$-8ab$
$(18a - 5b)(2a + b)$	$8ab$
$(18a + b)(2a - 5b)$	$-88ab$
$(18a - b)(2a + 5b)$	$88ab$
$(12a + 5b)(3a - b)$	$3ab$
$(12a - 5b)(3a + b)$	$-3ab$

Stop as soon as the correct pair is found.
$$36a^2 - 3ab - 5b^2 = (12a - 5b)(3a + b)$$

Stop as soon as the correct pair is found.
$$9x^2 + 4xy - 5y^2 = (9x - 5y)(x + y)$$

47. $x^2 + 4xy + 4y^2$

$1 = 1 \cdot 1 \qquad 4 = 4 \cdot 1$
$\qquad\qquad\qquad = 2 \cdot 2$

Notice all of the signs are positive.

Possible Factors	Middle Terms
$(x + 4y)(x + y)$	$5xy$
$(x + 2y)(x + 2y)$	$4xy$

$x^2 + 4xy + 4y^2 = (x + 2y)(x + 2y)$

49. $20x^2 - 20x - 15 = 5(4x^2 - 4x - 3)$
$\qquad\qquad\qquad\qquad = 5(2x - 3)(2x + 1)$

51. $8m^2 + 12m + 4 = 4(2m^2 + 3m + 1)$
$\qquad\qquad\qquad\qquad = 4(2m + 1)(m + 1)$

53. $15r^2 - 21rs + 6s^2 = 3(5r^2 - 7rs + 2s^2)$
$\qquad\qquad\qquad\qquad\quad = 3(5r - 2s)(r - s)$

55. $2x^3 - 2x^2 - 4x = 2x(x^2 - x - 2)$
$\qquad\qquad\qquad\qquad = 2x(x - 2)(x + 1)$

57. $2y^4 + 5y^3 + 3y^2 = y^2(2y^2 + 5y + 3)$
$\qquad\qquad\qquad\qquad = y^2(2y + 3)(y + 1)$

59. $36a^3 - 66a^2 + 18a = 6a(6a^2 - 11a + 3)$
$\qquad\qquad\qquad\qquad\quad = 6a(3a - 1)(2a - 3)$

61. $9p^2 + 30pq + 21q^2 = 3(3p^2 + 10pq + 7q^2)$
$\qquad\qquad\qquad\qquad\quad = 3(p + q)(3p + 7q)$

63. $10(x + y)^2 - 11(x + y) - 6$
$\qquad = [5(x + y) + 2][2(x + y) - 3]$
$\qquad = (5x + 5y + 2)(2x + 2y - 3)$

65. $5(x - 1)^2 - 15(x - 1) - 350$
$\qquad = 5[(x - 1)^2 - 3(x - 1) - 70]$
$\qquad = 5[(x - 1) - 10][(x - 1) + 7]$
$\qquad = 5(x - 1 - 10)(x - 1 + 7)$
$\qquad = 5(x - 11)(x + 6)$

67. $15 + 29x - 48x^2 = (1 + 3x)(15 - 16x)$

69. $-6x^2 + 19x - 15 = (3x - 5)(-2x + 3)$

Exercises 3.9

1. $x^2 + 2x - 3 \overset{?}{=} (x + 3)(x - 1);$ True
$(x + 3)(x - 1) = x^2 - x + 3x - 3$
$\qquad\qquad\qquad = x^2 + 2x - 3$

3. $x^2 - 10x - 24 \overset{?}{=} (x - 6)(x + 4);$ False
$(x - 6)(x + 4) = x^2 + 4x - 6x - 24$
$\qquad\qquad\qquad = x^2 - 2x - 24$

5. $x^2 - 16x + 64 \overset{?}{=} (x - 8)(x - 8);$ True
$(x - 8)(x - 8) = x^2 - 8x - 8x + 64$
$\qquad\qquad\qquad = x^2 - 16x + 64$

7. $25y^2 - 10y + 1 \overset{?}{=} (5y - 1)(5y + 1);$ False
$(5y - 1)(5y + 1) = (5y)^2 - 1^2$
$\qquad\qquad\qquad\quad = 25y^2 - 1$

9. $10p^2 - pq - 3q^2 \overset{?}{=} (5p - 3q)(2p + q);$ True
$(5p - 3q)(2p + q) = 10p^2 + 5qp - 6pq - 3q^2$
$\qquad\qquad\qquad\qquad = 10p^2 - pq - 3q^2$

11. $x^2 + 4x - 9;\ a = 1,\ b = 4,\ c = -9$

13. $x^2 - 3x + 8;\ a = 1,\ b = -3,\ c = 8$

15. $3x^2 + 5x - 8;\ a = 3,\ b = 5,\ c = -8$

17. $4x^2 + 8x + 11;\ a = 4,\ b = 8,\ c = 11$

19. $-3x^2 + 5x - 10;\ a = -3,\ b = 5,\ c = -10$

21. $x^2 + x - 6$
$a = 1 \qquad b = +1 \qquad c = -6$
$mn = ac = 1(-6) = -6$
$m + n = b = +1$

mn	$m + n$
$1(-6) = -6$	$1 + (-6) = -5$
$3(-2) = -6$	$3 + (-2) = 1$

We need look no further than 3 and −2. Because we found values for m and n, the trinomial is factorable.

m and n are −2 and +3.

23. $x^2 + x + 2$

$a = 1 \qquad b = 1 \qquad c = 2$

$mn = ac = 1(2) = 2$

$m + n = b = 1$

mn	$m + n$
$1(2) = 2$	$1 + 2 = 3$
$-1(-2) = 2$	$-1 + (-2) = -3$

None of these pairs has a sum of 1.
The trinomial is not factorable.

25. $x^2 - 5x + 6$

$a = 1 \qquad b = -5 \qquad c = 6$

$mn = ac = 1(6) = 6$

$m + n = b = -5$

mn	$m + n$
$1(6) = 6$	$1 + 6 = 7$
$2(3) = 6$	$2 + 3 = 5$
$-1(-6) = 6$	$-1 + (-6) = -7$
$-2(-3) = 6$	$-2 + (-3) = -5$

Because we found values for m and n, the trinomial is factorable.
m and n are -3 and -2.

27. $2x^2 + 5x - 3$

$a = 2 \qquad b = 5 \qquad c = -3$

$mn = ac = 2(-3) = -6$

$m + n = b = 5$

mn	$m + n$
$1(-6) = -6$	$1 + (-6) = -5$
$2(-3) = -6$	$2 + (-3) = -1$
$3(-2) = -6$	$3 + (-2) = 1$
$6(-1) = -6$	$6 + (-1) = 5$

Because we found values for m and n, the trinomial is factorable.
m and n are 6 and -1.

29. $6x^2 - 19x + 10$

$a = 6 \qquad b = -19 \qquad c = 10$

$mn = ac = 6(10) = 60$

$m + n = b = -19$

mn	$m + n$
$-1(-60) = 60$	$-1 + (-60) = -61$
$-2(-30) = 60$	$-2 + (-30) = -32$
$-3(-20) = 60$	$-3 + (-20) = -23$
$-4(-15) = 60$	$-4 + (-15) = -19$

We need look no further than -4 and -15.
Because we found values for m and n, the trinomial is factorable.

31. $\begin{aligned}[t] x^2 + 6x + 8 &= x^2 + 4x + 2x + 8 \\ &= (x^2 + 4x) + (2x + 8) \\ &= x(x + 4) + 2(x + 4) \\ &= (x + 2)(x + 4) \end{aligned}$

33. $\begin{aligned}[t] x^2 - 9x + 20 &= x^2 - 5x - 4x + 20 \\ &= (x^2 - 5x) + (-4x + 20) \\ &= x(x - 5) - 4(x - 5) \\ &= (x - 5)(x - 4) \end{aligned}$

35. $\begin{aligned}[t] x^2 - 2x - 63 &= x^2 - 9x + 7x - 63 \\ &= (x^2 - 9x) + (7x - 63) \\ &= x(x - 9) + 7(x - 9) \\ &= (x - 9)(x + 7) \end{aligned}$

37. $\begin{aligned}[t] x^2 + 8x + 15 &= x^2 + 5x + 3x + 15 \\ &= (x^2 + 5x) + (3x + 15) \\ &= x(x + 5) + 3(x + 5) \\ &= (x + 3)(x + 5) \end{aligned}$

39. $\begin{aligned}[t] x^2 - 11x + 28 &= x^2 - 7x - 4x + 28 \\ &= (x^2 - 7x) + (-4x + 28) \\ &= x(x - 7) - 4(x - 7) \\ &= (x - 4)(x - 7) \end{aligned}$

41. $\begin{aligned}[t] s^2 + 13s + 30 &= s^2 + 3s + 10s + 30 \\ &= (s^2 + 3s) + (10s + 30) \\ &= s(s + 3) + 10(s + 3) \\ &= (s + 10)(s + 3) \end{aligned}$

43. $a^2 - 2a - 48 = a^2 - 8a + 6a - 48$
$$= (a^2 - 8a) + (6a - 48)$$
$$= a(a - 8) + 6(a - 8)$$
$$= (a - 8)(a + 6)$$

45. $x^2 - 8x + 7 = x^2 - 7x - x + 7$
$$= (x^2 - 7x) + (-x + 7)$$
$$= x(x - 7) - (x - 7)$$
$$= (x - 1)(x - 7)$$

47. $x^2 - 6x - 40 = x^2 - 10x + 4x - 40$
$$= (x^2 - 10x) + (4x - 40)$$
$$= x(x - 10) + 4(x - 10)$$
$$= (x - 10)(x + 4)$$

49. $x^2 - 14x + 49 = x^2 - 7x - 7x + 49$
$$= (x^2 - 7x) + (-7x + 49)$$
$$= x(x - 7) - 7(x - 7)$$
$$= (x - 7)(x - 7)$$

51. $p^2 - 10p - 24 = p^2 - 12p + 2p - 24$
$$= (p^2 - 12p) + (2p - 24)$$
$$= p(p - 12) + 2(p - 12)$$
$$= (p - 12)(p + 2)$$

53. $x^2 + 5x - 66 = x^2 + 11x - 6x - 66$
$$= (x^2 + 11x) + (-6x - 66)$$
$$= x(x + 11) - 6(x + 11)$$
$$= (x + 11)(x - 6)$$

55. $c^2 + 19c + 60 = c^2 + 15c + 4c + 60$
$$= (c^2 + 15c) + (4c + 60)$$
$$= c(c + 15) + 4(c + 15)$$
$$= (c + 4)(c + 15)$$

57. $n^2 + 5n - 50 = n^2 + 10n - 5n - 50$
$$= (n^2 + 10n) + (-5n - 50)$$
$$= n(n + 10) - 5(n + 10)$$
$$= (n + 10)(n - 5)$$

59. $x^2 + 7xy + 10y^2 = x^2 + 5xy + 2xy + 10y^2$
$$= (x^2 + 5xy) + (2xy + 10y^2)$$
$$= x(x + 5y) + 2y(x + 5y)$$
$$= (x + 2y)(x + 5y)$$

61. $a^2 - ab - 42b^2 = a^2 - 7ab + 6ab - 42b^2$
$$= (a^2 - 7ab) + (6ab - 42b^2)$$
$$= a(a - 7b) + 6b(a - 7b)$$
$$= (a - 7b)(a + 6b)$$

63. $x^2 - 13xy + 40y^2 = x^2 - 8xy - 5xy + 40y^2$
$$= (x^2 - 8xy) + (-5xy + 40y^2)$$
$$= x(x - 8y) - 5y(x - 8y)$$
$$= (x - 5y)(x - 8y)$$

65. $6x^2 + 19x + 10 = 6x^2 + 4x + 15x + 10$
$$= (6x^2 + 4x) + (15x + 10)$$
$$= 2x(3x + 2) + 5(3x + 2)$$
$$= (3x + 2)(2x + 5)$$

67. $15x^2 + x - 6 = 15x^2 - 9x + 10x - 6$
$$= (15x^2 - 9x) + (10x - 6)$$
$$= 3x(5x - 3) + 2(5x - 3)$$
$$= (5x - 3)(3x + 2)$$

69. $6m^2 + 25m - 25 = 6m^2 - 5m + 30m - 25$
$$= (6m^2 - 5m) + (30m - 25)$$
$$= m(6m - 5) + 5(6m - 5)$$
$$= (6m - 5)(m + 5)$$

71. $9x^2 - 12x + 4 = 9x^2 - 6x - 6x + 4$
$$= (9x^2 - 6x) + (-6x + 4)$$
$$= 3x(3x - 2) - 2(3x - 2)$$
$$= (3x - 2)(3x - 2)$$

73. $12x^2 - 8x - 15 = 12x^2 + 10x - 18x - 15$
$$= (12x^2 + 10x) + (-18x - 15)$$
$$= 2x(6x + 5) - 3(6x + 5)$$
$$= (6x + 5)(2x - 3)$$

75. $3y^2 + 7y - 6 = 3y^2 - 2y + 9y - 6$
$$= (3y^2 - 2y) + (9y - 6)$$
$$= y(3y - 2) + 3(3y - 2)$$
$$= (3y - 2)(y + 3)$$

77. $8x^2 - 27x - 20 = 8x^2 + 5x - 32x - 20$
$$= (8x^2 + 5x) + (-32x - 20)$$
$$= x(8x + 5) - 4(8x + 5)$$
$$= (8x + 5)(x - 4)$$

79. $2x^2 + 3xy + y^2 = 2x^2 + xy + 2xy + y^2$
$$= (2x^2 + xy) + (2xy + y^2)$$
$$= x(2x + y) + y(2x + y)$$
$$= (2x + y)(x + y)$$

81. $5a^2 - 8ab - 4b^2 = 5a^2 + 2ab - 10ab - 4b^2$
$$= (5a^2 + 2ab) + (-10ab - 4b^2)$$
$$= a(5a + 2b) - 2b(5a + 2b)$$
$$= (5a + 2b)(a - 2b)$$

83. $9x^2 + 4xy - 5y^2 = 9x^2 - 5xy + 9xy - 5y^2$
$$= (9x^2 - 5xy) + (9xy - 5y^2)$$
$$= x(9x - 5y) + y(9x - 5y)$$
$$= (9x - 5y)(x + y)$$

85. $6m^2 - 17mn + 12n^2$
$$= 6m^2 - 8mn - 9mn + 12n^2$$
$$= (6m^2 - 8mn) + (-9mn + 12n^2)$$
$$= 2m(3m - 4n) - 3n(3m - 4n)$$
$$= (3m - 4n)(2m - 3n)$$

87. $36a^2 - 3ab - 5b^2 = 36a^2 - 15ab + 12ab - 5b^2$
$$= (36a^2 - 15ab) + (12ab - 5b^2)$$
$$= 3a(12a - 5b) + b(12a - 5b)$$
$$= (12a - 5b)(3a + b)$$

89. $x^2 + 4xy + 4y^2 = x^2 + 2xy + 2xy + 4y^2$
$$= (x^2 + 2xy) + (2xy + 4y^2)$$
$$= x(x + 2y) + 2y(x + 2y)$$
$$= (x + 2y)(x + 2y)$$
$$= (x + 2y)^2$$

91. $20x^2 - 20x - 15 = 5(4x^2 - 4x - 3)$
$$= 5(4x^2 - 6x + 2x - 3)$$
$$= 5[2x(2x - 3) + 1(2x - 3)]$$
$$= 5(2x - 3)(2x + 1)$$

93. $8m^2 + 12m + 4 = 4(2m^2 + 3m + 1)$
$$= 4(2m^2 + m + 2m + 1)$$
$$= 4[m(2m + 1) + (2m + 1)]$$
$$= 4(2m + 1)(m + 1)$$

95. $15r^2 - 21rs + 6s^2 = 3(5r^2 - 7rs + 2s^2)$
$$= 3(5r^2 - 2rs - 5rs + 2s^2)$$
$$= 3[r(5r - 2s) - s(5r - 2s)]$$
$$= 3(5r - 2s)(r - s)$$

97. $2x^3 - 2x^2 - 4x = 2x(x^2 - x - 2)$
$$= 2x(x^2 - 2x + x - 2)$$
$$= 2x[x(x - 2) + (x - 2)]$$
$$= 2x(x - 2)(x + 1)$$

99. $2y^4 + 5y^3 + 3y^2 = y^2(2y^2 + 5y + 3)$
$$= y^2(2y^2 + 3y + 2y + 3)$$
$$= y^2[y(2y + 3) + (2y + 3)]$$
$$= y^2(2y + 3)(y + 1)$$

101. $36a^3 - 66a^2 + 18a = 6a(6a^2 - 11a + 3)$
$$= 6a(6a^2 - 2a - 9a + 3)$$
$$= 6a[2a(3a - 1) - 3(3a - 1)]$$
$$= 6a(3a - 1)(2a - 3)$$

103. $9p^2 + 30pq + 21q^2 = 3(3p^2 + 10pq + 7q^2)$
$$= 3(3p^2 + 7pq + 3pq + 7q^2)$$
$$= 3[p(3p + 7q) + q(3p + 7q)]$$
$$= 3(p + q)(3p + 7q)$$

105. $x^2 + kx + 8 \Rightarrow mn = 8$ and $m + n = k$
$$2 \cdot 4 = 8 \text{ and } m + n = 6$$
$$1 \cdot 8 = 8 \text{ and } m + n = 9$$
$k = 6$ or $k = 9$

107. $x^2 - kx + 16 \Rightarrow mn = 16$ and $m + n = -k$
$$-4 \cdot (-4) = 16 \text{ and } m + n = -8$$
$$-2 \cdot (-8) = 16 \text{ and } m + n = -10$$
$$-1 \cdot (-16) = 16 \text{ and } m + n = -17$$
$-k = -8, -k = -10, -k = -17$
$k = 8$ or $k = 10$ or $k = 17$

109. $x^2 - kx - 5 \Rightarrow mn = -5$ and $m + n = -k$
$$-1 \cdot 5 = -5 \text{ and } m + n = 4$$
$$1 \cdot (-5) = -5 \text{ and } m + n = -4$$
$-k = -4$ gives $k = 4$

111. $x^2 + 3x + k \Rightarrow m + n = 3$ and $mn = k$
$$1 + 2 = 3 \text{ and } mn = 2$$
$$2 + 1 = 3 \text{ and } mn = 2$$
$k = 2$

113. $x^2 + 2x - k = (x+m)(x-n)$
$$= x^2 + (m-n)x - mn$$

$m - n = 2 \qquad k = mn$

$3 - 1 = 2 \qquad k = 3 \cdot 1 = 3$

$4 - 2 = 2 \qquad k = 4 \cdot 2 = 8$

$5 - 3 = 2 \qquad k = 5 \cdot 3 = 15$

$6 - 4 = 2 \qquad k = 6 \cdot 4 = 24$

$k = 3,\ 8,\ 15,\ 24,\ \ldots$

Exercises 3.10

1. $(x-3)(x-4) = 0$

$x - 3 = 0$ or $x - 4 = 0$

$x = 3$ or $\quad x = 4$

3. $(3x+1)(x-6) = 0$

$3x + 1 = 0$ or $x - 6 = 0$

$x = -\dfrac{1}{3}$ or $\quad x = 6$

5. $x^2 - 2x - 3 = 0$

$(x-3)(x+1) = 0$

$x - 3 = 0$ or $x + 1 = 0$

$x = 3$ or $\quad x = -1$

7. $x^2 - 7x + 6 = 0$

$(x-6)(x-1) = 0$

$x - 6 = 0$ or $x - 1 = 0$

$x = 6$ or $\quad x = 1$

9. $x^2 + 8x + 15 = 0$

$(x+5)(x+3) = 0$

$x + 5 = 0$ or $x + 3 = 0$

$x = -5$ or $\quad x = -3$

11. $x^2 + 4x - 21 = 0$

$(x+7)(x-3) = 0$

$x + 7 = 0$ or $x - 3 = 0$

$x = -7$ or $\quad x = 3$

13. $x^2 - 4x = 12$

$x^2 - 4x - 12 = 0$

$(x-6)(x+2) = 0$

$x - 6 = 0$ or $x + 2 = 0$

$x = 6$ or $\quad x = -2$

15. $x^2 + 5x = 14$

$x^2 + 5x - 14 = 0$

$(x+7)(x-2) = 0$

$x + 7 = 0$ or $x - 2 = 0$

$x = -7$ or $\quad x = 2$

17. $2x^2 + 5x - 3 = 0$

$(2x-1)(x+3) = 0$

$2x - 1 = 0$ or $x + 3 = 0$

$x = \dfrac{1}{2}$ or $\quad x = -3$

19. $4x^2 - 24x + 35 = 0$

$(2x-5)(2x-7) = 0$

$2x - 5 = 0$ or $2x - 7 = 0$

$x = \dfrac{5}{2}$ or $\quad x = \dfrac{7}{2}$

21. $\quad 4x^2 + 11x = -6$

$4x^2 + 11x + 6 = 0$

$(4x+3)(x+2) = 0$

$4x + 3 = 0$ or $x + 2 = 0$

$x = -\dfrac{3}{4}$ or $\quad x = -2$

23. $\quad 5x^2 + 13x = 6$

$5x^2 + 13x - 6 = 0$

$(5x-2)(x+3) = 0$

$5x - 2 = 0$ or $x + 3 = 0$

$x = \dfrac{2}{5}$ or $\quad x = -3$

25. $x^2 - 2x = 0$

$x(x-2) = 0$

$x = 0$ or $x - 2 = 0$

$\qquad\qquad x = 2$

27. $\quad x^2 = -8x$

$x^2 + 8x = 0$

$x(x+8) = 0$

$x = 0$ or $x + 8 = 0$

$\qquad\qquad x = -8$

29. $5x^2 - 15x = 0$

$5x(x-3) = 0$

$5x = 0$ or $x - 3 = 0$

$x = 0$ or $\quad x = 3$

31. $\quad x^2 - 25 = 0$

$(x+5)(x-5) = 0$

$x + 5 = 0$ or $x - 5 = 0$

$x = -5$ or $\quad x = 5$

33.
$$x^2 = 81$$
$$x^2 - 81 = 0$$
$$(x+9)(x-9) = 0$$
$$x+9 = 0 \quad \text{or} \quad x-9 = 0$$
$$x = -9 \quad \text{or} \quad x = 9$$

35.
$$2x^2 - 18 = 0$$
$$2(x^2 - 9) = 0$$
$$2(x+3)(x-3) = 0$$
$$x+3 = 0 \quad \text{or} \quad x-3 = 0$$
$$x = -3 \quad \text{or} \quad x = 3$$

37. $3x^2 + 24x + 45 = 0$
$$3(x^2 + 8x + 15) = 0$$
$$3(x+5)(x+3) = 0$$
$$x+5 = 0 \quad \text{or} \quad x+3 = 0$$
$$x = -5 \quad \text{or} \quad x = -3$$

39.
$$6x^2 + 28x = 10$$
$$6x^2 + 28x - 10 = 0$$
$$2(3x^2 + 14x - 5) = 0$$
$$2(3x - 1)(x + 5) = 0$$
$$3x - 1 = 0 \quad \text{or} \quad x + 5 = 0$$
$$x = \frac{1}{3} \quad \text{or} \quad x = -5$$

41. $(x+3)(x-2) = 14$
$$x^2 + x - 6 = 14$$
$$x^2 + x - 20 = 0$$
$$(x+5)(x-4) = 0$$
$$x+5 = 0 \quad \text{or} \quad x-4 = 0$$
$$x = -5 \quad \text{or} \quad x = 4$$

43. $x = 1^{st}$ integer
$x+1 = $ next integer
$$x(x+1) = 132$$
$$x^2 + x - 132 = 0$$
$$(x+12)(x-11) = 0$$
$$x = -12 \quad \text{or} \quad x = 11$$
$$x+1 = -11 \qquad x+1 = 12$$
The integers are $-12, -11$ or $11, 12$.

45. $x = $ the integer
$$x^2 + x = 72$$
$$x^2 + x - 72 = 0$$
$$(x+9)(x-8) = 0$$
$$x = -9 \quad \text{or} \quad x = 8$$
The integer is -9 or 8.

47. $x = $ side length of original square.
new area= original area+ 39
$$(x+3)^2 = x^2 + 39$$
$$x^2 + 6x + 9 = x^2 + 39$$
$$6x = 30$$
$$x = 5$$
The original square was 5 in. by 5 in.

49. $P = -20$
$$x^2 - 3x - 60 = -20$$
$$x^2 - 3x - 40 = 0$$
$$(x-8)(x+5) = 0$$
$$x = 8 \quad \text{or} \quad x = -5$$
There were 8 appliances sold.

51. Writing exercise

Exercises 3.11

1. $x^2 + 9x + 20 = 0$
$$x = \frac{-9 \pm \sqrt{9^2 - 4(1)(20)}}{2(1)}$$
$$x = \frac{-9 \pm 1}{2}$$
$$x = -5, -4$$

3. $x^2 - 4x + 3 = 0$
$$x = \frac{4 \pm \sqrt{(-4)^2 - 4(1)(3)}}{2(1)}$$
$$x = \frac{4 \pm 2}{2}$$
$$x = 1, 3$$

5. $3x^2 + 2x - 1 = 0$
$$x = \frac{-2 \pm \sqrt{2^2 - 4(3)(-1)}}{2(3)}$$
$$x = \frac{-2 \pm 4}{6}$$
$$x = -1, \frac{1}{3}$$

7. $x^2 + 5x = -4$
$$x^2 + 5x + 4 = 0$$
$$x = \frac{-5 \pm \sqrt{5^2 - 4(1)(4)}}{2(1)}$$
$$x = \frac{-5 \pm 3}{2}$$
$$x = -4, -1$$

9.
$$x^2 = 6x - 9$$
$$x^2 - 6x + 9 = 0$$
$$x = \frac{6 \pm \sqrt{(-6)^2 - 4(1)(9)}}{2(1)}$$
$$x = \frac{6 \pm 0}{2}$$
$$x = 3$$

11. $2x^2 - 3x - 7 = 0$
$$x = \frac{3 \pm \sqrt{(-3)^2 - 4(2)(-7)}}{2(2)}$$
$$x = \frac{3 \pm \sqrt{65}}{4}$$

13. $x^2 + 2x - 4 = 0$
$$x = \frac{-2 \pm \sqrt{2^2 - 4(1)(-4)}}{2(1)}$$
$$x = \frac{-2 \pm \sqrt{20}}{2}$$
$$x = \frac{-2 \pm 2\sqrt{5}}{2}$$
$$x = -1 \pm \sqrt{5}$$

15.
$$2x^2 - 3x = 3$$
$$2x^2 - 3x - 3 = 0$$
$$x = \frac{3 \pm \sqrt{(-3)^2 - 4(2)(-3)}}{2(2)}$$
$$x = \frac{3 \pm \sqrt{33}}{4}$$

17.
$$3x^2 - 2x = 6$$
$$3x^2 - 2x - 6 = 0$$
$$x = \frac{2 \pm \sqrt{(-2)^2 - 4(3)(-6)}}{2(3)}$$
$$x = \frac{2 \pm \sqrt{76}}{6}$$
$$x = \frac{2 \pm 2\sqrt{19}}{6}$$
$$x = \frac{1 \pm \sqrt{19}}{3}$$

19. $3x^2 + 3x + 2 = 0$
$$x = \frac{-3 \pm \sqrt{3^2 - 4(3)(2)}}{2(3)}$$
$$x = \frac{-3 \pm \sqrt{-15}}{6}$$
No real number solutions

21.
$$5x^2 = 8x - 2$$
$$5x^2 - 8x + 2 = 0$$
$$x = \frac{8 \pm \sqrt{(-8)^2 - 4(5)(2)}}{2(5)}$$
$$x = \frac{8 \pm \sqrt{24}}{10}$$
$$x = \frac{8 \pm 2\sqrt{6}}{10}$$
$$x = \frac{4 \pm \sqrt{6}}{5}$$

23.
$$2x^2 - 9 = 4x$$
$$2x^2 - 4x - 9 = 0$$
$$x = \frac{4 \pm \sqrt{(-4)^2 - 4(2)(-9)}}{2(2)}$$
$$x = \frac{4 \pm \sqrt{88}}{4}$$
$$x = \frac{4 \pm 2\sqrt{22}}{4}$$
$$x = \frac{2 \pm \sqrt{22}}{2}$$

25.
$$3x - 5 = \frac{1}{x}$$
$$3x^2 - 5x = 1$$
$$3x^2 - 5x - 1 = 0$$
$$x = \frac{5 \pm \sqrt{(-5)^2 - 4(3)(-1)}}{2(3)}$$
$$x = \frac{5 \pm \sqrt{37}}{6}$$

27. $(x - 2)(x + 1) = 3$
$$x^2 - x - 2 = 3$$
$$x^2 - x - 5 = 0$$
$$x = \frac{1 \pm \sqrt{(-1)^2 - 4(1)(-5)}}{2(1)}$$
$$x = \frac{1 \pm \sqrt{21}}{2}$$

29. $(x-1)^2 = 7$

$$x - 1 = \pm\sqrt{7}$$
$$x = 1 \pm \sqrt{7}$$

31. $x^2 - 5x - 14 = 0$

$$(x-7)(x+2) = 0$$
$$x - 7 = 0 \text{ or } x + 2 = 0$$
$$x = 7 \text{ or } x = -2$$

33. $6x^2 - 23x + 10 = 0$

$$(2x-1)(3x-10) = 0$$
$$2x - 1 = 0 \text{ or } 3x - 10 = 0$$
$$x = \frac{1}{2} \text{ or } x = \frac{10}{3}$$

35. $2x^2 - 8x + 3 = 0$

$$x = \frac{8 \pm \sqrt{(-8)^2 - 4(2)(3)}}{2(2)}$$
$$x = \frac{8 \pm \sqrt{40}}{4}$$
$$x = \frac{8 \pm 2\sqrt{10}}{4}$$
$$x = \frac{4 \pm \sqrt{10}}{2}$$

37. $x^2 - 9x - 4 = 6$

$$x^2 - 9x - 10 = 0$$
$$(x-10)(x+1) = 0$$
$$x - 10 = 0 \text{ or } x + 1 = 0$$
$$x = 10 \text{ or } x = -1$$

39. $4x^2 - 8x + 3 = 5$

$$4x^2 - 8x - 2 = 0$$
$$2(2x^2 - 4x - 1) = 0$$
$$2x^2 - 4x - 1 = 0$$
$$x = \frac{-(-4) \pm \sqrt{(-4)^2 - 4(2)(-1)}}{2(2)}$$
$$x = \frac{4 \pm \sqrt{24}}{4}$$
$$x = \frac{4 \pm 2\sqrt{6}}{4}$$
$$x = \frac{2 \pm \sqrt{6}}{2}$$

41. $\dfrac{3}{x} + \dfrac{5}{x^2} = 9$

$$3x + 5 = 9x^2$$
$$9x^2 - 3x - 5 = 0$$
$$x = \frac{3 \pm \sqrt{(-3)^2 - 4(9)(-5)}}{2(9)}$$
$$x = \frac{3 \pm \sqrt{189}}{18}$$
$$x = \frac{3 \pm 3\sqrt{21}}{18}$$
$$x = \frac{1 \pm \sqrt{21}}{6}$$

43. $\dfrac{x}{x+1} + \dfrac{10x}{x^2+4x+3} = \dfrac{15}{x+3}$

$$x(x+3) + 10x = 15(x+1)$$
$$x^2 + 3x + 10x = 15x + 15$$
$$x^2 - 2x - 15 = 0$$
$$(x-5)(x+3) = 0$$
$$x - 5 = 0 \quad \text{or} \quad x + 3 = 0$$
$$x = 5 \quad \text{or} \quad x = -3$$

Reject $x = -3$ since it gives division by zero.

$$x = 5$$

45.

$$4x = x^2 - 3$$
$$x^2 - 4x - 3 = 0$$
$$x = \frac{4 \pm \sqrt{(-4)^2 - 4(1)(-3)}}{2(1)}$$
$$= \frac{4 \pm 2\sqrt{7}}{2}$$
$$= 2 \pm \sqrt{7}$$
$$= 2 + \sqrt{7} \approx 4.646$$

Reject $2 - \sqrt{7} \approx -0.646$ since $x > 0$. Therefore the length of one side is ≈ 4.646.

47.

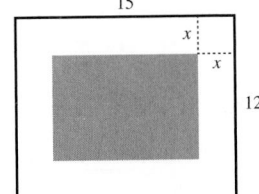

Let x be width of frame.

$$\text{Area of picture} = 140$$
$$(15 - 2x)(12 - 2x) = 140$$
$$180 - 54x + 4x^2 = 140$$
$$4x^2 - 54x + 40 = 0$$
$$2x^2 - 27x + 20 = 0$$
$$x = \frac{27 \pm \sqrt{(-27)^2 - 4(2)(20)}}{2(2)}$$
$$= \frac{27 \pm \sqrt{569}}{4}$$
$$\approx 0.787, 12.713$$

The width of the frame is ≈ 0.787 inches as a width of 12.713 is not possible.

49.

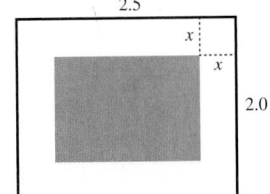

Let x be width of the frame.

$$\text{Area exposed} = 2.5$$
$$(2.5 - 2x)(2 - 2x) = 2.5$$
$$5 - 9x + 4x^2 = 2.5$$
$$4x^2 - 9x + 2.5 = 0$$
$$x = \frac{9 \pm \sqrt{(-9)^2 - 4(4)(2.5)}}{2(4)}$$
$$= \frac{9 \pm \sqrt{41}}{8}$$
$$\approx 0.325, 1.925$$

The width of the frame is ≈ 0.325 m or 32.5 cm.

51. Writing exercise

53. Writing exercise

Chapter 4 Algebraic Fractions

Exercises 4.1

1. $\dfrac{16}{24} = \dfrac{2 \cdot 2 \cdot 2 \cdot 2}{2 \cdot 2 \cdot 2 \cdot 3} = \dfrac{2}{3}$

3. $\dfrac{80}{180} = \dfrac{2 \cdot 2 \cdot 2 \cdot 2 \cdot 5}{2 \cdot 2 \cdot 3 \cdot 3 \cdot 5} = \dfrac{4}{9}$

5. $\dfrac{4x^5}{6x^2} = \dfrac{2 \cdot 2 \cdot x \cdot x \cdot x \cdot x \cdot x}{2 \cdot 3 \cdot x \cdot x} = \dfrac{2x^3}{3}$

7. $\dfrac{9x^3}{27x^6} = \dfrac{3 \cdot 3 \cdot x \cdot x \cdot x}{3 \cdot 3 \cdot 3 \cdot x \cdot x \cdot x \cdot x \cdot x \cdot x} = \dfrac{1}{3x^3}$

9. $\dfrac{10a^2b^5}{25ab^2} = \dfrac{2 \cdot 5 \cdot a \cdot a \cdot b \cdot b \cdot b \cdot b \cdot b}{5 \cdot 5 \cdot a \cdot b \cdot b} = \dfrac{2ab^3}{5}$

11. $\dfrac{42x^3y}{14xy^3} = \dfrac{2 \cdot 3 \cdot 7 \cdot x \cdot x \cdot x \cdot y}{2 \cdot 7 \cdot x \cdot y \cdot y \cdot y} = \dfrac{3x^2}{y^2}$

13. $\dfrac{2xyw^2}{6x^2y^3w^3} = \dfrac{2 \cdot x \cdot y \cdot w \cdot w}{2 \cdot 3 \cdot x \cdot x \cdot y \cdot y \cdot y \cdot w \cdot w \cdot w} = \dfrac{1}{3xy^2w}$

15. $\dfrac{10x^5y^5}{2x^3y^4} = \dfrac{2 \cdot 5 \cdot x \cdot x \cdot x \cdot x \cdot x \cdot y \cdot y \cdot y \cdot y \cdot y}{2 \cdot x \cdot x \cdot x \cdot y \cdot y \cdot y \cdot y}$

$= 5x^2y$

17. $\dfrac{-4m^3n}{6mn^2} = \dfrac{-2 \cdot 2 \cdot m \cdot m \cdot m \cdot n}{2 \cdot 3 \cdot m \cdot n \cdot n} = \dfrac{-2m^2}{3n}$

19. $\dfrac{-8ab^3}{-16a^3b} = \dfrac{-2 \cdot 2 \cdot 2 \cdot a \cdot b \cdot b \cdot b}{-2 \cdot 2 \cdot 2 \cdot 2 \cdot a \cdot a \cdot a \cdot b} = \dfrac{b^2}{2a^2}$

21. $\dfrac{8r^2s^3t}{-16rs^4t^3} = \dfrac{2 \cdot 2 \cdot 2 \cdot r \cdot r \cdot s \cdot s \cdot s \cdot t}{-2 \cdot 2 \cdot 2 \cdot 2 \cdot r \cdot s \cdot s \cdot s \cdot s \cdot t \cdot t \cdot t}$

$= \dfrac{-r}{2st^2}$

23. $\dfrac{3x+18}{5x+30} = \dfrac{3(x+6)}{5(x+6)} = \dfrac{3}{5}$

25. $\dfrac{3x-6}{5x-15} = \dfrac{3(x-2)}{5(x-3)}$

27. $\dfrac{6a-24}{a^2-16} = \dfrac{6(a-4)}{(a+4)(a-4)} = \dfrac{6}{a+4}$

29. $\dfrac{x^2+3x+2}{5x+10} = \dfrac{(x+2)(x+1)}{5(x+2)} = \dfrac{x+1}{5}$

31. $\dfrac{x^2-6x-16}{x^2-64} = \dfrac{(x-8)(x+2)}{(x+8)(x-8)} = \dfrac{x+2}{x+8}$

33. $\dfrac{2m^2+3m-5}{2m^2+11m+15} = \dfrac{(2m+5)(m-1)}{(2m+5)(m+3)} = \dfrac{m-1}{m+3}$

35. $\dfrac{p^2+2pq-15q^2}{p^2-25q^2} = \dfrac{(p+5q)(p-3q)}{(p+5q)(p-5q)} = \dfrac{p-3q}{p-5q}$

37. $\dfrac{2x-10}{25-x^2} = \dfrac{2(x-5)}{(5+x)(5-x)}$

$= \dfrac{2(x-5)}{-(x+5)(x-5)}$

$= \dfrac{-2}{x+5}$

39. $\dfrac{25-a^2}{a^2+a-30} = \dfrac{(5+a)(5-a)}{(a+6)(a-5)} = \dfrac{-(a+5)}{a+6} = \dfrac{-a-5}{a+6}$

41. $\dfrac{x^2+xy-6y^2}{4y^2-x^2} = \dfrac{(x+3y)(x-2y)}{(2y+x)(2y-x)}$

$= \dfrac{-(x+3y)}{x+2y}$

$= \dfrac{-x-3y}{x+2y}$

43. $\dfrac{x^2+4x+4}{x+2} = \dfrac{(x+2)(x+2)}{x+2} = x+2$

45. $\dfrac{xy-2y+4x-8}{2y+6-xy-3x} = \dfrac{y(x-2)+4(x-2)}{2(y+3)-x(y+3)}$

$= \dfrac{(x-2)(y+4)}{(y+3)(2-x)}$

$= \dfrac{-(y+4)}{y+3}$

47. $\dfrac{y-7}{7-y} = \dfrac{y-7}{-(y-7)} = -1$

49. $\dfrac{6x^2+19x+10}{3x+2} = \dfrac{(3x+2)(2x+5)}{3x+2}$

$= 2x+5$

The length is represented by $2x + 5$.

51. Writing exercise

53. Writing exercise

55. Writing exercise

Exercises 4.2

1. $\dfrac{7}{18} + \dfrac{5}{18} = \dfrac{7+5}{18} = \dfrac{12}{18} = \dfrac{2}{3}$

3. $\dfrac{13}{16} - \dfrac{9}{16} = \dfrac{13-9}{16} = \dfrac{4}{16} = \dfrac{1}{4}$

5. $\dfrac{x}{8} + \dfrac{3x}{8} = \dfrac{x+3x}{8} = \dfrac{4x}{8} = \dfrac{x}{2}$

7. $\dfrac{7a}{10} - \dfrac{3a}{10} = \dfrac{7a-3a}{10} = \dfrac{4a}{10} = \dfrac{2a}{5}$

9. $\dfrac{5}{x} + \dfrac{3}{x} = \dfrac{5+3}{x} = \dfrac{8}{x}$

11. $\dfrac{8}{w} - \dfrac{2}{w} = \dfrac{8-2}{w} = \dfrac{6}{w}$

13. $\dfrac{2}{xy} + \dfrac{3}{xy} = \dfrac{2+3}{xy} = \dfrac{5}{xy}$

15. $\dfrac{2}{3cd} + \dfrac{4}{3cd} = \dfrac{2+4}{3cd} = \dfrac{6}{3cd} = \dfrac{2}{cd}$

17. $\dfrac{7}{x-5} + \dfrac{9}{x-5} = \dfrac{7+9}{x-5} = \dfrac{16}{x-5}$

19. $\dfrac{2x}{x-2} - \dfrac{4}{x-2} = \dfrac{2x-4}{x-2} = \dfrac{2(x-2)}{x-2} = 2$

21. $\dfrac{8p}{p+4} + \dfrac{32}{p+4} = \dfrac{8p+32}{p+4} = \dfrac{8(p+4)}{p+4} = 8$

23. $\dfrac{x^2}{x+4} + \dfrac{3x-4}{x+4} = \dfrac{x^2+3x-4}{x+4} = \dfrac{(x+4)(x-1)}{x+4} = x-1$

25. $\dfrac{m^2}{m-5} - \dfrac{25}{m-5} = \dfrac{m^2-25}{m-5}$
$= \dfrac{(m+5)(m-5)}{m-5}$
$= m+5$

27. $\dfrac{a-1}{3} + \dfrac{2a-5}{3} = \dfrac{(a-1)+(2a-5)}{3}$
$= \dfrac{a-1+2a-5}{3}$
$= \dfrac{3a-6}{3} = \dfrac{3(a-2)}{3}$
$= a-2$

29. $\dfrac{3x-1}{4} - \dfrac{x+7}{4} = \dfrac{(3x-1)-(x+7)}{4}$
$= 3x-1-x-7$
$= \dfrac{2x-8}{4}$
$= \dfrac{2(x-4)}{4} = \dfrac{x-4}{2}$

31. $\dfrac{4m+7}{6m} + \dfrac{2m+5}{6m} = \dfrac{(4m+7)+(2m+5)}{6m}$
$= \dfrac{4m+7+2m+5}{6m}$
$= \dfrac{6m+12}{6m}$
$= \dfrac{6(m+2)}{6m}$
$= \dfrac{m+2}{m}$

33. $\dfrac{4w-7}{w-5} - \dfrac{2w+3}{w-5} = \dfrac{(4w-7)-(2w+3)}{w-5}$
$= \dfrac{4w-7-2w-3}{w-5}$
$= \dfrac{2w-10}{w-5}$
$= \dfrac{2(w-5)}{w-5}$
$= 2$

35. $\dfrac{x-7}{x^2-x-6} + \dfrac{2x-2}{x^2-x-6} = \dfrac{(x-7)+(2x-2)}{x^2-x-6}$
$= \dfrac{x-7+2x-2}{x^2-x-6}$
$= \dfrac{3x-9}{(x-3)(x+2)}$
$= \dfrac{3(x-3)}{(x-3)(x+2)}$
$= \dfrac{3}{x+2}$

37. $\dfrac{y^2}{2y+8} + \dfrac{3y-4}{2y+8} = \dfrac{y^2+3y-4}{2y+8}$
$= \dfrac{(y+4)(y-1)}{2(y+4)}$
$= \dfrac{y-1}{2}$

39. $\dfrac{7w}{w+3} + \dfrac{21}{w+3} = \dfrac{7w+21}{w+3} = \dfrac{7(w+3)}{w+3} = 7$

41. $\dfrac{x^2}{x^2+x-6} - \dfrac{6}{(x+3)(x-2)} + \dfrac{x}{x^2+x-6} = \dfrac{x^2}{(x+3)(x-2)} - \dfrac{6}{(x+3)(x-2)} + \dfrac{x}{(x+3)(x-2)}$

$$= \dfrac{x^2 - 6 + x}{(x+3)(x-2)}$$

$$= \dfrac{(x+3)(x-2)}{(x+3)(x-2)}$$

$$= 1$$

43. $\dfrac{2x}{x+3} + \dfrac{2x}{x+3} + \dfrac{6}{x+3} + \dfrac{6}{x+3} = \dfrac{2x+2x+6+6}{x+3}$

$$= \dfrac{4x+12}{x+3}$$

$$= \dfrac{4(x+3)}{x+3}$$

$$= 4$$

Exercises 4.3

1. $\dfrac{3}{7} \cdot \dfrac{14}{27} = \dfrac{3 \cdot 14}{7 \cdot 27} = \dfrac{2}{9}$

3. $\dfrac{x}{2} \cdot \dfrac{y}{6} = \dfrac{x \cdot y}{2 \cdot 6} = \dfrac{xy}{12}$

5. $\dfrac{3a}{2} \cdot \dfrac{4}{a^2} = \dfrac{3 \overset{1}{\cancel{a}} \cdot \overset{2}{\cancel{4}}}{\underset{1}{\cancel{2}} \cdot \underset{a}{\cancel{a}^2} } = \dfrac{6}{a}$

7. $\dfrac{3x^3 y}{10xy^3} \cdot \dfrac{5xy^2}{9xy^2} = \dfrac{3x^3 y \cdot 5xy^2}{10xy^3 \cdot 9xy^2} = \dfrac{x^2}{6y^2}$

Divide by the common factors of 15, x^2, and y^3.

9. $\dfrac{-4ab^2}{15a^3} \cdot \dfrac{25ab}{-16b^3} = \dfrac{-4ab^2 \cdot 25ab}{15a^3 \cdot (-16b^3)} = \dfrac{5}{12a}$

Divide by the common factors of -20, a^2, and b^3.

11. $\dfrac{-3m^3 n}{10mn^3} \cdot \dfrac{5mn^2}{-9mn^3} = \dfrac{-3m^3 n \cdot 5mn^2}{10mn^3 \cdot (-9mn^3)} = \dfrac{m^2}{6n^3}$

Divide by the common factors of -15, m^2, and n^3.

13. $\dfrac{x^2+5x}{3x^2} \cdot \dfrac{10x}{5x+25} = \dfrac{x(x+5)}{3x^2} \cdot \dfrac{10x}{5(x+5)}$

$$= \dfrac{\overset{1}{\cancel{x}}(x+5) \cdot \overset{2}{\cancel{10}} \overset{1}{\cancel{x}}}{\underset{1}{\cancel{3}} \cancel{x}^2 \cdot \underset{1}{\cancel{5}}(x+5)}$$

$$= \dfrac{2}{3}$$

15. $\dfrac{p^2-8p}{4p} \cdot \dfrac{12p^2}{p^2-64} = \dfrac{p(p-8)}{4p} \cdot \dfrac{12p^2}{(p-8)(p+8)}$

$$= \dfrac{\overset{1}{\cancel{p}}\overset{1}{\cancel{(p-8)}} \cdot \overset{3}{\cancel{12}} \, p^2}{\underset{1}{\cancel{4}} \, \underset{1}{\cancel{p}} \cdot \underset{1}{\cancel{(p-8)}}(p+8)}$$

$$= \dfrac{3p^2}{p+8}$$

17. $\dfrac{m^2-4m-21}{3m^2} \cdot \dfrac{m^2+7m}{m^2-49}$

$$= \dfrac{(m-7)(m+3)}{3m^2} \cdot \dfrac{m(m+7)}{(m+7)(m-7)}$$

$$= \dfrac{\overset{1}{\cancel{(m-7)}}(m+3) \cdot \overset{1}{\cancel{m}}\overset{1}{\cancel{(m+7)}}}{3 \underset{m}{\cancel{m}^2} \cdot \underset{1}{\cancel{(m+7)}} \underset{1}{\cancel{(m-7)}}}$$

$$= \dfrac{m+3}{3m}$$

19. $\dfrac{4r^2-1}{2r^2-9r-5} \cdot \dfrac{3r^2-13r-10}{9r^2-4}$

$= \dfrac{(2r-1)(2r+1)}{(2r+1)(r-5)} \cdot \dfrac{(3r+2)(r-5)}{(3r-2)(3r+2)}$

$= \dfrac{(2r-1)\cancel{(2r+1)}\cdot\cancel{(3r+2)}\cancel{(r-5)}}{\cancel{(2r+1)}\cancel{(r-5)}\cdot(3r-2)\cancel{(3r+2)}}$

$= \dfrac{2r-1}{3r-2}$

21. $\dfrac{x^2-4y^2}{x^2-xy-6y^2} \cdot \dfrac{7x^2-21xy}{5x-10y}$

$= \dfrac{(x-2y)(x+2y)}{(x-3y)(x+2y)} \cdot \dfrac{7x(x-3y)}{5(x-2y)}$

$= \dfrac{\cancel{(x-2y)}\cancel{(x+2y)}\cdot 7x\cancel{(x-3y)}}{\cancel{(x-3y)}\cancel{(x+2y)}\cdot 5\cancel{(x-2y)}}$

$= \dfrac{7x}{5}$

23. $\dfrac{2x-6}{x^2+2x} \cdot \dfrac{3x}{3-x} = \dfrac{2(x-3)}{x(x+2)} \cdot \dfrac{3x}{-1(x-3)}$

$= \dfrac{2\cancel{(x-3)}\cdot 3\cancel{x}}{\cancel{x}(x+2)\cdot(-1)\cancel{(x-3)}}$

$= \dfrac{-6}{x+2}$

25. $\dfrac{5}{8} \div \dfrac{15}{16} = \dfrac{5}{8} \cdot \dfrac{16}{15} = \dfrac{\cancel{5}\cdot\overset{2}{\cancel{16}}}{\cancel{8}\cdot\underset{3}{\cancel{15}}} = \dfrac{2}{3}$

27. $\dfrac{5}{x^2} \div \dfrac{10}{x} = \dfrac{5}{x^2} \cdot \dfrac{x}{10} = \dfrac{\cancel{5}\cancel{x}}{\underset{2}{\cancel{10}}\,\underset{x}{\cancel{x}^2}} = \dfrac{1}{2x}$

29. $\dfrac{4x^2y^2}{9x^3} \div \dfrac{8y^2}{27xy} = \dfrac{4x^2y^2}{9x^3} \cdot \dfrac{27xy}{8y^2} = \dfrac{3y}{2}$

Divide by the common factors of 36, x^3, and y^2.

31. $\dfrac{3x+6}{8} \div \dfrac{5x+10}{6} = \dfrac{3x+6}{8} \cdot \dfrac{6}{5x+10}$

$= \dfrac{3\cancel{(x+2)}\cdot\overset{3}{\cancel{6}}}{\underset{4}{\cancel{8}}\cdot 5\cancel{(x+2)}} = \dfrac{9}{20}$

33. $\dfrac{4a-12}{5a+15} \div \dfrac{8a^2}{a^2+3a} = \dfrac{4a-12}{5a+15} \cdot \dfrac{a^2+3a}{8a^2}$

$= \dfrac{\cancel{4}(a-3)\cdot\cancel{a}\cancel{(a+3)}}{5\cancel{(a+3)}\cdot\underset{2}{\cancel{8}}\,\underset{a}{\cancel{a}^2}}$

$= \dfrac{a-3}{10a}$

35. $\dfrac{x^2+2x-8}{9x^2} \div \dfrac{x^2-16}{3x-12} = \dfrac{x^2+2x-8}{9x^2} \cdot \dfrac{3x-12}{x^2-16}$

$= \dfrac{(x+4)(x-2)\cdot\overset{}{\cancel{3}}\cancel{(x-4)}}{\underset{3}{\cancel{9}}x^2\cdot\cancel{(x-4)}\cancel{(x+4)}}$

$= \dfrac{x-2}{3x^2}$

37. $\dfrac{x^2-9}{2x^2-6x} \div \dfrac{2x^2+5x-3}{4x^2-1}$

$= \dfrac{x^2-9}{2x^2-6x} \cdot \dfrac{4x^2-1}{2x^2+5x-3}$

$= \dfrac{\cancel{(x+3)}\cancel{(x-3)}\cdot\cancel{(2x-1)}(2x+1)}{2x\cancel{(x-3)}\cdot\cancel{(2x-1)}\cancel{(x+3)}}$

$= \dfrac{2x+1}{2x}$

39. $\dfrac{a^2-9b^2}{4a^2+12ab} \div \dfrac{a^2-ab-6b^2}{12ab}$

$= \dfrac{a^2-9b^2}{4a^2+12ab} \cdot \dfrac{12ab}{a^2-ab-6b^2}$

$= \dfrac{\cancel{(a-3b)}\cancel{(a+3b)}\cdot\overset{3}{\cancel{12}}\,\cancel{a}\,b}{\cancel{4}\,\cancel{a}\cancel{(a+3b)}\cdot\cancel{(a-3b)}(a+2b)}$

$= \dfrac{3b}{a+2b}$

41. $\dfrac{x^2-16y^2}{3x^2-12xy} \div (x^2+4xy)$

$= \dfrac{x^2-16y^2}{3x^2-12xy} \cdot \dfrac{1}{x^2+4xy}$

$= \dfrac{\overset{1}{\cancel{(x-4y)}}\,\overset{1}{\cancel{(x+4y)}}\cdot 1}{3x\cancel{(x-4y)}\cdot x\cancel{(x+4y)}}$

$= \dfrac{1}{3x^2}$

43. $\dfrac{x-7}{2x+6} \div \dfrac{21-3x}{x^2+3x} = \dfrac{x-7}{2x+6} \cdot \dfrac{x^2+3x}{21-3x}$

$= \dfrac{\overset{1}{\cancel{(x-7)}}\cdot x\overset{1}{\cancel{(x+3)}}}{2\cancel{(x+3)}(-3)\cancel{(x-7)}}$

$= \dfrac{-x}{6}$

45. $\dfrac{x^2-2x-8}{2x-8} \cdot \dfrac{x^2+5x}{x^2+5x+6} \div \dfrac{x^2+2x-15}{x^2-9}$

$= \dfrac{x^2-2x-8}{2x-8} \cdot \dfrac{x^2+5x}{x^2+5x+6} \cdot \dfrac{x^2-9}{x^2+2x-15}$

$= \dfrac{\overset{1}{\cancel{(x-4)}}\overset{1}{\cancel{(x+2)}}\cdot x\overset{1}{\cancel{(x+5)}}\cdot \overset{1}{\cancel{(x-3)}}\overset{1}{\cancel{(x+3)}}}{2\cancel{(x-4)}\cdot \cancel{(x+3)}\cancel{(x+2)}\cdot \cancel{(x+5)}\cancel{(x-3)}} = \dfrac{x}{2}$

47. $\dfrac{x^2+5x}{3x-6} \cdot \dfrac{x^2-4}{3x^2+15x} \cdot \dfrac{6x}{x^2+6x+8}$

$= \dfrac{\overset{1}{\cancel{x}}\overset{1}{\cancel{(x+5)}}\cdot \overset{1}{\cancel{(x+2)}}\overset{1}{\cancel{(x-2)}}\cdot \overset{2}{\cancel{6}}\,x}{\cancel{3}\cancel{(x-2)}\cdot 3\cancel{x}\cancel{(x+5)}\cdot (x+4)\cancel{(x+2)}}$

$= \dfrac{2x}{3(x+4)}$

49. $\dfrac{\frac{2}{3}}{\frac{6}{8}} = \dfrac{\frac{2}{3}\cdot 24}{\frac{6}{8}\cdot 24} = \dfrac{2\cdot 8}{6\cdot 3} = \dfrac{8}{9}$

51. $\dfrac{1+\frac{1}{2}}{2+\frac{1}{4}} = \dfrac{\left(1+\frac{1}{2}\right)\cdot 4}{\left(2+\frac{1}{4}\right)\cdot 4} = \dfrac{4+2}{8+1} = \dfrac{6}{9} = \dfrac{2}{3}$

53. $\dfrac{\frac{x}{8}}{\frac{x^2}{4}} = \dfrac{\frac{x}{8}\cdot 8}{\frac{x^2}{4}\cdot 8} = \dfrac{x}{2x^2} = \dfrac{1}{2x}$

55. $\dfrac{\frac{3}{a}}{\frac{2}{a^2}} = \dfrac{\frac{3}{a}\cdot a^2}{\frac{2}{a^2}\cdot a^2} = \dfrac{3a}{2}$

57. $\dfrac{\frac{y+1}{y}}{\frac{y-1}{2y}} = \dfrac{y+1}{y}\cdot \dfrac{2y}{y-1} = \dfrac{2(y+1)}{y-1}$

59. $\dfrac{2-\frac{1}{x}}{2+\frac{1}{x}} = \dfrac{\left(2-\frac{1}{x}\right)\cdot x}{\left(2+\frac{1}{x}\right)\cdot x} = \dfrac{2x-1}{2x+1}$

61. $\dfrac{3-\frac{x}{y}}{\frac{6}{y}} = \dfrac{\left(3-\frac{x}{y}\right)}{\left(\frac{6}{y}\right)\cdot y} = \dfrac{3y-x}{6}$

63. $\dfrac{\frac{x^2}{y^2}-1}{\frac{x}{y}+1} = \dfrac{\left(\frac{x^2}{y^2}-1\right)\cdot y^2}{\left(\frac{x}{y}+1\right)\cdot y^2}$

$= \dfrac{x^2-y^2}{xy+y^2}$

$= \dfrac{(x+y)(x-y)}{y(x+y)}$

$= \dfrac{x-y}{y}$

65. $\dfrac{1+\frac{3}{x}-\frac{4}{x^2}}{1+\frac{2}{x}-\frac{3}{x^2}} = \dfrac{\left(1+\frac{3}{x}-\frac{4}{x^2}\right)\cdot x^2}{\left(1+\frac{2}{x}-\frac{3}{x^2}\right)\cdot x^2}$

$= \dfrac{x^2+3x-4}{x^2+2x-3}$

$= \dfrac{(x+4)(x-1)}{(x+3)(x-1)}$

$= \dfrac{x+4}{x+3}$

67. $\dfrac{\frac{2}{x}-\frac{1}{xy}}{\frac{1}{xy}+\frac{2}{y}} = \dfrac{\left(\frac{2}{x}-\frac{1}{xy}\right)\cdot xy}{\left(\frac{1}{xy}+\frac{2}{y}\right)\cdot xy} = \dfrac{2y-1}{1+2x}$

69. $\dfrac{\frac{2}{x-1}+1}{1-\frac{3}{x-1}} = \dfrac{\left(\frac{2}{x-1}+1\right)\cdot (x-1)}{\left(1-\frac{3}{x-1}\right)\cdot (x-1)} = \dfrac{2+(x-1)}{(x-1)-3} = \dfrac{x+1}{x-4}$

71.
$$\frac{1-\frac{1}{y-1}}{y-\frac{8}{y+2}} = \frac{\left(1-\frac{1}{y-1}\right)\cdot(y-1)(y+2)}{\left(y-\frac{8}{y+2}\right)\cdot(y-1)(y+2)}$$

$$= \frac{(y-1)(y+2)-(y+2)}{y(y-1)(y+2)-8(y-1)}$$

$$= \frac{(y+2)[(y-1)-1]}{(y-1)[y(y+2)-8]}$$

$$= \frac{(y+2)(y-2)}{(y-1)(y^2+2y-8)}$$

$$= \frac{(y+2)(y-2)}{(y-1)(y+4)(y-2)}$$

$$= \frac{y+2}{(y-1)(y+4)}$$

73.
$$1+\frac{1}{1+\frac{1}{x}} = 1+\frac{1\cdot x}{\left(1+\frac{1}{x}\right)\cdot x}$$

$$= 1+\frac{x}{x+1}$$

$$= \frac{x+1}{x+1}+\frac{x}{x+1}$$

$$= \frac{x+1+x}{x+1}$$

$$= \frac{2x+1}{x+1}$$

75. $\dfrac{\frac{2}{3}}{\frac{1}{4}} = \dfrac{2}{3}\cdot\dfrac{4}{1} = \dfrac{8}{3}$

77. $\dfrac{\frac{7}{10}}{\frac{4}{5}} = \dfrac{7}{10}\cdot\dfrac{5}{4} = \dfrac{7}{8}$

79. The area of a rectangle is the product of the two sides.
$$\frac{2x+6}{12x-15}\cdot\frac{4x-5}{x+3} = \frac{2(x+3)\cdot(4x-5)}{3(4x-5)\cdot(x+3)} = \frac{2}{3}$$

81. Writing exercise

Exercises 4.4

1. $\dfrac{x}{15}$; None

3. $\dfrac{17}{x}$; $x = 0$ is the excluded value.

5. $\dfrac{3}{x-2}$; If $x - 2 = 0$, then $x = 2$. So, 2 is the excluded value.

7. $\dfrac{-5}{x+4}$; If $x + 4 = 0$, then $x = -4$. So, –4 is the excluded value.

9. $\dfrac{x-5}{2}$; None

11. $\dfrac{3x}{(x+1)(x-2)}$; If $(x + 1)(x - 2) = 0$, then
$x + 1 = 0$ or $x - 2 = 0$. So, $x = -1$ and $x = 2$ are the excluded values.

13. $\dfrac{x-1}{(2x-1)(x+3)}$; If $(2x - 1)(x + 3) = 0$, then
$2x - 1 = 0$ or $x + 3 = 0$. So, $x = \dfrac{1}{2}$ and $x = -3$ are the excluded values.

15. $\dfrac{7}{x^2-9} = \dfrac{7}{(x+3)(x-3)}$; If $(x + 3)(x - 3) = 0$,
then $x = -3$ or $x = 3$. So, –3 and 3 are the excluded values.

17. $\dfrac{x+3}{x^2-7x+12} = \dfrac{x+3}{(x-4)(x-3)}$;
If $(x - 4)(x -3) = 0$, then $x - 4 = 0$ or $x - 3 = 0$. So, 4 and 3 are the excluded values.

19. $\dfrac{2x-1}{3x^2+x-2} = \dfrac{2x-1}{(3x-2)(x+1)}$;
If $(3x - 2)(x + 1) = 0$, then $x = \dfrac{2}{3}$ or $x = -1$.
So, $\dfrac{2}{3}$ and –1 are the excluded values.

21. $\dfrac{x}{2}+3=6$
The LCD is 2.
$$2\cdot\frac{x}{2}+2\cdot3=2\cdot6$$
$$x+6=12$$
$$x=6$$

23. $\dfrac{3x}{4}-6=-3$
$$\underline{+6=+6}$$
$$\frac{3x}{4}=\frac{3}{1}$$
$$\frac{3x}{3}=\frac{12}{3}$$
$$x=4$$

25. $\dfrac{2x}{3} - 5 = -3$

$$\dfrac{+5 = +5}{\dfrac{2x}{3} = \dfrac{2}{1}}$$

$$\dfrac{2x}{2} = \dfrac{6}{2}$$

$$x = 3$$

27. $\dfrac{x}{2} - \dfrac{x}{3} = 2$

The LCD is 6.

$$6 \cdot \dfrac{x}{2} - 6 \cdot \dfrac{x}{3} = 6 \cdot \dfrac{2}{1}$$

$$3x - 2x = 12$$

$$x = 12$$

29. $\dfrac{x}{4} - \dfrac{x}{5} = 2$

The LCD is 20.

$$20 \cdot \dfrac{x}{4} - 20 \cdot \dfrac{x}{5} = 20 \cdot \dfrac{2}{1}$$

$$5x - 4x = 40$$

$$x = 40$$

31.

$$\dfrac{2x}{5} - \dfrac{x}{3} = \dfrac{7}{15}$$

$$15 \cdot \dfrac{2x}{5} - 15 \cdot \dfrac{x}{3} = \dfrac{7}{15}$$

$$6x - 5x = 7$$

$$x = 7$$

Check:

$$\dfrac{2 \cdot 7}{5} - \dfrac{7}{3} = \dfrac{7}{15}?$$

$$\dfrac{14}{5} - \dfrac{7}{3} = \dfrac{7}{15}?$$

$$\dfrac{42}{15} - \dfrac{35}{15} = \dfrac{7}{15}?$$

$$\dfrac{7}{15} = \dfrac{7}{15}$$

33. $15 \cdot \dfrac{2x}{3} - 15 \cdot \dfrac{4x}{5} = 15 \cdot \dfrac{2}{1}$

$$10x - 12x = 30$$

$$\dfrac{-2x}{-2} = \dfrac{30}{-2}$$

$$x = -15$$

35. $\dfrac{x}{5} - \dfrac{1}{3} = \dfrac{x-7}{3}$

The LCD is 15.

$$15 \cdot \dfrac{x}{5} - 15 \dfrac{1}{3} = 15 \cdot \dfrac{x-7}{3}$$

$$3x - 5 = 5(x-7)$$

$$3x - 5 = 5x - 35$$

$$30 = 2x$$

$$15 = x \text{ or } x = 15$$

37. $\dfrac{x}{4} - \dfrac{1}{5} = \dfrac{4x+3}{20}$

The LCD is 20.

$$20 \cdot \dfrac{x}{4} - 20 \cdot \dfrac{1}{5} = 20 \cdot \dfrac{4x+3}{20}$$

$$5x - 4 = 4x + 3$$

$$x = 7$$

39. $\dfrac{3}{x} + 2 = \dfrac{7}{x}$

The LCD is x.

$$x \cdot \dfrac{3}{x} + x \cdot 2 = x \cdot \dfrac{7}{x}$$

$$3 + 2x = 7$$

$$2x = 4$$

$$x = 2$$

41. $\dfrac{4}{x} + \dfrac{3}{4} = \dfrac{10}{x}$

The LCD is $4x$.

$$4x \cdot \dfrac{4}{x} + 4x \cdot \dfrac{3}{4} = 4x \cdot \dfrac{10}{x}$$

$$16 + 3x = 40$$

$$3x = 24$$

$$x = 8$$

43. $\dfrac{5}{2x} - \dfrac{1}{x} = \dfrac{9}{2x^2}$

The LCD is $2x^2$.

$$2x^2 \cdot \dfrac{5}{2x} - 2x^2 \cdot \dfrac{1}{x} = 2x^2 \cdot \dfrac{9}{2x^2}$$

$$5x - 2x = 9$$

$$3x = 9$$

$$x = 3$$

45. $\dfrac{2}{x-3} + 1 = \dfrac{7}{x-3}$

The LCD is $x - 3$.

$$(x-3) \cdot \dfrac{2}{x-3} + (x-3) \cdot 1 = (x-3) \cdot \dfrac{7}{x-3}$$

$$2 + (x-3) = 7$$

$$x - 1 = 7$$

$$x = 8$$

47. $\dfrac{12}{x+3} = \dfrac{x}{x+3} + 2$

The LCD is $x+3$.

$$(x+3) \cdot \dfrac{12}{x+3} = (x+3) \cdot \dfrac{x}{x+3} + (x+3) \cdot 2$$
$$12 = x + 2(x+3)$$
$$12 = x + 2x + 6$$
$$6 = 3x$$
$$2 = x \text{ or } x = 2$$

49. $\dfrac{3}{x-5} + 4 = \dfrac{2x+5}{x-5}$

The LCD is $x-5$.

$$(x-5) \cdot \dfrac{3}{x-5} + (x-5) \cdot 4 = (x-5) \cdot \dfrac{2x+5}{x-5}$$
$$3 + 4(x-5) = 2x + 5$$
$$3 + 4x - 20 = 2x + 5$$
$$2x = 22$$
$$x = 11$$

51. $\dfrac{2}{x+3} + \dfrac{1}{2} = \dfrac{x+6}{x+3}$

The LCD is $2(x+3)$.

$$2(x+3) \cdot \dfrac{2}{x+3} + 2(x+3) \cdot \dfrac{1}{2} = 2(x+3) \cdot \dfrac{x+6}{x+3}$$
$$4 + (x+3) = 2(x+6)$$
$$x + 7 = 2x + 12$$
$$-5 = x \text{ or } x = -5$$

53. $\dfrac{x}{3x+12} + \dfrac{x-1}{x+4} = \dfrac{5}{3}$

$$\dfrac{x}{3(x+4)} + \dfrac{x-1}{x+4} = \dfrac{5}{3}$$

The LCD is $3(x+4)$.

$$3(x+4) \cdot \dfrac{x}{3(x+4)} + 3(x+4) \cdot \dfrac{x-1}{x+4} = 3(x+4) \cdot \dfrac{5}{3}$$
$$x + 3(x-1) = 5(x+4)$$
$$x + 3x - 3 = 5x + 20$$
$$-23 = x \text{ or } x = -23$$

55. $\dfrac{x}{x-3} - 2 = \dfrac{3}{x-3}$

The LCD is $x-3$.

$$(x-3)\cdot\dfrac{x}{x-3} - 2(x-3) = (x-3)\cdot\dfrac{3}{x-3}$$
$$x - 2(x-3) = 3$$
$$x - 2x + 6 = 3$$
$$3 = x \text{ or } x = 3$$

But, $x = 3$ makes the fraction in the original equation undefined. Since 3 is an excluded value, the equation has no solution.

57. $\dfrac{x-1}{x+3} - \dfrac{x-3}{x} = \dfrac{3}{x^2+3x}$

$$\dfrac{x-1}{x+3} - \dfrac{x-3}{x} = \dfrac{3}{x(x+3)}$$

The LCD is $x(x+3)$.

$$x(x+3)\cdot\dfrac{x-1}{x+3} - x(x+3)\cdot\dfrac{x-3}{x} = x(x+3)\cdot\dfrac{3}{x(x+3)}$$
$$x(x-1) - (x-3)(x+3) = 3$$
$$x^2 - x - (x^2 - 9) = 3$$
$$-x + 9 = 3$$
$$6 = x \text{ or } x = 6$$

59. $\dfrac{1}{x-2} - \dfrac{2}{x+2} = \dfrac{2}{x^2-4}$

$$\dfrac{1}{x-2} - \dfrac{2}{x+2} = \dfrac{2}{(x+2)(x-2)}$$

The LCD is $(x+2)(x-2)$.

$$(x+2)(x-2)\cdot\dfrac{1}{x-2} - (x+2)(x-2)\cdot\dfrac{2}{x+2} = (x+2)(x-2)\cdot\dfrac{2}{(x+2)(x-2)}$$
$$(x+2) - 2(x-2) = 2$$
$$x + 2 - 2x + 4 = 2$$
$$6 - x = 2$$
$$4 = x \text{ or } x = 4$$

61. $\dfrac{3}{x-1} - \dfrac{1}{x+9} = \dfrac{18}{x^2+8x-9}$

$$\dfrac{3}{x-1} - \dfrac{1}{x+9} = \dfrac{18}{(x+9)(x-1)}$$

The LCD is $(x+9)(x-1)$.

$$(x+9)(x-1)\cdot\dfrac{3}{x-1} - (x+9)(x-1)\cdot\dfrac{1}{x+9} = (x+9)(x-1)\cdot\dfrac{18}{(x+9)(x-1)}$$
$$3(x+9) - (x-1) = 18$$
$$3x + 27 - x + 1 = 18$$
$$2x = -10$$
$$x = -5$$

63.
$$\frac{3}{x+3} + \frac{25}{x^2+x-6} = \frac{5}{x-2}$$
$$\frac{3}{x+3} + \frac{25}{(x+3)(x-2)} = \frac{5}{x-2}$$
The LCD is $(x+3)(x-2)$.
$$(x+3)(x-2) \cdot \frac{3}{x+3} + (x+3)(x-2) \cdot \frac{25}{(x+3)(x-2)} = (x+3)(x-2) \cdot \frac{5}{x-2}$$
$$3(x-2) + 25 = 5(x+3)$$
$$3x - 6 + 25 = 5x + 15$$
$$4 = 2x$$
$$2 = x \text{ or } x = 2$$

But, $x = 2$ makes a fraction in the original equation undefined. Since 2 is an excluded value, the equation has no solution.

65.
$$\frac{7}{x-5} - \frac{3}{x+5} = \frac{40}{x^2-25}$$
$$\frac{7}{x-5} - \frac{3}{x+5} = \frac{40}{(x+5)(x-5)}$$
The LCD is $(x+5)(x-5)$.
$$(x+5)(x-5) \cdot \frac{7}{x-5} - (x+5)(x-5) \cdot \frac{3}{x+5} = (x+5)(x-5) \cdot \frac{40}{(x+5)(x-5)}$$
$$7(x+5) - 3(x-5) = 40$$
$$7x + 35 - 3x + 15 = 40$$
$$4x = -10$$
$$x = -\frac{10}{4} = -\frac{5}{2}$$

67.
$$\frac{2x}{x-3} + \frac{2}{x-5} = \frac{3x}{x^2-8x+15}$$
$$\frac{2x}{x-3} + \frac{2}{x-5} = \frac{3x}{(x-3)(x-5)}$$
The LCD is $(x-3)(x-5)$.
$$(x-3)(x-5) \cdot \frac{2x}{x-3} + (x-3)(x-5) \cdot \frac{2}{x-5} = (x-3)(x-5) \cdot \frac{3x}{(x-3)(x-5)}$$
$$2x(x-5) + 2(x-3) = 3x$$
$$2x^2 - 10x + 2x - 6 = 3x$$
$$2x^2 - 11x - 6 = 0$$
$$(2x+1)(x-6) = 0$$
$$2x+1 = 0 \quad \text{or} \quad x-6 = 0$$
$$x = -\frac{1}{2} \quad \text{or} \quad x = 6$$

69.

$$\frac{2x}{x+2} = \frac{5}{x^2 - x - 6} - \frac{1}{x-3}$$

$$\frac{2x}{x+2} = \frac{5}{(x+2)(x-3)} - \frac{1}{x-3}$$

The LCD is $(x+2)(x-3)$.

$$(x+2)(x-3)\cdot\frac{2x}{x+2} = (x+2)(x-3)\cdot\frac{5}{(x+2)(x-3)} - (x+2)(x-3)\cdot\frac{1}{x-3}$$

$$2x(x-3) = 5 - (x+2)$$

$$2x^2 - 6x = 5 - x - 2$$

$$2x^2 - 5x - 3 = 0$$

$$(2x+1)(x-3) = 0$$

$$2x+1 = 0 \quad\text{or}\quad x-3 = 0$$

$$x = -\frac{1}{2} \quad\text{or}\quad x = 3$$

But since 3 is an excluded value, the solution is $-\dfrac{1}{2}$.

71. $\dfrac{7}{x-2} + \dfrac{16}{x+3} = 3$

The LCD is $(x-2)(x+3)$.

$$(x-2)(x+3)\cdot\frac{7}{x-2} + (x-2)(x+3)\cdot\frac{16}{x+3} = 3(x-2)(x+3)$$

$$7(x+3) + 16(x-2) = 3(x-2)(x+3)$$

$$7x + 21 + 16x - 32 = 3x^2 + 3x - 18$$

$$3x^2 - 20x - 7 = 0$$

$$(3x+1)(x-7) = 0$$

$$3x+1 = 0 \quad\text{or}\quad x-7 = 0$$

$$x = -\frac{1}{3} \quad\text{or}\quad x = 7$$

73. $\dfrac{11}{x-3} - 1 = \dfrac{10}{x+3}$

The LCD is $(x-3)(x+3)$.

$$(x-3)(x+3)\cdot\frac{11}{x-3} - 1(x-3)(x+3) = (x-3)(x+3)\cdot\frac{10}{x+3}$$

$$11(x+3) - (x-3)(x+3) = 10(x-3)$$

$$11x + 33 - x^2 + 9 = 10x - 30$$

$$x^2 - x - 72 = 0$$

$$(x-9)(x+8) = 0$$

$$x-9 = 0 \text{ or } x+8 = 0$$

$$x = 9 \text{ or } \quad x = -8$$

75. $\dfrac{x+1}{5} = \dfrac{20}{25}$

$25(x+1) = 100$

$25x + 25 = 100$

$25x = 75$

$x = 3$

77. $\dfrac{3}{5} = \dfrac{x-1}{20}$

$60 = 5(x-1)$

$60 = 5x - 5$

$65 = 5x$

$13 = x$ or $x = 13$

79. $\dfrac{3x+4}{5} = \dfrac{x}{2}$

$6x + 8 = 5x$

$\underline{-8 \quad -8}$

$6x = 5x - 8$

$\underline{-5x \quad -5x}$

$x = -8$

81. $\dfrac{x}{6} = \dfrac{x+5}{16}$

$16x = 6(x+5)$

$16x = 6x + 30$

$10x = 30$

$x = 3$

83. $\dfrac{x-3}{8} = \dfrac{x-2}{10}$

$10(x-3) = 8(x-2)$

$10x - 30 = 8x - 16$

$\underline{+30 = +30}$

$10x = 8x + 14$

$\underline{-8x \quad -8x}$

$\dfrac{2x}{2} = \dfrac{14}{2}$

$x = 7$

85. $\dfrac{x}{x+7} = \dfrac{10}{17}$

$17x = 10(x+7)$

$17x = 10x + 70$

$7x = 70$

$x = 10$

87. $\dfrac{2}{x-1} = \dfrac{6}{x+9}$

$2(x+9) = 6(x-1)$

$2x + 18 = 6x - 6$

$24 = 4x$

$6 = x$ or $x = 6$

89. $\dfrac{1}{x+3} = \dfrac{7}{x^2 - 9}$

$\dfrac{1}{x+3} = \dfrac{7}{(x-3)(x+3)}$

The LCD is $(x-3)(x+3)$.

$(x-3)(x+3) \cdot \dfrac{1}{x+3} = (x-3)(x+3) \cdot \dfrac{7}{(x-3)(x+3)}$

$x - 3 = 7$

$x = 10$

Section 4.5

1. $\dfrac{18x^6}{9x^2} = 2x^{6-2} = 2x^4$

3. $\dfrac{35m^3 n^2}{7mn^2} = 5m^{3-1}n^{2-2} = 5m^2$

5. $\dfrac{3a+6}{3} = \dfrac{3a}{3} + \dfrac{6}{3} = a+2$

7. $\dfrac{9b^2-12}{3} = \dfrac{9b^2}{3} - \dfrac{12}{3} = 3b^2-4$

9. $\dfrac{16a^3-24a^2}{4a} = \dfrac{16a^3}{4a} - \dfrac{24a^2}{4a} = 4a^2-6a$

11. $\dfrac{12m^2+6m}{-3m} = \dfrac{12m^2}{-3m} + \dfrac{6m}{-3m} = -4m-2$

13. $\dfrac{18a^4+12a^3-6a^2}{6a} = \dfrac{18a^4}{6a} + \dfrac{12a^3}{6a} - \dfrac{6a^2}{6a}$
$= 3a^3+2a^2-a$

15. $\dfrac{20x^4y^2-15x^2y^3+10x^3y}{5x^2y} = \dfrac{20x^4y^2}{5x^2y} - \dfrac{15x^2y^3}{5x^2y}$
$= 4x^2y-3y^2+2x$

17. Since the divisor is a binomial, use long division.

$$
\begin{array}{r}
x+3 \\
x+2\,\overline{\smash{)}\,x^2+5x+6} \\
\underline{x^2+2x} \\
3x+6 \\
\underline{3x+6} \\
0
\end{array}
$$

$\dfrac{x^2+5x+6}{x+2} = x+3$

19. Since the divisor is a binomial, use long division.

$$
\begin{array}{r}
x-5 \\
x+4\,\overline{\smash{)}\,x^2-x-20} \\
\underline{x^2+4x} \\
-5x-20 \\
\underline{-5x-20} \\
0
\end{array}
$$

$\dfrac{x^2-x-20}{x+4} = x-5$

21. Since the divisor is a binomial, use long division.

$$
\begin{array}{r}
x+3 \\
2x-1\,\overline{\smash{)}\,2x^2+5x-3} \\
\underline{2x^2-x} \\
6x-3 \\
\underline{6x-3} \\
0
\end{array}
$$

$\dfrac{2x^2+5x-3}{2x-1} = x+3$

23. Since the divisor is a binomial, use long division.

$$
\begin{array}{r}
2x+3 \\
x-3\,\overline{\smash{)}\,2x^2-3x-5} \\
\underline{2x^2-6x} \\
3x-5 \\
\underline{3x-9} \\
4
\end{array}
$$

$\dfrac{2x^2-3x-5}{x-3} = 2x+3+\dfrac{4}{x-3}$

25. Since the divisor is a binomial, use long division.

$$
\begin{array}{r}
4x+2 \\
x-5\,\overline{\smash{)}\,4x^2-18x-15} \\
\underline{4x^2-20x} \\
2x-15 \\
\underline{2x-10} \\
-5
\end{array}
$$

$\dfrac{4x^2-18x-15}{x-5} = 4x+2+\dfrac{-5}{x-5}$

27. Since the divisor is a binomial, use long division.

$$
\begin{array}{r}
2x+3 \\
3x-5\,\overline{\smash{)}\,6x^2-x-10} \\
\underline{6x^2-10x} \\
9x-10 \\
\underline{9x-15} \\
5
\end{array}
$$

$\dfrac{6x^2-x-10}{3x-5} = 2x+3+\dfrac{5}{3x-5}$

29. Since the divisor is a binomial, use long division.

$$
\begin{array}{r}
x^2 - x - 2 \\
x+2\overline{)x^3 + x^2 - 4x - 4} \\
\underline{x^3 + 2x^2} \\
-x^2 - 4x \\
\underline{-x^2 - 2x} \\
-2x - 4 \\
\underline{-2x - 4} \\
0
\end{array}
$$

$$\frac{x^3 + x^2 - 4x - 4}{x+2} = x^2 - x - 2$$

31. Since the divisor is a binomial, use long division.

$$
\begin{array}{r}
x^2 + 2x + 3 \\
4x-1\overline{)4x^3 + 7x^2 + 10x + 5} \\
\underline{4x^3 - x^2} \\
8x^2 + 10x \\
\underline{8x^2 - 2x} \\
12x + 5 \\
\underline{12x - 3} \\
8
\end{array}
$$

$$\frac{4x^3 + 7x^2 + 10x + 5}{4x-1} = x^2 + 2x + 3 + \frac{8}{4x-1}$$

33. Since the divisor is a binomial, use long division. The dividend $x^3 - x^2 + 5$ is missing a term in x, so write $0 \cdot x$.

$$
\begin{array}{r}
x^2 + x + 2 \\
x-2\overline{)x^3 - x^2 + 0x + 5} \\
\underline{x^3 - 2x^2} \\
x^2 + 0x \\
\underline{x^2 - 2x} \\
2x + 5 \\
\underline{2x - 4} \\
9
\end{array}
$$

$$\frac{x^3 - x^2 + 5}{x-2} = x^2 + x + 2 + \frac{9}{x-2}$$

35. Since the divisor is a binomial, use long division. The dividend $25x^2 + x$ is missing terms in x^2 and x^0, so write $0x^2$ and 0.

$$
\begin{array}{r}
5x^2 + 2x + 1 \\
5x-2\overline{)25x^3 + 0x^2 + x + 0} \\
\underline{25x^3 - 10x^2} \\
10x^2 + x \\
\underline{10x^2 - 4x} \\
5x + 0 \\
\underline{5x - 2} \\
2
\end{array}
$$

$$\frac{25x^2 + x}{5x-2} = 5x^2 + 2x + 1 + \frac{2}{5x-2}$$

37. Since the divisor is a binomial, use long division. Rearrange the dividend in descending-exponent form.

$$
\begin{array}{r}
x^2 + 4x + 5 \\
x-2\overline{)x^3 + 2x^2 - 3x - 8} \\
\underline{x^3 - 2x^2} \\
4x^2 - 3x \\
\underline{4x^2 - 8x} \\
5x - 8 \\
\underline{5x - 10} \\
2
\end{array}
$$

$$\frac{2x^2 - 8 - 3x + x^3}{x-2} = x^2 + 4x + 5 + \frac{2}{x-2}$$

39. Since the divisor is a binomial, use long division. The dividend $x^4 - 1$ is "missing" terms in x^3, x^2, and x, so write $0x^3 + 0x^2 + 0x$.

$$
\begin{array}{r}
x^3 + x^2 + x + 1 \\
x - 1 \overline{)\, x^4 + 0x^3 + 0x^2 + 0x - 1} \\
\underline{x^4 - x^3} \\
x^3 + 0x^2 \\
\underline{x^3 - x^2} \\
x^2 + 0x \\
\underline{x^2 - x} \\
x - 1 \\
\underline{x - 1} \\
0
\end{array}
$$

$$\frac{x^4 - 1}{x - 1} = x^3 + x^2 + x + 1$$

41. Since the divisor is a binomial, use long division.

$$
\begin{array}{r}
x - 3 \\
x^2 - 1 \overline{)\, x^3 - 3x^2 - x + 3} \\
\underline{x^3 - x} \\
-3x^2 + 3 \\
\underline{-3x^2 + 3} \\
0
\end{array}
$$

$$\frac{x^3 - 3x^2 - x + 3}{x^2 - 1} = x - 3$$

43. Since the divisor is a binomial, use long division. The dividend is missing terms in x^3 and x, so write $0x^3$ and $0x$.

$$
\begin{array}{r}
x^2 - 1 \\
x^2 + 3 \overline{)\, x^4 + 0x^3 + 2x^2 + 0x - 2} \\
\underline{x^4 + 3x^2} \\
-x^2 - 2 \\
\underline{-x^2 - 3} \\
1
\end{array}
$$

$$\frac{x^4 + 2x^2 - 2}{x^2 + 3} = x^2 - 1 + \frac{1}{x^2 + 3}$$

45. Since the divisor is a binomial, use long division. The dividend is missing terms in y^2 and y, so write $0y^2$ and $0y$.

$$
\begin{array}{r}
y^2 - y + 1 \\
y + 1 \overline{)\, y^3 + 0y^2 + 0y + 1} \\
\underline{y^3 + y^2} \\
-y^2 + 0y \\
\underline{-y^2 - y} \\
y + 1 \\
\underline{y + 1} \\
0
\end{array}
$$

$$\frac{y^3 + 1}{y + 1} = y^2 - y + 1$$

47. Since the divisor is a binomial, use long division. The dividend is missing terms in x^3, x^2, and x, so write $0x^3$, $0x^2$, and $0x$.

$$
\begin{array}{r}
x^2 + 1 \\
x^2 - 1 \overline{)\, x^4 + 0x^3 + 0x^2 + 0x - 1} \\
\underline{x^4 - x^2} \\
x^2 - 1 \\
\underline{x^2 - 1} \\
0
\end{array}
$$

$$\frac{x^4 - 1}{x^2 - 1} = x^2 + 1$$

49. $\dfrac{y^2 - y + c}{y + 1} = y - 2$ can be written as

$$y^2 - y + c = (y - 2)(y + 1)$$
$$y^2 - y + c = y^2 - y - 2$$
Therefore, $c = -2$.

51. Writing exercise

53. a.

$$\begin{array}{r} x+1 \\ x-1\overline{\smash{\big)}\,x^2+0x-1} \\ \underline{x^2-x} \\ x-1 \\ \underline{x-1} \\ 0 \end{array}$$

$$\frac{x^2-1}{x-1}=x+1$$

b.

$$\begin{array}{r} x^2+x+1 \\ x-1\overline{\smash{\big)}\,x^3+0x^2+0x-1} \\ \underline{x^2-x^2} \\ x^2+0x \\ \underline{x^2-x} \\ x-1 \\ \underline{x-1} \\ 0 \end{array}$$

$$\frac{x^3-1}{x-1}=x^2+x+1$$

c.

$$\begin{array}{r} x^3+x^2+x+1 \\ x-1\overline{\smash{\big)}\,x^4+0x^3+0x^2+0x-1} \\ \underline{x^4-x^3} \\ x^3+0x^2 \\ \underline{x^3-x^2} \\ x^2+0x \\ \underline{x^2-x} \\ x-1 \\ \underline{x-1} \\ 0 \end{array}$$

$$\frac{x^4-1}{x-1}=x^3+x^2+x+1$$

d. In each problem (a), (b), and (c) the quotient is a polynomial of degree one less than the degree of the dividend. The quotient has no missing terms and all of its coefficients are 1. Therefore, it would seem like

$$\frac{x^{50}-1}{x-1}=x^{49}+x^{48}+\cdots+x+1.$$

Exercises 4.6

1. $\sqrt{16}=\sqrt{4^2}=4$

3. $\sqrt{400}=\sqrt{20^2}=20$

5. $-\sqrt{100}=-\sqrt{10^2}=-10$

7. $\sqrt{-81}$ is not a real number, since $-81<0$.

9. $\sqrt{\dfrac{16}{9}}=\dfrac{\sqrt{16}}{\sqrt{9}}=\dfrac{4}{3}$

11. Not a real number, since $-\dfrac{4}{5}<0$

13. $\sqrt[3]{27}=\sqrt[3]{3^3}=3$

15. $\sqrt[3]{-27}=\sqrt[3]{(-3)^3}=-3$

17. $\sqrt[4]{-81}$ is not a real number, since $-81<0$.

19. $-\sqrt[3]{27}=-\sqrt[3]{3^3}=-3$

21. $\sqrt[4]{625}=\sqrt[4]{5^4}=5$

23. $\sqrt[3]{\dfrac{1}{27}}=\sqrt[3]{\left(\dfrac{1}{3}\right)^3}=\dfrac{1}{3}$

25. $\sqrt{19}$ is irrational because 19 is not a perfect square.

27. $\sqrt{100}=10$ is rational.

29. $\sqrt[3]{9}$ is irrational because 9 is not a perfect cube.

31. $\sqrt[4]{16}=2$ is rational.

33. $\sqrt{\dfrac{4}{7}}$ is irrational because $\dfrac{4}{7}$ is not the square of a rational number.

35. $\sqrt[3]{-27}=-3$ is rational.

37. $\sqrt{11}\approx3.32$

39. $\sqrt{7}\approx2.65$

41. $\sqrt{46}\approx6.78$

43. $\sqrt{\dfrac{2}{5}} \approx 0.63$

45. $\sqrt{\dfrac{8}{9}} \approx 0.94$

47. $-\sqrt{18} \approx -4.24$

49. $-\sqrt{27} \approx -5.20$

51. $-\sqrt{16} = -\sqrt{4^2} = -4$

53. $\sqrt[3]{-125} = \sqrt[3]{(-5)^3} = -5 = -\sqrt[3]{5^3} = -\sqrt[3]{125}$

55. $\sqrt[4]{10,000} = \sqrt[4]{10^4} = 10 = \sqrt[3]{10^3} = \sqrt[3]{1000}$

57. $\sqrt{16x^{16}} = \sqrt{(4x^8)^2} = 4x^8 \neq 4x^4$; False

59. True, because $16x^{-4}y^{-4} = \dfrac{16}{x^4 y^4} > 0$.

61. $\dfrac{\sqrt{x^2 - 25}}{x - 5} = \dfrac{\sqrt{(x-5)(x+5)}}{x-5} \neq \sqrt{x+5}$; False

63. $A = s^2$
$32 = s^2$
$\sqrt{32} = s$ so $s \approx 5.66$
The length of a side is 5.66 ft.

65. $A = \pi r^2$
$147 = \pi r^2$
$\dfrac{147}{\pi} = r^2$
$\sqrt{\dfrac{147}{\pi}} = r$ so $r \approx 6.84$
The radius is 6.84 ft.

67. $t = \dfrac{1}{4}\sqrt{s} = \dfrac{1}{4}\sqrt{800} \approx 7.07$
It would take 7.07 seconds.

69. $A = s^2$
$10 = s^2$, so
$s = \sqrt{10} \approx 3.16$ ft.

71. $A = s^2$
$17 = s^2$, so
$s = \sqrt{17} \approx 4.12$ ft.

73. Conjugate: $4 + \sqrt{7}$
Opposite: $-\left(4 - \sqrt{7}\right) = -4 + \sqrt{7}$

With the conjugate, only the sign on the radical changes. With the opposite, the sign on the entire expression changes.

75. $\left(\sqrt{3} - 2\right)\left(\sqrt{3} + 2\right)$
$= 3 + 2\sqrt{3} - 2\sqrt{3} - 4$
$= -1$
The answer is $\sqrt{3} + 2$.

77. Challenge exercise

79. (a) $T = 2\pi\sqrt{\dfrac{L}{g}} = 2\pi\sqrt{\dfrac{30}{980}} \approx 1.1$ s

(b) $T = 2\pi\sqrt{\dfrac{L}{g}} = 2\pi\sqrt{\dfrac{50}{980}} \approx 1.4$ s

(c) $T = 2\pi\sqrt{\dfrac{L}{g}} = 2\pi\sqrt{\dfrac{70}{980}} \approx 1.7$ s

(d) $T = 2\pi\sqrt{\dfrac{L}{g}} = 2\pi\sqrt{\dfrac{90}{980}} \approx 1.9$ s

(e) $T = 2\pi\sqrt{\dfrac{L}{g}} = 2\pi\sqrt{\dfrac{110}{980}} \approx 2.1$ s

Exercises 4.7

1. $\sqrt{18} = \sqrt{9 \cdot 2} = \sqrt{9} \cdot \sqrt{2} = 3\sqrt{2}$

3. $\sqrt{28} = \sqrt{4 \cdot 7} = \sqrt{4} \cdot \sqrt{7} = 2\sqrt{7}$

5. $\sqrt{45} = \sqrt{9 \cdot 5} = \sqrt{9} \cdot \sqrt{5} = 3\sqrt{5}$

7. $\sqrt{48} = \sqrt{16 \cdot 3} = \sqrt{16} \cdot \sqrt{3} = 4\sqrt{3}$

9. $\sqrt{200} = \sqrt{100 \cdot 2} = \sqrt{100} \cdot \sqrt{2} = 10\sqrt{2}$

11. $\sqrt{147} = \sqrt{49 \cdot 3} = \sqrt{49} \cdot \sqrt{3} = 7\sqrt{3}$

13. $3\sqrt{12} = 3\sqrt{4 \cdot 3} = 3 \cdot \sqrt{4} \cdot \sqrt{3} = 3 \cdot 2\sqrt{3} = 6\sqrt{3}$

15. $\sqrt{5x^2} = \sqrt{5} \cdot \sqrt{x^2} = x\sqrt{5}$

17. $\sqrt{3y^4} = \sqrt{3(y^2)^2} = \sqrt{3} \cdot \sqrt{(y^2)^2} = y^2\sqrt{3}$

19. $\sqrt{2r^3} = \sqrt{2r \cdot r^2} = \sqrt{2r} \cdot \sqrt{r^2} = r\sqrt{2r}$

21. $\sqrt{27b^2} = \sqrt{9b^2 \cdot 3} = \sqrt{9b^2} \cdot \sqrt{3} = 3b\sqrt{3}$

23. $\sqrt{24x^4} = \sqrt{4x^4 \cdot 6} = \sqrt{4x^4} \cdot \sqrt{6} = 2x^2\sqrt{6}$

25. $\sqrt{54a^5} = \sqrt{9a^4 \cdot 6a} = \sqrt{9a^4} \cdot \sqrt{6a} = 3a^2\sqrt{6a}$

27. $\sqrt{x^3y^2} = \sqrt{x^2y^2x} = \sqrt{x^2y^2} \cdot \sqrt{x} = xy\sqrt{x}$

29. $\sqrt{\dfrac{4}{25}} = \dfrac{\sqrt{4}}{\sqrt{25}} = \dfrac{2}{5}$

31. $\sqrt{\dfrac{9}{16}} = \dfrac{\sqrt{9}}{\sqrt{16}} = \dfrac{3}{4}$

33. $\sqrt{\dfrac{3}{4}} = \dfrac{\sqrt{3}}{\sqrt{4}} = \dfrac{\sqrt{3}}{2}$

35. $\sqrt{\dfrac{5}{36}} = \dfrac{\sqrt{5}}{\sqrt{36}} = \dfrac{\sqrt{5}}{6}$

37.
$$\sqrt{\dfrac{8a^2}{25}} = \dfrac{\sqrt{8a^2}}{\sqrt{25}}$$
$$= \dfrac{\sqrt{4a^2 \cdot 2}}{5}$$
$$= \dfrac{\sqrt{4a^2} \cdot \sqrt{2}}{5}$$
$$= \dfrac{2a\sqrt{2}}{5}$$

39. $\sqrt{\dfrac{1}{5}} = \dfrac{\sqrt{1}}{\sqrt{5}} = \dfrac{1 \cdot \sqrt{5}}{\sqrt{5} \cdot \sqrt{5}} = \dfrac{\sqrt{5}}{5}$

41. $\sqrt{\dfrac{3}{2}} = \dfrac{\sqrt{3}}{\sqrt{2}} = \dfrac{\sqrt{3} \cdot \sqrt{2}}{\sqrt{2} \cdot \sqrt{2}} = \dfrac{\sqrt{6}}{2}$

43. $\sqrt{\dfrac{3a}{5}} = \dfrac{\sqrt{3a}}{\sqrt{5}} = \dfrac{\sqrt{3a} \cdot \sqrt{5}}{\sqrt{5} \cdot \sqrt{5}} = \dfrac{\sqrt{15a}}{5}$

45.
$$\sqrt{\dfrac{2x^2}{3}} = \dfrac{\sqrt{2x^2}}{\sqrt{3}}$$
$$= \dfrac{\sqrt{2x^2} \cdot \sqrt{3}}{\sqrt{3} \cdot \sqrt{3}}$$
$$= \dfrac{\sqrt{x^2} \cdot \sqrt{2} \cdot \sqrt{3}}{3}$$
$$= \dfrac{x\sqrt{6}}{3}$$

47.
$$\sqrt{\dfrac{8s^3}{7}} = \dfrac{\sqrt{8s^3}}{\sqrt{7}}$$
$$= \dfrac{\sqrt{4s^2 \cdot 2s} \cdot \sqrt{7}}{\sqrt{7} \cdot \sqrt{7}}$$
$$= \dfrac{\sqrt{4s^2} \cdot \sqrt{2s} \cdot \sqrt{7}}{7}$$
$$= \dfrac{2s\sqrt{14s}}{7}$$

49. $\sqrt{10mn}$ is in simplest form.

51. $\dfrac{\sqrt{98x^2y}}{7x} = \dfrac{\sqrt{49x^2 \cdot 2y}}{7x} = \dfrac{7x\sqrt{2y}}{7x} = \sqrt{2y}$
Remove the perfect square factors from the radical and reduce the fraction.

53. Writing exercise

Exercises 4.8

1. $2\sqrt{2} + 4\sqrt{2} = (2+4)\sqrt{2} = 6\sqrt{2}$

3. $11\sqrt{7} - 4\sqrt{7} = (11-4)\sqrt{7} = 7\sqrt{7}$

5. $5\sqrt{7} + 3\sqrt{6}$; Cannot be simplified

7. $2\sqrt{3} - 5\sqrt{3} = (2-5)\sqrt{3} = -3\sqrt{3}$

9. $2\sqrt{3x} + 5\sqrt{3x} = (2+5)\sqrt{3x} = 7\sqrt{3x}$

11. $2\sqrt{3} + \sqrt{3} + 3\sqrt{3} = (2+1+3)\sqrt{3} = 6\sqrt{3}$

13. $5\sqrt{7} - 2\sqrt{7} + \sqrt{7} = (5-2+1)\sqrt{7} = 4\sqrt{7}$

15. $2\sqrt{5x} + 5\sqrt{5x} - 2\sqrt{5x} = (2+5-2)\sqrt{5x}$
$\qquad = 5\sqrt{5x}$

17.
$$2\sqrt{3} + \sqrt{12} = 2\sqrt{3} + \sqrt{4 \cdot 3}$$
$$= 2\sqrt{3} + \sqrt{4} \cdot \sqrt{3}$$
$$= 2\sqrt{3} + 2\sqrt{3}$$
$$= (2+2)\sqrt{3}$$
$$= 4\sqrt{3}$$

19.
$$\sqrt{20} - \sqrt{5} = \sqrt{4 \cdot 5} - \sqrt{5}$$
$$= \sqrt{4} \cdot \sqrt{5} - \sqrt{5}$$
$$= 2\sqrt{5} - \sqrt{5}$$
$$= (2-1)\sqrt{5}$$
$$= \sqrt{5}$$

21.
$$2\sqrt{6} - \sqrt{54} = 2\sqrt{6} - \sqrt{9 \cdot 6}$$
$$= 2\sqrt{6} - \sqrt{9} \cdot \sqrt{6}$$
$$= 2\sqrt{6} - 3\sqrt{6}$$
$$= (2-3)\sqrt{6}$$
$$= -\sqrt{6}$$

23.
$$\sqrt{72} + \sqrt{50} = \sqrt{36 \cdot 2} + \sqrt{25 \cdot 2}$$
$$= \sqrt{36} \cdot \sqrt{2} + \sqrt{25} \cdot \sqrt{2}$$
$$= 6\sqrt{2} + 5\sqrt{2}$$
$$= (6+5)\sqrt{2}$$
$$= 11\sqrt{2}$$

25.
$$3\sqrt{12} - \sqrt{48} = 3\sqrt{4 \cdot 3} - \sqrt{16 \cdot 3}$$
$$= 3 \cdot 2\sqrt{3} - 4\sqrt{3}$$
$$= 6\sqrt{3} - 4\sqrt{3}$$
$$= (6-4)\sqrt{3}$$
$$= 2\sqrt{3}$$

27.
$$2\sqrt{45} - 2\sqrt{20} = 2\sqrt{9 \cdot 5} - 2\sqrt{4 \cdot 5}$$
$$= 2 \cdot 3\sqrt{5} - 2 \cdot 2\sqrt{5}$$
$$= 6\sqrt{5} - 4\sqrt{5}$$
$$= (6-4)\sqrt{5}$$
$$= 2\sqrt{5}$$

29.
$$\sqrt{12} + \sqrt{27} - \sqrt{3} = \sqrt{4 \cdot 3} + \sqrt{9 \cdot 3} - \sqrt{3}$$
$$= 2\sqrt{3} + 3\sqrt{3} - \sqrt{3}$$
$$= (2+3-1)\sqrt{3}$$
$$= 4\sqrt{3}$$

31.
$$3\sqrt{24} - \sqrt{54} + \sqrt{6} = 3 \cdot 2\sqrt{6} - 3\sqrt{6} + \sqrt{6}$$
$$= 6\sqrt{6} - 3\sqrt{6} + \sqrt{6}$$
$$= (6-3+1)\sqrt{6}$$
$$= 4\sqrt{6}$$

33.
$$2\sqrt{50} + 3\sqrt{18} - \sqrt{32} = 2 \cdot 5\sqrt{2} + 3 \cdot 3\sqrt{2} - 4\sqrt{2}$$
$$= 10\sqrt{2} + 9\sqrt{2} - 4\sqrt{2}$$
$$= (10+9-4)\sqrt{2}$$
$$= 15\sqrt{2}$$

35.
$$a\sqrt{27} - 2\sqrt{3a^2} = a\sqrt{9} \cdot \sqrt{3} - 2\sqrt{a^2} \cdot \sqrt{3}$$
$$= 3a\sqrt{3} - 2a\sqrt{3}$$
$$= (3a-2a)\sqrt{3}$$
$$= a\sqrt{3}$$

37.
$$5\sqrt{3x^3} + 2\sqrt{27x} = 5\sqrt{x^2} \cdot \sqrt{3x} + 2\sqrt{9} \cdot \sqrt{3x}$$
$$= 5x\sqrt{3x} + 2 \cdot 3\sqrt{3x}$$
$$= (5x+6)\sqrt{3x}$$

39. $\sqrt{3} - \sqrt{2} \approx 0.32$

41. $\sqrt{5} + \sqrt{3} \approx 3.97$

43. $4\sqrt{3} - 7\sqrt{5} \approx -8.72$

45. $5\sqrt{7} + 8\sqrt{13} \approx 42.07$

47.
$$P = 2L + 2W$$
$$= 2\sqrt{36} + 2\sqrt{49}$$
$$= 2 \cdot 6 + 2 \cdot 7$$
$$= 12 + 14$$
$$= 26$$

49.
$$P = a + b + c$$
$$= \left(\sqrt{3} - \sqrt{2}\right) + \left(\sqrt{3} + \sqrt{2}\right) + 3$$
$$= \sqrt{3} + \sqrt{3} + 3$$
$$= 2\sqrt{3} + 3$$

Exercises 4.9

1.
$$\sqrt{x} = 2$$
$$\left(\sqrt{x}\right)^2 = 2^2$$
$$x = 4$$
Check:
$$\sqrt{4} \stackrel{?}{=} 2$$
$$2 = 2 \quad \text{True}$$
The solution is $x = 4$.

3.
$$\sqrt{x} = 6$$
$$(\sqrt{x})^2 = (6)^2$$
$$x = 36$$

5. $2\sqrt{y} - 1 = 0$

$\quad\quad 2\sqrt{y} = 1$

$\quad\quad \left(2\sqrt{y}\right)^2 = 1^2$

$\quad\quad\quad 4y = 1$

$\quad\quad\quad\quad y = \dfrac{1}{4}$

Check:

$2 \cdot \sqrt{\dfrac{1}{4}} - 1 \overset{?}{=} 0$

$2 \cdot \dfrac{1}{2} - 1 \overset{?}{=} 0$

$\quad 1 - 1 \overset{?}{=} 0$

$\quad\quad 0 = 0 \ \text{True}$

The solution is $y = \dfrac{1}{4}$.

7. $\sqrt{5x + 1} = 6$

$\quad (\sqrt{5x+1})^2 = (6)^2$

$\quad\quad 5x + 1 = 36$

$\quad\quad\quad \underline{-1 \quad -1}$

$\quad\quad\quad \dfrac{5x}{5} = \dfrac{35}{5}$

$\quad\quad\quad\quad x = 7$

9. $\sqrt{m + 5} = 3$

$\quad \left(\sqrt{m+5}\right)^2 = 3^2$

$\quad\quad m + 5 = 9$

$\quad\quad\quad m = 4$

Check:

$\sqrt{4 + 5} \overset{?}{=} 3$

$\quad \sqrt{9} \overset{?}{=} 3$

$\quad\quad 3 = 3 \ \text{True}$

The solution is $m = 4$.

11. $\sqrt{2x + 4} - 4 = 0$

$\quad\quad \sqrt{2x + 4} = 4$

$\quad \left(\sqrt{2x+4}\right)^2 = 4^2$

$\quad\quad 2x + 4 = 16$

$\quad\quad\quad 2x = 12$

$\quad\quad\quad\quad x = 6$

Check:

$\sqrt{2 \cdot 6 + 4} - 4 \overset{?}{=} 0$

$\quad \sqrt{16} - 4 \overset{?}{=} 0$

$\quad\quad 4 - 4 \overset{?}{=} 0$

$\quad\quad\quad\quad 0 = 0 \ \text{True}$

The solution is $x = 6$.

13. $\sqrt{3x - 2} + 2 = 0$

$\quad\quad \sqrt{3x - 2} = -2$

$\quad \left(\sqrt{3x-2}\right)^2 = \left(-2\right)^2$

$\quad\quad 3x - 2 = 4$

$\quad\quad\quad 3x = 6$

$\quad\quad\quad\quad x = 2$

Check:

$\sqrt{3 \cdot 2 - 2} + 2 \overset{?}{=} 0$

$\quad \sqrt{4} + 2 \overset{?}{=} 0$

$\quad\quad 2 + 2 \overset{?}{=} 0$

$\quad\quad\quad 4 \neq 0$

There are no solutions.

15. $\sqrt{x - 1} = \sqrt{1 - x}$

$\quad \left(\sqrt{x-1}\right)^2 = \left(\sqrt{1-x}\right)^2$

$\quad\quad x - 1 = 1 - x$

$\quad\quad 2x = 2$

$\quad\quad\quad x = 1$

Check:

$\sqrt{1 - 1} \overset{?}{=} \sqrt{1 - 1}$

$\quad \sqrt{0} \overset{?}{=} \sqrt{0}$

$\quad\quad 0 = 0 \quad\quad \text{True}$

The solution is $x = 1$.

17. $\sqrt{w + 3} = \sqrt{3 + w}$

$\quad \left(\sqrt{w+3}\right)^2 = \left(\sqrt{3+w}\right)^2$

$\quad\quad w + 3 = 3 + w$

$\quad\quad\quad 0 = 0$

The solution is all real numbers since this is always true.

19. $\sqrt{2x - 3} + 1 = 3$

$\quad\quad \sqrt{2x - 3} = 2$

$\quad \left(\sqrt{2x-3}\right)^2 = 2^2$

$\quad\quad 2x - 3 = 4$

$\quad\quad\quad 2x = 7$

$\quad\quad\quad\quad x = \dfrac{7}{2}$

Check:

$\sqrt{2 \cdot \dfrac{7}{2} - 3} + 1 \overset{?}{=} 3$

$\quad \sqrt{4} + 1 \overset{?}{=} 3$

$\quad\quad 2 + 1 \overset{?}{=} 3$

$\quad\quad\quad 3 = 3 \ \text{True}$

The solution is $x = \dfrac{7}{2}$.

21.

$$2\sqrt{3z+2} - 1 = 5$$
$$2\sqrt{3z+2} = 6$$
$$\sqrt{3z+2} = 3$$
$$\left(\sqrt{3z+2}\right)^2 = 3^2$$
$$3z+2 = 9$$
$$3z = 7$$
$$z = \frac{7}{3}$$

Check:
$$2 \cdot \sqrt{3 \cdot \frac{7}{3} + 2} - 1 \overset{?}{=} 5$$
$$2\sqrt{9} - 1 \overset{?}{=} 5$$
$$6 - 1 \overset{?}{=} 5$$
$$5 = 5 \quad \text{True}$$

The solution is $z = \frac{7}{3}$.

23.

$$\sqrt{15-2x} = x$$
$$\left(\sqrt{15-2x}\right)^2 = x^2$$
$$15 - 2x = x^2$$
$$x^2 + 2x - 15 = 0$$
$$(x-3)(x+5) = 0$$
$$x - 3 = 0 \quad \text{or} \quad x + 5 = 0$$
$$x = 3 \qquad\qquad x = -5$$

Check: $x = 3$ 　　　　Check: $x = -5$
$$\sqrt{15 - 2(3)} \overset{?}{=} 3 \qquad \sqrt{15 - 2(-5)} \overset{?}{=} 3$$
$$\sqrt{9} \overset{?}{=} 3 \qquad\qquad \sqrt{25} \overset{?}{=} 3$$
$$3 = 3 \quad \text{True} \qquad\qquad 5 \neq 3$$

The solution is $x = 3$.

25.

$$\sqrt{x+5} = x - 1$$
$$\left(\sqrt{x+5}\right)^2 = (x-1)^2$$
$$x + 5 = x^2 - 2x + 1$$
$$x^2 - 3x - 4 = 0$$
$$(x-4)(x+1) = 0$$
$$x - 4 = 0 \quad \text{or} \quad x + 1 = 0$$
$$x = 4 \qquad\qquad x = -1$$

Check: $x = 4$ 　　　　Check: $x = -1$
$$\sqrt{4+5} \overset{?}{=} 4 - 1 \qquad \sqrt{-1+5} \overset{?}{=} -1 - 1$$
$$\sqrt{9} \overset{?}{=} 3 \qquad\qquad \sqrt{4} \overset{?}{=} -2$$
$$3 = 3 \quad \text{True} \qquad\qquad 2 \neq -2$$

The solution is $x = 4$.

27.

$$\sqrt{3m-2} + m = 10$$
$$\sqrt{3m-2} = 10 - m$$
$$\left(\sqrt{3m-2}\right)^2 = (10-m)^2$$
$$3m - 2 = 100 - 20m + m^2$$
$$m^2 - 23m + 102 = 0$$
$$(m-6)(m-17) = 0$$
$$m - 6 = 0 \quad \text{or} \quad m - 17 = 0$$
$$m = 6 \qquad\qquad m = 17$$

Check: $m = 6$ 　　　　Check: $m = 17$
$$\sqrt{3 \cdot 6 - 2} + 6 \overset{?}{=} 10 \qquad \sqrt{3 \cdot 17 - 2} + 17 \overset{?}{=} 10$$
$$4 + 6 \overset{?}{=} 10 \qquad\qquad 7 + 17 \overset{?}{=} 10$$
$$10 = 10 \quad \text{True} \qquad\qquad 24 \neq 10$$

The solution is $m = 6$.

29.

$$\sqrt{t+9} + 3 = t$$
$$\sqrt{t+9} = t - 3$$
$$\left(\sqrt{t+9}\right)^2 = (t-3)^2$$
$$t + 9 = t^2 - 6t + 9$$
$$t^2 - 7t = 0$$
$$t(t-7) = 0$$
$$t = 0 \quad \text{or} \quad t = 7$$

Check: $t = 0$ 　　　　Check: $t = 7$
$$\sqrt{0+9} + 3 \overset{?}{=} 0 \qquad \sqrt{7+9} + 3 \overset{?}{=} 7$$
$$3 + 3 \overset{?}{=} 0 \qquad\qquad 4 + 3 \overset{?}{=} 7$$
$$6 \neq 0 \qquad\qquad 7 = 7 \quad \text{True}$$

The solution is $t = 7$.

31.

$$\sqrt{6x+1} - 1 = 2x$$
$$\sqrt{6x+1} = 2x + 1$$
$$\left(\sqrt{6x+1}\right)^2 = (2x+1)^2$$
$$6x + 1 = 4x^2 + 4x + 1$$
$$4x^2 - 2x = 0$$
$$2x(2x-1) = 0$$
$$x = 0 \quad \text{or} \quad x = \frac{1}{2}$$

Check: $x = 0$
$$\sqrt{6 \cdot 0 + 1} - 1 \overset{?}{=} 2 \cdot 0$$
$$\sqrt{1} - 1 \overset{?}{=} 0$$
$$1 - 1 \overset{?}{=} 0$$
$$0 = 0 \quad \text{True}$$

Check: $x = \frac{1}{2}$

$$\sqrt{6\cdot\frac{1}{2}+1}-1\overset{?}{=}2\cdot\frac{1}{2}$$
$$\sqrt{4}-1\overset{?}{=}1$$
$$2-1\overset{?}{=}1$$
$$1=1 \quad \text{True}$$

The solutions are $x=0$ and $x=\frac{1}{2}$.

33.
$$\sqrt[3]{x-5}=3$$
$$\left(\sqrt[3]{x-5}\right)^3=3^3$$
$$x-5=27$$
$$x=32$$
Check:
$$\sqrt[3]{32-5}\overset{?}{=}3$$
$$\sqrt[3]{27}\overset{?}{=}3$$
$$3=3 \quad \text{True}$$
The solution is $x=32$.

35.
$$\sqrt[3]{x^2-1}=2$$
$$\left(\sqrt[3]{x^2-1}\right)^3=2^3$$
$$x^2-1=8$$
$$x^2-9=0$$
$$(x+3)(x-3)=0$$
$$x+3=0 \quad \text{or} \quad x-3=0$$
$$x=-3 \qquad x=3$$

Check: $x=-3$ Check: $x=3$
$$\sqrt[3]{(-3)^2-1}\overset{?}{=}2 \qquad \sqrt[3]{3^2-1}\overset{?}{=}2$$
$$\sqrt[3]{8}\overset{?}{=}2 \qquad\qquad \sqrt[3]{8}\overset{?}{=}2$$
$$2=2 \text{ True} \qquad\quad 2=2 \text{ True}$$
The solutions are $x=-3$ and $x=3$.

37.
$$\sqrt{2x}=\sqrt{x+1}$$
$$\left(\sqrt{2x}\right)^2=\left(\sqrt{x+1}\right)^2$$
$$2x=x+1$$
$$x=1$$
Check:
$$\sqrt{2\cdot1}\overset{?}{=}\sqrt{1+1}$$
$$\sqrt{2}=\sqrt{2} \quad \text{True}$$
The solution is $x=1$.

39.
$$2\sqrt{3r}=\sqrt{r+11}$$
$$\left(2\sqrt{3r}\right)^2=\left(\sqrt{r+11}\right)^2$$
$$4(3r)=r+11$$
$$12r=r+11$$
$$11r=11$$
$$r=1$$
Check:
$$2\sqrt{3\cdot1}\overset{?}{=}\sqrt{1+11}$$
$$2\sqrt{3}\overset{?}{=}\sqrt{12}$$
$$2\sqrt{3}=2\sqrt{3} \quad \text{True}$$
The solution is $r=1$.

41.
$$\sqrt{x+2}+1=\sqrt{x+4}$$
$$\left(\sqrt{x+2}+1\right)^2=\left(\sqrt{x+4}\right)^2$$
$$x+2+2\sqrt{x+2}+1=x+4$$
$$2\sqrt{x+2}=1$$
$$\left(2\sqrt{x+2}\right)^2=1^2$$
$$4(x+2)=1$$
$$4x+8=1$$
$$4x=-7$$
$$x=-\frac{7}{4}$$
Check:
$$\sqrt{-\frac{7}{4}+2}+1\overset{?}{=}\sqrt{-\frac{7}{4}+4}$$
$$\sqrt{\frac{1}{4}}+1\overset{?}{=}\sqrt{\frac{9}{4}}$$
$$\frac{1}{2}+1\overset{?}{=}\frac{3}{2}$$
$$\frac{3}{2}=\frac{3}{2} \quad \text{True}$$

The solution is $x=-\frac{7}{4}$.

43.
$$\sqrt{4m-3} - 2 = \sqrt{2m-5}$$
$$\left(\sqrt{4m-3} - 2\right)^2 = \left(\sqrt{2m-5}\right)^2$$
$$4m - 3 - 4\sqrt{4m-3} + 4 = 2m - 5$$
$$2m + 6 = 4\sqrt{4m-3}$$
$$\left(2m+6\right)^2 = \left(4\sqrt{4m-3}\right)^2$$
$$4m^2 + 24m + 36 = 16\left(4m-3\right)$$
$$4m^2 + 24m + 36 = 64m - 48$$
$$4m^2 - 40m + 84 = 0$$
$$4\left(m^2 - 10m + 21\right) = 0$$
$$4\left(m-7\right)\left(m-3\right) = 0$$
$$\left(m-7\right)\left(m-3\right) = 0$$
$$m - 7 = 0 \quad \text{or} \quad m - 3 = 0$$
$$m = 7 \qquad m = 3$$

Check: $m = 7$
$$\sqrt{4\cdot 7 - 3} - 2 \overset{?}{=} \sqrt{2\cdot 7 - 5}$$
$$\sqrt{25} - 2 \overset{?}{=} \sqrt{9}$$
$$5 - 2 \overset{?}{=} 3$$
$$3 = 3 \qquad \text{True}$$

Check: $m = 3$
$$\sqrt{4\cdot 3 - 3} - 2 \overset{?}{=} \sqrt{2\cdot 3 - 5}$$
$$\sqrt{9} - 2 \overset{?}{=} \sqrt{1}$$
$$3 - 2 \overset{?}{=} 1$$
$$1 = 1 \qquad \text{True}$$
The solutions are $m = 3$ and $m = 7$.

45. $\sqrt{x+1} + \sqrt{x} = 1$
$$\sqrt{x+1} = 1 - \sqrt{x}$$
$$\left(\sqrt{x+1}\right)^2 = \left(1 - \sqrt{x}\right)^2$$
$$x + 1 = 1 - 2\sqrt{x} + x$$
$$2\sqrt{x} = 0$$
$$\sqrt{x} = 0$$
$$\left(\sqrt{x}\right)^2 = 0^2$$
$$x = 0$$
Check:
$$\sqrt{0+1} + \sqrt{0} \overset{?}{=} 1$$
$$\sqrt{1} + 0 \overset{?}{=} 1$$
$$1 = 1 \quad \text{True}$$
The solution is $x = 0$.

47. $\sqrt{5x+6} - \sqrt{x+3} = 3$
$$\sqrt{5x+6} = \sqrt{x+3} + 3$$
$$\left(\sqrt{5x+6}\right)^2 = \left(\sqrt{x+3} + 3\right)^2$$
$$5x + 6 = x + 3 + 6\sqrt{x+3} + 9$$
$$4x - 6 = 6\sqrt{x+3}$$
$$\left(4x - 6\right)^2 = \left(6\sqrt{x+3}\right)^2$$
$$16x^2 - 48x + 36 = 36\left(x+3\right)$$
$$16x^2 - 48x + 36 = 36x + 108$$
$$16x^2 - 84x - 72 = 0$$
$$4\left(4x^2 - 21x - 18\right) = 0$$
$$4\left(4x + 3\right)\left(x - 6\right) = 0$$
$$\left(4x + 3\right)\left(x - 6\right) = 0$$
$$4x + 3 = 0 \quad \text{or} \quad x - 6 = 0$$
$$x = -\frac{3}{4} \qquad x = 6$$

Check: $x = -\dfrac{3}{4}$
$$\sqrt{5\left(-\frac{3}{4}\right) + 6} - \sqrt{-\frac{3}{4} + 3} \overset{?}{=} 3$$
$$\sqrt{\frac{9}{4}} - \sqrt{\frac{9}{4}} \overset{?}{=} 3$$
$$0 \neq 3$$
Check: $x = 6$
$$\sqrt{5\cdot 6 + 6} - \sqrt{6 + 3} \overset{?}{=} 3$$
$$\sqrt{36} - \sqrt{9} \overset{?}{=} 3$$
$$6 - 3 \overset{?}{=} 3$$
$$3 = 3 \quad \text{True}$$
The solution is $x = 6$.

49. $\sqrt{y^2 + 12y} - 3\sqrt{5} = 0$
$$\sqrt{y^2 + 12y} = 3\sqrt{5}$$
$$\left(\sqrt{y^2 + 12y}\right)^2 = \left(3\sqrt{5}\right)^2$$
$$y^2 + 12y = 9\cdot 5$$
$$y^2 + 12y - 45 = 0$$
$$\left(y + 15\right)\left(y - 3\right) = 0$$
$$y + 15 = 0 \quad \text{or} \quad y - 3 = 0$$
$$y = -15 \qquad y = 3$$
Check: $y = -15$
$$\sqrt{\left(-15\right)^2 + 12\left(-15\right)} - 3\sqrt{5} \overset{?}{=} 0$$
$$\sqrt{45} - 3\sqrt{5} \overset{?}{=} 0$$
$$3\sqrt{5} - 3\sqrt{5} \overset{?}{=} 0$$
$$0 = 0 \quad \text{True}$$
Check: $y = 3$

$$\sqrt{3^2 + 12 \cdot 3} - 3\sqrt{5} \stackrel{?}{=} 0$$
$$\sqrt{45} - 3\sqrt{5} \stackrel{?}{=} 0$$
$$3\sqrt{5} - 3\sqrt{5} \stackrel{?}{=} 0$$
$$0 = 0 \quad \text{True}$$

The solutions are $y = -15$ and $y = 3$.

51.
$$\sqrt{\frac{x-3}{x+2}} = \frac{2}{3}$$
$$\left(\sqrt{\frac{x-3}{x+2}}\right)^2 = \left(\frac{2}{3}\right)^2$$
$$\frac{x-3}{x+2} = \frac{4}{9}$$
$$9(x-3) = 4(x+2)$$
$$9x - 27 = 4x + 8$$
$$5x = 35$$
$$x = 7$$

Check:
$$\sqrt{\frac{7-3}{7+2}} \stackrel{?}{=} \frac{2}{3}$$
$$\sqrt{\frac{4}{9}} \stackrel{?}{=} \frac{2}{3}$$
$$\frac{2}{3} = \frac{2}{3} \quad \text{True}$$

The solution is $x = 7$.

53.
$$\sqrt{\sqrt{t}+5} = 3$$
$$\left(\sqrt{\sqrt{t}+5}\right)^2 = 3^2$$
$$\sqrt{t}+5 = 9$$
$$\sqrt{t} = 4$$
$$\left(\sqrt{t}\right)^2 = 4^2$$
$$t = 16$$

Check:
$$\sqrt{\sqrt{16}+5} \stackrel{?}{=} 3$$
$$\sqrt{4+5} \stackrel{?}{=} 3$$
$$\sqrt{9} \stackrel{?}{=} 3$$
$$3 = 3 \quad \text{True}$$

The solution is $t = 16$.

55. $\sqrt{(x-1)^2} = |x-1| = x-1$ for $x-1 \geq 0$ or $x \geq 1$.

The solution set is $\left\{ x \mid x \geq 1 \right\}$.

57.
$$h = \sqrt{pq}$$
$$h^2 = \left(\sqrt{pq}\right)^2$$
$$h^2 = pq$$
$$\frac{h^2}{p} = \frac{pq}{p}$$
$$\frac{h^2}{p} = q$$
$$q = \frac{h^2}{p}$$

59.
$$v = \sqrt{2gR}$$
$$v^2 = \left(\sqrt{2gR}\right)^2$$
$$v^2 = 2gR$$
$$\frac{v^2}{2g} = \frac{2gR}{2g}$$
$$\frac{v^2}{2g} = R$$
$$R = \frac{v^2}{2g}$$

61.
$$r = \sqrt{\frac{S}{2\pi}}$$
$$r^2 = \left(\sqrt{\frac{S}{2\pi}}\right)^2$$
$$r^2 = \frac{S}{2\pi}$$
$$r^2 \cdot 2\pi = \frac{S}{2\pi} \cdot 2\pi$$
$$2\pi r^2 = S$$
$$S = 2\pi r^2$$

63.
$$r = \sqrt{\frac{2V}{\pi h}}$$
$$r^2 = \left(\sqrt{\frac{2V}{\pi h}}\right)^2$$
$$r^2 = \frac{2V}{\pi h}$$
$$\frac{\pi h}{2} \cdot r^2 = \frac{2V}{\pi h} \cdot \frac{\pi h}{2}$$
$$\frac{\pi r^2 h}{2} = V$$
$$V = \frac{\pi r^2 h}{2}$$

65.
$$d = \sqrt{(x-1)^2 + (y-2)^2}$$
$$d^2 = \left(\sqrt{(x-1)^2 + (y-2)^2}\right)^2$$
$$d^2 = (x-1)^2 + (y-2)^2$$
$$d^2 - (y-2)^2 = (x-1)^2$$
$$\sqrt{d^2 - (y-2)^2} = \sqrt{(x-1)^2}$$
$$\pm\sqrt{d^2 - (y-2)^2} = x - 1$$
$$1 \pm \sqrt{d^2 - (y-2)^2} = x$$
$$x = 1 \pm \sqrt{d^2 - (y-2)^2}$$

67.
$$t = 2\pi\sqrt{\frac{0.9}{10}}$$
$$t = 2\pi(0.3)$$
$$t = 0.6\pi$$
$$t \approx 1.88$$

To the nearest hundredth of a second, the period is 1.88 s.

69.
$$t = 2\pi\sqrt{\frac{l}{g}}$$
$$\frac{t}{2\pi} = \sqrt{\frac{l}{g}}$$
$$\left(\frac{t}{2\pi}\right)^2 = \left(\sqrt{\frac{l}{g}}\right)^2$$
$$\frac{t^2}{4\pi^2} = \frac{l}{g}$$
$$\frac{t^2 g}{4\pi^2} = l$$
$$l = \frac{t^2 g}{4\pi^2}$$

71. Let x = the integer.
$$x + \sqrt{x} = 12$$
$$\sqrt{x} = 12 - x$$
$$\left(\sqrt{x}\right)^2 = (12 - x)^2$$
$$x = 144 - 24x + x^2$$
$$x^2 - 25x + 144 = 0$$
$$(x - 9)(x - 16) = 0$$
$$x - 9 = 0 \quad \text{or} \quad x - 16 = 0$$
$$x = 9 \qquad\qquad x = 16$$

Check: $x = 9$ 　　　　Check: $x = 16$
$9 + \sqrt{9} \overset{?}{=} 12$ 　　$16 + \sqrt{16} \overset{?}{=} 12$
$9 + 3 \overset{?}{=} 12$ 　　　$16 + 4 \overset{?}{=} 12$
$12 = 12$ True 　　　$20 \neq 12$

The integer is 9.

73. Let x = the integer.
$$x + 2\sqrt{x} = 24$$
$$2\sqrt{x} = 24 - x$$
$$\left(2\sqrt{x}\right)^2 = (24 - x)^2$$
$$4x = 576 - 48x + x^2$$
$$x^2 - 52x + 576 = 0$$
$$(x - 16)(x - 36) = 0$$
$$x - 16 = 0 \quad \text{or} \quad x - 36 = 0$$
$$x = 16 \qquad\qquad x = 36$$

Check: $x = 16$ 　　　　Check: $x = 36$
$16 + 2\sqrt{16} \overset{?}{=} 24$ 　　$36 + 2\sqrt{36} \overset{?}{=} 24$
$16 + 2 \cdot 4 \overset{?}{=} 24$ 　　$36 + 2 \cdot 6 \overset{?}{=} 24$
$16 + 8 \overset{?}{=} 24$ 　　　$36 + 12 \overset{?}{=} 24$
$24 = 24$ True 　　　$48 \neq 24$

The integer is 16.

75.
$$d(h) = \sqrt{2h}$$
$$d(30,000) = \sqrt{2(30,000)}$$
$$= \sqrt{60,000}$$
$$\approx 245$$

The horizon is approximately 245 mi away.

77.
$$d = \sqrt{2h}$$
$$d^2 = \left(\sqrt{2h}\right)^2$$
$$d^2 = 2h$$
$$\frac{d^2}{2} = \frac{2h}{2}$$
$$\frac{d^2}{2} = h$$
$$h = \frac{d^2}{2}$$

79. $s(65) = 2\sqrt{5(65)}$

$\quad\quad = 2\sqrt{325}$

$\quad\quad \approx 36$

The skidding distance is approximately 36 ft.

81. $s(40) = 2\sqrt{5(40)}$

$\quad\quad = 2\sqrt{200}$

$\quad\quad \approx 28$

The skidding distance is approximately 28 ft.

83. $x = \dfrac{s^2}{20}$

$\quad = \dfrac{(35)^2}{20}$

$\quad = \dfrac{1225}{20}$

$\quad \approx 60$

The car's speed was approximately 60 mi/h.

85. $Y_1 = \sqrt{2-x}$, $Y_2 = x+4$

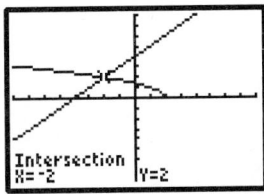

Intersection
X=-2   Y=2

The solution is –2, the x-value of the intersection.

87. $Y_1 = 5 - 3\sqrt{2-x}$, $Y_2 = 3 - 4x$

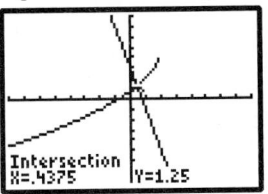

Intersection
X=.4375   Y=1.25

The solution is 0.44, the x-value of the intersection.

Exercises 4.10

1. $\sqrt{-16} = \sqrt{16}\,i = 4i$

3. $-\sqrt{-64} = -\sqrt{64}\,i = -8i$

5. $\sqrt{-21} = \sqrt{21}\,i$ or $i\sqrt{21}$

7. $\sqrt{-12} = \sqrt{12}\,i = 2\sqrt{3}\,i$ or $2i\sqrt{3}$

9. $-\sqrt{-108} = -\sqrt{108}\,i = -6\sqrt{3}\,i$ or $-6i\sqrt{3}$

11. $(3+i)+(5+2i) = (3+5)+(1+2)i = 8+3i$

13. $(3-2i)+(-2+7i) = (3-2)+(-2+7)i = 1+5i$

15. $(5+4i)-(3+2i) = (5-3)+(4-2)i = 2+2i$

17. $(8-5i)-(3+2i) = (8-3)+(-5-2)i = 5-7i$

19. $(5+i)+(2+3i)+7i = (5+2)+(1+3+7)i$

$\quad\quad = 7+11i$

21. $(2+3i)-(3-5i)+(4+3i)$

$\quad = (2-3+4)+[3-(-5)+3]i$

$\quad = 3+(3+5+3)i$

$\quad = 3+11i$

23. $(7+3i)-[(3+i)-(2-5i)]$

$\quad = (7+3i)-[(3-2)+(1-(-5))i]$

$\quad = (7+3i)-(1+6i)$

$\quad = (7-1)+(3-6)i$

$\quad = 6-3i$

25. $(5+3i)+(-5-3i) = (5-5)+(3-3)i = 0+0i$

27. $3i(3+5i) = 3i \cdot 3 + 3i \cdot 5i$

$\quad\quad = 9i + 15i^2$

$\quad\quad = 9i + 15(-1)$

$\quad\quad = -15 + 9i$

29. $4i(3-7i) = 4i \cdot 3 + 4i(-7i)$

$\quad\quad = 12i - 28i^2$

$\quad\quad = 12i - 28(-1)$

$\quad\quad = 28 + 12i$

31. $-2i(4-3i) = -2i \cdot 4 - 2i(-3i)$

$\quad\quad = -8i + 6i^2$

$\quad\quad = -8i + 6(-1)$

$\quad\quad = -6 - 8i$

33. $6i\left(\dfrac{2}{3}+\dfrac{5}{6}i\right) = 6i\left(\dfrac{2}{3}\right)+6i\left(\dfrac{5}{6}i\right)$

$\quad\quad = 4i + 5i^2$

$\quad\quad = 4i + 5(-1)$

$\quad\quad = -5 + 4i$

35. $(3+2i)(2+3i) = 3(2+3i) + 2i(2+3i)$
$$= 6 + 9i + 4i + 6i^2$$
$$= 6 + 13i + 6(-1)$$
$$= 0 + 13i$$
$$= 13i$$

37. $(4-3i)(2+5i) = 4(2+5i) - 3i(2+5i)$
$$= 8 + 20i - 6i - 15i^2$$
$$= 8 + 14i - 15(-1)$$
$$= 23 + 14i$$

39. $(-2-3i)(-3+4i) = -2(-3+4i) - 3i(-3+4i)$
$$= 6 - 8i + 9i - 12i^2$$
$$= 6 + i - 12(-1)$$
$$= 18 + i$$

41. $(5-2i)^2 = (5)^2 - 2(5)(2i) + (2i)^2$
$$= 25 - 20i + 4i^2$$
$$= 25 - 20i + 4(-1)$$
$$= 21 - 20i$$

43. The conjugate of $3 - 2i$ is $3 + 2i$.
$$(3-2i)(3+2i) = 3^2 - (2i)^2$$
$$= 9 - 4i^2$$
$$= 9 - 4(-1)$$
$$= 9 + 4$$
$$= 13$$

45. The conjugate of $2 + 3i$ is $2 - 3i$.
$$(2+3i)(2-3i) = 2^2 - (3i)^2$$
$$= 4 - 9i^2$$
$$= 4 - 9(-1)$$
$$= 4 + 9$$
$$= 13$$

47. The conjugate of $-3 - 2i$ is $-3 + 2i$.
$$(-3-2i)(-3+2i) = (-3)^2 - (2i)^2$$
$$= 9 - 4i^2$$
$$= 9 - 4(-1)$$
$$= 9 + 4$$
$$= 13$$

49. The conjugate of $5i$ is $-5i$.
$$(5i)(-5i) = -25i^2 = -25(-1) = 25$$

51. $\dfrac{3+2i}{i} = \dfrac{(3+2i)(-i)}{(i)(-i)}$
$$= \dfrac{-3i - 2i^2}{-i^2}$$
$$= \dfrac{-3i - 2(-1)}{-(-1)}$$
$$= \dfrac{-3i + 2}{1}$$
$$= 2 - 3i$$

53. $\dfrac{6-4i}{2i} = \dfrac{(6-4i)(-2i)}{(2i)(-2i)}$
$$= \dfrac{-12i + 8i^2}{-4i^2}$$
$$= \dfrac{-12i + 8(-1)}{-4(-1)}$$
$$= \dfrac{-8 - 12i}{4}$$
$$= -2 - 3i$$

55. $\dfrac{3}{2+5i} = \dfrac{3(2-5i)}{(2+5i)(2-5i)}$
$$= \dfrac{3(2-5i)}{4 - 25i^2}$$
$$= \dfrac{6 - 15i}{4 - 25(-1)}$$
$$= \dfrac{6 - 15i}{4 + 25}$$
$$= \dfrac{6 - 15i}{29}$$
$$= \dfrac{6}{29} - \dfrac{15}{29}i$$

57. $\dfrac{13}{2+3i} = \dfrac{13(2-3i)}{(2+3i)(2-3i)}$
$$= \dfrac{13(2-3i)}{4 - 9i^2}$$
$$= \dfrac{26 - 39i}{4 - 9(-1)}$$
$$= \dfrac{26 - 39i}{4 + 9}$$
$$= \dfrac{26 - 39i}{13}$$
$$= 2 - 3i$$

59. $\dfrac{2+3i}{4+3i} = \dfrac{(2+3i)(4-3i)}{(4+3i)(4-3i)}$

$= \dfrac{8-6i+12i-9i^2}{16-9i^2}$

$= \dfrac{8+6i-9(-1)}{16-9(-1)}$

$= \dfrac{8+6i+9}{16+9}$

$= \dfrac{17+6i}{25}$

$= \dfrac{17}{25} + \dfrac{6}{25}i$

61. $\dfrac{3-4i}{3+4i} = \dfrac{(3-4i)(3-4i)}{(3+4i)(3-4i)}$

$= \dfrac{3^2 - 2(3)(4i) + (4i)^2}{9-16i^2}$

$= \dfrac{9-24i+16i^2}{9-16(-1)}$

$= \dfrac{9-24i+16(-1)}{9+16}$

$= \dfrac{-7-24i}{25}$

$= -\dfrac{7}{25} - \dfrac{24}{25}i$

63. writing exercise

65. $\sqrt{-5} \cdot \sqrt{-7} = (i\sqrt{5})(i\sqrt{7})$

$= i^2\sqrt{35}$

$= (-1)\sqrt{35}$

$= -\sqrt{35}w$

67. $\sqrt{-2} \cdot \sqrt{-18} = (i\sqrt{2})(i\sqrt{18})$

$= i^2\sqrt{36}$

$= (-1)\sqrt{36}$

$= -6$

69. $\sqrt{-6} \cdot \sqrt{-15} = (i\sqrt{6})(i\sqrt{15})$

$= i^2\sqrt{90}$

$= (-1)\sqrt{90}$

$= -3\sqrt{10}$

71. $\sqrt{-10} \cdot \sqrt{-10} = (i\sqrt{10})(i\sqrt{10})$

$= i^2\sqrt{100}$

$= (-1)\sqrt{100}$

$= -10$

73. $i^{10} = i^8 \cdot i^2 = (i^4)^2 \cdot i^2 = 1^2(-1) = -1$

75. $i^{20} = (i^4)^5 = 1^5 = 1$

77. $i^{38} = i^{36} \cdot i^2 = (i^4)^9 \cdot i^2 = 1^9 \cdot (-1) = -1$

79. $i^{51} = i^{48} \cdot i^3 = (i^4)^{12} \cdot i^2 \cdot i = 1^{12} \cdot (-1) \cdot i = -i$

81. challenge exercise

Chapter 4